Using Financial Accounting: An Introduction

Using Financial Accounting: An Introduction

Dennis Murray, Professor of Accounting
University of Colorado at Denver

Bruce R. Neumann, Professor of Accounting
University of Colorado at Denver

Pieter Elgers, Professor of Accounting
University of Massachusetts at Amherst

South-Western College Publishing
Thomson Learning™

Australia • Canada • Denmark • Japan • Mexico • New Zealand • Philippines
Puerto Rico • Singapore • South Africa • Spain • United Kingdom • United States

Using Financial Accounting: An Introduction, 2e, by Dennis Murray, Bruce Richard Neumann, and Pieter Elgers

Acquisitions Editor: Maureen L. Riopelle
Senior Developmental Editor: Ken Martin
Marketing Manager: Dan Silverburg
Media & Technology Editor: Diane Van Bakel
Media Production Editor: Lora Craver
Production Editor: Mike Busam
Manufacturing Coordinator: Doug Wilke
Internal Design: Michael H. Stratton
Cover Design: Matulionis Design
Cover Image: copyright Corbis images
Production House: D&G Limited, LLC
Printer: Westgroup

Printed in the United States of America
1 2 3 4 5 02 01 00 99

For more information contact South-Western College Publishing, 5101 Madison Road, Cincinnati, Ohio, 45227. Or you can visit our Internet site at http://www.swcollege.com

For permission to use material from this text or product contact us by
- **telephone: 1-800-730-2214**
- **fax: 1-800-730-2215**
- **web: http://www.thomsonrights.com**

Library of Congress Cataloging-in-Publication Data
Murray, Dennis Francis.
Using financial accounting : an introduction / Dennis Murray, Bruce R. Neumann, Pieter Elgers.
p. cm.
Includes bibliographical references and index.
ISBN 0-324-00636-5 (hardcover)
1. Accounting. I. Neumann, Bruce R. II. Elgers, Pieter T. III. Title.
HF5635.M9679 2000
657-dc21 99-30148
CIP

This book is printed on acid-free paper.

preface

This is an exciting time in accounting education. Various constituencies have emphasized the need for change and accounting educators have been quick to respond. Colleges and universities have developed innovations in their curricula, methods of instructional delivery, and course materials. We believe this book will assist those students and faculty members seeking an innovative approach to introductory financial accounting.

For several years now, nearly all introductory texts have offered new and various pedagogical features that proclaim to follow a "user" approach. We have attempted to advance this trend. *Using Financial Accounting* is truly written from the user's perspective. We emphasize (1) the effects of transactions on financial statements, (2) the interrelationships among the financial statements, and (3) the interpretation of financial statement information.

The mechanical aspects of the accounting process, such as journals, ledgers, debits/credits, trial balances, etc., are virtually eliminated from the text. Beginning students too frequently become immersed in detailed bookkeeping procedures and lose sight of the underlying objective of accounting: to assist in making business and economic decisions.

By taking an analytical and interpretative approach, students are able to understand and use financial statements. They will retain this ability longer than the knowledge of detailed accounting procedures. This approach "adds value" to students' potential contributions as business professionals.

TARGET AUDIENCE

This text is intended to serve both accounting majors and nonmajors. Nonmajors view a rules-based presentation as procedural rather than conceptual. Majors are also limited by a mechanical approach in that they do not really understand the goals and purposes of financial accounting until much later in their academic or professional careers. The target audience for this text includes:

1. Undergraduate accounting majors
2. Students other than accounting majors who want to interpret financial statements and interact with accounting professionals. This student group includes business majors and students in nonbusiness disciplines, such as engineering, health services, and law.
3. MBA students, who are particularly well served by an interpretative approach.

FEATURES

This text's distinctive combination of features enhances value to students. These features include (1) the use of transaction analysis, rather than journal entries, to describe business events; (2) incorporation of "Reality Checks" that relate the text material to current real-world companies; (3) attention to international issues and accounting conventions for non-U.S. firms; (4) discussions and problem materials dealing with ethical issues facing managers and accountants; (5) evaluations of economic consequences associated with accounting policy decisions; (6) inclusion of an unusually large, diverse, and flexible set of end-of-chapter assignment material; and (7) a host of Internet-based problems in each chapter.

Transaction Analysis

To understand and interpret financial statements, students must gain an understanding of how transactions affect financial statements. This is accomplished by using the basic accounting equation:

ASSETS = LIABILITIES + SHAREHOLDERS' EQUITY

Transaction analysis, using the accounting equation, provides students with the background and tools to analyze financial statements. In addition to showing how business events affect the accounting equation, significant parts of each chapter are devoted to analysis and interpretation. Ratio analysis is introduced as early as Chapter 3, "The Balance Sheet," and appears in every subsequent chapter.

Reality Checks

Because we focus on the uses of financial accounting information, each chapter includes numerous real-world illustrations. These illustrations show how financial statements provide insights into a firm's performance. As part of this real-world orientation, Reality Checks are interspersed throughout the text. Reality checks are self-contained, limited-scope problems (with solutions), based on actual financial statements and other disclosures. They help students see how financial statements can be used to answer important questions.

International Coverage

International issues are interwoven into the discussion of financial statement analysis. The reader is shown how international differences in accounting standards can affect the inferences drawn from financial statements. For example, the discussion of noncurrent assets indicates that firms in some countries (such as Australia) report the market value of property, plant, and equipment. Moreover, problems involving non-U.S. firms are included at the end of several chapters. International accounting issues are summarized in Chapter 13, "Reporting Issues for Affiliated and International Companies."

Ethics

Ethical issues are considered throughout the text. Ethical dilemmas are presented, and the reader is asked to identify the proper course of action. We use a flag called "What Would You Do?" to alert readers to these ethical issues as they arise.

Economic Consequences

During the past 20 years, we have become more aware of the economic consequences and managerial motivations related to accounting policy decisions. Sophisticated users of financial statements should know that motivations stemming from compensation plans and debt covenants can affect the relevance and reliability of financial accounting information. These discussions are relatively self-contained so that they can be included at the instructor's option.

End-of-Chapter Material

Each chapter ends with questions, exercises, and problems. The questions and exercises are relatively short, straightforward applications of the text material. Problems are longer and more involved than the exercises. Many involve writing or research assignments. Some problems are long enough, and sufficiently complex, to be treated as mini-cases.

Extended discussion problems have been included to challenge students' understanding of how financial statements can be used. They often require qualitative, narrative responses; some require research and writing. Our focus on the user orientation, real-world information, international issues, and ethics is carried through to the end-of-chapter material. Much of this material is based on actual financial statements from companies from around the world.The end-of-chapter material also contains situations requiring the application of ethics and Internet searches.

ORGANIZATION

This book is arranged into four major components that make it readily adaptable for use in quarter, semester, or modular-type programs.

Chapters 1 through 5 introduce financial accounting and three primary financial statements: the balance sheet, the income statement, and statement of cash flows.

Chapters 6 through 10 examine in more detail current and noncurrent assets, current and noncurrent liabilities, and shareholder's equity.

Chapter 11 is a synthesis of financial statement analysis. Although all chapters focus on the analysis and interpretation of financial statements, Chapter 11 provides an overall framework for financial statement analysis. Most instructors will use this chapter to unify the topics covered earlier in the text.

Chapters 12 through 14 consist of several self-contained modules that explore relatively complex topics such as leases, pensions, consolidated reporting, and international reporting. Many instructors will choose to cover only a subset of these topics.

Appendix A contains an overview of the accounting process. Journal entries, adjusting entries, closing entries, and other procedural aspects of accounting are discussed. This appendix is intended primarily for those students (such as accounting majors) who wish to engage in further study of financial accounting. Most instructors who elect to utilize this appendix would likely use it in an end-of-course module to prepare students for intermediate financial accounting.

Appendix B examines various career options in accounting. This material would be of interest to a wide array of readers.

Appendix C reviews the basic concepts of the time value of money.

In keeping with our real-world approach, Appendixes D and E contain the annual reports of Wendy's International, Inc. and Reebok International Limited, respectively. These reports serve as the basis for a number of exercises and problems.

SUPPLEMENTS

The following supplements are available for use with this text:

Solutions/Instructor's Manual. Prepared by Elizabeth C. Conner of the University of Colorado at Denver, this manual provides solutions to the text's extensive end-of-chapter review material. It also includes chapter overviews, learning objectives, and material designed to encourage group work. Sheila Viel of the University of Wisconsin—Milwaukee, carefully verified the solutions.

Test Bank. Prepared by Linda Kidwell of Niagara University, the Test Bank provides a variety of true/false, multiple-choice, matching, fill-in, and essay problems—80 to 100 per chapter in both the printed and computerized versions. Each chapter includes a page linking the problems to the learning objectives and providing a difficulty level for each problem.

PowerPoint Presentation Slides. Prepared by Anthony Zambelli of the University of Redlands, these slides highlight the major concepts of each chapter.

Study Guide. Prepared by Cecilia M. Fewox of the College of Charleston, the Study Guide for students provides an overview for each chapter, a review of each specific chapter objective, and self-test material that utilizes matching, completion, and multiple-choice formats, as well as demonstration problems.

ACKNOWLEDGMENTS

We thank our colleagues who took the time to provide us with helpful comments on the manuscript for this text. The reviewers include:

Mel Auerbach
California State University–Dominguez Hills

Ronnie Burrows
University of Dayton

K. Michael Geary
University of Dayton

Linda Hadley
University of Dayton

James Livingston
Southern Methodist University

Ronald Mannino
University of Massachusetts at Amherst

Aileen Ormiston
Mesa Community College

Don Pagach
North Carolina State University

Ronald Reed
University of Northern Colorado

James Sander
Butler University

Douglas Sharp
Wichita State Unibversity

Karen Smith
Arizona State University

DENNIS MURRAY
BRUCE R. NEUMANN
PIETER ELGERS

about the authors

DENNIS MURRAY, Ph.D., CPA, is Professor of Accounting at the University of Colorado—Denver. He received his doctoral degree from the University of Massachusetts—Amherst and his undergraduate and masters degrees from the State University of New York at Albany. Professor Murray has published articles in a number of journals including *The Accounting Review, Journal of Accounting and Economics, Journal of Accounting Research,* and *Accounting Organzations and Society.* He also serves on the editorial boards of *Advances in Accounting* and *The Journal of Managerial Issues.* Professor Murray has public accounting experience with KPMG Peat Marwick and is a member of the American Accounting Association and the American Institute of CPAs. He has received several awards recognizing his academic accomplishments.

BRUCE R. NEUMANN, Ph.D., is Professor of Accounting and Health Administration at the University of Colorado—Denver. He received his doctoral degree from the University of Illinois and his undergraduate and masters degrees from the University of Minnesota. Dr. Neumann's primary research interests focus on analyses of costs in public and private organizations and on behavioral issues related to the interpretation and use of financial reports. His work has appeared in the *Jounal of Accounting Reseach, Journal of Accountancy, Management Accounting,* and *Accounting and Business Research.* He has held visiting professorships at Bond University (Australia), Murdoch University (Australia), and the University of Auckland. He has also served as a research fellow at the National Center for Health Services Research (Washington, DC) and at the Health Services Management Unit at the University of Manchester (U.K.).

PIETER ELGERS, Ph.D., is Professor of Accounting at the University of Massachusetts at Amherst, and has previously served on the faculties of the College of William and Mary and Boston University, and visited at Yale University and the University of Auckland. His research has appeared in the *Journal of Accounting Research, The Accounting Review, Journal of Accounting and Economics, Journal of Finance, Management Science,* and various other academic and professional journals in accounting and finance. He has co-authored and edited books in the areas of financial management, accounting theory, lease-buy analysis, and financial accounting.

brief contents

contents

chapter 1

Financial Accounting and Its Environment

LEARNING OBJECTIVES

1. Define accounting and identify its objectives.
2. Distinguish among the three major types of accounting.
3. List the three primary financial statements and briefly summarize the information contained in each.
4. Identify financial statement users and the decisions they make.
5. Define generally accepted accounting principles and explain how they are determined.
6. Describe the role of auditing.
7. List the economic consequences of accounting principle choice.
8. Assess the importance of ethics in accounting.

INTRODUCTION

Jane Johnson is considering selling T-shirts in the parking lot during her university's football games. Jane, of course, will do this only if she expects to make a profit. To estimate her profits, Jane needs certain pieces of information, such as the cost of a shirt, the university's charge for the right to conduct business on its property, the expected selling price, and the expected sales volume. Suppose Jane has developed the following estimates:

Sales price per shirt	$ 12
Cost per shirt	$ 7
Number of shirts sold per game day	50
University fee per game day	$100

Although developing estimates is tricky, let's take these estimates as given. Based on the estimates, Jane would earn a profit of $150 per game day.

Sales ($12 × 50)		$600
Less expenses:		
Cost of merchandise ($7 × 50)	$350	
University fee	100	
Total expenses		450
Net income		$150

Since this looks like a reasonable profit, Jane puts her plan into action. After her first game day, Jane needs to assess her success (or failure). Based on her actual results, Jane prepares the following information:

Sales ($12 × 40)		$480
Less expenses:		
Cost of merchandise ($7 × 40)	$280	
University fee	100	
Total expenses		380
Net income		$100

Jane's business was profitable, but not as profitable as she planned. This is because Jane sold fewer shirts than she hoped, but Jane is confident that she can sell any remaining shirts on the next game day.

The preceding illustration shows two ways in which accounting can be used. First, Jane used accounting to help plan her business. That is, she used accounting to project her expected profit. Second, after Jane operated her business for a day, she used accounting to determine if, in fact, she had made a profit. In general, accounting is used during all phases of planning and operating a business.

ACCOUNTING

Accounting is the systematic process of measuring the economic activity of a business to provide useful information to those who make economic decisions. Accounting information is used in many different situations. The illustration in the introductory section shows how a business owner (Jane) can use accounting information. Bankers use accounting information when deciding whether or not to make a loan. Stockbrokers and other financial advisers base investment recommendations on accounting information, while government regulators use accounting information to determine if firms are complying with various laws and regulations.

TYPES OF ACCOUNTING

The examples mentioned in the last section explained how accounting information can be helpful in a number of situations. In fact, the field of accounting consists of several specialty areas that are based on the nature of the decision. The following sections describe the three major types of accounting, which are summarized in Exhibit 1-1.

Financial Accounting

Financial accounting provides information to decision makers who are external to the business. To understand the role of financial accounting, consider a large corporation such as IBM. The owners of corporations are called shareholders, and IBM has more than 600,000 shareholders. Obviously, each shareholder cannot participate directly in the running of IBM, and because IBM needs to maintain various trade secrets, its many thousands of shareholders are not permitted access to much of the firm's information. Because of this, shareholders delegate most of their decision-making power to the corporation's board of directors and officers. Exhibit 1-2 contains an organizational chart for a typical corporation. Shareholders, however, need information to evaluate (1) the performance of the business and (2) the advisability of retaining their investment in the business. Financial accounting provides some of the information for this purpose; such information is also used by potential shareholders who are considering an investment in the business.

EXHIBIT 1-1 The Three Major Types of Accounting

Accounting Specialty	Decision Maker	Examples of Decisions
Financial accounting	Shareholders	Buy shares Hold shares Sell shares
	Creditors	Lend money Determine interest rates
Managerial accounting	Managers	Set product prices Buy or lease equipment
Tax	Managers	Comply with tax laws Minimize tax payments Assess the tax effects of future transactions

EXHIBIT 1-2 Organizational Chart of a Typical Corporation

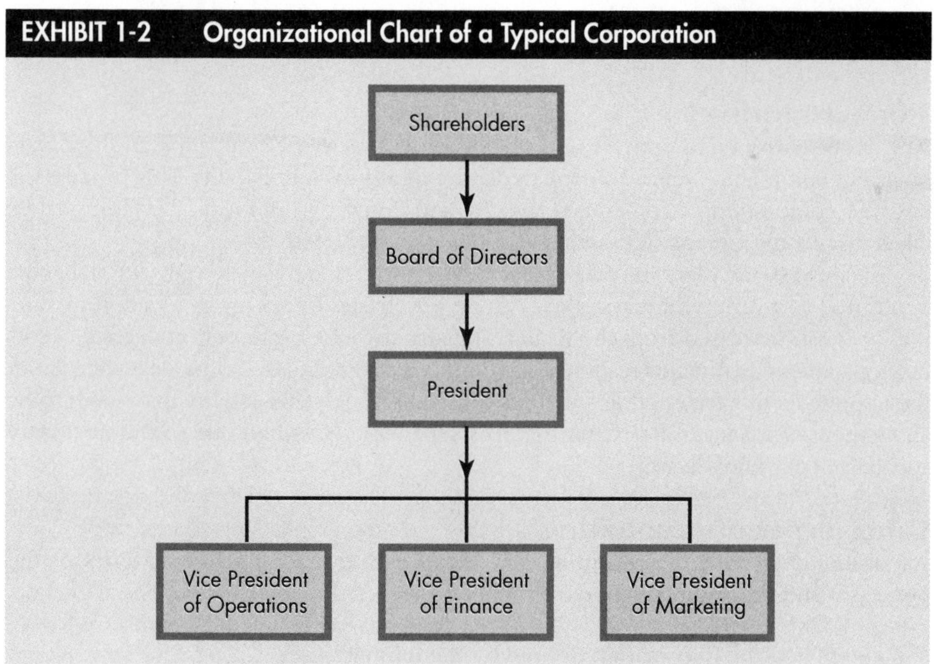

Creditors and potential creditors are also served by financial accounting. Firms often seek loans from banks, insurance companies, and other lenders. Although creditors are not internal parties of those firms, they need information about them so that funds are loaned only to credit-worthy organizations. Financial accounting will usually provide at least some of the information needed by these decision makers.

Managerial Accounting

Managers make numerous decisions. These include (1) whether to build a new plant, (2) how much to spend for advertising, research, and development, (3) whether to lease or buy equipment and facilities, (4) whether to manufacture or buy component parts for inventory production, or (5) whether to sell a certain product. Managerial accounting provides information for these decisions. This information is usually more detailed and more tailor-made to decision making than financial accounting information. It is also proprietary; that is, the information is not disclosed to parties outside the firm.

Sterling Collision Centers, Inc. provides a good illustration of managerial accounting at work. Although Sterling only has 18 shops, it hopes to put a major dent in the automotive body shop business through aggressive expansion and the introduction of innovative management techniques. One of its strategies is to use computers to better track repair times, which will provide both standards for different types of repair jobs as well as measures of how individual workers perform relative to the standards. By tying pay to performance, Sterling hopes to improve worker productivity. Knowledge of repair times will also help Sterling to determine estimated bids for its repair jobs. Managerial accountants play a major role in all these activities.

Although distinguishing between financial and managerial accounting is convenient, the distinction is somewhat blurred. For example, financial accounting provides information about the performance of a firm to outsiders. Because this information is essentially a performance report on management, managers are appropriately interested in and influenced by financial accounting information. Accordingly, the distinction between financial and managerial accounting depends on who is the primary user of the information.

Tax Accounting

Tax accounting encompasses two related functions: tax compliance and tax planning. Tax compliance refers to the calculation of a firm's tax liability. This process entails the completion of sometimes lengthy and complex tax forms. Tax compliance takes place after a year's transactions have been completed.

In contrast, tax planning takes place before the fact. A business transaction can be structured in a variety of ways; a car can be purchased by securing a loan, for example, or it can be leased from the dealer. The structure of a transaction determines its tax consequences. A major responsibility of tax accountants is to provide advice about the tax effects of a transaction's various forms. Although this activity may seem to be an element of managerial accounting, it is separately classified due to the necessary specialized tax knowledge.

Other Types of Accounting

A few additional types of accounting exist. **Accounting information systems** are the processes and procedures required to generate accounting information. These include

1. identifying the information desired by the ultimate user,
2. developing the documents (such as sales invoices) to record the necessary data,
3. assigning responsibilities to specific positions in the firm, and
4. applying computer technology to summarize the recorded data.

Another type of accounting deals with **nonbusiness organizations**. These organizations do not attempt to earn a profit and have no owners. They exist to fulfill the needs of certain groups of individuals. Nonbusiness organizations include

1. hospitals,
2. colleges and universities,
3. churches,

4. the federal, state, and local governments,
5. many other organizations such as museums, volunteer fire departments, and disaster relief agencies.

Nonbusiness organizations have a need for all the types of accounting we have just reviewed. For example, a volunteer fire department might need to borrow money to purchase a new fire truck. Its banker would then require financial accounting information to make the lending decision.

Nonbusiness organizations are fundamentally different from profit-oriented firms: They have no owners and they do not attempt to earn a profit. Because of this, the analysis of the financial performance of business and nonbusiness organizations is considerably different. This text addresses only business organizations. Most colleges and universities offer an entire course devoted to the accounting requirements of nonbusiness organizations.

A CLOSER LOOK AT FINANCIAL ACCOUNTING

This text is primarily concerned with financial accounting, which summarizes the past performance and current condition of a firm. An overview of financial accounting is presented in Exhibit 1-3. Each element of the exhibit is discussed in the following sections.

Past Transactions and Other Economic Events

Past transactions and events are the raw materials for the financial accounting process. **Transactions** typically involve an *exchange* of resources between the firm and other parties. For example, purchasing equipment with cash is a transaction that would be incorporated in the firm's financial accounting records. Purchasing equipment on credit is also a transaction; equipment is obtained in *exchange* for a promise to pay for it in the future.

Financial accounting also incorporates significant economic events that do not involve exchanges with other parties. For example, assume that a firm owns an uninsured automobile that is completely destroyed in an accident. Financial accounting would reflect the effect of this event.

Keep in mind that financial accounting deals with *past* transactions and events. It provides information about the past performance and current financial standing of a firm. Financial accounting itself does not usually make predictions about the future. Although financial statement users need to assess a firm's future prospects, financial accounting does not make these predictions, but it does provide information about the past and present that is useful in making predictions about the future.

EXHIBIT 1-3 Overview of Financial Accounting

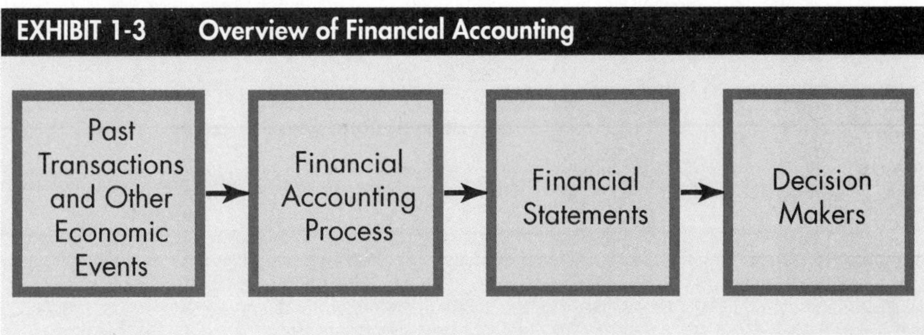

The Financial Accounting Process

The financial accounting process consists of

1. *categorizing* past transactions and events,
2. *measuring* selected attributes of those transactions and events, and
3. *recording* and *summarizing* those measurements.

The first step places transactions and events into categories that reflect their type or nature. Some of the categories used in financial accounting include (1) purchases of inventory (merchandise acquired for resale), (2) sales of inventory, and (3) wage payments to workers.

The next step assigns values to the transactions and events. The attribute measured is the fair value of the transaction on the exchange date. This is usually indicated by the amount of cash that changes hands. If equipment is purchased for a $1,000 cash payment, for example, the equipment is valued at $1,000. The initial valuation is not subsequently changed. (Some exceptions are discussed in later chapters.) This original measurement is called **historical cost**.

The final step in the process is to record and meaningfully summarize these measurements. Summarizing is necessary because, otherwise, decision makers would be overwhelmed with an extremely large array of information. Imagine, for example, that an analyst is interested in Ford Motor Company's sales for 1998. Providing a list of every sales transaction and its amount would yield unduly detailed information. Instead, the financial accounting process summarizes the dollar value of all sales during a given time period and this single sales revenue number is included in the financial statements.

Financial Statements

Financial statements are the end result of the financial accounting process. Firms prepare three major financial statements: the balance sheet, the income statement, and the statement of cash flows. The following sections briefly describe these statements.

The Balance Sheet The **balance sheet** shows a firm's assets, liabilities, and owners' equity. **Assets** are valuable resources that a firm owns or controls. The simplified balance sheet shown in Exhibit 1-4 includes four assets. **Cash** obviously has value. **Accounts receivable** are amounts owed to Newton Company by its customers; these

EXHIBIT 1-4 A Balance Sheet

The Newton Company
Balance Sheet
December 31, 2000

Assets		**Liabilities and Owners' Equity**	
Cash	$ 5,000	Liabilities	
Accounts receivable	7,000	Accounts payable	$ 8,000
Inventory	10,000	Notes payable	2,000
Equipment	7,000	Total liabilities	10,000
		Owners' equity	19,000
Total assets	$29,000	Total liabilities and owners' equity	$29,000

have value because they represent future cash inflows. **Inventory** is merchandise acquired that is to be sold to customers. Newton expects its inventory to be converted into accounts receivable and ultimately into cash. Finally, **equipment** (perhaps delivery vehicles or showroom furniture) enables Newton to operate its business.

Liabilities are obligations of the business to convey something of value in the future. Newton's balance sheet shows two liabilities. Accounts payable are unwritten promises that arise in the ordinary course of business. An example of this would be Newton purchasing inventory on credit, promising to make payment within a short period of time. Notes payable are more formal, written obligations. Notes payable often arise from borrowing money.

The final item on the balance sheet is **owners' equity**, which refers to the owners' interest in the business. It is a residual amount that equals assets minus liabilities. The owners have a positive financial interest in the business only if the firm's assets exceed its obligations.

The Income Statement Just as each of us is concerned about our income, investors and creditors are interested in the ability of an organization to produce income (sometimes called earnings or profits). The **income statement** summarizes the earnings generated by a firm during a specified period of time. Exhibit 1-5 contains Newton Company's income statement for 2000.

Income statements contain at least two major sections: revenues and expenses. **Revenues** are inflows of assets from providing goods and services to customers. Newton's income statement contains one type of revenue: sales to customers. This includes sales made for cash and sales made on credit.

Expenses are the costs incurred to generate revenues. Newton's income statement includes three types of expenses. Cost of goods sold is the cost to Newton of the merchandise that was sold to its customers. General and administrative expenses include salaries, rent, and other items. Tax expense reflects the payments that Newton must make to the Internal Revenue Service and other taxing authorities. The difference between revenues and expenses is **net income** (or **net loss** if expenses are greater than revenues).

The Statement of Cash Flows From a financial accounting perspective, income is not the same as cash. For example, suppose that a sale is made on credit. Will this sale be recorded on the income statement? Yes. It meets the definition of a revenue

EXHIBIT 1-5 An Income Statement

The Newton Company
Income Statement
For the Year Ended December 31, 2000

Revenues		
Sales		$63,000
Expenses		
Cost of goods sold	$35,000	
General and administrative	20,000	
Tax	3,000	
Total expenses		58,000
Net Income		$ 5,000

transaction: an inflow of assets (the right to receive cash in the future) in exchange for goods or services. Moreover, including this transaction in the income statement provides financial statement readers with useful information about the firm's accomplishments. However, no cash has been received. Thus, the income statement does not provide information about cash flows.

Financial statement users, though, are also interested in a firm's ability to generate cash. After all, cash is necessary to buy inventory, pay workers, purchase equipment, and so on. The **statement of cash flows** summarizes a firm's inflows and outflows of cash. Exhibit 1-6 illustrates Newton Company's statement of cash flows, which has three sections. One section deals with cash flows from **operating activities**, such as the buying and selling of inventory. The second section contains information about **investing activities**, such as the acquisition and disposal of equipment. The final section reflects cash flows from **financing activities**. These activities include obtaining and repaying loans, as well as obtaining financing from owners.

Notes to Financial Statements A full set of financial statements includes a number of **notes** that clarify and expand the material presented in the body of the financial statements. The notes indicate the accounting principles (rules) that were used to prepare the statements, provide detailed information about some of the items in the financial statements, and, in some cases, provide alternative measures of the firm's assets and liabilities.

Notes to financial statements are not illustrated in this chapter because they are highly technical and apply to specific accounting topics covered in subsequent chapters. Notes are, however, emphasized throughout much of this book.

Annual Reports All large firms, and many smaller ones, issue their financial statements as part of a larger document referred to as an **annual report**. In addition to the financial statements and their accompanying notes, the annual report includes descriptions of significant events that occurred during the year, commentary on future plans and strategies, and a discussion and analysis by management of the year's results. Appendixes C and D of this text contain substantial portions of two annual reports.

EXHIBIT 1-6 A Statement of Cash Flows

The Newton Company
Statement of Cash Flows
For the Year Ended December 31, 2000

Cash flows from operating activities:		
Cash received from customers	$61,000	
Cash paid to suppliers	(37,000)	
Cash paid for general and administrative functions	(19,900)	
Taxes paid	(3,000)	
Net cash provided by operating activities		1,100
Cash flows from investing activities:		
Purchase of equipment		(2,000)
Cash flows from financing activities:		
Net borrowings		1,000
Net increase in cash		100
Cash at beginning of year		4,900
Cash at end of year		$ 5,000

Decision Makers

Recall that the primary goal of financial accounting is to provide decision makers with useful information. This section identifies the major users of financial statements and describes the decisions they make.

Owners Present and potential owners (investors) are prime users of financial statements. They continually assess and compare the prospects of alternative investments. The assessment of each investment is often based on two variables: expected return and risk.

Expected return refers to the increase in the investor's wealth that is expected over the investment's time horizon. This wealth increase is comprised of two parts: (1) increases in the market value of the investment and (2) dividends (periodic cash distributions from the firm to its owners). Both of these sources of wealth depend on the firm's ability to generate cash. Accordingly, financial statements can improve decision making by providing information that helps current and potential investors estimate a firm's future cash flows.

Risk refers to the uncertainty surrounding estimates of expected return. The term *expected* implies that the return is not guaranteed. For most investments, numerous alternative future returns are possible. For example, an investor may project that a firm's most likely return for the upcoming year is $100,000. However, the investor recognizes that this is not the only possibility. There is some chance that the firm might generate returns of $90,000 or $110,000. Still other possibilities might be $80,000 and $120,000. The greater the difference among these estimates, the greater the risk. Financial statements help investors assess risk by providing information about the historical pattern of past income and cash flows.

Investment selection involves a trade-off between expected return and risk. Investments with high expected returns generally have a high risk. Each investor must assess whether investments with greater risk offer sufficiently higher expected returns.

To illustrate the trade-off between risk and expected return, assume that an investor has two choices: Investment A and Investment B. Each investment costs $100. The return provided by the investments during the next year depends on whether the economy experiences an expansion or recession. The following chart summarizes the possibilities:

	Expected Return	
	Investment A	Investment B
Expansion	$10	$4
Recession	$ 0	$2

Assuming that expansion and recession are equally as likely, the expected return of the two investments can be calculated as follows:

Investment A ($10 × .5) + ($0 × .5) = $5
Investment B ($4 × .5) + ($2 × .5) = $3

Although Investment A has the higher expected return, it also has the higher risk. Its return next year can vary by $10, while Investment B's return can vary by only $2. Investors must decide for themselves whether Investment A's higher expected return is worthwhile, given its greater risk.

Creditors The lending decision involves two issues: whether or not credit should be extended, and the specification of a loan's terms. For example, consider a bank loan officer evaluating a loan application. The officer must make decisions about the amount of the loan (if any), interest rate, payment schedule, and collateral. Because repayment of the loan and interest will rest on the applicant's ability to generate cash, lenders need to estimate a firm's future cash flows and the uncertainty surrounding those flows. Although investors generally take a long-term view of a firm's cash generating ability, creditors are concerned about this ability only during the loan period.

Lenders are not the only creditors who find financial statements useful. Suppliers often sell on credit, and they must decide which customers will or will not honor their obligations.

Other Users A variety of other decision makers find financial statements helpful. Some of these decision makers and their decisions include the following:

1. *Financial analysts and advisors*. Many investors and creditors seek expert advice when making their investment and lending decisions. These experts use financial statements as a basis for their recommendations.
2. *Customers*. The customers of a business are interested in a stable source of supply. They can use financial statements to identify suppliers that are financially sound.
3. *Employees and labor unions*. These groups have an interest in the viability and profitability of firms that employ them or their members. As described in Reality Check 1-1, unions in the airline industry have recently made several important decisions based, in part, on financial statements.
4. *Regulatory authorities*. Federal and state governments regulate a large array of business activities. The Securities and Exchange Commission (SEC) is a prominent example. Its responsibility is to ensure that capital markets, such as the New York Stock Exchange, operate smoothly. To help achieve this, corporations are required to make full and fair financial disclosures. The SEC regularly reviews firms' financial statements to evaluate the adequacy of their disclosures. Reality Check 1-2 describes another regulatory use of accounting information.

The accounting profession views financial statements as being *general purpose*. They are intended to meet the common information needs of a wide variety of users, such as those in the preceding list.

REALITY CHECK 1-1

United Airlines: Employees of United Airlines gained controlling ownership of United's parent, UAL Corporation, by agreeing to billions of dollars in wage and benefit concessions. The employees needed to estimate the value of UAL so that they could determine the extent of the wages and benefits to sacrifice. Financial statements are frequently used in valuing businesses.

Northwest Airlines: In 1993, Northwest asked its pilots to forgo $886 million in wages and benefits over three years. Northwest's reported 1993 loss of $115 million played a role in securing the pilots' agreement. However, in 1997, Northwest reported a profit of $597 million. As you might imagine, the pilots became much more assertive in their bargaining, asking for wage increases, profit sharing, and bonuses.

REALITY CHECK 1-2

California has perhaps the country's toughest standards for vehicle emissions. One aspect of its program requires the major automakers to generate 10% of their California sales from electric vehicles by 2003. Compliance with this regulation will be assessed from financial accounting information.

GENERALLY ACCEPTED ACCOUNTING PRINCIPLES

Decision makers often wish to compare the financial statements of several firms. To permit valid comparisons, the firms' statements need to be based on the same set of accounting principles, which are the rules and procedures used to produce the financial statements.

To illustrate how one event might be accounted for in more than one way, consider a movie production company that has just produced a new film costing $25,000,000. Assume that a balance sheet is to be prepared before the film is marketed. Does the firm have a $25,000,000 asset? The real value of the film rests on its capability to generate future revenues. A successful film will generate revenue that is many times greater than its cost; an unsuccessful film may not even cover its cost. At the balance sheet date, the future revenue is unknown.

As a potential investor or creditor, how would you prefer that this film be reflected on the balance sheet? Two obvious alternatives are $25,000,000 and $0. The latter is clearly more conservative; it results in a lower asset value. Some financial statement readers would prefer this conservative approach. Others would maintain that management expects to reap at least $25,000,000 in revenue; otherwise, they would not have undertaken the project. Thus, they feel that $25,000,000 is the most reasonable figure. There is no obvious answer to this issue. However, to permit valid comparisons of various firms' balance sheets, the same accounting principle should be used. Current accounting practice, in general, is to record assets at historical cost; in this case, the movie would be recorded at $25,000,000.

The Financial Accounting Standards Board

The most widely used set of accounting principles is referred to as generally accepted accounting principles (GAAP). GAAP is currently set by the Financial Accounting Standards Board (FASB). The FASB is a private organization located in Norwalk, Connecticut. The board is comprised of seven voting members who are supported by a large staff. As of June 1, 1998, the FASB issued 132 Statements of Financial Accounting Standards (SFASs). These standards are the primary source of GAAP.

The FASB's predecessor was the **Accounting Principles Board (APB)**. The APB issued 31 *Opinions*, which are still part of GAAP, unless they have been superseded by an SFAS.

The FASB faces a difficult task in setting GAAP. Financial accounting is not a natural science; no fundamental accounting laws have been proven to be correct. Accounting exists to provide information useful for decision making. The FASB's responsibility is to specify the accounting principles that will result in highly useful information. However, given that financial statement users are rather diverse, this is not a simple task.

The FASB employs an elaborate due process procedure prior to the issuance of an SFAS. Exhibit 1-7 summarizes the FASB's procedures. This process is designed to ensure that all those who wish to participate in the setting of accounting standards have an opportunity to do so.

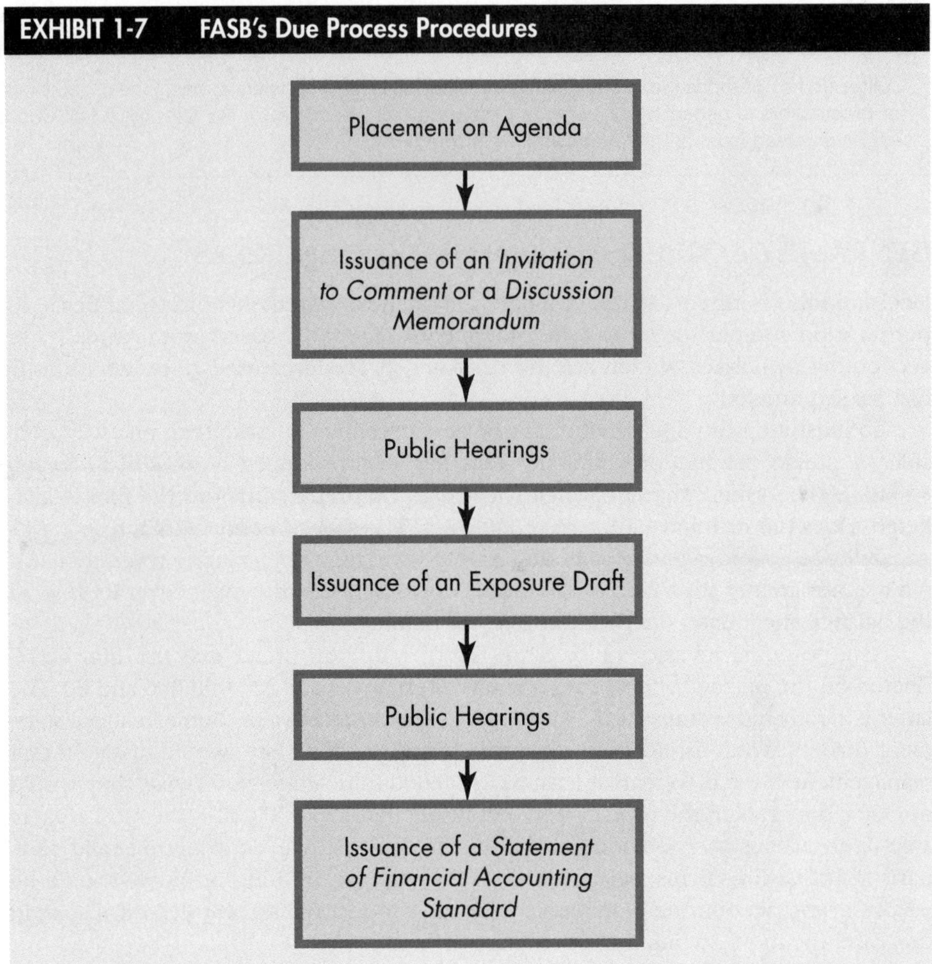

The FASB publishes several preliminary documents during its deliberations on each SFAS. The documents include an *Invitation to Comment* or a *Discussion Memorandum* that identify the fundamental accounting issues to be addressed. An *Exposure Draft* is the FASB's initial attempt at resolving such issues. These documents are widely disseminated, and interested parties are invited to communicate with the board, both in writing and by making presentations at public hearings. An affirmative vote of five of the seven FASB members is needed to issue a new SFAS.

An interesting aspect of GAAP is that more than one accounting method (or principle) is acceptable for some transactions. For example, there are several acceptable inventory accounting methods. This provides managers with considerable discretion in preparing their financial statements.

Several accountants, judges, and legislators have criticized this situation. They believe that only a single method should be allowed for a given transaction. In general, the FASB is attempting to narrow the availability of multiple acceptable accounting procedures.

The Securities and Exchange Commission

The **Securities and Exchange Commission (SEC)** was created by the Securities Exchange Act of 1934. The act empowered the SEC to set accounting principles and financial disclosure requirements for the corporations that it regulates. These corporations are quite large and have ownership interests that are widely dispersed among the public. Such corporations are referred to as ***publicly held***. Thus, for at least publicly held corporations, the SEC has legislative authority to set GAAP. This raises a question about the relationship between the SEC and the FASB.

The FASB is a private (nongovernment) organization whose authority to set GAAP derives from two sources. First, the business community and the accounting profession, by accepting FASB rulings, provide one source of support. In the United States, accounting principles have traditionally been set in the private sector, and the FASB's standards have received a reasonable amount of support. At the same time, not everyone is entirely happy with the FASB's pronouncements. Some people criticize the FASB for issuing standards that are too complex and too costly to implement. Part of the FASB's responsibility is to balance financial statement users' demands for better information with the costs incurred by those who provide that information.

The second source of the FASB's standard-setting authority is the SEC. Although the SEC has legislative authority to set GAAP for publicly held corporations, it prefers to rely on the accounting profession's private rule-making bodies to do this. In fact, the SEC has formally indicated that it will recognize GAAP as prescribed by the FASB. The SEC does, however, retain the right to overrule FASB pronouncements, and it occasionally exercises this right. Exhibit 1-8 shows the relationships among the different organizations involved in setting accounting standards.

THE ROLE OF AUDITING

A firm's management is primarily responsible for preparing its financial statements. Yet the financial statements can be viewed as a report on the performance of management. The conflict of interest in this situation is apparent. As a result, the financial statements of all corporations reporting to the SEC must be audited. **Audits** are required because they enhance the credibility of the financial statements. The financial statements of many privately held businesses are also subject to an audit. Banks, for

EXHIBIT 1-8 Groups Involved in Setting Accounting Standards

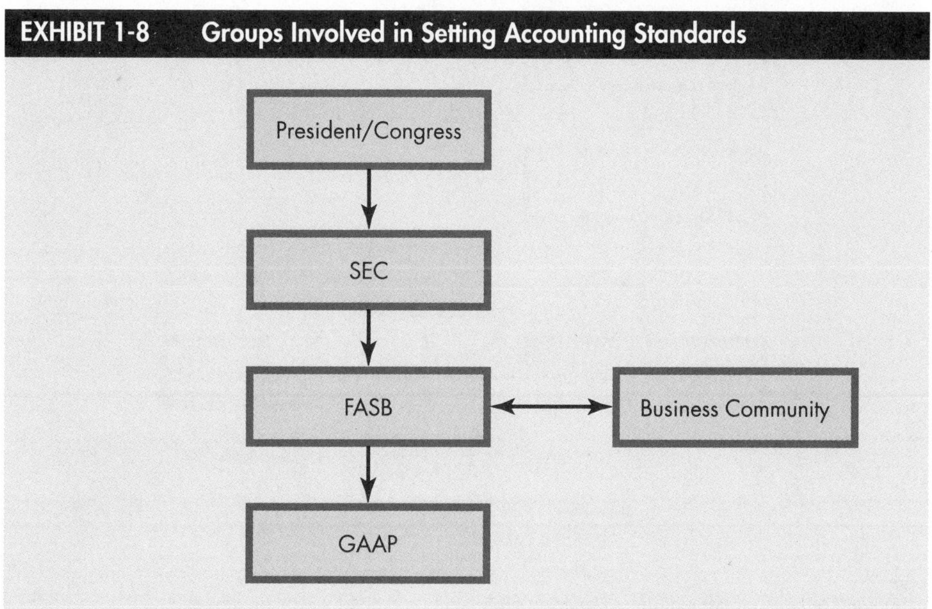

example, require many loan applicants to submit audited financial statements so that lending decisions can be based on credible financial information.

One of the most important auditing relationships, which are depicted in Exhibit 1-9, is the role of the independent certified public accountant (CPA) who conducts the audit. CPAs are licensed by the individual states by meeting specified educational and experience requirements and passing the uniform CPA exam, which takes two days to complete. CPAs are also required to attend continuing professional education classes and participate in a peer review process, whereby one CPA firm reviews and critiques the work of another firm.[1]

Exhibit 1-10 contains an auditor's report. The wording has been carefully chosen by the accounting profession to communicate precisely what an audit does and does not do. The first paragraph identifies the company, the specific financial statements that were audited, and the years of the audit. Management's responsibility for the financial statements is also acknowledged.

The second paragraph states that the audit has been conducted in accordance with **generally accepted auditing standards (GAAS)**. These standards have been developed by the accounting profession to provide guidance in the performance of an audit, which consists of an examination of evidence supporting the financial statements. Because audits are costly, auditors cannot retrace the accounting for every transaction. Accordingly, only a sample of a corporation's many transactions are reviewed. Based on the results of these tests, the auditor draws an inference about the fairness of the financial statements.

The second paragraph also notes that audits provide reasonable (not absolute) assurance that financial statements are free of material error. The lesser standard of reasonable assurance is employed for two reasons. First, auditors do not examine every transaction and thus they are unable to state conclusions in too strong a fashion. Sec-

EXHIBIT 1-9 Auditing Relationships

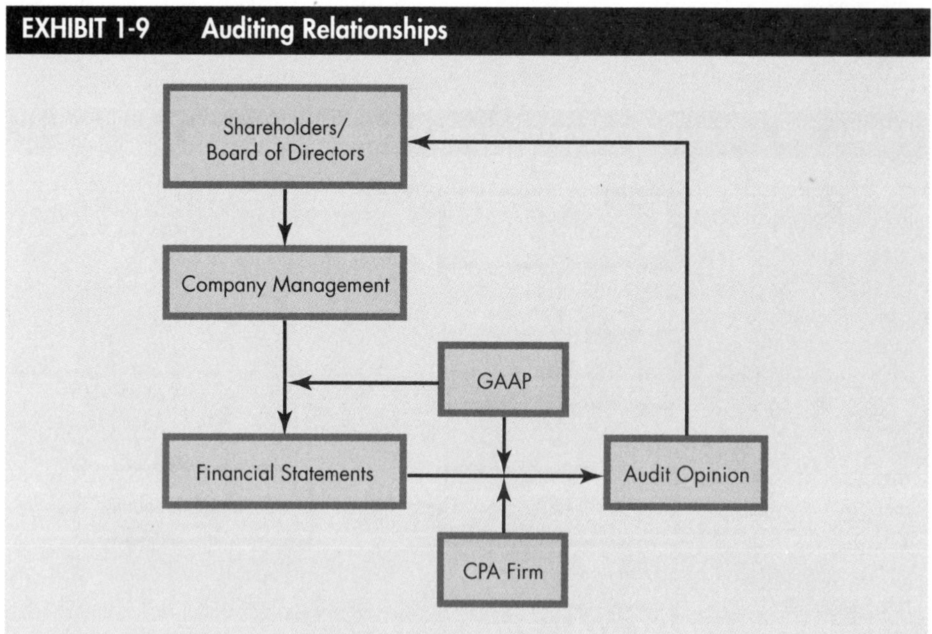

[1]More detailed descriptions of the accounting profession are provided in Appendix B.

EXHIBIT 1-10 An Auditor's Report

To the Stockholders and
Board of Directors of Merck & Co., Inc.:

We have audited the accompanying consolidated balance sheet of Merck & Co., Inc. (a New Jersey corporation) and subsidiaries as of December 31, 1997 and 1996, and the related consolidated statements of income, retained earnings, and cashflows for each of the three years in the period ended December 31, 1997. These financial statements are the responsibility of the company's management. Our responsibility is to express an opinion on these financial statements based on our audits.

We conducted our audits in accordance with generally accepted auditing standards. Those standards require that we plan and perform the audit to obtain reasonable assurance about whether the financial statements are free of material misstatement. An audit includes examining, on a test basis, evidence supporting the amounts and disclosures in the financial statements. An audit also includes assessing the accounting principles used and significant estimates made by management, as well as evaluating the overall financial statement presentation. We believe that our audits provide a reasonable basis for our opinion.

In our opinion, the financial statements referred to above present fairly, in all material respects, the financial position of Merck & Co., Inc. and subsidiaries as of December 31, 1997 and 1996, and the results of their operations and cash flows for each of the three years in the period ended December 31, 1997, in conformity with generally accepted accounting principles.

New York, New York ARTHUR ANDERSEN LLP
January 27, 1998

ond, even if auditors were to examine every transaction, collusion between two parties could make the detection of an error virtually impossible.

The third paragraph contains the **auditor's opinion**. The opinion reflects the auditor's professional judgment regarding whether the financial statements are fairly presented in accordance with GAAP. Some readers mistakenly assume that auditors "certify" the financial statements. Auditors do not provide financial statement readers with that level of assurance. Auditors do not guarantee the correctness of the financial statements. Auditors merely express an educated professional judgment based on audit tests conducted according to acceptable professional standards.

An analogy can be drawn to a medical doctor diagnosing a patient. Based on a series of appropriate tests, the doctor develops a diagnosis. In many cases, the doctor cannot be absolutely certain of the diagnosis. This is why, for example, exploratory surgery is sometimes necessary. Doctors do not issue guarantees, and neither do auditors.

The report that appears in Exhibit 1-10 is an unqualified opinion, indicating that Arthur Andersen has no reservations about the reasonableness of Merck's financial statements. However, a variety of concerns may arise that would cause the auditor to qualify the opinion or to include additional explanatory material. We know, for example, that there are several acceptable methods of accounting for inventory. If a company were to change its inventory method from one year to the next, the comparability of the financial statements for those years would be impaired, and financial statement readers would certainly want to be aware of such a situation. Because of this, changes in accounting methods are noted in the auditor's report.

ECONOMIC CONSEQUENCES AND MANAGERIAL PREFERENCES FOR ACCOUNTING PRINCIPLES

The selection of accounting principles occurs at two levels. First, the FASB determines which principles constitute GAAP. In a number of instances, however, the FASB allows the use of more than one method. Thus, corporate managers also make accounting policy decisions. Which criteria are used by the FASB and corporate managers to select accounting principles?

The FASB's primary objective is to select accounting principles that provide useful information to financial statement readers. However, businesses incur costs to generate the information required by the FASB. Thus, the FASB attempts to balance the costs and benefits of its rulings.

Some members of the financial community suggest that corporate managers act in the same way. For example, in choosing an inventory method, managers balance the costs of implementing each method with the quality of the information that each method yields. A more sophisticated view recognizes that accounting principles have economic consequences to managers and their firms, and that these consequences are considered by managers when choosing accounting principles. Beyond implementation costs, accounting principles can affect the wealth of managers and firms via (1) compensation plans, (2) debt contracts, and (3) political costs.

Compensation Plans

Many corporations pay their top managers a fixed salary plus an annual bonus, which is often a percentage of reported net income. A number of bonus agreements include a floor and a ceiling on the bonus. The floor requires that net income must exceed a predetermined amount before the bonus is activated. The ceiling places a limit on the size of the bonus; once the annual bonus reaches the ceiling, additional increases in net income no longer increase the bonus.

Bonus plans are intended to align the interests of managers and shareholders. Managers frequently face alternative courses of action, where one course is in their best interest, and another course is in the shareholders' best interest. For example, a manager's career might be aided by expanding the business (empire building), even when such expansion is not particularly profitable and is not in the shareholders' best interest. Expansion may result in more prestige and visibility for the firm and its managers, thus enhancing a manager's employment opportunities. Because (1) bonus plans motivate managers to make decisions that increase net income and (2) increased net income is usually in the shareholders' best interest, the goals of these two groups come more in line when a manager's compensation depends on reported net income.

Given that managers' compensation is tied to reported accounting earnings, how would we expect managers to select accounting principles? Most managers probably consider the effect that different accounting principles have on net income, and consequently on their compensation. In particular, bonuses often motivate managers to select accounting methods that increase reported net income.

Debt Contracts

Lenders are concerned about limiting their risk and maximizing the probability that principal and interest will be paid. **Debt contracts** between borrowers and lenders can help accomplish this. Many of these contracts impose constraints on the behavior of borrowers. For example, some contracts limit the total amount of debt a borrower can incur. In such cases, measurement of the borrower's debt is based on the liabilities reported in the balance sheet. As another example, some contracts limit the cash dividends a borrower can distribute. This limitation is defined in terms of retained earnings, a component of owners' equity that appears on the balance sheet. Penalties exist for violating debt contracts. These include

1. an interest rate increase,
2. an increase in collateral (assets pledged to secure the debt),
3. a one-time renegotiation fee, and
4. an acceleration in the maturity date.

Because these contracts are defined in terms of financial statement numbers, the use of accounting principles that increase reported net income can reduce the chances of contract violation. Accordingly, the likelihood of violating debt contracts is another influence on managers' accounting policy choices.

Political Costs

Federal and state governments have the power to regulate many operations of a business. Pollutant emissions and employment practices are just two illustrations. Governments also have the power to tax corporations. Because regulation and taxation are costly to firms, managers can be expected to take actions that minimize these costs. Because these costs are imposed via the political process, they are referred to as **political costs**.

Some accountants suggest that highly profitable firms are more exposed to political costs than less profitable ones. Relatively profitable firms are more likely to be the target of antitrust investigations or special tax assessments. For example, in the mid-1970s, firms in the oil industry earned unusually high profits due to a steep rise in oil prices. As a result, Congress enacted the Windfall Profits Tax, which subjected these companies to an additional tax on their earnings. More recently, Microsoft, Inc. has been the target of intense scrutiny by federal regulators because of its dominance in the computer operating system market and its resultant profitability.

Some accountants also argue that larger firms are more susceptible to regulation and taxation because their size attracts more attention. Accordingly, the managers of larger firms are particularly motivated to undertake actions that minimize political costs. One of these actions is the selection of accounting principles that reduce reported net income. Note that compensation plans and debt contracts motivate managers to select accounting principles that increase reported income, whereas political costs have the opposite effect.

The Two Roles of Financial Accounting

At the beginning of this chapter, the informational role of financial accounting was emphasized. From this perspective, both the FASB and corporate managers select accounting principles that yield the most useful information. However, as shown above, accounting principles also have economic consequences. These consequences arise in several ways. First, accounting serves as a basis for contracting. That is, some contracts (compensation plans and debt contracts) are based on accounting numbers. Because different accounting principles result in different accounting numbers, the choice of accounting principles can modify the terms of these contracts. Second, accounting principles may affect a firm's exposure to political costs, such as taxes and regulation. Finally, the costs to implement different accounting principles vary. Some accounting principles are quite complex and costly, whereas others are rather simple.

For all these reasons, accounting principles can affect the wealth of a firm and its managers. The managers have an obvious incentive to select the principles that increase their wealth. Such an incentive may conflict with the notion that managers select accounting principles to provide useful information. This implies that financial statement readers must carefully evaluate the accounting principles used by a firm. The selection may not result in the most useful financial statement information. In subsequent chapters, managers' selections of accounting principles will be examined from both informational and economic incentive perspectives.

The Political Nature of Accounting Standard Setting

Economic incentives associated with accounting principles might motivate an additional element of managerial behavior. As mentioned in an earlier section, the FASB conducts an elaborate due process procedure prior to issuing an accounting standard. This process provides corporate managers an opportunity to lobby the FASB. What underlies their comments to the board? Again, two possibilities exist. The comments may reflect managers' assessments of which principles generate the most useful financial statement information. Alternatively, their comments may also reflect, perhaps in a disguised way, how the various accounting principles will affect their wealth.

Some observers believe that the FASB has been overly responsive to the latter arguments. Of course, others believe that the FASB is not sufficiently sensitive to the effects its pronouncements have on individual managers or firms. Thus, accounting standards setting is now widely recognized as a political process in which various parties argue for the selection of the accounting principles that further their own self-interest. Some accountants believe that self-interest arguments have had a negative effect on the usefulness of the information required by some FASB rulings.

ETHICS AND ACCOUNTING

Accountants have a significant responsibility to the public. This responsibility exists because outside shareholders, creditors, employees, and others rely on financial statements in making various business decisions. Business organizations employ internal accountants to prepare financial statements. These statements are then audited by a firm of independent CPAs. Both the internal accountants and the external auditors have a responsibility to perform their tasks with integrity and due care.

Various accounting organizations promote high standards of ethical behavior. One example is the American Institute of Certified Public Accountants (AICPA), which is a professional organization that serves CPAs who work for public accounting firms or other organizations (such as corporations). Its *Code of Professional Conduct* emphasizes the obligation of CPAs to serve the public interest, and their responsibility to act with integrity, objectivity, independence, and due professional care.

In a given situation, formalized codes of ethics can often help in deciding the proper course of action. However, some situations are sufficiently complex that the codes do not provide clear guidance. Fortunately, ethicists have developed frameworks for examining ambiguous ethical situations. Two of these frameworks, utilitarianism and deontology, are briefly described next.

WHAT WOULD YOU DO?

Lifetime Products, Inc., sold part of its business to its chief executive and to the wife of its board of directors' chairman. Some of Lifetime's shareholders subsequently filed a lawsuit seeking to rescind the sale.

Why might Lifetime's shareholders be upset? Would you have authorized the sale?

Utilitarianism judges the moral correctness of an act based solely on its consequences. According to this perspective, the act that should be taken is the one that maximizes overall favorable consequences (net of unfavorable ones). Consequences not only to the actor but to all parties should be considered.

The proponents of **deontology** assert that the consequences of an act do not exclusively dictate moral correctness. They believe that the underlying nature of the act itself influences its correctness. However, within deontology are two different perspectives. Some deontologists feel that the nature of an act is the only thing to be considered in assessing its moral correctness. For example, they believe that killing and lying are morally wrong under any circumstances. Other deontologists assert that the nature of the act and its consequences in a particular situation should both be considered.

To illustrate these approaches, imagine you are in the process of filling out an expense report after having just completed a business trip. Your employer does not reimburse child-care costs while away from home, yet most of your colleagues (including your immediate supervisor) feel that child care is a legitimate expense. They recoup this expenditure by overstating the cost of meals (most restaurants provide you with a blank receipt). Is it ethically correct for you to overstate your meal cost?

Many deontologists would assert that the act of lying is ethically wrong, and that falsifying an expense report is the equivalent of lying. Utilitarians, on the other hand, would examine the consequences of the action, and it is not clear that their analysis would reach the same conclusion. An assessment would need to be made of how you versus the shareholders would be affected by the falsification.

To develop a strong personal code of ethics, each of us must understand how we think about ethical situations. We suggest that you consider how utilitarianism and deontology can be used to analyze ethical situations, and that you assess which of those approaches, if either, is consistent with your own moral framework.

KEY TERMS

Accounting 2
Accounting information systems 4
Accounting Principles Board (APB) 11
Annual report 8
Assets 6
Audit 14
Auditor's opinion 15
Balance sheet 6
Compensation plans 16
Debt contracts 16
Deontology 19
Expected return 9
Expenses 7
Financial accounting 2
Financial Accounting Standards Board (FASB) 11
Financing activities 8
Generally accepted accounting principles (GAAP) 11
Generally accepted auditing standards (GAAP) 14
Historical cost 6
Income statement 7
Investing activities 8
Liabilities 7
Managerial accounting 4
Net income 7
Net loss 7
Nonbusiness organizations 4
Notes 8
Operating activities 8
Owners' equity 7
Political costs 17
Revenues 7
Risk 9
Securities and Exchange Commission (SEC) 12
Statement of cash flows 8
Statements of Financial Accounting Standards (SFASs) 11
Tax accounting 4
Transactions 5
Utilitarianism 18

SUMMARY OF LEARNING OBJECTIVES

1. **Define accounting and identify its objectives.**
   Accounting is the systematic process of measuring the economic activity of an entity. The primary objective of accounting is to provide useful information to those who make business and economic decisions. Users of accounting information include present and potential investors and creditors, investment advisers, corporate managers, employees, unions, and government regulators. A secondary objective of accounting is to help develop and enforce contracts. That is, in certain instances, people and organizations find the use of accounting numbers in contracts to be quite helpful.
2. **Distinguish among the three major types of accounting.**
   The three major types of accounting are based on the identity of the user of the information. Financial accounting provides information to outsiders who do not have access to the firm's confidential records. This includes shareholders, creditors, employees, unions, and government regulators. Managerial accounting provides information to corporate managers to help them with their decisions. Tax accounting has two elements: (1) Tax compliance involves the periodic preparation of tax forms as required by various taxing authorities. The purpose of this is to calculate a firm's tax liability. It takes place after transactions have been completed. (2) Tax planning takes place before transactions have been undertaken. Its purpose is to structure transactions so as to minimize their tax effect.
3. **List the three primary financial statements and briefly summarize the information contained in each.**
   The balance sheet, income statement, and statement of cash flows are the three primary financial statements. The balance sheet shows a firm's assets, liabilities, and owners' equity at a point in time. The income statement summarizes a firm's revenues and expenses for a period of time. The difference between revenues and expenses is net income (or loss). The statement of cash flows shows a firm's inflows and outflows of cash for a period of time. The three categories of this statement are cash flows from (1) operating activities, (2) investing activities, and (3) financing activities.
4. **Identify financial statement users and the decisions they make.**
   The main users of financial statements are shareholders, creditors, management, and government regulators. Shareholders decide whether to buy, hold, or sell shares in the firm. Creditors must determine whether to extend credit and on what terms. Because financial statements are a performance report on corporate management, managers are concerned about the effect of their decisions on the financial statements. Government regulators use financial statements to determine if firms are complying with various laws and regulations.
5. **Define generally accepted accounting principles and explain how they are determined.**
   Generally accepted accounting principles (GAAP) are the most widely used set of accounting rules. Currently, the FASB sets GAAP. The FASB's authority rests on (1) the acceptance of its rulings by the financial community and (2) the delegation by the SEC of its legislative authority to determine GAAP for large, publicly held corporations. Prior to issuing a new ruling, the FASB conducts an elaborate process that permits participation by all interested parties.
6. **Describe the role of auditing.**
   A firm's management is responsible for preparing financial statements. Yet those same statements are a performance report on management. Because of

this conflict of interest, the financial statements of many organizations are audited by a firm of independent CPAs. Auditors examine a sample of an organization's transactions to provide a reasonable basis for expressing an opinion on the fairness of the financial statements. CPAs do not certify financial statements; they merely express a professional opinion regarding their fairness in conformity with GAAP.

7. **List the economic consequences of accounting principles.**
Accounting principles not only affect the quality of the information contained in financial statements, but they also affect the wealth of various parties. Accounting principles have economic consequences because of implementation costs, compensation plans, debt contracts, and political costs. Managers therefore have certain preferences for accounting principles that are not necessarily related to the inherent quality of the resulting information. Accordingly, care must be taken in interpreting both financial statements and managers' recommendations about accounting standards.

8. **Assess the importance of ethics in accounting.**
Accountants have an important responsibility to the public that arises because financial statements are used by large numbers of people for a variety of purposes. It is essential that accountants adhere to the highest levels of ethical conduct.

QUESTIONS

1-1 The chapter discussed two general functions of financial accounting. Briefly describe them.

1-2 List the three types (specialty areas) of accounting. Who are the users of each type of accounting? How do the needs of these users differ?

1-3 Compare the cash flows of a business to its profits. How do cash flows differ from income or profits?

1-4 Describe the financial accounting process. Discuss its relationship to decision makers.

1-5 List the three major financial statements. What information do they contain? How are they different?

1-6 Write a short essay describing four different users of accounting reports and indicate their particular interests.

1-7 What decisions do present and future owners of a business need to make? How are financial statements helpful?

1-8 What information do present and potential creditors need to make decisions? How are financial statements helpful?

1-9 The selection of accounting principles can affect a firm's manager's wealth. Describe these effects.

1-10 An old joke goes as follows:
- Questioner: What is 2 + 2?
- Accountant: Whatever you want it to be.

What do you think this joke is designed to communicate?

1-11 Accounting principle selection has economic effects. How might this affect managers' behavior?

1-12 Is accounting standard setting an art or a science? Why?

1-13 What considerations are used by the FASB in setting GAAP?

1-14 What is the relationship between the FASB and the SEC? What role does Congress play in setting accounting standards?

1-15 Why do many businesses that are not regulated by the SEC elect to have their financial statements audited?

1-16 A number of situations exists where more than one accounting principle is acceptable. Why is this advisable?

EXERCISES

Critical Thinking

Conceptual Distinctions: Maps Versus Financial Statements

1-17 Some accountants draw an analogy between developing financial statements and cartography (map making). They maintain that just as maps reflect the geographical reality of the area under study, so should financial statements reflect the economic reality of the organization. Critique this position by discussing the differences between a map and a financial statement.

Critical Thinking

Essay: Measurement Criteria

1-18 Write a short essay identifying three measurement criteria that should be followed by accountants. Indicate why each criterion is important.

Identification of Accounting Transactions

1-19 Which of the following transactions or events should be recorded in the firm's accounting records? Explain your answer.

a. Cash is received from a sale previously made on credit.
b. A year after obtaining a bank loan, a business owes the bank interest charges. These charges remain unpaid at the end of the year.
c. A professional baseball player, hitting .425, expects a bonus under his incentive contract for leading the league in hitting for the season. The bonus was "pegged" at $1,000 for every point that he exceeded the batting target of .375. How much should the baseball player record in his checkbook at the end of the season?
d. An employer and a labor union sign a new collective bargaining agreement.
e. An item of factory equipment is removed from service. The item has a book value of $10,000. It is determined that the equipment is worthless.

PROBLEMS

Critical Thinking

Conceptual Discussion: Audits and Loan Applications

1-20 Refer to the T-shirt business described at the beginning of this chapter. The owner has decided to expand her business by trying to secure a bank loan. After meeting with the bank loan officer, she asked for your help in answering several questions before proceeding with the loan application.

a. Required: What is an audit, and why would a bank require an audit before granting a loan?
b. Are audits expensive? Are they time-consuming? Will an audit delay her application? Why?
c. Identify several alternative types of loans that the owner might consider.
d. The owner is considering whether to purchase and install a computer-based accounting system to replace the checkbook that she has been using. What information should the owner gather?

Review of Auditor's Opinion

1-21 Following is the auditor's opinion expressed on the financial statements of Kleen-ware, Inc.:

AN AUDITOR'S REPORT
The Board of Directors
Kleen-ware, Incorporated and Subsidiaries (the Company)

We have audited the accompanying consolidated balance sheets of Kleen-ware, Inc. and subsidiaries (the company) as of December 31, 1997 and 1998, and the related consolidated statements of income, changes in shareholders' equity, and cash flows for years then ended. These financial statements are the responsibility of the company's management. Our responsibility is to express an opinion on these financial statements based on our audits.

We conducted our audits in accordance with generally accepted auditing standards. Those standards require that we plan and perform the audit to obtain reasonable assurance about whether the financial statements are free of material misstatement. An audit includes examining, on a test basis, evidence supporting the amounts and disclosures in the financial statements. An audit also includes assessing the accounting principles used and significant estimates made by management, as well as evaluating the overall financial statement presentation. We believe that our audits provide a reasonable basis for our opinion.

In our opinion, the 1997 and 1998 financial statements referred to above present fairly, in all material respects, the consolidated financial position of the Company at December 31, 1997 and 1998, and the consolidated results of its operations and its cash flows for the years then ended in conformity with generally accepted accounting principles.

Max Ernst & Company
Milwaukee, Wisconsin
February 14, 1999

Required

Review the following auditor's opinion. Identify the specific sentence indicating the auditor's opinion. What other useful information is shown in this opinion? Why is it useful?

Ethics

Company Perquisites and Cash Transactions

1-22 Assume that you are employed by a law firm as a staff accountant. The firm has purchased four season tickets for the Colorado Rockies (a baseball franchise). Your boss, one of the partners in the firm, has offered individual tickets to you, but also asked you to pay $10 for each ticket. Since they are $14 tickets, you are happy to get a bargain. You are even happier to get a chance to go to the game because tickets are in short supply.

Next month, while reviewing the financial statements for your department, you are unable to find the $40 of cash receipts for these tickets. Since you know that the firm has purchased these tickets, you wonder what happened to your $40 payment. After discussing this matter with several other junior staff members who had also paid the partner for tickets to Rockies' games, you guess that the partner has pocketed the money and not reported the revenue to the other partners.

Required

a. What should or would you do? Why?
b. Would it make any difference if the firm were a single proprietorship and not a partnership? Why?
c. Would it make any difference if all the partners followed the same procedure and pocketed the ticket money? Why?
d. Is this an issue that should be reported to any other parties such as the Internal Revenue Service, the State Auditor, or the Attorney General? Why?

Conceptual Discussion: Choosing Accounting Principles

1-23 The Homestead Furniture Store has just begun selling a new line of inventory. Management must now decide on an inventory method to use. Method A results in higher net income and higher assets than Method B. Method A is more costly to implement. What advice would you give to the chief executive officer?

Essay: Users of Accounting Information

1-24 Write a short essay describing how information requirements might differ between internal and external users of accounting.

Conceptual Discussion: Historical Information Versus Forecasts

1-25 Some members of the financial community believe that annual reports should not only contain historical financial statements but should also contain forecasts by management of future results. Evaluate this proposal.

Ethics

Reporting Errors in Wages

1-26 At the end of every year, all employers send W-2 forms to their employees. These forms report the employees' wages and the amount of tax withheld by the employer. These forms are the government's only record of earned wages. Assume that an employee receives a W-2 form that understates the wages but correctly states the withholding amount. Ethically, how should the employee handle this situation?

Essay (or Discussion): Identifying Useful Information

1-27 The auditor's report, shown in Exhibit 1-10, contains much useful information. Write a short essay, or form small groups in your class, discussing the kinds of information you think auditors should provide. You may identify specific kinds of information that you think would be helpful to an investor or creditor. Indicate why you think such information would be helpful.

Personal Experience: Uses of Accounting Information

1-28 Describe two ways that you have already used accounting information in your personal decisions.

Essay: Expectations and Uses of Accounting Information

1-29 Write a short essay indicating how you might use accounting in a professional or business capacity.

Essay: Changes in Accounting Disclosure Requirements

1-30 The accounting profession considered increasing its required disclosures and the type of information that is required from public companies. The following paragraphs appeared in The Wall Street Journal (August 26, 1993, p. A4):

A key accounting group calls for a sharp increase in the amount of information companies must disclose in their annual reports. The prospect alarms corporate financial officers.

If adopted, the recommendations could force companies to change the way they figure profits. It could make them disclose more data about the competitive pressures they face. They could transform the auditor's report from the current boilerplate message to a longer and much more revealing statement about the company's health. Information about changes in the firm's product prices in response to competitive price shifts would be required.

The new requirements would favor more segmenting of data so that sales and profits for each company unit would be shown. More meaningful breakdowns of company data would be required. Much more data would be required from larger companies than from small companies.

Required

Write a short memo to the key accounting group noted in the article from the perspective of a company president, responding to the proposed changes in accounting disclosures.

Essay: Changing How Profits Are Measured

1-31 An accounting group has adopted new definitions of earnings or profits. These changes include the following:

- Reporting comprehensive earnings, along with net income, for the company. This could result in several new profit numbers for most companies.
- Comprehensive earnings include external market effects of changes in the value of foreign currency and changes in the prices of investments (shares) in other companies.

Required

Write a short essay supporting or criticizing these changes in the definitions of income or profit.

Internet

Internet Search: CPA Firms

1-32 Bowling Green State University maintains the following two Web sites containing a "Directory of CPA Firms":

www.cpafirms.com
(www.eyi.com)

Access one of these sites and locate the Web page for Ernst & Young, a large ("Big Five") accounting firm.

Required

a. List six countries (other than the United States, Canada, and the United Kingdom) where Ernst and Young (E&Y) has a presence.
b. On a worldwide basis, list the services that E&Y member firms can provide to their clients and list the industries on which E&Y focuses.
c. In the United States, list the services that E&Y member firms can provide to their clients and list the industries on which E&Y focuses.

continued

d. Within the United States, identify the career paths available at E&Y.
e. The E&Y office nearest to your university is located in which city?

Internet Search: SEC

1-33 Go to the home page of the United States Securities and Exchange Commission (SEC) located at:

www.sec.gov/

Required

a. Briefly describe the role of the SEC. Which laws does it enforce?
b. How many commissioners sit on the board of the SEC? Who is the current chairperson of the SEC? Who has the authority to appoint the chairperson?
c. List three cities where regional or district offices of the SEC are located. (Hint: Washington, D.C., is not a regional or district office.)
d. Identify the principal divisions of the SEC.

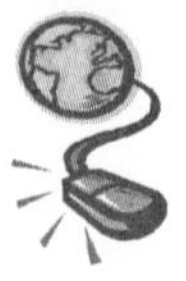

Internet Search: Accounting Careers

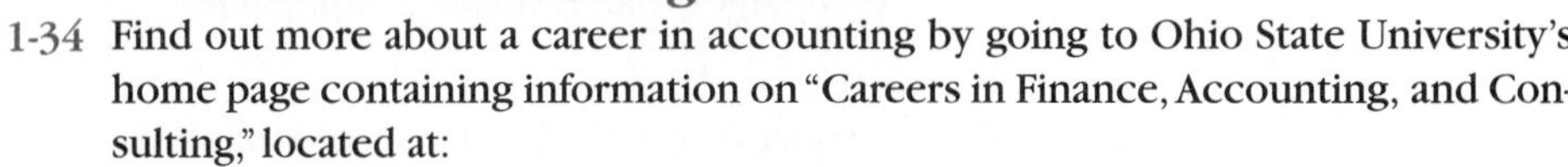

1-34 Find out more about a career in accounting by going to Ohio State University's home page containing information on "Careers in Finance, Accounting, and Consulting," located at:

www.cob.ohio-state.edu/dept/acctmis/students/careers.html

Required

a. List the key job functions in accounting.
b. List the key job skills required for a career in accounting.
c. List the key job contexts in accounting.

Internet Search: CPA, CIA, CMA

1-35 Certifications in accounting include the Certificate of Public Accounting (CPA), Certificate of Internal Auditing (CIA), and Certificate of Management Accounting (CMA). Certification examinations must be passed before gaining these professional qualifications. Go to the following Web sites and identify the subject areas covered in each exam.

Exam	Site
CPA	**www.ais-cpa.com**
CIA	**www.theiia.org**
CMA	**www.rutgers.edu/Accounting/raw/ima/ima.htm**

c h a p t e r

2

Basic Concepts of Financial Accounting

LEARNING OBJECTIVES

1. Define the terms assets, liabilities, and owners' equity.
2. Explain why the balance sheet must balance.
3. Describe revenues and expenses.
4. Use the basic accounting equation to analyze transactions.
5. Prepare simple balance sheets and income statements.
6. Describe the relationship between the balance sheet and the income statement.
7. Distinguish between the accrual basis and the cash basis of accounting.
8. Explain the differences between the balance sheets of sole proprietorships and those of corporations.

INTRODUCTION

This chapter describes the financial accounting process. It shows how information about transactions and events is accumulated to produce the balance sheet and the income statement. This early presentation is quite basic; subsequent chapters will present more complex issues. Also, although the cash flow effects of various transactions are addressed in this chapter, the statement of cash flows is actually covered in detail in Chapter 5, "Statement of Cash Flows."

THE BASIC ACCOUNTING EQUATION

A balance sheet, illustrated in Exhibit 2-1, contains three sections: assets, liabilities, and owners' equity. The total of the left side (assets) equals the total of the right side (liabilities and owners' equity).

Financial accounting is based on one simple, three-element equation, referred to as the **basic accounting equation:**

ASSETS = LIABILITIES + OWNERS' EQUITY

The basic accounting equation is simply an algebraic form of the balance sheet. The following sections elaborate on the definitions of the equation's elements.

EXHIBIT 2-1 A Balance Sheet

Newton Company
Balance Sheet
December 31, 2000

Assets		**Liabilities and Owners' Equity**	
Cash	$ 5,000	Liabilities	
Accounts receivable	7,000	Accounts payable	$ 8,000
Inventory	10,000	Notes payable	2,000
Equipment	7,000	Total liabilities	10,000
		Owners' equity	19,000
Total assets	$29,000	Total liabilities and owners' equity	$29,000

Assets

Assets are valuable resources that are owned or controlled by a firm. They represent probable future economic benefits and arise as the result of past transactions or events. Examples of assets include cash, accounts receivable (the right to receive cash in the future), inventory (merchandise manufactured or acquired for resale to customers), equipment, land, and investments.

Two aspects of the definition deserve emphasis. First, the term probable suggests that in some situations accountants are not certain that future economic benefits exist. Many business owners, for example, feel that a loyal customer base and a highly skilled workforce enhance a firm's competitive advantage. Although few would argue with this, the link in any particular situation between customer loyalty or workforce skill and future benefits is sufficiently uncertain that these factors are not recognized as assets.

Second, assets must be owned or controlled by the firm. This component of the definition is designed to exclude public goods from balance sheets. Although many firms benefit from roadways, sewers, national defense, and the public education system, for example, these items are not owned by individual firms. Because of this, they do not appear on balance sheets of individual firms.

Liabilities

Liabilities are present obligations of the firm. They are probable future sacrifices of economic benefits (usually cash) that arise as the result of past transactions or events. Common examples of liabilities are notes payable (written obligations), accounts payable (obligations to suppliers arising in the normal course of business), and taxes payable.

Two aspects of the definition of liabilities need elaboration. First, as with assets, the term probable is used. This is an important part of the definition. Although in some instances, the existence of a liability is virtually certain (as when one arises from obtaining a bank loan), other situations are less clear. For example, consider a firm that has been sued. At the inception of the suit, the outcome may be highly uncertain, but as the litigation proceeds, it may seem more likely (but not certain) that the firm will be forced to pay some amount. Accountants need to exercise judgment in determining the existence of a liability. They do so by assessing whether a potential future sacrifice is probable.

Second, the definition requires that liabilities arise from past transactions or events. Consider a definition that did not include this criterion. Most firms expect to be in existence for a considerable period of time. They anticipate employing workers, buying inventory, and so on. These planned activities may well result in probable future sacrifices of economic benefits, yet the organization is not obliged to make those payments until a transaction has occurred.

Because of the "past transaction" criterion, financial accounting does not reflect **executory contracts,** which are contracts that initially involve merely an exchange of promises. For example, David Letterman's three-year contract to host a late night show for CBS stipulated that Letterman's compensation for each year was to be $14 million. At the time of contract signing, a substantive exchange had not taken place. Neither side had actually done anything. Letterman had not yet hosted the shows, and CBS had not provided payment. This type of contract is not incorporated in the financial accounting process. Subsequently, when one or both parties have performed, a substantive exchange has occurred, and then it is appropriate to reflect the transaction in the financial statements.

Owners' Equity

Owners' equity represents the owners' interest in the assets of the business. Owners can obtain an interest in their business either by making direct investments or by operating the business at a profit and retaining the profits in the firm.

Owners' equity is also referred to as the **residual interest,** a term that implies the owners' interest is what remains after creditors' claims have been honored. This can most easily be seen by rearranging the basic accounting equation:

OWNERS' EQUITY = ASSETS − LIABILITIES

This version of the equation shows that at a given point in time, if assets exceed liabilities, the excess (residual) amount is attributed to the owners. Other terms used to refer to assets minus liabilities are **net assets** and **net worth.**

The balance sheet and the original form of the basic accounting equation can be interpreted as providing two views of the business. The left side details the composition of the firm's assets: cash, inventory, and the like. It shows "what the firm has." The right side indicates the amount of financing supplied by the creditors and the amount supplied by the owners. It shows how assets were acquired. It also shows the extent to which the creditors and the owners have a claim against the assets. This will become clearer after you study the next section on transaction analysis.

TRANSACTION ANALYSIS

Transaction analysis is the central component of the financial accounting process. During this phase, the accountant identifies transactions (exchanges with other organizations), assigns monetary values (usually an exchange amount), and records the effects of the transactions on the three elements of the basic accounting equation. The remainder of this section analyzes a number of transactions.

Owners' Original Investment

Harry Jacobs has decided to open a golf and tennis store. The business is organized as a sole proprietorship. Sole proprietorships are businesses owned and operated by one individual. Keep in mind that we are concerned about the records of Harry's business; we are not interested in Harry's personal affairs. The **entity assumption** indicates that accounting records are kept for business units (entities) distinct from their owners.

Harry opens a bank account in the name of the business, Jacobs Golf and Tennis (JG&T), and deposits $50,000 of his own money. From the firm's perspective, the $50,000 deposit is a transaction (an exchange between the business and its owner), and it would be analyzed by increasing cash and owners' equity by $50,000 each. Increasing owners' equity indicates that the owner has invested $50,000 and that he has an interest in or claim against the assets to the extent of $50,000. The word **capital** is conventional terminology in sole proprietorships. It simply denotes the owners' interest in (or claim on) the assets of the business.

ASSETS	=	LIABILITIES	+	OWNERS' EQUITY
Cash				H. Jacobs, capital
(1) +$50,000				+$50,000

Notice that the equation balances for this transaction, as it does for all transactions.

Exhibit 2-2, shown later, contains a summary of all the transactions to be reviewed in this section. For simplicity, assume that all transactions occur on January 1, 2000.

Bank Loan

Harry realizes that his new business needs more cash than the $50,000 he invested. The firm applies for and is granted a $20,000 bank loan. The loan carries an interest rate of 8%, and both principal and interest are due on January 1, 2001.

This transaction increases cash and liabilities by $20,000. Liabilities increase because JG&T is obligated to repay the loan in the future; this constitutes a virtually certain sacrifice of future economic benefits. Additionally, the obligation has arisen as the result of a past transaction (having obtained the cash on January 1, 2000). The liability item that increases is notes payable. Banks usually require borrowers to sign written promises to repay loans, and the word notes indicates that JG&T has a written obligation to repay the loan.

ASSETS	=	LIABILITIES	+	OWNERS' EQUITY
Cash		Notes payable		
(2) +$20,000		+$20,000		

The equation balances for this transaction, too. Because the equality holds for all transactions, it holds for the sum of all transactions. After the first two transactions, JG&T has cash of $70,000, which equals liabilities of $20,000 plus owners' equity of $50,000.

You might be wondering about the interest on the loan. Interest is a charge for borrowing money during a specified period of time. Because this time period has just begun, no interest is immediately recorded. As you will see, interest is recorded periodically throughout the life of the loan.

Rent

JG&T enters into an agreement to lease retail space from another company. The lease is for one year, and the entire $12,000 rent is paid on January 1, 2000, the date the lease is signed. Cash obviously declines by $12,000. However, what other equation item is affected? JG&T has acquired another asset: the right to occupy the retail space for a year. This enables JG&T to carry on its normal business operations. The asset is referred to as **prepaid rent** and is assigned a value equal to its **historical cost** (exchange price on the date of acquisition). *Assets are usually recorded at their historical cost.*

	ASSETS		=	LIABILITIES	+	OWNERS' EQUITY
	Cash	Prepaid rent				
(3)	−$12,000	+$12,000				

Inventory

Inventory is merchandise acquired for resale to customers. It is an asset because firms expect to receive cash from selling it to customers.

JG&T is in the business of buying and selling sporting goods. Assume JG&T purchases goods for $30,000, **on account** (on credit). This transaction increases inventory, and because payment is not made immediately, liabilities increase. Because notes are not used for ongoing purchases from suppliers, another liability item, **accounts payable,** is increased. Accounts payable are unwritten obligations that arise in the normal course of business.

	ASSETS	=	LIABILITIES	+	OWNERS' EQUITY
	Inventory		Accounts payable		
(4)	+$30,000		+$30,000		

Equipment

Because the retail space that JG&T leased contains no equipment (cash registers, display cases, and so on), equipment must be purchased. JG&T makes a purchase for $25,000. Cash decreases, equipment increases, and total assets are unchanged.

	ASSETS		=	LIABILITIES	+	OWNERS' EQUITY
	Cash	Equipment				
(5)	−$25,000	+$25,000				

Preparation of the Balance Sheet

The last two lines in Exhibit 2-2 reflect the cumulative effect of JG&T's transactions. This summary is equivalent to the balance sheet. To prepare a balance sheet, simply summarize the various equation elements into the appropriate balance sheet format. The balance sheet for JG&T as of January 1, 2000, is shown in Exhibit 2-3 and is based directly on the last two lines of Exhibit 2-2.

Evaluation of Historical Cost

An asset's historical cost is a very good indication of its economic value to the firm at the time of acquisition. As times goes on, however, the historical cost becomes outdated. That is, it no longer reflects the asset's economic value.

Instead of valuing assets at historical cost, accountants could use other measures. For example, current replacement cost could be used. Current replacement cost is the cost of replacing the asset on the balance sheet date. Many analysts feel that this amount better reflects the value of an asset to the firm. They feel that current replacement cost is more *relevant* to financial statement readers.

EXHIBIT 2-2 Transaction Analysis

	ASSETS				LIABILITIES		OWNERS' EQUITY
	Cash	Prepaid Rent	Inventory	Equipment	Accounts Payable	Notes Payable	H. Jacobs, Capital
(1)	+50,000						+50,000
(2)	+20,000					+20,000	
(3)	−12,000	+12,000					
(4)			+30,000		+30,000		
(5)	−25,000			+25,000			
Totals	33,000	12,000	30,000	25,000	30,000	20,000	50,000
		100,000				100,000	

EXHIBIT 2-3 JG&T Balance Sheet

Jacobs Golf and Tennis
Balance Sheet
January 1, 2000

Assets		**Liabilities and Owners' Equity**	
Cash	$ 33,000	Liabilities	
Prepaid rent	12,000	Accounts payable	$ 30,000
Inventory	30,000	Notes payable	20,000
Equipment	25,000	Total liabilities	50,000
Total assets	$100,000	H. Jacobs, capital	50,000
		Total liabilities and owners' equity	$100,000

Why then does financial accounting use historical cost? Primarily because it is *reliable.* Historical cost is the result of an actual bargained transaction between two independent parties. Moreover, supporting documents, such as canceled checks, contracts, or invoices, exist to verify the amount. In contrast, current replacement cost is based on appraisals and estimates, which accountants view as "soft" numbers. In general, the accounting profession believes that the use of historical cost provides the best trade-off between relevance and reliability.

REVENUES AND EXPENSES

The transactions examined thus far are related to start-up activities. Businesses are organized to earn a profit, and this section discusses revenue and expense transactions. All transactions reviewed in this section are summarized in Exhibit 2-4.

Revenues

Revenues are inflows of assets (or reductions in liabilities) in exchange for providing goods and services to customers. Suppose that during January JG&T provides services (golf lessons) to customers and charges them $600. The customers pay $200 immediately and agree to pay the remaining $400 in February. This transaction meets both aspects of the preceding definition. First, JG&T has received assets of $600. The receipt of the $200 is obviously an asset inflow. The $400 to be received next month is also an asset and is called an **account receivable.** Second, the services were provided by the end of January. That is, they have been earned; JG&T has done everything it has promised to do. Accordingly, revenue of $600 is recorded in January.

This transaction increases cash by $200, accounts receivable by $400, and owners' equity by $600. Why has owners' equity increased by $600? The assets of the business have expanded, and it must be decided who has a claim against (or an interest in) those assets. Because this transaction has not increased the creditors' claims, the owners' interests must have increased. This conclusion makes sense. Owners are the primary risk-takers, and they do so with the hope of expanding their wealth. If the firm enters into a profitable transaction, the owners' wealth (their interest in the business) should expand.

	ASSETS		=	LIABILITIES	+	OWNERS' EQUITY
	Cash	Accounts receivable				H. Jacobs, capital
(6)	+$200	+$400				+$600 (service revenue)

Of course, we cannot be absolutely certain that the customers will eventually pay the additional $400. This concern will be addressed in a subsequent chapter. For now, assume we are quite confident about this future receipt.

This transaction holds an important lesson. Although revenue equals $600, only $200 of cash has been received. Thus, from an accounting perspective, revenue does not necessarily equal cash inflow. Although revenue is recorded when assets are received in exchange for goods and services, the asset received need not be cash. This underscores the need for both an income statement to summarize earnings and a statement of cash flows to identify the sources and uses of cash.

EXHIBIT 2-4 Revenue and Expense Transactions

	ASSETS					LIABILITIES				OWNERS' EQUITY	
	Cash	Accts. Receivable	Prepaid Rent	Inventory	Equipment	Accts. Payable	Notes Payable	Unearned Revenue	Util. Payable	H. Jacobs, Capital	
Bal	33,000	0	12,000	30,000	25,000	30,000	20,000	0	0	50,000	
(6)	+200	+400								+600	(service revenue)
(7)	+100							+100			
(8)	−700									−700	(salary expense)
(9)									+120	−120	(utility expense)
(10)		+4,000								+4,000	(sales revenue)
				−2,200						−2,200	(cost of goods sold)
Totals	32,600	4,400	12,000	27,800	25,000	30,000	20,000	100	120	51,580	
	101,800					101,800					

As another illustration, assume that on January 10 a customer pays $100, in advance, for golf lessons. The lessons are to be rendered during the last week in January and the first week in February. Has a revenue transaction occurred on January 10? No. A requirement for revenue recognition is that the services must be rendered. As of January 10, this has not yet occurred. The transaction increases cash, but the owners' claim on assets has not increased. Instead, the *customer* now has a claim on the assets. If JG&T does not provide the lessons, the customer has the right to expect a refund; JG&T has a liability. It is obligated to either provide the lessons, which have a $100 value, or return the $100 payment. In either case, a $100 liability exists on January 10. **Unearned revenue** is the liability that has increased. Another appropriate name is **advances from customers.**

Reality Check 2-1 illustrates a revenue situation in the franchising industry.

	ASSETS	=	LIABILITIES	+	OWNERS' EQUITY
	Cash		Unearned revenue		
(7)	+$100		+$100		

Expenses

Expenses occur when resources are consumed in order to generate revenue. For example, during January, JG&T employed salespersons and golf instructors. Assume these employees earned total wages of $700, which were paid in cash by JG&T. Because JG&T used the employees' services during January, this is an expense transaction for that month.

The transaction decreases cash and owners' equity by $700. The decrease in cash is obvious. Why does owners' equity decrease? An analogy can be drawn to revenue.

REALITY CHECK 2-1

Franchisors are firms that sell the right to market their products. McDonald's Corporation, for example, sells the right to operate its restaurants to other businesses and individuals. These franchisees usually pay a fee at the time of signing the contract, plus ongoing fees based on the amount of their sales.

In exchange for the initial fee at the time of contract signing, a franchisor is required to help the franchisee select an appropriate site, supervise construction, train employees, and install the franchisee's accounting system.

Required

When should the franchisor recognize the revenue associated with the initial fee?

Solution

Many franchisors prefer to recognize the revenue when the cash is received at the time of contract signing. This enables them to show improved performance. However, are the revenue recognition rules met at that point in time? In particular, has the franchisor performed the promised services? No, it has not. Because of this, the FASB has ruled that revenue from the initial franchise fee cannot be recognized as revenue until all the initial services have been performed. In general, this occurs when the franchisee opens for business.

When assets increase because of profitable operations, the owners' interest in the firm's assets expands. With expenses, when assets decrease in order to generate revenue, the owners' interest in the firm's assets declines.

	ASSETS	=	LIABILITIES	+	OWNERS' EQUITY
	Cash				H. Jacobs, capital
(8)	– $700				– $700 (salary expense)

Exhibit 2-5 graphically depicts this analysis. The first rectangle reflects JG&T's assets, liabilities, and owners' equity before the salary expense transaction. The second rectangle reflects the situation after the expense transaction. Assets and the owners' claim have both decreased.

EXHIBIT 2-5 Expense Transation Analysis

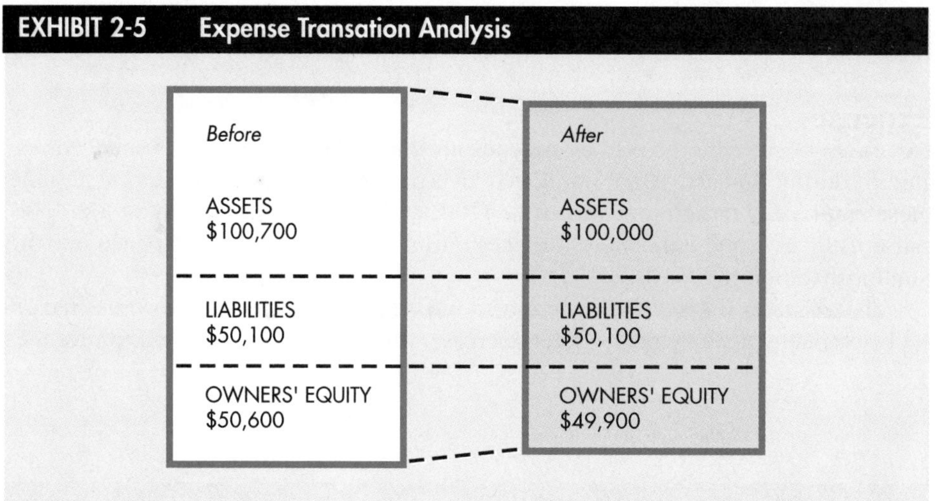

Consider another example. Assume that JG&T receives its utility bill on January 31 for electricity used during January. The bill is for $120. JG&T elects not to pay immediately. Even though cash has not been paid, an expense transaction has occurred in January. JG&T has consumed resources (electricity) in order to generate revenue.

Because JG&T is now obligated to the utility company, liabilities increase by $120, and owners' equity decreases by $120. Owners' equity decreases because assets have not changed, yet the creditors' claims have increased by $120. There is no alternative but to recognize that owners' equity has decreased by $120.

	ASSETS	=	LIABILITIES	+	OWNERS' EQUITY
			Utilities payable		H. Jacobs, capital
(9)			+ $120		– $120 (utility expense)

Exhibit 2-6 displays the analysis graphically. It shows the assets remaining fixed while (1) the creditors' claims increase and (2) the owners' claims decrease. Also note that expenses do not necessarily equal cash outflows. Goods and services can be consumed to generate revenue without a cash outflow.

EXHIBIT 2-6 Expense Transaction Analysis

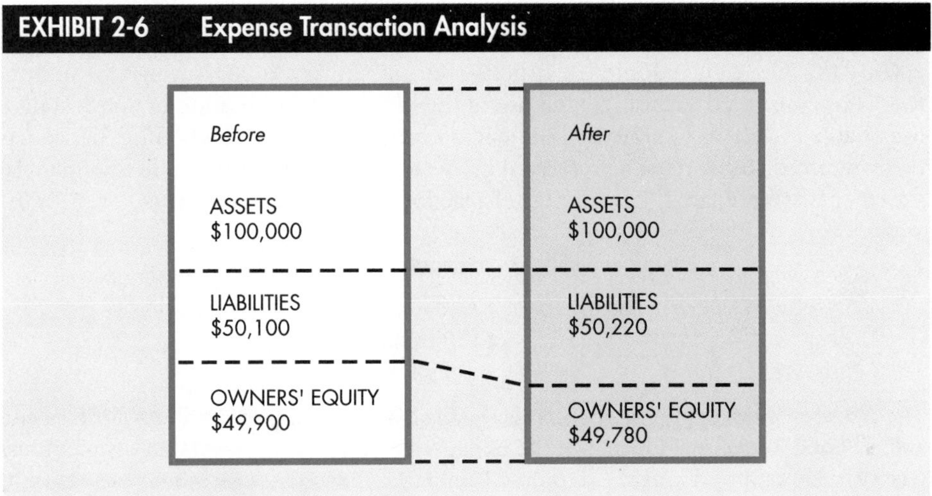

Sales of Inventory

Sales of inventory contain both revenue and expense components. Assume that JG&T makes sales on account (credit) during the month totaling $4,000. The cost of the inventory to JG&T was $2,200.

A revenue transaction exists because an asset (accounts receivable) has been obtained, and the goods have been provided to customers. An expense transaction exists because the asset inventory has been consumed to generate the revenue. That is, JG&T has fewer assets because the inventory has been transferred to its customers. This expense is called **cost of goods sold** (CGS). The net increase in assets and owners' equity is $1,800.

	ASSETS		=	LIABILITIES	+	OWNERS' EQUITY
	Accounts receivable	Inventory				H. Jacobs, capital
(10)	+$4,000					+$4,000 (sales revenue)
		−$2,200				−$2,200 (cost of goods sold)

ADJUSTMENTS

At the end of January, Harry Jacobs wishes to prepare a balance sheet and an income statement. Before doing so, several adjustments must be made to the accounting records. These adjustments are necessary because certain events do not have normally occurring source documents, such as sales tickets or checks, to trigger their accounting recognition. At the end of each period (usually each month or year), the accountant undertakes a deliberate search to identify and record these items. All adjustments reviewed in this section are summarized in Exhibit 2-7.

Interest

As previously mentioned, on January 1, 2000, JG&T borrowed $20,000 at 8% interest (on an annual basis). Although the interest payment is not required until January 1, 2001, JG&T has incurred interest expense during January 2000. During that month, JG&T has consumed a resource: the use of the money. The utilization of that resource has enabled JG&T to operate and to generate revenues. Accordingly, an expense has been incurred, and it must be reflected in the accounting records before the financial statements are prepared. The interest charge for January is calculated as

$$\begin{aligned}\text{Interest expense} &= \text{Principal} \times \text{Rate} \times \text{Time}\\ &= \$20{,}000 \times .08 \times 1/12\\ &= \$133 \text{ (rounded)}\end{aligned}$$

The principal is the amount borrowed, in this case, $20,000. The annual interest rate is 8%. Stated in decimal form, it is .08. Because the interest rate is stated on an annual basis, the time period must be expressed similarly. Given that one month has elapsed, the time period is 1/12 of a year.

The general form of the analysis is similar to the earlier utility bill situation. Because the bank's services (use of the bank's money) have been consumed, JG&T has an additional obligation (interest payable) in the amount of $133. Further, because assets have remained constant and liabilities have increased, owners' equity must decrease.

	ASSETS	=	LIABILITIES	+	OWNERS' EQUITY
			Interest payable		H. Jacobs, capital
(11)			+$133		−$133 (interest expense)

Rent

On January 1, JG&T paid a year's rent in advance. The amount was $12,000, and an asset (prepaid rent) was appropriately recorded. By January 31, one month of the payment had been consumed; thus, an expense should be reflected in the accounting records. The analysis is

	ASSETS	=	LIABILITIES	+	OWNERS' EQUITY
	Prepaid rent				H. Jacobs, capital
(12)	−$1,000				−$1,000 (rent expense)

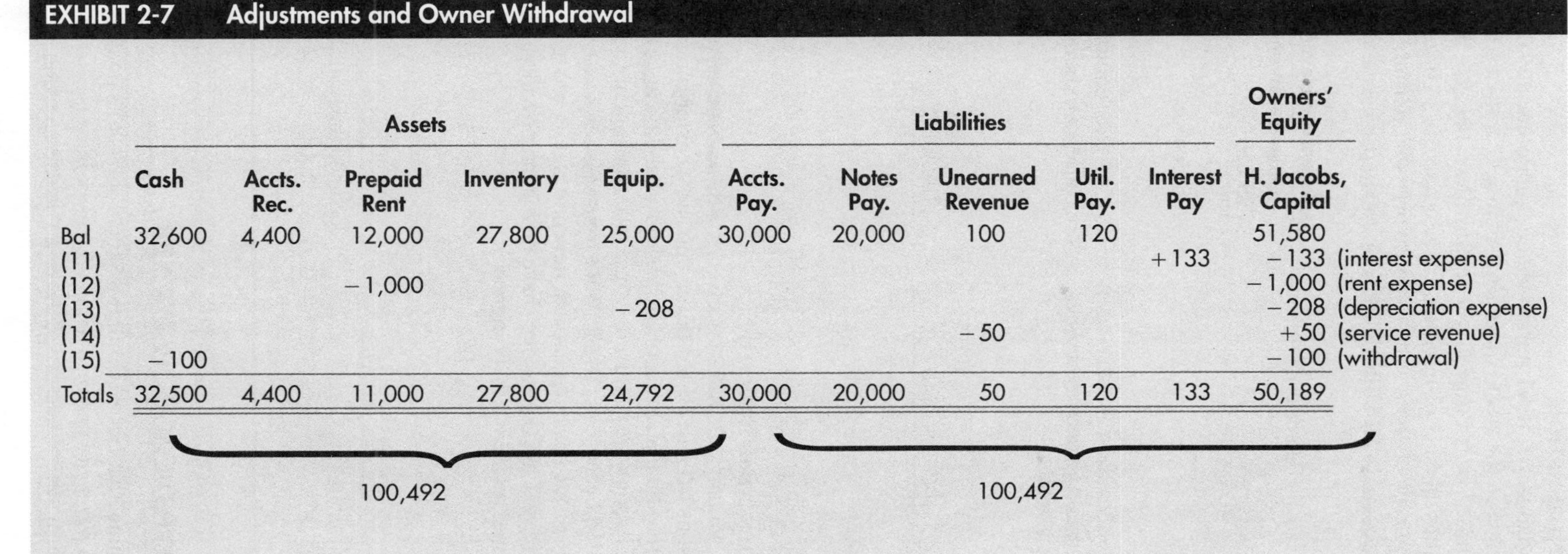

EXHIBIT 2-7 Adjustments and Owner Withdrawal

	Assets					Liabilities					Owners' Equity	
	Cash	Accts. Rec.	Prepaid Rent	Inventory	Equip.	Accts. Pay.	Notes Pay.	Unearned Revenue	Util. Pay.	Interest Pay	H. Jacobs, Capital	
Bal	32,600	4,400	12,000	27,800	25,000	30,000	20,000	100	120		51,580	
(11)										+133	−133	(interest expense)
(12)			−1,000								−1,000	(rent expense)
(13)					−208						−208	(depreciation expense)
(14)								−50			+50	(service revenue)
(15)	−100										−100	(withdrawal)
Totals	32,500	4,400	11,000	27,800	24,792	30,000	20,000	50	120	133	50,189	
	100,492					100,492						

Depreciation

On January 1, JG&T purchased equipment for $25,000. As you recall, this transaction increased the asset equipment. Assume that the estimated life of the equipment is 10 years, at which time it will be worthless. Because the service potential of the equipment will be consumed over the course of its 10-year life, the cost of the equipment should be charged as an expense over that period. This expense is referred to as **depreciation.** Monthly depreciation expense is calculated as:

$$\text{Depreciation expense} = \frac{\text{Historical cost (less anticipated salvage value)}}{\text{Number of months in the useful life}}$$

$$= \frac{\$25{,}000}{120}$$

$$= \$208 \text{ (rounded)}$$

Because the service potential of the equipment has declined, the asset's recorded value is decreased, and because an expense has been incurred, owners' equity declines.

	ASSETS	=	LIABILITIES	+	OWNERS' EQUITY
	Equipment				H. Jacobs, capital
(13)	−$208				−$208 (depreciation expense)

Unearned Revenue

On January 10, JG&T received a $100 advance payment from a customer for golf lessons to be delivered during the last week of January and the first week in February. At that time, cash increased, as did a liability, unearned revenue. Assume that half of the lessons were given in January. An adjustment to the accounting records is now required because (1) JG&T's obligation to its customer has declined by $50, and (2) $50 of revenue has been earned. Revenue is now recognized because assets have already increased and the services have now been provided. Because $50 of revenue has been earned, owners' equity increases.

	ASSETS	=	LIABILITIES	+	OWNERS' EQUITY
			Unearned revenue		H. Jacobs, capital
(14)			−$50		+$50 (service revenue)

WITHDRAWAL BY OWNER

Assume that Harry withdraws $100 from JG&T's bank account on January 31 so that he can pay some personal living expenses. Because Harry worked in the shop during the month, the withdrawal could be viewed as an expense to the business (Harry's salary).

Because the owner of a sole proprietorship cannot really establish an independent relationship with the business, however, the "salary" amount does not have a great deal of reliability. For example, Harry could simply withdraw amounts based on his personal needs, rather than on the value of the services he contributed to the business. Because of this, owner withdrawals are not viewed as salary expenses. Instead, they are considered to be capital transactions, which involve investments or disinvestments by the owner. Thus, the analysis is exactly the opposite of a contribution by the owner.

WHAT WOULD YOU DO?

In the 1990s, Woolworth Corporation experienced some accounting irregularities. Although its yearly results were accurate, Woolworth initially reported quarterly figures that subsequently needed to be restated. An investigation into this matter determined that senior management created an environment that prompted the inaccurate reporting. Senior management placed great emphasis on never reporting a quarterly loss.

One way in which reporting a quarterly loss might be avoided is by delaying expense recognition. At the end of any quarter, a corporation will have consumed resources (say, utilities or interest) for which it has not made payment. By overlooking these expenses during the adjustment process, reported quarterly net income can be increased. Of course, when these payments are made, the next quarter's net income will be decreased.

Imagine that you work for a large corporation whose senior managers are quite intent on never reporting a quarterly loss. Assume that you supervise the quarterly adjustment process. What would you do if the chief executive officer and the chief financial officer instructed you to delay recognizing some expenses for the most recent quarter?

	ASSETS	=	LIABILITIES	+	OWNERS' EQUITY
	Cash				H. Jacobs, capital
(15)	−$100				−$100 (withdrawal)

TRANSACTIONS THAT AFFECT OWNERS' EQUITY

Note that four types of transactions affect owners' equity:

1. owner contributions,
2. owner withdrawals,
3. revenues, and
4. expenses.

FINANCIAL STATEMENTS

All transactions and events for JG&T have now been properly recorded. The accounting records are correct and up to date, so they can be used to prepare the financial statements.

The Balance Sheet

The cumulative effect of all transactions and events on the various equation items is shown in the last two lines of Exhibit 2-7. The **balance sheet** is prepared by simply rearranging the numbers so that they appear in the proper format. The balance sheet as of January 31 appears in Exhibit 2-8. Each item on the balance sheet is often referred to as an **account.**

Note the date on the balance sheet: January 31, 2000. All balance sheets summarize a firm's assets, liabilities, and owners' equity at a discrete point in time.

The Income Statement

The **income statement** summarizes a firm's revenues and expenses for a period of time. Net income is computed by subtracting expenses from revenues. JG&T's income statement for the month of January appears in Exhibit 2-9.

The income statement is prepared by compiling information from the owners' equity account. Recall that all revenue transactions increase owners' equity and that all expense transactions reduce owners' equity. This makes owners' equity a convenient place to look for information about revenues and expenses. To help you see that JG&T's income statement summarizes its revenue and expense transactions for the month of January, Exhibit 2-10 summarizes all of JG&T's transactions for that month.

EXHIBIT 2-8 JG&T Balance Sheet

Jacobs Golf and Tennis
Balance Sheet
January 31, 2000

Assets		**Liabilities and Owners' Equity**	
Cash	$ 32,500	Liabilities	
Accounts receivable	4,400	Accounts payable	$ 30,000
Prepaid rent	11,000	Unearned revenue	50
Inventory	27,800	Utilities payable	120
Equipment	24,792	Interest payable	133
Total assets	$100,492	Notes payable	20,000
		Total liabilities	50,303
		H. Jacobs, capital	50,189
		Total liabilities and owners' equity	$100,492

EXHIBIT 2-9 JG&T Income Statement

Jacobs Golf and Tennis
Income Statement
For the Month Ended January 31, 2000

Revenue		
Sales	$4,000	
Service	650	
Total revenue		$4,650
Expenses		
Cost of goods sold	2,200	
Rent	1,000	
Salary	700	
Depreciation	208	
Interest	133	
Utilities	120	
Total expenses		4,361
Net income		$ 289

EXHIBIT 2-10 Transaction Analysis Summary

	Assets					Liabilities					Owners' Equity	
	Cash	Accts. Rec.	Prepaid Rent	Inventory	Equip.	Accts. Pay.	Notes Pay.	Unearned Revenue	Util. Pay.	Interest Pay	H. Jacobs, Capital	
(1)	+50,000										+50,000	
(2)	+20,000						+20,000					
(3)	−12,000		+12,000									
(4)				+30,000		+30,000						
(5)	−25,000				+25,000							
(6)	+200	+400									+600	(service revenue)
(7)	+100							+100				
(8)	−700										−700	(salary expense)
(9)									+120		−120	(utility expense)
(10)		+4,000									+4,000	(sales revenue)
				−2,200							−2,200	(cost of goods sold)
(11)										+133	−133	(interest expense)
(12)			−1,000								−1,000	(rent expense)
(13)					−208						−208	(depreciation expense)
(14)								−50			+50	(service revenue)
(15)	−100										−100	(withdrawal)
Totals	32,500	4,400	11,000	27,800	24,792	30,000	20,000	50	120	133	50,189	

Assets total: 100,492 — Liabilities and Owners' Equity total: 100,492

An alternative method that can be used to prepare the income statement is to examine asset and liability accounts. However, such an approach would be much more cumbersome. For example, some revenue transactions affect cash, other revenue transactions affect accounts receivable, and still others affect unearned revenue. Thus, the information about revenue transactions appears in a variety of asset and liability accounts. Moreover, many nonrevenue transactions affect assets and liabilities, complicating the identification of revenue transactions. An easier approach is simply to examine owners' equity. A similar argument can be made for expenses.

Care must be taken, however, not to include in the income statement all transactions that affect owners' equity. Direct contributions by owners increase owners' equity, but they do not constitute revenue. Similarly, withdrawals by owners reduce owners' equity, but they are not viewed as expenses.

The income statement provides financial statement readers with information about the profitability of the organization for a past period of time. It indicates how successful the organization was in generating revenues and controlling costs. During January, JG&T earned a net income of $289. Although this amount might not seem very impressive in light of total revenues of $4,650 and an investment of $50,000 by Harry, January was JG&T's first month of operation. Simply operating above breakeven (a zero profit or loss) is an accomplishment.

Within the context of a large corporation, an income statement can also be thought of as a report on management's performance. One of management's major responsibilities is to enhance shareholder wealth. Managers serve as agents of the shareholders, and they must be held accountable for their performance. Because profitable operations are essential to adding value to the firm, the income statement can be used to assess how well managers have performed.

Reported net income is an extremely useful figure to investors and plays a major role in their decisions. To illustrate, when Nordstrom Inc. reported healthy second-quarter earnings, the value of the company's stock surged $4.34 per share (14%). On the other hand, Adobe Systems' stock fell $3.44 per share (11%) on the day it warned of a possible small loss for its third quarter.

Note that income statements are prepared for periods of time, usually a month, quarter, or year. Income must be related to a specific period of time to be interpretable. For example, assume that you apply for a job and are told the job pays $5,000. An evaluation of the job's desirability would be impossible without knowing if you would earn $5,000 per week, month, year, or some other time period. For this reason, the income statement in Exhibit 2-9 contains the caption "For the Month Ended January 31, 2000."

Many firms prepare income statements for calendar years, that is, for the period January 1 through December 31. Other firms use 12-month periods that do not end on December 31. These firms usually select an ending date that corresponds to a low point in their activity. For example, many clothing stores, such as the Gap, have **fiscal** years that run from February 1 through January 31. January 31 is selected as the end of the fiscal year because it shortly follows the busy holiday period and provides time for refunds and exchanges to take place.

Statement of Owners' Equity

In addition to the balance sheet and the income statement, firms also prepare a **statement of owners' equity.** This statement summarizes the changes that took place in owners' equity during the period under review. Because investments and withdrawals by the owners affect owners' equity, they appear on this statement. Revenue and expense transactions also affect owners' equity. Instead of listing each revenue and expense transaction separately, their difference (net income) is included in the statement of owners' equity.

Exhibit 2-11 contains JG&T's statement of owners' equity for the month of January. Now refer back to Exhibit 2-10. As you can see, the statement of owners' equity reflects all of JG&T's transactions that affected owners' equity.

Relationship Between the Balance Sheet and the Income Statement

As you know, the balance sheet reports assets, liabilities, and owners' equity at a moment in time. The income statement summarizes revenue and expense transactions that occur during a period of time. Since revenue and expense transactions affect owners' equity, net income explains most of the change that takes place in owners' equity during a period. Contributions and withdrawals by owners also affect owners' equity. Thus, the change in owners' equity is explained by net income, owner contributions, and owner withdrawals. Because owners' equity must equal assets minus liabilities (net assets), the changes in one side of the equation must equal the changes in the other side. Therefore, changes in net income, owner contributions, and owner withdrawals also explain changes in net assets.

THE ACCRUAL BASIS OF ACCOUNTING

An important aspect of a financial accounting system is the decision about when to record revenue and expense transactions. Recording a transaction in the accounting records is referred to as **recognition.** Consider JG&T's first revenue transaction in January. Customers were given golf lessons and charged $600. The customers paid $200 in January and promised to pay the remainder in February. (Keep in mind our assumption that the customers will honor this pledge.) There is little argument that at least $200 of revenue should be recorded in January. But when should the other $400 be recorded? In January when the services were provided, or in February when the cash is ultimately collected?

The **accrual basis of accounting** records revenues when goods or services have been delivered or provided, regardless of when cash is received. At the time of rendering the service, JG&T has earned the revenue; the entire $600 is recognized as revenue at that time under the accrual basis. All of JG&T's previous transactions have used the accrual basis.

EXHIBIT 2-11 Statement of Owners' Equity

Jacobs Golf and Tennis
Statement of Owners' Equity
For the Month Ended January 31, 2000

Balance, January 1	$ 0
Investment by owner	50,000
Net income	289
Withdrawal by owner	100)
Balance, January 31	$50,189

The **cash basis of accounting** records revenue when cash is received. Under that approach, JG&T recognizes $200 of revenue in January and $400 of revenue in February.

Let's evaluate these two approaches. Which provides the most useful information to financial statement readers? If the income statement is viewed as providing information about increases in a firm's wealth, the accrual basis seems to be the preferable approach. In January, JG&T received not only $200 in cash, but also the right to receive $400 in the future. Recording $600 of revenue in January is appropriate.

Income statements can also be viewed as reports on a firm's performance. Which number, $600 or $200, is a better indicator of JG&T's accomplishments in January? Because $600 of golf lessons were provided in January, $600 seems a better measure of accomplishment (or performance).

Now consider one of JG&T's expense transactions. During January, $120 of utility services were consumed. This amount will be paid in February. Should a $120 expense be recorded in January or February? The accrual basis records expenses when resources are consumed (regardless of when payment is made), while the cash basis records expenses when the cash is actually paid. The utility's services were used in January, and the accrual basis would record the $120 as an expense in that month. The cash basis would defer recognition until JG&T pays the utility company in the following month.

Again, let's evaluate the usefulness of the information produced by the two approaches. Consumption of the utility services took place in January. At that time, the firm's liabilities increased, and its net worth decreased. This reduction in the firm's value should be reflected in January's income statement; the accrual basis would do this. Moreover, in measuring a firm's performance, all resources consumed in generating revenue should be shown on the same income statement as that revenue. Accountants refer to this as the **matching principle.** The utility services were consumed in January to help generate the revenue reported on January's income statement. Accordingly, the accrual basis provides a better portrayal of a firm's performance.

GAAP requires the use of the accrual basis, yet as previously discussed, cash flow information is also important to financial statement readers. Accordingly, GAAP also requires the statement of cash flows, which is discussed in Chapter 5, "Statement of Cash Flows." Also note that some small businesses, which do not need audited financial statements, use the cash basis.

FORMS OF BUSINESS ORGANIZATION

Financial accounting is used by a wide variety of organizations, including businesses organized to earn a profit, nonprofit organizations, and governmental entities. This book focuses on profit-oriented enterprises, which can be organized in one of the four ways described next.

Sole Proprietorships

Sole proprietorships are businesses that are owned by one individual and usually operated by that individual. They are not separate legal entities apart from the owner, and no special legal steps are required to launch or operate this form of business. Jane's T-shirt business, discussed in Chapter 1, "Financial Accounting and Its Environment," would probably be organized as a sole proprietorship. As another example, if you decided to earn money by mowing lawns during the summer, your business would probably be organized as a sole proprietorship.

Because no legal procedures are needed to begin operating sole proprietorships, their primary advantage is ease of formation. The major disadvantage is unlimited legal liability. Because owners are not legally distinct from their businesses, any claims against sole proprietorships are also claims against the owners' personal assets.

Although sole proprietorships are not separate legal entities, they are separate accounting (or economic) entities. The entity assumption indicates that the actions of the owner, serving as an agent of the business, can be (and should be) separated from the personal affairs of the owner. Based on this distinction, information about the transactions of the business can be accumulated via the financial accounting process. This enables the owner to assess the status and performance of the business on a stand-alone basis.

Partnerships

Partnerships are very similar to sole proprietorships, except that partnerships have more than one owner. Partnerships are not separate legal entities apart from their owners, but they are separate accounting entities. They are almost as easy to form as sole proprietorships, yet because of multiple owners, care must be taken to specify the rights and responsibilities of each owner. This is usually done in a partnership agreement, which is a legal contract among the partners.

Corporations

Corporations differ substantially from sole proprietorships and partnerships because they are separate legal entities. They are granted their right to exist by the individual states. A corporation must develop bylaws governing its operation, issue stock to its owners (shareholders) to represent their ownership interests, elect a board of directors who are responsible for the management of the corporation, pay taxes, and adhere to a variety of laws and regulations. Most large and many smaller businesses are organized as corporations.

As might be expected, forming a corporation is a relatively cumbersome and expensive process. Costs include filing fees paid to the state of incorporation, legal fees, and amounts paid for corporate records, such as stock certificates, bylaws, and so on. Corporations, unlike sole proprietorships and partnerships, must pay income taxes. Moreover, shareholders are also taxed on any dividends paid to them. Thus, corporations are subject to **double taxation.** Because sole proprietorships and partnerships are not separate legal entities, they do not pay income taxes; sole proprietors and partners include the income of their businesses on their individual income tax returns.

The corporate form of organization has certain advantages that can outweigh the costs. Perhaps the primary benefit is the limited liability offered to shareholders. Because the corporation is a legal entity, the corporation itself is responsible for its actions. Although shareholders risk losing their investment, their personal assets are protected from claims against the corporation. Such is not the case for sole proprietorships and partnerships.

Hybrid Forms of Organization

Many states are now offering forms of organization that combine certain characteristics of partnerships and corporations. These forms include professional corporations, limited liability companies, and limited liability partnerships. Although an evaluation of the advantages and disadvantages of these forms of organization is beyond our scope, keep in mind that careful consideration must be given to this issue when starting a new business.

Accounting Implications

The accounting differences among these three organizational forms lie mainly in the owners' equity section of the balance sheet. The accounting for partnerships is very similar to that for sole proprietorships. Because each partner is an owner, each partner has a capital account where his or her interest in the firm is shown. The accounting for corporations is slightly more complex and is described in the following section.

ACCOUNTING FOR CORPORATIONS

Two differences exist in the accounting for owners' equity in corporations. First, because shareholders are the owners of the corporation, this section is called shareholders' equity. Second, the shareholders' equity section is divided into two subcategories. One category is **invested capital.** It reflects the shareholders' interest in the firm that arises from direct contributions by the shareholders. If Harry Jacobs had formed a corporation when he started his golf and tennis shop, for example, his initial investment would be recorded by increasing both cash and the invested capital part of shareholders' equity.

ASSETS	=	LIABILITIES	+	OWNERS' EQUITY
Cash				Invested capital
+ $50,000				+ $50,000

The other category of shareholders' equity is **retained earnings.** This section contains the effect of revenue and expense transactions on shareholders' equity. That is, it reflects the increase (or decrease) in the shareholders' interest in the firm that arose from operations since the firm's inception.

Consider again transaction (10) from earlier in this chapter. Inventory that was previously purchased for $2,200 was sold, on account, for $4,000. The only change in the analysis for a corporation is that the retained earnings component of shareholders' equity reflects the effect of this transaction on the shareholders' interest in the firm.

ASSETS		=	LIABILITIES	+	SHAREHOLDER'S EQUITY
Accounts receivable	Inventory				Retained earnings
+ $4,000					+ $4,000 (revenue)
	− $2,200				− $2,200 (cost of goods sold)

SUMMARY OF LEARNING OBJECTIVES

1. **Define the terms *assets, liabilities, and owners' equity.***
   Assets are valuable resources owned by a firm. They represent probable future economic benefits. Liabilities are present obligations of a firm. They represent probable future sacrifices of economic benefits. Owners' equity reflects the owners' interest in the firm.
2. **Explain why the balance sheet must balance.**
   The balance sheet shows two views of the same thing: the resources of the firm. The left side of the balance sheet shows the composition of a firm's resources (cash, inventory, and so on). The right side shows the amount of resources supplied by creditors and the amount supplied by owners. Because resources must be supplied by either creditors or owners, the total of the left side of the balance sheet must equal the total of the right side.
3. **Describe revenues and expenses.**
   Revenues are inflows of assets (or reductions in liabilities) in exchange for providing goods and services to customers. Expenses occur when resources are consumed in order to generate revenue.
4. **Use the basic accounting equation to analyze transactions.**
   The basic accounting equation is

   ASSETS = LIABILITIES + OWNER'S EQUITY

   The financial accounting process consists of analyzing a transaction's effect on the elements of this equation. The equation balances for each transaction and for the summation of all transactions.
5. **Prepare simple balance sheets and income statements.**
   Balance sheets are prepared by cumulating the effect of all transactions on the elements of the basic accounting equation. Income statements summarize all revenue and expense transactions that took place during a period of time. The difference between revenues and expenses is net income.
6. **Describe the relationship between the balance sheet and the income statement.**
   Revenue and expense transactions affect owners' equity. Therefore, the income statement summarizes the impact these transactions have on the balance sheet item owners' equity.
7. **Distinguish between the accrual basis and the cash basis of accounting.**
   The accrual basis recognizes revenues when they are earned, that is, when the goods are delivered or the service is rendered. The cash basis recognizes revenues when cash is received from the customer. The accrual basis recognizes expenses when resources are consumed. The cash basis recognizes expenses when cash is paid. The accrual basis provides a better measure of performance. GAAP requires use of the accrual basis.
8. **Explain the differences between the balance sheets of sole proprietorships and those of corporations.**
   The primary difference involves owners' equity. In sole proprietorships, only one component of owners' equity is used; it is referred to as capital, and it reflects the owners' interests that arise from both direct contributions and profitable operations. Corporations use two components: invested capital, which reflects owners' direct contributions, and retained earnings, which show the owners' interest that arose from profits.

KEY TERMS

QUESTIONS

2-1 Describe each part of the basic accounting equation. Identify one example of each item or term in this equation and describe why it fits in that particular category.

2-2 Using the definition of assets in this chapter, describe why each of the following items should not be listed as an asset on the firm's balance sheet:
- a. Favorable location
- b. Skilled employees
- c. Reputation for honesty and fairness
- d. Brand recognition in the market
- e. Steady customers
- f. Customers' names, addresses, and product preferences

2-3 Executory contracts.
- a. Discuss the concept of an executory contract. Why might a firm sign such a contract?
- b. How should such a contract be recorded in the firm's financial statements?

2-4 Identify two forms of business organizations and list a major advantage and disadvantage of each.

2-5 Indicate whether each of the following statements concerning possible organization structures is true or false. If a statement is false, indicate why.
- a. A sole proprietorship and its owner are legally the same entity.
- b. The partners in a partnership are not liable for the debts of the partnership.
- c. All partners in a partnership must agree on all decisions.
- d. A sole proprietorship and its owner are the same entity for financial reporting.
- e. A partnership is less risky (for the partners) than a sole proprietorship.
- f. Two people can form a sole proprietorship.
- g. Twenty people cannot form a partnership.
- h. It is more expensive to form a partnership than a sole proprietorship.
- i. Any group of people (less than five) canform a partnership by oral agreement.

2-6 Indicate whether each of the following statements concerning possible organization structures is true or false. If a statement is false, indicate why it is false.
- a. A corporation and its investors are legally the same entity.
- b. The shareholders of a corporation are not liable for the debts of the corporation.
- c. A publicly held corporation usually sends its financial statements to all of its owners (investors).
- d. A corporation is less risky (for its owners) than a partnership or sole proprietorship.
- e. It is more expensive to form a corporation than a sole proprietorship.
- f. Shareholders are taxed on the corporation's net income.

2-7 Define accrual accounting. Contrast accrual accounting with cash basis accounting.

2-8 Define an asset. Define a liability. How can one firm's asset be another firm's liability?

2-9 Define owners' equity. How does this differ from retained earnings? How can one firm's asset be another firm's equity?

EXERCISES

2-10 Indicate the effects [(1) increase, (2) decrease, (0) no effect] on the accounting equation from the following transactions:

a. Owner invested cash in the business.
b. Performed services for cash.
c. Purchased equipment by signing a note payable.
d. Customers paid in advance for services to be performed.
e. Purchased a two-year insurance policy.
f. Paid employees for the period's work.
g. Purchased supplies on account.
h. Performed services referred to in part d.
i. Paid note from part c in full, plus interest.
j. Recorded depreciation adjustment.

Identifying Transactions: Cash Versus Accrual Method

2-11 Identify which of the following events should be reported on financial statements under

1. the cash basis of accounting,
2. the accrual basis of accounting,
3. both methods, or
4. neither method.

Explain each choice.

a. Agreed (verbally) to purchase a used car from Slee-Z-Auto.
b. Paid $300 for a warranty on the used car.
c. Took the car on a test drive, found it faulty, and asked the salesperson for a different car.
d. The sales manager helped choose another car.
e. The sales manager kindly transferred the warranty to the second vehicle.
f. Paid $6,500 for the vehicle.
g. Paid license and taxes of $275.
h. Bought new tires for $450 on account.
i. On a cold winter morning, the car failed to start.
j. Purchased a new battery for $65 on account.
k. Filed a warranty claim for the new battery.
l. Received $45 payment under the warranty.

Analyzing Transactions: Cash and Accrual Bases

2-12 Use pluses and minuses (or NA for not applicable) to show how the following events should be analyzed using the accounting equation under

1. the cash basis of accounting and
2. the accrual basis of accounting.

a. Signed a contract for the purchase of land.
b. Paid a deposit on the land purchase.
c. Received money in advance from a customer.
d. Listed land for sale with a local realtor.
e. Used equipment, such as a computer, in the business.
f. Had a computer repaired; the repair person just leaves a bill, but cannot accept payment for the repair.
g. Paid the repair bill.

h. Provided services to customers who will not pay until next month.
i. Received compliments from customers about excellent customer services.
j. Hired a well-trained accountant to prepare financial statements and provide financial advice. (Assume no payments have been made.)
k. Collected money from customers who have already been billed.
l. Employees worked this month, but the payroll (payment) was delayed until the following month.
m. Failed to pay suppliers for three months because there is not enough money in the bank.
n. Received supplies from a vendor, along with a bill.
o. Sold land under a contract for 10 future payments.
p. Collected one of the contract payments from the land sale.

Valuing Contract Terms

2-13 A professional baseball player signs a contract for next season to play for the Colorado Rockies. The contract includes payment terms of $7,000,000 over the next two years. The player receives an extra "signing bonus" of $1,000,000. How should each of these two amounts be recorded by the Rockies? Note that the $7,000,000 is contingent on the player "making" the team.

Identifying Accounting Transactions

2-14 R & R Travel entered into the following transactions. Which of these transactions or events should be recorded in R & R's accounting process? Explain your answer.

a. Obtained a bank loan.
b. Repaid a bank loan.
c. Signed a one-year agreement to rent office space. The first month's rent is paid at this time.
d. Signed a one-year agreement to rent office space. No cash is transferred at this time.
e. Purchased office equipment on credit.
f. Agreed with the local newspaper to place advertising in next month's special travel section. No cash yet paid.

Transaction Analysis

2-15 The Western Fittings Corporation began business on July 1, 1999. The following transactions occurred during its first six months:

1. Three individuals each invested $30,000 in exchange for capital stock.
2. One year's rent was paid for $12,000 on July 1.
3. On August 1, several pieces of property, plant, and equipment were purchased for $75,000 on account.
4. During the six months, clothing, boots, and accessories were purchased for $60,000 cash.
5. The corporation had sales revenue of $85,000, of which $35,000 has not yet been collected in cash.
6. The cost of the clothing, boots, and accessories sold in item 5 was $55,250.
7. Employees were paid $24,000 in wages.
8. The corporation paid utilities and telephone expenses of $5,000.

Required

a. Analyze and record these transactions using the basic accounting equation.
b. Record the following adjustments for the six months ended December 31, 1999: rent expense and depreciation expense. Assume a 10-year life and zero residual value.
c. What is the net income (loss) for the six months ended December 31, 1999?

Transaction Analysis

2-16 John Hasty opened his bakery on March 1, 1999, as a sole proprietor. The following transactions took place at the beginning of March:

1. Deposited $10,000 into a checking account in the name of the Hasty Bakery.
2. Rented a small kitchen and paid the first month's rent of $500.
3. Purchased kitchen equipment for $3,000 cash.
4. Purchased baking ingredients for $6,000 on account.
5. Obtained a $2,000, 9%, one-year loan.
6. Obtained a one-year insurance policy on the kitchen equipment. Paid the entire premium of $500.

Required

a. Analyze the above transactions for March, using the basic accounting equation.
b. Record necessary adjustments: interest expense, insurance expense, and depreciation expense. (Assume a 60-month life and zero residual value.)
c. What additional information is needed to fully analyze Hasty Bakery results for March?

Fill in the Blanks

2-17 Find the missing elements in the following (independent) cases:

ASSETS	=	LIABILITIES	+	SHAREHOLDERS' EQUITY
a. $100,000		$ 30,000		?
b. ?		$450,000		$200,000
c. $350,000		$450,000		?
d. $675,000		?		$310,000

Fill in the Blanks

2-18 Ascertain the missing items (*A*, *B*, and *C*) in the following situation:

Assets, January 1	$10,000
Assets, December 31	$14,000
Liabilities, January 1	A
Liabilities, December 31	$ 7,000
Owners' equity, January 1	$ 8,000
Owners' equity, December 31	B
Owners' contributions	0
Owners' withdrawals	C
Net income	$ 2,000

Transaction Analysis

2-19 Record the following business transactions in the basic accounting equation. Use column headings for Cash, Accounts Receivable, Land, Accounts Payable, Unearned revenue, Notes Payable, Invested Capital, and Retained Earnings.

a. Three individuals each invested $70,000 in a newly formed corporation in exchange for capital stock.
b. Paid $12,500 for land.
c. Performed services for customers, all on account; billed the customers $24,300.
d. Received a utility bill for $850 and immediately paid it.
e. Received $11,200 for services not yet performed.
f. Received a telephone bill for $650, but did not pay it yet.
g. Borrowed $34,000 cash from a bank and signed the loan documents.
h. Received $10,000 from customers on account.
i. Performed the services described in part e.

PROBLEMS

Transaction Analysis: Income Statement and Balance Sheet Effects

2-20 Identify the effects of the following events on the first year's income statement and balance sheet:

a. A company paid a $2,000 bill for a fire insurance policy that covers the current year and the next year.
b. A company purchased a trash compactor for $200 that has an expected life of five years. What are the balance sheet effects of treating the $200 as an expense this year versus the effects of depreciating the trash compactor over five years? What are the effects on net income?
c. Two attorneys, working together under a corporate structure, decide that a ski chalet at Vail is necessary to entertain current and prospective clients. At the same time, they are considering the addition of a third attorney as another owner of their company. This third attorney has a ski chalet that she purchased five years ago for $120,000. Its current market value is $200,000. How should the ski chalet be reflected on the corporation's financial statements, assuming that the new attorney is hired and the ski chalet is transferred to the corporation?

Transaction Analysis

2-21 Jane Goodrum established a sole proprietorship to sell and service personal computers. Use the balance sheet equation to analyze the effects of the following transactions:

a. Invested $50,000 in the business.
b. Purchased a four-wheel drive pickup truck for $22,000 (on account) that will be used in the business.
c. The truck's fuel and repair annual costs were $1,750 (paid in cash).
d. Shortly after buying the truck, it proved to be a "lemon" and Jane pushed it over a cliff! Explain to Jane how the loss of this truck affects her balance sheet. If Jane had not ever paid for the truck, who is responsible for the loss of the truck?

Transaction Analysis: Accrual Adjustments

2-22 The accounting firm Seaver & Co. prepares its own financial statements at the end of each year. Based on the following information, prepare any adjustments that are needed for the accounting records as of December 31, 1999 in terms of the basic accounting equation.

a. As of December 31, Seaver & Co. has rendered $20,500 worth of services to clients for which they have not yet billed the client and for which they have not made any accounting entry.
b. Seaver & Co. owns equipment (computers and so on) having an original cost of $12,000. The equipment has an expected life of six years.
c. On January 1, 1999, Seaver borrowed $15,000. Both principal and interest are due on December 31, 2000. The interest rate is 11%.
d. On January 1, 1999, Seaver rented storage space for three years. The entire three-year charge of $15,000 was paid at this time. Seaver (correctly) created a prepaid rent account in the amount of $15,000.
e. As of December 31, workers have earned $10,200 in wages that are unpaid and unrecorded.

Transaction Analysis: Preparing Financial Statements

2-23 The following account balances are shown on November 30, 1999, for the Clever Bookstore:

Cash	$ 8,000	Accounts payable	$ 4,000
Accounts receivable	9,000	Salaries payable	2,000
Inventory	60,000	Notes payable	35,000
Supplies	3,000	J. Clever, capital	39,000
Total	$80,000	Total	$80,000

The following transactions occurred during December.

1. Paid workers the $2,000 owed them on November 30.
2. Made sales totaling $40,000. Half of the sales were for cash. The other half were on account. The cost of goods sold was $25,000.
3. Purchased inventory on account, $15,000.
4. Collected in cash $22,000 of receivables.
5. Used supplies totaling $800.
6. Paid accounts payable of $12,000.
7. Paid all December's interest on the note payable in the amount of $300.

Required

a. Analyze all transactions using the basic accounting equation. Begin your analysis by entering the November 30 account balances into a worksheet. Then enter each of the transactions above into your worksheet.
b. Prepare a balance sheet as of December 31, 1999.
c. Prepare an income statement for the month ended December 31, 1999.

Transaction Analysis: Preparing Financial Statements

2-24 Susan's Sweets, a candy shop, opened on January 1, 1999, with the following transactions:

1. Susan deposited $100,000 in cash on January 1, 1999, and began business as a sole proprietorship.
2. Susan transferred a rental agreement for commercial premises to the candy shop. She personally had paid $20,000 rent for the next six months on De-

cember 31 of the prior year, and now transferred all rights under the six-month agreement. This agreement is renewable for another six months on July 1. (*Note:* Increase owners' equity capital account.)

3. Susan purchased candy and other "sweetments" at a cost of $40,000 in cash.
4. Susan purchased store fixtures at a cost of $15,000, paying $5,000 in cash and the balance on account. These store fixtures have a useful life of five years, with no expected salvage value.
5. The six-month rental agreement expired. She renewed it for another six months and paid $20,000.
6. During the first year of operations, Susan's sales totaled $132,000 on account.
7. Collections from customers totaled $130,500.
8. During the first year, her other operating expenses were $37,300 on account. In addition, she received "salaries" of $10,000, which were really a withdrawal or drawing.
9. At the end of the first year, Susan's Sweets had $2,000 of inventory.
10. Record depreciation for the first year.
11. Record the adjustment to prepaid rent.

Required

a. Use the basic accounting equation to show the effects of the transactions and any necessary accruals during Susan's first year of business.

b. Based on that analysis, prepare a balance sheet and an income statement for the first year.

Transaction Analysis: Preparing Financial Statements

2-25 Susan's Shoe Shop opened on January 1. The following transactions took place during the first month:

1. Deposited $30,000 in the firm's checking account.
2. Purchased shoes, boots, socks, and other inventory for $45,000 on account.
3. Purchased display shelving, chairs, and other fixtures for $10,000 cash and $40,000 on account. Assume a useful life of five years.
4. Obtained $20,000 and signed a three-year, $20,000 bank loan at 8% annual interest.
5. Had sales revenue during January of $75,000. Of this amount, $25,000 was received in cash and the balance was on account.
6. The cost of the merchandise sold in item 5 was $32,000.
7. Paid $10,000 to each of two different creditors.
8. Signed an application for a one-year insurance policy and paid the year's premium of $2,400.
9. Paid three employees a monthly salary of $2,000 each.
10. Collected $35,000 from (accounts receivable) customers.

Required

a. Analyze these transactions, including any appropriate adjustments, using the basic accounting equation.

b. Prepare a simple income statement for the firm.

c. Identify any significant missing elements in your income statement.

d. Prepare a simple balance sheet for Susan's Shoe Shop.

Fill in the Blanks

2-26 Ascertain the missing items (*A-L*) in the following *independent* situations. (*Note:* You do *not* have to find the answers in any particular sequence.)

	1	2	3
Assets, January 1	$ 5,000	*E*	*I*
Assets, December 31	$ 8,000	*F*	$ 9,000
Liabilities, January 1	*A*	$ 2,000	$ 3,000
Liabilities, December 31	$ 3,000	$ 2,200	*J*
Owners' equity, January 1	$ 3,000	$ 4,000	*K*
Owners' equity, December 31	*B*	$ 4,800	$ 7,000
Revenues	$20,000	$15,000	*L*
Expenses	$18,500	*G*	$20,000
Contributions by owners	$ 1,000	*H*	$ 1,000
Withdrawals by owners	*C*	1,200	$ 3,000
Net income	*D*	2,000	$ 5,000

Note: The solutions for Situation 1 are shown below:

January 1:	Assets	=	Liabilities	+	Owners' equity
	$5,000	=	(A)	+	$3,000
	$5,000	=	$2,000	+	$3,000
December 31:	Assets	=	Liabilities	+	Owners' equity
	$8,000	=	$3,000	+	(B)
	$8000	=	$3,000	+	$5,000

Revenues	−	Expenses	=	Net Income
$20,000	−	$18,500	=	Net income
$20,000	−	$18,500	=	$1,500

Beginning owners' equity + Contributions by owners − Withdrawals by owners + Net Income = Ending owners' equity

$3,000 + $1,000 − (C) + $1,500 = $5,000
$3,000 + $1,000 − $500 + $1,500 = $5,000

Fill in the Blanks

2-27 Ascertain the missing items (*A-L*) in the following *independent* situations. (*Note:* You do *not* have to find the answers in any particular sequence. See the previous assignment for an explanation of how to find these missing items.)

	1	2	3
Assets, January 1	$12,000	*E*	*I*
Assets, December 31	$ 9,000	*F*	$ 9,500
Liabilities, January 1	*A*	$ 5,000	$ 3,200
Liabilities, December 31	$ 7,500	$ 5,200	*J*
Owners' equity, January 1	$ 7,500	$ 3,200	*K*
Owners' equity, December 31	*B*	$ 5,300	$ 8,000
Revenues	$25,000	$12,000	*L*
Expenses	$16,200	*G*	$22,000
Contributions by owners	$ 2,000	*H*	$ 2,000
Withdrawals by owners	*C*	$ 1,200	$ 3,500
Net income	*D*	$ 3,000	$ 4,000

Analyzing Investment Alternatives

2-28 Assume that you inherit $10,000, which according to the terms of the bequest must be invested in a single company. After much research, you find two attractive alternatives: The Salt Company and The Pepper Company.

Required

a. On the basis of the following limited information, which of the following would you prefer (M = millions of dollars)?

	Salt Co.	Pepper Co.
Total assets	$40M	$25M
Net income	$4M	$4M

b. If you then find the following additional information about each company's liabilities, which company would you prefer? Why?

	Salt Co.	Pepper Co.
Total liabilities	$20M	$23M

c. If you then read a newspaper article predicting each firm's future income prospects, which firm is now preferable? Why?

	Salt Co.	Pepper Co.
Next year's predicted net income	$1M	$10M

d. Write a short memo describing any additional information that you might find helpful in making an investment in either of the two companies.

Recording Transactions Using Cash and Accrual Methods

2-29 Use a balance sheet equation to show how each of the following events would be treated under

1. the cash basis of accounting and
2. the accrual basis of accounting.

   a. Ordered airline tickets, hotel accommodations, and tour guidance from Hugo's U-Go Travel at a cost of $5,000.
   b. Changed the airline reservation.
   c. Paid a $35 fee to a travel advisor.
   d. Paid $2,000 for the airline tickets, room, and tour.
   e. Arrived at the hotel and checked in.
   f. Found the room to be next to the hotel laundry and facing the noisy loading zone. Furthermore, the room only had two cheap radios and no television! Asked the hotel manager for a more suitable room.
   g. Tipped the bellhop $5 after luggage was moved to an upgraded room.
   h. Charged $257 for meals and telephone calls during the week.
   i. Upon checking out of the hotel at the end of the week, found a $40 per day (for five days) upgrade charge on the hotel bill.
   j. Paid for the meals and phone charges on the hotel bill, but denied responsibility for the upgrade charges.
   k. The hotel manager insisted that the upgrade charges were not covered by the prepaid vouchers from Hugo's, and they would be charged to the Visa credit card account number on file with the hotel.
   l. Took vacation film to a photo shop for developing. Charges for developing and printing this film were expected to be $45, not yet paid.
   m. Paid the $45 two weeks later.

Transaction Analysis

2-30 Use the accounting equation to analyze the effects of the following events. Assume that the beginning balances are zero. Prepare an income statement and balance sheet after recording each transaction.

a. Sugar Loaf Enterprises bought inventory for resale at a cost of $350,000 on account.
b. Half the inventory was sold to customers for $525,000, all on account.
c. Customers paid $200,000 on account.
d. A particularly interested customer paid $10,000 in advance to reserve an especially desirable item.
e. The item was shipped at an invoiced charge of $2,500 more than the deposit. The inventory cost was $6,000.
f. The customer paid the $2,500 invoice, after reducing the invoice by the $55 freight cost, which, in the customer's opinion, should have been waived because of the $10,000 advance payment.

Transaction Analysis: Simple Interest

2-31 Identify the effects of the following events on the income statement and the balance sheet for each year:

a. Sunshine House borrowed $20,000 at 5% interest per annum.
b. Interest for the first year was accrued, but not paid.
c. Two months into the next year, the interest was paid for the first year.
d. At the end of the second year, the loan was repaid, plus the second year's interest.

Transaction Analysis: Simple Interest

2-32 Heidi's Golf and Swim Club borrowed $500,000 at 12% per annum.

Required

a. Calculate Heidi's expected monthly and annual interest expense.
b. Show the effect of the $500,000 loan on Heidi's accounting equation.
c. Show the effects of the first and second months' interest accruals.
d. Show the effects of Heidi's payment of two months' interest.
e. Show the effects of the interest accruals for the remainder of the first year.

Transaction Analysis: Liabilities and Interest Accruals

2-33 John's Anti-Mediation League (JAML), a sole proprietorship, engaged in the following transactions in 1999:

1. On January 1, JAML borrowed $100,000 at 6% per year with interest due quarterly.
2. JAML paid a $1,000 kickback to a good friend who helped obtain the loan.
3. JAML had not yet paid any interest after the loan had been in effect for three months.
4. On June 30, JAML paid the interest due.
5. On July 1, JAML renegotiated the terms of the loan, which increased the interest rate to 9% per year.
6. At the end of September, John paid the interest on the loan from his personal account.
7. At the end of December, JAML accrued the interest due.
8. On January 1, 2000, JAML paid the interest due to the lender and to John's personal account.

Required

Record these transactions, using the accounting equation.

Transaction Analysis: Liabilities and Interest Accruals

2-34 Sharon's Affairs and Parties (SAAP), a sole proprietorship, engaged in the following transactions in 1999:

1. SAAP borrowed $150,000 at 10% per year to begin operations.
2. SAAP accrued the first month's interest on the loan.
3. SAAP accrued the second month's interest.
4. SAAP paid the interest due.
5. Sharon loaned SAAP $10,000 at 24% interest per year.
6. SAAP accrued interest for the next month on both loans.
7. SAAP paid the accrued interest.
8. SAAP repaid Sharon's loan, along with a loan "cancellation" fee of $2,500.
9. SAAP accrued interest for the next month.
10. SAAP repaid the original loan, along with the accrued interest.

Required

Record these transactions, using the accounting equation.

Transaction Analysis: Describing Underlying Events

2-35 Shown below are several transactions recorded by Beth's coffee shop, The Bitter Bean (TBB):

	ASSETS	=	LIABILITIES	+	OWNER'S EQUITY
a.	Cash, +$30,000				Capital, +$30,00
b.	Inventory, +$12,000		Accounts payable, +$12,000		
c.	Cash, −$3,000		Loans, −$3,000		
d.			Loans, −$27,000		Capital, +$27,000
e.	Accounts receivable, +$10,000				Revenue, +$10,000
f.	Inventory, −$3,000				Cost of goods sold, −$3,000
g.	Cash, +$8,000 Accounts receivable, −$8,000				
h.			Accounts payable, +$30,000		Operating expenses, −$30,000

Required

For each transaction, describe the event or activity that occurred. For example: *Answer:* The firm borrowed $20,000.

Transaction Analysis: Describing Underlying Events

2-36 Following are several transactions recorded by Bruce's tea shop, The Better Leaf (TBL):

	ASSETS	=	LIABILITIES	+	OWNER'S EQUITY
a.	Cash, +$50,000				Capital, +$50,000
b.	Inventory, +$22,000		Accounts payable, +$22,000		
c.	Cash, +$3,000		Loans, +$3,000		
d.			Loans, −$23,000		Capital, +$23,000
e.	Accounts receivable, +$32,000				Revenue, +$32,000
f.	Inventory, −$13,000				Cost of goods sold, −$13,000
g.	Cash, +$28,000, Accounts receivable, −$28,000				
h.	Inventory, +$30,000		Loans, +$30,000		

Required

For each transaction, describe the event or activity that occurred. For example: *Answer:* The firm borrowed $20,000.

Analyzing Effects of Cash and Accrual Accounting

2-37 Assume that you are auditing a small bank that uses the cash basis of accounting to record interest on its customers' accounts and uses the accrual basis of accounting for interest earned on its investments.

a. If most of the bank's investments were earning daily interest, while most of the bank's customers had their money invested in five-year certificates of deposit, do you think that the income reported by the bank represents a fair or useful measure of accomplishment? Why?

b. Reconsider your prior answer. What if you find out that most of the five-year certificates of deposit had just been issued? What if you find out that the bank issued and redeemed the same number of five-year certificates every month? How do the issues of timing or renewal cycles affect your view of this situation?

Analyzing Transactions: Effects of Missing Information

2-38 Answer each of the following *independent* questions:

a. Dennis Company has assets of $125,000 and owners' equity of $40,000. What are its liabilities? If these liabilities include an outstanding mortgage of $60,000, identify some of the other liabilities that Dennis Company might have.

b. Bruce Company has assets of $300,000 and liabilities of $110,000. Suppose that the original owners invested $200,000 in this business. What might account for the difference between the original investment and the current balance in owners' equity?

c. Pieter Company has liabilities of $400,000 and owners' equity of $155,000. What are its assets? Suppose that Pieter has conducted an appraisal and has found that its assets are valued at $1,000,000. How can such a difference occur?

d. Elizabeth Company has assets of $500,000 and liabilities of $600,000. What conclusions can you draw about this firm?

Identifying Accounting Transactions

2-39 Refer to the T-shirt business first described in Chapter 1, "Financial Accounting and Its Environment." The firm now has a small store near the football stadium to display and sell various sporting goods. During the first week that the shop is open, the following events occur. Should they be recorded in the financial statements of the firm? Why or why not?

a. A famous football player gives a signed football to the store owner's daughter.
b. The firm received a bill from the Public Service Co. for gas and electricity used by the prior tenants in the store.
c. The owner bought three lottery tickets for $6.
d. One of the three lottery tickets won $150. (In this case, assume that you did not originally record the purchase of the tickets and that the owner did not want to record the winnings.)
e. The owner learned that the Super Bowl will be held at the nearby stadium in three years.

Ethics

Cash Versus Accrual Accounting

2-40 Suppose that Tina's Frame Shop is anticipating applying for a bank loan in the near future. Although Tina's has been using accrual accounting, the bookkeeper suggests that the firm switch to a cash basis in order to improve its financial picture.

Required

a. Assuming that the bank requires financial statements on a cash basis, what actions could the bookkeeper and the firm take to report more favorable results under the cash basis?
b. How might the bank react when it compares any of Tina's earlier statements under the accrual method with statements that are much more favorable under the cash basis?
c. Is Tina's auditor obligated to provide both sets of statements to the bank and explain any differences? Why?
d. Now assume that the bank permits either cash or accrual accounting. Is it ethical for Tina's to try to "fool" the bank with statements prepared using the most favorable accounting procedures? Why?
e. If you were Tina's bookkeeper, would you expect to be fired if you gave the bank both sets of financial statements? How would this possibility change your views?

Critical Thinking

Conceptual Discussion: Objectivity

2-41 Financial statements, and the underlying accounting processes, rely on many subjective estimates. Review the sample transactions described in this chapter and indicate which of them are objective. Which are subjective? Which could be more objective if additional information was available? Why?

Writing

Essay: Measuring Liabilities

2-42 Write a one- to two-paragraph essay assessing the following statement:

Liabilities must be precisely measured because the firm needs to know how much is owed to its creditors. If such amounts are not precisely known, the firm risks bankruptcy or other liquidity crises whenever the actual liabilities may have been underestimated.

Writing

Essay: Asset Valuation

2-43 Write a one- to two-paragraph essay defending the following statement: Assets need not be objectively measured and valued because they can be sold at any time. If the firm feels that asset values are going to decline, it can avoid any potential losses merely by selling the assets before they decline.

Critical Thinking

Conceptual Discussion: Effects of Overstating Expenses

2-44 Consider a situation in which you learn that your employer's accounting staff has consistently overestimated the firm's expenses (such as depreciation or bad debts). As a manager in the firm, what action could you take in response to this knowledge? Why?

Critical Thinking

Conceptual Discussion: Contracts

2-45 Often, when a highly-regarded athlete joins a new team, his/her contract is recorded at a value well beyond the payments due in the first year.

a. Since a person cannot be owned, how can an athlete's contract be recorded in the team's financial statements?
b. What measurement rules might apply to the valuation of such athletic contracts? When should this contract be recorded by the team? When has either party actually performed (executed) its part of the contract?
c. How do you think accountants might handle the uncertainties associated with the length of a player's career, possible injuries, trades, and so on?
d. How would the existence of guarantees in the contract affect your view of these uncertainties?

Ethics

Identifying Unusual Transactions and Events

2-46 As the staff accountant for Gil's Plumbing, you notice that a $1,000 check is drawn (payable to "Cash") on the third Monday of each month and is charged to miscellaneous expenses. You also notice that a sleazy character with a canvas bag comes into the office on the third Tuesday of each month for a 30-second meeting with Gil. After inquiring about what the $1,000 check is for and to which account it might more properly be charged, Gil suggests that you should "mind your own business" and just record the expenses where you are told.

Required

a. What would you guess is really happening in this situation?
b. Is the $1,000 properly recorded in Gil's accounts? Why?
c. Is this a personal transaction or a business transaction?
d. Since Gil is the sole owner of the plumbing business, can he do whatever he wants with his money? How would this situation differ if Gil were merely the manager who was making these payments without the owner's knowledge? What should you do in this case? Why?

Ethics

Overstating Expenses

2-47 In 1999, Woolies, Inc. reported some accounting irregularities. Although its yearly results were accurate, Woolies initially reported interim results that were incorrect. An investigation into this matter determined that senior management created an environment that prompted the inaccurate reporting. Senior management placed great emphasis on never reporting a quarterly loss. The accounting staff was encouraged to be creative in meeting this goal!

One way in which reporting a quarterly loss might be avoided is by recognizing revenues prior to shipment. At the end of any quarter, a corporation will have a variety of unfilled orders. By "booking" these orders during the adjustment process, reported quarterly net income could be increased. Of course, when these shipments are actually made, the next quarter's net income will require some form of adjustment.

Imagine that you work for a large corporation whose senior managers are quite intent on never reporting a quarterly loss. Assume that you supervise the quarterly adjustment process. What would you do if the chief executive officer and the chief financial officer instructed you to recognize some unfilled orders as sales revenues for the current quarter?

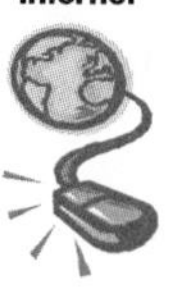

Creating Accounting Equations

2-48 Select two of the following companies (your instructor might specify which two) and locate the most recent set of financial statements. You may use either the 10-K available at EDGAR (**www.sec.gov/edgarhp.htm**) or the annual report available at the company page on the Web. The annual report is usually located in the Investor Information section.

Corporation	WWW Page Location
Xerox	**www.xerox.com**
Ben & Jerry's	**www.benjerry.com**
Lewis Galoob Toys	**www.galoob.com**
Microsoft	**www.microsoft.com** (go to index)
Compaq	**www.compaq.com** (go to overview)
Eli Lilly	**www.lilly.com**

Required

a. Obtain the following information for each corporation: Total Assets, Total Liabilities, Total Shareholders' Equity, Net Income.

b. Verify the accounting equation for each corporation.

Finding Balance Sheet Information

2-49 A major asset for most companies is facilities. Use the SEC's EDGAR corporate database (**www.sec.gov/edaux/searches.htm.**) to locate the 10-K for Rockwell International dated September 30, 1995, and filed on December 21, 1995.

Required

a. Locate and read Item 2, properties (pp. 7-8). For the United States, Europe, South America, and Canada, identify the types of operations for which facilities are maintained.

b. Scroll down to the Balance Sheet. Net Property, Plant, and Equipment represents what percentage of total assets on September 30, 1995?

Identifying Core Activities

2-50 This assignment is based on a report by the Jenkins Committee. The Jenkins Committee was formed to analyze users' needs in financial reporting and to suggest improvements in financial reporting, keeping in mind these needs.

Required

a. Locate Chapter Six of the Jenkins Committee report (located at **www.rutgers.edu/Accounting/raw/aicpa/business/chap6.htm**), and scroll down to Recommendation 4. How does the Committee define the core activities of a firm?

b. List the core activities for the following corporations:

Corporation	WWW Page Location
Kodak	**www.kodak.com**
Ryder	**www.ryder.inter.net**
Rockwell International	**www.rockwell.com**
Rohm and Haas Company	**www.rohmhaas.com**

chapter

3

The Balance Sheet

LEARNING OBJECTIVES

1. Identify the basic elements of the balance sheet.
2. Recognize the types of assets, liabilities, and owners' equity that are found on the balance sheets of most business firms.
3. Comprehend the ordering and classification of items on the balance sheet.
4. Appreciate why balance sheets differ for firms in different industries.
5. Use balance sheet relationships to obtain information useful to investors and lenders.
6. Be alert to the limitations as well as the usefulness of balance sheet information.

INTRODUCTION

This chapter focuses solely on the balance sheet, which is often called the statement of financial position. Beginning with formal definitions of the basic elements of the balance sheet, the discussion describes the types of assets, liabilities, and owners' equity that are found on the balance sheets of most business firms. A variety of balance sheet ratios are presented to show how managers and investors use balance sheet information in making decisions.

ELEMENTS OF THE BALANCE SHEET

The previous two chapters introduced you to the three basic financial statements. They showed how transactions and other events affecting business firms cause changes in the elements reported in the financial statements. This chapter focuses solely on the balance sheet, which is often called the **statement of financial position.** At any given date, the balance sheet shows the sources from which the firm has obtained its resources and the ways in which those resources are currently employed. Recall the basic accounting equation:

ASSETS = LIABILITIES + OWNERS' EQUITY

Another way to state this relationship is

Uses of resources = Sources of resources

In other words, liabilities and owners' equity are the sources from which the firm has obtained its funds, and the listing of assets shows the way in which the firm's managers have put those funds to work. This relationship is illustrated as follows, based on the balance sheet for Sample Company at the end of 2000, which is presented in Exhibit 3-1.

Uses of resources	=	Sources of resources
Assets	=	Liabilities + Owners' Equity
$2,057,000	=	$1,199,000 + $858,000
$2,057,000	=	$2,057,000

Viewed in this manner, there is no mystery to the fact that both sides of the balance sheet have the same total; they are merely two sides of a single coin, or two ways of describing the total wealth of the firm. The firm's wealth can be viewed in terms of sources of financing (from creditors and owners) and in terms of uses of resources (owning or controlling assets).

Another useful way to view the balance sheet is as the cumulative result of the firm's past activities. Liabilities represent the total amount the firm has borrowed during its existence, minus the amounts that have been repaid to date. The owners' equity

EXHIBIT 3-1 A Balance Sheet

Sample Company Balance Sheet
at December 31, 2000

Assets			**Liabilities and Owners' Equity**		
Current assets			Current liabilities		
Cash	$110,000		Accounts payable	$260,000	
Accounts receivable	466,000		Notes payable	225,000	
Inventories	812,000		Warranty obligations	112,000	
Prepaid expenses	32,000		Accrued expenses	75,000	
Total current assets		$1,420,000	Taxes payable	27,000	
Noncurrent assets			Total current liabilities		$ 699,000
Land	$ 85,000		Noncurrent liabilities		
Buildings and equipment (net of accumulated depreciation of $313,000)	552,000		Bonds payable	$350,000	
			Mortgage payable	150,000	
			Total noncurrent liabilities		500,000
			Total liabilities		$1,199,000
Total noncurrent assets		637,000	Shareholders' equity		
			Paid-in capital	$600,000	
			Retained earnings	258,000	
			Total shareholders' equity		858,000
Total assets		$2,057,000	Total liabilities and shareholders' equity		$2,057,000

items show the total amount invested by owners, plus the total profits earned by the firm during previous periods, minus any amounts that have been distributed to owners. Similarly, the assets of the firm represent the total resources obtained by the firm from lenders and owners, minus those that have been consumed in the firm's operations, repaid to lenders, or distributed to owners.

Definitions of Assets, Liabilities, and Owners' Equity

The Financial Accounting Standards Board (FASB) has identified the essential characteristics of assets, liabilities, and owners' equity. The FASB definitions, which were introduced in Chapter 2, "The Basic Concepts of Financial Accounting," and are summarized in Exhibit 3-2, provide a frame of reference that helps accountants identify the items to be included in the balance sheet. They will be referred to frequently during the remaining discussions in this chapter. For now, note that according to the FASB's definitions, ***assets*** represent future benefits, ***liabilities*** represent future sacrifices, and ***owners' equity*** is the residual amount, or difference, between assets and liabilities.

The following pages introduce you to the types of individual assets, liabilities, and owners' equity to be found on the balance sheets of most business firms. In studying these individual balance sheet items, keep in mind the FASB's definitions shown in Exhibit 3-2.

Assets

As noted in Exhibit 3-2, assets represent "probable future economic benefits obtained or controlled by a particular entity as a result of past transactions or events." Future economic benefits come in many forms. For example, cash is an asset because it represents purchasing power; the firm can use cash to acquire goods and services, to repay debts, or to make distributions to owners. Inventories are assets because they are merchandise intended for sale to customers for cash and other assets. The firm's buildings and equipment are assets because they enable the firm to perform its operations and to earn profits in the future.

Assets typically represent tangible economic resources, such as cash, buildings, and trucks. On the other hand, some economic resources are intangible, such as patent rights and copyrights to a text or musical score. Assets may also be represented by promises of future payments from customers who bought goods or services on credit. Assets can be created by contract or acquisition of property rights, and yet they may not be visible to the human eye. All assets, however, have a common characteristic in that they represent probable future economic benefits to the firm.

EXHIBIT 3-2 FASB Definitions of Assets, Liabilities, and Owners' Equity

Assets are probable future economic benefits obtained or controlled by a particular entity as a result of past transactions or events.

Liabilities are probable future sacrifices of economic benefits arising from present obligations of a particular entity to transfer assets or provide services to other entities in the future as a result of past transactions or events.

Equity is the residual interest in the assets of an entity that remains after deducting liabilities. In a business enterprise, the equity is the ownership interest.

SOURCE: Statement of Financial Accounting Concepts No. 6, "Elements of Financial Statements" (Stamford, CT: FASB, 1980).

Asset Classifications Assets are classified into two overall categories: current assets and noncurrent assets. This distinction is based on the length of time before the asset is expected to be consumed or converted to cash. **Current assets** include cash and other assets that will typically become cash or be consumed in one year or one operating cycle, whichever is longer. Current assets are used quickly and repeatedly during a firm's normal operations. This notion of using assets on a cyclical basis corresponds to a concept called *turnover*. Current assets turn over quickly, anywhere from daily to annually, and are usually generated in the normal course of business operations. The notion of turnover is used to differentiate current assets from other asset categories that are used (turn over) much more slowly over a number of years.

To illustrate, Sample Company's balance sheet in Exhibit 3-1 shows that the firm's total assets of $2,057,000 are comprised of $1,420,000 in current assets and $637,000 in noncurrent assets. The balance sheet equation is easily expanded to show this additional detail:

ASSETS		=	LIABILITIES	+	OWNERS' EQUITY
Current	Noncurrent				
$1,420,000 +	$637,000	=	$1,199,000	+	$858,000
$2,057,000		=	$2,057,000		

This classification of assets is useful to the analyst concerned with the liquidity of the firm. **Liquidity** reflects the ability of the firm to generate sufficient cash to meet its operating cash needs and to pay its obligations as they become due. This focus on liquidity will become clear as we discuss the ordering and valuation of individual current assets in the next section.

Current Assets Current assets are listed in the order in which they are expected to be consumed or converted to cash. For example, Sample Company's current assets are listed (in Exhibit 3-1) in the following typical order of maturity or collectibility:

- cash and cash equivalents,
- accounts receivable,
- inventories, and
- prepaid expenses.

Cash and cash equivalents include currency, bank deposits, and various marketable securities that can be turned into cash on short notice merely by contacting a bank or broker. These amounts are presently available to meet the firm's cash payment requirements. Note that only securities that are purchased within 90 days of their maturity dates, or are scheduled to be converted to cash within the next 90 days, may be classified as cash equivalents.

Accounts receivable represent credit sales that have not been collected yet. They are converted into cash as soon as the customers or clients pay their bills (their accounts). Accounts receivable should turn over, or be collected, within the firm's normal collection period, which is usually 30 or 60 days. A slower accounts receivable turnover embodies more risk to the organization because the probability of nonpayment usually increases as turnover decreases. Overdue accounts may imply that the customer is either unable to pay or is unwilling to pay because of disagreement over the amounts billed. Both cases imply that the amount of cash that will ultimately be collected is less than the amount originally billed to the customer.

Managers are interested less in the total amount of accounts receivable than in the estimated cash to be generated from collections of the accounts. For this reason, accounts receivable are listed on the balance sheet at the amounts estimated to be actually collectible. This amount is termed the **net realizable value** of the receivables. For example, if management estimates that some portion of the amounts billed to customers will ultimately be uncollectible, then the estimated uncollectible portion will be deducted in valuing the accounts receivable on the balance sheet. The uncollectible portion of the receivables is termed an *allowance account* and is discussed in Chapter 6, "Current Assets."

Inventory represents items that have been purchased or manufactured for sale to customers. That is, inventory can either be created through the manufacturing and assembly efforts of the organization or be acquired from others and held for resale. Inventory is the "stuff of commerce" dating back to merchants on camels and pirates raiding the high seas looking for bounty. Inventory can be as prosaic as black tea or salt, or it can be as glamorous as gold bullion or silver coins. Today, inventory is often "high tech," such as silicon wafers, memory chips, or disk drives. Should the company discover that some of its inventory is unsalable, or marketable only at a greatly reduced price, the reported value of the inventory should be reduced accordingly.

Prepaid expenses, the final category of current assets shown in Exhibit 3-1, represents unexpired assets such as insurance premiums.Insurance policies, for example, are frequently paid ahead on an annual basis. The unexpired portion, the portion of the policy paid for but not yet used, is shown as part of prepaid expenses, which are interpreted as current assets. Prepaids are usually minor elements of the balance sheet, and, in the usual course of events, prepaids will not be converted or turned into cash. Instead, the rights to future benefits will be used up in future periods.

The Operating Cycle and Liquidity Manufacturing and merchandising firms' **operating cycles** include turning inventory into cash. Using three of the current assets discussed earlier, the operating cycle evolves from the purchase of inventory, to the exchange of inventory for a promised payment by a customer (an account receivable), and finally to the conversion of the receivable into cash. Operating cycles may vary in length from just a few days (in the case of food retailers) to months (consumer appliance sellers) or even years (defense contractors). Exhibit 3-3 illustrates the operating cycle.

The more quickly this cycle is completed, the more quickly the inventory is turned into cash, and liquidity is higher. When the operating cycle becomes longer, the firm's liquidity usually is lower. Should the operating cycle become too long, the firm will be forced to incur debt in order to pay its suppliers of inventory. To some extent, the length of the operating cycle is outside management's control. The length of time permitted customers to pay their accounts, for example, may be governed by industry practice. To attract and retain customers, the firm may need to offer credit terms as liberal as those offered by its competitors. Likewise, the amount of inventory that the firm keeps on hand may be related to the length of its "production pipeline." Some products require a lengthy production process that entails a substantial investment in inventory at various stages of completion.

On the other hand, the turnover of accounts receivable and inventory may be influenced by management. For instance, managers may have considerable leeway in of-

EXHIBIT 3-3 The Operating Cycle

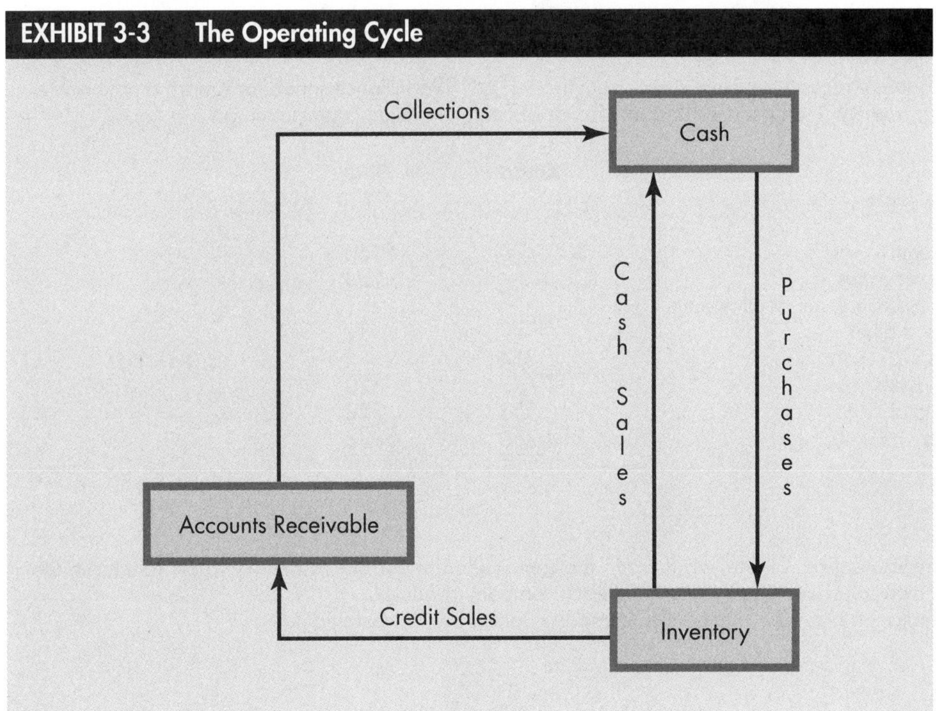

fering credit terms to customers or in deciding how much inventory to keep on hand. The analyst, in attempting to assess the firm's liquidity, needs to understand these underlying factors that cause differences in the amounts of accounts receivable and inventories across firms and industries. Reality Check 3-1 illustrates how the composition of current assets differs for two firms engaged in different industries.

Noncurrent Assets Noncurrent assets are long-term assets that are used in the conduct of the business. Whereas current assets are liquid and turn over in relatively short time periods, noncurrent assets usually turn over very slowly, on the order of once in several years. In other words, while the operating cycle for current assets is usually less than a year, the replacement cycle for noncurrent assets is longer than a year. In a high-tech organization, however, some noncurrent assets may be replaced more frequently.

All noncurrent assets are recorded on the balance sheet at their historical acquisition costs. The disadvantage of this is that as time passes the historical costs of many noncurrent assets become out of date relative to their current market values. Consequently, they indicate little about the market value of the organization and about the future resources necessary to replace the assets. However, the historical costs listed on the balance sheet do represent the costs of these assets that will eventually be consumed by future operations.

Property, Plant, and Equipment. For most firms, noncurrent assets consist mainly of **property, plant, and equipment.** These assets are widely referred to as **fixed assets**. **Property** usually represents the land on which the firm's offices, factories, and other facilities are located. In most cases, property is a relatively minor portion of the total noncurrent assets, yet in some cases, such as firms engaged in mining, logging,

REALITY CHECK 3-1

The following schedule summarizes the current assets from the end of 1996 balance sheets for Kmart, a national retailer of consumer products, and HBO, a producer and distributor of cable television programming:

	Kmart	HBO
(Dollars in millions)		
Current assets		
Cash and equivalents	$ 406	$160
Investment securities	—	23
Accounts receivable, net of allowance	—	291
Prepaids and other	973	39
Inventories	6,354	7
Total current assets	7,733	520
Noncurrent, total	6,553	328
Total assets	$14,286	$848

Required

a. Identify the major differences between these two firms in the composition of current assets. Try to explain these differences in terms of the types of goods and services that each company produces.
b. Based solely on the information provided here, which company appears to be more liquid?

Solution

a. The major differences in the composition of current assets are the amounts invested in inventories and accounts receivable.
   - Inventories: Kmart is a retailer of consumer products and maintains inventories of merchandise in regional warehouses and retail stores. HBO is a service firm and, hence, does not require inventories.
   - Accounts receivable: HBO invests about 34.3% of its total assets in customer accounts receivable ($291/$848 = 34.3%), and Kmart has no significant accounts receivable. Providers of subscription cable services such as HBO sell primarily on credit and have relatively large accounts receivable balances, while retailing firms such as Kmart derive much of their revenues from cash and credit card sales and require smaller (if any) accounts receivable balances.
b. Kmart's current assets include a substantial proportion in inventories, while HBO's current assets consist primarily of cash and accounts receivable. As a result, most analysts would consider HBO to be more liquid, based solely on the information provided.

or oil and gas exploration, property constitutes a major operating asset. Property is also valued on the balance sheet at its historical acquisition cost, and because property is usually one of the oldest assets held by an organization, its recorded historical cost is often the most out of date in terms of current market values.

Buildings and equipment represent the largest category of noncurrent assets, as shown in Exhibit 3-1. **Buildings** or **plant** may be office, retail, or factory buildings; warehouses or supply depots; or hospitals or health clinics. **Equipment** includes office desks and chairs, tools, drill presses, robots, computers, x-ray and other scanners, podiums, and so on. In other words, buildings and equipment are the primary productive assets of many organizations. Whether widgets or rings are produced, whether knowledge or health is improved, buildings and equipment are necessary to produce most goods and services.

Because buildings and equipment are long-lived assets, it would not make sense to treat their entire cost as expenses in the year they are acquired. On the other hand, because buildings and equipment gradually lose their economic value over time, it does not make sense to wait until the end of their service lives to recognize their declining usefulness to the firm. As a consequence, accountants gradually and systematically reduce the reported values of buildings and equipment on successive balance sheets in order to allocate expenses to individual years of asset use. The reduction in the reported value of buildings and equipment during a period is called **depreciation expense**.

On the balance sheet, the total amount of depreciation expense recognized to that date is called **accumulated depreciation.** It is subtracted from the initial cost of the asset. The resulting carrying value is referred to as the **net book value** of the asset. In Exhibit 3-1, the net book value of $552,000 for buildings and equipment is calculated by subtracting the $313,000 of accumulated depreciation from the original cost of $865,000:

Buildings and equipment	$865,000
Less: Accumulated depreciation	−313,000
Net book value	$552,000

In other words, of the original cost of $865,000, a total of $313,000 has been expensed, or written off, in previous periods. The net book value of these assets is unlikely to reflect their current resale value because of changes in technology, price inflation, and many other factors. Accumulated depreciation is not an attempt to adjust carrying values to current resale values. It also does not represent any cash or other investments that the company has set aside for replacing the buildings and equipment. Rather, depreciating an asset is an attempt to apportion or allocate its original cost as an expense to the periods that benefit from the asset's use.

The net book value of buildings and equipment can be used to estimate the remaining productive capacity of the organization. For example, Sample Company's buildings and equipment are about 36% depreciated ($313,000 accumulated depreciation divided by $865,000 initial cost). If Sample Company does not purchase additional buildings and equipment, then each successive balance sheet will show a lower net book value for these assets. Such a declining net book value will signal to analysts that Sample Company is not replenishing its productive capacity on a regular basis.

As a practical matter, most firms regularly invest in new plant and equipment and, as a result, the net book value of these assets usually increases over time. The percentage relationships between the initial cost and the accumulated depreciation of these assets may give analysts a rough gauge of the overall age of the firm's productive capacity. However, the analyst must usually refer to other disclosures in the financial statements to evaluate the firm's productive capacity.

Other Noncurrent Assets. In addition to property, plant, and equipment, many firms possess other noncurrent assets such as intangibles. **Intangibles** are noncurrent assets that lack physical substance and yet are important resources in the regular operations of a business. Intangibles often consist of legal rights, such as patents or copyrights. Such legal rights are vital to the operations of many firms and, in some cases, may be the most valuable resources owned by the organization.

Consider, for example, the importance of copyrights to computer software developers or book publishers. The value of such firms depends almost entirely on the value of the copyrights that protect their legal rights to the products they have developed. Accounting for intangible assets is similar to that of buildings and equipment because the initial costs are systematically recognized as expenses over the years that benefit from the use of the assets. Intangible assets are valued on the balance sheet at their historical costs, minus any amounts subsequently recognized as expenses. The term **amortization** is used in place of depreciation when referring to the consumption of intangible assets.

Another important type of intangible asset is goodwill. **Goodwill** is a general label used by accountants to denote the economic value of an acquired firm in excess of the value of its identifiable net assets (assets minus liabilities). Goodwill reflects the adage that "the value of the whole differs from the sum of its parts." This economic value is largely due to factors such as customer loyalty, employee competence and morale, management expertise, and so on. In other words, the value of a successful business firm is usually much greater than the total values of its individual assets.

The balance sheet recognition of goodwill depends on whether the firm's goodwill is internally generated or externally acquired. **Internally generated goodwill** evolves gradually as the firm develops a good reputation and customer base. It also evolves as the firm cultivates successful relationships with its suppliers, trains and retains a skilled labor force, and conducts other value-enhancing activities. The costs incurred in generating this goodwill are generally not recorded as assets by the firm and instead are recognized as expenses when incurred. The argument used to support the immediate expensing of these costs is the uncertainty and subjectivity involved in identifying future benefits. **Externally acquired goodwill**, on the other hand, usually arises when one business firm acquires another. In this case, the amount that the purchaser is paying for the goodwill of the seller can be more objectively determined by appraisers. Externally acquired goodwill is discussed more extensively in Chapter 13, "Reporting Issues for Affiliated and International Companies," which deals with various business combinations.

The composition of noncurrent assets, and the relative amounts of current to noncurrent assets, varies across industries. Reality Check 3-2 shows how noncurrent assets differ between two firms in different industries.

Assets: Summary and Evaluation Before leaving the asset side of the balance sheet, it is helpful to summarize the conventions used by accountants to define and value the firm's assets. We also identify here some of the limitations faced by analysts who must use asset values shown in the balance sheet to evaluate the firm's liquidity and productive capacity.

As we have seen, accountants classify assets into two broad groups: current and noncurrent. In reporting current assets, the focus is on liquidity. For this reason, current assets are generally valued at the lower of their acquisition costs or present resale values. An exception to this rule is made for investments in the securities of other firms, as we discuss in Chapter 6. These practices are useful to the analyst concerned with the ability of the firm to meet its short-term cash needs.

Noncurrent assets, on the other hand, are generally valued at their acquisition costs minus amounts that have been recognized as expenses in previous periods. These previously recognized expenses will have been shown as depreciation of buildings and equipment or as amortization of intangibles such as patents or good-

REALITY CHECK 3-2

The following schedule summarizes the noncurrent assets reported in the end-of-1997 balance sheets of Hewlett-Packard, a company that designs, manufactures, and services electronic data and communications systems, and Bethlehem Steel, a major steel fabricator.

	Hewlett-Packard	Bethlehem Steel
	(Dollars in millions)	
Current assets (total)	$20,947	$1,464
Noncurrent assets		
Property, plant, and equipment (at cost)	11,776	6,454
Less: Accumulated depreciation	(5,464)	(4,096)
Net	6,312	2,358
Long-term receivables and other	4,490	981
Total noncurrent assets	10,802	3,339
Total assets	$31,749	$4,803

Required

a. Identify the major differences between these two firms in the composition of noncurrent assets. Try to explain these differences based on the types of products that each company produces.
b. Based solely on the information provided here, which company appears to have the older assets?

Solution

a. Bethlehem Steel invests 69.5% of its resources in noncurrent assets ($3,339/$4,803 = 69.5%), and the corresponding amount for Hewlett-Packard is just 34.0% ($10,802/$31,749 = 34.0%). Bethlehem Steel is a highly capital-intensive firm because the technology of steel production requires large investments in plant and equipment. Steel firms also usually invest in properties containing natural resources (such as coal or iron ore) used in steel fabrication. In comparison, Hewlett-Packard is moderately capital intensive because of the property, plant, and equipment required by its product development and manufacturing activities.
b. Bethlehem Steel appears to have the older assets, which are about 63.5% depreciated ($4,096/$6,454 = 63.5%), while Hewlett-Packard's are about 46.4% depreciated ($5,464/$11,776 = 46.4%). These percentages are only approximations, however, because these amounts include property (land) that is not being depreciated.

will. In reporting noncurrent assets, the focus is on the **operating capacity** of the firm; that is, the firm must focus on the structure of its long-lived assets, both tangible and intangible, which are necessary in order for the firm to produce goods or services. The carrying values of these noncurrent assets represent the portion of their original acquisition costs that will be recognized as expenses in future periods. The carrying values of noncurrent assets rarely reflect their market values because inflation has usually caused asset replacement costs to increase beyond their reported values.

The experienced financial statement analyst is alert to two central issues in examining a firm's asset structure as reported on the balance sheet:

1. Different valuation methods are used for various types of assets (cost, market values, lower of cost or market value).

2. Many assets that are critical to the firm's successful operations are not shown on the balance sheet.

With respect to these "missing" assets, chief executive officers (CEOs) are fond of proclaiming:

- "Our employees are our most important resource."
- "Research today provides profits tomorrow."
- "Our reputation for quality ensures our success."

Regardless of these lofty statements, resources such as employee morale, productivity, research and development expertise, and a loyal and satisfied network of customers and suppliers are absent from the balance sheet. Accountants justify these omissions either because these valuable resources do not meet the conditions stated in the FASB's definition of assets (refer to Exhibit 3-2) or because there is no reliable method for measuring or valuing such resources.

Liabilities

As noted in Exhibit 3-2, liabilities represent "probable future sacrifices of economic benefits" that are the result of past transactions or events. Many times they entail cash payments to other entities, such as repayment to lenders of amounts that have been previously borrowed. The concept of a liability is somewhat broader than this. Liabilities include any probable obligation that the firm has incurred as a consequence of its past activities. For example, many firms warranty their products and consequently are obliged to perform repairs or pay refunds when defects are later uncovered, so, as you can see, not all liabilities require that the firm repay specific dollar amounts on specified dates. Moreover, some liabilities require estimation and judgment in order to determine their amounts. All liabilities, however, have a common characteristic: They represent probable future economic sacrifices by the firm.

Liability Classifications Just as with assets, liabilities are classified into two overall categories: current liabilities and noncurrent liabilities. The distinction is based on the length of time before the liability is expected to be repaid or otherwise satisfied by the firm and on whether payment will require the use of assets that are classified as current. **Current liabilities** are short-term obligations that are expected to utilize cash or other current assets within a year or an operating cycle, whichever is longer. **Noncurrent liabilities** represent obligations that generally require payment over periods longer than a year.

To illustrate, Sample Company's balance sheet in Exhibit 3-1 shows that the firm's total liabilities of $1,199,000 are comprised of $699,000 in current liabilities and $500,000 in noncurrent liabilities. The following balance sheet equation shows this additional detail:

ASSETS		=	LIABILITIES		+	OWNERS' EQUITY
Current	Noncurrent		Current	Noncurrent		
$1,420,000 +	$637,000	=	$699,000 +	$500,000	+	$858,000
$2,057,000		=		$2,057,000		

Current Liabilities The current liabilities of Sample Company, shown in Exhibit 3-1, consist of accounts payable, notes payable, warranty obligations, accrued expenses, and taxes payable. These liabilities represent various claims against the firm's economic resources.

Accounts payable usually represents debts that the firm incurs in purchasing inventories and supplies for manufacturing or resale purposes. Accounts payable also includes amounts that the firm owes for other services used in its operations, such as rentals, insurance, utilities, and so on. Accounts payable are often called *trade debt* because they represent debt that occurs in the normal course of any trade or business.

Notes payable, the next current liability shown in Exhibit 3-1, are more formal current liabilities than the accounts payable. A note may be signed on the borrowing of cash from a local bank. The note represents a legal document that a court can force the firm to satisfy.

Warranty obligations represent the firm's estimated future costs to fulfill its obligations for repair or refund guarantees. These obligations refer to any products sold or services provided prior to the balance sheet date. Unlike accounts and notes payable, the exact amount of the firm's obligations for warranties cannot be determined by referring to purchase documents, formal contracts, or similar evidence. Instead, the amount reported for the warranty obligation is based on management's judgment about future claims for repairs and refunds that may arise from past sales. The amount reported is an estimate, based in part on the past experience of the firm and its competitors. Recall that the FASB defines liabilities in terms of "probable future economic sacrifices" (refer to Exhibit 3-2). If Sample Company's products have required warranty repairs in the past, then it is probable that items sold recently will also require warranty repairs in the future. Because the sales have already occurred, the obligation exists at the balance sheet date, and these estimated amounts must be reported as liabilities.

The next item listed among Sample Company's current liabilities is **accrued expenses**, which represent liabilities for services already consumed but not yet paid for or included elsewhere in liabilities. These accrued liabilities usually constitute only a minor part of current liabilities.

Taxes payable comprise the final account listed among the current liabilities of Sample Company. **Taxes payable** represents unpaid taxes that are owed to the government and will be paid within a year. Taxes payable may include employee withholding taxes, unemployment taxes, employer income taxes, or any number of other taxes that are incurred in the normal course of operations. Taxes payable are typically a relatively minor portion of current liabilities because governmental units require that taxes be paid on a timely basis.

The current liabilities of Sample Company are a representative sample of many short-term liabilities. Businesses engage in many credit-based transactions; most sales to businesses involve accounts receivable, and most purchases by businesses correspondingly involve accounts payable. As a result, the largest of the current liabilities usually consists of trade accounts payable. The other liability items, although less significant in dollar amount, also represent common business transactions and circumstances.

Noncurrent Liabilities Noncurrent liabilities generally have longer maturities than the current liabilities discussed in the preceding section. Their maturity date is more than one year. Most noncurrent liabilities represent contracts to repay debts at specified future dates. In addition, these borrowing agreements often place some restrictions on the activities of the firm until the debt is fully repaid. In Chapter 9, "Noncurrent Liabilities," we discuss a variety of different borrowing arrangements that are widely used.

Exhibit 3-1 shows that Sample Company has two types of noncurrent liabilities: bonds payable and mortgage payable. These liabilities are similar because they require Sample Company to make future payments of interest and principal. Yet they differ in terms of the **collateral** that Sample Company used to obtain the loan.

Bonds payable are a major source of funds for larger business firms. They represent liabilities that the firm incurs by selling a contract called a bond. A **bond** contains the firm's promise to pay interest periodically (usually every six months) and to repay the money originally borrowed **(principal)** when the bond matures. The amount of money that the firm receives from investors for its bonds depends on investors' views about the riskiness of the firm and the prevailing rate of interest. Investors rely on the ability of the firm to generate sufficient cash flows from its operations to meet the payments as they become due.

Mortgage payable is similar to bonds payable because firms must also make principal and interest payments as they are due. Unlike most bonds, a mortgage represents a pledge of certain assets that will revert to the lender if the debt is not paid. The simplest example of a mortgage is that of a bank holding title to your house until your loan is fully paid. If the loan is not paid, the bank can sell the house and use the proceeds to pay off the debt. Mortgages on factories and hospitals are very similar. The problem in such cases is that there are often very few buyers of specialized assets such as factory buildings and equipment. In such cases, possible mortgage default represents more risk and higher costs to lenders. It also indicates that most lenders will cooperate with borrowers to find alternative solutions to avoid defaults. From an analytical perspective, the analyst or manager must make sure that mortgage terms are being satisfied and that payments have been promptly remitted. For both bonds and mortgages, analysts will try to discern whether cash flows from operations are sufficient to pay the interest and principal.

Liabilities: Summary and Evaluation Before leaving the liabilities or "borrowed resources" part of the balance sheet, it is useful to summarize various liabilities and to point out some limitations faced by analysts in assessing the firm's liabilities.

Liabilities are classified as either current or noncurrent, based on their maturity dates. The current liabilities of the firm are closely related to its operations. As examples, trade accounts payable arise as a direct consequence of purchasing inventory; accrued expenses and taxes payable result from the firm's operating and tax expenses; and product warranty obligations occur because the firm has sold products covered by warranties. For this reason, analysts often refer to these types of obligations as *spontaneous* or *operating liabilities*.

In contrast, noncurrent liabilities consist mainly of long-term borrowing contracts that managers have negotiated with investors, banks, and other parties. This type of borrowing reflects a deliberate decision by managers to obtain funds from lenders, rather than to obtain additional investments from owners. The decision about how much of the firm's resources should be provided by long-term borrowing and how much should be invested by owners is a fundamental issue faced by all firms.

Financial statement users are concerned with the firm's ability to pay both its short-term and long-term obligations as they mature. Later in this chapter, we discuss some ratios that are useful for making these assessments. The analyst is aware of two important features of liability reporting. First, not all liabilities result from promises by the firm to repay specific amounts at determinable future dates. Instead, many liabilities require estimates of future events, such as the warranty obligations reported in Sample Company's balance sheet. Many other obligations reported by business firms entail similar liability estimates, as we discuss later in Chapter 8, "Accounts Payable, Commitments, Contingencies, and Risks," and Chapter 9.

Second, the analyst is aware that some potential obligations of business firms either are not reported on the balance sheet or are reported at amounts that do not adequately reflect their potential future claims against the assets of the firm. Consider, for example, lawsuits against the firm. At present, tobacco firms are disputing a lengthy list of ailments allegedly associated with cigarette smoking. Similarly, large chemical and nuclear industry firms are being sued over toxic wastes. In these cases, the potential damages awarded to plaintiffs could result in awards of billions of dollars. Although these potentially ruinous lawsuits are based on business activities prior to the current balance sheet date, none of these firms reports significant contingent liabilities because the loss cannot be reliably estimated at this time. Contingent liabilities are discussed further in Chapter 8.

Owners' Equity

This final element of the balance sheet represents the equity of the firm's owners. As shown in Exhibit 3-2, the FASB defines **owners' equity** simply as the "residual interest in the assets of an entity that remains after deducting liabilities." This definition makes it clear that the balance sheet's valuation of owners' equity is determined by its valuations of assets and liabilities. This view of owners' equity as a *residual amount* is apparent when we rearrange the balance sheet equation in the following way:

OWNERS' EQUITY = ASSETS − LIABILITIES

Sample Company's balance sheet in Exhibit 3-1 shows a firm that has been organized as a **corporation**, which is an entity that is owned by a group of shareholders. Although a corporation's owners' equity may be called shareholders' equity, in Sample Company, it comprises both **paid-in capital**, which represents direct investments by the owners of the firm, and **retained earnings**, which represents the earnings of the firm that have been reinvested in the business. Sample Company's balance sheet in Exhibit 3-1 shows that owners have paid $600,000 for shares of stock of the company. Sample Company has received this invested capital (probably in cash from investors) in exchange for its shares of stock. In addition, the firm has been profitable in the past, and Sample Company has reinvested $258,000 of those profits in the business. This $258,000 represents Sample's retained earnings.

If in the next year, Sample Company reports profits of $200,000 and pays dividends to shareholders of $75,000, then retained earnings will increase by $125,000 ($200,000 − $75,000). Bear in mind, however, that retained earnings do not represent cash available for the payment of dividends. Rather, retained earnings reflect the amount of resources that a firm has obtained as a result of operations. The firm

REALITY CHECK 3-3

The following schedule summarizes the components of shareholders' equity reported in the end-of-1997 balance sheets of Bethlehem Steel and Lear Corporation:

	Bethlehem Steel	Lear Corporation
	(Dollars in millions)	
Shareholders' equity:		
Paid-in capital	$1,923	$ 852
Retained earnings (deficit)	(708)	401
Other	—	(46)
Total shareholders' equity	$1,215	$1,207

Required

a. Which firm has obtained the larger amount of capital through sale of stock to investors?
b. Which firm has obtained the larger amount of capital through reinvestment of earnings?
c. Explain why Bethlehem reports a negative (deficit) balance in retained earnings at the end of 1997.
d. Suppose that Lear earns $150 and pays dividends of $90 during 1998. What would be the firm's ending balance in retained earnings? (All dollars are in millions.)

Solution

a. Paid-in capital represents the amount that each firm has received through the sale of stock to investors. Bethlehem Steel has obtained $1,923 million, and Lear obtained $852 million from this source.
b. Lear has obtained $401 million of its investment in net assets through retention of earnings. Bethlehem Steel, on the other hand, has a negative balance in its retained earnings. For this reason, Bethlehem has not obtained any of its capital through reinvestment of earnings.
c. Retained earnings are increased when a firm is profitable and decreased when a firm pays dividends to shareholders or incurs losses. The negative (deficit) balance in Bethlehem's retained earnings indicates that since the firm began operations, its total dividends and losses have exceeded its total income.
d. Lear would report a balance in retained earnings at the end of 1998 of $461 (in millions), computed as follows:

Retained earnings, end of 1997	$401
Add: Net income for 1998	150
Less: Dividends in 1998	(90)
Retained earnings, end of 1998	$461

has retained this increase for use in its operations, rather than returning it immediately to the investors as dividends. Those resources are presently invested as shown on the asset side of the balance sheet. For this reason, it is possible that a firm may have a large retained earnings balance, but have insufficient cash available for dividends.

Reality Check 3-3 illustrates the reporting of shareholders' equity for two firms, one of which reports a negative (deficit) balance in retained earnings.

This discussion of owners' equity completes our tour of Sample Company's balance sheet, and, at this point, you are aware of the typical components of the balance sheets of most business firms. In future chapters, we will generally use the term shareholders' equity, rather than the more generic term owners' equity. The following section illustrates a variety of balance sheet relationships that are of interest to analysts.

Balance Sheet Analysis

Various ratios are used to help interpret and understand financial statements. These ratios are guides to understanding changes in financial performance for one company from year to year and differences in financial performance between two or more companies. Ratios are most useful when comparisons are made, either between time periods or among different companies. Ratios are useful shortcuts that permit the analyst to collapse the myriad details in financial statements into a few simple numbers. But remember that the ratio calculations are not the answers; they just show relationships. The analyst or manager must understand those relationships and make decisions on the basis of a host of information.

Ratios are just one input to those decisions. In other words, ratios are one indicator of financial health and viability, but they do not tell the whole story. Users of financial statements must be careful not to become too enamored of the ratios themselves and should not forget to look for other indicators that will permit better decision making. Also, ratios are historical. Judgment is needed to use them for decision making because future conditions may change. Bear in mind that ratios are only as good as the data that comprise them. The discussions in later chapters will help you be aware of differences in accounting policies that can cause differences in ratios.

Balance sheet ratios aid the analyst in assessing a firm's liquidity, asset management, and debt management policies, each of which is discussed in this section.

Vertical Analysis Analysts usually begin with a review of the firm's assets, as well as its liabilities and owners' equity. This review begins with the preparation of a common-size balance sheet, which shows the percentage component of each major section to the grand totals on each side of the balance sheet. This analysis is called **vertical analysis**, or **vertical percentage analysis**, because it is based on the percentage relationship of each line in the balance sheet to the total. Exhibit 3-1 has been revised as Exhibit 3-4, showing the vertical percentages for each account on the balance sheet. These percentages are calculated by dividing each line by the total assets ($2,057,000). Note that either total assets or total liabilities plus owners' equity can be used as the denominator for this calculation because the number is the same ($2,057,000).

Liquidity Ratios Liquidity represents the ability of a company to convert its assets to cash, and **liquidity ratios** are often calculated from balance sheet data. Although there are many types of liquidity ratios, we focus here on a few of the more basic ones.

Current Ratio. The most popular liquidity ratio is the current ratio. The **current ratio** is calculated by dividing all current assets by all current liabilities:

$$\text{Current ratio} = \frac{\text{Current assets}}{\text{Current liabilities}}$$

For the data in Exhibit 3-1,

$$\text{Current ratio} = \frac{\$1{,}420{,}000}{\$699{,}000} = 2.03$$

Current ratios that represent good liquidity and financial health vary widely across firms and industries. Currently, many companies have a current ratio between 1.3 and

EXHIBIT 3-4 Vertical Analysis

Sample Company Balance Sheet: Vertical Analysis at December 31, 2000

Assets			**Liabilities and Owners' Equity**		
Current assets			Current liabilities		
Cash	5.3%		Accounts payable	12.6%	
Accounts receivable	22.6		Notes payable	10.9	
Inventories	39.5		Warranty obligations	5.4	
Prepaid expenses	1.6		Accrued expenses	3.6	
Total current assets		69.0%	Taxes payable	1.3	
Noncurrent Assets			Total current liabilities		33.8%
Land	4.1%		Noncurrent liabilities		
Buildings and equipment (net of accumulated depreciation of $313,000)	26.9		Bonds payable	17.1%	
			Mortgage payable	7.3	
			Total noncurrent liabilities		24.4
			Total liabilities		58.2%
Total noncurrent assets		31.0	Shareholders' equity		
			Paid-in capital	29.3%	
			Retained earnings	12.5	
			Total shareholders' equity		41.8
Total assets		100.0%	Total liabilities and shareholders' equity		100.0%

1.5. Many companies have short-term lines of credit and other borrowing capacities that permit them to operate with a nearly balanced amount of current assets and current liabilities. In any event, the analyst would be worried to find current liabilities substantially in excess of current assets (in other words, when the current ratio is considerably less than 1). Declining trends in the current ratio would also cause concern, especially in conjunction with declining trends in other ratios.

Quick Ratio. Another major liquidity ratio is the quick ratio, which is often called the *acid test.* In this context, "quick" means close to cash. To calculate this ratio, cash and receivables are added and then divided by all current liabilities. In computing the quick ratio, the net realizable value of the accounts receivable should be used.

The purpose of the **quick ratio** is to indicate the resources that may be available quickly, in the short term, for repaying the current liabilities. For this reason, inventory and prepaid expenses are left out. In other words, the quick ratio is a type of "disaster" ratio that is used to indicate a worst case scenario that might apply if no other resources are available to pay the current liabilities that are due within the next year.

$$\text{Quick ratio} = \frac{(\text{Cash} + \text{Receivables})}{\text{Current liabilities}}$$

For the data in Exhibit 3-1,

$$\text{Quick ratio} = \frac{(\$110{,}000 + \$466{,}000)}{\$699{,}000}$$
$$= .82$$

Values for the quick ratio are often less than 1.0, and a rule of thumb used by some analysts is that the quick ratio should not be less than .30. Again, declining trends should cause the most concern. When comparing two companies, a lower quick ratio and a lower current ratio do not, in and of themselves, indicate that the company with the lower values is in worse financial condition. Lower liquidity may be offset by a variety of other financial indicators, such that the company with lower liquidity ratios could still rank higher on its overall financial stability and financial health.

Information useful for calculating the current and quick ratios for a firm at two successive dates is shown in Reality Check 3-4.

Asset Management Ratios **Asset management ratios** focus on the composition of the firm's assets and on changes in the composition of assets over time (changes between successive balance sheets). A vertical analysis of the left side of the balance sheet allows the analyst to examine the percentages of the total assets devoted to each

REALITY CHECK 3-4

The following schedule summarizes the composition of current assets and current liabilities reported in Apple Computer's end-of-1996 and 1995 balance sheets:

	1996	1995
	(Dollars in millions)	
Total current assets	$4,515	$5,224
Inventories included in current assets	662	1,775
Prepayment and supplies included in current assets	612	566
Total current liabilities	2,003	2,325

Required

a. Based on the information given here, determine the firm's current ratio and quick ratio at the end of 1996 and 1995.
b. In which year do you consider the firm to be in better financial condition? Explain.

Solution

a. Calculation of current ratio and quick ratio:

		1996	1995
Current ratio =	$\frac{\text{Current assets}}{\text{Current liabilities}}$	$\frac{\$4,515}{\$2,003}$ = 2.25	$\frac{\$5,224}{\$2,325}$ = 2.25
Quick ratio =	$\frac{\text{Quick assets*}}{\text{Current liabilities}}$	$\frac{\$3,240}{\$2,003}$ = 1.62	$\frac{\$2,883}{\$2,325}$ = 1.24

b. Apple Computer has about the same current ratio in each year. Apple's quick ratio, however, has increased from 1.24 to 1.62. Although Apple appears to be more liquid in 1996, the analyst would seek additional information from the financial statements and elsewhere before making a final judgment.

*Quick assets are estimated as current assets, minus the amounts in inventories, prepayments, and supplies.

category. This examination gives some indication of the resources used for current assets relative to those used to provide operating capacity.

In reviewing the **percentage composition** of a firm's assets, the analyst keeps several factors in mind. First, to a large extent, the composition of assets depends on the industry in which the firm operates. In some cases, comparisons between industries may be meaningless. "Smokestack" industries, for example, such as metal fabrication, require large investments in factory buildings and heavy equipment, such that a major portion of these firms' assets are noncurrent. On the other hand, merchandising industries, such as department stores, require large amounts of accounts receivable and also substantial investments in inventories available for resale, but relatively minor investment in buildings and equipment. Financial firms such as banks and insurance companies have relatively little in the way of inventories, factory buildings, and equipment. Instead, the assets of financial firms consist mainly of loans receivable and investments in securities (stocks and bonds) of other firms. A first step for the analyst in assessing a firm's asset composition is to be aware of any peculiar industry norms or special circumstances.

In addition to industry characteristics, the analyst knows that managers may have sound business reasons for structuring a firm's assets differently than those of its competitors. For example, some managers may extend liberal credit terms to customers as a way of improving sales and, as a result, may have a large accounts receivable balance. Other managers may carry large inventories for customer convenience or may stockpile inventories in anticipation of rising price or supply bottlenecks. On the other hand, large amounts of accounts receivable may indicate that a firm has difficulty collecting its accounts. Similarly, large inventories may reflect obsolete items or declining product sales. In short, increases or decreases in specific components of a firm's total assets may be either good news or bad news. Any ratio computations are only the first step for the analyst. The creative art in ratio analysis is understanding the reasons for ratio differences among firms and over time.

Debt Management Ratios The most inclusive and most useful **debt management ratios** are the composition ratios drawn from a vertical analysis of the right side of the balance sheet. Note the liability and equity composition ratios in the right-hand column of Exhibit 3-4. These percentage composition ratios indicate the relative proportions of various forms of debt and owners' equity used to finance the organization.

The vertical analysis of Sample Company's sources of funds shows that 33.8% of all financing came from current liabilities. A smaller amount (24.4%) came from long-term liabilities, and the largest portion (41.8%) came from owners. Of the 41.8% portion that came from owners, 29.3% was in the form of direct investment, and 12.5% was in the form of profits reinvested in the business.

The ratio of total debt to total assets, also called the **debt-to-assets ratio**, is often used as a primary indicator of the firm's debt management. Exhibit 3-4 shows that Sample Company's total liabilities are equal to 58.2% of total assets. As this key ratio increases or decreases, it indicates the firm's changing reliance on borrowed resources. The lower the ratio, the lower the firm's risk because the organization will usually be better able to meet its obligations for interest and debt payments. A lower debt-to-assets ratio also suggests a lower risk of default. Default on a firm's liabilities is a costly event from both a lender's and a borrower's perspective and should be avoided if at all possible.

The fact that Sample Company's owners' equity provides 41.8% of the firm's resources suggests that the owners' equity of this firm offers substantial protection to lenders. Suppose, for example, Sample Company was unable to continue its operations and had to **liquidate** its assets, or, in other words, convert its assets to cash. In such a situation, Sample Company could incur losses of 41.8% of the assets' carrying value, and the cash received would still be sufficient to pay off all the firm's debts. Of course, nothing would then be left for the owners.

Limitations of Balance Sheet Analysis Although the ratios reviewed in this section provide a useful starting point for assessing a firm's financial management policies, several limitations must be considered. First, ratio calculations are only the initial step in analyzing a firm's condition. They merely provide the analyst with a point of departure for asking further questions. Second, individual financial statements such as the balance sheet are seldom analyzed separately from other statements described in the next two chapters. In fact, many of the most useful ratios used by analysts measure relationships among financial statements, rather than relationships within a single financial statement. For this reason, we will expand and enrich our study of ratio analysis after first describing the other primary financial statements. Third, information useful for analyzing and clarifying financial statements is contained in other parts of a company's financial reports.

An important limitation in comparing financial ratios across firms is the fact that their accounting methods may differ. Later chapters discuss the varieties of different methods that firms may use in measuring assets, liabilities, shareholders' equity, revenues, and expenses. For now, be aware that financial ratios may be significantly affected by alternative accounting methods. The analyst attempts to adjust for differences caused by accounting methods in order to make valid ratio comparisons among different firms. The notes to the financial statements alert the analyst to the principal methods being used.

KEY TERMS

Accounts payable 77
Accounts receivable 69
Accrued expenses 77
Accumulated depreciation 73
Amortization 74
Asset management ratios 83
Bond 78
Bonds payable 78
Buildings 72
Cash and cash equivalents 69
Collateral 78
Corporation 79
Current assets 69
Current liabilities 76
Current ratio 81
Debt management ratios 84
Debt-to-assets ratio 84
Depreciation expense 73
Equipment 72
Externally generated goodwill 74
Fixed assets 71
Goodwill 74
Intangibles 73
Internally generated goodwill 74
Inventory 70
Liquidity 69
Liquidity ratio 81
Mortgage payable 78
Net book value 73
Net realizable value 70
Noncurrent assets 71
Noncurrent liabilities 76
Notes payable 77
Operating capacity 75
Operating cycles 70
Owners' equity 79
Paid-in capital 79
Percentage composition 84
Plant 72
Prepaid expenses 70
Principal 78
Property 71
Property, plant, and equipment 71
Quick ratio 82
Retained earnings 79
Statement of financial position 66
Taxes payable 77
Vertical analysis 81
Vertical percentage analysis 81
Warranty obligations 77

SUMMARY OF LEARNING OBJECTIVES

1. **Identify the basic elements of the balance sheet.**
The basic elements of the balance sheet are assets, liabilities, and owners' equity. Liabilities and owners' equity are the sources from which a firm has obtained its funds, and assets show the way that the firm's managers have invested those funds.
2. **Recognize the types of assets, liabilities, and owners' equity that are found on the balance sheets of most business firms.**
Assets are resources that are expected to benefit the firm in future periods, including cash, accounts receivable, inventories held for production and sale, prepayments of expenses, and property, plant, and equipment. Liabilities are obligations to provide future services or to make future payments, and include trade accounts payable, short- and long-term borrowings, and other debts. Owners' equity is the difference between assets and liabilities. For a corporation, owners' equity consists of invested capital, which has been paid by investors to obtain ownership shares, and retained earnings, which represent earnings that have been reinvested in the business.
3. **Comprehend the ordering and classification of items on the balance sheet.**
Both assets and liabilities are listed in order of liquidity or maturity on the balance sheet. They are further classified into current and noncurrent portions. Current assets will become cash or be consumed in a year or an operating cycle, whichever is longer; current liabilities require payment from current assets.
4. **Appreciate why balance sheets differ for firms in different industries.**
"Smokestack" industries require large investments in factory buildings and heavy equipment, and a major portion of their assets are noncurrent. Merchandising industries, however, require large investments in accounts receivable and inventories and relatively minor investments in buildings and equipment. Financial firms such as banks have relatively little investment in inventories, factory buildings, and equipment. Instead, their assets consist mainly of loans receivable and investments in securities (stocks and bonds) of other firms.
5. **Use balance sheet relationships to obtain information useful to investors and lenders.**
Various ratios help assess a firm's liquidity, asset management, and debt management policies. Liquidity ratios aid in assessing how the firm may pay its debts and meet its other short-term cash requirements. Asset management ratios show how the funds invested in the firm are being used. Debt management ratios show the firm's reliance on borrowed capital and the buffer or "safety zone" provided by owners' equity.
6. **Be aware of the limitations as well as the usefulness of balance sheet information.**
Balance sheet relationships do not provide direct answers to the analyst in assessing the firm's potential risks and returns; they merely provide a base for further questions. The balance sheet is also rarely analyzed separately from the other financial statements, which will be discussed in subsequent chapters. Moreover, an important limitation in comparing financial relationships across firms is the fact that their accounting methods may differ.

QUESTIONS

3-1 Rearrange the balance sheet equation into several variations. Why are these differences helpful? How might each version be used? Should an analyst always use the simplest version possible? Why or why not?

3-2 Discuss the role and purpose of the balance sheet. How is it different from an income statement?

3-3 Explain why both sides of the balance sheet must have the same total dollar amount. Does this equality imply that the balance sheet is "correct" as a measure of financial position? Discuss.

3-4 The balance sheet may be viewed as *the cumulative result of the firm's past activities*. Explain how the assets, liabilities, and equity amounts may be interpreted in this way.

3-5 All assets represent probable future economic benefits to the firm. Identify the probable future benefit associated with each of the following: (a) inventories, (b) accounts receivable, and (c) building and equipment.

3-6 Compare and contrast current assets and current liabilities. How and why are they different? In what ways are they similar?

3-7 Compare and contrast prepaid expenses and accrued expenses. How and why are they different? Could they be easily confused? How are they being kept separate?

3-8 Differentiate between current and noncurrent assets, and explain why this distinction may be useful to readers of financial reports.

3-9 Compare and contrast noncurrent assets and long-term liabilities. How and why are they different? In what ways are they similar?

3-10 Describe the concept of an operating cycle. Identify reasons why operating cycles may differ for firms in different industries, and also for firms in the same industry.

3-11 What is meant by the term *net book value* of a firm's building and equipment? Explain why net book value differs from the initial cost of these assets and is also likely to differ from current market (resale) values.

3-12 Differentiate between tangible and intangible assets. Do you believe that both types of assets are equally important in measuring a firm's financial position? Discuss.

3-13 Define the term *net realizable value* as it refers to accounts receivable. Why would a financial analyst or manager be interested in the net realizable value of receivables, as compared to the gross amount of such receivables?

3-14 Distinguish between unreported assets and unreported liabilities. Why are items that are unreported on a balance sheet important to financial analysts or managers? Would a banker or other creditor be interested in such items? Why?

3-15 Distinguish between internally generated and externally acquired goodwill. Which of these is reported on the balance sheet? State and defend your agreement or disagreement with this accounting convention.

3-16 Analysts often attempt to estimate the values of assets that are "missing" from the balance sheet. Identify at least two kinds of missing assets and discuss reasons for this omission from the balance sheet.

3-17 Identify several examples of liabilities that do not require payments of specific dollar amounts to lenders.

3-18 Discuss the differences between bonds payable and mortgages payable. As a potential lender, which type of debt is preferable?

3-19 Discuss the concept of owners' equity on the balance sheet. In what ways does owners' equity represent a *residual* interest? Why is owners' equity called a *residual* amount?

3-20 Is it possible for a firm to report a substantial amount of retained earnings on its balance sheet and still be unable to pay its shareholders a cash dividend? Explain.

3-21 Compare and contrast the current ratio and the quick ratio.
   a. When might these two ratios be similar in amount?
   b. When will they be different in amount?
   c. If the current ratio is at an acceptable level but the quick ratio is weak, what factors might cause this?
   d. Why might some firms prefer to have low current and quick ratios?

3-22 How much flexibility should the analyst or manager accept in constructing ratio definitions for use within the same company or organization? For example, why might the analyst be more flexible in defining the quick ratio but not the current ratio? On the other hand, would the same flexibility be associated with a vertical analysis? Why not?

3-23 Discuss the process of calculating balance sheet vertical (composition) ratios. How are such ratios used? Why are these ratios important?

Reclassifying Liabilities

3-24 Suppose that a supervisor asks you to reclassify a short-term note payable as a long-term liability.
   a. What effect will this have on the current ratio?
   b. Could such an effect be viewed beneficially by a current or prospective lender?
   c. How would your answer change if the lender agreed to extend the due date on the loan by 18 months?
   d. How would your answer in part b change if a prospective lender also held other long-term liabilities? Why?
   e. Consider the ethical implications of reclassifying the note, assuming that you know the note's maturity is at the end of the current fiscal year. You may assume that the size of the note is significant (or material). As an accountant within the firm, what should/would you do? As the firm's auditor, how would you view this reclassification?

EXERCISES

Classifying Accounts

3-25 Classify each account listed below into one of the following categories:
   1. current assets,
   2. noncurrent assets,
   3. current liabilities,
   4. noncurrent liabilities, and
   5. owners' equity.
      a. cash
      b. retained earnings
      c. land
      d. invested capital
      e. accounts payable
      f. accounts receivable

g. mortgage payable
h. marketable securities
i. prepaid expenses
j. wages payable
k. unemployment taxes payable
l. accumulated depreciation
m. inventory
n. prepaid insurance
o. patents (or copyrights)
p. externally acquired goodwill

Arranging Accounts in Balance Sheet Order

3-26 Rearrange the following accounts in the order in which you would expect to find them in a typical balance sheet and explain why you put them in that order:

a. Mortgage payable
b. Accounts payable
c. Taxes payable
d. Owner's Equity
e. Inventory
f. Cash
g. Land
h. Building
i. Accrued expenses
j. Long-term notes payable

Sorting Balance Sheet Information

3-27 The account balances given below are shown on the balance sheet of a corporation.

Marketable securities	$ 20,000
Invested capital	200,000
Buildings and equipment	400,000
Accounts receivable	80,000
Prepaid rent	17,000
Bonds payable	230,000
Inventories	85,000
Taxes payable	30,000
Accounts payable	16,000
Advance payments from customers	3,000
Interest payable	9,000
Land	19,000
Retained earnings	133,000

Required

Arrange three columns corresponding to the balance sheet equation:

ASSETS = LIABILITIES + OWNERS' EQUITY

Finding Missing Balance Sheet Information

3-28 The following balances appear in the records of May Co. at the end of its first month of operations:

Cash	$12,000	Land	$100,000
Equipment	6,500	Accounts payable	3,400
Supplies	2,700	Accounts receivable	7,500
Taxes payable	2,110	Truck	22,500
Mortgage	80,000	Owners' equity	?

Required

a. Determine the missing item by preparing a balance sheet.

b. Identify two other typical accounts that might appear on May's balance sheet but are not shown here.

PROBLEMS

Critical Thinking

Preparing a Balance Sheet with Missing or Inconsistent Information

3-29 The following information is provided for Tom's Track Shoe Store at the end of 2000:

Accounts receivable	$ 6,500
Accounts payable	106,500
Bonds payable	180,000
Invested capital	300,000
Cash	14,500
Equipment	88,000
Income taxes payable	11,500
Inventory	497,500
Other long-term assets	110,000
Notes payable	50,000
Prepaid rent	54,000
Retained earnings, 12-31-99	94,500
Retained earnings, 12-31-00	?

Required

a. Prepare a balance sheet, and make it balance. Discuss the steps necessary to balance it along with any necessary assumptions.

b. What conclusions can be drawn regarding this business? Why?

Integration of Concepts

Preparing and Evaluating Balance Sheet Information

3-30 The following data are available:

Cash	$100,000
Accounts payable	55,000
Retained earnings	?
Invested capital	150,000
Buildings and equipment	600,000
Mortgage payable	400,000

Required

a. Prepare a balance sheet.

b. Would most businesses, in reality, have such a limited balance sheet? Why not?

c. What other accounts might usually be found in a balance sheet for a service company? Discuss the differences between balance sheets for companies providing services versus those manufacturing products. Why are these differences essential? How are they useful to the financial analyst?

Effects of Transactions on Balance Sheet

3-31 The following transactions are given:

a. A corporation issued common stock for cash.
b. The firm bought land with part of the cash.
c. The firm issued common stock in exchange for a building and equipment.
d. The firm purchased inventory on account.
e. The firm collected cash from a customer for merchandise sold several months previously.
f. A corporation issued some of its common stock in exchange for a parcel of land.
g. The firm paid cash to its creditors.
h. The firm sells obsolete equipment at its net book value.

Required:

Indicate the effects of the transactions on the balance sheet equation:

ASSETS = LIABILITIES + OWNERS' EQUITY

Transaction Analysis

3-32 The following transactions are given:

a. A corporation issued capital stock in exchange for land valued at $300,000.
b. A corporation issued capital stock for $200,000.
c. The corporation hired a chief executive officer (CEO) at $180,000 per year.
d. The firm agreed to rent office space at $2,000 per month.
e. The firm paid the first month's rent.
f. The firm paid the last month's rent as a security deposit.
g. The firm bought supplies for $2,500.
h. The firm ordered office equipment costing $15,000 (assume no obligation has occurred yet).
i. The CEO finished her first month's work.
j. The firm paid the CEO her first month's salary.
k. The firm received the office equipment and the bill. The equipment is expected to last five years.
l. The firm recorded depreciation for the first month, using straight-line depreciation.

Required:

Analyze the transactions, using the balance sheet equation, and prepare a simple balance sheet:

ASSETS = LIABILITIES + OWNERS' EQUITY

Transaction Analysis

3-33 The following transactions are given:

a. A law firm was formed by 10 lawyers, each investing $200,000.
b. The firm charged its clients $1,200,000 for services rendered in May.
c. The law firm collected $900,000 from its clients.

d. One disgruntled client sued the law firm for malfeasance in the amount of $5,000,000. The firm believes the lawsuit is frivolous.
e. The law firm paid its lawyers $333,000 for work performed in May.
f. The law firm ordered and received supplies costing $33,000 on account. However, 10% of the order was damaged, so the firm returned the damaged supplies for credit.
g. The law firm paid $155,000 for rent and other administrative costs.
h. The law firm settled the suit by paying the disgruntled client $10,000.

Required:

Analyze the transactions, using the balance sheet equation, and prepare a simple balance sheet:

ASSETS = LIABILITIES + OWNERS' EQUITY

Calculating Liquidity Ratios

Critical Thinking

3-34 The following schedule summarizes the composition of current assets and current liabilities reported in the year-end balance sheets from Triangle Air Lines and Nazareth Steel:

	Triangle Air Lines	Nazareth Steel
	(Dollars in millions)	
Total current assets	$2,821,920	$1,591,100
Inventories included in current assets	0	852,500
Prepayment and supplies included in current assets	586,751	6,500
Total current liabilities	2,972,831	914,200

Required

a. Based on the information given here, determine each firm's current ratio and quick ratio at the end of the year.
b. Which firm do you consider to be in better financial condition? Explain.

Liquidity Analysis: Current Ratio and Quick Ratio

Critical Thinking

3-35 Wesfarmers Limited is a major diversified Australian public company with interests in fertilizer and chemicals manufacturing, gas processing and distribution, coal mining and production, building materials, hardware and forest products, rural and country services, transport, country supermarkets, and insurance. The following schedule summarizes the composition of current assets and current liabilities reported on its June 30, 1996 and June 30, 1997 balance sheets:

	Wesfarmers Limited	
	1997	1996
	(Dollars in millions)	
Total current assets	$761	$688
Inventories included in current assets	368	1
Receivables included in current assets	362	685
Total current liabilities	822	155

Required

a. Based on the information given here, determine the firm's current ratio and quick ratio at the end of 1997 and 1996.
b. In which year do you consider the firm to be in better financial condition? Explain.

Transaction Analysis: Expanded Accounting Equation

Integration of Concepts

3-36 The following transactions are given:

1. Owners invested $500,000 in this business for capital stock.
2. Buildings and equipment are purchased for $200,000 cash and a mortgage of $600,000.
3. Inventory purchased on account for $100,000.
4. Insurance for two years paid in advance, $8,000.
5. Interest of $60,000 paid on the mortgage.
6. Defective merchandise costing $5,000 returned to a supplier for credit.
7. Customers paid $10,000 in advance as a deposit against an order to be delivered later.
8. Recorded depreciation of $80,000.
9. One year of insurance expired.

Required

a. Arrange columns corresponding to the following expanded balance sheet equation (assume zero beginning balances):

CASH + PREPAID INSURANCE + INVENTORY + BUILDING AND EQUIPMENT − ACCUMULATED DEPRECIATION = ACCOUNTS PAYABLE + UNEARNED REVENUE + MORTGAGE PAYABLE + INVESTED CAPITAL + RETAINED EARNINGS

Enter transactions 1 through 9 into the columns of the equation. Total each column and verify that the balance sheet equation does balance. Prepare a classified balance sheet from the totals of your spreadsheet.
b. What conclusions can be drawn about the liquidity of this firm?
c. What conclusions can be drawn about its financial position?

Using Ratios to Evaluate Performance

3-37 The following balance sheet data are given:

	2000	1999
Cash	$ 45,000	$ 35,000
Fixed assets	330,000	270,000
Current liabilities	95,000	45,000
Long-term liabilities	300,000	320,000
Accounts receivable	115,000	95,000
Invested capital	100,000	100,000
Inventories	100,000	80,000
Retained earnings	95,000	15,000

Required

a. Prepare a balance sheet for each year.

b. Compute the liquidity ratios described in this chapter, along with the asset management and debt management ratios. Evaluate the company's liquidity. Evaluate its asset management and debt management.

c. What strategies does the company seem to be following in managing its finances?

Preparing a Balance Sheet and Ratio Analysis

3-38 Given the following data:

	2001	2000
Cash	$ 30,000	$ 40,000
Retained earnings	175,000	225,000
Current liabilities	17,000	16,000
Invested capital	600,000	600,000
Accounts receivable	27,500	38,000
Inventories	45,000	47,000
Fixed assets, net	?	?

Required

a. Rearrange these data into classified balance sheets.

b. Find the missing Fixed Assets amounts necessary to balance each balance sheet.

c. Evaluate the firm's liquidity, using the ratios described in this chapter.

d. Calculate the firm's asset management and debt management ratios. Evaluate the results.

Preparing a Balance Sheet and Ratio Analysis

3-39 Given the following data:

	2001	2000
Cash	$300,000	$340,000
Retained earnings	?	?
Accounts payable	20,000	11,000
Wages payable	7,000	5,000
Interest payable	10,000	30,000
Bonds payable	40,000	100,000
Mortgage payable	60,000	300,000
Invested capital	500,000	600,000
Accounts receivable	37,500	118,000
Inventories	55,000	87,000
Fixed assets, net	165,000	320,000

Required

a. Rearrange these data into classified balance sheets.

b. Find the missing Retained Earnings amounts necessary to balance each balance sheet.

c. Evaluate the firm's liquidity, using the ratios described in this chapter.

d. Calculate the firm's asset management and debt management ratios. Evaluate the results.

Transaction Analysis: Expanded Accounting Equation

3-40 Consider these transactions:

1. Investors purchased $900,000 of common stock from the firm.
2. The firm purchased land, buildings, and equipment valued at $1,300,000; paid $300,000 in cash; and signed a mortgage for the balance due.
3. Paid rent of $10,000 for five automobiles.
4. The auto rental covers two months, one of which is the current month.
5. Purchased supplies on account for $55,000.
6. Provided services on account to customers at a retail value of $3,200,000.
7. Collected $3,000,000 from customers on account.
8. Paid its supplies.
9. Recorded monthly depreciation of $22,000.
10. Accrued one month's (mortgage) interest at 12% per annum.

Required

a. Arrange columns in a spreadsheet, corresponding to the balance sheet equation using these balance sheet accounts: Cash, Accounts Receivable, Prepaid Rent, Supplies, Property Plant and Equipment, Accumulated Depreciation, Accounts Payable, Interest Payable, Mortgage Payable, Common Stock, Retained Earnings. Enter transactions 1 through 10 into the columns. Total each column and verify that the balance sheet equation does indeed balance.

b. Prepare a classified balance sheet, using the column totals from your spreadsheet.

c. Analyze the firm's liquidity, using the ratios from this chapter.

d. Evaluate the firm's asset management and debt management. Provide an overall performance assessment.

e. What important information is missing that would further assist in evaluating these results? Even though the firm's performance seems spectacularly good, could the missing information change your opinion? Why?

Transaction Analysis: Expanded Accounting Equation

3-41 Given these transactions:

1. An engineering firm was formed when three engineers each invested $50,000 (cash).
2. Each founder also invested an assortment of utility trucks, inclinometers, and other specialty equipment, valued at $10,000 (each).
3. Borrowed $50,000 to provide additional operating funds.
4. Rented office space at $1,000 per month.
5. Paid the first month's rent.
6. Paid a security deposit of $2,000.
7. A wealthy individual also wanted to invest in the firm, but not as an owner, so the firm borrowed $500,000 from this individual at 18% per year.
8. Two additional staff members were hired at $6,000 per month.
9. The staff earned their first month's salary of $6,000 but were not yet paid.
10. Supplies costing $45,000 were purchased.
11. Recorded depreciation for the first month. Assume that the equipment (in transaction 2) has useful lives of five years.
12. Accrued interest on the loan for one month.

Required

a. Arrange five columns in a worksheet or spreadsheet, corresponding to the following expanded balance sheet equation (assume zero beginning balances):

CURRENT ASSETS + FIXED ASSETS = CURRENT LIABILITIES + LONG-TERM LIABILITIES + OWNERS' EQUITY

Enter transactions 1 through 12 in the five columns. Total each column and verify that the balance sheet does indeed balance. Prepare a classified balance sheet, using the column totals from your spreadsheet.

b. Evaluate the firm's liquidity, using the ratios described in this chapter.

c. Evaluate the firm's asset management and debt management.

d. On an overall basis, evaluate the firm's performance. What important information is missing? Even though the firm's performance seems somewhat questionable, could the missing information change your opinion? Why?

Interpreting Financial Statements: Ratio Analysis

Integration of Concepts

3-42 Comparative balance sheets for Creative Cabinetry, Inc. are shown below:

Assets	**12-31-01**	**12-31-00**
Cash	$ 95,000	$ 33,000
Accounts receivable	23,160	22,500
Inventory	30,000	123,650
Prepaid rent	3,840	5,850
Total current assets	152,000	185,000
Land	83,000	72,000
Equipment	800,000	600,000
Accumulated depreciation	(140,000)	(90,000)
Total long-term assets	743,000	582,000
Total assets	$895,000	$767,000
Liabilities and Shareholders' Equity		
Current Liabilities		
Accounts payable	$ 83,300	$ 48,100
Accrued liabilities	23,500	24,200
Short-term notes payable	62,000	51,000
Total current liabilities	168,800	123,300
Mortgage payable	547,200	383,500
Shareholders' Equity		
Common stock	150,000	150,000
Retained earnings	29,000	110,200
Total shareholders' equity	179,000	260,200
Total liabilities and shareholders' equity	$895,000	$767,000

Required

a. Conduct a vertical analysis (common-size) of Creative Cabinetry's balance sheets for each year.

b. Calculate the liquidity ratios for each year.

c. Calculate asset management and debt management ratios for each year.

d. What conclusions can be drawn about Creative Cabinetry's financial management?

Integration of Concepts

Transaction Analysis: Expanded Equation Including Fund Balances (non-profit hospital)

3-43 Given these transactions:

1. Community donations of $150,000 are received.
2. A mortgage of $1.5M is secured and a hospital is constructed.
3. Donated land worth $1M is received.
4. Short-term lines of credit are used to acquire supplies of $50,000.
5. Obstetrics clients pay $20,000 in advance as a deposit.
6. Operating lease payments of $30,000 on x-ray equipment are made.
7. Donations of $1,000 by the hospital to the American Cancer Society are recorded.
8. Half of the land is sold for $2M.
9. Depreciation expense of $6,250 on the hospital building is recorded.

Required

a. Arrange five columns corresponding to the following expanded balance sheet equation for a nonprofit hospital (assume zero beginning balances), where FUND BALANCES is used instead of OWNERS' EQUITY:

CURRENT ASSETS + FIXED ASSETS = CURRENT LIABILITIES + LONG-TERM LIABILITIES + FUND BALANCES

Enter transactions 1 through 9 into the five columns. Total each column and verify that the balance sheet does balance. Note that FUND BALANCES can be used in the same manner as OWNERS' EQUITY for a commercial firm. Prepare a simple balance sheet from the totals of your spreadsheet.

b. Calculate appropriate liquidity ratios. Evaluate the results.

c. Evaluate the hospital's asset management and debt management.

d. What conclusions can be drawn about the overall financial condition of this hospital ?

Composition of Current Assets

3-44 The following schedule summarizes the current assets reported in the 1997 balance sheets of Wendy's and Reebok:

	Wendy's	Reebok
	(Dollars in millions)	
Current Assets		
Cash and equivalents	$ 234	$ 210
Notes receivable	14	—
Accounts receivable, net of allowance	67	562
Prepaids and other		54
Inventories	36	564
Deferred income taxes	31	75
Total current assets	382	1,465
Noncurrent, total	1,560	291
Total assets	$1,942	$1,756

Required

a. Identify the major differences between these two firms in their composition of current assets. Try to explain these differences in terms of the types of goods and services that each company produces.

b. On the basis of the liquidity ratios, which company appears to be more liquid?

c. Conduct a vertical analysis for each company. Do these results support your earlier conclusions in part b? Why?

Composition of Current Assets

3-45 The following schedule summarizes the current assets reported in the year-end balance sheets of Costello Laboratories, a company that develops, manufactures, and markets health care products, and Triangle Air Lines, a major provider of passenger, freight, and mail air transportation:

	Costello Laboratories	Triangle Air Lines
	(Dollars in thousands)	
Current Assets		
Cash and equivalents	$ 300,676	$ 1,180,364
Investment securities	78,149	—
Accounts receivable, net of allowance	1,336,222	1,024,869
Supplies	—	90,593
Inventories	940,533	—
Prepaids and other	929,955	526,094
Total current assets	3,585,535	2,821,920
Noncurrent, total	4,103,034	9,049,103
Total assets	$7,688,569	$11,871,023

Required

a. Identify the major differences between these two firms in the composition of current assets. Try to explain these differences in terms of the types of goods and services that each company produces.

b. Based solely on the information provided here, which company appears to be more liquid?

Composition of Noncurrent Assets

3-46 The following schedule summarizes the noncurrent assets reported in the year-end balance sheets of Packard Computers, a company that designs and manufactures electronic data and communications systems, and Nazareth Steel, a major steel fabricator:

	Packard Computers	Nazareth Steel
	(Dollars in millions)	
Current assets (total)	$10,236	$1,591
Noncurrent assets		
Property, plant, and equipment (at cost)	7,527	6,741
Less: Accumulated depreciation	(3,347)	(4,107)
Net	4,180	2,634
Other long-term receivables and other	2,320	1,652
Total noncurrent assets	6,500	4,286
Total assets	$16,736	$5,877

Required

a. Identify the major differences between these two firms in the composition of noncurrent assets. Try to explain these differences based on the types of products that each company produces.
b. Based solely on the information provided here, which company appears to have the older assets? Calculate the asset management ratios. Evaluate the results.

Composition of Noncurrent Assets

3-47 The following schedule summarizes the noncurrent assets reported in the 1997 balance sheets of Wendy's and Reebok:

	Wendy's	Reebok
	(Dollars in millions)	
Current assets (total)	$ 382	$1,465
Noncurrent assets		
Property, plant, and equipment (at cost)	1,803	354
Less: Accumulated depreciation	(538)	(197)
Net	1,265	157
Other long-term receivables	179	—
Goodwill, net	51	68
Other noncurrent assets	65	66
Total noncurrent assets	1,560	291
Total assets	$1,942	$1,756

Required

a. Identify the major differences between these two firms in their composition of noncurrent assets. Try to explain these differences based on the types of products that each company produces.
b. Based solely on the information provided here, which company appears to have the older assets? Calculate the asset management ratios. Evaluate the results.

Composition of Shareholders' Equity

3-48 The following schedule summarizes the components of shareholders' equity reported in the 1997 balance sheets of Wendy's and Reebok:

	Wendy's	Reebok
	(Dollars in millions)	
Shareholders' equity:		
Invested capital	$1	$365
Retained earnings	1,145	839
Other	(639)	(20)
Total shareholders' equity	$ 507	$1,184

Required

a. Which firm has obtained the larger amount of capital through sale of stock to investors?
b. Which firm has obtained the larger amount of capital through reinvestment of earnings?
c. Explain why Wendy's reports a much higher balance in retained earnings at the end of 1997.
d. Suppose that Reebok earns $250 and pays dividends of $95 during 1998. What would be the firm's ending balance in retained earnings? (All dollars are in millions.)

Evaluating the Composition of Shareholders' Equity

3-49 The following schedule summarizes the components of shareholders' equity reported in the year-end balance sheets of Nuclear Holdings and Hellmorgen:

	Nuclear Holdings	Hellmorgen
	(Dollars in millions)	
Shareholders' equity:		
Paid-in capital	$13,905	$50,322
Retained earnings (deficit)	29,132	(30,166)
Other	—	(12,571)
Total shareholders' equity	$43,037	$ 7,585

Required

a. Which firm has obtained the larger amount of capital through sale of stock to investors?

b. Which firm has obtained the larger amount of capital through reinvestment of earnings?

c. Explain why Hellmorgen reports a negative (deficit) balance in retained earnings at the end of the year.

d. Suppose Nuclear Holdings earns $15,000 and pays dividends of $9,000 during the next year. What would be the firm's ending balance in retained earnings? (All dollars are in thousands.)

Using Vertical Analysis Data to Reconstruct a Balance Sheet

3-50 A vertical analysis was previously conducted, using the Edgar Elgar, Inc. balance sheet. The results are shown below.

Assets		**Liabilities and Owners' Equity**	
Current assets		Current liabilities	
Cash	5.3%	Accounts payable	22.6%
Accounts receivable	12.6	Notes payable	16.3
Inventories	39.5	Accrued expenses	3.6
Prepaid expenses	1.6	Taxes payable	1.3
Total current assets	59.0%	Total current liabilities	43.8%
Property, plant, and equipment		Noncurrent liabilities	
Land	14.1%	Bonds payable	17.1
		Mortgage payable	7.3
Buildings and equipment	42.0	Total noncurrent liabilities	24.4%
Less: Accumulated		Total liabilities	68.2%
depreciation	−15.1	Shareholders' equity	
Net book value	26.9%	Invested capital	29.3%
Total property, plant, and		Retained earnings	2.5
equipment assets	41.0%	Total shareholders' equity	31.8%
Total assets	100.0%	Total liabilities and	
		shareholders' equity	100.0%

NOTE: Assume that this balance sheet was in balance before the vertical analysis was conducted.

Required

Using these results, reconstruct Edgar Elgar's balance sheet, assuming that the total assets are known to be $4M.

Reconstructing a Balance Sheet

3-51 Van Gogh's fragmentary balance sheet is shown below.

Assets		**Liabilities and Owners' Equity**	
Current assets		Current liabilities	
Cash	$ 210,000	Accounts payable	$ 250,000
Accounts receivable	466,000	Notes payable	?
Inventories	812,000	Accrued expenses	275,000
Prepaid expenses	?	Total current liabilities	?
Total current assets	1,520,000	Noncurrent liabilities	
Property, plant, and equipment		Bonds payable	350,000
		Mortgage payable	250,000
Land	?	Total noncurrent liabilities	?
Buildings and equipment	865,000	Total liabilities	1,600,000
Less: Accumulated depreciation	−313,0000	Shareholders' equity	
Net book value	552,000	Invested capital	500,000
Total property, plant, and equipment	938,000	Retained earnings	?
Total assets	?	Total shareholders' equity	858,000
		Total liabilities and shareholders' equity	?

Required

Determine the missing figures and reconstruct the balance sheet in its proper format.

Balance Sheet Analysis

Critical Thinking

3-52 The balance sheet for Wendy's International Inc. is shown in Appendix C.

Required

a. Conduct a vertical analysis of the balance sheet for each year, 1996 and 1997.
b. Calculate the liquidity, asset management, and debt management ratios.
c. Evaluate Wendy's' liquidity in each year.
d. Evaluate Wendy's' asset management and debt management strategies.
e. In which year was Wendy's most successful? Why?

Balance Sheet Analysis

Critical Thinking

3-53 The balance sheet for Reebok International LTD is shown in Appendix D.

Required

a. Conduct a vertical analysis of the balance sheet for each year, 1996 and 1997.
b. Calculate the liquidity, asset management, and debt management ratios.
c. Evaluate Reebok's liquidity in each year.
d. Evaluate Reebok's asset management and debt management strategies.
e. In which year was Reebok most successful? Why?

Identifying Transactions from Worksheet Entries

3-54 The following worksheet entries have been retrieved from a corrupt data file.

	Cash	Inventory	Buildings	Trucks	Accts. Pay	Mortgage	Inv. Cap.
a.	1,000						1,000
b.	−2,000			2,000			
c.	−8,000		8,000				
d.		4,000			4,000		
e.	−22,000			22,000			
f.	−4,000				−4,000		
g.		8,000			6,000		2,000
h.			18,000			18,000	
i.	−6,000				−6,000		
h.				12,000			12,000

Required:

Identify the transactions that correspond to each entry in the worksheet. Discuss the underlying business reasons associated with each transaction.

Interpreting Financial Statements

3-55 XYZ Corporation's 2000 and 1999 balance sheets are summarized below (dollars in millions):

	12-31-00	12-31-99
Current Assets		
Cash and temporary investments	$ 535	$ 499
Receivables, less allowances	706	668
Materials and supplies	211	199
Prepaid and other	213	215
Total current assets	1,665	1,581
Property, plant, and equipment		
Net property, plant and equipment	11,044	10,778
Investment in affiliates and other companies	302	268
Other assets and deferred charges	713	793
Total assets	$13,724	$13,420
Current Liabilities		
Debt maturing within one year	312	146
Accounts payable and other current liabilities	1,992	1,965
Short-term debt	201	164
Total current liabilities	2,505	2,275
Long-term debt	2,618	3,133
Deferred income taxes	2,570	2,341
Long-term liabilities and deferred gains	2,300	2,491
Shareowners' equity		
Common stock and retained earnings	3,731	3,180
Total liabilities and shareowners' equity	$13,724	$13,420

Required

a. With regard to XYZ's balance sheet, identify any unusual or unfamiliar terms. Describe your understanding of each new or unfamiliar term.

b. Calculate the current and quick ratios for each year and analyze XYZ's liquidity.

c. What recommendations would you suggest to XYZ about its liquidity?

d. Calculate and evaluate XYZ's debt-to-asset ratios for each year. Calculate any other appropriate asset management or debt management ratios.

e. How has XYZ changed its financial management strategies? Do these changes seem to be appropriate? Why?

Critical Thinking

Interpreting Financial Statements: Ratio Analysis

3-56 Consider Sigma Designs' balance sheets for 1993 and 1992 (dollars in thousands). Sigma Designs is a high-tech software development company specializing in imaging and multimedia computer applications.

Assets	**1993**	**1992**
Current Assets		
Cash and equivalents	$ 5,086	$ 9,283
Marketable securities	14,326	19,537
Accounts receivable, net of allowances	6,471	2,987
Inventories	12,275	10,066
Prepaid expenses and other	435	753
Income taxes receivable	1,582	2,428
Total current assets	40,175	45,054
Equipment, net	1,626	1,607
Other assets	2,466	2,388
Total assets	$44,267	$49,049
Liabilities and Shareholders' Equity		
Current liabilities		
Accounts payable	$ 4,933	$ 1,826
Accrued salary and benefits	809	594
Other accrued liabilities	737	1,119
Total current liabilities	6,479	3,539
Other long-term liabilities	—	755
Total liabilities	6,479	4,294
Shareholders' Equity		
Common stock	19,287	19,088
Retained earnings	18,501	25,667
Shareholders' equity	37,788	44,755
Total liabilities and shareholders' equity	$44,267	$49,049

Required

a. Conduct a vertical analysis of Sigma Designs' balance sheets. What conclusions can be drawn from these ratios?
b. Calculate the current and quick ratios for each year.
c. Does it seem that Sigma Designs has any liquidity problems? What major changes in current assets and current liabilities may contribute to these liquidity comparisons?
d. Calculate and evaluate the debt-to-assets ratio for Sigma Designs.
e. Concentrate on the equity section of the balance sheet. What may have caused the changes shown, as in the decrease in Retained Earnings and in Shareholders' Equity?
f. Examine the Income Taxes Receivable section. How can a company have income taxes that are receivable and not payable? How are such receivables usually satisfied? Will the government just issue a refund check to Sigma Designs?

Internet

Vertical Analysis

3-57 Locate the most recent set of financial statements for the companies listed below. You may use either the 10-K available at EDGAR (**www.sec.gov/edaux/searches.htm**) or the annual report available at the company page on the Web. The annual report is usually located in the Investor Information section.

Corporation	WWW Page Location
Xerox (office products)	**www.xerox.com**
Ben & Jerry's (food)	**www.benjerry.com**
Lewis Galoob Toys (toys)	**www.galoob.com**
Eli Lilly (pharmaceutical)	**www.lilly.com**

Required

a. For each company, perform a vertical analysis for the four major categories of assets (Current Assets; Investments; Property, Plant, and Equipment; and Other).
b. Discuss the impact that different types of business have on the composition of total assets.

Internet

Ratio Calculations

3-58 Locate the most recent set of financial statements for the corporations listed below. You may use either the 10-K available at EDGAR (**www.sec.gov/edaux/searches.htm**) or the annual report available at the company page on the Web. The annual report is usually located in the Investor Information section.

Corporation	WWW Page Location
Ameritech	**www.ameritech.com**
U S West	**www.uswest.com**
Bell Atlantic	**www.bell-atl.com**
Pacific Bell	**www.pacbell.com**

Required

For each company compute the:

a. current ratio
b. quick ratio
c. property, plant, and equipment as a percent of total assets
d. debt-to-assets ratio

Internet

Balance Sheet Comparisons

3-59 Locate the balance sheet for IBM and Bank One. You can use either the 10-K available at EDGAR (**www.sec.gov/edaux/searches.htm**) or the annual report available at the company page on the Web. The annual report is usually located in the Investor Information section.

Corporation	WWW Page Location
IBM	**www.ibm.com**
Bank One	**www.bankone.com**

Required

a. Discuss the similarities and differences between the two balance sheets.
b. Property, plant, and equipment is used directly by companies such as IBM to generate earnings. However, property, plant, and equipment is classified by banks as Other Assets. Why?

chapter 4

The Income Statement

LEARNING OBJECTIVES

1. Explain when to recognize revenues.
2. Explain when to recognize expenses.
3. Interpret the components of the income statement.
4. Analyze income statement information using various ratios.
5. Describe the effects that reported earnings have on managers' wealth and, consequently, on their accounting policy decisions.

INTRODUCTION

The **income statement** summarizes the results of a firm's operations for a period of time. Four major types of items appear on income statements: revenues, expenses, gains, and losses.

Revenues are inflows of assets (or reductions in liabilities) that result from providing goods and services to customers; they arise from a firm's ongoing operations. Sales of inventory to customers, for example, generate assets (cash or accounts receivable) and constitute revenues. **Expenses** arise from consuming resources in order to generate revenues. The cost of inventory sold to customers illustrates an expense.

Gains, as with revenues, increase assets or decrease liabilities, yet they arise from activities that are not central to a firm's major operations. For example, a gain would result from selling land for more than its carrying (book) value. **Losses** are similar to expenses in that they decrease assets or increase liabilities, but they are not central to a firm's major activities. The sale of land at an amount less than its carrying value would result in a loss.

AN ILLUSTRATED INCOME STATEMENT

Exhibit 4-1 contains the 1997 income statement for Altron Incorporated, a manufacturer of component parts used in advanced electronics equipment. The income statement is for the year ended January 3, 1998. Although most firms use a calendar year-end of December 31, Altron uses a 52-week year and prepares its financial statements as of the Saturday closest to December 31. A 52-week year enhances comparisons across quarterly reports because each quarter will have 13 weeks. Some firms use a natural year-end instead of a calendar year-end. That is, the financial statements are prepared shortly after the firm's busy season. Wal-Mart, for example, prepares its

EXHIBIT 4-1 Multiple Step Income Statement

Altron Incorporated
Income Statement
For the Year Ended January 3, 1998
(Dollars in thousands)

Net sales	$172,428
Cost of sales	134,373
Gross profit	38,055
Selling, general and administrative expenses	14,844
Income from operations	23,211
Other income	1,503
Interest expense	31
Income before provision for income taxes	24,683
Provision for income taxes	10,016
Net income	$ 14,667

annual financial statements on January 31, which is a good fiscal year-end for them because December is their busiest time of year. By the end of January, Wal-Mart has completed its busy season; it has made any exchanges or refunds, and its inventory levels are probably rather low. This is a good time to tally results.

Altron's income statement, similar to the income statements of many corporations, is highly condensed. It contains two revenue items, four expense items, and no gains or losses. However, Altron almost certainly did experience gains and losses, but their relative sizes were probably so small that they were combined with other items on the income statement. This is an application of the **materiality principle,** which states that separate disclosure is not required if an item is so small that knowledge of it would not affect the decision of a reasonable financial statement reader. This principle can actually improve the usefulness of financial statements by eliminating the disclosure of inconsequential items, which helps analysts concentrate on items of importance.

The major revenue line on Altron's income statement is labeled **Net sales.** Note that the terms *sales* and *revenue* are used interchangeably by many firms, while the term **net** implies that certain items have been deducted from the gross (or full) sales price. For example, most firms allow their customers to return merchandise within a specified period, and customers are usually offered a full refund upon returning the merchandise. The original sales amount is included in gross sales. The refund amount is termed a **sales return,** and it is subtracted from gross sales in calculating net sales. Even if the term *net* is omitted, reported sales on the income statement are usually net sales.

Cost of sales is often referred to as **cost of goods sold.** It reflects the cost to Altron of the goods sold to its customers. The difference between sales and cost of goods sold is called **gross profit** or **gross margin.**

Altron has elected to combine selling, general, and administrative expenses, although some companies report separate figures. **Selling expenses** include advertising costs, commissions to salespersons, depreciation of equipment used in the selling function, and a number of other items. **General and administrative expenses** consist of senior managers' salaries, accounting and auditing costs, insurance, depreciation of administrative offices, and so on.

Operating income equals sales minus all costs and expenses incurred by normal operations. Operating income is a primary indicator of how well a firm has managed its operations and, as you will see, serves as a basis for comparing firms within the same industry.

Altron's income statement contains several other items. Other income can arise from a variety of sources, such as interest on investments. **Interest expense** reflects the firm's cost of borrowing money from creditors. **Income taxes** are imposed by the federal government, state and local governments, and foreign jurisdictions. Neither interest nor income taxes directly relate to a firm's operations. For example, interest expense is largely a function of how much the firm has borrowed to finance its operations. Differences in interest expense between firms are determined primarily by choices the firms have made in financing their businesses. Some firms elect to borrow heavily, which results in large interest charges. Other firms rely on investments by owners; Interest charges are not paid on these funds and, because of this, interest expense is deducted after operating income is calculated.

The **bottom line** of the income statement is called **net income, earnings,** or **profit.** Although interest and income tax expenses do not affect operating income, they are appropriate deductions in the calculation of overall profitability. Because net income reflects the increase in net assets from all profit-oriented activities, it is the focus of much scrutiny by analysts, investors, and other financial statement readers.

Keep in mind the difference between *revenue* and *profit*. Revenue refers to the total inflow of assets (or reduction in liabilities) from customers. Profit is the net increase in a firm's recorded wealth after deducting expenses from revenue.

Altron's income statement presented in Exhibit 4-1 is in the **multiple-step format.** Multiple-step income statements calculate certain subtotals for the reader. Altron's statement contains subtotals for gross profit and operating income. In contrast, income statements using the **single-step format** summarize all revenues in one section and all expenses in another. Exhibit 4-2 illustrates a single-step income statement. Whereas the single-step approach is simpler, the multiple-step approach provides more information.

USES OF THE INCOME STATEMENT

A major purpose of the income statement is to show a firm's profitability, yet it also provides a number of additional performance measures. Revenue, for example, is a key measure of growth that reflects a firm's success in expanding its market. Additionally, comparisons of expense numbers from year to year indicate a firm's success in controlling costs. As previously mentioned, operating income measures managers' performance in conducting a firm's operations.

Income statement information provides the basis for a variety of decisions. Because earnings underlie a firm's ability to generate cash flows for dividends and growth, equity investors are interested in the income statement. Lenders are also interested in the income statement because a firm's ability to pay principal and interest in a timely manner ultimately depends on its profitability.

A firm's management can use income statement information to make a variety of decisions. For example, managers must constantly evaluate the prices they set for the firm's products and services. Pricing affects both profitability and growth. The income

EXHIBIT 4-2 Single-Step Income Statement

Altron Incorporated
Income Statement
For the Year Ended January 3, 1998
(Dollars in thousands)

Revenues		
Net sales	$172,428	
Other income	1,503	
		$173,931
Expenses		
Cost of sales	134,373	
Selling, general and administrative expenses	14,844	
Interest expense	31	
Provision for income taxes	10,016	
		159,264
Net income		$ 14,667

statement tells managers and investors how well the firm's pricing strategy has accomplished stated objectives.

Corporations always strive to reduce the costs of their operations, and the income statement can also measure the success of cost-cutting initiatives. However, cost-cutting, such as employee layoffs, do not ensure increased profitability. Apple Computer Inc. cut thousands of jobs in 1996 and 1997, yet continued to post losses. Continued competition from industry rivals and the loss of human talent are issues that must also be addressed.

As a final illustration, managers often use the income statement when setting dividends. Net income is a primary measure of a firm's ability to pay dividends. In fact, some firms set a dividend target equal to a certain percentage of net income.

REVENUE RECOGNITION

A firm's earnings process often takes place over an extended period of time. A manufacturer's typical earnings process, which is depicted in Exhibit 4-3, entails purchasing raw materials, manufacturing, storing and selling the finished product, and collecting cash from the customer. The manufacturer creates value through all these steps, but for accounting purposes, firms usually select a discrete point in time to recognize (record) revenue.

General Rule

The **revenue recognition principle** states that revenue should be recognized in the accounting records when

1. the earnings process is substantially complete, and
2. the amount to be collected is reasonably determinable.

EXHIBIT 4-3 Time Line of a Manufacturer's Earnings Process

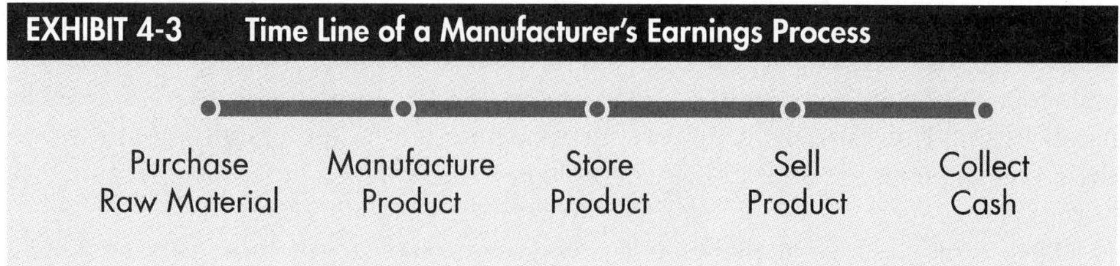

The first criterion prevents the recognition of revenue before a firm has fulfilled its obligation to the customer. The second criterion indicates that the sales price has been set and that the customer will probably pay the amount due. Both criteria ensure that revenue is not recognized prematurely. If revenue is recognized too soon, the income statement will indicate that the firm has accomplished activities that it has not, which would mislead financial statement users.

In most situations, these criteria are met at the point of sale, that is, when a product is delivered or a service is rendered to a customer. Even if payment is not immediately received, a claim to cash (an account receivable) has been obtained, and revenue recognition is proper.

Two additional comments need to be made about revenue recognition at the point of sale. First, many sellers guarantee their products' performance for a period of time. If a product malfunctions, the seller is obligated to incur the cost of correcting the problem. Does the existence of such a warranty indicate that the earnings process is not substantially complete at the time of sale? No, it does not. For most sellers, the warranty cost is relatively minor. Thus, the earnings process is ***substantially*** complete at the time of sale. Chapter 8, "Accounts Payable, Commitments, Contingencies, and Risks," discusses warranty costs in more depth.

Second, when accounts receivable are obtained at the point of sale, can we be certain that cash will ultimately be collected? In most cases, absolute assurance cannot be obtained, but if the seller has done a good job of checking customers' credit histories, a reasonable estimate of worthless accounts receivable can be made. This estimate is used to adjust both the income statement and the balance sheet. Chapter 6, "Current Assets," discusses this issue in more detail.

Exceptions

A number of exceptions exist to the general rule of thumb that revenue is recognized at the point of sale. One exception deals with the collectibility of receivables. If the seller is highly uncertain about the collectibility of a receivable, revenue recognition should be delayed beyond the point of sale to the point when cash is actually collected. This approach is sometimes used in the real estate industry.

Another exception deals with long-term construction contracts (for bridges, highways, and so on). These projects can take several years to complete. If revenue recognition is delayed until the earnings process is substantially complete, no revenue is recognized in any contract year except the final one, at which point all the revenue is recognized. Such an uneven pattern of revenue recognition would contrast with the actual earnings process, which takes place throughout the life of the contract. Accordingly, if (1) a binding contract exists between the buyer and the seller and (2) the seller can reasonably estimate the costs to complete the project, then revenue, the related costs, and the resultant profit should be estimated and recognized each year by the **percentage of completion method.** This method recognizes a portion of the revenue, cost, and profit each year according to the percentage of the job completed.

A similar situation exists with some service contracts. For example, consider a health club that sells one-year memberships for an immediate payment of $600. Revenue recognition at the point of sale is inappropriate because the earnings process has barely begun. However, delaying revenue recognition until the twelfth month, when the earnings process is substantially complete, is also inadvisable. GAAP permits proportional revenue recognition each month over the contract's life.

Most firms describe their revenue recognition policies in a note to the financial statements. Reality Check 4-1 contains an excerpt from the financial statements of *Reader's Digest*, which frequently receives payments for subscriptions at the inception of a contract. Because the earnings process has just begun at that point, the magazine records a liability instead of revenue. Recording a liability recognizes that *Reader's Digest* has an obligation to provide its customers something of value: either the magazine or a refund. Revenue is recognized as the magazines are mailed to the customers.

EXPENSE RECOGNITION

The **matching principle** governs expense recognition. It states that all costs that were incurred to generate the revenue appearing on a given period's income statement should appear as an expense on the same income statement. In other words, we should match expenses against revenues. Revenues are first recognized and expenses are then matched with those revenues. By doing this, the income statement contains measures of both accomplishment (revenue) and effort (expenses), thereby enabling an assessment of firm performance. The matching principle is implemented in one of three ways, explained below.

REALITY CHECK 4-1

Reader's Digest records sales of magazine subscriptions as unearned revenue at the gross subscription price at the time the orders are received. Proportionate shares of the gross subscription price are recognized as revenue when the subscriptions are fulfilled.

Required

a. Assume that *Reader's Digest* receives $48 from a customer for a two-year subscription. Analyze this transaction in terms of the basic accounting equation.
b. Assume that the subscription is for 24 monthly issues. In terms of the basic accounting equation, what analysis would *Reader's Digest* undertake when each issue is mailed?

Solution

a.

ASSETS	=	LIABILITIES	+	SHAREHOLDERS' EQUITY
Cash		Unearned revenue		
+$48		+$48		

b.

ASSETS	=	LIABILITIES	+	SHAREHOLDERS' EQUITY
		Unearned Revenue		Retained earnings
		−$2		+$2 (subscription revenue)

Associating Cause and Effect

One method of implementing the matching principle is known as **associating cause and effect.** This implies that a clear and direct relationship exists between the expense and the associated revenue. Cost of goods sold is a good example. A retail store certainly cannot generate sales revenue without consuming inventory. Salespersons' commissions are another example. Because commissions are usually paid as a percentage of sales revenue, commission expense is tied directly to revenue.

Systematic and Rational Allocation

Another method used to implement the matching principle is **systematic and rational allocation.** Many costs cannot be directly linked to specific revenue transactions. They can, however, be tied to a span of years and allocated as an expense to each of those years. Sales equipment, as an example, is essential to generate revenue. However, linking the cost of each display case, piece of furniture, and the like to specific sales transactions is difficult. Instead, the equipment's cost is systematically allocated as depreciation expense to the years during which the equipment helps generate revenue.

Immediate Recognition

The final method of applying the matching principle is **immediate recognition.** Some expenditures have no discernible *future* benefit. In these cases, the expenditure is expensed immediately. Officers' salaries, utilities, and interest are treated in this manner.

Reality Check 4-2 addresses revenue and expense issues for Cendant Corporation.

REALITY CHECK 4-2

Cendant Corporation markets memberships in discount purchasing clubs. Typical subscriptions last one year. The first month is a trial membership; members pay no fee. After the first month, members are billed monthly. However, at any time during the year-long subscription period, a member can terminate the agreement and receive a refund for all amounts paid. Cendant also incurs marketing costs in attracting new members (such as mailings and phone solicitations).

Required

a. Describe two methods that Cendant could use to recognize revenue. Which method is the most conservative?
b. For each of the two revenue recognition methods described above, suggest a method of expense recognition that adheres to the matching principle.
c. Because Cendant has experienced significant accounting regularities, the SEC has forced Cendant to use certain revenue and expense methods. Which methods do you suspect these are?

Solution

a. Cendant could recognize revenue ratably over the 11-month period following the trial membership. This method is supported by the fact that Cendant provides the services over this period. However, Cendant would also need to establish an allowance for its estimate of the number of memberships that will be canceled. Alternatively, Cendant could recognize revenue at the end of the twelfth month, when cancellation is no longer possible. This method defers revenue recognition as long as possible, requires no estimates, and is the most conservative.
b. The first method of revenue recognition would be accompanied by deferring the marketing costs and expensing them over months two through 12. The second method would be accompanied by deferring the marketing costs and expensing them at the end of the twelfth month. In both cases, a portion of the marketing costs should be expensed more quickly to reflect the canceled subscriptions.
c. The SEC has required Cendant to use the most conservative methods possible. Accordingly, revenue is recognized at the end of the twelfth month. Expenses are recognized when incurred because they cannot be recovered in the event of cancellation.

WHAT WOULD YOU DO?

Software Programs International (SPI) designs and markets several software packages. SPI's word processing program has not generated as many sales as management had forecast. Because of this, SPI is evaluating two alternative strategies. One strategy is to discontinue the product. The other strategy involves a renewed effort to improve the product and make it more attractive to potential customers. SPI's consideration of these strategies began in October of 2000. A final decision will be made around July 2001.

SPI is a calendar year-end firm. SPI realizes that its financial statement readers would find information about these plans useful. On the other hand, disclosing that the word processing product might be discontinued would probably make customers hesitant to purchase the product. They would also be reluctant to buy and learn a system that will never be upgraded or improved. The decline in sales would, of course, negatively affect SPI's shareholders.

Should SPI disclose its strategy evaluation in its 2000 financial statements?

A CLOSER LOOK AT THE INCOME STATEMENT

As indicated earlier, income statements summarize *past* transactions and events. Many users of income statements are interested in the past only to the extent that it can help predict the future. Financial statement users are concerned about earnings **sustainability,** which refers to the likelihood that earnings will persist in the future.

Historical income statements will be less useful for predicting the future if the results of ongoing operations are combined with the effects of events that are unusual or are not expected to recur in the future. Consequently, GAAP requires that income statements separately report certain items. This section describes these items and shows how they are displayed on the income statement.

Discontinued Operations

If a firm ceases to operate (or plans to cease operating) a major segment of its business, separate income statement disclosure is required of its (1) continuing operations and (2) **discontinued operations.** Exhibit 4-4 contains the income statement

EXHIBIT 4-4 Income Statement with Discontinued Operations

Hahn Automotive Warehouse, Inc.
Statement of Operations
For the Year Ended September 30, 1997
(Dollars in thousands)

Net sales	$142,242
Cost of products sold	86,967
Gross profit	55,275
Selling, general and administrative expense	46,717
Depreciation and amortization	2,005
Income from operations	6,553
Interest expense	(4,670)
Other income	719
Income before provision for income taxes	2,602
Provision for income taxes	1,011
Income from continuing operations	1,591
Loss from discontinued operations:	
Write-down of investment, net of tax benefit	**(18,789)**
Loss from discontinued operations, net of tax benefit	**(3,937)**
Total loss from discontinued operations	**(22,726)**
Net loss	($ 21,135)

of Hahn Automotive Warehouse, Inc., which sells replacement auto parts. Hahn traditionally had sold to both commercial concerns, such as automotive repair shops, and to retail customers (do-it-yourselfers) via its AUTOWORKS retail division, which Hahn decided to dispose of in 1997 because of poor profitability.

The first 11 lines of Hahn's income statement reflect the results of continuing operations. The discontinued operations section contains two line items; the first line reports the loss from the AUTOWORKS division, and the second line indicates the results of operating the segment. In making predictions about future earnings, most analysts would ignore the effects of these items by focusing on income from continuing operations. To qualify for separate reporting, the discontinued operation must represent an *entire* major line of business. Many divestitures do not qualify as an entire line of business and do not necessitate separate reporting.

For example, a *Wall Street Journal* article stated: "HCA-Hospital Corporation of America, bowing to weakness in the psychiatric hospital industry, said it will sell 22 hospitals and take an after-tax charge of as much as $300 million in the third quarter." The charge reflects operating losses and anticipated losses on the sale. Because HCA retained ownership of 26 psychiatric hospitals and 73 general hospitals, it did not dispose of an entire line of business. Treatment as a discontinued operation would be inappropriate. The $300 million charge would be included in continuing operations. Thus, financial statement readers must be aware that continuing operations might contain revenues, expenses, gains, and losses that will not persist in the future. Some analysts would prefer to remove the $300 million charge from the current quarter's earnings when making projections about the future. On the other hand, some analysts might view HCA's sale of hospitals as a normally recurring modification of the firm's strategy. Because these modifications are expected to occur periodically, these analysts would not remove the $300 million from reported earnings.

Reality Check 4-3 describes a disposal by Ford Motor Company.

REALITY CHECK 4-3

Ford Motor Company reported a first quarter profit of $904 million. However, that profit included a $440 million loss from the sale of First Nationwide, a financial institution. Because Ford did not dispose of its entire financial services unit, this disposal does not qualify as a discontinued operation, but some analysts might prefer to exclude the disposal loss from Ford's earnings when making projections about future earnings.

Required

Eliminate the First Nationwide loss from Ford's reported net income.

Solution

Reported net income	$ 904,000,000
Plus loss on disposal	440,000,000
Adjusted income	$1,344,000,000

Extraordinary Items

Extraordinary items are events and transactions that are unusual in nature and infrequent in occurrence. Unusual in nature implies that the event or transaction is, at most, incidentally related to a firm's typical operations. Infrequent in occurrence suggests that the item is not expected to recur in the foreseeable future. Extraordinary items usually include natural disasters and actions by foreign governments, such as expropriation of assets. Separate disclosure of extraordinary items enables analysts to make better projections of a firm's future operations.

Exhibit 4-5 shows a partial income statement for a California-based company, American Enterprises, Inc. (AE) and an accompanying note. It shows that AE lost a building in an earthquake, which meets the criterion of being unusual in nature. A question arises as to whether they are expected to recur in the foreseeable future. In California, earthquakes continue to occur with some regularity. This is another accounting situation that requires judgment. Evidently, AE and its auditors feel that earthquakes in their area occur with sufficient irregularity that they are not expected to recur in the foreseeable future. Based on the footnote disclosures, analysts can exercise their own judgment about reported extraordinary items.

EXHIBIT 4-5 Partial Income Statement

American Enterprises, Inc.
Partial Income Statement
For the Year Ended October 31, 2001
(Dollars in thousands)

Income before extraordinary gain	$ 9,846
Extraordinary gain (net of income taxes of $1,047)	1,387
Net income	$11,233

Note:
The Company's former headquarters building in San Francisco was severely damaged by an earthquake. After the settlement with the insurers, the Company retired the building and recognized an extraordinary gain of $1,387,000, net of income taxes of $1,047,000.

Note also that AE recognized a gain. A gain arose because the proceeds from the insurance settlement exceeded the carrying value of the building. Recall that buildings are carried in the accounting records at depreciated historical cost, which does not reflect current market values.

When making predictions about AE's future income levels, most analysts would remove the extraordinary gain from AE's reported net income:

Reported net income	$11,233,000
Less extraordinary gain	1,387,000
Adjusted net income	$ 9,846,000

Income Taxes

Given that many income statements have several major sections (continuing operations, discontinued operations, and extraordinary items), a decision must be made about where to report income tax expense. GAAP takes the reasonable position that taxes should be allocated to each major section. Consider again Exhibit 4-4; one item listed is provision for income taxes. This is not Hahn's total income tax expense, however. It is the income tax associated with continuing operations. The tax effects associated with discontinued operations are included in the calculation of those reported losses. This format shows discontinued operations **net of tax.**

Note that discontinued operations generated a loss and that the tax effect is labeled a **tax benefit.** Losses yield tax benefits because they lower the taxes a firm must pay.

Consider a simple example. In 2001, Crimp Corporation earned, before taxes, a profit of $10,000 on continuing operations. It also incurred a $2,000 loss on discontinued operations. Assume a tax rate of 30%. Had the $2,000 loss not been incurred, Crimp's total tax expense would have been $3,000:

$$\text{Total tax expense} = \$10{,}000 \times .3 = \$3{,}000$$

However, given that Crimp did incur the $2,000 loss, its total tax expense is $2,400:

$$\text{Total tax expense} = (\$10{,}000 - \$2{,}000) \times .3 = \$2{,}400$$

Thus, the loss from discontinued operations reduced income tax expense by $600. The tax expense allocated to continuing operations is $3,000, and the tax benefit allocated to discontinued operations is $600. A partial income statement would appear as follows:

Crimp Corporation
Partial Income Statement
For the Year Ended December 31, 2001

Earnings before taxes	$10,000
Income tax expense	3,000
Net earnings from continuing operations	7,000
Loss from discontinued operations (less income tax benefit of $600)	1,400
Net income	$ 5,600

Earnings per Share

Many financial numbers are stated on a per-share basis. Price per share and dividends per share are widely quoted in the financial press. Because a share of stock is the basic ownership unit in corporations, this mode of expression is quite useful. Consequently, GAAP requires that publicly held companies state net income on a per-share basis. In general terms, this requires dividing net income by the average number of shares of stock outstanding. The result is **earnings per share (EPS):**

$$\text{EPS} = \frac{\text{Net income}}{\text{Shares outstanding}}$$

Per-share amounts make it easier to relate the dividends, prices, and earnings of a given firm.

ANALYZING THE INCOME STATEMENT

As you've seen by now, the income statement contains a great deal of useful information about a firm. This section shows how to extract and interpret that information.

The income statements of OshKosh B'Gosh, Inc. (OB) for the years 1997 and 1996, which are summarized in Exhibit 4-6, serve as the basis for this section.

One item on OB's income statement deserves special mention. In 1996, OB incurred a $32,900,000 special charge. The charge includes costs to close facilities, write down assets, and lay off employees (see the Note in Exhibit 4-6). Because OB did not discontinue an entire line of business, these changes do not qualify as a discontinued operation, yet this charge might not recur in the near future. Consequently, some analysts would delete this $32,900,000 loss in calculating ratios and evaluating trends. Such adjustments are demonstrated later in the chapter.

Vertical Analysis

Vertical analysis examines relationships within a given year. To do this with the income statement, divide each line by the first item, net sales. Net sales are a summary measure of a firm's total activities, so evaluating each income statement item relative to net sales makes sense. The result yields **common-size income statements** in percentage terms. OB's common-size statements appear in Exhibit 4-7.

The first line of a common-size income statement is always 100% because the net sales figure is divided by itself. The second line of the common-size income statement, cost of products sold divided by net sales, is referred to as the **cost of goods sold percentage.** For a firm that is a **merchandiser,** one that simply buys and resells goods without changing their shape or form, this percentage reflects the relationship between the price the firm pays for the goods and the price it charges customers. For a **manufacturer,** a firm that buys raw materials and component parts and reshapes them into a finished product, the cost of goods sold percentage can also indicate the efficiency of the manufacturing process.

EXHIBIT 4-6 Income Statements for 1997 and 1996

OshKosh B'Gosh, Inc.
Income Statements
(Dollars in thousands)

	Year Ended December 31, 1997	1996
Net sales	$395,196	$444,766
Cost of products sold	250,815	300,495
Gross profit	144,381	144,271
Selling, general, and administrative expenses	115,439	122,055
Special charges and plant closings	—	32,900
Royalty income, net	(7,945)	(6,100)
Operating income (loss)	36,887	(4,584)
Interest expense	(305)	(1,088)
Other income	1,605	1,575
Income (loss) before taxes	38,187	(4,097)
Income taxes (benefit)	15,629	(5,216)
Net income	$ 22,558	$ 1,119

Note:
During 1996, the Company recorded special charges of $32,900,000 to close facilities, discontinue the Company's Genuine Kids retail store chain, and wind down the Company's European subsidiaries. Special charges (net of income tax benefit) reduced net income by $15,200,000 ($1.23 per share) in 1996.

EXHIBIT 4-7 Common-Size Income Statements

OshKosh B'Gosh
Common-Size Income Statements

	Year Ended December 31, 1997	1996
Net sales	100.0%	100.0%
Cost of products sold	63.5	67.6
Gross profit	36.5	32.4
Selling, general, and administrative expenses	29.2	27.4
Special charges and plant closings	—	7.4
Royalty income, net	(2.0)	(1.4)
Operating income (loss)	9.3	(1.0)
Interest expense	(.1)	(.2)
Other income	.5	.3
Income (loss) before taxes	9.7	(.9)
Income taxes (benefit)	4.0	(1.2)
Net income	5.7%	.3%

In assessing a firm's ability to generate cash flows, low costs and consequently low cost of goods sold percentages are desirable. This provides a larger profit per item sold. For every dollar of revenue in 1997, OB paid about $0.64 to manufacture the associated clothing.

The third line, **gross profit** (or **gross margin) percentage,** is calculated either by dividing gross profit by net sales or by subtracting the cost of goods sold percentage from 100%. It reflects the percentage of the sales price that exceeds the cost of goods sold. It measures the percentage of revenue that is available to cover expenses other than cost of goods sold and to contribute toward profits. In 1997, about $0.36 of every OB sales dollar was available for these purposes. Given that a lower cost of goods sold percentage is desirable, a higher gross profit percentage is preferable.

Two basic strategies exist to increase the gross profit percentage (or, in other words, to decrease the cost of goods sold percentage). First, unit selling prices could be increased. This option is limited because of competition from other companies in the firm's industry. Second, efforts can be made to reduce the cost of goods sold. This can be done, for example, through more astute purchasing (such as buying in bulk to obtain a discount) or a more efficient manufacturing process.

The fourth line of OB's common-size income statement reflects the relationship between selling, general, and administrative expenses and net sales. Managers have substantial control over these costs, and percentages that increase over time are usually viewed with disfavor.

Of the remaining items in Exhibit 4-7, the two most important are the **operating income percentage** and the **net income percentage.** The operating income percentage is an indicator of management's success in operating the firm. The numerator, operating income (or loss), excludes both interest expense and taxes. Because these expenses are not directly affected by operating (buying and selling) decisions, the operating income percentage is a better reflection of how management handles the day-to-day affairs of the firm. The net income percentage reflects the firm's overall profitability, after interest and taxes, relative to its level of activity (net sales). Both ratios are indicators of a firm's financial success.

Exhibit 4-8 graphically depicts the information contained in Exhibit 4-7.

EXHIBIT 4-8 OshKosh B'Gosh Graphic Depiction of Common-Size Income Statements

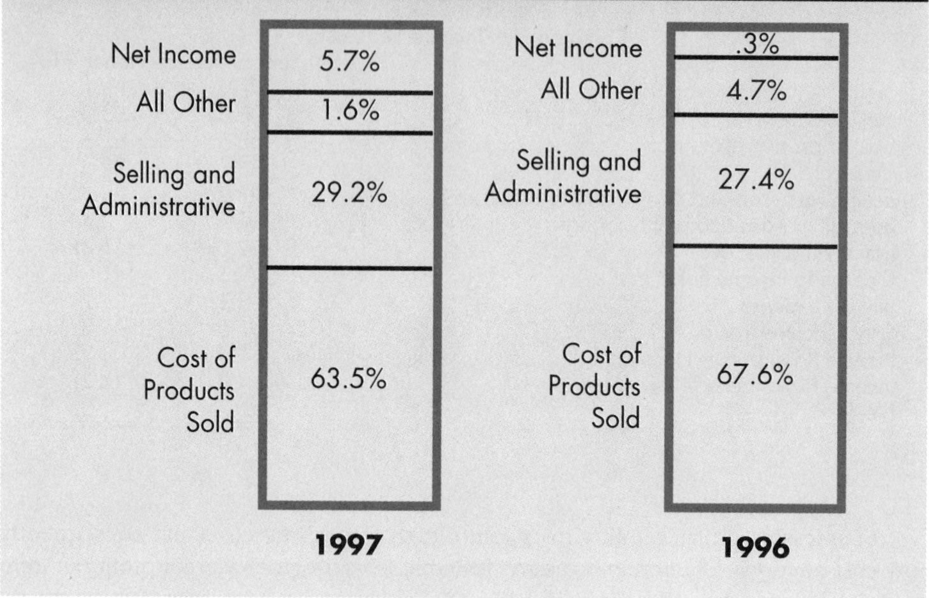

	1997	1996
Net Income	5.7%	.3%
All Other	1.6%	4.7%
Selling and Administrative	29.2%	27.4%
Cost of Products Sold	63.5%	67.6%

Trend Analysis

Trend analysis involves comparing financial statement numbers over time. One way to implement this is to compare the common-size income statement items over time. The trends in OB's cost of goods sold percentage and its gross profit percentage are favorable. For example, the cost of goods sold percentage decreased from 67.6% in 1996 to 63.5% in 1997. This decrease could reflect decreases in the prices of raw materials, increased demand for its products (allowing an increase in selling prices) or efficiencies in the manufacturing process.

The trend in selling, general, and administrative expenses as a percentage of net sales is not favorable. They have increased from 27.4% of sales to 29.2% of sales. However, as Exhibit 4-6 shows, the total dollar amount of these costs has declined.

Both operating income and net income show very desirable trends. However, if OB's special charge is not expected to recur, the operating income percentage and net income percentage should be adjusted for purposes of assessing performance and forecasting future results. To adjust the 1996 operating income percentage, the special charge should be added to operating income because it has already been subtracted in arriving at that number.

$$\text{Adjusted operating income percentage} = \frac{\text{Operating income} + \text{Special charge}}{\text{Net sales}}$$

$$= \frac{-\$4{,}584 + \$32{,}900}{\$444{,}766} = 6.4\%$$

Because net income is an after-tax figure, the adjusted net income percentage must be modified on an after-tax basis. Exhibit 4-6 indicates that the after-tax effect of the special charge was $15,200,000. The after-tax cost is smaller than the pre-tax cost of $32,900,000 because it reflects the benefit of a reduction in taxes due to the loss. The adjustment is accomplished by adding the $15,200,000 after-tax loss to net income.

$$\text{Adjusted net income percentage} = \frac{\text{Net income} + \text{After-tax special charge}}{\text{Net sales}}$$

$$= \frac{\$1{,}119 + \$15{,}200}{\$444{,}766} = 3.7\%$$

Using these adjusted percentages for 1996 as a benchmark, OB's performance in 1997 has still improved, but not to the degree as the unadjusted percentages indicated.

Horizontal Analysis

Horizontal analysis is another form of trend analysis. It uses the figures from a prior year's income statement as the basis for calculating percentage increases and decreases over time. Exhibit 4-9 contains a horizontal analysis of OB's income statements. The figures in the exhibit are obtained by dividing the items in the 1997 income statement by their corresponding amounts in the 1996 income statement.

The exhibit shows that net sales decreased 11.1% (100% − 88.9%) between 1996 and 1997. A decrease in sales is often a cause of major concern. A sales decline could reflect a decrease in sales activity (number of units sold) or a decrease in unit selling prices. Either of these causes could have adverse effects on profitability. Additional research regarding OB indicates that the sales decline was due primarily to two other factors. First, OB intentionally adopted the strategy of reducing its reliance on wholesalers, who are intermediaries that purchase the company's products and resell them to retail vendors, such as department stores. OB concluded that its relationship with certain wholesalers was not sufficiently profitable to warrant continuation.

The other major reason for the decline in sales was that OB discontinued its own European operations, which had a negative effect on sales. To replace these operations, however, OB granted a license to another organization that is more familiar with the European market. The license permits this organization to sell OB products in exchange for royalty payments. Exhibit 4-9 shows that royalty income increased by 30%. Thus, OB's strategy was to trade the profit generated by its own European operations for the royalty income generated by its licensee.

The strategies of OB, described above, that affected sales should also have impacted expenses. Cost of products sold is the largest single expense item. Exhibit 4-9 shows that this item declined 16.5% (100% − 83.5%) from 1996 to 1997. The decrease in cost of products sold is larger than the decrease in sales (11.1%). This suggests that the actions taken by OB will have a positive effect on profitability. The decline in cost of products sold is also attributable to two other reasons; OB was able to find less expensive sources of raw materials, and OB improved the efficiency of its manufacturing operations. The latter was accomplished, in part, by plant closings, the costs of which were contained in the 1996 income statement. Also note that the decline in cost of products sold relative to sales is consistent with the results of the common-size income statements (refer to Exhibit 4-7) that showed that the cost of products sold had decreased as a percentage of sales.

EXHIBIT 4-9 Horizontal Analysis of Income Statements

OshKosh B'Gosh
Income Statements—Horizontal Analysis

	Year Ended December 31,	
	1997	**1996**
Net sales	88.9%	100%
Cost of products sold	83.5	100
Gross profit	100.1	100
Selling, general, and administrative expenses	94.6	100
Special charges and plant closings	—	100
Royalty income, net	130.2	100
Operating income	NA	100
Interest expense	28.0	100
Other income	101.9	100
Income before taxes	NA	100
Income taxes	NA	100
Net income	2,015.9%	100%

NA = Not available

Exhibit 4-9 indicates that the percentage change in operating income for 1997 is not available. This is due to the fact that an operating *loss* was generated in 1996 and operating *income* was generated in 1997. Although the 1997 figure can be calculated (36,887 / −4,584 = −805%), care must be exercised when dealing with negative numbers. The negative denominator yields a negative percentage, yet the income in 1997 is much more positive than the 1996 loss. Even if absolute values are used, knowing that the 1997 operating income is eight times as large as the 1996 operating loss is not particularly insightful. Regardless of the difficulties with this calculation, the trend in operating income is extremely favorable.

The trend in net income is also quite favorable. Net income in 1997 is 20 times greater than 1996 net income. This result underscores another pitfall in calculating ratios: the small denominator problem. The large percentage increase is not primarily due to 1997 being so superlative. Rather, the small net income generated in 1996 has the effect of inflating the calculated value. Although net income improved substantially in 1997, a percentage increase of 2,015.9% probably overstates the improvement.

Other Ratios

Several ratios link the income statement and the balance sheet. **Return on shareholders' equity (ROE)** is of utmost importance to shareholders. To calculate ROE, divide net income by average shareholders' equity:

$$\text{ROE} = \frac{\text{Net income}}{\text{Average shareholders' equity}}$$

ROE relates the earnings generated by a firm to the assets invested by its shareholders. It is obviously in the shareholders' best interest to have larger earnings generated on their investments. A potential investor, faced with competing investment choices, will use ROE to help identify the preferred investment.

The denominator of ROE is *average* shareholders' equity. Because net income is earned over the course of a year, it makes sense to use the firm's average shareholders' equity during the year. As a practical matter, average shareholders' equity is usually calculated by averaging beginning and end-of-year shareholders' equity amounts, which are found on the balance sheet. Exhibit 4-10 summarizes certain items from OB's balance sheet.

OB's 1997 ROE is:

$$\text{ROE} = \frac{\$22{,}558}{(\$138{,}077 + \$113{,}157)/2} = 18.0\%$$

A ROE of 18% is very close to OB's industry average. The 1997 ROE compares extremely favorably to the 1996 ROE of .8%.

Another important ratio is **return on assets (ROA).** This ratio relates a firm's earnings to *all* the assets the firm has available to generate those earnings. ROA differs from ROE in that ROE utilizes only the assets that the shareholders supplied. ROE measures management's success in using the assets invested by shareholders, whereas ROA measures how successfully management utilized all the assets entrusted to it. To calculate ROA, divide net income, adjusted for interest expense, by average total assets:

$$\text{ROA} = \frac{\text{Net income} + \text{Interest expense } (1 - \text{tax rate})}{\text{Average total assets}}$$

Why is interest expense added to net income in the numerator? Recall that a firm can acquire assets from two sources: owners and creditors. Interest expense is a cost incurred to acquire assets from creditors (e.g., interest expense on bank borrowings). It arises from a financing decision (obtaining funds from creditors rather than owners), not an operating decision (utilizing assets). Because ROA is designed to measure managers' success in utilizing assets, interest expense is irrelevant. Its effect on net income should be eliminated when calculating ROA.

Interest expense has direct and indirect effects on net income, and both effects should be eliminated. Regarding the direct effect, because interest expense has already been subtracted in calculating net income, it is now added back. The indirect effect relates to taxes. Because interest expense is a deduction for tax purposes, tax expense is lower and net income is higher by an amount equal to interest expense multiplied by the tax rate. Therefore, to adjust fully for the elimination of interest expense, net income must be increased by interest expense and decreased by interest expense multiplied by the tax rate. The difference between these two amounts is interest expense multiplied by 1 minus the tax rate):

EXHIBIT 4-10 Summary of Selected Information

OshKosh B'Gosh
Selected Balance Sheet Information
(Dollars in thousands)

	1997	1996
Total shareholders' equity	$113,157	$138,077
Total assets	$217,211	$229,131

$$\begin{array}{l} + \text{ Interest expense} \\ - \text{ Interest expense} \times \text{tax rate} \\ \hline \text{Interest expense} \times (1 - \text{tax rate}) \end{array}$$

Eliminating the effects of interest expense facilitates the comparison of asset utilization across firms that have different amounts of debt.

Financial statements disclose, in the notes, firms' tax rates. OB's effective rate in 1997 was 40.9% and its ROA for 1997 was

$$\text{ROA} = \frac{\$22,558 + \$305\,(1 - .409)}{(\$196,033 + \$174,788)/2} = 12.3\%$$

OB's 1997 ROA greatly exceeds its performance in 1996. The dramatic improvements in OB's ROE and ROA reflect the success of its operational changes mentioned above.

The final ratio discussed in this section is **times interest earned**. Because profits ultimately are a source of cash, and because cash is necessary for the payment of interest charges, creditors are concerned about the relationship between profits and interest expense. The times interest earned ratio shows how many times interest expense is covered by resources generated from operations, and creditors prefer higher times interest earned ratios. It is calculated by dividing earnings before interest and taxes by interest expense:

$$\text{Times interest earned} = \frac{\text{Earnings before interest and taxes}}{\text{Interest expense}}$$

Earnings before interest and taxes, not net income, is used in the numerator. Because interest expense is already deducted in calculating net income, net income understates the resources available to cover interest expense. Tax expense should not reduce the numerator because, in a worst case scenario, as income declines, taxes would be eliminated.

OB's income statement, presented in Exhibit 4-6, does not contain a line item for income before interest and taxes. The easiest way to calculate this figure, given OB's income statement format, is to add interest expense to income before taxes. In 1997, OB's income before interest and taxes would be determined as follows:

Income before taxes	$38,187,000
Interest expense	305,000
Income before interest and taxes	$38,492,000

OB's 1997 times interest earned ratio is 126.2:

$$\text{Times interest earned} = \frac{\$38,492}{\$305} = 126.2$$

This ratio indicates that interest expense is covered 126.2 times at present income levels. This is an outstanding ratio and reflects that OB has little outstanding debt. Given that potential creditors would look very favorably on a ratio this large, OB would likely have little problem securing additional financing, if it so desires.

LIMITATIONS OF ACCOUNTING INCOME

Although financial statement readers find reported accounting income very useful, it does have several limitations. Conceptually, we often think of income as an increase in wealth. If our bank account grows by $100 because of interest, we feel as though our income is $100. For many assets, however, accounting does not recognize an increase in value when it occurs. Instead, the value increase and the associated income are recognized at the time of the asset's disposal.

Sometimes the difference between historical cost and current value can be quite large. Consider Hiroshi Fujishige, who owns a 58-acre farm across the street from Disneyland. The farm was purchased in 1953 for $2,500. Southern California real estate experts estimate its value to be $55,000,000. In spite of this estimate, the Fujishige Farm balance sheet reflects the land at $2,500, and the increase in value has not appeared on any of Fujishige's income statements. In general, to recognize a value increase, accounting rules require the occurrence of a transaction for verification purposes.

Financial statements do not reflect still other accomplishments of a firm. For example, the *Wall Street Journal* reported that the Food and Drug Administration planned to approve an anticlotting drug developed by COR Therapeutics, Inc. This was extremely good news for COR; in fact, its stock soared 79% on the news. However, this event was not included in its accounting records when the announcement was made. At that time, COR had not engaged in any transaction; no sales had been made. The financial statement effects of the drug sales will be recognized in the accounting records as they occur.

Accounting's **conservatism principle** can also limit the extent to which accounting income reflects changes in wealth. This principle states that when doubt exists about the accounting treatment for a given transaction, a conservative alternative should be selected. In other words, select the alternative that reports lower asset values and lower net income. For example, expenditures for research and development are immediately expensed, even when they result in valuable products or patents. Spending on employee training is expensed immediately, even though its objective is to create a more highly skilled workforce. These examples suggest that the balance sheets of some companies may have undervalued or unrecorded assets; this, of course, implies that the net income figure on the income statement does not necessarily reflect changes in wealth. On the other hand, most accountants support the conservatism principle because it helps avoid overly optimistic financial statements.

In summary, to ensure that reliable and verifiable financial statements emerge from the accounting process, GAAP precludes the recognition of certain potential value changes. Because of this, accounting income does not strictly measure changes in wealth. However, it is a very useful performance measure on which the business community relies heavily.

ACCOUNTING INCOME AND ECONOMIC CONSEQUENCES

Recall from Chapter 2, "The Basic Concepts of Financial Accounting," that the managers of many publicly-held corporations receive bonuses that are based on reported accounting net income. These bonus plans typically include a floor and a ceiling. The floor requires that net income must reach a certain level before the bonus is activated, while the ceiling places a limit on the size of the bonus. That is, the bonus is not increased as net income increases above the ceiling. Thus, managers prefer that net income falls at the high end of the range between the floor and the ceiling.

Bonuses can motivate managers to undertake actions that will improve the operations of the firm, thereby increasing profits. Unfortunately, bonuses can also motivate managers to make accounting-related decisions that do not affect the underlying profitability of the firm, but that do affect *reported* accounting income.

For example, firms occasionally engage in **big baths.** These are accounting decisions that result in large losses in a single year. If reported earnings would otherwise have been below a bonus plan's floor, such losses have no effect on the current year's bonus. Moreover, by taking the losses all at one time, subsequent periods are relieved of those charges, and the chances of higher reported profits and bonuses in the future are maximized. Reality Check 4-4 describes a big bath taken by Waste Management, Inc.

The actions taken by Waste Management are within the bounds of allowable managerial discretion. Other corporations, however, have been accused of much more questionable actions. For example, Miniscribe, a bankrupt disk-drive manufacturer, is alleged to have recognized revenue prematurely on shipments that customers had not ordered, improperly estimated uncollectible accounts receivable, and falsified inventory.

The application of GAAP requires the exercise of judgment. At the same time, manager's self-interest is affected by reported accounting income. Accordingly, financial statement users should not be surprised that managers' self-interests influence their accounting policy judgments. As a result, financial statements may not be unbiased reflections about the underlying economic activities of firms.

REALITY CHECK 4-4

Waste Management, Inc. recently took several large charges totaling $1.6 billion. These charges included asset write-downs, the cost of severance packages, costs to discontinue serving several large customers because of lost contracts, and other items. These charges contributed to Waste Management's 1997 loss of $1.2 billion. Perhaps more than coincidentally, Waste Management had recently selected a new chairman. Some analysts suggest that new corporate administrations are inclined to take big baths.

Required

List two reasons why recently installed corporate managers might want to take a big bath.

Solution

First, these charges can easily be blamed on the former management. Second, they help the company report favorable earnings in the future, which reflects well on the new management team. Moreover, the higher reported net income might increase the bonuses paid to the new managers.

SUMMARY OF LEARNING OBJECTIVES

1. **Explain when to recognize revenues.**
Revenue should be recognized when the earnings process is substantially complete and the amount to be collected is reasonably determinable. These criteria ensure that revenue is not recognized before the firm has honored its obligation to the customer and is reasonably assured of collecting cash from the customer. Revenue is usually recognized at the point of sale.
2. **Explain when to recognize expenses.**
The matching principle states that expenses should be recognized when resources have been consumed to help generate revenue. Showing revenues and the related expenses on the same income statement results in a net income figure that best reflects a firm's performance for the period. The matching principle is implemented in one of three ways: associating cause and effect, systematic allocation, and immediate recognition.
3. **Interpret the components of the income statement.**
Income statements may contain several major sections: income from continuing operations, income from discontinued operations, and extraordinary items. This format helps financial statement users assess the past performance of a firm and predict the results of future operations. When making forecasts based on historical information, the effect of transactions and events that are not expected to recur in the future should be eliminated from net income. Because of the way accounting definitions have been developed, even income from continuing operations may include nonrecurring items.
4. **Analyze income statement information using various ratios.**
The income statement contains a number of measures related to a firm's ability to generate earnings. This helps analysts assess a firm's expected return. Vertical analysis examines relationships within the income statement of one period; each line of the income statement is expressed as a percentage of sales. Horizontal analysis shows the trend over time in income statement numbers. Return on shareholders' equity and return on assets are good summary measures of a firm's performance. Finally, the times interest earned ratio provides creditors with an indication of the firm's ability to pay interest charges.
5. **Describe the effects that reported earnings have on managers' wealth and, consequently, on their accounting policy decisions.**
Many corporations tie the compensation of their top officers to reported accounting earnings. These bonus plans often contain a floor and a ceiling. The floor is the level of net income that must be exceeded before the bonus is activated, while the ceiling limits the amount of the bonus, regardless of how large net income is. This situation motivates managers to report a net income figure that is at the high end of the floor-ceiling range. Managers are also motivated to undertake "big baths." Taking large charges in one year relieves future years' income of those expenses and paves the way for higher reported earnings and higher bonuses for management.

KEY TERMS

QUESTIONS

4-1 Describe the differences between revenues and gains. Also distinguish between expenses and losses. Explain why these items are usually disclosed separately on income statements.

4-2 Explain why a firm might elect to report its annual income using a fiscal year-end that doesn't end on December 31.

4-3 In deciding which items to disclose on the income statement, managers are guided by the materiality principle. Explain how this principle would affect a decision about whether to disclose a firm's research expenses separately.

4-4 Often the first item on a firm's income statement is labeled "Net sales" or "Sales revenue." Discuss the measuring of these terms. Why do you think this is displayed so prominently on the income statement? Why are managers concerned with determining when the earnings process is *substantially complete*?

4-5 Why do most companies disclose the cost of goods sold as a separate item on the income statement? How might this item differ for merchandising firms versus manufacturing firms? Why might some firms not want to disclose this item?

4-6 Explain why interest expense is not considered to be an operating expense by most firms. Identify several types of businesses where interest expense might be reported as an operating expense?

4-7 Distinguish between a single-step and a multiple-step income statement. Why is a multiple-step format usually more informative to the reader?

4-8 Identify and discuss several decisions that managers make based on information from the income statement. Include a discussion of the basic purpose and objectives of an income statement.

4-9 Identify and discuss the kinds of information that investors in a firm's debt and equity securities may seek when reading the income statement. What decisions will usually be of interest to such investors?

4-10 Explain the two criteria that must be met for a firm to recognize revenue in its income statement. Discuss how these criteria might be applied to revenue recognition by (a) a fast-food restaurant and (b) a home appliance merchandiser.

4-11 Discuss the purpose of the matching principle, and explain the three ways in which this principle is implemented.

4-12 Determine how the matching principle would affect recognition of the following items: (a) cost of inventory sold, (b) depreciation expense of production equipment, and (c) expenditures for new product development.

4-13 Income statements are often used in order to provide a historical measure of a firm's performance, and are also used as a basis for predicting future profitability. How are income statements useful for both purposes? Discuss.

4-14 Why are extraordinary items reported separately in the income statement? Identify an event that would be classified by one firm as an ordinary item and by another firm as an extraordinary item? Discuss.

4-15 Discuss the differences between *revenues* and *profits*. Where do each appear on the income statement? Why is it important to keep these two separate?

4-16 Discuss the differences between *profits* and *profitability*. In what context might they be used interchangeably? When must they be kept separate?

4-17 Define the accounting principle of *conservatism*. Why would a manager or owner prefer conservative profits? When would a manager or owner prefer that income or profit not be measured conservatively?

4-18 Explain why GAAP requires that income taxes be allocated to each major section of the income statement.

4-19 Under what circumstances might an income statement report a tax *benefit*?

4-20 Discuss the meaning of a "restructuring charge" and explain why you believe that such charges should (or should not) be reported as extraordinary items in the income statement. How does the concept of *sustainability* affect how extraordinary items are reported on the income statement?

4-21 Describe the construction of a common-size income statement. Why is the selection of the base (the number selected as the 100% figure) so important? Discuss how common-size statements are used in a vertical analysis of the income statement.

4-22 Identify three reasons why a firm's gross profit (gross margin) percentage might change over time.

4-23 Discuss several reasons why a firm's net income percentage might change over time. Discuss how financial statements help explain the reasons for changes in the net income percentage over time?

4-24 Distinguish between vertical analysis and trend analysis of the income statement. Describe two ways of implementing a trend analysis.

4-25 Provide two examples of ratios that link the income statement and the balance sheet. In each case, explain why it is useful to relate the items that appear in the numerator and the denominator of the ratio.

4-26 The ratios discussed in this chapter include return on assets, return on shareholders' equity, and times interest earned. In each case, a different measure of income is used. Identify and discuss those differences. Explain why income is measured differently in each of these ratio calculations.

4-27 The chapter states that "accounting income does not strictly measure changes in wealth." Provide two examples of changes in wealth that would not be reported currently in the income statement. In each case, evaluate whether reporting these changes would improve the usefulness of the income measure.

4-28 Describe the nature of a *big bath* reported in the income statement. How would a big bath affect reported income in later years? What is the likely effect of a *big bath* on a firm's stock price in the year that the losses are reported?

EXERCISES

Vertical Analysis, Single Year's Data

4-29 Conduct a vertical analysis of the income statement for Hahn Automotive Warehouse in Exhibit 4-4. Discuss Hahn's profitability (or lack thereof).

Matching Income Statement Items

4-30 For each numbered item, indicate (by letter) where in the income statement it belongs.

a. Revenues
b. Cost of Goods Sold
c. Selling Expenses
d. General and Administrative Expenses
e. Other Income and Expenses
f. Separate Line Item, Net of Tax After Income from Continuing Operations
g. Not on the Income Statement

_____ 1. Commissions expense
_____ 2. Gain on sale of land
_____ 3. Dividends declared and paid
_____ 4. Prepaid rent
_____ 5. Depreciation expense for office equipment
_____ 6. Interest expense
_____ 7. Tornado loss (business located in Kansas)
_____ 8. Merchandise inventory
_____ 9. Income tax payable
_____ 10. Loss on discontinued operations

Preparing an Income Statement

4-31 Woodway Company's annual report contained the following data (dollars in millions) on its income statement

Interest expense	$ 2,489
Investment income	11,218
Other income	9,033
Depreciation	1,257
Revenues	591,762
Other expenses	8,482
Cost of sales	482,355
Operating expenses	98,576
Income taxes	522

Required

a. Prepare an income statement using a multiple-step format similar to Exhibit 4-1.

b. Revise your income statement (from part a above) to include the following two additional items from Woodway's annual report (dollars in millions):

Loss on discontinued operations, net of tax	$1,025
Extraordinary loss, net of tax	314

Interpreting Financial Statements

4-32 The Woodway Company included the following note in its 2000 annual report: In June 2000, Woodway Company and its principle subsidiaries filed for protection under Chapter 11 of the United States Bankruptcy Code. Woodway recorded a provision for possible impairment of $24 million at December 31, 1999, and recorded an additional provision of $19 million in the second quarter of 2000.

Required

a. Do you think that this $19 million loss should be reported on Woodway's 2000 income statement? Why or why not?

b. Based on the data in Exercises 4-31 and 4-32, what estimate would you make regarding Woodway's adjusted income (sustainable operating profit or sustainable earnings)?

Calculating Adjusted Income (Sustainable Earnings)

4-33 James Hardie Industries Ltd. is an Australian company specializing in building materials. It also has several plants in the USA specializing in producing fibre-cement roofing materials. It reported the following financial results on its 1998 income statement:

	1998	**1997**
Total revenues (($bn)	1.29	1.62
Net profit ($m)	41.6	83.0
Abnormals ($m)	(41.7)	31.7
EBIT ($m)	132.0	87.4
EPS	.206	. 131

(Results shown for the 12 months ended March 31, 1998; net profit is after tax and after abnormals.)

Required

a. Calculate adjusted income by eliminating the abnormal items from James Hardie's reported net profits.
b. Discuss how this adjusted income figure is more useful and more representative than the reported net profits.
c. Discuss the concept of adjusted income as it relates to sustainable earnings or sustainable operating profit for each year.
d. Given the decreasing level of total revenues, explain why you think it is still likely that James Hardie will show an increase in its 1999 net profit.

Sorting Accounting Information: Income Statement Versus Balance Sheet

4-34 Sort the following account titles according to whether they would appear on the income statement or the balance sheet:

Supplies expense	Salaries payable
Accounts payable	Cost of goods sold
Land	Trucks
Capital stock	Sales revenue
Interest earned	Interest expense
Accrued taxes payable	Tax expense
Interest payable	Retained earnings
Rent expense	Rent revenue
Cash sales	Cash
Depreciation expense	Wages expense

Financial Ratios

4-35 Answer each of the following *independent* questions:

a. The return on equity for the Hammond Corporation for the year ended December 31, 1999, is 9%. The owners' equity balances on December 31, 1998 and 1999 were $180,000 and $200,000, respectively. What is the net income for 1999?
b. The Beachfront Resort Company had the following income statement information:

Sales revenue	$500,000
Gross profit percentage	30%
Net income percentage	5%

What is the cost of goods sold? What is the total operating and other expenses?

c. The return on assets for the Wicker Chair Company is 12%. The average total assets is $230,000 and net income is $20,100. What is interest expense, net of tax? What is gross interest expense if the income tax rate is 25%?

Income Statement

4-36 The following data were provided by Bluebird Company for calendar year 1999:

Sales	$350,000
Gross margin percentage	45%
Net income percentage	8%
Income tax percentage	25%

Required

a. Based on the previous data, determine the following:
   1. Cost of goods sold
   2. Net income
   3. Income taxes
   4. Operating expenses (assume no "other expenses and revenues")

b. Prepare a multiple-step income statement for the year ended December 31, 1999.

Recording Transactions and Preparing an Income Statement

Integration of Concepts

4-37 Spinner Sewing Corporation was incorporated on January 1, 2000. Three investors *each* invested $150,000 in exchange for $150,000 of common stock of the corporation. The following transactions took place during 2000:

1. Purchased merchandise inventory on account, $200,000.
2. Rent paid on January 2 for a two-year period, $48,000.
3. Borrowed $100,000 on March 31 at a 10% annual interest rate for one year.
4. Sold goods at retail, $300,000; half for cash, half on account. The cost of goods sold was $135,000.
5. Paid $120,000 on outstanding bills owed to inventory suppliers.
6. Received $80,000 from receivables customers.
7. Incurred operating expenses of $36,000, of which $14,000 was paid in cash and the balance on account.

Required

a. Record the above transactions, including the initial investment, in the accounting equation. Set up separate account columns for assets, liabilities, and shareholders' equity.

b. Record the following year-end accruals (adjust the figures from part a):
   1. Expired portion of prepaid rent
   2. Accrued interest expense
   3. Accrued income tax. Assume 20% tax rate.

c. Prepare a multiple-step income statement for the year ended December 31, 2000.

d. Calculate:
   1. Gross profit percentage
   2. Operating income percentage
   3. Net income percentage

e. Calculate:
   1. Return on assets
   2. Return on equity

f. Evaluate the performance of the corporation. What other transactions would you typically expect to see?

g. What if the corporation discontinued part of its operations during the year and incurred a loss of $45,000 on the disposal? What impact would this have on the income statement?

Integration of Concepts

Recording and Analyzing Transactions

4-38 Boomingdales, Inc., reported the following transactions:

1. Purchased $150 of equipment on account. The corporation has over $1 million in assets.
2. Sold merchandise at retail of $150,000 during the year on account. Customers returned $10,000 of merchandise at retail for credit on their accounts. (Ignore cost of goods sold.)
3. Received $40,000 *in advance* from customers.
4. Recorded annual depreciation of $280,000.

Required

a. Record the above transactions in the accounting equation. Set up separate account columns as needed.

b. Discuss the generally accepted accounting principles that guide accountants in recording each of these transactions properly.

Interpreting Income Statements: Ratio Analysis

4-39 Use the following comparative income statements to evaluate Clarkson Brewery's performance for the year ended December 31, 1999 and 1998.

	1999	1998
Net sales	$405,000	$378,000
Operating expenses:		
Cost of goods sold	163,250	154,400
Selling expense	81,000	48,360
General and administrative expense	121,500	102,650
Total operating expenses	365,750	305,410
Operating income	39,250	72,590
Other income:		
Gain on sale of property	34,000	—
Income before tax	73,250	72,590
Income tax expense	21,975	21,777
Income before extraordinary item	51,275	50,813
Extraordinary loss net of tax	—	(25,000)
	$ 51,275	$ 25,813

Required

a. Calculate a horizontal and vertical analysis, using the data from Clarkson Brewery.

b. In which year was the company more successful?

c. What underlying business reasons might have resulted in differences in the company's gains and losses each year?

Income Tax Expense and Income Statement Classifications

4-40 Amherst Trucking Co. had the following pre-tax amounts of revenues, expenses, gains, and losses during 2000. All items are subject to an income tax rate of 40%.

Revenues	$1,500,000
Operating expenses	$ 900,000
Extraordinary loss	$ 400,000

Required

a. Determine the firm's total income tax expense during 2000.
b. What amount would be reported as operating income after tax?
c. What is the amount of tax benefit (tax reduction) associated with the extraordinary loss?
d. What is the net of tax amount of the extraordinary loss?
e. What amount would the firm report as net income for 2000?

Trend Analysis: Net Income and EPS

4-41 Equity Cushion Co. reports the following items in its financial statements:

	1998	1999
Net income	$16,000,000	$24,000,000
Common shares outstanding	1,000,000 shares	1,200,000 shares

Required

a. Determine the firm's earnings per share (EPS) in both 1998 and 1999.
b. Determine the percentage change in net income and EPS from 1998 to 1999.
c. Based on your answers to part b, what would you expect Equity Cushion's net income and EPS to be in 2000? Clearly state any assumptions made in developing your answers.

Vertical Analysis of the Income Statement

Critical Thinking

4-42 P-Town O'Malley's 2000 income statement reported net income of $6 million. A vertical analysis of the income statement shows the following:

Net sales percentage	?%
Cost of products sold percentage	?
Gross profit percentage	48
Selling and administrative expense percentage	?
Operating income percentage	?
Income tax* percentage	?
Net income percentage	6

*Income tax rate: 40% of operating income.

Required

Determine the missing percentages and the dollar amounts that are reported in P-Town's income statement for each of the above items.

Horizontal and Vertical Analysis of the Income Statement

Critical Thinking

4-43 The Miami Rockies, a recently transplanted baseball franchise, reported the following income statement and horizontal percentages:

	1999 Amount (Hundreds of $)	Percentage Changes During 2000
Revenues	$ 6,500	+10%
Operating expenses	(4,800)	+ 8%
Operating income	$ 1,700	?
Income tax (40%)	(680)	?
Net income	$ 1,020	?

Required

a. Complete the "Percentage Changes during 2000" column and determine the dollar amounts reported in the Rockies' 2000 income statement.
b. Prepare a vertical analysis of the income statements for both 1999 and 2000.
c. Comment on any apparently favorable or unfavorable changes between 1999 and 2000, revealed by your analyses in parts a and b.

Gross Margin Changes: Two-Product Firm

4-44 Ben-Shien's Wonton Works produces two grades of dumpling wrappers, standard and deluxe. Sales and cost of sales for both products for 1999 and 2000 were:

	1999		2000	
	(Dollars in thousands)			
	Standard	Deluxe	Standard	Deluxe
Sales	$600	$900	$900	$600
Cost of sales	$500	$600	$750	$400

Required

a. Determine Ben-Shien's total sales, gross profit, and gross profit percentage in each year.

b. Conduct a horizontal (percentage change) analysis of the sales, cost of sales, and gross margin amounts.

c. Explain why Ben-Shien's overall gross profit declined during 2000.

Revenue Recognition

4-45 The following transactions are given:

1. Rent for two months of $1,200 was paid in advance.
2. A customer's order was received for a bridal veil that will be billed at delivery for $120.
3. Supplies, purchased three months ago at a cost of $300, were used in the current month.
4. An etching by Picasso was purchased in 1960 for $400. A similar etching just sold at Sotheby's for $45,000.
5. Equipment purchased 10 years ago had monthly depreciation recorded of $900. The equipment had an original useful life of five years and is still in use.
6. An architect was paid a $2,000 retainer for preparing designs and plans for a new office.
7. Wages of $120, earned by employees on New Year's Eve, will be paid on January 5.
8. A mortgage loan was issued last year, but the creditors are now three months delinquent in their monthly payments.

Required:

Discuss how the matching and revenue recognition principles would be used to determine the revenue or expense in each of the transactions:

Revenue Recognition

4-46 Consider the following transactions for the publishers of *Mobile Home Improvement*. This magazine is produced monthly and sold on newsstands and to annual subscribers.

1. *Mobile Home Improvement* received cash for 100 two-year subscriptions ($48 each) and 3,000 one-year subscriptions ($36 each).
2. *Mobile Home Improvement* sold 30,000 copies of the January issue to newsstand vendors at $1.50 each and received payment.
3. In February, the same vendors ordered and received 30,000 copies, but payment was not received until March.
4. In March, the same vendors ordered and received 30,000 copies, but payment was not received until April.
5. In addition, in March, a new vendor placed a standing order for 40,000 copies for each month for the rest of year. The vendor paid in advance for one

month's supply, which is to be kept on deposit to reflect the purchase commitment. In return, the publishers of *Mobile Home Improvement* reduced the purchase price by 10 cents per copy. The publishers shipped March's 40,000 copies to the vendor on account.

Required:

Determine the amount of revenue that should be recorded on an accrual basis in each circumstance.

Determining Revenues and Expenses

4-47 McGucken's Software sold $1,354,000 of merchandise for cash and had credit sales totaling $2,658,000. It collected cash from customers in the amount of $3,396,000. McGucken's received merchandise from suppliers invoiced at $1,100,000 and paid suppliers $900,000.

Required

a. Determine the amount of revenue that should be recognized this year.
b. Determine the cost of goods sold (amount) that should be matched with this year's revenue, assuming no change in inventory (that is, beginning inventory equals ending inventory).

PROBLEMS

Vertical and Horizontal Analysis of the Income Statement

Critical Thinking

4-48 Denny's CPA School provided the following vertical analysis of its income statements for 1999 and 2000:

	Percentage of Revenues 1999	2000
Revenues	100%	100%
Salaries expense	40	45
Rentals expense	20	25
Books and supplies	10	10
Advertising	10	15
Operating income	20	5
Income tax	8	2
Net income	12	3

In addition, Denny's tuition revenues were $500,000 in 1999 and $400,000 in 2000.

Required

a. Based on the above information, prepare the firm's income statements for 1999 and 2000.
b. Provide a horizontal analysis of the changes in each item in the income statement.
c. Based on your analysis, comment about the expected future performance of Denny's CPA School.

Critical Thinking

Transaction Analysis: Preparing an Income Statement, Cash Versus Accrual

4-49 Jill Zimmer wants to evaluate the success of her restaurant, Planet Broadway. She has assembled the following 2000 data:

1. Wages were $270,000, paid in cash.
2. Collections from customers were $675,000. (Assume that half the customers paid their bills by year-end).
3. A $5,000 deposit for a future wedding reception is included in these collections.
4. Insurance expense was $3,500, paid in cash.
5. Rental expense was $120,000, paid half in cash and half in promissory notes due in 2001.
6. Food costs were $85,000, paid in cash.
7. Advertising bills of $13,000 were paid; however, Jill had only agreed to pay $1,000 each month under her contract with the advertising firm. The extra $1,000 payment pertained to 1999.
8. Interest revenues were $350, collected in cash.
9. Cab fares (for inebriated customers) were $875.
10. Jill's salary was $10,000 per month, but due to concerns about cash flow, she was only paid $5,000 each month.
11. The income tax rate is 28% of income before taxes.

Required

a. Prepare a single-step income statement, using the accrual basis of accounting.
b. Prepare a similar income statement, using the cash basis of accounting.
c. Discuss the differences between these two statements.
d. What managerial concerns might Jill have upon seeing your income statement?
e. What additional items usually appear in such an income statement for a small business?
f. Which costs do you feel are high, relative to Jill's volume of business?
g. On which costs should she concentrate most in order to improve her profitability?
h. What else could she do to improve her net income?

Revenue Recognition: Cash Versus Accrual

4-50 Consider the following transactions:

1. A firm sold merchandise for $1,000, but no cash was received.
2. A firm collected the $1,000 from transaction 1.
3. A medical clinic provided treatment for a patient and billed the patient's insurance company for $65. The patient is responsible for any deficiency not paid by insurance.
4. An insurance company paid the medical clinic only $49.
5. The physician billed the patient for the balance due.
6. The patient paid the physician $11.
7. Safeway Market sold three bags of groceries for $110, but the customer paid for the groceries with a credit card.
8. Shannon Engineers signed a contract with the State of Arkansas for $10,000,000 to design and build a bridge over the Arkansas River. It will take Shannon two years to complete this project, and no work will be started until next year.

9. The state of Arkansas paid Shannon a deposit of $1,000,000 after the contract was signed but before any other work commenced.
10. The state of Arkansas paid $4,000,000 to Shannon during the first year of work, even though two-thirds of the bridge was completed-way ahead of schedule.
11. The state of Arkansas paid the remaining $5,000,000 at the end of the second year, long after the bridge was completed.

Required

a. For each transaction, determine the amount of revenue that would be recognized under accrual accounting.
b. For each transaction, determine the amount of revenue that would be recognized under cash basis accounting.
c. Discuss the differences between the revenue amounts recognized on each basis.

Revenue Recognition

4-51 Consider the following transactions, which are independent, except as noted:

1. Sarah Jones, R.N., provided home nursing services to her clients and billed them for 20 hours of service at $65 per hour.
2. Ms. Jones collected $60 per hour from her state's Medicaid program for the services in transaction 1. Patients are not required to make up any shortfall for the 20 hours of service. Therefore, Sarah wrote off (canceled) the balance in the receivable account.
3. Quick-Shop Grocery sold food and other merchandise for $3,500, on account. (Ignore the cost of goods sold.)
4. Quick-Shop Grocery contracted with Bob's Bakery to provide flour, sugar, and other ingredients at a standard fee of $100 per day.
5. Andy's Aerobic Aerie sold annual memberships to exercise fanatics at $30 per month. This entitles members to unlimited access to aerobics classes, workouts, and so on. On January 1, Andy signed 100 members, who pay the first month's fee.
6. Andy signed an agreement with Sarah Jones to provide discounted memberships to 10 of her impoverished clients at $20 per month. Half paid at the end of the first month.
7. Andy decided to prepare and distribute a monthly aerobics magazine, which is available to members at $5 per issue. Only half of Andy's 110 members took advantage of this offer and paid the annual subscription.
8. Andy put 30 copies of the aerobics magazine on display in Quick-Shop. These copies were "consigned" to Quick-Shop, and payment is not due until the issues are sold.
9. All 30 copies of the guide sold. Andy collected $4 per issue from Quick-Shop ($5 minus 20% consignment fee).

Required

a. Determine the revenue associated with each item that would be recognized during the first month under the accrual method.
b. Determine the revenue that would be recognized for each item under the cash basis of accounting.

Integration of Concepts

Transaction Analysis: Preparing an Income Statement, Accrual Basis

4-52 The Lick Skillet Bakery provides deli meals, bakery goods, and espresso to restaurant customers. It also sells take-out specialty foods, including bakery goods, hot and cold entrees, and so on. The owners of Lick Skillet want to know how successful the bakery was in 2000, based on the following information:

1. Lick Skillet sold food items and collected $400,500 (cash) from restaurant customers. (Ignore the cost of goods sold until transaction 8.)
2. Lick Skillet contracted with local firms to provide it with catering services totaling $560,000 during 2000.
3. Lick Skillet provided the contract catering services and collected $456,000 from its catering clients.
4. Lick Skillet purchased (with cash) restaurant equipment, expected to last three years, at a cost of $30,000.
5. Lick Skillet paid employees $475,000 during 2000.
6. Lick Skillet owed employees $55,000 for work performed near the end of December 2000.
7. Lick Skillet owed employment taxes of $67,500 for the entire year of 2000, but had not obtained the appropriate forms from the state and federal governments.
8. Lick Skillet purchased food and other consumable supplies costing $236,700 and paid cash. Although it had no inventory at the beginning of 2000, its inventory on December 31, 2000, was estimated at $6,500.
9. Items returned by disgruntled customers resulted in refunds totaling $3,550.
10. Lick Skillet purchased an insurance policy on January 1, 2000, costing $4,400 and provided insurance for both 2000 and 2001.

Required

a. Record these business transactions in the basic accounting equation, including any necessary adjustments, using the accrual basis of accounting. Set up headings as follows: Cash, Accounts Receivable, Inventory, Prepaid Insurance, Equipment, Accumulated Depreciation, Accrued Liabilities, and Owners' Equity.
b. Prepare a multistep income statement.
c. Evaluate Lick Skillet's success in 2000.
d. What important items might Lick Skillet be ignoring in its income statement?
e. If you now find that Mr. and Mrs. Lick have worked the entire year at no salary, how would that change the analysis?
f. If you then find that the bakery is located in the Lick personal residence, how does that affect your analysis? Assume that the Licks pay rent of $3,000 per month, and that the bakery covers about two-thirds of the unit's total floor space.

Integration of Concepts

Transaction Analysis

4-53 The Bichette Company had the following transactions during the year ended December 31, 2000:

1. Sales on account were $155,000. Cash sales were $38,000.
2. Cost of goods sold during the year was $42,000.
3. Wages earned by employees were $32,000. Three-quarters of the amount was paid during the year as the wages were incurred. The remainder was accrued at year end.
4. A two-year insurance policy was purchased on January 1, 2000, for $4,800.
5. Equipment with a five-year life was acquired on June 30, 2000, for $10,000, with a note bearing interest at an annual rate of 9%. The interest and principal are not due until June 30, 2001.
6. Rent and other operating expenses paid in cash were $14,500.
7. The company sold a short-term investment and recorded a gain of $800.
8. Dividends declared and paid were $24,015.
9. The income tax rate was 30%.

Required

a. Prepare a multi-step income statement similar to Exhibit 4-1 for the year ended December 31, 2000. *Note:* Make the necessary adjustments before preparing the income statement.

b. Assume that stockholders' equity at the beginning of the year was $740,000. The only changes recorded in stockholders' equity during 2000 were net income and dividends. Calculate return on equity and evaluate your results.

c. Calculate earnings per share. Assume that 140,000 shares were outstanding.

d. Calculate times interest earned.

Income Statement Preparation, Calculate EPS

4-54 Revenue, expenses, and related accounts of Stackwell Enterprises Inc. for the year ended December 31, 1999, were

Cost of goods sold	$135,000	Utilities expense	$4,800
Depreciation expense	12,000	Income tax rate	30%
Dividends declared and paid	4,000	Earthquake loss (gross amount; assume not in an earthquake area)	$15,000
Advertising expense	1,600	Interest expense	10,000
Office wages expense	28,000	Repairs and maintenance expense	1,700
Insurance expense	2,400	Interest income	2,000
Gain on sale of short-term investments	3,500	Sales revenue	230,000
Commission expense	15,000		

Required

a. Prepare a multi-step income statement similar to Exhibit 4-1 for the year ended December 31, 1999. Selling expenses include advertising and commission expense.

b. Calculate earnings per share. Assume that 100,000 shares were outstanding.

Critical Thinking

Analyzing Financial Statements

4-55 Consider the following income statement (dollars in thousands):

	2000	1999
Net revenues		
Software sales	$ 77,350	$ 66,450
Customer support and service	48,500	39,040
Total net revenues	125,850	105,490
Operating expenses		
Cost of goods sold	4,700	4,580
Sales and marketing	60,650	40,235
Research, development, and support	31,990	25,102
General and administrative	19,036	19,438
Total operating expenses	116,376	89,355
Income from operations	$ 9,474	$ 16,135

Required

a. Conduct horizontal and vertical analyses of the firm's income statement.

b. Describe several possible reasons for the firm's decline in income from operations?

c. In what areas was the firm successful in 2000?

d. Based on the approximate trends shown here, is it likely that the firm's income from operations will increase or decrease in 2001? Why?

Critical Thinking

Analyzing Financial Statements

4-56 Consider the following income statement (dollars in thousands):

	1999	1998
Net revenues:		
Computer sales	$ 75,250	$ 62,250
Software sales	45,400	38,600
Net revenues	120,650	100,850
Operating expenses:		
Cost of sales	4,205	4,500
Marketing	63,520	45,542
Research and development	30,100	21,587
General and administrative	20,026	19,000
Total operating expenses	117,851	90,629
Income from operations	$ 2,799	$ 10,221

Required

a. Conduct horizontal and vertical analyses of the firm's income statement.

b. Evaluate the firm's profitability in 1999 versus 1998?

c. In what areas was the firm successful in either year?

d. Based on the approximate trends shown here, is it likely that the firm's income from operations will increase or decrease in 2000? Why?

e. Identify the underlying business reasons as to why revenues are increasing but the cost of sales is decreasing. Why might some of the other expenses be dramatically increasing while others are almost constant?

Preparing Financial Statements: Performance Evaluation

4-57 Susan's Drawing Studio has been very successful, with annual sales and profits at a record high. Susan wants to evaluate and better understand the studio's profitability and performance based on the following year-end account balances:

Sales	$400,000	Supplies used	$ 25,600
Property tax expense	2,550	Cash	32,300
Supplies inventory	12,400	Building and equipment	110,000
Accounts payable	2,450	Wages payable	1,200
Wages expense	13,240	Shareholders' equity	?
Receivables	2,200	Advertising expense	2,400
Taxes payable	2,670	Miscellaneous expenses	120,000

Required

a. Prepare a balance sheet and a multiple-step income statement.

b. Evaluate Susan's net income relative to her sales volume.

c. What is Susan's net income as a percentage of sales? Why do you think most firms do not have net income ratios this high?

d. Would your conclusions about Susan's net income change if you learned that she had been withdrawing $10,000 every month and charging these payments to Miscellaneous Expenses? Why?

e. How would your conclusions change if you learned that Susan, who is a gifted artist, could be earning $40,000 a month by working for her former employer, the Degas Drawing Corporation?

f. Given that Susan has a Building and Equipment account, what basic type of expense is missing from her income statement? Would calculation of that item change your conclusions about her relative profitability? How large would this item have to be to change your views about Susan's profitability? Why? What other information would you need before drawing firm conclusions about this issue?

g. Why do you think shareholders' equity has a lower balance than the net income (part a)?

h. Are there any other major elements of information missing? If so, what are they, and why would you like more information about these items?

Determining Expected Revenues and Expenses and Preparing an Income Statement

4-58 Beth's Espresso Cart Inc. sells coffee, pastries, and mineral water at the Boulder Mall. Last year, Beth leased a coffee cart and opened her business. She initially felt that cash flows were a useful measure of her performance. The cart's owner is now running a competitive coffee cart on the next block. Beth has heard about accrual accounting and is hoping to develop a better measure of her performance this year.

1. Beth paid $5,200 for a coffee cart, which she expects to use for the next four years.
2. She purchased coffee pots, cups, and other supplies at a cost of $2,000 and paid cash. Half of these supplies will be replaced each year.
3. Electricity and propane costs averaged $40 per month.
4. Beth started and ended the year with negligible amounts of coffee beans and mineral water.
5. Each month, Beth was paid a salary of $500 to cover personal living expenses.

6. Last year, Beth purchased a three-year insurance policy for liability and related incidents costing $1,200.
7. Beth expects to have six really good months of sales revenue during the summer and six slower months. Based on last year, her purchases of coffee, pastries, and mineral water during the peak months averaged about $2,000 each month. During the slower months, these items cost about $1,400 each month.
8. During peak months, Beth generally collected $4,500 each month, and during slower months she collected $3,000.

Required

a. Identify the amount of annual revenues and expenses that would be expected for each of the items above. Construct a single-step income statement for Beth's Espresso Cart for the next year.
b. What should Beth consider as she makes plans for next year? What other items should be considered for inclusion in her income statement? Why?
c. Why is an income statement useful to Beth? Discuss how the income statement may be more useful than a checkbook listing each cash inflow and outflow?

Interpreting Financial Statements

4-59 Consider the following income statement:

Commission revenue	$120,000	
Rental revenue	9,900	
Interest income	4,100	
Total revenue		$134,000
Salaries expense	54,000	
Depreciation expense	23,000	
Interest expense	2,550	
Miscellaneous expense	10,400	(89,950)
Operating income		44,050
Income taxes		(16,825)
Extraordinary items, net of tax		12,000
Net income		$39,225

Required

a. Review and analyze this income statement, using vertical analysis.
b. What other items might usually be found in such an income statement (what is missing)?

Ethics

Revenue Recognition

4-60 Consider the following cases:

1. Banana Republic sells clothes for cash or on credit card vouchers, which are collected from banks within a few days after the sale.
2. Micropoint Computer Systems sells hardware and software on installment or time-payment plans. Micropoint runs a credit check on every customer and only extends credit to customers with high credit ratings.
3. Backdoor Appliances sells used and new household appliances on installment or time-payment plans. They sell on credit to anyone who signs a purchase agreement, even though many of their customers have dubious credit histories. Accordingly, Backdoor experiences many customer defaults, incurs substantial collection costs, and is rarely able to recover its merchandise.

4. Ball Aerospace manufactures satellites and satellite parts under contract to NASA. NASA requires Ball to maintain certain inventories of spare parts as well as the expertise to provide consultants and technical assistance as needed. Their contract obligates NASA to buy all parts, such as satellites, produced by Ball. Under the contract, Ball produced spare parts at a cost of $2 million and billed NASA for $3 million.
5. Assume that the correct accounting was conducted for part 4. Now assume that the sales manager at Ball is trying to boost her performance for 1998 and sells a complete weather satellite to Russia for $5 million, in violation of the NASA contract. What revenue should be recognized and what should the firm's controller do when informed of this situation?

Required:

Identify when, and how much, revenue should be recognized in each of the previous cases.

Income Statement Analysis

4-61 Review the Income Statement from Wendy's International Inc. in Appendix D.

Required

a. Conduct a horizontal and vertical analysis of the income statement for each year from 1995 to1997.
b. Calculate the other profitability ratios described in Chapter 4, "The Income Statement."
c. Evaluate Wendy's profitability in each year. In which year was Wendy's most successful? Why?

Income Statement Analysis

4-62 Review the Income Statement from Reebok International Ltd. in Appendix D.

Required

a. Conduct a horizontal and vertical analysis of the income statement for each year from 1995 to1997.
b. Calculate the other profitability ratios described in Chapter 4.
c. Evaluate Reebok's profitability in each year. In which year was Reebok most successful? Why?

Identifying Transactions from Worksheet Entries

Critical Thinking

4-63 The following worksheet has been retrieved from a company's files that were destroyed by fire. Identify the underlying transactions that occurred during the month. Write a brief (one to two sentence) description of each transaction.

	Cash	Equipment	Buildings	Prepaids	Accts. Pay.	Sh. Equity	Revs.	Exps.
a.	10,000					10,000		
b.	−2,000	2,000						
c.	−5,000			5,000				
d.	90,000					90,000		
e.	50,000		50,000					
f.	3,500						3,500	
g.	−1,200							−1,200
h.	− 400							− 400
i.				−500				− 500
j.		8,000			8,000			

Critical Thinking

Interpreting Financial Statements

4-64 SILLA, Inc., is a producer and supplier of natural gas and petroleum-based products. Its condensed statements of operations for the first quarters of 1998 and 1999 are shown below (dollars in thousands):

	1999	1998
Revenues:		
Natural gas, oil, and other liquids	$63,405	$59,088
Other	1,065	176
	64,470	59,264
Costs and expenses:		
Operating, exploration, and taxes	19,099	18,844
General and administrative	5,780	5,819
Depreciation, etc.	29,450	25,650
	54,329	50,313
Operating income	$10,141	$ 8,951

Required

a. Based on this (partial) income statement, evaluate SILLA's first quarter performance for 1999. To accomplish this objective, conduct horizontal and vertical analyses.

b. What other information would help you evaluate SILLA's profitability?

c. Now consider the remainder of SILLA's income statement as follows:

	1999	1998
Operating income	$ 10,141	$ 8,951
Interest expense, net of interest income	(32,259)	(32,575)
Securities gains	5,509	3,280
Other	(370)	(1,851)
Net loss	$ (16,979)	$ (22,195)
Average total assets	$542,500	$553,000
Average total stockholders' equity	105,345	106,950
Interest expense, net of tax	42,400	43,200

Complete Silla's income statement (see part a) and evaluate SILLA's first-quarter performance for 1999.

d. To better understand Silla's performance, calculate the return on assets and return on equity for both periods.

e. How has this new information changed the evaluation of SILLA's performance? What issues will most concern SILLA's board of directors? Why? What suggestions could be made to SILLA's Board?

Critical Thinking

Interpreting Financial Statements

4-65 Microbyte Corporation's consolidated statement of operations (dollars in thousands) follows. Note that Microbyte is a computer company, specializing in data storage devices.

	2000	1999
Sales	$184,355	$92,642
Cost of goods sold	102,453	53,344
Gross profit	81,902	39,298
Operating expenses:		
Selling, general, and administrative	20,188	12,272
Research and development	15,669	6,785
Total operating expenses	35,857	19,057
Income from operations	46,045	20,241
Other income	1,831	1,744
Income before income taxes and extraordinary item	47,876	21,985
Income taxes	(17,040)	(8,056)
Income before extraordinary item	30,836	13,929
Extraordinary item	—	1,049
Net income	$30,836	$14,978

Required

a. Identify any unusual trends or categories of information. Identify any potential problems or questions based on this analysis. What other information would be helpful? Why?

b. Conduct horizontal and vertical analyses for each year. Identify any potential problems or issues based on this analysis.

c. Would you consider Microbyte as a very profitable company? Why or why not?

d. Assume that Microbyte's annual report contained the following footnote:

   Because research is so important to the future of Microbyte, the corporation has budgeted $23,000,000 for research and development for 2001. These funds are presently committed to a new facility under construction and to 42 engineers and computer analysts who have been hired to begin work January 1, 2001.

   On the basis of this footnote, estimate what would have happened to 2000 earnings if these charges had been incurred in 2000. Construct a simple balance sheet equation including these charges, as though they happened in 2000.

e. Assume that the annual report also contained the following footnote:

   Because interest rates are expected to be low during 2001, Microbyte Corporation has signed commitments and pledges to effectively refinance all its short term and long-term liabilities. Accordingly, Microbyte expects to recognize a $12 million gain (on debt refinancing) in 2001.

   On the basis of this footnote, estimate what would have happened to 2000 earnings, assuming that this gain had been recognized in 2000. Construct a simple balance sheet equation, as though the gain had been recognized in 2000.

Ethics

Interpreting Financial Statements

4-66 Pioneer Resource Inc.'s 1999 income statement (dollars in millions) is summarized on the next page. Pioneer Resource is involved in telecommunications.

	1999	1998
Revenues	$13,932.3	$13,231.1
Costs and expenses		
Network operations	3,787.1	3,642.3
Selling, general, and administrative	4,219.7	4,007.5
Taxes, other than income taxes	661.0	570.2
Interest expense	481.9	410.6
Depreciation expense	1,951.7	1,818.9
Other income, net	(87.4)	(55.4)
Subtotal	11,014.0	10,394.1
Income before income taxes	2,918.3	2,837.0
Income taxes	897.3	855.6
Net income	$ 2,021.0	$ 1,981.4

Required

a. Conduct horizontal and vertical analyses of Pioneer Resource's income statement.

b. Were Pioneer Resource's operating activities stable or unstable across these two years? Why?

c. What types of costs were probably included in "Network operations"? In "Selling, general, and administrative"? Why were the latter costs so much larger than the former?

d. Why is "Other income, net" shown in parentheses? Are these items significant? Would it change your opinion about Pioneer Resource's operations if these amounts had been included in "Revenues"? Why?

e. Your vertical analysis should have indicated that depreciation expenses are more than 15% of revenues. In this case, depreciation is the third largest expense category. Would you consider that unusual for many companies? Why? Why do you suppose that Pioneer Resource has such high depreciation expenses?

f. Suppose that you were Pioneer Resource's controller and suppose that the board members had forecast and widely publicized their goal of increasing net income by 5% in 1999. Your horizontal analysis should have indicated that net income only increased by 2%, whereas revenues increased by almost 5% (actually 5.3%). What explanations might you offer as to why the 5% net income goal was not achieved?

g. Suppose that Pioneer Resource's chairman of the board and the CEO met with you, the controller, prior to publishing this income statement. In this meeting, they strongly encouraged you to make some accounting adjustments in order to achieve the 5% goal. They suggested that interest expense be recalculated at a lower rate of interest, which would cut the "Interest expense" by 50%. Interest rates in the external market were declining rapidly. The chairman and CEO's rationale was that Pioneer Resource was refinancing its debts and would soon enjoy the lower interest rates. They also suggested that some revenues from January 2000, which had already been realized, should be transferred to the 1999 income statement. Their rationale was that Pioneer Resource did the work to get the sales in 1999; therefore, the revenues should be properly matched with other revenues and expenses in 1999 and should be shown on the 1999 income statement. Write a short paragraph to the chairman and the CEO indicating your response to their suggestions.

Integration of Concepts

Research Project: Comparing Two Computer Companies

4-67 IBM is a well-known U.S. company specializing in computer hardware. Several U.S. companies are comparable to IBM.

Required

a. Using library resources (or the Internet), obtain income statements for IBM and one other comparable company (Digital or Compaq) for similar fiscal periods.

b. Conduct horizontal and vertical analyses of IBM and your identified company. Use the results of your analysis to identify any unusual trends or patterns in the firms' operating costs. Note that even if the report dates are not identical, the relative cost comparisons may be instructive.

c. Write a short report examining the relative profitability of these two companies. Identify the major similarities and differences in the cost structures of these two companies. For example, are the depreciation expenses relatively high in each company? Are the operating costs in the same proportion to revenues across the two companies? Is the growth rate in revenues and net income the same? Why might such similarities or differences exist?

Interpreting Financial Statements

4-68 Sigma Designs is a high-tech software development company specializing in imaging and multimedia computer applications. Sigma's balance sheets are reproduced below (dollars in thousands):

Assets	**1993**	**1992**
Cash and equivalents	$ 5,086	$ 9,283
Marketable securities	14,326	19,537
Accounts receivable, net of allowances	6,471	2,987
Inventories	12,275	10,066
Prepaid expenses	435	753
Income taxes receivable	1,582	2,428
Total current assets	40,175	45,054
Equipment, net	1,626	1,607
Other assets	2,466	2,388
Total assets	$44,267	$49,049
Liabilities and Shareholders' Equity		
Current liabilities		
Accounts payable	$ 4,933	$ 1,826
Accrued salary and benefits	809	594
Other accrued liabilities	737	1,119
Total current liabilities	6,479	3,539
Other long-term liabilities	—	755
Total liabilities	6,479	4,294
Shareholders' Equity		
Common stock	19,287	19,088
Retained earnings	18,501	25,667
Total shareholders' equity	37,788	44,755
Total liabilities and shareholders' equity	$44,267	$49,049

Sigma's 1991-1993 statements of operations are summarized below (dollars in thousands):

	1993	1992	1991
Net sales	$27,058	$27,567	$35,968
Costs and expenses:			
Cost of sales	23,045	20,255	23,438
Sales and marketing	7,476	7,261	6,840
Research and development	5,043	5,105	3,323
General and administrative	1,951	1,788	1,722
Total cost and expenses	37,515	34,409	35,323
Income (loss) from operations	(10,457)	(6,842)	645
Interest income, net	1,207	1,742	1,964
Other, net	(67)	(6)	59
Income (loss) before income taxes	(9,317)	(5,106)	2,688
Provision for income taxes	2,151	1,663	(880)
Net income (loss)	$ (7,166)	$ (3,443)	$ 1,788

Required

a. Before making any calculations, state in your own words what each item in the income statement means. In particular, identify which items are positive or negative and why.

b. Using information from both statements, evaluate Sigma's profitability and operating performance. To accomplish this objective, conduct the following analyses:

   1. Conduct horizontal and vertical analyses.
   2. Calculate operating income ratios and net income ratios for each year.
   3. Calculate Sigma's return on assets ratio for 1992 and 1993. Assume that the average total assets for 1992 was $51,000 and assume that the interest expense included in the line item "Interest income, net" for 1993 and 1992 was $35 and $105. All numbers are in the thousands.
   4. Calculate Sigma's return on equity ratio for 1992 and 1993. Assume that the average total equity for 1992 was $46,000. All numbers are in the thousands.

c. Identify any unusual items and information that are typically found in an income statement, but not included in Sigma's. How would access to this information affect your analysis of Sigma's performance?

d. How does the information shown in the categories of "Interest income, net" and "Other, net" affect your conclusions about Sigma's performance? What other information might be helpful?

Interpreting Expense Reclassifications

Writing

4-69 Borden, Inc., in response to pressure from the Securities and Exchange Commission, restated its 1993 and 1992 earnings. It restated the effects of a $642 million restructuring charge taken in 1992, which contributed significantly to Borden's reported 1992 loss of $439.6 million. It reclassified $145.5 million of the restructuring charge as operating expenses in 1992, and it reversed $119.3 million, for a total restatement of $264.8 million. Therefore, the entire restatement was more than 40% of the original restructuring charge, which is a very large change. The original restructuring charge must have included some very aggressive accounting procedures, which have now been largely restated.

The after-tax effects of these restatements on Borden's net income are:

	1992	1993
Net loss, as originally reported	$(439.6)	$(593.6)
1994 restatements, reported net of tax	75.2	(37.1)
Net loss, as adjusted	$(364.4)	$(630.7)

According to the *Wall Street Journal* (March 22, 1994, p. B8), Borden reported that these restatements would have no further effect on 1994 earnings. Borden further reported that the expenses included in the original 1992 charge of $642 million were "truly incremental and related to one-time advertising and promotion programs not occurring in the normal course of business."

Required

a. Write a short memo to a manager at Borden, Inc., justifying these restatements.

b. Write a short memo to an investor, explaining why these restatements would affect the investor's decision to purchase (or sell) shares of Borden's common stock.

c. Explain in your own words why you think Borden was so aggressive in taking the original $642 million restructuring charge. What will it accomplish by restating its 1992 and 1993 net losses?

Conceptual Analysis: Revenue Recognition and Forecasting

Critical Thinking

4-70 The following scenario illustrates several issues concerning revenue recognition, particularly impacting sustainable earnings or operating profits. You should also consider the managerial implications associated with these issues.

A computer firm designs, builds, and sells a microcomputer, called a PEAR, for $1,800. The design costs of the computer are well in excess of $30,000,000 and only 10,000,000 computers are expected to be sold before they are obsolete. A Korean company is currently selling identical computers for $1,500. A Japanese company has just invested a new cursor device to replace the mouse (they call it a RAT). This new RAT will only work with computers sold by the Japanese company. The Japanese computers perform very similar functions to each of the computers described earlier. It sells for $1,200. Discounters have been selling the PEAR for $1,100 via telephone and catalog sales. The PEAR and the Korean clone are essentially obsolete, but will still reach their original volume projections. The primary developer of the PEAR has just resigned and formed a new company that is expected to design a competitive computer that will be superior to any of these other three models (PEAR, Korean clone, Japanese computer).

Required

Indicate how the PEAR managers might view each of these issues in forecasting their operating income for the next year.

Critical Thinking

Interpreting Financial Statements: Effects of Asset Write-Downs

4-71 Byte City, Inc., is a leading independent provider of systems and network management software. Its income statements are abbreviated as follows:

	2000	1999
Net revenues		
Software products	$64,282,171	$ 52,392,108
Product support and enhancements	32,545,876	27,419,766
Total net revenues	96,828,047	79,811,874
Operating expenses		
Cost of goods sold	3,614,919	3,215,778
Sales and marketing	45,782,349	38,372,418
Research, development, and support	23,582,478	27,652,020
General and administrative	14,622,594	14,887,923
Write-down of marketing rights and restructuring expenses	0	17,236,845
Total operating expenses	87,602,340	101,364,984
Income (loss) from operations	$ 9,225,707	($21,553,110)

Required

a. Conduct a horizontal and vertical analysis of Byte City's income statement.

b. Identify any major unusual items in either year. How might these items affect the future? How might they have been reflected in prior years? How might they have been caused by events in prior years?

c. Discuss why Byte City's cost of goods sold is so low relative to other expenses, and also with respect to revenues.

d. Restate 1999's income (loss) from operations by excluding the $17,236,845 write-down. What does this restated amount indicate about possible trends in Byte City's total operating expenses? How does this affect the trend in income from operations?

e. Based only on the information provided, would you predict that Byte City would have a positive income from operations in 2001? Why? By extending the trends in net revenues and in operating expenses to 2001, what amount of income from operations would you predict?

Critical Thinking

Interpreting Financial Statements: Horizontal Analysis

4-72 Consider the following horizontal analysis of a firm's income statement (assume that 1998 is the base year used for comparison, when all items equal 100%):

	2000	1999
Net revenues		
Product sales	116.4%	118.2%
Product support and enhancement	124.2	177.9
Total net revenue	119.3	134.9
Operating expenses		
Cost of goods sold	102.8	40.2
Sales and marketing	120.7	172.1
Research, development and support	91.1	181.8
General and administrative	97.9	161.3
Total operating expenses	103.5	132.2
Income (loss) from operations	114.3	101.5

Required

a. Evaluate the firm's performance.
b. In which year was it more successful? Why?
c. In which year did it control costs most effectively? Why?
d. In which year did the market respond best to the firm's products and services? Why?
e. In which area of expenses should management concentrate the most attention? Why?
f. Did this firm have a positive or a negative income from operations in 1999? Why? In 2000? Why?

Writing

Revenue Recognition

4-73 Contact local firms with which you are familiar, or review several annual reports from firms in the same industry, and examine their revenue recognition principles and procedures. Review the notes to their financial statements to see how they describe their principles. Write a short description and critique their revenue recognition policies.

Ethics

Timing and Revenue Recognition

4-74 You are the chief accountant for the Seal Company, which produces candy bars. You like your job very much, and one reason is that your best friend, Stacy Monroe, is a salesperson for Seal.

Seal primarily markets its candy bars to grocery chains, which buy in large quantities. As December 31 (Seal's year-end) approaches, your friend Stacy worries that she will not achieve her sales quota. If the quota is not met, Stacy will not receive the rather large bonus she had been counting on.

With just one week to go before year-end, Stacy receives a big order; in fact, the order will enable her to meet her quota and receive her bonus. There's just one problem. Seal's sales terms are that the customer takes title to the candy when Seal transfers the candy to an independent trucker. At that point, Seal records the revenue and Stacy gets credit for the sale. You assure Stacy that one week is plenty of time to process the order. Stacy is so elated that she celebrates by buying a $20,000 car.

On December 31, Stacy's order is ready to be shipped and is awaiting the trucker. Although this particular trucker is usually reliable, he phones to say that a blizzard will prevent him from arriving until January 2.

Stacy is understandably upset. She purchased a new car based on your assurance that she would receive her bonus, and it now appears that her bonus will not materialize.

Required

Describe how the sale on December 31 should be recorded, thus enabling Stacy to receive (or not receive) the bonus.

Internet

Ratio Calculations

4-75 Locate the most recent set of financial statements for the regional telecommunications companies listed below. You may use either the 10-K available at EDGAR **(www.sec.gov/edaux/searches.htm)** or the annual report available at the company page on the Web. The annual report is usually located in the Investor Information section.

Corporation	Home Page Location
Ameritech	**www.ameritech.com**
U S West	**www.uswest.com**
Bell Atlantic	**www.bell-atl.com**
Pacific Bell	**www.pacbell.com**

Required

Calculate the following for each corporation (for each year shown in their financial statements):

a. cost of goods sold percentage
b. gross profit percentage
c. operating income percentage
d. net income percentage
e. return on equity
f. return on assets
g. times interest earned

Internet

Ratio Calculations and Interpretation

4-76 Locate the most recent 10-K filing by Wal-Mart and Kmart in the EDGAR archives **(www.sec.gov/edaux/searches.htm).** Scroll down to the Summary of Financial Information (in the financial report section).

Required

a. Calculate the following ratios or amounts for each of the most recent three years:
   1. percentage change in net sales for each year
   2. percentage change in net income for each year
   3. net income percentage
   4. return on equity (use the beginning of the year balance for the denominator)
   5. return on assets (use the beginning of the year balance for the denominator)
   6. times interest earned
b. Based on the above calculations, which company in your opinion has been more successful during the last five years?

Internet

Ratio Calculations and Strategic Marketing Data

4-77 Locate the most recent 10-K filing by Toys 'R' Us and Gillette in the EDGAR archives **(www.sec.gov/edaux/searches.htm).**

Required

a. What is each company's major product line? (This information should be near the beginning of the 10-K.) For each company, do you expect sales to be fairly constant throughout the year or to exhibit seasonal cycles? Why?
b. Find (by scrolling through) the "annual calculations data" that both companies included at the end of their Notes to Financial Statements. Based on these data, calculate:
   1. percentage change in net sales, cost of goods sold, gross profit, and net income for each quarter
   2. the gross profit percentage for each quarter
   3. the net income percentage for each quarter
c. Does your response in part a match the sales pattern you observed in part b? If not, why not?

chapter

5 Statement of Cash Flows

LEARNING OBJECTIVES

1. Describe the objectives of the statement of cash flows.
2. Explain the complementary nature of accrual earnings and cash flows.
3. Identify the three types of activities that generate and use cash.
4. Explain the difference between the direct and the indirect methods of presenting a statement of cash flows.
5. Draw inferences about the financial performance of a firm from the statement of cash flows.

Appendix: Calculate cash flow from operating activities by using relationships among income statement and balance sheet items.

INTRODUCTION

Thus far, our focus has been on the two long-standing, conventional financial statements: the balance sheet and the income statement. We now turn our attention to the **statement of cash flows.** This chapter describes the statement of cash flows, indicates how cash flow information can be used in analyzing the financial performance of a business, and explains the relationships among this statement, the balance sheet, and the income statement.

OVERVIEW

The statement of cash flows is designed to provide information about a firm's inflows and outflows of cash during a period of time. It also explains the change in cash from the beginning of a period to the end of the period. Exhibit 5-1 contains an illustration of a statement of cash flows.

Objectives

According to SFAS No. 95, the statement of cash flows is intended to help financial statement readers assess

1. a firm's ability to generate positive future net cash flows;
2. a firm's ability to meet its obligations, its ability to pay dividends, and its need for external financing;

EXHIBIT 5-1 Statement of Cash Flows—Direct Approach

The Peak Company
Statement of Cash Flows
(Direct Approach)
For the Year Ended December 31, 2000

Cash flows from operating activities:		
Cash received from customers	$68,200	
Interest received	1,300	
Payments to employees	(17,100)	
Payments to suppliers	(40,500)	
Interest paid	(800)	
Taxes paid	(2,000)	
Net cash provided from operating activities		$ 9,100
Cash flows from investing activities:		
Purchase of equipment	(3,500)	
Purchase of IBM stock	(12,000)	
Net cash used in investing activities		(15,500)
Cash flows from financing activities:		
Proceeds from issuing long-term debt	25,000	
Proceeds from issuing common stock	5,000	
Payment of short-term debt	(12,000)	
Net cash provided by financing activities		18,000
Net increase in cash		11,600
Cash at beginning of year		22,000
Cash at end of year		$33,600

3. the reasons for differences between net income and associated cash receipts and payments; and
4. the effects on a firm's financial position of both its cash and its noncash investing and financing transactions.

Ultimately, a firm's cash-generating ability affects its solvency, its capacity to pay dividends and interest, and the price of its securities. Accordingly, a firm's ability to generate cash is important to financial statement users.

Accrual Earnings Versus Cash Flow as a Performance Measure

Keep in mind that accrual earnings (net income from the income statement) do not necessarily reflect cash flows. Many revenue and expense transactions have no *immediate* cash flow effect. Nevertheless, net income is a very useful performance measure. It reflects accomplishments by the firm (such as credit sales that will subsequently result in cash inflows) as well as resources consumed by the firm in generating revenue (for example, employee salaries that remain unpaid at the end of a period).

If net income is a useful performance measure, why is cash flow information needed? An analogy to baseball can be drawn. Many aspects of a baseball player's performance are measured. For example, home runs measure power hitting, while on-base percentage reflects the ability to reach base safely. Similarly, earnings and cash flows are different performance measures of a business organization. They should be viewed as complements, rather than substitutes. Each measure contains information not necessarily reflected in the other. In particular, the statement of cash flows provides information about a firm's liquidity and financial flexibility (the ability to respond to unexpected events by altering the amounts and timing of its cash flows).

Cash and Cash Equivalents

Firms can elect to focus their statement of cash flows on either (1) cash or (2) cash and cash equivalents. The term **cash** includes cash on hand and cash in bank accounts that can be withdrawn on demand. **Cash equivalents** are short-term, highly liquid financial instruments with maturities of less than three months; they are quickly convertible into cash. Examples include money market funds, treasury bills, and certificates of deposit (CDs). Because cash equivalents are so similar to cash, many firms prefer to combine them with cash, rather than with other investments.

Firms must consistently apply a policy of using either cash or cash and cash equivalents. Additionally, the beginning and ending balances that appear on the statement of cash flows must correspond to similarly titled items on the balance sheet.

CLASSIFICATION OF ACTIVITIES

As illustrated in Exhibit 5-1, a firm's cash flows are placed in one of three categories: operating, investing, or financing. This section describes each of these categories. Examples of each activity are given in Exhibit 5-2.

EXHIBIT 5-2 Summary of Activities Generating Cash Flows

Operating Activities

Cash Inflows	Cash Outflows
From customers	To employees
From interest	To suppliers
From dividends	For interest
All other cash inflows not defined as an investing or financing activity	For taxes
	All other cash outflows not defined as an investing or financing activity

Investing Activities

Cash Inflows	Cash Outflows
Sale of property, plant, and equipment	Purchase of property, plant, and equipment
Collections of loans	Making of loans
Sale of investments	Acquisition of investments

Financing Activities

Cash Inflows	Cash Outflows
Issuing common stock	Reacquiring common stock
Obtaining loans	Repaying loans
	Paying dividends

Operating Activities

Operating activities typically involve transactions related to providing goods and services to customers. They reflect the cash flow effects of the typical and recurring transactions that appear on the income statement. Examples of operating cash inflows are receipts from customers and the receipt of interest and dividends from investments. Operating cash outflows include payments to employees and suppliers and payments for interest and taxes.

Investing Activities

Investing activities usually involve cash flows from the acquisition and disposal of noncurrent assets. Cash outflows arise from purchasing (investing in) property, plant, and equipment, making loans, and acquiring investments in other corporations. Cash inflows result from disposing of property, plant, and equipment; collecting loans (other than the interest); and selling investments.

Financing Activities

Financing activities include cash flows from obtaining and repaying financing. Cash inflows result from contributions by owners (issuing stock to shareholders in exchange for cash) and from loans. Cash outflows arise from payments to shareholders (as dividends or payments to repurchase their shares) and the repayment of loans (but not the associated interest).

Exhibit 5-1 shows that the net cash provided (or used) in each of the three classifications is summarized in the far right column of the statement. The sum of these amounts equals the change in the cash balance that occurred during the period. This change is added to the cash balance at the beginning of the year to compute the ending cash balance. These beginning and ending cash amounts must, of course, correspond to the cash figures appearing on the balance sheet.

The remainder of this section addresses two additional format issues: (1) the direct versus the indirect approach to preparing the operating activities section and (2) noncash investing and financing activities.

Direct Versus Indirect Approach

The operating activities section of Peak's statement of cash flows in Exhibit 5-1 is prepared based on the **direct approach.** Under the direct approach, a separate line item is provided for each type of operating cash inflow and outflow. These items usually correspond to categories on the income statement. For example, cash received from customers corresponds to sales revenue on the income statement. Keep in mind, however, that the income statement and the statement of cash flows provide different information. For example, the income statement discloses sales made to customers during the year, regardless of whether cash has been collected during the year. The statement of cash flows indicates the amount of cash collected during the year from customers for the current year's sales, past years' sales, and even future sales if the firm has collected cash prior to the point of sale.

An acceptable alternative in preparing the operating activities section is the **indirect approach.** This method begins with net income and makes adjustments to it in order to arrive at cash generated by operating activities. The indirect approach is illustrated in Exhibit 5-3.

Although both the direct and indirect approaches produce the same figure for cash provided from operating activities, the internal compositions of the statements differ substantially. A major advantage of the direct method is that the primary sources

EXHIBIT 5-3 Statement of Cash Flows—Indirect Approach

The Peak Company
Statement of Cash Flows
(Indirect Approach)
For the Year Ended December 31, 2000

Cash flows from operating activities:		
Net income	$ 5,300	
Adjustments to net income		
Depreciation expense	2,000	
Increase in accounts receivable	(500)	
Decrease in interest receivable	200	
Increase in inventory	(1,000)	
Increase in accounts payable	3,000	
Decrease in salaries payable	(100)	
Increase in interest payable	200	
Net cash provided from operating activities		$ 9,100
Cash flows from investing activities:		
Purchase of equipment	(3,500)	
Purchase of IBM stock	(12,000)	
Net cash used in investing activities		(15,500)
Cash flows from financing activities:		
Proceeds from issuing long-term debt	25,000	
Proceeds from issuing common stock	5,000	
Payment of short-term debt	(12,000)	
Net cash provided by financing activities		18,000
Net increase in cash		11,600
Cash at beginning of year		22,000
Cash at end of year		$33,600

and uses of cash are listed. As will be seen in a later section, this is highly useful information. A major advantage of the indirect method is that the reasons for the difference between net income and cash generated by operations is detailed. This can help reduce uncertainties or answer questions raised by financial statement readers.

As Exhibit 5-3 shows, under the indirect approach, depreciation expense is added to net income. Because of this, some financial statement readers erroneously believe that depreciation expense is a source of cash. It is not. Depreciation expense is added to net income in arriving at cash provided from operating activities because (1) it has already been subtracted in the computation of net income and (2) it does not involve any cash outflow. Adding depreciation expense to net income therefore eliminates the effect of this noncash expense.

The FASB has expressed a preference for the direct approach. In spite of that, the indirect approach is used more frequently. This is partly due to historical convention; the indirect approach is similar to the statement that was required prior to SFAS No. 95. Additionally, a firm using the direct approach must provide a schedule that reconciles net income with cash provided by operating activities. This reconciliation essentially consists of the information contained in the indirect approach. Thus, a firm that opts for the direct approach must really provide both methods. Some firms are reluctant to do this, either because additional costs are involved or because they feel that the statement will become too cluttered and, therefore, less informative. (For brevity, the reconciliation has been omitted from Peak's statement of cash flows appearing in Exhibit 5-1.)

Noncash Investing and Financing Activities

A firm may engage in investing and financing activities that do not involve cash. For example, a firm might acquire property by issuing common stock. Although no cash is involved, this transaction is both an investing activity (the acquisition of a noncurrent asset) and a financing activity (the issuance of stock). Because these transactions do not involve cash, they do not appear in the major sections of the statement of cash flows. However, **noncash investing and financing activities** are summarized in a schedule that appears at the end of the statement. This provides readers of the cash flow statement with a complete picture of a firm's investing and financing activities.

USING CASH FLOW INFORMATION: OPERATING ACTIVITIES

Many financial statement users find the operating activities section to be quite informative. Creditors, for example, recognize that loans can only be repaid with cash and that a firm's operations are a likely source of cash for debt repayment.

Because the ability to generate cash determines dividends and share price, shareholders and their advisors are interested in cash provided by operating activities. Moreover, some analysts believe that because reported net income can be manipulated by accounting ploys, cash flow from operating activities is a more reliable performance measure than net income. We will subsequently discuss how managers can also manipulate cash flow figures.

Keep in mind, however, that not all healthy firms have a large positive cash flow from operations. Firms that experience growth in sales invariably need to expand their accounts receivable and inventory. These asset acquisitions must be financed, and cash generated by operations is a frequently used source.

For example, Digital Power Corp., which designs, develops, and manufactures component parts for computers and other electronic equipment, increased its sales from $13,835,008 in 1996 to $18,884,259 in 1997. Digital's 36% increase in sales was accompanied by a $1,673,340 increase in accounts receivable and inventory. So even though net income increased 21% to $1,400,790, the increased investment in receivables and inventory resulted in a net cash outflow from operating activities of $80,252 in 1997. In Digital's case, the cash outflow does not indicate poor operating performance. Instead, it reflects growth. In general, however, a negative cash flow from operating activities should prompt further investigation.

To illustrate the insights that can be drawn from cash flow numbers, consider Exhibit 5-4, which contains Altron Incorporated's statement of cash flows. Recall that Altron's income statement appears in Exhibit 4-1. Additional information that will be helpful in interpreting the cash flow statement is in Exhibit 5-5.

First, note that Altron chose the indirect format for the operating section of the cash flow statement. Because of this, the specific sources and uses of cash are not detailed. We will soon show how to estimate some of these numbers. The bottom of the operating section shows that a positive cash flow of $14,428,000 was generated by operating activities. Keep in mind, however, that this figure does not reflect the cash spent to replace worn-out equipment.

EXHIBIT 5-4 Statement of Cash Flows

Altron Incorporated
Statement of Cash Flows
For the Year Ended January 3, 1998
(Dollars in thousands)

Cash flows from operating activities:		
Net income	$14,667	
Adjustments to reconcile net income to net cash		
Depreciation and amortization	6,637	
Deferred taxes	2,345	
Changes in current assets and liabilities:		
Accounts receivable	(941)	
Increase in inventory	(10,072)	
Other current assets	(529)	
Accounts payable	3,490	
Accrued payroll and other employee benefits	(543)	
Other accrued expenses	(626)	
Net cash provided by operating activities		$14,428
Cash flows from investing activities:		
Purchases of investments	(14,920)	
Proceeds from sale of investments	21,577	
Capital expenditures	(25,944)	
Net cash used in investing activities		(19,287)
Cash flows from financing activities:		
Proceeds from issuance of common stock	1,086	
Income tax benefit of stock options	750	
Net cash provided by financing activities		1,836
Net change in cash and cash equivalents		(3,023)
Cash and cash equivalents at beginning of year		14,949
Cash and cash equivalents at end of year		$11,926
Supplemental disclosures:		
Cash paid during the year for:		
Interest		$ 533
Taxes		7,256

EXHIBIT 5-5 Selected Financial Information Used to Illustrate Cash Flow Ratios

Altron Incorporated
Selected Financial Statement Information
(Dollars in Thousands)

	1997	1996
Total assets	$155,603	$134,561
Accounts receivable	25,781	24,840
Inventory	28,626	18,554
Investments	17,438	24,095
Property, plant, and equipment	65,311	45,727

Ratios

This section describes several ratios that can be computed from the statement of cash flows. Because the statement of cash flows is a relatively recent addition to GAAP, the development of cash flow ratios is at an early stage, and there is no general consensus about which ratios are the most informative. Also note that some of these ratios require information disclosed only by the direct approach for preparing the operating activities section. We will illustrate ways to estimate this information from statements of cash flows using the indirect approach.

Cash Return on Assets The **cash return on assets ratio** is calculated by adding interest payments to cash flow from operating activities (CFOA) and then dividing by average total assets:

$$\text{Cash return on assets} = \frac{\text{CFOA} + \text{Interest paid}}{\text{Average total assets}}$$

Cash return on assets measures management's success, given the assets entrusted to it, in generating cash from operating activities. Because CFOA is available to pay dividends and to finance investments, a high ratio is desirable.

Interest payments are added to CFOA in the numerator for the same reason that interest expense was added to net income in the return on assets calculation discussed in Chapter 4. That is, cash return on assets is designed to measure management's success in making operating decisions. Because interest payments are determined by financing decisions, and because they have already been subtracted in calculating CFOA, they are added back.

Altron's 1997[1] cash return on assets is:

$$\begin{aligned}\text{Cash return on assets} &= \frac{\text{CFOA} + \text{Interest paid}}{\text{Average total assets}} \\ &= \frac{\$14{,}428 + \$533}{(\$155{,}603 + \$134{,}561)/2} \\ &= 10.3\%\end{aligned}$$

Altron's cash return on assets appears reasonable, but it does not compare very favorably to the prior year when operating activities generated $22,686,000 and the cash return on assets was 18.7%. What caused the decline in cash flow? Statements of cash flows prepared under the indirect approach show the adjustments needed to convert net income to cash generated by operations. Altron's largest adjustment is $10,072,000 for inventory. That is, inventory increased by approximately $10 million and that inventory expansion was essentially funded from operations. The advisability of increasing inventory holdings is usually assessed by comparing the percentage increase in sales to the percentage increase in inventory. Sales increased only 4.3% [($172,428/$165,248) − 1], while inventory increased 54.3% ($28,626/$18,554 − 1). Thus, the decline in Altron's cash return on assets raises concerns about its inventory management or the salability of its inventory.

[1]Even though Altron's statement of cash flows is dated 1998, it is usually referred to as the 1997 statement of cash flows, since the majority of days included in it are from 1997.

Some analysts question the use of CFOA in cash return on assets and other ratios. Their reservation is that CFOA makes no provision for replacing worn-out equipment. These expenditures are necessary to maintain productive capacity and current operating levels. Because CFOA is not reduced for these expenditures, it overstates the amount of discretionary cash flow generated from operations.

Instead of using CFOA in ratio calculations, some analysts use **free cash flow.** One way to calculate free cash flow is to subtract from CFOA the cash payment necessary to replace worn-out equipment. Unfortunately, firms rarely disclose this figure. Although the investing activities section of the statement of cash flows shows total payments for the acquisition of productive assets, the amounts spent to (1) replace assets and (2) expand productive capacity are not detailed. Because of this, depreciation expense is sometimes used as an imperfect estimate of the cash expenditure needed to maintain productive capacity. Because depreciation expense is based on historical cost, it probably understates the cash necessary to replace productive assets.

Quality of Sales The **quality of sales ratio** is computed by dividing cash received from customers by sales (revenue):

$$\text{Quality of sales} = \frac{\text{Cash received from customers}}{\text{Sales}}$$

All other things being equal, a firm is in a more advantageous position if a large portion of its sales is collected in cash. Not only is final realization of the transaction assured, but the investment in accounts receivable is minimized.

This ratio is particularly useful for analyzing firms that use liberal revenue recognition policies or firms that, of necessity, employ revenue recognition policies that require the use of judgment. In both of these situations, a deterioration of this ratio over time might indicate that a firm is inflating earnings by the use of questionable accounting judgments. For example, some of Altron's sales arise from firm contracts with other businesses for the design and manufacture of custom-made products. Although Altron records revenue at the time goods are shipped, it could argue for using the more liberal percentage-of-completion method. Utilizing this procedure too aggressively would likely result in recognizing significant amounts of revenue before cash is collected and would be reflected in a low quality of sales ratio.

The quality of sales ratio can also reflect a firm's performance in making collections from customers. Suppose that a firm increases sales by the questionable strategy of reducing the credit standards that customers must meet. These customers are likely to be relatively tardy in making payments. This situation will be revealed to financial statement readers by a declining quality of sales ratio.

Altron's quality of sales ratio cannot be computed from the information shown in Exhibit 5-4. Why not? The numerator, cash received from customers, is available only from the cash flow statement under the direct approach. However, this figure can be approximated by the following relationship:

$$\text{Cash received from customers} = \text{Beginning balance in Accounts Receivable} + \text{Sales} - \text{Ending balance in Accounts Receivable}$$

To understand this relationship, recognize that both the beginning balance in accounts receivable and sales for the year might potentially be collected in cash during the current year. In fact, the sum of these two amounts is collected in cash, except for the balance that remains in accounts receivable at the end of the year.

Altron's estimated cash collections from customers is $171,487 (in thousands).

Cash received from customers	=	Beginning balance in Accounts Receivable	+	Sales	−	Ending balance in Accounts Receivable
$171,487	=	$24,840	+	$172,428	−	$25,781

Altron's quality of sales ratio for 1997 is 99.5%.

$$\text{Quality of sales} = \frac{\text{Cash received from customers}}{\text{Sales}}$$

$$= \frac{\$171{,}487}{\$172{,}428}$$

$$= 99.5\%$$

This is a very high quality of sales ratio and reflects good accounts receivable management and conservative revenue recognition policies.

Reality Check 5-1 describes how the quality of sales ratio provides useful insights into the software industry.

Quality of Income The **quality of income ratio** is computed by dividing CFOA by net income:

$$\text{Quality of income} = \frac{\text{CFOA}}{\text{Net income}}$$

This ratio indicates the proportion of income that has been realized in cash. As with quality of sales, high levels for this ratio are desirable. The quality of income ratio has a tendency to exceed 100% because (1) depreciation expense has reduced the denominator and (2) cash spent to replace productive assets has not been subtracted in calculating the numerator. Altron's 1997 quality of income ratio is 98.4%.

$$\text{Quality of income} = \frac{\$14{,}428}{\$14{,}667} = 98.4\%$$

Altron's 1997 ratio is less than 100% and does not compare favorably to its 1996 ratio of 128%. The decline in this ratio is largely due to the growth in inventories that was mentioned previously.

In the discussion of quality of sales, we indicated that revenue recognition may be judgmental. The same is true with expense recognition. A variety of alternatives for expense allocations are available to firms, and firms have considerable discretion in the selection of these alternatives. The quality of income ratio can provide an overall in-

REALITY CHECK 5-1

Several firms in the software industry have been criticized for their revenue recognition policies. The allegations suggest that these firms have recognized revenue prematurely. Such a practice would not only overstate sales, but net income as well.

Revenue overstatements can be achieved in various ways. Some companies were said to double-bill customers. Other companies booked revenue when they shipped goods to their own warehouses in foreign countries. Ultimately, such practices catch up with companies. For example, Oracle Corporation recently paid $24,000,000 to settle shareholder lawsuits, and Cambridge Biotech Corporation was forced to file for bankruptcy.

The quality of sales ratio can help investors detect and avoid such situations. Consider the following information for two software companies.

	Cambridge Biotech	Kendall Square Research
	(Dollars in thousands)	
Accounts receivable		
Beginning of year	$ 5,951	$ 804
End of year	10,520	2,785
Sales for year	28,981	10,066

Required

a. Estimate the cash collected from customers for each firm.
b. Compute the quality of sales ratio for each firm.
c. What do you conclude from these ratios?

Solution

a.

	Cambridge Biotech	Kendall Square Research
Sales	$28,981	$10,066
Plus: Beginning accounts receivable	5,951	804
Less: Ending accounts receivable	(10,520)	(2,785)
Cash collected from customers	$24,412	$ 8,085

b. Quality of sales $= \dfrac{\$24{,}412}{\$28{,}981}$ (Cambridge Biotech) ; $\dfrac{\$8{,}085}{\$10{,}066}$ (Kendall Square Research)

$=$ 84% (Cambridge Biotech) ; 80% (Kendall Square Research)

c. These ratios are considerably below 100%. This should certainly prompt financial statement readers to undertake further investigation.

dication of how liberal a firm's accounting judgments have been. Reality Check 5-2 provides information about quality of income ratios in the software industry.

You should realize that cash flows can be manipulated by management. For example, customers can be induced to remit payments early if they are provided with a sufficiently large cash discount. Although the short-term consequences of this action may be to increase net cash flow, large discounts might not be in the shareholders' best long-term interest.

Cash Interest Coverage The **cash interest coverage ratio** is used by creditors to assess a firm's ability to pay interest. It is calculated by summing CFOA, interest payments, and tax payments and then dividing by interest payments. Interest and tax pay-

REALITY CHECK 5-2

As with the quality of sales ratio, the quality of income ratio can help detect situations involving questionable accounting judgments. Reality Check 5-1 showed that the quality of sales ratios for Cambridge Biotech and Kendall Square Research were both below 85%. Consider the following information:

	Cambridge Biotech	**Kendall Square Research**
	(Dollars in thousands)	
Cash provided by operating activities	($5,696)	($27,194)
Net income (loss)	$ 348	($21,619)

Required

a. Compute the quality of income ratio for each firm.
b. What inferences can you draw from these ratios?

Solution

a.

		Cambridge Biotech	**Kendall Square Research**
Quality of sales	=	($5,696) / $ 348	($27,194) / ($21,619)
	=	−1,637%	126%

b. Cambridge's negative quality of income ratio results from a negative numerator and a positive denominator. This indicates that although Cambridge generated a positive net income, its operations resulted in a net cash outflow. The ratio is quite large (in absolute terms), which should be rather alarming to financial statement readers.

Regarding Kendall Square, interpreting ratios generated from negative numbers is often difficult. A ratio of 126% usually indicates that a firm generated more cash than income. However, when a 126% ratio is computed from two negative numbers, it indicates that the firm's cash outflow exceeded its reported loss. Both the loss and the cash outflow from operations should concern financial statement readers.

ments are added to CFOA because they have been subtracted in the calculation of CFOA and because those payments are available to cover interest. In particular, tax payments are added because in the unfortunate case of zero profitability, those payments would not be made and would provide another measure of relief for the creditors. Interest and taxes paid are usually summarized at the bottom of the statement of cash flows.

$$\text{Cash interest coverage} = \frac{\text{CFOA} + \text{Interest paid} + \text{Taxes paid}}{\text{Interest paid}}$$

The cash interest coverage ratio reflects how many times greater cash provided by operations is than the interest payment itself. Creditors prefer high levels of this ratio.

Altron's 1997 cash interest coverage ratio is 4,168% or 41.68 to 1:

$$\text{Cash interest coverage} = \frac{\$14{,}428 + \$533 + \$7{,}256}{\$533} = 4{,}168\%$$

This ratio is quite high and should provide creditors with considerable assurance that Altron is currently generating more than enough cash to meet its interest payments.

WHAT WOULD YOU DO?

As a successful college student, you feel that you can make money by sharing your secrets of success with others. Specifically, you decide to begin a Scholastic Aptitude Test (SAT) review course. The course will be taught by yourself and several of your friends. Classroom space can be rented at a local community college.

Because of the costs you will incur, a minimum of 20 students is necessary to generate a positive cash flow from operations. If fewer than 20 students enroll, you intend to cancel the course.

Marketing is, of course, a key to the success of any new business. Attracting new students is essential. This presents you with a dilemma. On the one hand, you cannot afford to run the course with less than 20 students. On the other hand, potential students always ask if you are certain that the course will be offered. Understandably, they prefer to enroll in a course that will not be canceled. You have many competitors; students can choose from several review courses.

How would you respond to the students' questions about course cancellation? Keep in mind that being perfectly honest may result in the failure of your business.

USING CASH FLOW INFORMATION: INVESTING AND FINANCING ACTIVITIES

The investing activities section of the statement of cash flows summarizes the cash inflows from disposing of investments, and the cash outflows from purchasing investments. Altron's investments (both short-term and long-term) consist primarily of government and municipal bonds. The short-term investments, in particular, are highly liquid and readily available to satisfy pending cash needs. In 1997, Altron purchased investments for $14,920,000 and liquidated investments of $21,577,000, resulting in a net decline in investments of $6,657,000.

The investing activities section also shows that Altron spent $25,944,000 on capital expenditures. Most of this amount was for a new 100,000 square foot manufacturing plant. The 1996 year-end balance sheet shows a property, plant, and equipment (PPE) figure of $45,727,000. Thus, Altron made a considerable investment in PPE during 1997. Altron is in an industry that requires firms to stay up-to-date in terms of technology. However, Altron should not increase its investment in high technology facilities to such an extent that its profitability and/or cash flows are ultimately compromised. Cause for concern is further heightened by the 1996 cash flow statement, which shows capital expenditures of $21,175,000. Summing over 1996 and 1997, Altron has spent about $47 million on capital improvements. This amount is approximately equal to 70% of the PPE figure on the 1997 balance sheet! Questions certainly arise regarding the necessity for Altron to continue such expenditures, as well as its ability to do so.

So far, we have learned the following about Altron's 1997 cash flows:

Cash provided by operating activities	$14,428,000
Net cash generated by liquidating investments	6,657,000
Cash paid for capital improvements	(25,944,000)
Net cash outflow (excluding financing activities)	$ (4,859,000)

The financing activities section shows two items. Altron issued common stock in exchange for approximately $1,086,000. Altron also received an income tax benefit related to its stock option plans. These two financing activities were not sufficient to fund the $4,859,000 outflow. Consequently, the cash balance declined:

Net cash outflow (excluding financing activities)	$(4,859,000)
Net cash provided by financing activities	1,836,000
Net change in cash and cash equivalents	$(3,023,000)

A $3 million decline in cash and cash equivalents is not an extremely large drop. Moreover, Altron has a considerable investment in government securities that can be liquidated. Also, Altron does not have much debt outstanding, and therefore would likely have little trouble in securing additional borrowings. Nevertheless, management's plans for funding future capital expenditures should be examined.

SUMMARY OF LEARNING OBJECTIVES

1. **Describe the objectives of the statement of cash flows.**
   The statement of cash flows explains the change in cash from the beginning to the end of a period. It provides financial statement users with information to assess a firm's ability to generate positive future net cash flows, to meet its obligations, to pay dividends, and to generate financing internally.
2. **Explain the complementary nature of accrual earnings and cash flows.**
   Accrual earnings reflect a firm's success in providing goods and services to customers. Cash flow figures show a firm's solvency and its capacity to pay dividends and interest.
3. **Identify the three types of activities that generate and use cash.**
   Operating activities include providing goods and services to customers (for example, collecting cash from customers and paying cash to suppliers). Investing activities involve acquiring or disposing of noncurrent assets (such as property, plant, and equipment and investments in other corporations). Financing activities include the obtaining of funds from shareholders and returning funds to shareholders; financing activities also include obtaining and repaying loans.
4. **Explain the difference between the direct and indirect methods of presenting a statement of cash flows.**
   This distinction lies in the operating section. Under the direct method, a separate line item is provided for each major operating inflow and outflow of cash. In contrast, the indirect approach starts with net income and makes various adjustments to arrive at cash generated by operating activities. Although the direct method provides the most useful information, most firms use the indirect method.
5. **Draw inferences about the financial performance of a firm from the statement of cash flows.**
   Much of the information included in the statement of cash flows can be extracted by the use of ratios. These ratios provide insights into a firm's ability to generate cash in light of the assets it has, the quality of the firm's sales and net income, and the ability of the firm to generate cash to meet its interest payments.

KEY TERMS

Cash 154
Cash equivalents 154
Cash interest coverage ratio 163
Cash return on assets ratio 158
Direct approach 155
Financing activities 155
Free cash flow 160
Indirect approach 155
Investing activities 155
Noncash investing and financing activities 157
Operating activities 155
Quality of income ratio 161
Quality of sales ratio 160
Statement of cash flows 152

QUESTIONS

5-1 The income statement and the cash flow statement focus on various aspects of profitability and liquidity. Distinguish between these concepts and discuss their importance to users of financial statements.

5-2 Describe how a firm's financial statements help meet these objectives:

a. To evaluate a firm's ability to generate future cash flows available to pay dividends to shareholders.

b. To evaluate a firm's ability to meet its short-term obligations and its needs for external financing.

5-3 Contrast cash and cash equivalents? Why would managers want to include both when preparing a statement of cash flows?

5-4 Why are managers and creditors often more concerned about cash and cash flows, as compared to nonmonetary assets?

5-5 Discuss three major business activities that usually produce cash inflows or outflows.

5-6 What information is provided in a statement of cash flows that is not disclosed in a balance sheet or an income statement?

5-7 Identify three types of operating, financing, and investing activities. Contrast these with several noncash investing or financing activities.

5-8 How could a firm report positive amounts of net income and negative cash flows from operating activities? Identify specific instances where this might occur.

5-9 Define the following cash flow concepts in your own words as you would describe them to the owner of a small business:

a. Cash flow from operating activities
b. Cash used to purchase investments
c. Cash obtained from bank loans
d. Cash collected from clients
e. Cash paid to vendors
f. Taxes paid to federal, state, and local governments
g. Loan repayments to bank (including principal and interest)

5-10 Compare and contrast the two methods of preparing cash flow statements: the direct vs. the indirect method. What are the essential differences between these two methods? The similarities?

5-11 Identify each of the following activities as either operating, investing, or financing activities:

a. Cash received from customers
b. Cash paid to acquire operating equipment
c. Cash paid as dividends to shareholders
d. Cash received from issuing common stock
e. Cash paid for income taxes

5-12 Under the indirect method of preparing the statement of cash flows, each of the following items would be added to net income in measuring cash flows from operating activities (CFOA). Which (if any) of these items may be considered to be a source of cash?

a. Depreciation expense
b. Loss on sale of plant and equipment
c. Reductions in customer accounts receivable
d. Increases in supplier accounts payable

5-13 Describe two investing and financing activities that do not involve cash receipts or payments. Why might a financial analyst want to know about such noncash transactions?

5-14 Evaluate the following conventions in preparing a statement of cash flows:

a. Dividend payments to shareholders are reported as a financing activity, and interest payments on debt are reported as an operating activity.
b. Purchases of inventory are operating activities, but purchases of plant and equipment are investing activities.
c. Accounts payable transactions are operating activities, but most other liability transactions are treated as financing activities.

5-15 In each of the following cases, indicate whether the amount of cash inflow (or outflow) is greater or less than the related revenue (or expense):

a. A firm's accounts receivable balance has increased during the period.
b. A firm's salaries payable balance has increased during the period.
c. A firm's accumulated depreciation balance has increased during the period.
d. A firm's inventory balance has increased during the period, and the supplier accounts payable balance has also increased by a greater amount.

5-16 Discuss how cash return on assets (CROA) can be used as a measure of managerial performance. Distinguish between CROA and "free cash flow."

5-17 A government agency once reported to one of the authors that it could not extend a job offer because it was "financially embarrassed." What do you suppose this term meant? Could a commercial company also be financially embarrassed? What mechanisms might a firm have that a government agency would not have to avoid financial embarrassment?

5-18 Consider the differences between owning and managing an apartment building or a retail store. Would the owner of one prefer a cash-based measure of performance? Would one prefer an accrual-based performance measure? Would either have an advantage if only the income statement, or only the statement of cash flows, were used to evaluate annual operations? Why?

EXERCISES

Effects of Transactions: Cash Versus Accrual

5-19 Consider the following transactions or events:

1. Sold merchandise on account.
2. Sold a used computer for cash.
3. Paid a supplier's overdue account.
4. Recorded depreciation expense on a building.
5. Signed a mortgage and received cash.
6. Purchased inventory on account.
7. Gave a refund after hearing a customer's complaint.
8. Received payment from a customer.
9. Sold shares of IBM stock for cash and recorded a gain.
10. Recorded a loss after discarding obsolete inventory.
11. Received a personal cash gift from a friend.
12. Made an "even" swap of a used truck for another truck.
13. Paid quarterly unemployment taxes.
14. Received a tax refund after sending duplicate checks to the IRS.

Required

a. Show the effects on cash of each transaction or event, using the format below:

Effects on Cash		
Increase	**Decrease**	**No Change**

b. Show the effects of each transaction or event on net income, using a similar format:

Effects on Net Income		
Increase	**Decrease**	**No Change**

Effects of Transactions: Cash Versus Accrual

5-20 Consider the following events or transactions:

1. Delivered groceries and received a personal check.
2. Took a taxi and paid the fare.
3. Gave a refund for defective merchandise.
4. Recorded depreciation.
5. Sold a building, received a note receivable in exchange, and recorded a gain.
6. Made a donation to the Youth Services Community Foundation.
7. Received proceeds of a bank loan.
8. Received title to a classic Corvette in settlement of a customer's account.
9. Returned merchandise to a supplier for credit.
10. Traded in a used truck and acquired a new truck with the balance owed on account.
11. Found securities in the bottom of an old trunk in the attic that are now worth $100,000.
12. Filed an insurance claim for water damage to inventory.
13. Recorded a loss due to water damage.
14. Received a refund from a supplier who had been overpaid.

Required

a. Show the effects on cash of each transaction or event, using the format below:

Effects on Cash		
Increase	**Decrease**	**No Change**

b. Show the effects of each transaction or event on revenues or expenses, using a similar format:

Effects on Shareholders' Equity		
Revenues (Increase)	**Expenses (Decrease)**	**No Change**

Effects of Transactions on Cash Flows

5-21 The following transactions were reported by Colorado Company in its statement of cash flows. Indicate whether each transaction is an operating (O), a financing (F), an investing (I), or a transaction that has no effect on cash flows (X) activity.

1. Office supplies were purchased and paid for.
2. Land was sold for cash.
3. Employees' salaries and wages were paid.
4. The firm made a short-term loan to its president.
5. A short-term bank loan was obtained.
6. Interest on this loan was paid.
7. The maturity date on this loan was extended.
8. Depreciation for the year was recorded.
9. The firm's tax return was filed with a request for a refund.
10. The firm paid its unemployment taxes to the state.

Transaction Analysis

5-22 Indicate where each of the following transactions would be reported on the statement of cash flows (operating section, investing section, financing section, or not a cash flow item):

1. Purchased inventory on account.
2. Issued common stock for cash.

3. Paid loan principle.
4. Paid interest on the loan.
5. Lent money to a customer.
6. Received cash from sales.
7. Paid inventory suppliers.
8. Sold a building for cash.
9. Recorded a gain on the sale of the building in transaction
10. Received a dividend from short-term investments.
11. Recorded depreciation for the period.

Interpreting Cash Flow Concepts

5-23 Discuss the differences in the following terms:

a. Cash received from customers versus sales revenue
b. Cash paid to suppliers versus cost of goods sold
c. Cash proceeds from the sale of equipment versus gain on the sale of equipment
d. Cash paid to employees versus wages expense
e. Cash paid for equipment versus depreciation expense

Critical Thinking

Performance Evaluation, Alternative Scenarios

5-24 Evaluate the following two scenarios and identify the possible sources of information that would be used by a union in asserting its demands to two different bargaining units (employers).

1. Firm 1 reported record high earnings, but also told its union representatives that it could not afford even a small increase in wages.
2. Firm 2 reported huge decreases in its earnings and, at the same time, was considering accepting its union's proposed 15% average increase in wages.

PROBLEMS

Integration of Concepts

Transaction Analysis: Expanded Accounting Equation

5-25 The following transactions were recorded by May G&M Retail Stores:

1. Merchandise inventory was sold on account for $120,000.
2. The cost of merchandise sold in transaction 1 was $62,500.
3. Collections from customers were $125,000.
4. A $900,000 long-term note payable was paid by check.
5. A $10,000 loan to the company's president was due, but not yet paid.
6. One hundred thousand dollars was invested in short-term certificates of deposit.
7. Merchandise inventory was purchased on account for $65,000.
8. Payments of $62,500 were made to suppliers.
9. Interest of $9,000 is due on a long-term note payable.
10. Paid half the interest (transaction 9).
11. A $45,000 refund from a supplier was received unexpectedly.
12. Land was purchased for $95,000 cash and a $300,000 note.
13. Salaries and wages due at the end of the fiscal period were accrued at $7,800.
14. Recorded depreciation of $4,650 on equipment.

Required

Classify each transaction into the following balance sheet equation and, if an item affects cash, note next to the cash item where it would appear in the statement of cash flows (using the direct method).

CASH + OTHER ASSETS = LIABILITIES + SHAREHOLDER' EQUITY

Integration of Concepts

Recording Transactions and Preparing a Simple Income Statement and Partial Cash Flow Statement

5-26 The following transactions were made by Manning, Inc.:

1. Merchandise was purchased for $180,000 cash.
2. Sales during the year (half received in cash) were $250,000.
3. Cost of goods sold in transaction 2 was $130,000.
4. Wages earned by employees was $42,000, of which $20,000 was still unpaid at year-end.
5. Prepaid rent at the beginning of the year was $36,000. This represented rent for 18 months.
6. Utilities incurred during the year totaled $8,500. Three-fourths of this was paid by year-end.

Required

a. Record these transactions using the accounting equation. Set up separate columns for assets, liabilities, and shareholders' equity.
b. Prepare an income statement.
c. Prepare the operating activities section of the statement of cash flows (using the direct method).
d. Comment on any differences in net income and cash flow from operating activities.

Integration of Concepts

Transaction Analysis

5-27 The following transactions were recorded by Macintosh Corporation:

1. Purchased a building and took on a mortgage for $150,000.
2. Purchased merchandise for $12,000 cash.
3. Collected an account receivable of $4,000.
4. Recorded depreciation of $20,000.
5. Paid dividends of $8,000 to shareholders.
6. Received $15,000 cash from the sale of a short-term investment, and recorded a loss of $2,000 on the sale.
7. Issued additional common stock and received $5,000.
8. Paid interest of $11,000 on the mortgage.

Required

Classify these transactions in terms of the balance sheet equation given below and indicate which transactions would be reported on the statement of cash flows by labeling the transaction as an operating, investing, or financing activity.

CASH + OTHER ASSETS = LIABILITIES + SHAREHOLDER' EQUITY

Critical Thinking

Converting from Cash Flows to Revenues and Expenses

5-28 Determine the amounts of revenue or expense associated with each of the following cash flows:

1. Cash received from customers was $8.5 million; accounts receivable increased by $1.6 million.
2. Paid salaries of $3 million; salaries payable decreased by $.6 million.
3. Paid cash of $4.5 million to suppliers; supplier accounts payable increased by $.5 million. Inventories decreased by $1 million.

Critical Thinking

Converting from Revenues and Expenses to Cash Flows

5-29 Determine the amounts of cash flows associated with each of the following:

1. Sales revenue was $20 million; accounts receivable decreased by $2 million.
2. Salary expense was $7.5 million; salaries payable decreased by $1 million.
3. Cost of goods sold was $9 million; inventories decreased by $1.2 million. Supplier accounts payable increased by $1.6 million.

Effects of Asset Disposals on Cash Flows

5-30 The Shifting Sands Company reported an increase in its property (land) account of $4 million during 1999. During 1999, the firm sold land with an initial cost of $12 million for cash proceeds of $9 million and purchased additional land for $16 million. Determine the effects of these transactions on the following elements of the firm's 1999 financial statements:

a. Net income (ignore income tax effects)
b. Adjustments to net income to compute cash flows from operations (as in the indirect method)
c. Cash flows from investing activities

Critical Thinking

Preparing a Cash Flow Statement from a Listing of Transactions

5-31 Haywire Systems had the following cash receipts and payments during 2000 (dollars in millions):

1. Cash received from customers	$130
2. Cash paid to inventory suppliers	42
3. Cash paid to employees as wages	38
4. Paid income taxes	31
5. Cash paid for other operating expenses	17
6. Cash dividends paid to shareholders	10
7. Cash paid to acquire equipment and vehicles	75
8. Cash paid to retire bank loans	25
9. Cash received from sale of land	8
10. Cash received by a company issuing common stock	85

Required

Based on the above information, using the direct method:

a. Determine cash flow from operations.
b. Determine cash flow from investments.
c. Determine cash flow from financing.
d. Calculate Haywire's net income for 2000. If this is not possible, identify additional information that would be needed to determine net income.

Computing Quality of Sales Ratios

5-32 Consider the following information for two hi-tech companies:

	Oxford, LTD	Kendall, LTD
	(Dollars in thousands)	
Accounts receivable		
Beginning of year	$ 9,915	$ 408
End of year	11,250	7,258
Sales for year	21,891	11,606

Required

a. Calculate the cash collected from customers for each firm.
b. Compute the quality of sales ratio for each firm.
c. What do these ratios indicate?

Computing Quality of Income Ratios

5-33 Consider the following information for two high-tech companies:

	Oxford, LTD	Kendall, LTD
	(Dollars in thousands)	
Cash provided by operating activities	$5,600	$ 7,419
Net income	$ 684	$12,916

Required

a. Compute the quality of income ratio for each firm.
b. What inferences can be drawn from these ratios?

Computing Cash-Based Ratios

5-34 Consider the following information:

Windbag International, Inc.
Selected Financial Statement Information
(Dollars in Millions)

	2000	1999
Total assets	$1,086	$ 996
Total owners' equity	681	660
Debt	145	201
Sales	1,256	1,199
Accounts receivable	28	27
Depreciation expense	74	69
Interest paid	19	22
Taxes paid	53	42
Purchases of property, plant, and equipment	142	117
Net cash outflow from investing activities	95	107
Cash flow from operating activities	166	147
Net income	97	79

Required

a. Calculate the following ratios, for each year:
   1. Cash return on assets (2000 only)
   2. Quality of sales
   3. Quality of income
   4. Cash interest coverage

b. Based on your ratios, evaluate Windbag's performance. In what areas do the cash flow ratios indicate positive or negative performances?

Interpreting Cash Flow Statement

Critical Thinking

5-35 The following cash flow statement was prepared by the Brainard Music Company for the year ended December 31, 2000:

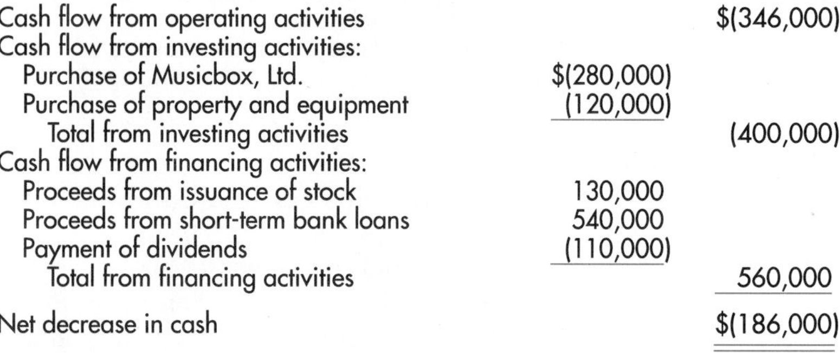

Cash flow from operating activities		$(346,000)
Cash flow from investing activities:		
Purchase of Musicbox, Ltd.	$(280,000)	
Purchase of property and equipment	(120,000)	
Total from investing activities		(400,000)
Cash flow from financing activities:		
Proceeds from issuance of stock	130,000	
Proceeds from short-term bank loans	540,000	
Payment of dividends	(110,000)	
Total from financing activities		560,000
Net decrease in cash		$(186,000)

Required

a. Give three reasons why Brainard engaged in these investing and financing activities.

b. Assume that Brainard received dividends from Musicbox, Ltd. Why aren't they reported as part of investing activities?

c. Discuss the concept of depreciation as it affects cash flows and as it affects Brainard Music Co.

d. Do you think the future outlook for this company is optimistic? Why or why not?

Interpreting Financial Statements: Cash Flow Effects

Critical Thinking

5-36 The following statement of cash flows has been provided by Davo's Surf Shop of Malibu, California:

Davo's Surf Shop
Statement of Cash Flows
For the Year Ended December 31, 2000

Cash flows from operating activities		$ 225,000
Cash flows from investing activities:		
Investment in Susie's Swim-Wear, Ltd.	$ (215,000)	
Purchase of marketable securities	(550,000)	
Proceeds from sale of building	1,000,000	235,000
Cash flows from financing activities:		
Proceeds from debt issuance	$ 600,000	
Gift from friends and family	400,000	
Payment of dividends	(200,000)	800,000
Net increase in cash		$1,260,000

Required

a. Explain and discuss each item that resulted in a change in cash for Davo's Surf Shop.
b. Based on this limited information for only one year, evaluate Davo's future prospects.
c. What other information would be helpful in evaluating Davo's prospects?

Critical Thinking

Interpreting Financial Statements: Cash Flow Effects

5-37 Byte City, Inc., provided the following cash flow information in the form of subtotals on its cash flow statements:

	2000	1999
Net cash provided by operating activities	$ 2,956,020	$ 587,249
Net cash used in investing activities	(8,123,648)	(33,942,808)
Net cash provided by financing activities	3,880,973	31,672,955
Net decrease in cash and cash equivalents	$(1,286,655)	$ (1,682,604)

Required

a. Did Byte City's cash and cash equivalents increase or decrease in 1999? In 2000? Why?
b. How would you assess Byte City's cash flows from operating activities?
c. What financing and investing strategies was Byte City apparently following in 1999? How did this strategy change in 2000?
d. If Byte City purchased other companies in 1999 for more than $47 million, and borrowed almost $37 million, what does this new information indicate about its financing and investing strategies.
e. If Byte City made zero payments on long-term debt in 1999, but its payments in 2000 totaled more than $26 million, reevaluate its financing strategies?
f. What other information would be helpful in answering these types of questions?

Critical Thinking

Calculate Cash Flow Ratios

5-38 Given the following information extracted from Byte City's financial statements, calculate and evaluate its cash flow ratios:

	2000	1999
Interest paid	$ 4,186,532	$ 3,695,431
Interest received	718,574	1,218,940
Income taxes paid	150,000	1,997,600
Total assets	107,219,075	103,542,717
Long-term debt	58,742,916	62,671,335
Shareholders' equity	42,827,531	35,912,651
Net income (loss)	7,459,828	(32,818,050)
Net revenues	129,485,952	109,948,716
Net cash provided by operations	2,956,020	587,249
Cash received from customers	118,158,941	101,879,383

Required

a. Discuss the differences between net cash provided by operations and cash received from customers.
b. Discuss the differences between net revenues and cash received from customers.

c. Using the previous data, estimate Byte City's overall cash flows or cash balances at the end of each year. Justify your conclusions.
d. Refer to the data in the previous problem (5-37). Revise your conclusions about Byte City's overall cash flows or cash balances at the end of each year. Again, justify your revised answer.
e. Calculate the following ratios for each year:
   1. Cash return on assets (2000 only)
   2. Quality of sales
   3. Quality of income
   4. Cash interest coverage
f. Based on these ratios, evaluate Byte City's performance each year. In what areas do the cash flow ratios indicate positive or negative performances?
g. What additional information would be useful in evaluating Byte City's performance?

Interpreting Financial Statements: Cash Flow Effects

5-39 The following summary information has been extracted from the financial statements of Hi-Tech Vaporware (dollars in thousands):

	2000	1999
Total net revenues	$126,000	$106,000
Operating expenses	(105,100)	(93,500)
Interest income	700	950
Interest expense	(3,560)	(3,815)
Provision for income taxes	(355)	(215)
Net income	$17,685	$ 9,420
Total assets	$131,900	$101,500
Total long-term debt	30,150	36,450
Total shareholders' equity	99,759	62,420
Cash received from customers	116,580	98,987
Cash paid to suppliers	(114,371)	(94,641)
Income taxes paid	4,965	(702)
Interest paid	(1,474)	(1,886)
Net cash provided by operating activities	5,700	1,758
Sale of marketable securities	716	3,873
Capital expenditures	(9,608)	(48,017)
Net cash used in investing activities	(8,892)	(44,144)
Proceeds from bank loans	11,467	40,593
Payments on bank loans	(16,380)	—
Proceeds from issuing common stock	13,794	1,875
Net cash provided by financing activities	8,881	42,468
Net increase in cash and cash equivalents	$ 5,689	$ 82

Required

a. Discuss the differences between net cash provided by operating activities and cash received from customers.
b. Discuss the differences between net revenues and cash received from customers.
c. From the data above, evaluate Hi-Tech's overall cash flows during the year. Similarly evaluate its cash balances at the end of each year.

(Continued)

d. What part of the balance sheet or cash flow statement would improve your evaluations of Hi-Tech's overall cash flows or cash balances at the end of either year? Why?
e. Calculate the following ratios for each year:
   1. Cash return on assets (2000 only)
   2. Quality of sales
   3. Quality of income
   4. Cash interest coverage
f. Based on these ratios, evaluate Hi-Tech's performance. In what areas do the cash flow ratios represent positive or negative performances?
g. What additional information would be useful in evaluating Hi-Tech's performance?

Interpreting Financial Statements: Cash Flow Effects

Critical Thinking

5-40 United States Surgical Corporation (USSC) provided the following consolidated statement of cash flows, as abbreviated:

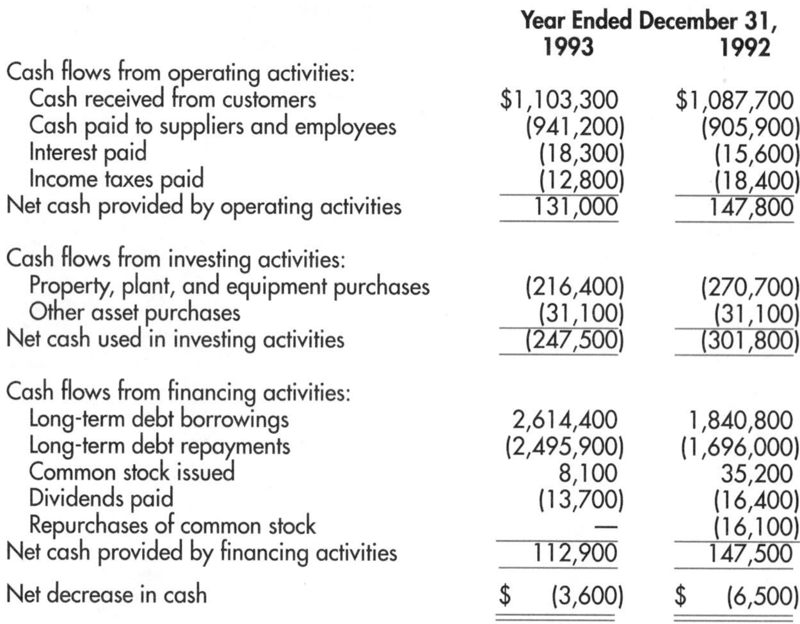

	Year Ended December 31, 1993	1992
Cash flows from operating activities:		
Cash received from customers	$1,103,300	$1,087,700
Cash paid to suppliers and employees	(941,200)	(905,900)
Interest paid	(18,300)	(15,600)
Income taxes paid	(12,800)	(18,400)
Net cash provided by operating activities	131,000	147,800
Cash flows from investing activities:		
Property, plant, and equipment purchases	(216,400)	(270,700)
Other asset purchases	(31,100)	(31,100)
Net cash used in investing activities	(247,500)	(301,800)
Cash flows from financing activities:		
Long-term debt borrowings	2,614,400	1,840,800
Long-term debt repayments	(2,495,900)	(1,696,000)
Common stock issued	8,100	35,200
Dividends paid	(13,700)	(16,400)
Repurchases of common stock	—	(16,100)
Net cash provided by financing activities	112,900	147,500
Net decrease in cash	$ (3,600)	$ (6,500)

Required

a. Identify and discuss any unfamiliar terms or unusual treatments in USSC's cash flow statement.
b. Discuss the differences between net cash provided by operating activities and cash received from customers.
c. From the data above, evaluate USSC's overall cash flows or cash balances at the end of each year.
d. What part of the balance sheet or cash flow statement would help you better evaluate USSC's overall cash flows or cash balances at the end of either year? Why?
e. Given the following additional balance sheet and income statement data:

(Continued)

	1993	1992
Net sales	$1,037,200	$1,197,200
Net income (loss)	(138,700)	138,900
Interest expense	18,500	14,700
Income taxes	1,300	54,000
Total assets	1,170,500	1,168,000
Long-term debt	137,500	110,700
Stockholders' equity	443,900	590,000

Calculate the following ratios, for each year:

1. cash return on assets (1993 only)
2. quality of sales
3. quality of income
4. cash interest coverage

f. Based on these ratios, evaluate USSC's performance. In what areas do the cash flow ratios represent positive or negative performances?

g. What additional information would be useful in evaluating USSC's performance?

Interpreting Financial Statements: Cash Flow Effects

5-41 StorageTek's consolidated statement of cash flows contained the following information, as abbreviated (dollars in thousands):

	Year Ended December 31, 1993	Year Ended December 25, 1992
Operating Activities		
Cash received from customers	$1,532,183	$1,572,892
Cash paid to suppliers and employees	(1,446,321)	(1,456,835)
Interest received	54,251	67,136
Interest paid	(40,519)	(47,751)
Income taxes paid	(12,048)	(28,327)
Net cash from operating activities	87,546	107,115
Investing Activities		
Short-term investments, net	(15,377)	40,227
Purchase of property, plant, and equipment	(67,720)	(106,119)
Business acquisitions, net of cash	—	(51,761)
Other assets, net	(6,945)	(4,136)
Net cash used in investing activities	(90,042)	(121,789)
Financing Activities		
Proceeds from preferred stock offering	166,479	—
Proceeds from nonrecourse borrowings	87,508	114,935
Repayments of nonrecourse borrowings	(147,647)	(169,005)
Proceeds from other debt	79,740	21,320
Repayments of other debt	(44,144)	(27,538)
Other financing activities	2,009	61,050
Net cash from financing activities	143,945	762
Effect of exchange rate changes	(4,341)	(4,884)
Increase (decrease) in cash	$ 137,108	$ (18,796)

Required

a. Identify and discuss any unfamiliar terms or unusual treatments in StorageTek's cash flow statement.

b. Discuss the differences between net cash provided by operating activities and cash received from customers.

c. From the data above, evaluate StorageTek's overall cash flows or cash balances at the end of each year.

d. What part of the balance sheet or cash flow statement would help you better evaluate StorageTek's overall cash flows or cash balances at the end of either year? Why?

e. Given the following additional balance sheet and income statement data (dollars in thousands):

	1993	1992
Net sales	$ 902,482	$1,079,130
Net income (loss)	(77,796)	9,334
Interest expense	43,670	48,706
Income taxes	5,000	17,700
Total assets	1,793,009	1,739,043
Long-term debt	361,718	369,988
Stockholders' equity	1,017,303	927,913

Calculate the following ratios for each year:

1. Cash return on assets (1993 only)
2. Quality of sales
3. Quality of income
4. Cash interest coverage

f. Based on these ratios, evaluate StorageTek's performance. In what areas do the cash flow ratios indicate positive or negative performances?

g. What additional information would be useful in evaluating StorageTek's performance?

h. StorageTek's 1991 fiscal year ended on December 27. Would the difference in the number of days or number of weeks in each fiscal year affect any of the above analyses? Why?

Interpreting Financial Statements: Cash Flow Effects

5-42 The following (summary) statement of cash flows has been provided by Sigma Designs, which specializes in diversified graphic systems, document imaging, and multimedia markets.

Sigma Designs, Inc.
Statement of Cash Flows (abbreviated)
For the Years Ended January 31, 1993 and 1992
(Dollars in Thousands)

	1993	1992
Cash flows from operating activities:		
Net loss	$(7,166)	$(3,443)
Summary of adjustments to net loss activities	(659)	4,731
Net cash provided by (used for) operating activities	(7,825)	1,288
Cash flows from investing activities:		
Purchases of marketable securities	(25,367)	(28,598)
Sales of marketable securities	30,518	23,189
Equipment additions	(801)	(702)
Software development costs (capitalized)	(551)	(1,070)
Other asset transactions	(339)	87
Net cash provided by (used for) investing activities	3,460	(7,094)
Cash flows from financing activities:		
Common stock sold	312	329
Repayment of long-term debt	(39)	(35)
Other financing transactions	(105)	24
Net cash provided by (used for) financing activities	168	318
Decrease in cash and equivalents	$(4,197)	$(5,488)

Required

a. Explain and discuss each item that resulted in a change in cash for Sigma Designs.
b. Based on this information, evaluate Sigma's future prospects.
c. Indicate whether Sigma used the direct or indirect method to calculate its cash flows from operations. How can you tell?

Interpreting Financial Statements: Cash Flow Effects, Trends in Cash Flow, and Net Income

5-43 The following (summary) statement of cash flows has been provided by Sigma Designs, which specializes in diversified graphic systems, document imaging, and multimedia markets.

Sigma Designs, Inc.
Statement of Cash Flows (abbreviated)
For the Years Ended January 31, 1995 and 1994
(Dollars in Thousands)

	1995	1994
Cash flows from operating activities:		
Net loss	$(1,000)	$(2,145)
Summary of adjustments to net loss activities	2,997	2,731
Net cash provided by (used for) operating activities	1,997	586
Cash flows from investing activities:		
Purchases of marketable securities	(20,547)	(23,288)
Sales of marketable securities	35,245	32,155
Equipment additions	(625)	(502)
Software development costs (capitalized)	(300)	(1,200)
Other asset transactions	(273)	215
Net cash provided by (used for) investing activities	13,500	7,380
Cash flows from financing activities:		
Common stock sold	594	450
Repayment of long-term debt	(47)	(40)
Other financing transactions	(252)	(75)
Net cash provided by (used for) financing activities	295	335
Decrease in Cash and Equivalents	$15,792	$ 8,301

Required

a. Explain and discuss each item that resulted in a change in cash for Sigma Designs.

b. Based on this information, evaluate Sigma's future prospects.

c. Did Sigma use the direct or indirect method? What evidence indicates which method Sigma used?

d. With reference to the data in this assignment, and in the preceding assignment (5-42), prepare a graph showing the trends in Sigma Designs' cash flow from operations. On the same graph, show Sigma's net income (loss). Discuss these trends, along with your estimate of Sigma's future prospects.

e. Write a short memo to Sigma Designs' controller regarding the effects of net losses on operating cash flows during the period 1992 through 1995. Evaluate the dramatic turnaround in Sigma's cash balances. What factors caused this reversal (1992-95)?

Interpreting Financial Statements: Cash Flow Effects

Critical Thinking

5-44 A condensed version of Microbyte Corporation's consolidated statements of cash flows for 1999 and 2000 are shown below (dollars in thousands):

	2000	1999
Cash flows from operating activities:		
Cash received from customers	$164,177	$82,152
Cash paid to suppliers and employees	(142,336)	(69,507)
Interest received	2,622	722
Interest paid	(87)	(224)
Income taxes paid	(16,121)	(5,187)
Net cash provided by operating activities	8,255	7,956
Cash flows from investing activities:		
Sale (purchase) of short-term investments	600	(16,200)
Capital expenditures	(9,740)	(1,932)
Net cash used for investing activities	(9,140)	(18,132)
Cash flows from financing activities:		
Proceeds from issuing common stock	496	22,114
Payments under capital leases	(472)	(347)
Other	(9)	31
Net cash provided by financing activities	15	21,798
Net increase (decrease) in cash	(870)	11,622
Cash balances at beginning of year	14,808	3,186
Cash balances at end of year	$ 13,938	$14,808

Required

a. Is Microbyte's statement of cash flows based on the direct or indirect method? What evidence supports this view?

b. By how much did Microbyte's cash flow from operations increase?

c. During these two years, how much did Microbyte spend to purchase marketable securities and other short-term investments? Did Microbyte buy or sell securities each year? Show any relevant calculations.

d. How much did Microbyte spend on capital expenditures during the two years? Did Microbyte purchase or sell capital assets each year? How do you know?

e. During these two years, how much money did Microbyte receive by issuing common stock? Given these proceeds, what do you suppose Microbyte did with it? Why would Microbyte take these actions?

f. By how much did Microbyte's collections from customers increase between 1999 and 2000? Does this increase represent modest or significant growth? Is the increase in cash paid to suppliers and employees consistent with this growth? Why?

g. By how much did Microbyte's cash balances increase between the beginning of 1999 and the end of 2000? Is this increase significant? Does it represent a significant increase in Microbyte's liquidity? Why?

h. Why do you think the amounts shown for interest payments are so low? Why is interest received so much larger than interest payments? Under what circumstances is this a favorable relationship?

i. During 1999, Microbyte's cash increased by $11,622,000. On the other hand, during 2000 its cash decreased by $870,000. Is this trend alarming? Does it indicate any problems for Microbyte?

j. How would an analyst evaluate the relationship between Microbyte's cash provided by operations of $8,255,000 and its cash used for investing activities of $9,140,000? How is this relationship affected by Microbyte's financing activities? Has Microbyte been a prudent manager of its cash during 2000? Why?

continued

k. Compute the following ratios or amounts for Microbyte Corporation for 2000. Discuss each ratio in the context of Microbyte's statement of cash flows.
   1. Cash flow from operating activities
   2. Cash return on assets, assuming average total assets are $81,613,000
   3. Cash return on stockholders' equity, assuming average stockholders' equity is $60,386,000
   4. Quality of sales, assuming sales revenues are $170,290,000
   5. Quality of income, assuming net income is $40,513,000
   6. Cash interest coverage

l. Compute the following ratios or amounts for Microbyte Corporation for 1999 and discuss each ratio in the context of Microbyte's statement of cash flows.
   1. Cash flow from operating activities
   2. Quality of sales, assuming sales revenues are $88,655,000
   3. Quality of income, assuming net income is $17,848,000
   4. Cash interest coverage

m. Evaluate the trends in these ratios over the two years.

n. Evaluate Microbyte's future prospects.

Interpreting Financial Statements: Cash Flow Effects

Critical Thinking

5-45 Consider the following (summary) consolidated statements of cash flows from Pioneer Resource, Inc., for 1999 and 2000:

Consolidated Statements of Cash Flows
Pioneer Resource, Inc.
For the years ending December 31, 2000 and 1999
(Dollars in Millions)

	2000	1999
Cash flows from operating activities:		
Net cash from operating activities	$ 2,989.5	$3,125.7
Cash flows from investing activities:		
Acquisitions of property, plant, and equipment	$(2,454.0)	(2,111.9)
Acquisitions of new companies	(796.3)	(65.4)
Other investing activities, net	125.8	(185.6)
Net cash from investing activities	(3,124.5)	(2,362.9)
Cash flows from financing activities:		
Net change in short-term debt	818.4	17.5
Issuance of long-term debt	97.5	32.9
Retirements of long-term debt	(102.3)	(89.2)
Dividend payments	(825.4)	(776.4)
Repurchase of common stock	(588.1)	(807.2)
Other financing activities, net	205.3	895.7
Net cash from financing activities	(394.6)	(726.7)
Net increase (decrease) in cash and temporary investments	$ (529.6)	$ 36.1

Required

a. Identify and discuss each item that caused a change in Pioneer Resource's net cash flows for each year.

b. Using only the cash flow statement, evaluate Pioneer Resource's cash flow prospects for 2001.

continued

c. Describe and evaluate Pioneer Resource's apparent strategy for financing its acquisitions. How do its dividend payments and its repurchases of common stock affect its financing strategies?
d. If Pioneer Resource's net income figures for 2000 and 1999 were, respectively, $1,253.8 and $1,238.2 (dollars in millions), write a short essay explaining the relationship between net income and net cash flow provided by operating activities. Draw a simple graph to show how these amounts relate to each other. What conclusions can be drawn from the graph?
e. Compare Pioneer Resource's net income and cash provided by operating activities with the net income and cash flow trends for another company. Unless your instructor designates another company, use the data from Sigma Designs' net income (loss) and cash provided (or used) by operating activities (see problem 5-43). Although these are two distinctly different companies, how do your conclusions about cash flows differ? Why do you think there are such vast differences?

Interpreting Financial Statements: Cash Flow Effects

5-46 Mitronics Corporation reported the following items (which are only partial excerpts) in its 1997 statement of cash flows (dollars in thousands).

	1997	1996
Net earnings	$788	$845
Increases (decreases) in current liabilities	(512)	532
Cash provided by operating activities	276	1,377

In the financial review section of Mitronics' annual report, management reported the following:

Cash provided by operations was $276,000 in 1997 compared with $1,377,000 in 1996. The reduction was primarily due to lower earnings from operations and a reduction in current liabilities.

Required

a. Explain in your own words what Mitronics is communicating in this note. Why might Mitronics' managers manage its cash in this manner?
b. What else would a financial analyst like to know about Mitronics' cash flow from operating activities?

Interpreting Financial Statements: Cash Flow Effects

5-47 SILLA, Inc., reported the following items (which are partial excerpts) in its 1999 statement of cash flows (dollars in thousands):

	2000	1999
Net loss	$(81,542)	$(202,144)
Interest payments, net	(114,000)	(132,000)
Debt repayments	(214,000)	(7,100)
Cash provided by operating activities	36,548	15,432

Included in management's discussion of SILLA's annual results was the following:

During 1999, cash flows from operating activities included $31 million relating to net reductions in operating receivables and payables relating primarily to property sales of $35 million. Accordingly, operations provided enough cash flow for net interest costs but did not provide substantial additional cash for debt principal repayment or capital expenditures.

Required

a. Has SILLA improved its cash flow in 2000 (versus the prior year)? What actions has it taken that resulted in significant changes in cash flow?

b. On what grounds would you agree, or disagree, with management's assertions about its cash flow from operating activities?

Interpreting Financial Statements: Cash Flow Effects

5-48 Woodway Company reported the following data in its 2000 statement of cash flows (dollars in thousands):

	2000	1999
Net earnings	$ 1,654	$6,215
Cash provided by operating activities	26,118	1,984

Required

a. What are some likely explanations for the trend in cash provided by operating activities relative to the trend in net earnings?

b. Would you expect Woodway's cash balance at the end of 2000 to be higher or lower than that at the end of 1999? Why? What other information would you need before drawing definitive conclusions in this regard?

Interpreting Financial Statements: Cash Flow Effects

Writing

5-49 The following cash flow statement from Low-Down Industries is causing concern to its president, Ms. High-Flyer. She can't understand why Low-Down is having trouble meeting its debt obligations on a timely basis. She is further concerned about the long-term prospects of the company, especially because last year's net income was only $100,000.

Low-Down Industries
Statement of Cash Flows (abbreviated)
For the year ended November 30, 1999

Net cash used by operating activities		$(23,000)
Proceeds from sale of building	125,000	
Purchase of equipment	(47,000)	
Net cash provided by investing activities		78,000
Dividends paid	(31,000)	
Payment on long-term note payable	(90,000)	
Net cash used by financing activities		(121,000)
Decrease in cash		$(66,000)

Required

a. Write a memo to Ms. High-Flyer addressing her concerns and your recommendations.

b. Assume that Low-Down Industries has no more land or buildings or other tangible assets to sell. Suppose also that Low-Down's operations will not substantially change.

   1. Prepare an approximate forecast of next year's cash flows, assuming no other major changes.
   2. Identify several viable strategies for Ms. High-Flyer to consider for future years in order to alleviate these potential cash shortages.

Writing

Effects of Discounts on Net Income

5-50 Assume that you are the controller of a publicly held company called Spring Corporation. The CEO and the CFO are quite concerned about financial analysts' assessments of Spring's prospects. Analysts have publicized their doubts about Spring's ability to generate cash from operating activities.

As is common, Spring pays for all of its inventory purchases almost immediately upon receipt of the appropriate bills. Because finance charges in this industry are exorbitant, you, as controller, are careful to make all payments within the allowable interest-free period. At year end, the CFO orders you to suspend temporarily all payments to suppliers. The obvious reason for this suspension is to enhance, that is to "window dress," Spring's CFOA in its statement of cash flows. It is also obvious that this action will cost Spring substantial future interest charges.

Required

Write a short response to the CFO's request.

Integration of Concepts

Preparing an Income Statement and a Statement of Cash Flows

5-51 Beth's Espresso Cart, first introduced in Chapter 4, "The Income Statement," finished its second year of operations.

1.	Cash collections from clients	$35,505
2.	Payments to suppliers (beans, etc.)	17,347
3.	Replacement of cups, pots, etc.	1,000
4.	Depreciation of coffee cart	1,300
5.	Withdrawals for personal use	6,000
6.	Purchases of propane, electricity, etc.	510
7.	Amortization of insurance (final year)	400
8.	Repaid start-up loan (to her father)	4,000
9.	Paid interest on loan, two years at 10% simple interest (for last year and this year)	

Required

a. Prepare an income statement and a statement of cash flows on the basis of the data (assuming that all sales and purchases are for cash). Assume there have been no significant inventory changes (supplies, fuel, coffee beans, etc.) during the past year.

b. Write a short memo evaluating the year's operating performance of Beth's Espresso Cart. Provide suggestions for next year.

Writing

Effects on Net Income and Cash Flows

5-52 Jane Stallings is the vice-president of operations for the Floppy Disk Computer Company, which produces a wide variety of hardware and software for personal computers. This equipment is sold to other manufacturers and is also sold to business and personal (retail) customers through specialty computer suppliers in shopping malls and business centers throughout the United States and Europe.

Floppy Disk has been in business for about 15 years and its overall operating results have been generally satisfactory. However, because the product life cycle for floppy disks is reaching its end, the manufacturing of floppy disks is almost completely conducted in the Far East due to lower labor costs, and the Floppy Disk Division has had zero profits for the past three years, Jane Stallings has proposed eliminating the Floppy Disk Division.

Max Marcker, son of Floppy Disk's founder and holder of 45% of the company's shares, objected to this proposal at the last meeting of the board of directors. Max believes that a resurgence of interest in floppy disk technology will soon occur and that such products will soon be produced at a cost of two cents each. He suggested to the board that this division is still integral to the company's future, that it contributes to its cash flows, and that better planning and budgeting will improve the company's future cash flows.

Required

a. Write a short memo to Max from Jane, explaining the difference between cash flows and profits.

b. Each of Floppy Disk's divisions has, in the past, been evaluated on the basis of net income and return on shareholders' equity. Jane Stallings has suggested that cash flows should now be viewed as just as important a performance measure as net income. Write a short response to Jane. Suggest some cash-based ratios that would be more helpful and useful for annual performance evaluation of the divisions.

c. Jane has also suggested that each division be required to use the direct method in its cash flow statements. Again, write a short response to Jane. Explain why the direct method may be more helpful to managers in each division, as well as for anyone who might be evaluating the divisions.

Effects on Net Income and Cash Flows

Writing

5-53 Write a short essay describing the advantages and disadvantages of using the income statement and the cash flow statement as a basis for evaluating the performance of a firm. Specifically comment on the distinction between operating performance, based on cash provided by operations and on income from continuing operating activities and "bottom line" results on either the income statement or the cash flow statement.

Interpreting Financial Statements: Cash Flow Effects Versus Effects on Net Income

5-54 Four Square Computer Company has provided the following (partial) income statement for the year ended December 31, 2001:

Revenues	
Cash sales	$1,600,000
Sales on account	3,335,000
Subtotal	4,935,000
Expenses	
Salary expense	2,259,900
Supplies expense	300,550
Advertising expense	969,430
Rent	1,200,000
Miscellaneous	31,260
Subtotal	$4,761,140

Required

a. Calculate income before taxes, tax expense (at 28%), and net income after taxes.

b. About half of the sales on account have still not been collected and are expected to be collected in January of the next fiscal year. On what basis are they included in this year's income statement?

(Continued)

c. Given that about half of this year's sales have not yet been collected and represent all the accounts receivable that are still outstanding, evaluate Four Square's profitability. On the basis of this limited information, what would you conclude about its operating cash flows?
d. Assuming that all the nonsalary expenses have been paid as incurred, and assuming that salaries for December have not been paid or accrued, evaluate Four Square's profitability and its operating cash outflows. Assume that salaries were earned by employees evenly throughout the year.
e. Now, assume that half of the advertising expense was incurred in December for a promotional campaign that was designed to boost sales in the post-holiday period. Should these expenses have been omitted from this year's income statement and deferred until the following year? Why? If GAAP required that such advertising costs be expensed (that is, shown in this year's income statement), how might Four Square's managers now view the results of 2001's operations? Why?
f. On December 31, Four Square purchased 1,000 shares of Microcell (a computer software company) at $121 per share. Why isn't this purchase reflected in the income statement?
g. In November, Four Square purchased 100,000 disk drive units at $12 per unit. These are very advanced disk drives that have not yet been sold. Why isn't this purchase shown on the income statement?
h. When the outstanding accounts receivable are collected in the next year, should those collections be shown on next year's income statement? Why?
i. When the disk drives are used to manufacture computers, should their cost be shown on the income statement for the month and year in which they are assembled into the finished product? Or should they be shown on the income statement in the month and year when the computers (and their associated disk drives) are sold? Why?

Ethics

Effects of Timing on Revenue Recognition

5-55 Key, Inc., manufactures key rings and "dummy" keys for football fans to shake and rattle at opportune times during football games. These items are sold to sports specialty shops and sidewalk vendors during the football season. The company's fiscal year ends December 31 each year. In 1999, just before the "bowl" season, the company received orders and payment for $23,000 worth of keys and key rings. The goods will be manufactured and shipped on January 1, 2000, just in time for the major bowl games later that day. The effects these orders have in December 1999 on key's balance sheet equation is as follows:

ASSETS	=	LIABILITIES	+	SHAREHOLDERS' EQUITY
Cash + $23,000				Sales Revenue + $23,000

The company's overall financial results, summarized under the accounting equation, were

ASSETS	=	LIABILITIES	+	SHAREHOLDERS' EQUITY
$275,000		$266,000		$9,000

Key's summarized income statement for 1999 is as follows:

Revenues	$115,000
Expenses	109,000
Net income	$ 6,000

Required

a. Show how the $23,000 in December 1999 orders should have been recorded.
b. Reconstruct the income statement, showing how it might have appeared without the inclusion of the $23,000 in December orders. For this purpose, assume that the expenses associated with the orders were $11,000.
c. Show how the balance sheet would have changed if the $23,000 in orders had been recorded correctly. Why might Key management be unhappy with these results?
d. Discuss the ethical problems inherent in this situation for the company, for its financial managers, and for its auditors.

Ethics

Effects of Returns on Net Income

5-56 VaporWare II, Inc. (VWIII), had spectacularly good financial results in 1999. However, in 2000, the millenium bug, other defects, and general customer dissatisfaction resulted in returns of $3 million. These products had originally been expensed for $1 million. It cost $5 million to satisfy VWIII's irate customers. VWIII chose not to report any returns in 2000, while showing the $5 million as sales revenue in 2000.

Required

a. Show how the $3 million of returns should have been recorded.
b. If the defects had been properly anticipated, what impact would this have had on VWIII's 1999 income statement?
c. Show how the 1999 balance sheet would have changed if the returns had been recorded correctly. Why might VWIII's management be unhappy with these results?
d. Discuss how the 2000 financial statements will be affected by VWIII's treatment of these returns.
e. Discuss the ethical problems inherent in this situation, for the company, for its financial managers, and for its auditors.

Interpreting Financial Statements: Cash Flow Effects

5-57 From Appendix D, "Wendy's International, Inc.," review Wendy's cash flow statement and income statement.

Required

a. Evaluate Wendy's cash flow from operations. Calculate the relevant, cash-based ratios from this chapter.

continued

b. Compare Wendy's cash flow from operations to "income before taxes" (alternatively, you could calculate its operating income from the data shown on the income statement). Prepare a graph to help show trends in each.
c. Describe Wendy's cash management strategies as revealed in the operating, financing, and investing activities sections of its cash flow statement.
d. Write a short memo to a potential investor in which you critique Wendy's cash management strategies. Contrast predicted cash flow from operations with predicted income before taxes. What evidence supports the view that Wendy's will increase its operating cash flows and its income before taxes?

Interpreting Financial Statements: Cash Flow Effects

5-58 From Appendix E, "Reebok International Ltd.," review Reebok's cash flow statement and income statement.

Required

a. Evaluate Reebok's cash flow from operations. Calculate the relevant cash-based ratios from this chapter.
b. Compare Reebok's cash flow from operations to its "income before income taxes and minority interest." Prepare a graph to help show trends in each.
c. Describe Reebok's cash management strategies as revealed in the operating, financing, and investing activities sections of its cash flow statement.
d. Write a short memo to a potential investor in which you critique Reebok's cash management strategies. Contrast predicted cash flow from operations with predicted income before income taxes and minority interest. What evidence supports the view that Reebok will increase its operating cash flows and its income before income taxes and minority interest?

Analyzing Financial Statements of Several Companies

Critical Thinking

5-59 Obtain recent financial statements for two or three companies. If possible, these companies should be in the same industry and they should use the same method in reporting their cash flows from operating activities. Ideally, they will all use the direct method, though it will be hard to identify three such companies in the same industry who are otherwise comparable.

Required

a. Summarize each company's cash flow from operations in tabular and graphical formats. Calculate the relevant cash-based ratios from this chapter.
b. Summarize each company's net operating income in tabular and graphical formats.
c. Identify the cash flow strategies of each company by examining the operating, financing, and investing activities sections of each cash flow statement.
d. Write a short memo to a potential investor in which you critique the cash flow strategies of each company. Identify which company might offer the most favorable prospects for increasing its operating cash flows.

Cash Flow Issues

Writing

5-60 Scan recent business publications or use a business index in your library to locate an article discussing a company's cash flow issues. Read the article and write a short summary discussing the managerial implications of the company's cash flow issues.

Writing

Cash Flow Issues

5-61 Obtain the cash flow statements for a company that has been described in a recent business article as having cash flow problems. Conduct your own analysis of the company's cash flows, using the ratios described in this chapter. Write a short essay, clearly showing why you agree or disagree with the article's author regarding the company's cash flow problems.

Writing

Using CFO and/or NI for Performance Evaluation

5-62 Write a short memo discussing the advantages of using operating cash flows as an indicator of success. Contrast the use of operating cash flows as a performance measure, with accrual-based net income measures. Indicate the circumstances under which managers might prefer to use both measures simultaneously.

Critical Thinking

Identify Underlying Reasons for Changes in CFOA

5-63 The following financial statements from SOS Staffing Services, Inc. were downloaded from the SEC's EDGAR database:

SOS STAFFING SERVICES, INC.
CONSOLIDATED STATEMENTS OF CASH FLOWS

For the Fiscal Years Ended December 28, 1997, December 29, 1996 and December 31, 1995
Increase (Decrease) in Cash and Cash Equivalents

	Fiscal Year (52 Weeks) Ended		
	1997	1996	1995
CASH FLOWS FROM OPERATING ACTIVITIES:			
Net income	$7,526,227	$4,029,160	$2,939,942
Adjustments to reconcile net income to net cash used in operating activities:			
Depreciation and amortization	2,156,882	854,902	374,114
Deferred income taxes	(596,604)	(825,941)	274,352
Loss on disposition of assets	26,927	63,030	3,554
Changes in operating assets and liabilities:			
Accounts receivable, net	(12,448,572)	(8,785,524)	(10,740,788)
Workers' compensation deposit	134,924	(6,021)	1,277,178
Prepaid expenses and other	(288,556)	(127,943)	(128,033)
Amounts due from related parties	(17,521)	54,521	(445,881)
Deposits and other assets	(312,348)	(84,969)	7,667
Accounts payable	371,271	391,177	29,742
Accrued payroll costs	1,456,305	529,247	685,683
Workers' compensation reserve	1,196,488	957,338	(35,989)
Accrued liabilities	(624,956)	219,439	57,650
Income taxes payable	479,885	301,961	74,576
Net cash used in operating activities	(939,648)	(2,429,623)	(5,626,233)

Net cash used in operating activities (from page 190)	(939,648)	(2,429,623)	(5,626,233)
CASH FLOWS FROM INVESTING ACTIVITIES:			
Cash paid for acquisition of businesses	(38,574,952)	(10,162,026)	(1,340,707)
Principal payment of note related to acquisition	--	(1,450,000)	--
Purchases of property and equipment	(1,829,547)	(683,889)	(684,092)
Payments on acquisition earnouts	(3,955,275)	(239,139)	(29,800)
Deposits related to acquisition of certain assets	--	--	236,078
Proceeds from sale of property and equipment	2,743	--	--
Net cash used in investing activities	(44,357,031)	(12,535,054)	(1,818,521)
CASH FLOWS FROM FINANCING ACTIVITIES:			
Proceeds from issuance of common stock, net	$ 59,831,875	$ 18,098,350	$ 12,629,345
Proceeds from exercise of employee stock options	142,800	39,130	--
Repayments on line of credit, net	--	--	(2,530,251)
Proceeds from long-term debt	13,000,000	11,000,000	--
Principal payments on long-term debt	(13,000,000)	(11,105,541)	(550,000)
Capital contribution from shareholders	--	--	750,000
Distributions to shareholders	--	--	(750,000)
Net cash provided by financing activities	59,974,675	18,031,939	9,549,094
NET INCREASE IN CASH AND CASH EQUIVALENTS	14,677,996	3,067,262	2,104,340
CASH AND CASH EQUIVALENTS AT BEGINNING OF YEAR	5,784,651	2,717,389	613,049
CASH AND CASH EQUIVALENTS AT END OF YEAR	$ 20,462,647	$ 5,784,651	$ 2,717,389
SUPPLEMENTAL CASH FLOW INFORMATION:			
Cash paid during the year for:			
Income taxes	$ 5,168,820	$ 2,902,393	$ 1,117,214
Interest	225,776	280,018	134,917

SUPPLEMENTAL DISCLOSURES OF NONCASH INVESTING AND FINANCING ACTIVITIES:

The following information relates to the Company's acquisitions:

Fair value of assets acquired	$ 39,553,495	$ 14,980,167	$ 3,433,773

During fiscal year 1995 the Company distributed approximately $8 million of its accounts receivable to its SOS Corporation shareholders.

SOS STAFFING SERVICES, INC.
CONSOLIDATED BALANCE SHEETS
As of December 28, 1997 and December 29, 1996

ASSETS

	1997	1996
CURRENT ASSETS:		
Cash and cash equivalents	$20,462,647	$5,784,651
Accounts receivable, less allowances of $678,000 and $459,000, respectively	32,982,075	19,114,117
Current portion of workers' compensation deposit	475,549	610,473
Prepaid expenses and other	729,697	305,151
Deferred tax asset	1,238,955	661,645
Amounts due from related parties	--	406,376
Total current assets	55,888,923	26,882,413
PROPERTY AND EQUIPMENT, at cost:		
Computer equipment	2,852,320	1,399,408
Office equipment	2,241,392	1,461,945
Leasehold improvements and other	1,286,134	969,208
	6,379,846	3,830,561
Less accumulated depreciation and amortization	(2,353,511)	(1,698,080)
Total property and equipment, net	4,026,335	2,132,481
OTHER ASSETS:		
Workers' compensation deposit, less current portion	106,369	106,369
Intangible assets, less accumulated amortization of $1,941,000 and $457,000, respectively	57,456,417	17,798,588
Deposits and other assets	811,527	372,973
Total other assets	58,374,313	18,277,930
Total assets	$118,289,571	$47,292,824

LIABILITIES AND SHAREHOLDERS' EQUITY

	1997	1996
CURRENT LIABILITIES:		
Accounts payable	$971,775	$600,504
Accrued payroll costs	3,566,859	2,110,554
Current portion of workers' compensation reserve	2,537,995	1,501,669
Accrued liabilities	663,042	408,027
Income taxes payable	946,611	466,726
Accrued acquisition earnouts	4,412,658	4,782,689
Total current liabilities	13,098,940	9,870,169
LONG-TERM LIABILITIES:		
Workers' compensation reserve, less current portion	535,580	375,418
Deferred income tax liability	193,762	213,056
Deferred compensation liability	126,206	--
Total long-term liabilities	855,548	588,474
COMMITMENTS AND CONTINGENCIES (Notes 2, 3, and 5)		
SHAREHOLDERS' EQUITY:		
Common stock $0.01 par value 20,000,000 shares authorized; 12,653,002 and 8,706,020 shares issued and outstanding, respectively	126,530	87,060
Additional paid-in capital	91,152,122	31,216,917
Retained earnings	13,056,431	5,530,204
Total shareholders' equity	104,335,083	36,834,181
Total liabilities and shareholders' equity	$118,289,571	$ 47,292,824

Required

a. Contrast SOS's positive net income with its negative CFOA.
b. Draw a simple graph showing the trends in net income and CFOA. Evaluate these trends.
c. From the data above, what is the primary reason for SOS's negative CFOA?
d. Use balance sheet data to verify or confirm your answer from part (c). Explain why these data are confirmatory.
e. Calculate the following ratios, for each year:
   1. cash return on assets (1997 and 1996 only)
   2. quality of income
   3. cash interest coverage
f. Based on these ratios, evaluate SOS's performance each year. In what areas, do the cash flow ratios indicate positive or negative performances?
g. What additional information would be useful in evaluating SOS's performance?

Critical Thinking

Compare and Contrast CFOA for Two Companies

5-64 The following financial statements from Eli Lilly and Company and Pfizer INC. were downloaded from the SEC's EDGAR database:

Consolidated Statements of Cash Flows
ELI LILLY AND COMPANY AND SUBSIDIARIES
(Dollars in millions)

Year Ended December 31	1997	1996	1995
Cash Flows From Operating Activities			
Net income (loss).........................	$(385.1)	$1,523.5	$2,290.9
Adjustments To Reconcile Net Income (Loss) to Cash Flows From Operating Activities			
Depreciation and amortization............	509.8	543.5	553.7
Change in deferred taxes.................	(293.0)	207.3	144.0
Gain on sale of DowElanco, net of tax.....	(303.5)	--	--
Asset impairment, net of tax.............	2,429.6	--	--
Net gain on disposition of discontinued operations...........................	--	--	(921.5)
Other noncash income--net................	(37.8)	(97.8)	(9.8)
	1,920.0	2,176.5	2,057.3
Changes in operating assets and liabilities:			
Receivables--(increase) decrease.......	(4.7)	104.4	(189.3)
Inventories--(increase)..............	(65.8)	(42.2)	(22.1)
Other assets--(increase).............	(22.2)	(51.7)	(114.5)
Accounts payable and other liabilities--increase (decrease)....	573.1	(195.6)	93.2
	480.4	(185.1)	(232.7)
Net Cash From Operating Activities.........	2,400.4	1,991.4	1,824.6
Cash Flows From Investing Activities			
Acquisitions..............................	--	(97.1)	(36.8)
Additions to property and equipment........	(366.3)	(443.9)	(551.3)
Disposals of property and equipment........	11.5	11.2	21.5
Additions to other assets.................	(34.2)	(40.8)	(54.1)
Reductions of investments.................	365.7	396.9	430.8
Additions to investments..................	(388.5)	(294.3)	(372.9)
Proceeds from sale of DowElanco...............	1,221.5	--	--
Net Cash From (Used for) Investing Activities............................	809.7	(468.0)	(562.8)

Net Cash From (Used for) Investing Activities (from page 194).............	809.7	(468.0)	(562.8)
Cash Flows From Financing Activities			
Dividends paid............................	(818.0)	(753.2)	(747.2)
Purchases of common stock and other capital transactions...................	(351.3)	(314.5)	(156.0)
Issuances under stock plans................	205.4	218.4	54.7
Proceeds from issuance of subsidiary stock.	160.0	--	--
Decrease in short-term borrowings..........	(1,146.0)	(801.4)	(967.7)
Additions to long-term debt................	2.8	--	1,019.5
Reductions of long-term debt...............	(7.5)	(10.4)	(17.0)
Net Cash Used for Financing Activities.....	(1,954.6)	(1,661.1)	(813.7)
Effect of exchange rate changes on cash....	(121.7)	(48.1)	14.5
Net increase (decrease) in cash and cash equivalents.......................	1,133.8	(185.8)	462.6
Cash and cash equivalents at beginning of year..............................	813.7	999.5	536.9
Cash and cash equivalents at end of year....	$1,947.5	$ 813.7	$ 999.5
Cash payments of interest..................	243.9	292.9	271.7
Cash payments of taxes.....................	542.0	289.0	449.0

PFIZER INC AND SUBSIDIARY COMPANIES
CONSOLIDATED STATEMENT OF CASH FLOWS

	Year ended December 31 (millions of dollars)		
	1997	1996	1995
Operating Activities			
Net income	$2,213	$1,929	$1,573
Adjustments to reconcile net income to net cash provided by operating activities:			
Depreciation and amortization of intangibles	502	430	374
Deferred taxes and other	24	89	64
Changes in assets and liabilities, net of effect of businesses acquired and divested:			
Accounts receivable	(503)	(255)	(290)
Inventories	(375)	(149)	(25)
Prepaid and other assets	(138)	(208)	(171)
Accounts payable and accrued liabilities	(26)	66	320
Income taxes payable	(127)	23	88
Other deferred items	59	142	(112)
Net cash provided by operating activities	1,629	2,067	1,821

Net cash provided by operating activities (from page 195)	1,629	2,067	1,821
Investing Activities			
Purchases of property, plant, and equipment	(943)	(774)	(696)
Purchases of short-term investments	(221)	(2,851)	(2,611)
Proceeds from redemptions of short-term investments	29	3,490	2,185
Purchases of long-term investments	(76)	(820)	(151)
Purchases and redemptions of short-term investments by financial subsidiaries	45	(11)	(30)
(Increase)/decrease in loans and long-term investments by financial subsidiaries	(20)	52	330
Acquisitions, net of cash acquired	--	(451)	(1,521)
Proceeds from the sale of businesses	21	353	--
Other investing activities	143	75	151
Net cash used in investing activities	(1,022)	(937)	(2,343)
Financing Activities			
Proceeds from issuances of long-term debt	57	636	502
Repayments of long-term debt	(269)	(804)	(52)
Increase/(decrease) in short-term debt	370	259	(444)
Purchases of common stock	(586)	(27)	(108)
Cash dividends paid	(881)	(771)	(659)
Stock option transactions	411	280	205
Other financing activities	50	45	37
Net cash used in financing activities	(848)	(382)	(519)
Effect of exchange rate changes on cash and cash equivalents	(32)	(1)	(14)
Net increase/(decrease) in cash and cash equivalents	(273)	747	(1,055)
Cash and cash equivalents at beginning of year	1,150	403	1,458
Cash and cash equivalents at end of year	$ 877	$ 1,150	$ 403
Supplemental Cash Flow Information			
Cash paid during the period for:			
Income taxes	$ 856	$ 709	$ 646
Interest	151	139	175

Required

a. Contrast Lilly's CFOA with Pfizer's CFOA.

b. Draw a simple graph showing these trends in CFOA. Evaluate these trends. Which company exhibits more variability in its CFOA trends? Discuss these trends.

c. How are these two company's cash flow management strategies different? Similar?

d. What other data would be helpful in evaluating cash flows for these two companies?

e. Calculate the following ratios for each year:

   1. Quality of income
   2. Cash interest coverage

f. Evaluate each company's performance, using only the information in the cash flow statement. In what areas do the cash flow ratios indicate positive or negative performances?

g. What additional information would be useful in evaluating each company's performance?

Internet

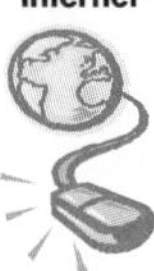

Identifying Cash Flows

5-65 Locate the most recent financial statements for the computer manufacturing companies listed below. You may use either the 10-K available at EDGAR **(www.sec.gov/edgarhp.htm)** or the annual report available at the company page on the Web. The annual report is usually located in the Investor Information section.

Corporation	Home Page Location
Digital	**www.digital.com**
IBM	**www.ibm.com**
Apple	**www.apple.com**
Compaq	**www.compaq.com**

Required:

a. Identify the amount of cash flow from operating activities.
b. Identify the amount of cash flow from investing activities.
c. Identify the amount of cash flow from financing activities.
d. Identify the amount of net cash flow.
e. Identify the amount of interest paid.
f. Identify the amount of taxes paid.
g. Compute cash return on assets.
h. Compute quality of sales.
i. Compute quality of income.
j. Compute cash interest coverage.

Comparing Net Income with Cash Flow

Internet

5-66 The 10-K for Oncogene Science, a biotechnology company, contains a thorough description of its main products. Locate the most recent 10-K from the EDGAR archives **(www.sec.gov/edgarhp.htm).**

Required

a. What are the main products of Oncogene Science?
b. Scroll down to the most recent set of financial statements. Using the income statement and the statement of cash flows, answer the following questions:
   1. What is the reported amount of net income?
   2. How much are net cash flows from operating activities?
   3. How much are net cash flows from investing activities? What is the primary component of this item?
   4. How much are net cash flows from financing activities?
   5. How does Oncogene Science cover its shortfall in cash flows from operating activities?

Internet

Identify Strategic Information

5-67 Locate the three 10-Q filings and the 10-K for the most recently completed fiscal year for Cedar Fair, L.P., and H&R Block. These statements can be retrieved from the EDGAR archives **(www.sec.gov/edgarhp.htm).**

Required

a. What is the main business of these two companies? What is the peak season for each of these two companies? Which quarter do you think will reflect this peak level of activity?
b. From the financial statements in the 10-K, identify the starting and ending dates for the most recently completed fiscal year.

a p p e n d i x

5 Preparing a Statement of Cash Flows

INTRODUCTION

Conceptually, the statement of cash flows could be prepared by analyzing the cash flow effects of each transaction and accumulating that information. Most accounting systems, however, are not designed to implement such an approach. Instead, cash flows are inferred from items on the balance sheet and income statement.

Operating Activities

This section examines the income statement and balance sheet relationships that are relevant to determining cash flows from operating activities under the direct approach. The income statement and comparative balance sheets for the Peak Company that appear in Exhibits 5A-1 and 5A-2, respectively, are used to illustrate these relationships and to generate the statement of cash flows that appears in Exhibit 5-1.

Collections from Customers Peak began 2000 with an accounts receivable balance of $4,000. Let us assume that Peak collected these receivables in 2000. (This is a reasonable assumption, but our result would not be affected by changing it.) The $4,000 is a cash inflow in 2000. Peak then made sales of $68,700 in 2000. What portion of these sales was collected in cash in 2000? Because we assumed that the beginning balance in accounts receivable has already been collected, the ending balance must have been part of 2000 sales. Therefore, all of 2000 sales have been collected in cash, except for the ending balance in accounts receivable. Accordingly, cash collected from customers can be computed as the beginning balance in accounts receivable plus the portion of 2000 sales that has been collected in 2000.

Cash received from customers	=	Beginning balance in Accounts Receivable	+	Sales	−	Ending balance in Accounts Receivable
$68,200	=	$4,000	+	$68,700	−	$4,500

Interest Received A similar relationship can be used for cash collected in the form of interest on the firm's investments.

Interest received from customers	=	Beginning balance in Interest Receivable	+	Interest Revenue	−	Ending balance in Interest Receivable
$1,300	=	$300	+	$1,100	−	$100

EXHIBIT 5A-1 Income Statement

The Peak Company
Income Statement
For the Year Ended December 31, 2000

Revenues:		
Sales	$68,700	
Interest revenue	1,100	
		$69,800
Expenses:		
Cost of goods sold	42,500	
Salary expense	17,000	
Depreciation expense	2,000	
Interest expense	1,000	
Tax expense	2,000	
		64,500
Net Income		$ 5,300

EXHIBIT 5A-2 Balance Sheet

The Peak Company
Balance Sheet

	December 31 2000	1999
Cash	$33,600	$22,000
Accounts receivable	4,500	4,000
Interest receivable	100	300
Inventory	11,000	10,000
Property, plant, and equipment (net)	31,500	30,000
Investments	12,000	0
Total assets	$92,700	$66,300
Accounts payable	$ 6,000	$ 3,000
Salaries payable	300	400
Interest payable	200	0
Short-term debt	0	12,000
Long-term debt	30,000	5,000
Common stock	35,000	30,000
Retained earnings	21,200	15,900
Total liabilities and shareholders' equity	$92,700	$66,300

Payments to Employees During 2000, Peak incurred a salary expense of \$17,000. But how much cash did it actually pay to its employees in 2000? At the beginning of 2000, Peak had a liability to its employees of \$400. Let us make the reasonable assumption that this amount was paid to employees in the early part of 2000, and thus constitutes a cash outflow in that year. This implies that the ending balance in salaries payable must have arisen from 2000's expense and reflects that part of the expense that has not been paid at the end of 2000. Accordingly, cash payments to employees can be computed as the beginning balance in salaries payable plus the amount paid in 2000 for 2000's salary expense (salary expense minus the ending balance in salaries payable).

Payments to employees	=	Beginning balance in Salaries Payable	+	Salary Expense	−	Ending balance in Salaries Payable
\$17,100	=	\$400	+	\$17,000	−	\$300

Payments to Suppliers Calculating cash paid to suppliers (for merchandise) is a bit more complex than the preceding illustrations. First, note that cost of goods sold is the income statement item related to cash paid to suppliers. However, the purchases for a period are more closely related to cash outflows than is cost of goods sold. How can purchases be computed based on the information contained in the financial statements? The following equation can help:

Cost of goods sold = Beginning Inventory + Purchases − Ending Inventory

The sum of beginning inventory plus purchases reflects the cost of goods available for sale. That is, this sum equals the cost of goods on hand during the year that could have been sold. All of these goods will have been sold by year-end, except for those that remain on hand at the end of the year (ending inventory). Thus, subtracting ending inventory from the sum of beginning inventory plus purchases yields the cost of goods that have been sold during the year.

The equation can be rearranged to solve for purchases:

Purchases	=	Cost of Goods Sold	+	Ending Inventory	−	Beginning Inventory
\$43,500	=	\$42,500	+	\$11,000	−	\$10,000

Because purchases can be made on credit, they do not necessarily reflect cash outflows. Assume that accounts payable relate solely to the acquisition of merchandise and that the beginning balance is paid in early 2000. This represents a cash outflow in 2000. Moreover, the ending balance in accounts payable must have arisen from 2000 purchases. Thus, all the purchases made in 2000 have been paid for in that year, except for the ending balance in accounts payable. Therefore, cash paid to suppliers equals the beginning balance in accounts payable plus the portion of 2000's purchases that was paid in 2000 (purchases minus the ending balance in accounts payable).

Payments to suppliers	=	Beginning balance in Accounts Payable	+	Purchases	−	Ending balance in Accounts Payable
$40,500	=	$3,000	+	$43,500	−	$6,000

Payments for Interest The previous discussions can be used to justify the following relationship regarding cash paid for interest:

Interest paid	=	Beginning balance in Interest Payable	+	Interest Expense	−	Ending balance in Interest Payable
$800	=	$0	+	$1,000	−	$200

Depreciation Although Peak's income statement contains a $2,000 depreciation charge, depreciation expense does not appear on the statement of cash flows prepared under the direct approach. This is because depreciation expense does not involve a cash outflow. Recall the analysis of depreciation:

ASSETS	=	LIABILITIES	+	SHAREHOLDERS' EQUITY
Equipment −$2,000				Retained earnings −$2,000 (depreciation expense)

Because cash is not affected, depreciation expense has no place in the direct approach to the statement of cash flows.

Taxes Peak's 2000 tax expense of $2,000 happens to equal the amount of taxes paid on the statement of cash flows. Because no tax liability appears on either the beginning or the ending balance sheet, this makes sense. More generally, if the related balance sheet item has the same balance at the beginning and the end of the year, the cash flow statement amount will equal the expense reported on the income statement.

Other Items Peak's income statement and balance sheets contain only a sampling of the accounts that could possibly appear. For example, the income statement could include selling expenses and the balance sheet could include prepaid expenses and accrued liabilities. Accordingly, Peak's situation is only an illustration of the steps needed to adjust income statement numbers to cash flow figures.

As a general guide to preparing the operating activities section of the statement of cash flows under the direct approach, the following steps should be taken:

1. Ignore income statement items that are unrelated to cash flows (such as depreciation expense).
2. Ignore gains and losses associated with nonoperating activities (such as extraordinary gains and losses or gains and losses on disposals of noncurrent assets).
3. Adjust all the remaining income statement items by the changes in related balance sheet accounts. Be sure to include in the adjustments all balance sheet accounts related to operating activities.

Indirect Approach As you know, the operating activities section can also be prepared under the indirect approach. This approach starts with net income and makes adjustments to convert net income to cash flow from operating activities. Exhibit 5-3 contains Peak's cash flow statement using the indirect approach. The first adjustment is depreciation expense, which has been subtracted in calculating net income. Yet it does not result in a cash outflow. Accordingly, net income understates the cash flow generated from operating activities. Therefore, to modify net income so that it reflects cash flow, depreciation expense must be added back.

The next adjustment relates to accounts receivable. Recall how Peak's sales were converted to a cash flow figure under the direct method:

Cash received from customers	=	Beginning balance in Accounts Payable	+	Sales	−	Ending balance in Accounts Payable
$68,200	=	$4,000	+	$68,700	−	$4,500

Rearranging the equation slightly yields:

Cash received from customers	=	Sales	+	Beginning balance in Accounts Receivable	−	Ending balance in Accounts Receivable
	=	$68,700	+	$4,000	−	$4,500
$68,200	=	$68,700			− $500	

If the ending balance in accounts receivable is greater than the beginning balance, combining these components results in a negative number. Thus, to convert sales to a cash flow figure, sales must be reduced by the increase in accounts receivable. Because sales are included in net income, net income must be reduced by the increase in accounts receivable to compute a cash flow figure. More intuitively, an increase in accounts receivable suggests that not all the current year's sales have been collected in cash. Therefore, sales (or net income) must be reduced by an increase in accounts receivable.

The other adjustments in Exhibit 5-3 are handled in a similar fashion.

INVESTING AND FINANCING ACTIVITIES

Although the information for preparing the operating activities section can often be obtained from the income statement and balance sheets, this is not usually the case for investing activities and financing activities. A detailed analysis of the relevant accounts is needed to identify the inflows and outflows of cash. This information is usually readily available to a firm's accountants, because relatively few transactions are involved and documentation (such as bank notes) is easily accessible. Also note that the investing and financing activities sections are the same under both the direct and indirect approaches.

SUMMARY OF LEARNING OBJECTIVES

Calculate cash flow from operating activities by using relationships among income statement and balance sheet items.

Under the direct approach, individual income statement line items are adjusted by their related balance sheet accounts. For example, sales are adjusted by the change in accounts receivable. Under the indirect approach, net income is adjusted for the change in these same balance sheet accounts. Additionally, nonoperating items and items with no cash flow consequence must also be eliminated from net income.

Using Direct Method to Calculate Cash Flow from Operating Activities

5A-1 The following financial statements for Lucy Enterprises are provided:

Income Statement for Year Ending December 31, 1999

Sales revenues	$550,000	
Cost of goods sold	210,000	
Gross margin		$340,000
Salary expenses	(115,000)	
Interest expense	(15,000)	
Interest revenue	20,000	110,000
Net income before taxes		230,000
Tax expense		92,000
Net income		$138,000

Balance Sheet at Year-End

	1999	1998		1999	1998
Cash	$225,000	$100,000	Accounts payable	$ 30,000	$ 20,000
Accounts receivable	124,000	135,000	Salaries payable	5,000	4,000
Inventory	35,000	21,000	Interest payable	3,000	12,000
			Taxes payable	2,500	3,500
	384,000	256,000		40,500	39,500
Property, plant, and equipment	101,000	134,000	Shareholders' equity	444,500	350,500
Totals	$485,000	$390,000		$485,000	$390,000

Required

Prepare the cash flow from operating activities section of the statement of cash flows, using the direct method and the indirect method. The following amounts must first be calculated when using the direct method:

- Cash collections from customers
- Cash payments to suppliers
- Cash payments to employees
- Taxes paid
- Interest paid
- Interest collected
- Purchases

Using Direct Method to Calculate Cash Flow from Operating Activities

5A-2 The following condensed information (dollars in thousands) is available from Mary's Muffins. Assume that all sales are credit sales (accounts receivable) and all purchases are also on credit (accounts payable).

	December 31 Year 1	Year 2
Balance Sheet Data:		
Accounts receivable	$55	$ 53
Prepaid expenses	13	15
Salaries payable	22	25
Taxes payable	17	13
Inventory	32	26
Accounts payable	27	21
Income Statement Data:		
Sales revenues		$550
Cost of goods sold		210
Salaries expense		112
Tax expense		57
Depreciation expense		29
Other expense		$ 21

Required

Prepare the operating activities section of Year 2's statement of cash flows, using the direct method.

Preparing a Statement of Cash Flows

5A-3 The following are comparative balance sheets for the Paulino Corporation for 2000 and 1999 and the income statement for the year ended December 31, 2000:

Paulino Corporation
Comparative Balance Sheets
December 31

	2000	1999
Assets		
Cash	$ 89,000	$ 60,000
Accounts receivable	65,000	50,000
Inventory	200,000	90,000
Land	100,000	225,000
Equipment, net	371,000	380,000
	$825,000	$805,000
Liabilities and Shareholders' Equity		
Accounts payable	54,000	32,000
Dividends payable	15,000	0
Interest payable	6,000	8,000
Mortgage payable	130,000	305,000
Invested capital	280,000	280,000
Retained earnings	340,000	180,000
	$825,000	$805,000

Paulino Corporation
Income Statement
For the Year Ended December 31, 2000

Sales		$1,200,000
Cost of goods sold		(720,000)
Gross profit		480,000
Operating and other expenses		
Depreciation	(9,000)	
Other operating expenses	(275,000)	
Gain on sale of land	15,000	
Interest expense	(10,000)	(279,000)
Net income		$ 201,000

Additional Information:

1. Dividends declared during the year were $41,000.
2. Land at a cost of $125,000 was sold for $140,000.
3. The only change in equipment was the depreciation expense.
4. All other balance sheet account changes are from normal transactions.

Required

Use the direct method to prepare a statement of cash flows for Paulino Corporation.

Preparing a Statement of Cash Flows

5A-4 The following financial statements for Swale, LTD are provided:

Swale Limited
Income Statement
For the Year Ended December 31, 2000

Revenues:		
Sales	$97,800	
Interest revenue	1,300	
		$99,100
Expenses:		
Cost of goods sold	56,500	
Salary expense	19,000	
Depreciation expense	3,000	
Interest expense	1,500	
Tax expense	2,500	82,500
Net Income		$ 16,600

Swale Limited
Balance Sheet

	December 31	
	2000	**1999**
Cash	$35,600	$24,000
Accounts receivable	5,500	3,000
Inventory	21,000	11,000
Property, plant, and equipment (net)	21,500	20,000
Investments	12,000	0
Total assets	$95,600	$58,000
Accounts payable	$5,000	$2,000
Salaries payable	600	500
Short-term debt	0	12,000
Long-term debt	25,000	6,000
Common stock	36,000	25,100
Retained earnings	29,000	12,400
Total liabilities and shareholders' equity	$95,600	$58,000

Required

Prepare a statement of cash flows.

Working from Operating Cash Flows to Net Income

5-A5 The Blunt Instrument Company reports cash flow from operations of $65 million for 2001. You are provided the following additional information for the year:

1. Customer accounts receivable increased by $6 million.
2. Dividends paid to common shareholders were $20 million.
3. Depreciation expense was $24 million.
4. Noncurrent debt was increased by $35 million.
5. Supplier accounts payable decreased by $8 million.
6. Inventory balances increased by $18 million.
7. Income tax payable increased by $9 million.

Required

Based on the above information, determine the amount of net income reported by Blunt for 2001.

Preparing a Cash Flow Statement Using Comparative Balance Sheets

5-A6 The Limpid Pool Company reports net income of $25 million for 2000. Balance sheets at the beginning and end of the year are shown below.

	December 31	
	1999	**2000**
	(Dollars in millions)	
Cash	$ 50	$ 70
Other current assets	80	145
Property, plant, and equipment (net)	170	135
Total assets	$300	$350
Current liabilities	$20	$15
Noncurrent liabilities	180	195
Common stock	80	110
Retained earnings	20	30
Total liabilities and shareholders' equity	$300	$350

The firm did not acquire any noncurrent assets during 2000.

Required

Determine the following amounts for 2000:

a. Dividends paid
b. Cash flow from operating activities
c. Cash flow from investing activities
d. Cash flow from financing activities

chapter 6

Current Assets

LEARNING OBJECTIVES

1. Identify the items included in cash.
2. Understand the need for cash planning and how firms exercise control over cash.
3. Comprehend the basic accounting for marketable securities and the limitations of generally accepted accounting principles in this area.
4. Determine if a firm is properly managing its accounts receivable.
5. Assess if a firm's allowance for uncollectible accounts is adequate.
6. Understand the various inventory cost flow assumptions and the effect that the firm's choice of inventory method has on its taxes, the quality of information in its financial statements,its management compensation, its loan covenants, and its stock price.
7. Analyze a firm's inventory management practices.
8. Understand the nature of prepaid expenses.

Appendix: Prepare a bank reconciliation.

INTRODUCTION

This chapter examines five prominent current assets:

1. cash and cash equivalents,
2. marketable securities,
3. accounts receivable,
4. inventories, and
5. prepaid expenses.

For each asset, we examine the accounting issues and the information contained in the financial statements.

CASH AND CASH EQUIVALENTS

Cash is the most liquid asset a business can own. Most firms devote considerable effort to the management and control of cash. Because a firm's creditors expect payment in cash, a sufficient amount of cash must always be available to meet obligations as they become due. This necessitates careful scheduling of cash inflows and outflows.

Although an adequate cash balance is essential, excessive holdings of cash should be avoided. Cash deposited in checking accounts (or even savings accounts) usually does not earn very much, if any, interest. Cash amounts over and above those needed to meet obligations due in the near future should be invested in assets earning higher returns.

The liquidity of cash also makes it easily pilfered. Firms must institute internal control procedures so that cash is properly accounted for and safeguarded. Failure to do so may tempt employees to misappropriate the firm's cash and may also result in various accounting errors.

Composition of Cash

Cash is composed of funds that are readily available. This includes cash on hand and cash on deposit in bank accounts that do not restrict the withdrawal of cash. Deposits in checking accounts would qualify because those balances can be withdrawn on demand. Because banks rarely enforce restrictions on withdrawals from savings accounts, they are usually classified as cash. Also classified as cash are money market funds permitting withdrawal by check, checks from customers awaiting deposit, and foreign currency (converted to dollars). Items not classified as cash include certificates of deposit, stamps, and postdated checks.

Large corporations may have hundreds of checking accounts. Multiple accounts are needed because firms have numerous physical locations and each location makes expenditures. Firms also find it convenient to use separate accounts for specific purposes. Many firms use one or more checking accounts solely for payroll purposes, for example. All checking accounts are condensed into the one cash item on the balance sheet.

Many firms keep **petty cash funds** on hand to pay for small, incidental expenditures, such as cab fare or delivery charges. These funds are included in the cash amount on the balance sheet. Many retailers also keep **change funds.** These funds enable cashiers to make change for their customers. Change funds are also included in the cash item on the balance sheet.

As a part of borrowing agreements with banks, firms sometimes agree to maintain **compensating balances.** These are minimum amounts the firm agrees to keep on deposit at the lending bank in accounts that pay little or no interest. As a result, the bank is able to use these funds interest free. This provides the bank with additional compensation for lending funds to the firm. Compensating balances are usually included in the balance sheet cash amount and are disclosed in the notes to the financial statements.

Instead of showing a cash item on their balance sheets, some firms use the term *cash and cash equivalents*. Recall from previous chapters that **cash equivalents** are short-term, highly liquid investments that will mature within three months. Examples include certificates of deposit, treasury bills, and commercial paper (short-term obligations of corporations). Because cash equivalents can readily be converted into known amounts of cash, reporting a combined cash and cash equivalents figure is probably as informative as reporting each figure separately.

OshKosh B'Gosh (OB) follows the practice of reporting a combined figure for cash and cash equivalents. Exhibit 6-1 contains an excerpt from its financial statement note describing this policy.

Control of Cash

As previously mentioned, because cash is so liquid and so easily transported, special care must be exercised to ensure that it is properly recorded and safeguarded. Most

EXHIBIT 6-1 Disclosure of Cash Reporting Policy

OshKosh B'Gosh, Inc.
1997 Annual Report
Note 1 (Partial)

Cash equivalents consist of highly liquid debt instruments such as money market accounts and commercial paper with original maturities of three months or less. The Company's policy is to invest cash in conservative instruments as part of its cash management program and to evaluate the credit exposure of any investment. Cash and cash equivalents are stated at cost, which approximates market value.

corporations follow several sound management practices that enhance their control over cash. Employees who are permitted access to cash, for example, should not also have access to the accounting records for cash. Access to both cash and the accounting records might enable an employee to misappropriate cash and to conceal the theft by altering the records.

As an illustration, retail clerks (who have ready access to cash) should not "read" the cash register. That is, they should not have the responsibility of ascertaining the daily sales total from the register's internal record and recording this amount in the accounting records. As shown in Exhibit 6-2, clerks with such dual access could take some cash and hide the theft by reducing the firm's recorded cash collections.

Checking accounts with banks provide firms with several cash control advantages. First, cash receipts can be deposited daily. Limiting the amount of time that cash is on the firm's premises reduces the possibility that it will be misappropriated.

Second, checks provide a written record of a firm's disbursements. Such a record would not necessarily exist if disbursements were made in currency. Moreover, most firms require that checks be supported by underlying documentation such as pur-

EXHIBIT 6-2 Poor Control Over Cash

chase orders, invoices, and receiving reports. This helps ensure that only valid expenditures are made and provides the basis for an analysis of costs and expenses.

Third, by limiting the number of people authorized to sign checks, firms restrict access to cash and reduce the possibility that cash will be used for unintended purposes.

Finally, bank statements provide a monthly listing of deposits and withdrawals. So not only does the firm keep track of its cash flows, but so does the bank. Thus, the bank statement can be used to verify the firm's cash records.

This verification process is accomplished via a **bank reconciliation,** which is a detailed comparison of the firm's records and the bank statement. Because the bank reconciliation may uncover errors related to cash, it should be prepared by an employee who has no other cash-related responsibilities. The preparation of a bank reconciliation is illustrated in the appendix to this chapter.

Analysis of Cash

The most informative analysis of cash pertains to cash flows. Chapter 5, "Statement of Cash Flows," examined the statement of cash flows, which summarized the inflows and outflows of cash. A firm's ability to generate cash enables it to pay obligations as they become due, replace and expand productive assets, and provide a return to investors. Chapter 5 described analyses that provide insights into this ability.

The balance sheet does not contain information about a firm's cash *flows*. It simply indicates the amount of cash a firm holds on a given date. Nevertheless, some useful information about cash can be obtained from the balance sheet. The amount of cash on hand and the trend in the cash balance over time can be ascertained. Also, because most current liabilities are paid in cash, many analysts relate the cash balance to current liabilities. This is done via the cash to current liabilities ratio:

$$\text{Cash to Current liabilities ratio} = \frac{\text{Cash}}{\text{Current liabilities}}$$

Exhibit 6-3 contains cash-related information for OB. OB's cash position decreased substantially from 1996 to 1997. The cash balance declined from $31,201,000 to $13,779,000. The cash to current liabilities ratio also decreased significantly, from 70.4% in 1996 to 28.5% in 1997.

	1997	1996
Cash to Current liabilities ratio	$\frac{\$13{,}779}{\$48{,}286} = 28.5\%$	$\frac{\$31{,}201}{\$44{,}293} = 70.4\%$

EXHIBIT 6-3 Financial Statement Information

OshKosh B'Gosh
Selected Cash-Related Information
(Dollars in thousands)

	1997	1996
Cash and cash equivalents	$ 13,779	$ 31,201
Current assets	$131,048	$148,934
Current liabilities	$ 48,286	$ 44,293

The decline in the cash balance and the cash to current liabilities ratio is potentially worrisome. What caused this decline? OB has attempted to operate more efficiently by utilizing a smaller cash balance. Recall that although firms need to maintain a cash balance sufficient to meet their obligations, excessive cash balances are undesirable because idle cash earns, at best, a modest return. Given that OB has virtually no debt, has unused lines of credit available, and has strong cash flow from operations, the decline in the cash balance should not cause alarm.

Note that the cash to current liabilities ratio is a severe test of liquidity. To see this, compare OB's 1997 cash to current liabilities ratio of 28.5% to its current ratio, which was discussed in Chapter 3, "The Balance Sheet."

$$\text{Current ratio} = \frac{\text{Current assets}}{\text{Current liabilities}} = \frac{\$131{,}048}{\$48{,}286} = 2.71$$

Both ratios contain current liabilities in the denominator. However, because the cash to current liabilities ratio has a much smaller numerator, a lower ratio results.

Implications for Managers

Financial statements provide managers and others with historical information about cash. Managers must ensure that sufficient cash is available on an ongoing basis to enable the firm to meet its commitments. As in many cases, managers must be proactive, not reactive, and the historical information can help with decision making.

The management of cash begins with projecting the amount and timing of future cash flows. This enables firms to forecast their cash balances over the course of a specified time period. If positive net cash flows are expected, managers must identify profitable uses of that cash. Alternatively, if negative net cash flows are projected, managers must identify additional sources of cash. Possibilities include short-term debt, long-term debt, additional investments by owners, and the liquidation of assets. Other strategies might include attempting to speed up cash collections from customers and delaying payments to suppliers.

MARKETABLE SECURITIES

Many firms experience uneven cash flows during a year. Department stores, for example, make a large portion of their sales during November and December, resulting in significant cash inflows. In many instances, such large amounts of cash are not immediately needed to fund operations. Many firms elect to put excess cash balances into short-term investments. These investments, known as **marketable securities,** typically produce higher earnings than those available from bank accounts, thus enabling firms to increase their earnings.

Types of Investments

Firms can choose from two general types of securities. **Equity securities** represent ownership interests in other corporations. For example, General Motors (GM) can purchase shares of IBM stock, which would be reflected on GM's balance sheet as an asset.

Firms can also invest in **debt securities,** which result from lending transactions. For example, if GM were to lend funds to IBM, IBM would probably issue a debt security as written evidence of the indebtedness. The security might be commercial paper (indicating short-term borrowing) or a bond (indicating long-term borrowing). In either case, the security would appear on GM's balance sheet as an asset.

This chapter deals primarily with investments in equity securities that are classified as current assets. As you know, current assets are either consumed or converted into cash within one year. Thus, we cover only investments that will be held a relatively short period of time. Long-term investments are covered in Chapter 13, "Reporting Issues for Affiliated and International Companies."

Marketability

This chapter is also restricted to securities that are **marketable.** A security is marketable if it is traded on a securities exchange registered with the Securities and Exchange Commission (SEC) or if its price is available through the National Association of Securities Dealers Automated Quotations systems or the National Quotation Bureau. Securities traded on foreign exchanges may also qualify.

Securities that are not readily marketable are unlikely candidates for short-term investments of excess cash. Nonmarketable securities cannot necessarily be liquidated when the investor desires to do so. Investments in nonmarketable securities are usually classified as long-term investments.

Basic Accounting

SFAS No. 115, *Accounting for Certain Investments in Debt and Equity Securities*, governs the accounting for short-term investments in marketable securities. This standard requires that a firm classify such investments as either **trading securities** or **available-for-sale securities.** Trading securities are intended to be held for brief periods of time to generate profits from short-term differences in price. For example, investment banks will often buy an entire stock issue from a corporation with the intent of almost immediately selling the stock to the public. The investment bank would classify the stock as a trading security.

Marketable equity securities not classified as trading securities are classified as available-for-sale. Nonfinancial organizations classify most of their investments in marketable equity securities as available-for-sale. Proper classification is important because the accounting treatment differs for the two categories. Because most corporations classify their securities as available-for-sale, this chapter emphasizes the accounting procedures for that classification.

Available-for-Sale Securities Marketable equity securities classified as available-for-sale should be accounted for at market value on the balance sheet date. The difference between a security's historical cost and its market value is an *unrealized* gain or loss. The term *unrealized* indicates that the gain or loss has not been confirmed by an actual sale. However, because the securities are highly marketable, the value change is virtually certain, and, accordingly, the gain or loss is a valid and useful measure of a change in wealth.

Unrealized gains and losses on available-for-sale securities do not, however, appear on the income statement. Instead, these gains and losses appear in a special section of shareholders' equity that is distinct from invested capital or retained earnings. Also note that the marketable securities account continues to reflect the historical cost of the securities. The adjustment to market value is made to a valuation account, often labeled **allowance for unrealized gain/loss.**

To illustrate, assume that on December 1, 2000, Mega Company purchased marketable securities for $1,000. This analysis is straightforward.

	ASSETS		=	LIABILITIES	+	SHAREHOLDERS' EQUITY
	Cash	Marketable securities				
Dec. 1	− $1,000	+ $1,000				

On December 31, the securities are still on hand and have a market value of $980. To record the value change, reduce marketable securities by $20 via the allowance for unrealized loss and reduce shareholders' equity by $20.

	ASSETS		=	LIABILITIES	+	SHAREHOLDERS' EQUITY
	Marketable securities	Allowance for unrealized loss				Unrealized loss on marketable securities
Bal.	$1,000					
Dec. 31		− $20				− $20

In the asset section of the balance sheet, the $20 balance in allowance for unrealized loss is subtracted from marketable securities to show a net asset of $980. The account **unrealized loss on marketable securities** is a separate component of shareholders' equity. Keep in mind that it is *not* an income statement account.

Assume further that the securities are sold on January 10, 2001, for $990. Looking at the purchase and sale together, a $10 loss has been incurred. Because no loss was recognized on the income statement when the securities were revalued at the end of 2000, a $10 loss must now be reflected on the income statement.

The analysis is most easily completed in two steps. First, because the $20 loss is no longer unrealized, the entry to record that loss should be reversed. Second, cash is increased by $990, marketable securities are reduced by $1,000, and a $10 loss is recognized. This loss is termed *realized* because it has been confirmed by a cash transaction. This loss appears on the 2001 income statement.

	ASSETS			=	LIABILITIES	+	SHAREHOLDERS' EQUITY	
	Cash	Marketable securities	Allowance for unrealized loss				Unrealized loss on marketable securities	Retained earnings
Bal.		$1,000	− $20				− $20	
Jan. 10			+ $20				+ $20	
Jan. 10	+ $990	− $1,000						− $10 (realized loss)

Trading Securities Trading securities are also accounted for at market value. One major difference exists between the accounting for trading securities and that for securities classified as available-for-sale. Unrealized gains and losses on trading securities *are included* in net income, as opposed to being reflected in a special section of shareholders' equity. The FASB believes that, because trading securities are purchased to generate profits on short-term price changes, all unrealized gains and losses should be immediately reflected on the income statement.

Debt Securities The accounting for debt securities is a bit more complex. If a firm intends to hold a debt security until its maturity date, the security is valued at historical cost. Debt securities not intended to be held until maturity appear on the balance sheet at market value. However, because debt securities classified as current assets will be liquidated within the next year, a large discrepancy between cost and market value is unlikely. Thus, in most cases, financial statement readers can view the marketable debt securities figure in the current asset section as a very close approximation to market value.

Analysis of Marketable Securities

Marketable securities are reflected on the balance sheet at market value. Because these securities can be readily converted into known amounts of cash, such a valuation rule seems quite reasonable. Analysts evaluate the liquidity of a firm, in part, by examining current assets. The amount of cash a marketable security can be transformed into is likely to be much more relevant for liquidity assessment than is a security's historical cost.

Your accounting common sense probably suggests that all unrealized gains and losses on marketable securities should appear on the income statement. SFAS No. 115 precludes this treatment for securities classified as available-for-sale. The FASB's justification for this position relates to liabilities. The FASB tried but failed to agree on how to measure changes in the value of liabilities. Because net income might be distorted by including asset value changes in income while excluding similar changes for liabilities, the FASB decided to exclude changes in asset values from reported income.

The FASB's required procedures can be challenged on at least three grounds. First, some argue that two wrongs do not make a right. Changes in the value of marketable securities are valid gains and losses and should be included in net income, regardless of how liabilities are treated. Not doing so reduces the usefulness of net income as a measure of wealth changes and as an indicator of managerial performance.

Second, the FASB's procedures provide an opportunity for profit manipulation by management. By selecting to sell those securities that have either risen or fallen in value, managers can dictate whether gains or losses will be reported.

Third, the FASB created a new element of shareholders' equity (unrealized gain/loss on marketable securities) in order to exclude changes in the value of marketable securities from net income. This element is a new (and somewhat unusual) addition to the conventional financial accounting framework. Its existence compromises the basic notion that the change in shareholders' equity for a period equals net income plus the effects of direct contributions/withdrawals by the shareholders.

ACCOUNTS RECEIVABLE

Revenue transactions are usually undertaken for cash or on credit. Firms obviously prefer to make sales for cash because funds are immediately available to meet obligations, invest in productive endeavors, pay dividends, and so on. Moreover, cash sales entail no uncertainty about collectibility.

Credit Sales

Many firms, however, make a significant portion of their sales on credit. They do so because customers prefer deferring their payments. Credit transactions enable purchasers to use their cash for a longer period of time before paying the seller. Moreover, credit transactions permit the purchaser to inspect and actually use the goods prior to payment. Industry practices and competitive pressures force many firms to sell on credit, and credit sales to customers in the ordinary course of business give rise to **accounts receivable (trade receivables).**

Before making a credit sale, the credit standing of the customer should be assessed. Credit-worthiness is an important consideration in making a credit sale because it bears directly on a potential customer's ability and willingness to ultimately make payment. Various credit bureaus (such as Dun & Bradstreet and Equifax) provide credit ratings and other information for this purpose.

Selling only to customers with high credit ratings, however, will not necessarily maximize profits. Although such a policy would minimize receivables that prove to be uncollectible, a number of potentially profitable sales might be eliminated and the profit on these sales may well overshadow the expense of uncollectible accounts. Thus, a firm must decide how much credit to grant and to whom credit should be offered. Selecting a credit-rating cutoff in some middle range is probably optimal.

Accounting for Credit Sales

The analysis of credit sales is quite straightforward. The credit sale of merchandise for $100 would increase accounts receivable and shareholders' equity.

ASSETS	=	LIABILITIES	+	SHAREHOLDERS' EQUITY
Accounts receivable +$100				Retained earnings +$100 (sales)

When the cash is ultimately collected, the balance in cash is increased, and the accounts receivable balance is decreased.

ASSETS		=	LIABILITIES	+	SHAREHOLDERS' EQUITY
Cash +$100	Accounts receivable −$100				

Notice that revenue is recognized when the sale is made. The collection of cash does not result in the recognition of revenue. Rather, it merely transforms one asset (accounts receivable) into another (cash).

Discounts

When selling on credit, many firms offer discounts for early payment. Such discounts are offered primarily for two reasons. First, early payment by the customer enables the seller to have access to cash sooner. Second, the sooner an account is paid, the less opportunity there is for nonpayment.

Typical discount terms are 2/10, net 30. This indicates that a 2% discount will be granted if payment is made within 10 days of sale; otherwise, full payment is due within 30 days of sale.

These particular terms offer a significant inducement for early payment. To see this, consider the 2% to be a finance charge assessed for extending credit from the 10th to the 30th day after sale. That is, the customer must pay 2% more than otherwise required if payment is delayed for those 20 days. Because there are about 18 20-day periods in a year (365/20), the quoted discount implies an approximate annual interest rate of 36% (2% × 18), which is quite high relative to other sources of financing.

Factoring Accounts Receivable

In some industries, sellers extend very generous credit terms to their customers. For example, furniture retailers sometimes do not require any payment until six months after sale. To obtain cash more quickly, these firms sell **(factor)** their receivables. In most cases, the receivables are factored to a financial institution that charges a fee as compensation for the cost of collection, the delayed receipt of the cash, and potential uncollectible accounts.

To illustrate, assume that a furniture store has previously made a credit sale for $1,500. If the receivable is subsequently factored for $1,300, cash would increase by $1,300, accounts receivable would decrease by $1,500, and a $200 expense would be incurred.

ASSETS		=	LIABILITIES	+	SHAREHOLDERS' EQUITY
Cash	Accounts receivable				Retained earnings
+$1,300	−$1,500				−$200 (financing expense)

Uncollectible Accounts

As noted earlier, revenue is recognized at the time a credit sale is made. Recognizing revenue increases a firm's assets and net income. However, given that some of the receivables may ultimately prove to be uncollectible, assets and net income might be overstated.

Year-End Adjustment To avoid this possibility, firms make year-end adjustments to recognize that some of their accounts receivable will probably not be collected. Because firms are unlikely to know which particular accounts will prove to be uncollectible, the amount of the adjustment is an estimate.

To illustrate, assume that on December 31, 2000, at the end of its first year of operation the Box Company estimates that $2,400 of its year-end accounts receivable balance of $100,000 will be uncollectible. Keep in mind that this is an overall estimate and that Box is currently unable to identify which particular customers will not fulfill their obligations. Accordingly, the adjustment does not directly reduce accounts receivable. Instead, a negative (contra) asset, **allowance for uncollectible accounts,** is used.

An expense is also recorded, which is consistent with the matching principle. One cost of generating sales is the receivables that will ultimately prove to be uncollectible. This cost (even though it must be estimated) should be deducted from the sales revenue that gave rise to those receivables. The analysis follows.

	ASSETS		=	LIABILITIES	+	SHAREHOLDERS' EQUITY
	Accounts receivable	Allowance for uncollectible accounts (contra asset)				Retained earnings
Bal.	$100,000					
Dec. 31		−$2,400				−$2,400 (uncollectible accounts expense)

The net difference between the balances in accounts receivable and the allowance for uncollectible accounts is net accounts receivable, which is included in total assets on the balance sheet.

Accounts receivable, gross	$100,000
Less allowance for uncollectible accounts	(2,400)
Accounts receivable, net	$ 97,600

Exhibit 6-4 contains OB's partial balance sheet. It shows the balance in the allowance account, as well as the net accounts receivable included in total assets.

EXHIBIT 6-4 Partial Balance Sheet

OshKosh B'Gosh
Partial Balance Sheet
(Dollars in thousands)

	December 31, 1997	1996
Accounts receivable, less allowances of $4,225 in 1997 and $5,474 in 1996	$23,278	$20,504

From the information provided, gross accounts receivable on December 31, 1997, can be computed as $27,503,000:

Net receivable	=	Gross receivable	−	Allowance
$23,278,000	=	Gross receivable	−	$4,225,000
$23,278,000	=	$27,503,000	−	4,225,000

Write-Offs When a firm subsequently ascertains that a **particular** customer will not pay, that customer's account is written off. This is done by reducing the balances in accounts receivable and in the allowance for uncollectible accounts. Continuing with the Box Company illustration, assume that on February 11, 2001, Box becomes aware that a customer who owes $450 has just gone out of business and that collection is extremely unlikely. The balances in the accounts receivable and allowance accounts would each be reduced by $450.

ASSETS			=	LIABILITIES	+	SHAREHOLDERS' EQUITY
	Accounts receivable	Allowance for uncollectible accounts				
Bal.	$100,000	−$2,400				
Feb. 11	−$ 450	+$ 450				
	$ 99,550	−$1,950				

Because the balance in accounts receivable is reduced, as is the accompanying contra asset, the write-off has no effect on total assets or expenses. This is proper, because the asset reduction and expense were previously recorded. Box's net receivable is $97,600, both before and after the write-off.

	Before	After
Accounts receivable, gross	$100,000	$99,550
Less allowance	2,400	1,950
Accounts receivable, net	$ 97,600	$97,600

The effect of the write-off is depicted graphically in Exhibit 6-5.

Estimation Methods Firms can estimate the year-end adjustment for uncollectible accounts in several ways. One approach is the **aging method.** In its simplest form, the aging method classifies the year-end accounts receivable balance into two categories: (1) current and (2) past due. Suppose, for example, that a firm's sales terms are 2/10, net 30. This indicates that all accounts are due within 30 days of sale. On the balance sheet date, accounts that have been outstanding for 30 or fewer days are classified as current. The remainder are classified as past due.

Based on a firm's past experience, industry norms, and current trends, the firm estimates the percentage of each category that will not be collected. This is the step that

EXHIBIT 6-5 Effect of Write-Offs on Accounts Receivable

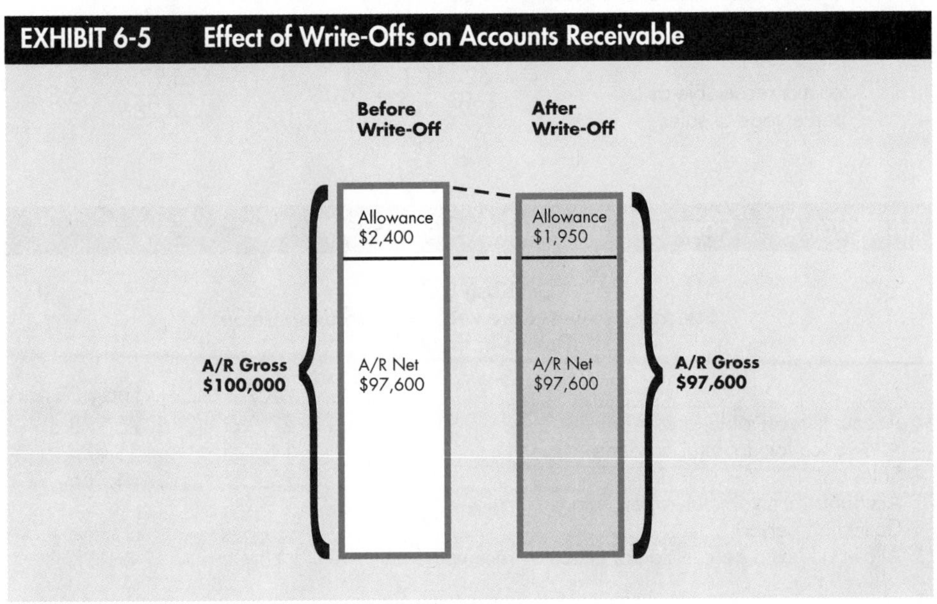

requires the most judgment. Also, because older accounts are more likely not to be collected, the past-due category has a higher percentage of uncollectibles than the current category. These percentages are multiplied by each category's balance to estimate the allowance for uncollectible accounts.

Recall that Box Company estimated its allowance to be $2,400 at the end of 2000. The aging analysis that resulted in this estimate is as follows:

Age Category	Balance	×	Percentage Estimated to Be Uncollectible	=	Estimated Amount Uncollectible
Current	$ 90,000		2%		$1,800
Past due	10,000		6%		600
Total	$100,000				$2,400

Although other estimation methods can yield different results on a year-to-year basis, over the long run their results will be quite similar.

Analysis of Accounts Receivable

The analysis of accounts receivable involves two issues: the relative size of accounts receivable and the adequacy of the allowance for uncollectible accounts. The financial statements of OB are used to illustrate these issues. Exhibit 6-6 contains some basic information about OB's receivables.

Size of Accounts Receivable Because accounts receivable earn no return after the discount period has expired, firms should limit their investment in this asset. The size of accounts receivable is usually assessed relative to the amount of credit sales. This seems appropriate because credit sales give rise to accounts receivable. Most firms do not separately disclose credit sales, so net sales are usually used. A straightforward analysis divides gross accounts receivable by sales:

$$\text{Accounts receivable as a percentage of sales} = \frac{\text{Accounts receivable (gross)}}{\text{Sales}}$$

OB's percentage increased from 5.8% in 1996 to 7.0% in 1997:

$$\text{Accounts receivable as a percentage of sales} = \quad \underset{\textbf{1997}}{\frac{\$27{,}503}{\$395{,}196} = 7.0\%} \qquad \underset{\textbf{1996}}{\frac{\$25{,}978}{\$444{,}766} = 5.8\%}$$

EXHIBIT 6-6 Financial Statement Information

OshKosh B'Gosh
Selected Accounts Receivable-Related Information
(Dollars in thousands)

	1997	1996
Accounts receivable, gross	$ 27,503	$ 25,978
Allowance for doubtful accounts	$4,225	$5,474
Sales	$395,196	$444,766
Accounts receivable as a percentage of sales	7.0%	5.8%
Collection period	25 days	21 days
Allowance as a percentage of accounts receivable	15.4%	21.1%

OB's trend is not favorable. Notice that although sales declined from 1996 to 1997, the balance in accounts receivable actually increased. Although the unfavorable trend might be due to less effective management of accounts receivable, it could also be due to a changing sales pattern. If, in 1997, OB made a relatively larger proportion of its sales near year-end, we would expect to see an increase in year-end accounts receivable.

An alternative analysis involves calculating the average length of time it takes to collect a receivable. This is known as the **collection period.** It is calculated in two steps. First, calculate the average sales per day:

$$\text{Average sales per day} = \frac{\text{Sales}}{365}$$

Next, the collection period is calculated by dividing gross accounts receivable by average sales per day.

$$\text{Collection period} = \frac{\text{Accounts receivable (gross)}}{\text{Average sales per day}}$$

This ratio indicates the number of days sales in accounts receivable.

OB's collection period increased from 21 to 25 days. This is consistent with the analysis of accounts receivable as a percentage of sales.

	1997	1996
Average sales per day =	$\frac{\$395,196}{365} = \$1,083$	$\frac{\$444,766}{365} = \$1,219$
Collection period =	$\frac{\$27,503}{\$1,083} = 25$ days	$\frac{\$25,978}{\$1,219} = 21$ days

Exhibit 6-7 contains a comparison of OB's ratios with Hartmarx Corporation, another apparel manufacturer, and, as a point of contrast, with Albertson's, a food store. OB's accounts receivable as a percentage of sales and its collection period are about one-third as large as those of Hartmarx. At least four interpretations are possible: (1) OB is doing much better than Hartmarx in quickly collecting its receivables and minimizing its investment in this asset; (2) OB's sales pattern during the year differs markedly from that of Hartmarx (that is, OB makes substantially fewer sales at year-end than Hartmarx does); (3) OB is inducing its customers to pay quickly either through strong pressure or steep discounts; or (4) OB factors more accounts receivable than does Hartmarx.

EXHIBIT 6-7 Comparisons of Accounts Receivable Ratios

Accounts Receivable Ratios
Interfirm Comparisons
1997

	OB	Hartmarx Corp.	Albertsons
Accounts receivable as a percentage of sales	7.0%	20.4%	.8%
Collection period	25 days	75 days	3 days
Allowance as a percentage of accounts receivable	15.4%	6.7%	1.0%

Also note that food stores have a much shorter collection period than apparel manufacturers, which is due to the nature of food stores' credit sales. Most credit sales are made via customers' credit cards at major banks and food stores are able to collect these receivables from the banks very quickly. Some credit sales are made to businesses (such as restaurants and caterers), but these customers pay by check within a reasonable period of time.

Reality Check 6-1 summarizes an accounts receivable issue that arose for Topps Co., Inc., the sports card producer.

REALITY CHECK 6-1

Topps Co., Inc., produces sports cards. During two consecutive quarters, Topps' accounts receivable increased by more than 50%, while sales declined. Such a trend might indicate that Topps is experiencing difficulty collecting from its customers.

Topps asserts, however, that receivables have increased because of a change in its shipping schedule. It has begun to ship 50% of its cards in the final few weeks of a quarter. Thus, many of its accounts receivable are outstanding at quarter's end, and at the same time, are not yet past due.

Required

a. Does Topps' explanation make sense?
b. Can Topps' claim be verified with publicly available information?

Solution

a. Topps' explanation may well make sense. Because sales and accounts receivable are recorded when goods are shipped, making shipments closer to a quarter's close increases the accounts receivable balance on the balance sheet date. Topps' explanation, however, raises the question of why its shipping schedule has changed. Some firms who have difficulty meeting sales expectations pressure customers to place orders toward the end of a quarter.
b. Verifying Topps' claim would be difficult. Firms do not publish shipping schedules or any other information that might indicate when shipments occurred during a quarter. Perhaps the best source of information is Topps' customers. They would certainly know if shipping schedules have changed and the reason for any change.

Adequacy of Allowance for Uncollectible Accounts Recall that writing off a specific account as uncollectible has no effect on total assets or net income. Assets and income are affected by the year-end adjustment in which uncollectible accounts are **estimated**. A great deal of judgment and discretion is used by management in making this estimate. Accordingly, analysts must carefully assess the reasonableness of the allowance for uncollectible accounts.

Few firms disclose their uncollectible accounts expense, yet most firms do disclose the year-end balance in the allowance for uncollectible accounts. The adequacy of this balance is usually assessed relative to the year-end accounts receivable balance. This is done by dividing the allowance by gross accounts receivable:

$$\text{Allowance for uncollectible accounts as a percentage of accounts receivable} = \frac{\text{Allowance for uncollectible accounts}}{\text{Accounts receivable (gross)}}$$

OB's percentage decreased from 21.1% in 1996 to 15.4% in 1997.

	1997	1996
Allowance for uncollectible accounts as a percentage of accounts receivable =	$\frac{\$4,225}{\$27,503} = 15.4\%$	$\frac{\$5,474}{\$25,978} = 21.1\%$

The reason for such a decrease is not entirely apparent. Perhaps OB made a conscious decision to decrease its sales to customers with dubious credit ratings. Such a change in the customer base would allow a decrease in the allowance for uncollectible accounts. Alternatively, recall from Chapter 4, "The Income Statement," that in 1997 OB ceased its European operations and terminated its relationship with certain domestic distributors. These changes altered the composition of OB's customer base and might justify the decline in the allowance for uncollectible accounts.

Exhibit 6-6 shows that OB's uncollectible accounts estimate is much more conservative than that of its competitor Hartmarx. Most analysts view conservative accounting practices with favor and feel that they result in earnings numbers of high quality.

Implications for Managers

As with any asset, managers should attempt to maximize the return on accounts receivable. One way to do this is to reduce the firm's investment in accounts receivable. Managers can employ several strategies to do this. Sales terms can be set so that the customer is obligated to make payment in a relatively short period of time. Managers should closely monitor accounts receivable collections to ensure that customers are paying within the agreed period.

Discounts for early payment can also induce customers to pay quickly. However, discounts large enough to prompt early payment may prove to be quite expensive for the seller.

Also keep in mind that sales terms may be constrained by industry practices. That is, a firm must provide terms that are competitive with those offered by its rivals. In general, sales terms are just one product attribute in a firm's overall promotional strategy.

Managers must also decide which customers will be granted credit. As mentioned previously, a trade-off exists between the amount of sales that can be generated and the level of uncollectible accounts expense incurred. Managers should set minimum credit ratings for its customers so that profitability is maximized.

INVENTORY

Inventory consists of products acquired for resale to customers. For many companies, inventory is a major asset and a significant source of revenue.

Basic Accounting

Assume that several items of inventory are acquired for a total price of $100. This transaction results in an increase in inventory and a decrease in cash.

ASSETS		=	LIABILITIES	+	SHAREHOLDERS' EQUITY
Cash	Inventory				
– $100	+$100				

Now assume that half the inventory is sold for $75. This transaction is analyzed in two steps. The revenue part increases cash and shareholders' equity by $75. The expense part decreases inventory and shareholders' equity by $50 (half of the $100 historical cost).

ASSETS		=	LIABILITIES	+	SHAREHOLDERS' EQUITY
Cash	Inventory				Retained earnings
+$75					+$75 (sales)
	−$50				−$50 (cost of goods sold)

The difference between the sales price of $75 and the **cost of goods sold** (CGS) of $50 is the **gross profit** or **gross margin.**

Cost Flow Assumptions

Most firms purchase inventory items on an ongoing basis. Usually, these purchases are not made at a uniform price. This poses an accounting problem when inventory is sold: What is the cost of the goods that were sold and what is the cost of the goods that remain on hand?

Some firms find it advantageous to keep a record of the cost of individual inventory items. These situations involve inventory units with a high dollar value and relatively few sales. Car dealerships are good illustrations. When negotiating with a customer over the selling price of a given car, for example, the cost of that particular car is important information for the dealer. Thus, these firms are motivated to keep a record of each car's cost. Moreover, a dealer's inventory consists of perhaps no more than 100 cars, and the dealer makes only a few sales per day. Such activity levels do not present a significant record-keeping challenge. The **specific identification method** maintains accounting records showing the cost of each inventory item.

For most businesses, however, the number of inventory units and the volume of purchases and sales are so large that the specific identification method would be very costly to implement. A grocery store, for example, may sell 1,000 cereal boxes in one day. This requires firms to use a cost flow assumption.

Consider the following summary of inventory acquisitions:

	# of Units	×	Unit Price	=	Total Cost
Beginning inventory	30		$4		$120
Purchase on February 18	10		5		50
Purchase on June 8	20		6		120
Purchase on October 22	20		8		160
Totals	80				$450

Assume that 48 units were sold during the year and 32 units remain on hand at year-end. To prepare the financial statements, the cost of the ending inventory and the cost of goods sold must be determined.

Average Cost The **average-cost method** calculates the weighted-average cost of an inventory item on hand during the period and applies this cost to the units sold and to the ending inventory. The average cost is calculated by dividing the cost of goods available for sale by the number of units available for sale. The **cost of goods available for sale** equals the cost of the beginning inventory plus the cost of all purchases during a period. It reflects the total cost of goods that were on hand at any time during the period and that were available for sale:

$$\text{Average cost} = \frac{\text{Cost of goods available for sale}}{\text{Number of units available for sale}}$$

$$\frac{\$450}{80} = \$5.625$$

To calculate the cost of the 48 units that have been sold, multiply the average cost of \$5.625 by 48:

$$\text{Cost of goods sold} = \$5.625 \times 48 = \$270$$

To calculate the cost of the 32 units in ending inventory, multiply the average cost of \$5.625 by 32:

$$\text{Ending inventory} = \$5.625 \times 32 = \$180$$

Alternatively, once either cost of goods sold or ending inventory has been calculated, the following equation can be used to compute the other.

$$\text{CGS} = \text{Beginning inventory} + \text{Purchases} - \text{Ending inventory}$$

Adding beginning inventory and purchases yields the cost of goods available for sale. Subtracting the cost of goods that have not been sold (the ending inventory) from the cost of all goods available for sale results in CGS (the cost of the goods that have been sold). If ending inventory is calculated first, the cost of goods sold can be computed as follows:

CGS	=	Beginning inventory	+	Purchases	−	Ending inventory
\$270	=	\$120	+	\$330	−	\$180

On the other hand, assuming that cost of goods sold is computed first, the equation can be rearranged and ending inventory can be calculated as follows.

Ending inventory	=	Beginning inventory	+	Purchases	−	CGS
\$180	=	\$120	+	\$330	−	\$270

This general equation can be used with all the inventory methods described in this section.

First-In, First-Out Another commonly used inventory method is the First-in, First-out (or **FIFO**) method. This method **assumes** that **inventory costs** move on a first-in, first-out basis. This implies that the cost of the beginning inventory and the cost of purchases made early in the period are the first to flow out of the firm and comprise the cost of goods sold.

In our illustration, the cost of goods sold under the FIFO method is based on the cost of the 48 units that were acquired first.

	# of Units	×	Unit Price	=	Total Cost
Beginning inventory	30		$4		$120
February 18	10		5		50
June 8	8		6		48
CGS	48				$218

Because the cost of goods sold under the FIFO method is based on the cost of the earliest acquisitions, ending inventory must consist of the costs from the most recent purchases (those made closest to the period's end). Based on the inventory and purchase data given in the last subsection, ending inventory consists of the costs associated with the 32 units acquired closest to the end of the year. This includes the 20 units purchased on October 22 and 12 of the units purchased on June 8. Only 12 of the 20 units purchased on June 8 are included because the ending inventory consists of 32 units.

	# of Units	×	Unit Price	=	Total Cost
June 8	12		$6		$ 72
October 22	20		8		160
Ending Inventory	32				$232

Last-In, First-Out The Last-in, First-out **(LIFO)** inventory method **assumes** that the **costs** associated with the purchases made closest to the period's end comprise the cost of goods sold. Therefore, the cost of goods sold is based on the cost of the 48 units acquired most recently.

	# of Units	×	Unit Price	=	Total Cost
October 22	20		$8		$160
June 8	20		6		120
February 18	8		5		40
CGS	48				$320

Ending inventory, therefore, must be composed of the beginning inventory cost and the cost of the period's earliest acquisitions. Based on the preceding illustration, ending inventory is calculated by identifying the cost of the 32 units acquired the earliest.

	# of Units	×	Unit Price	=	Total Cost
Beginning inventory	30		$4		$120
February 18	2		5		10
Ending Inventory	32				$130

The difference between FIFO and LIFO can be described by examining the cost of goods available for sale. Recall that the cost of goods available for sale equals the cost of beginning inventory plus the cost of the year's purchases. By year end, each inventory item either will have been sold or will remain on hand. FIFO assumes that the cost of goods sold consists of the costs of the beginning inventory and the earliest purchases, and that the ending inventory is comprised of the more recent costs. In contrast, LIFO assumes that the cost of goods sold consists of the most recent costs and that the costs of beginning inventory and the earliest purchases are included in ending inventory. These partitions of cost of goods available for sale are depicted in Exhibit 6-8.

Financial Statement Effects of Inventory Method The choice of inventory method can have significant effects on financial statements. In the Exhibit 6-8 illustration, the effects of inventory method choice can be summarized as follows:

WHAT WOULD YOU DO?

You are the sole owner of a local CPA firm. Your firm has been quite successful, primarily because of your hard work.

It is December 31 and you are working on the audit of The Boot Warehouse. Part of your audit program requires that you test count Boot's inventory. You have decided that counting seven sections of Boot's warehouse would provide sufficient assurance that the inventory is correctly stated.

There's just one problem. Because you have been so successful, and because you are so busy, you arrived at the warehouse late. Because Boot is scheduled to make a number of large shipments soon after midnight, there is not enough time to count the seven sections as you planned. Delaying the shipments would be very costly. In fact, Boot's lost profits would probably be greater than your audit fee. What would you do?

	FIFO	Average Cost	LIFO
Cost of goods sold	$218	$270	$320
Ending inventory	$232	$180	$130

Notice that the illustration reflects a period of rising inventory costs, which is the typical situation for many firms. The conclusions drawn in this section are dependent on rising prices. Opposite conclusions would be warranted in periods of price declines.

EXHIBIT 6-8 Partitioning Cost of Goods Available for Sale: FIFO Vs LIFO

FIFO

Beginning inventory	Purchase of February 18	Purchase of June 8	Purchase of October 22
30 × $4	10 × $5	20 × $6	20 × $8

Cost of goods sold:

30 × $4 =		$120
10 × 5 =		50
8 × 6 =		48
48		$218

Ending inventory:

12 × $6 =		$ 72
20 × 8 =		160
32		$232

LIFO

Beginning inventory	Purchase of February 18	Purchase of June 8	Purchase of October 22
30 × $4	10 × $5	20 × $6	20 × $8

Ending Inventory:

30 × $4 =		$120
2 × 5 =		10
32		$130

Cost of Goods Sold:

20 × $8 =		$160
20 × 6 =		120
8 × 5 =		40
48		$320

LIFO results in the highest cost of goods sold because (1) it assumes that the more recent costs are the first ones sold, and (2) these most recently acquired costs are the most expensive ones. FIFO results in the lowest cost of goods sold, and the average-cost method yields results between LIFO and FIFO. Because LIFO reports the highest cost of goods sold figure, it results in the lowest reported net income number.

LIFO results in the lowest ending inventory value because it assumes that the earliest costs remain on hand at year-end, and these costs are the least expensive. FIFO yields the highest inventory value, and average cost falls between the two.

The Choice of Inventory Method

FIFO, LIFO, specific identification, and average cost are all acceptable inventory methods. Firms are free to choose one of these methods and consistently apply it across periods. Interestingly, GAAP does not require that the assumed flow of costs corresponds to the actual flow of goods. Supermarkets, for example, put their older products on the front of shelves so that they will be sold before items acquired more recently; this helps preserve the general freshness of the merchandise available to customers. In this case, goods actually flow on a FIFO basis. However, supermarkets are not required to use FIFO in the preparation of their financial statements.

This raises a question about the factors that are considered by managers in selecting an inventory method. Because LIFO and FIFO yield the most dissimilar results, the following discussion focuses on them.

Taxes The example we used to illustrate the various inventory methods was characterized by a period of rising prices. Many industries have experienced decades of inflation in inventory costs. In such periods, LIFO assigns the higher, recently acquired inventory costs to cost of goods sold. Of course, a higher cost of goods sold results in lower reported income. Thus, the selection of LIFO in inflationary periods reduces both reported pre-tax income and income taxes. Because a smaller check will be written to the IRS, the use of LIFO actually increases a firm's cash flow, even though reported net income is lower than under FIFO.

In general, firms are not required to select the same accounting principle for financial reporting and for taxes. Because financial statements and tax returns serve different purposes, this makes sense. LIFO, however, is an exception to this general rule. If LIFO is used for tax purposes, it must be used for financial reporting. Many firms prepare their tax return using LIFO to obtain the associated tax savings and are thus required to use it for their financial statements.

Implementation Costs Although we need not be concerned about the details, simply note that LIFO is more costly to implement than FIFO or average cost, especially for small firms. This may help explain why large firms tend to adopt LIFO more often than small firms. Managers must balance the tax savings from LIFO with the costs of implementation.

Quality of Financial Statement Information LIFO and FIFO result in different financial statement numbers for inventory, cost of goods sold, and net income. Which method results in the most useful information? The answer is not clear-cut.

FIFO's ending inventory calculation is based on a firm's most recent acquisition costs. Thus, the inventory amount on the balance sheet is likely to be very close to current value. In contrast, LIFO's ending inventory is based on the costs of beginning inventory and the earliest acquisitions. Keep in mind that this occurs each year and that the beginning inventory may contain components carried forward from many years ago. Thus, in a period of rising prices, LIFO ending inventory values may be dramatically understated.

On the other hand, LIFO provides more informative income statement numbers because it matches current inventory costs with revenues. Cost of goods sold under LIFO consists of the costs of the most recent acquisitions. These costs approximate amounts necessary to replace inventory as it is depleted. Because of this, LIFO is more consistent with the matching principle. Furthermore, gross profit under LIFO is a useful measure of the resources generated from inventory sales that are available to cover other expenses and provide for net income. Managers can then view the gross profit measure as an indicator of "spendable" resources.

LIFO and Loan Agreements As mentioned in previous chapters, many firms have loan agreements that require them to maintain certain levels of financial ratios. The current ratio is one example. Given that during a period of rising prices, LIFO results in a lower inventory figure, current assets will also be lower. This results in a lower current ratio and a greater likelihood of loan agreement violations. A number of other ratios will be similarly affected. When adopting LIFO, managers must be confident that the use of LIFO will not result in levels of financial ratios that violate existing loan agreements.

LIFO and Management Compensation Because LIFO reduces reported net income in a period of rising prices, LIFO may also reduce the compensation of managers who have bonuses based on reported income. This could limit management's motivation to adopt LIFO.

LIFO and Stock Prices LIFO results in lower **reported** net income during a period of rising prices. Some managers may fear that the stock market will react negatively to a lower income stream. A more sophisticated view, however, recognizes that LIFO results in lower taxes, thereby increasing a firm's cash flow. The increased cash flow benefits the firm and its shareholders, and should result in higher stock prices. Research evidence is ambiguous regarding the stock market reaction to LIFO adoptions.

Actual Usage of Inventory Methods **Accounting Trends and Techniques** conducts an annual survey of 600 major U.S. corporations to ascertain their financial reporting practices. Exhibit 6-9 shows the number of firms using various inventory methods.

FIFO is the most frequently used method, followed by LIFO, with the average-cost method a distant third. The total number of firms exceeds the 600 that were surveyed because many firms use multiple inventory methods. Keep in mind that the results are for major corporations; as mentioned, because LIFO is relatively expensive to implement, smaller businesses utilize LIFO less frequently. Also, LIFO is not widely used outside the United States.

Valuation of Inventories at Lower of Cost or Market

GAAP requires that inventories be valued at **lower of cost or market (LCM).** Inventory cost is determined based on one of the cost flow assumptions discussed earlier. Market is defined as the current replacement cost, which is the amount that would be required to replace the firm's inventory on the balance sheet date.

The LCM rule is based on the rationale that a decline in replacement cost indicates that the inventory's utility to the firm has decreased. Conservatism would dictate that this loss should be reflected immediately in the financial statements, rather than

EXHIBIT 6-9 Inventory Method Usage

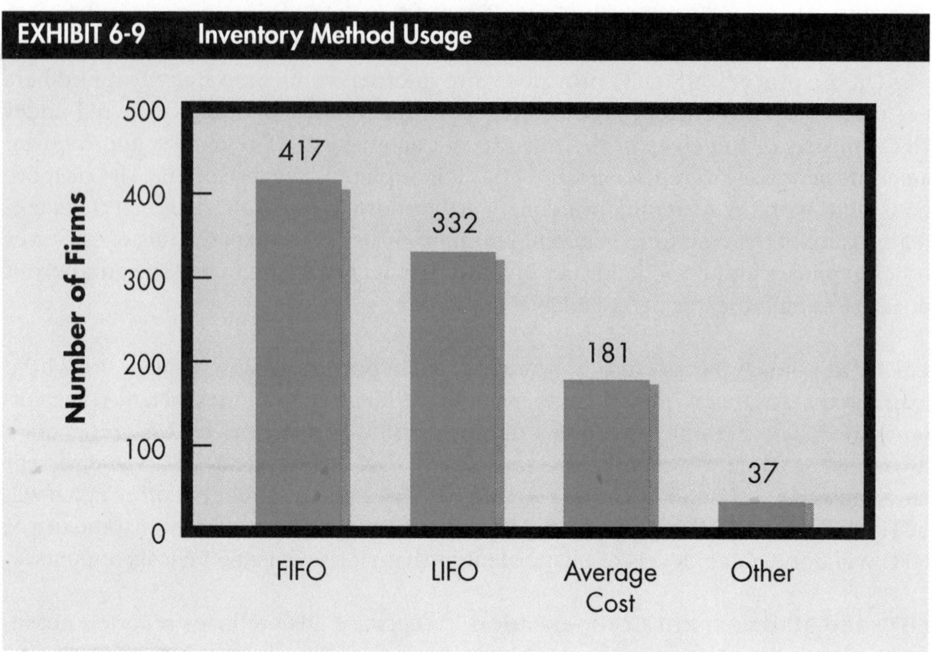

SOURCE: *Accounting Trends and Techniques,* 1997.

postponing such recognition until the time of sale. When inventory is written down to market, the loss is sometimes disclosed separately on the income statement, but more frequently, it is included in the cost of goods sold.

Manufacturers

The inventories of manufacturers are comprised of three broad categories. **Raw materials** are the basic components of the inventory items produced by the firm. **Work-in-process** inventory consists of inventory items that are partially completed on the balance sheet date. **Finished goods** are completed inventory items that are awaiting sale.

Firms usually report just one total inventory figure on the balance sheet. The composition of the inventory is found in the notes to the financial statements. Exhibit 6-10 contains OB's inventory note. It shows the breakdown of inventory into the three basic components.

Analysis of Inventories

The income statement contains information about profitability and the balance sheet contains useful information about inventory levels.

Profitability The income statement contains information about cost of goods sold and gross profit. Gross profit is often expressed as a percentage of sales:

$$\text{Gross profit \%} = \frac{\text{Gross profit}}{\text{Sales}}$$

A higher gross profit percentage helps cover other expenses and contributes to net income. Exhibit 6-11 contains inventory-related information for OB. The gross profit percentages in Exhibit 6-11 are calculated as follows:

$$\text{Gross profit \%} = \frac{\$144{,}381}{\$395{,}196} = 36.5\% \quad (1997) \qquad \frac{\$144{,}271}{\$444{,}766} = 32.4\% \quad (1996)$$

OB's gross profit percentage showed a reasonable increase between 1996 and 1997. Several factors may have caused this. First, OB's inventory costs may have fallen. Second, competitive forces may have enabled OB to increase its selling prices. Finally, keep in mind that OB's different products probably have varying gross profit percentages. A change in the mix of products sold can affect the gross profit percentage. OB's gross profit percentage compares favorably to other apparel manufacturers.

Industries differ with respect to gross profit percentage. For example, the pharmaceutical industry's average gross profit percentage exceeds 50%. Drug companies incur substantial costs when researching and developing their products. Accordingly, they must sell their goods at relatively high markups so that they can cover these costs and remain profitable.

EXHIBIT 6-10 Financial Statement Inventory Note

OshKosh B'Gosh
Inventory Note
(Dollars in thousands)

A summary of inventories follows:

	December 31, 1997	1996
Finished goods	$49,400	$51,584
Work in process	14,782	10,698
Raw materials	4,044	4,517
Total	$68,226	$66,799

The replacement cost of inventory exceeds the above LIFO costs by $14,138 and $15,100 at December 31, 1997 and 1996, respectively. Partial liquidation of certain LIFO layers in 1997 and 1996 increased net income by approximately $577 and $660, respectively.

EXHIBIT 6-11 Financial Statement Information

OshKosh B'Gosh
Selected Inventory-Related Information
(Dollars in thousands)

	1997	1996
Inventory	$ 68,226	$ 66,799
Sales	$395,196	$444,766
Cost of goods sold	$250,815	$300,495
Gross profit	$144,381	$144,271
Gross profit %	36.5%	32.4%
Number of days' sales in ending inventory	99	81

Reality Check 6-2 examines the effect on gross profit of applying the LCM inventory valuation rule.

Inventory Levels The balance sheet contains information about the cost of inventories remaining on hand at year-end. This provides insights into whether the level of inventory is adequate to meet customer demands. Inadequate levels may result in lost sales and reduced profitability, while excessive levels increase carrying

REALITY CHECK 6-2

California Micro Devices Corporation (CMD) manufactures and markets integrated thin-film, silicon-based termination and filtering components and active electronic circuitry. During the year ended March 31, 1998, CMD recorded inventory write-downs of $900,000. The write-downs were due to potential obsolescence and severe price competition by Asian manufacturers. CMD reported the following results (in thousands):

	For the year ended March 31, 1998	
	1998	**1997**
Revenue	$33,043	$32,936
Cost of sales	24,701	21,255
Gross profit	8,342	11,681

Assume that the write-down is reflected in cost of sales.

Required

a. Calculate CMS's gross profit percentages for 1998 and 1997.
b. Recalculate the 1998 gross profit percentage, assuming that the write-down did not occur.
c. What concerns are raised by the trend in gross profit percentages and the effect of the write-down?

Solution

a.

		1998	**1997**
Gross profit percentage	$= \dfrac{\text{Gross profit}}{\text{Sales}}$	$= \dfrac{\$8{,}342}{\$33{,}043}$	$\dfrac{\$11{,}681}{\$32{,}936}$
		= 25.2%	35.5%

b. Had the write-down not occurred, gross profit would have been:

Gross profit, as reported	$8,342,000
Plus: Write-down	900,000
Cost of sales, adjusted	$9,242,000

Based on this, an adjusted gross profit percentage can be calculated.

$$\text{Gross profit percentage} = \frac{\text{Gross profit}}{\text{Sales}} = \frac{\$9{,}242}{\$33{,}043} = 28\%$$

As can be seen, the write-down reduced the 1998 gross profit percentage by almost three percentage points.

c. CMD would have experienced a significant decline in gross profit percentage even in the absence of the inventory write-down. The decline in gross profit percentage, coupled with the causes for the write-down (obsolescence and pricing pressures from Asian manufacturers) suggest that CMD is in a rapidly changing and competitive industry. CMD must develop a plan to increase its profitability.

costs, which also has a negative impact on profitability. Carrying costs include storage, handling, insurance, and the opportunity cost of the funds invested in inventory. An opportunity cost exists because cash invested in inventory that remains on hand for several months cannot be invested in more profitable alternative opportunities.

The **number of days' sales in ending inventory (NDS)** is frequently used to measure inventory levels. It is computed in two steps. First, divide cost of goods sold by 365. This indicates the cost of inventory sold in one day.

$$\text{CGS per day} = \frac{\text{CGS}}{365}$$

Next divide ending inventory by CGS per day to obtain NDS.

$$\text{NDS} = \frac{\text{Ending inventory}}{\text{CGS per day}}$$

NDS reflects inventory size relative to the level of sales activity. OB's NDS for 1997 and 1996 are calculated as follows:

	1997	1996
CGS per day = (in thousands)	$\frac{\$250,815}{365} = \$687$	$\frac{\$300,495}{365} = \$823$
NDS =	$\frac{\$68,226}{\$687} = 99$ days	$\frac{\$66,799}{\$823} = 81$ days

OB's NDS increased from 81 days in 1996 to 99 days in 1997. This occurred because inventory levels increased while sales (and cost of goods sold) declined. Recall that OB ceased dealing with certain wholesalers and curtailed its European operations, which resulted in a smaller scale of operations. OB does not seem to have fully adjusted its inventory levels to this smaller scale.

It is interesting to contrast apparel manufacturers' NDS with that of food stores, who maintain about 40 days' sales of inventory on hand. This reflects the perishable nature of food stores' inventories, coupled with their high volume of sales.

Comparing LIFO and FIFO Firms

Comparing the financial statements of firms that use different inventory methods is troublesome. In these situations, differences in ratios might be due to the different accounting methods or to the different underlying economic conditions of the firms. Whenever possible in making interfirm comparisons, financial statement numbers should be recast to reflect the use of a uniform accounting method.

Although firms do not usually make disclosures enabling such analyses, companies using LIFO often reveal their FIFO-based inventory values. In all likelihood, these firms are motivated to do this because FIFO usually results in a lower CGS number than LIFO. Regardless of the motivation, the disclosures provide the basis to generate ratios on a FIFO basis for firms that actually use LIFO.

OB, which uses LIFO, elected to disclose the replacement cost of its inventories. Replacement cost approximates the FIFO cost of inventories and allows the analyst to adjust OB's financial ratios for purposes of comparisons to FIFO firms. Recall the calculation for cost of goods sold:

$$\text{CGS} = \text{Beginning inventory} + \text{Purchases} - \text{Ending inventory}$$

Under LIFO, the calculation for 1997 was:

CGS	=	Beginning inventory	+	Purchases	–	Ending inventory
$250,815,000	=	$66,799,000	+	$252,242,000	–	$68,226,000

The inventory disclosures indicate that under FIFO (or replacement cost), the beginning inventory would have been higher by $15,100,000 and the ending inventory would have been higher by $14,138,000. The only differences in the cost of goods sold calculations relate to the valuation of beginning and ending inventory. Therefore, FIFO-based cost of goods sold can be computed by adjusting LIFO-based cost of goods sold by these inventory valuation differences.

CGS under LIFO	$250,815,000
Plus the increase in the beginning inventory valuation under FIFO	15,100,000
Less the increase in the ending inventory valuation under FIFO	(14,138,000)
CGS under FIFO	$251,777,000

Notice that in this particular situation CGS under FIFO is higher than under LIFO. This is rather unusual. Firms typically employ LIFO to capture the tax benefit of higher CGS and lower taxable income. OB's lower LIFO-based CGS could be due to two factors. First, the unit cost of its inventory items might be declining. Under LIFO, these recently acquired, lower-priced goods are the ones assumed sold. Alternatively, recall that OB scaled back some operations. In the process, OB might have liquidated certain lines of apparel. If these lines had been held for a number of years, their recorded LIFO cost was likely based on rather old (and low) prices. In fact, OB's inventory note appearing in Exhibit 6-10 references such a situation by using the phrase "liquidation of certain LIFO layers."

Exhibit 6-10 provides sufficient information to recalculate OB's ratios on a FIFO basis. OB's FIFO-based and LIFO-based ratios are summarized in Exhibit 6-12. As often happens, little difference exists in the gross profit percentages generated by the two methods. This occurs because the beginning and ending inventories are higher under FIFO by roughly the same amount; the previous calculation of FIFO cost of goods sold showed that these two inventory increases tend to cancel each other.

Inventory method has a more dramatic effect on NDS. The FIFO ratio indicates that OB has more inventory on hand than suggested by the LIFO ratio. Given that many analysts believe FIFO yields more relevant balance sheet numbers, OB's inventory levels may be more problematic than they first appeared.

EXHIBIT 6-12 Inventory Ratio

OshKosh B'Gosh
Inventory Ratios

	1997	
	LIFO	**FIFO**
Gross profit %	36.5%	36.3%
Number of days' sales in ending inventory	99 days	119 days

PREPAID EXPENSES

In many situations, firms pay for goods and services in advance. Insurance is a good example. Quite often, firms make full payment at the inception of a policy's term. The accounting issue involves the proper treatment of assets and expenses. At the beginning of a policy's term, an asset has been acquired: the right to be covered by insurance for the next year (or other time period). As the policy's term progresses, the asset is used up and an expense is incurred.

Prepaid expenses are recorded at their historical cost. Because prepaids usually have a short life, their cost corresponds closely to market value, and few analysts would object to this valuation practice.

Prepaid expenses generally constitute a very small proportion of a firm's assets. For example, in 1997, OB's prepaid expenses comprised less than 1% of its assets. Consequently, prepaids are not subjected to extensive analysis. Recall, however, that they are included in the numerator of the current ratio. Because prepaids will be utilized in the near future, most analysts feel that this is proper. Note that prepaids are not a source of future cash inflows, but they do reflect the reduced need for future cash outflows.

Summary of Learning Objectives

1. **Identify the items included in cash.**
Cash includes funds on hand and cash on deposit in bank accounts that do not restrict withdrawals. Most firms also classify as cash amounts in money market funds on which checks can be drawn.
2. **Understand the need for cash planning and how firms exercise control over cash.**
Firms must carefully plan their cash inflows and outflows so that sufficient cash is available to meet obligations as they become due. At the same time, because cash earns virtually no return, excessive balances should be avoided. Also, because cash is easily misappropriated, management should take steps to safeguard cash and to ensure that the accounting for cash is proper. This can be accomplished through effective internal control procedures, including the use of checking accounts and bank reconciliations.
3. **Comprehend the basic accounting for marketable securities and the limitations of generally accepted accounting principles (GAAP) in this area.**
Marketable securities are shown on a balance sheet at market value. Revaluing marketable securities from their historical cost to market value requires that unrealized gains/losses be recorded. Most industrial firms own securities classified as available-for-sale. The rule for these securities requires that unrealized gains/losses not be shown on the income statement. Instead, they appear on the balance sheet in a separate component of shareholders' equity. This rule's major shortcoming is that the value change is not reflected in net income.
4. **Determine if a firm is properly managing its accounts receivable.**
Collections of accounts receivable should be made in a timely manner. This reduces the firm's investment in a nonproductive asset and reduces the opportunity for nonpayment. A firm's success at doing this is measured by its collection period.
5. **Assess if a firm's allowance for uncollectible accounts is adequate.**
On the balance sheet date, an adequate allowance for uncollectible accounts should be established. This is assessed by dividing the allowance by the ending accounts receivable balance.
6. **Understand the various inventory cost flow assumptions and the effect that the firm's choice of inventory method has on its taxes, the quality of information in its financial statements, its management compensation, its loan covenants, and its stock price.**
The most commonly used inventory cost flow assumptions are average cost, FIFO, and LIFO. FIFO (LIFO) assumes that the oldest (newest) costs are the first ones sold. The choice of inventory method can have a significant effect on the reported financial statement numbers. In a period of rising prices, LIFO results in the highest cost of goods sold and the lowest inventory value. The reverse is true for FIFO. The average cost method yields results between LIFO and FIFO. Because LIFO has an adverse effect on net income and financial ratios, the adoption of LIFO may reduce managerial compensation and increase the likelihood of loan covenant violations. However, a lower reported net income number also reduces taxes. Regardless of the direction of inventory prices, LIFO results in a cost of goods sold figure that reflects current costs, and FIFO results in an ending inventory value that reflects current costs.

KEY TERMS

7. **Analyze a firm's inventory management practices.**
To be profitable, a firm must sell inventory for more than its cost. The gross profit percentage measures a firm's success in doing this. A firm should also have an adequate, but not excessive, supply of inventory on hand. The amount of inventory on hand is measured by the number of days' sales in ending inventory.
8. **Understand the nature of prepaid expenses.**
Prepaid expenses reflect payments made prior to the time that services are actually used. Prepayments often occur for insurance and rent. Prepayments are usually small in dollar amount and, accordingly, do not require detailed examination by analysts.

QUESTIONS

6-1 What does the term *cash*, as shown on financial statements, usually include? Discuss *cash* and *cash equivalents* separately.

6-2 Why would a business usually want to have a positive cash balance? What does a firm usually do with cash? Describe how a firm might operate with a cash balance of zero in its accounting records.

6-3 Under what circumstances could a firm's cash balance be negative? Why?

6-4 Describe how market valuations are applied to short-term equity investments.

6-5 Explain the relationship between inventory cost flows and the actual flow of goods into and out of the firm's storeroom.

6-6 Why would a firm extend credit to its customers? Identify some firms that rarely offer credit terms. How have bank credit cards changed some of these credit practices? Identify some industries where credit is an essential part of daily business.

6-7 Discuss the typical relationship between inventory and accounts receivable. How are the dollar amounts reported in inventory related to those reported as accounts receivable? Are the dollar amounts comparable or related to each other in any systematic manner? Under what circumstances could a firm have inventory and not accounts receivable? What types of firms might have neither?

6-8 Does a firm's recognition of revenue depend on whether the transaction is a cash sale or a credit sale? Why?

6-9 What policies (within the firm) will help determine how quickly a firm collects cash on its credit sales? What customer attributes will also affect cash collections?

6-10 Describe one method that can be used to estimate a firm's uncollectible accounts expense.

6-11 Describe two different methods of accounting for marketable securities. Why is one method preferable?

6-12 Under what circumstances might cash not be considered a current asset?

6-13 Under what circumstances can accounts receivable be turned into cash, almost "overnight"?

6-14 Discuss the criterion "available-for-sale" as it is used in determining how marketable securities are reported in the firm's financial statements.

6-15 What steps can a firm take to protect cash held on its premises?

6-16 Discuss the relationships between "lower of cost or market" and the various methods that might be used to determine inventory costs, such as FIFO and LIFO.

6-17 Describe how LIFO provides better matching of revenues and expenses than FIFO. Why would such an attribute be desirable for income measurement?

6-18 Describe five general types of current assets. Why do you think managers and analysts might prefer that firms generally use these categories and definitions for current assets?

6-19 Define prepaid expenses and identify examples of two types of prepaid expenses.

6-20 If a firm purchased a three-year fire insurance policy on July 1, 1999, how would this policy be shown on the firm's balance sheet at December 31, 2000?

6-21 With regard to accounts receivable, explain how the average sales per day ratio and collection period ratio could be used. As a company relaxes its credit policies, how would the values of these ratios usually change? Why?

6-22 Discuss how and why accountants might use the accounts receivable contra asset account Allowance for Uncollectible Accounts. Does such an account seem useful for managers and analysts? Why?

6-23 Describe the circumstances under which a manager might want to change her firm's inventory method from FIFO to LIFO. Similarly, describe why a change from LIFO to FIFO might be desirable.

6-24 Identify the best answer to each of the following multiple-choice questions, and explain why it is the best answer:

1. To help achieve internal control over the assets of a company:
   a. Segregate authorization and execution
   b. Segregate authorization and review
   c. Segregate custody and record keeping
   d. Segregate custody and payment
2. Which of the following internal control statements is correct?
   a. Internal control does not ensure that collusion will be detected.
   b. Internal control design is the responsibility of the outside auditors.
   c. The costs of internal control often exceed the benefits.
   d. A strong system of internal control should be enough to show that the financial statements "present fairly."

EXERCISES

Describing Inventory Methods

Writing

6-25 Compare and contrast each of the following methods used to value inventories:

a. FIFO
b. LIFO
c. Weighted average
d. Specific identification
e. Lower of cost or market

Identifying Cash

6-26 Classify each of the following items as either a cash or a noncash item.

a. Savings accounts
b. Postage stamps
c. Traveler's checks
d. Handwritten notes from employees promising to repay the firm for lunch money taken from the cash register
e. Travel advances provided to employees

f. Cash in a drawer waiting to be deposited at the bank
g. Customers' checks that have arrived in today's mail
h. A petty cash fund of $50 that is rarely used
i. Foreign currency
j. Foreign coins
k. U.S. savings bonds
l. 100 shares of IBM common stock

Interpreting Financial Statements: Inventories

6-27 Examine the financial statements for Wendy's and Reebok in the appendices. Read Note 1 for each firm. Identify the inventory valuation method used by each. Do these methods seem appropriate for each firm? Why? Examine the relative amount of inventories reported by each firm. Why would one firm have much larger inventories than the other? Why is it reasonable to expect such differences?

Interpreting Financial Statements: Current Assets

6-28 Refer to Reebok's financial statements in Appendix E. Review the balance sheet to determine how and where current assets were reported.

Required

a. Read Note 1. Why does Reebok report cash and cash equivalents?
b. What is the gross amount of accounts receivable at the end of 1997 and 1996? Why do you suppose the allowance for doubtful accounts has increased?
c. Discuss how "other current assets" may differ from "prepaid expenses." In your opinion, should they be disclosed separately? Why?
d. Discuss any other unusual concerns regarding Reebok's current assets. What other related information might an external analyst require or prefer?

Interpreting Financial Statements: Current Assets

6-29 Refer to Wendy's financial statements in Appendix D. Review the balance sheet to determine how and where current assets were reported.

Required

a. Read Note 1. Identify and discuss any unusual terms.
b. Why does Wendy's separate cash equivalents from notes receivable? Which are reported at market value? Why?
c. Discuss how "inventories" may differ from "other current assets." In your opinion, should they be disclosed separately? Does the distinction seem to be significant? Why?
d. Discuss any other unusual concerns regarding Wendy's current assets.

Accounts Receivable Management : Contrast Two Firms

6-30 Firm A has an accounts receivable balance of $126,000 and a balance in its allowance for uncollectible accounts of $29,000. Contrast this situation with Firm B, which has corresponding balances of $963,000 and $865,000. Which firm is riskier? Why? Which firm do you think is doing a better job of managing its accounts receivable? Why?

Analysis: Marketable Securities

6-31 The Amber Corporation purchased three different stocks during the year as follows:

- 100 shares of Fancy Corporation, cost $23 per share
- 250 shares of Traylor Corporation, cost $15 per share
- 180 shares of Sensor Corporation, cost $7 per share

Amber Corporation intends to sell these soon when its cash flow gets low. On the balance sheet date, these securities had a market price as follows:

1. Fancy Corporation: $24 per share
2. Traylor Corporation: $12 per share
3. Sensor Corporation: $9 per share

Required

a. Assuming that these securities are considered available-for-sale, what would be the effect on the financial statements of holding these securities?

b. Assuming that these securities are considered trading securities, what would be the effect on the financial statements?

c. What if, after the balance sheet date, Amber decides to sell Traylor Corporation stock for a market price of $14 per share? What would be the effect on the financial statements if the security is (1) available-for-sale or (2) trading?

Cash, Cash Equivalents, and Short-Term Investment Classifications

6-32 The Simmons Corporation had the following investments at December 31:

1. 1000 shares of Hollings, Inc., purchased early in the year at $40 per share and held as available-for-sale and with a year-end fair market value of $38 per share
2. $25,000 in U.S. three-month Treasury Bills
3. $15,000 commercial deposit with a maturity date of April 30 of the next year
4. $2,500 in postage stamps
5. $1,600 petty cash fund
6. $3,000 IOU from the president of Simmons Corporation
7. $12,000 money market account

Required

a. Describe where each item would be classified on the balance sheet.

b. At what amount should cash, cash equivalents, and short-term investments be reported?

Transactions Related to Accounts Receivable: Effects on Selected Financial Statement Items

6-33 Spit-Spot Cleaners, Inc., recognized the following events related to customer accounts receivable during the firm's first year of operation:

1. Sales on credit totaled $4,000,000 for the year.
2. The firm estimated that 2% of its credit sales would ultimately prove to be uncollectible.
3. Cash collections of accounts receivable totaled $3,480,000 during the year.
4. The firm wrote off uncollectible accounts of $75,000.

Required

a. Determine the effects of each of these events on the following financial statement items:

- Accounts receivable (net of allowance)
- Total assets
- Revenues
- Expenses

b. Determine the firm's balance of accounts receivable (net) at December 31 (year-end).

Transactions Related to Accounts Receivable: Effects on Selected Financial Statement Items

6-34 Shard Crockery Co. recognized the following events related to customer accounts receivable during 2000. At the start of the year, the firm reported gross accounts receivable of $22,000,000 and an allowance for uncollectible accounts of $2,000,000.

1. Sales on credit totaled $60,000,000 for the year.
2. The company factored $18,000,000 of its receivables to a financial institution and paid a fee of $700,000.
3. Uncollectible customer accounts totaling $3,200,000 were written off during the year.
4. Based on an aging of its remaining accounts receivable at year-end, the company estimates that 10% of its remaining receivables will ultimately be uncollectible.

Required

a. Determine the balance of accounts receivable (net of allowance) to be reported in Shard Crockery's balance sheet at the end of 2000.

b. Determine the effects of each of the events described above on the company's accounts receivable (net), total assets, revenues, and expenses.

c. How would the factoring of accounts receivable during the year affect your calculation or interpretation of the company's accounts receivable collection period (if at all)? Discuss.

Interpreting Financial Statements: Accounts Receivable

6-35 DSE is a world leader in the application of information technology. Excerpts from its financial statements disclosed the following information (dollars in millions):

	Years Ended December 31		
	1999	1998	1997
Total revenues	$8,463.9	$8,154.3	$6,998.2
Accounts receivable	$1,325.6	$1,200.5	—

Required

a. Because DSE did not separately disclose its allowance account balances, what interpretation must be given to the reported balances in accounts receivable?

b. What conclusions, based on the information available, can be drawn regarding DSE's management of accounts receivable?

Ratio Calculations: Accounts Receivable

6-36 Frosty King, Inc., reported the following information in its 2000 financial statements:

	Years Ended November 30	
	2000	1999
Net sales	$228,542,157	$231,845,632
Accounts receivable, net	21,402,613	19,280,407
Allowance for uncollectible accounts	650,811	1,018,416

Required

a. Calculate the adequacy of Frosty King's allowance account for each year.
b. Calculate its average sales per day for each year.
c. Calculate its collection period for each year.
d. Calculate its accounts receivable as a percentage of sales for each year.
e. Based on your analyses, discuss Frosty King's management of accounts receivable.

Gross Profit Ratio Calculations

6-37 Calculate the gross profit percentages for each of the following situations and, based on these results, identify which situations are most preferable:

a. Sales of $500,000, cost of goods sold of $300,000
b. Sales of $600,000, gross profit of $300,000
c. Sales of $600,000, cost of goods sold of $250,000
d. Sales of $500,000, cost of goods sold of $100,000

Gross Profit Ratio Calculations

6-38 Calculate the gross profit percentages for each of the following situations and, based on these results, identify which situations are most preferable:

a. Sales of $450,000, cost of goods sold of $300,000
b. Sales of $660,000, gross profit of $230,000
c. Sales of $700,000, gross profit of $330,000
d. Sales of $800,000, gross profit ratio of 25%

Turnover Ratios for Accounts Receivable and Inventory

6-39 Ken's and Den's Recreational Products, Inc., reports the following information in its 2000 financial statements:

	Balance (dollars in millions)	
	January 1, 2000	December 31, 2000
Accounts receivable (gross)	$14	$12
Allowance for uncollectible accounts	1	2
Inventory	20	26
During 2000:		
Sales		80
Cost of goods sold		55

Required

Determine Ken's and Den's accounts receivable collection period ratio and the number of days' sales in ending inventory during 2000.

Inventory Valuation Error Effects on Financial Statements

6-40 Illusory Products Co. began operations early in 1999 and reported the following items in its financial statements at the ends of 1999 and 2000 (dollars in millions):

	1999	2000
Ending inventory	$18	$22
Gross margin	62	75
Retained earnings	54	66

Early in 2001, management discovered that the ending inventory for 1999 was overstated by $7 million, and the ending inventory for 2000 was correctly measured. The company's income tax rate in both years was 40 percent.

Required

Determine the effects, if any, of the overstatement of 1999's ending inventory on Illusory Products' gross margin and retained earnings for 1999 and 2000.

PROBLEMS

Footnote Disclosures: Convert from LIFO to FIFO-Based Measures of Cost of Goods Sold

6-41 Dolo's Building Block Company uses LIFO costing and reports the following information in a footnote to its financial statements: "If Dolo had used FIFO costing during 2000, the beginning and ending inventories would have been higher by $50 million and $70 million, respectively."

Required

a. Determine how much higher or lower Dolo's cost of goods sold would be during 2000 if the firm had used FIFO in costing its inventories.
b. Assume that all of Dolo's income is taxed at 40%. How much higher or lower would Dolo's income tax expense be during 2000 if the firm had used FIFO?
c. What was Dolo's tax savings for the year due to the use of LIFO?
d. What was Dolo's *cumulative* tax savings through the end of the year 2000?

Financial Statement Effects of Inventory Costing Methods, First Year of Operations

6-42 Tom Hanky, a financial analyst specializing in the toy industry, has provided the following comments concerning the 1999 financial statements of Toys-U-Must:

Toys-U-Must began operations in 1999 and uses the LIFO method in costing its inventories. Because the typical firm in the industry uses FIFO costing, it is desirable to adjust the company's financial statements "as if" FIFO costing had been used. Footnotes to the financial statements reveal that the use of FIFO would increase the company's inventory valuation by $150 million, and that the company's income is taxed at 40%.

Required

Based on Hanky's comments, explain how each of the following items would be adjusted in Toys-U-Must's 1999 financial statements:

a. Inventory
b. Working capital (current assets less current liabilities)
c. Gross margin
d. Income tax expense
e. Net income
f. Retained earnings
g. At the end of 2000, Toys-U-Must's financial statement footnotes reveal that the use of FIFO costing would increase the company's ending inventory valuation by $200 million (the effects on the beginning inventory were described above). Explain how each of the following items would be adjusted in order to convert the company's reported accounts "as if" the firm had used FIFO costing during 2000:
   1. Inventory
   2. Working capital
   3. Gross margin
   4. Income tax expense
   5. Net income
   6. Retained earnings

Ratio Calculations: LIFO and FIFO

6-43 Teddie Bower, Inc., reported the following data in its annual financial statements (dollars in thousands):

	1999	2000
Sales	$333,667	$313,456
Cost of goods sold—LIFO	32,587	44,690
Cost of goods sold—FIFO	30,198	45,833
Ending inventory—LIFO	11,189	10,567
Ending inventory—FIFO	15,999	14,234
Net income—LIFO	34,000	33,500
Net income—FIFO	38,980	37,765

Required

a. Calculate the number of days' sales in ending inventory (NDS) under both LIFO and FIFO.
b. Calculate the gross profit percentage under both LIFO and FIFO.
c. Discuss the differences in inventory levels, income, and gross profit under both LIFO and FIFO.
d. Discuss why a firm might prefer LIFO under these circumstances.

Income Differences: FIFO and LIFO

6-44 Jeans R'Us, Inc., reported the following data in its annual financial statements (dollars in thousands):

	2000	2001
Cost of goods sold—LIFO	31,678	44,690
Cost of goods sold—FIFO	31,089	41,656
Ending inventory—LIFO	12,298	13,365
Ending inventory—FIFO	14,888	18,989
Net income—LIFO	30,500	37,775
Net income—FIFO	37,895	40,876

Required

a. Discuss the differences in inventory values and net income under both LIFO and FIFO.
b. Discuss why a firm might prefer LIFO under these circumstances.

Potential LIFO Liquidation: Effect on Profits

6-45 El Puerto Company uses LIFO for its inventories. Information regarding 2000's beginning inventory and purchases up until December 15, 2000 is shown below:

Beginning inventory (January 1, 2000) 500,000 units @ $10	$5 million
Purchases during 2000: 1,200,000 units @ an average cost of $20	$24 million

El Puerto sold 1,500,000 units up to December 15 and expects that very few, if any, additional sales will occur before year-end. Inventory purchase costs are $25 per unit at December 15, and prices are not expected to change over the remainder of 2000. The company's income tax rate is 40%.

Required

a. Determine El Puerto Company's ending inventory value and cost of goods sold for 2000, assuming that (1) no additional purchases are made during 2000 and (2) an additional 400,000 units are purchased at $25 per unit before year-end.
b. Based on these calculations, would you advise the company to purchase additional inventory before year-end? Explain.

Comprehensive Marketable Securities, Accounts Receivable, Inventory

6-46 Pratsky, Inc., had the following account balances:

December 31, 1999

Assets		**Liabilities**	
Cash	$12,500	Accounts payable	$10,000
Accounts Receivable	22,400		
Allowance for		**Stockholders' Equity:**	
uncollectible accounts	(3,400)	Invested capital	20,000
Inventory	17,500	Retained earnings	19,000
		Total stockholders' equity	39,000
	$49,000		$49,000

During 2000, the corporation had the following transactions:

1. Issued common stock for $40,000 cash.
2. Purchased inventory on account; 200 units @ $38, then 150 units @ $39. Note: Beginning inventory was comprised of 500 units @ $35.
3. Purchased 200 shares of IBM for $45/share and purchased 100 shares of Microsoft for $90/share.
4. Sales at retail during 2000 were $75,000 (half received in cash, and the balance on account).
5. Write-offs of uncollectible accounts totaled $2,600.
6. Received $38,000 from receivable customers.
7. Paid creditors on account, $18,000. Paid operating expenses for the current period of $51,000.

8. At year-end, a physical inventory equaled 225 units. The company uses the LIFO inventory costing method.
9. Assume that marketable securities are "available-for-sale," and the market price at December 31, 2000, for IBM is $42/share, and for Microsoft $102/share.
10. Based on the accounts receivable aging, management feels that the allowance for uncollectible accounts should have a balance of $5,700 at year-end.

Required

a. Set up the beginning balances in the balance sheet equation. Leave enough room to add new columns as necessary.
b. Record transactions 1 through 10 using the balance sheet equation.
c. Calculate the following ratios for 1999 and 2000 and evaluate the company's management of its accounts receivable:
   - Accounts receivable/sales (assume that sales in 1999 were $125,786)
   - Sales/day
   - Collection period
   - Allowance as a percentage of accounts receivable

Ratio Calculations: Comprehensive Problem Including LIFO and FIFO

Critical Thinking

6-47 Two similar companies use different inventory valuation methods. In fact, the companies are identical except for their inventory methods. L Co. uses the LIFO inventory valuation method, and F Co. uses FIFO.

Income Statements	**L Co.**	**F Co.**
Sales	$ 30,000	$30,000
Cost of goods sold	(21,280)	(19,200)
Gross profit	8,720	10,800
Selling, general, and administrative	(6,000)	(6,000)
Income before interest expense	2,720	4,800
Interest expense (12%)	(960)	(960)
Income before taxes	$ 1,760	$ 3,840
Balance Sheets		
Assets		
Cash	$ 4,000	$ 4,000
Accounts receivable	5,000	5,000
Inventory	2,720	4,800
Total current assets	11,720	13,800
Fixed assets (net)	30,000	30,000
Total assets	$ 41,720	$43,800
Equities		
Current liabilities	$ 3,200	$ 3,200
Long-term liabilities	8,000	8,000
Total liabilities	11,200	11,200
Shareholders' equity	30,520	32,600
Total equities	$ 41,720	$43,800

Required

Using the financial statements from L Co. and F Co., calculate the following ratios (assume an income tax rate of 20%):

a. Current ratio
b. Accounts receivable as a percentage of sales
c. Average sales per day
d. Collection period
e. Gross profit percentage
f. Cost of goods sold per day
g. Number of days sales' in ending inventory
h. Operating income ratio
i. Return on equity (assume that average shareholders' equity for L and F Co. are $30,000 and $32,000, respectively)
j. Return on assets (assume that average total assets for L and F Co. are $41,000 and $43,000, respectively)

Based on these results (a through j, above), which company represents

k. The best lending alternative? Why?
l. The best investment alternative? Why?
m. The best acquisition alternative? Why?

Ratio Calculations: Effects of FIFO and LIFO

6-48 Two similar companies use different inventory valuation methods. LL Co. uses the LIFO inventory valuation method, and FF Co. uses FIFO. Ignore the effect of income taxes on each company.

Income Statements	**LL Co.**	**FF Co.**
Sales	$ 35,000	$35,000
Cost of goods sold	(20,350)	(18,200)
Gross profit	14,650	16,800
Selling, general, and administrative	(6,000)	(6,000)
Income before interest expense	8,650	10,800
Interest expense (12%)	(960)	(960)
Income before taxes	$ 7,690	$ 9,840
Balance Sheets		
Total current assets	10,320	12,870
Fixed assets (net)	29,000	31,000
Total assets	$ 39,320	$43,870
Equities		
Current liabilities	$ 3,120	$ 3,270
Long-term liabilities	8,000	8,000
Total liabilities	11,120	11,270
Shareholders' equity	28,200	32,600
Total equities	$ 39,320	$43,870

Required

Using the financial statements from LL Co. and FF Co., calculate the following ratios:

a. Current ratio
b. Average sales per day
c. Gross profit percentage

(Continued)

d. Cost of goods sold per day
e. Operating income ratio
f. Return on equity (use ending shareholders' equity in the denominator)
g. Return on assets (use ending total assets in the denominator)
h. Based on these results (above), which company seems to be better managed? In which company would you prefer to make an equity investment? Explain.

Accounts Receivable: Effects on Allowance for Uncollectibles

6-49 Becca's Finance and Collection Company has had a lot of trouble collecting its receivables recently. Discuss how each of the following circumstances might be reflected in the Allowance for Uncollectible Accounts:

1. Dagwood Bumpstead has an "open" account that is always overdue. Dagwood makes regular payments of $500 each month, but the balance in his account is always about $4,000.
2. Blondie purchased a car using $4,000 borrowed from Becca's. Blondie has not made any payments for six months, and her overdue balance exceeds $1,200.
3. Sad Sack has just borrowed $4,000 from Becca's, has excellent credit references, and after borrowing the money has sent Becca's a change-of-address notification showing a new address in Brazil.
4. Blondie paid her overdue balance.
5. Dagwood's son purchased a car using $4,000 borrowed from Becca's. He has no credit references, other than the family connections and circumstances discussed earlier. Becca's is unable to get Dagwood to cosign the note!
6. Blondie's daughter purchased a new sound system for her house and car, using $4,000 borrowed from Becca's. She has an excellent credit history, but after purchasing the sound system, it failed; she informed Becca's that because the seller provided no warranty, she was not going to make any payments on the defective sound system.

Accounts Receivable: Effects on Allowance for Uncollectibles

6-50 Becca's Finance and Collection Company had the following year-end balances in its financial statements:

	1999	2000
Accounts receivable	$300,000	$500,000
Allowance for uncollectibles	(50,000)	(50,000)
Interest and finance revenue	150,000	300,000

Required

a. Assess the adequacy of the 2000 balance in the allowance for uncollectibles.
b. Describe the interest and finance revenue account. What does this account include? On which financial statement does it appear?
c. Calculate the accounts receivable as a percentage of revenues for each year. Evaluate the trends in this ratio.
d. Assume that the credit-worthiness of Becca's customer base significantly deteriorated at the end of 2000. Assess the adequacy of its allowance for uncollectibles under these new circumstances.

Transaction Analysis: Accounts Receivable

6-51 S. Claus Company ended the 2000 season with an accounts receivable balance of $375,000, less allowance for uncollectible accounts of $37,500. Use the accounting equation to reflect each of the following situations and calculate the 2001 season's ending balance in accounts receivable and the allowance account.

1. Revenues in 2001 were $4,500,000, half of which were collected in cash, with the balance on account.
2. Cash collections of accounts receivable in 2001 were $2,375,000.
3. Write-offs of delinquent accounts in 2001 were $2,000. (Most people are not willing to offend S. Claus!)
4. S. Claus wants its allowance account, at the end of 2001, to have the same proportionate relationship reflected at the end of 2000.

Analyzing Accounts Receivable

6-52 The Atlas Tile Company has an accounts receivable balance at December 31 of $376,000. Its allowance for uncollectible accounts, before adjustment, has a balance of $37,000. Credit sales for Atlas, for the year just ended, were $2,700,000. Using its credit history, Atlas decides to increase its allowance account by 3% of credit sales.

Required

a. Calculate the allowance for uncollectible accounts as a percentage of the accounts receivable ratio, both before and after the 3% adjustment was made.

b. Now assume that the firm's auditors have conducted an aging analysis and recommend that the allowance account balance be increased to $96,000. Recalculate the allowance for uncollectible accounts as a percentage of accounts receivable ratio after this alternative adjustment has been made.

c. Compare and contrast these results.

Calculating Ending Inventory: FIFO, LIFO, and Average-Cost Method

6-53 S. Claus Company makes toys and gifts. At the beginning of July, it owned 200 gallons of red paint, which were recorded on the balance sheet at $4.00 per gallon. The following events occurred in the next quarter.

1. Purchased 300 gallons on July 1 at $4.25 each.
2. Purchased 500 gallons on August 1 at $4.50 each.
3. Purchased 800 gallons during September at $4.75 each.
4. Used 1,450 gallons during July through September.

Required

a. Calculate the inventory balance at the end of September and the cost of goods sold (given away!) during these three months, using FIFO accounting.

b. Calculate the inventory balance at the end of September and the cost of goods sold (given away!) during these three months, using LIFO accounting.

c. Calculate the inventory balance at the end of September and the cost of goods sold (given away!) during these three months, using the average cost method to determine inventory balances.

d. Explain and discuss the differences shown under each method. Explain why the total costs of goods available for sale (delivery!) must be identical under all methods.

e. Under what circumstances would S. Claus prefer one method to the others? Under what circumstances would S. Claus prefer one result to the others? Discuss how S. Claus might make a choice between inventory costing methods.

Financial Statement Effects: Prepaid Insurance

6-54 Firefly Beach Cottages, Inc., purchased a three-year fire insurance policy for $4,800. The policy was purchased on July 1, 1999, and financial statements are prepared as of December 31 each year.

Required

a. Show the effects of this insurance policy on the balance sheets for each of the following years during which this policy would have an effect.
b. Similarly, calculate the effects on the income statement in each year.

Interpreting Financial Statements: Current Assets

6-55 Refer to Reebok's financial statements in Appendix E. Review the financial statements to determine how and where current assets have been reported.

Required

a. Calculate the following accounts receivable ratios:
   - Accounts receivable as a percentage of sales
   - Average sales per day
   - Collection period
   - Allowance for uncollectible accounts as a percentage of accounts receivable
b. Based on these results, what conclusions can be drawn regarding Reebok's accounts receivable?
c. Calculate the following inventory ratios:
   - Gross profit percentage
   - Cost of goods sold per day
   - Number of days sales' in ending inventory (NDS)
d. Based on these results, what conclusions can be drawn regarding Reebok's inventories and cost of goods sold?
e. Discuss any other unusual concerns regarding Reebok's current assets. What other related information might an external analyst require or prefer?

Interpreting Financial Statements: Current Assets

6-56 Refer to Wendy's financial statements in Appendix D. Review the financial statements to determine how and where current assets have been reported.

Required

a. Did Wendy's disclose how it calculated the allowance for uncollectible accounts? Is it essential for a financial analyst to know which method has been used? What reliance can an analyst place on the firm's disclosure of its allowances?
b. If the allowance amounts were not separately disclosed, discuss how they have been included in the firm's balance sheet.
c. Calculate the following accounts receivable ratios (assume that the doubtful account amounts pertaining to royalties are netted in the accounts receivable):
   - Accounts receivable as a percentage of sales
   - Average sales per day
   - Collection period (*Note:* Wendy's uses a 52/53 week year.)
   - Allowance for uncollectible accounts as a percentage of accounts receivable

(Continued)

d. Based on these results, what conclusions can be drawn regarding Wendy's accounts receivable?
e. Calculate the following inventory ratios:
   - Gross profit percentage
   - Cost of goods sold per day
   - Number of days' sales in ending inventory (NDS) (use the caption "inventory and other" line item for inventory)
f. Based on these results, what conclusions can be drawn regarding Wendy's inventories and cost of goods sold?
g. Discuss any other unusual concerns regarding Wendy's current assets. What other related information might an external analyst require or prefer?

Critical Thinking

Conceptual Discussion: Marketable Securities

6-57 Marketable securities are usually shown on the balance sheet as current assets. Based on what you have learned, under what circumstances might they be shown as noncurrent assets? Why do you think a firm might hold its investments in marketable securities for more than a year?

Critical Thinking

Conceptual Discussion: Credit Management

6-58 The manager of Rob's Shoe Store has been congratulated by her division manager for almost completely eliminating all bad debts. She instituted a policy of conducting extensive credit checks on all prospective credit customers and, consequently, rejects most applications. The cost of each credit report is $50 and the store's profits have declined significantly since she adopted this policy.

Required

a. Identify the circumstances under which this might be an acceptable policy. Under what circumstances might this be an unwise or unacceptable policy?
b. The manager of Rob's Shoe Store is considering conducting her own credit checks and preparing her own credit reports in order to avoid the $50 cost of credit reports on each prospective credit customer. Why might this not be a cost-effective practice?
c. Why would the manager of Rob's Shoe Store want to have large inventories on hand? Why would her division manager want to curtail these desires? Could a firm ever have too much inventory? If so, what undesirable consequences might occur?

Critical Thinking

Interpreting Financial Statements: Liquidity

6-59 Kesler Inc. is a research-based health care company whose objectives include the application of scientific knowledge to help people enjoy longer, healthier, and more productive lives. Its balance sheets for 2000 and 1999 show the following amounts (dollars in millions):

	2000	1999
Cash and cash equivalents	$1,295.0	$1,384.7
Short-term investments	502.4	307.6

In the Summary of Significant Accounting Policies in its Notes to Consolidated Financial Statements, Kesler reported:

The Company considers demand deposits, certificates of deposit, and certain time deposits with maturities of three months or less at the date of purchase to be cash equivalents. Certain items that meet the definition of cash equivalents but are part of a larger pool of investments are included in Short-term investments.

Required

a. Describe, in your own words, what Kesler may have done with some of its cash equivalents between 1999 and 2000.
b. Is Kesler's reporting of cash and cash equivalents consistent with most company's use of the balance sheet category "Cash and cash equivalents"? Why?
c. How do your conclusions change if you later learn that Kesler's *second* category of cash equivalents, described as "Certain items... included in Short-term investments," was only about $2.5 (million) each year? What if it were more than $200 (million) each year?
d. Evaluate Kesler's treatment of cash and cash equivalents if the following amounts had been reported?:

	2000	1999
Cash and cash equivalents	$880	$ 165
Short-term investments, *at cost*	$445	$1,257

e. Based on this hypothetical situation, what actions did Kesler probably take in 2000 to improve its cash position?
f. Given Kesler's inclusion of some cash and cash equivalents on *two separate lines* of its balance sheet, how should an external analyst use these data in analyzing Kesler's liquidity? In other words, what should an analyst do to comprehensively interpret Kesler's liquidity?

Integration of Concepts

Interpreting Financial Statements: Inventory Methods

6-60 Pioneer Resource, Inc., reported the following in its Notes to Consolidated Financial Statements for 1999.

Material and Supplies: Inventories of new and reusable material and supplies are stated at the lower of cost or market with cost determined on a FIFO or average cost basis. For certain large individual items, however, cost is determined on a specific identification basis.

Required

a. Identify and explain, in your own words, all of the inventory costing methods used by Pioneer Resource.
b. Why might Pioneer Resource use these different methods? Do these various inventory methods enhance the internal consistency and usability of Pioneer Resource's financial data? Why?
c. If inventories comprised only 1% of Pioneer Resource's assets, how would that change your views on Pioneer's use of these different inventory costing methods? What if inventories were 15% of Pioneer Resource's assets?
d. If the inventory balances reported by Pioneer Resource in 1999 and 1998 were $212.3 and $212.2 million, respectively, how would that change your view of Pioneer Resource's choice of reporting methods? Note that Pioneer Resource's 1999 total assets exceeded $22.4 billion. If in subsequent years you found that Pioneer Resource's inventories had increased by 300%, how would that change your views of these diverse inventory costing methods?

Critical Thinking

Interpreting Financial Statements: Current Assets

6-61 Entertainment Office Group is a leading producer of film (and video) entertainment. Its 1999 and 1998 consolidated balance sheets reported the following assets (dollars in thousands):

	1999	1998
Cash and short-term investments	$ 37,015	$ 38,402
Accounts receivable, net	66,241	32,659
Film costs and program rights, net	180,501	130,204
Property, plant, and equipment, net	5,231	7,124
Other assets	—	14,050
Current liabilities	120,507	156,419

Required

a. Evaluate Entertainment's liquidity on the basis of the above information.

b. Assume that Entertainment's revenues doubled between 1998 and 1999. Reevaluate the change in accounts receivable. If Entertainment's revenues were constant, reconsider your conclusions about accounts receivable.

c. What does the term "net" mean in each of the cases shown above?

d. Why might "Other assets" disappear in 1999?

e. What is meant by the term "Film costs and program rights"? Could this be viewed as a type of inventory? If these were stocks of films and scripts, how would the fickle nature of public opinion and personal tastes affect your evaluation of Entertainment's assets and its liquidity? Why?

f. Entertainment's Notes to Consolidated Financial Statements contained the following item:

Program Rights

Advance payments to producers are recorded as program rights in the balance sheet and are stated at the lower of cost or estimated net realizable value.

i. How does this knowledge of how program rights are created affect your prior conclusions? Can its program rights still be viewed as inventory? Why?

ii. If these advance payments will not be refunded by the producers, under any circumstances, how does that change your opinion concerning the program rights?

iii. What other information about the producers, the films, and the scripts would you need to have before coming to a final conclusion about the program rights?

iv. How does the relative proportion of program rights to other assets affect your conclusions? Note that Entertainment's total assets were between $450 million and $475 million, each year.

v. If the program rights were less than $10,000,000 each year, would that change your conclusions about Entertainment's assets?

g. Assume that a further note in Entertainment's annual report includes the following information:

Film Costs and Program Rights:
Film costs and program rights, net of amortization, comprised the following at December 31 (dollars in thousands):

	1999	1998
Film costs:		
Released	$ 68,304	$ 60,028
In process and other	8,863	13,723
Program rights	103,334	56,453
	$180,501	$130,204

It is estimated that approximately half of the film cost associated with the released product will be amortized in the next three years.

In October 1999, Entertainment purchased domestic television rights from Oroco Television, Inc. to their film library of more than 142 feature films and related receivables for approximately $45 million, plus the assumption of approximately $10 million in liabilities.

i. How does this new information about program rights affect your conclusions? Does the fact that a substantial portion of these amounts relates to released films affect your conclusions? How?
ii. Explain, in your own words, what happened in October 1999. Indicate how the Oroco purchase was recorded in Entertainment's assets?
iii. Given this new knowledge about the Oroco purchase, what final conclusions can be drawn about Entertainment's film costs and program rights?

Conceptual Discussion: Factoring Accounts Receivable

Writing

6-62 Describe the concept of factoring accounts receivable. If necessary, conduct further research in a finance text to determine what functions a factor performs. Consider the following factoring issues:

a. Why would a company sell its receivables to a factor?
b. If these receivables were 180 days old, why might a factor not be interested in purchasing them?
c. Who bears the risk in factoring? How can these risks be shifted?
d. What industries might use factoring more extensively (than other industries)?
e. Why wouldn't a convenience store or a discount store be able to factor its accounts receivable, even if it had such receivables?

Disclosure of Compensating Balances

Critical Thinking

6-63 Discuss the implications of the following note. How will it affect the company's liquidity? How will it affect the company's overall asset management policies?

Conry Publishing Company
1999 Annual Report
Note 5 (Partial)

At December 31, 1999, the Company has a $10,000,000 Line of Credit Agreement ("Credit Agreement") with a bank. The Credit Agreement provides for a short-term, variable-rate line of credit under which the Company may borrow and repay from time to time until maturity on May 31, 2002. The Credit Agreement requires the Company to maintain compensating balances of $200,000 with the bank in lieu of annual commitment fees. No borrowings were outstanding under the Credit Agreement as of December 31, 1999.

Critical Thinking

Comparisons of Accounts Receivable Ratios

6-64 Financial analysts have computed the following ratios for Firm X and several industries where Firm X has significant operations. Evaluate Firm X's performance relative to each industry. What factors might account for the differences observed?

Accounts Receivable Ratios
Industry Comparisons

	Firm X	**Apparel Manufacturers**	**Food Stores**
Accounts receivable as a percentage of sales	7.6%	13.5%	1.4%
Collection period	28 days	48 days	5 days
Allowance as a percentage of accounts receivable	13.4%	2.5%	0.9%

Critical Thinking

Evaluating Management's Explanations

6-65 Topps Co., Inc., produces sports cards. During two quarters in the same year, Topps' accounts receivable increased by more than 50%, while sales declined. Such a trend might indicate that Topps is experiencing difficulty collecting from its customers.

Topps asserts, however, that receivables have increased because of a change in its shipping schedule. It has begun to ship 50% of its cards in the final few weeks of a quarter. Thus, many of its accounts receivable are outstanding at quarter's end, and at the same time, are not yet past due.

Required

a. How might Firm X's managers react to these data?
b. What recommendations would you make to Firm X?

Critical Thinking

Inventory Write-downs

6-66 Storage Technology Corporation (StorageTek) is a manufacturer of computer storage devices. StorageTek continually modifies its existing products and develops new ones. These improvements permit larger amounts of data to be stored and accessed more quickly.

One of StorageTek's new products was called Iceberg. An Iceberg system comprised many small storage devices designed to work together. StorageTek was quite optimistic about Iceberg's future success.

Because Iceberg held clear advantages over other systems that StorageTek sells, StorageTek needed to reduce the selling price of these other systems. Because of this, StorageTek must also ensure that the recorded value of its inventory is not overstated. In fact, in the first quarter of 1994, shortly before Iceberg was marketed to the public, StorageTek reduced the recorded value of its older storage systems by $7,500,000. Write-downs such as this are rather common in industries that experience rapid technological change.

For the first quarter in 1994, StorageTek reported the following:

Revenue	$335,623,000
Cost of goods sold	$234,315,000

Assume that the $7,500,000 charge was included in cost of goods sold.

Required

a. What effect did the write-down have on
   i. gross profit?
   ii gross profit percentage?
b. Under these circumstances, what issues will be of concern to StorageTek's managers? What recommendations would you make to StorageTek? Justify your recommendations.

Ethics

Accounts Receivable Management

6-67 Sheila Glow sells advertising for KBOL, a local radio station. She receives a small monthly salary plus a commission of 20% of all advertising contracts that she negotiates and that are billed by KBOL. KBOL conducts an informal credit review on all new clients, but relies extensively on the salesperson's recommendations.

Because Sheila interviews the owner and chief financial officer (CFO) of all her new clients, she feels that her credit screening should be an adequate basis on which KBOL could reliably determine whether to accept or reject a potential client's credit request.

One potential new client, Atlas Tile Company, has been experiencing financial difficulties and several letters to the editors from disgruntled customers have recently appeared in the local newspaper. Although Sheila knows that Atlas needs many new customers, her commissions have not been strong this month compared to prior months.

KBOL always has the right to reject Atlas's credit application. Sheila knows that if the credit application contains favorable information, it is likely to be accepted. In the process of helping Atlas' CFO complete the application, she suggests that City Bank's rejection of Atlas' loan application for $5,000 worth of working capital not be shown on the current application for KBOL's credit. She reasons that Atlas needs her help, and it is not her job to collect the bills; it is only her job to sell radio advertising.

Required

a. What are the ethical ramifications of Sheila's actions?
b. What are the likely business results of Sheila's actions?
c. How does KBOL's commission policy affect Sheila's incentives?
d. How might the commission policy be changed to more closely align Sheila's incentives with KBOL's goals?
e. If the radio station's managers find that Sheila helped falsify the credit report, what should they do? Why?

Critical Thinking

Comparative Intercompany Analysis: Current Assets and Current Liabilities

6-68 The following balance sheet segments were extracted from the SEC's EDGAR data base:

Consolidated Balance Sheets
ELI LILLY AND COMPANY AND SUBSIDIARIES
(Dollars in millions)

December 31	1997	1996
Current Assets		
Cash and cash equivalents	$ 1,947.5	$ 813.7
Short-term investments	77.1	141.4
Accounts receivable, net of allowances of $53.3 (1997) and $82.4 (1996)	1,544.3	1,474.6
Other receivables	338.9	262.5
Inventories (Note 1)	900.7	881.4
Deferred income taxes (Note 12)	325.7	145.2
Prepaid expenses	186.5	172.5
Total current assets	5,320.7	3,891.3

December 31	1997	1996
Current Liabilities		
Short-term borrowings (Note 7)	$ 227.6	$ 1,212.9
Accounts payable	985.5	829.3
Employee compensation	456.6	388.4
Dividends payable	221.7	198.8
Income taxes payable (Note 12)	1,188.0	691.8
Other liabilities	1,112.2	901.0
Total current liabilities	4,191.6	4,222.2

PFIZER INC AND SUBSIDIARY COMPANIES
CONSOLIDATED BALANCE SHEET

December 31 (millions, except per share data)	1997	1996	1995
Current Assets			
Cash and cash equivalents	$ 877	$ 1,150	$ 403
Short-term investments	712	487	1,109
Accounts receivable, less allowance for doubtful accounts: 1997--$51; 1996--$58; 1995--$61	2,527	2,252	2,024
Short-term loans	115	354	289
Inventories			
Finished goods	677	617	564
Work in process	852	695	579
Raw materials and supplies	244	277	241
Total inventories	1,773	1,589	1,384
Prepaid expenses, taxes, and other assets	816	636	943
Total current assets	6,820	6,468	6,152

Current Liabilities			
Short-term borrowings, including current portion of long-term debt	$ 2,255	$ 2,235	$ 2,036
Accounts payable	765	913	715
Income taxes payable	785	892	822
Accrued compensation and related items	477	436	421
Other current liabilities	1,023	1,164	1,193
Total current liabilities	5,305	5,640	5,187

Required:

a. Conduct a liquidity analysis for each company.
b. Identify which company is more liquid. Justify your answer.
c. Which company seems to manage its accounts receivable better? Why?
d. Which company seems to manage its inventories better? Why?
e. Discuss any unusual issues concerning the current assets or current liabilities of either company.

Internet

Computing Liquidity Ratios

6-69 Owens-Corning values its inventories using LIFO. This presents a problem when comparing its current ratio against that of a company using FIFO. Locate the latest financial statements for Owens-Corning at the company page **(www.owens-corning.com)** or from the 10-K filed in the EDGAR archives **(www.sec.gov/edgarhp.htm).**

Required

a. Compute the current ratio and the number of days' sales (NDS) in ending inventory based on numbers reported on the balance sheet.
b. Find the FIFO value of inventory reported in the Notes to the Financial Statements and recompute the current ratio and NDS.
c. Compare the ratios based on LIFO to those based on FIFO. How different are they? Do you think that the observed differences are great enough to have an impact on a decision?

Internet

Evaluating Company Disclosures Regarding Marketable Securities

6-70 Locate the latest available set of financial statements for Oncogene Science, Inc., from the 10-K on file in the EDGAR archives.

Required

a. In what types of short-term securities does Oncogene invest? (The information needed to answer this question can be found in the Notes to the Financial Statements.)
b. According to SFAS No. 115, what alternatives are available to Oncogene for reporting its investments in short-term securities?
c. Does Oncogene classify its short-term investments as trading securities, available-for-sale securities, or held-to-maturity securities?
d. Describe how Oncogene's investments are reflected on the income statement, balance sheet, statement of shareholders' equity, and statement of cash flows.

Internet

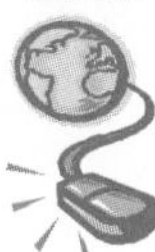

Evaluating Industry Inventory Data

6-71 The Center for Inventory Management (CIM) publishes quarterly inventory ratios for manufacturing industry groups.

Required

a. How does CIM **(www.inventorymanagement.com)** compute its inventory ratio? What shortcomings are implicit in its calculations?
b. How would you convert CIM's inventory ratio to the number of days' sales in ending inventory described by this textbook?
c. Access the latest Inventory Ratio Study reported on the CIM home page **(www.inventorymanagement.com)** and identify the inventory ratios for two types of transportation equipment industries: motor vehicles and aircraft. Why are the ratios so different?

Internet

Evaluating Accounts Receivable

6-72 In the HMO industry, accounts receivable represent one of the major assets. HMOs provide medical services to patients and then bill insurance companies and Medicare/Medicaid agencies. Timely collection is important to maintaining adequate liquidity. Locate the latest 10-K filings for Columbia/HCA Healthcare and FHP International, using the EDGAR archives.

Required

a. What is the value of net accounts receivable? What percent of total assets and current assets do they represent for each company?
b. What is the value of allowance for uncollectible accounts and what percentage of gross accounts receivable does it represent?
c. What are the net revenues for each HMO? Which HMO is larger?
d. Calculate the accounts receivable collection period for both companies.
e. Which company is doing a better job with its accounts receivable?

a p p e n d i x

6

Bank Statements and Reconciliations

An earlier part of the chapter noted that bank statements provide an accounting of cash that is independent of the accounting undertaken by the firm. Exhibit 6A-1 contains an illustration of Quick Company's bank statement for the month of April. One column shows withdrawals, one column reflects deposits, and the final column keeps a running total of the account's balance. This particular bank statement contains check numbers, which makes comparing the bank statement and the accounting records much easier. Notice that two withdrawals were not made by check. One withdrawal was preauthorized, which means that Quick has previously instructed the bank to make certain payments. A monthly loan payment is a good example. The other direct withdrawal was the service charge assessed by the bank for processing checks, making preauthorized payments, and so on.

As of any given date (such as April 30), the cash balance reported on the bank statement might not agree with the balance in the firm's accounting records (often called the book balance). This situation can arise for three general reasons. First, some transactions may be reflected in the accounting records, but not on the bank statement. For example, after a check is written and mailed to the payee, several days (or weeks) may elapse before the payee cashes the check and the check clears through the banking system. Until this happens, the bank is unaware of the check. Checks that are included in the accounting records but not shown on the bank statement are called **outstanding checks.**

EXHIBIT 6A-1 Bank Statement

Quick Company
Bank Statement
April 2000

Date	Description	Withdrawals	Deposits	Balance
4-1	Balance			$7,780
4-6	Check # 210	$ 180		7,600
4-10	Check # 212	500		7,100
4-13	Check # 213	1,000		6,100
4-15	Deposit		$2,300	8,400
4-21	Check # 215	200		8,200
4-25	Check # 216	400		7,800
4-30	Preauthorized	140		7,660
4-30	Service charge	10		7,650

A **deposit-in-transit** is another reconciling item that is recorded in the accounting records but not yet recorded on the bank statement. Most banks delay, by one business day, processing deposits made after a certain time of day (say, 3 P.M.). These cash receipts, however, are already recorded in the firm's accounting records. Therefore, deposits made after 3 P.M. on the last business day of a month will be included in the month-end book balance, but not the bank balance.

The second major reason why the bank balance and the book balance might differ is that the bank statement may reflect items not yet shown in the accounting records. For example, prior to receiving the bank statement, firms usually will not have made entries in the accounting records for bank service charges and preauthorized withdrawals.

Errors, either in the accounting records or on the bank statement, are the third reason why the bank balance and the book balance might differ. If errors are unintentional and occur infrequently, they are not a cause for alarm; they simply need to be corrected. However, frequent or intentional errors involving cash warrant careful investigation.

Exhibit 6A-2 contains Quick Company's April accounting records for cash, and Exhibit 6A-3 illustrates Quick's April 30 bank reconciliation. Several valid approaches exist for preparing a bank reconciliation. The approach in Exhibit 6A-3 modifies both the bank and the book balances to obtain a corrected balance. The goal of the reconciliation is for the two corrected balances to agree. If this is accomplished, all the differences between the two sets of records have been identified, and the firm can have increased confidence that the accounting for cash is proper.

To prepare a reconciliation, compare the bank statement and the accounting records to identify those items appearing on one but not the other. These items result in differences between the book and the bank balances and must be included in the reconciliation.

Exhibit 6A-2 shows that Quick received $1,000 on April 30. That amount does not appear on the bank statement. Evidently, it was deposited after the close of business on April 30. This deposit-in-transit must be added to the bank balance.

EXHIBIT 6A-2 Accounting Records for Cash

Quick Company
Internal Cash Records

Date	Description	Amount
4-1	Balance	$7,780
4-2	Check # 210	– 180
4-3	Check # 211	– 750
4-5	Check # 212	– 500
4-8	Check # 213	– 1,000
4-12	Check # 214	– 300
4-14	Deposit	2,300
4-17	Check # 215	– 200
4-22	Check # 216	– 400
4-26	Check # 217	– 50
4-28	Check # 218	– 250
4-30	Deposit	1,000
4-30	Balance	$7,450

EXHIBIT 6A-3 Bank Reconciliation

Quick Company
Bank Reconciliation
April 30, 2000

Bank Balance		$7,650
Plus: Deposit-in-transit		1,000
		$8,650
Less: Outstanding checks		
# 211	$750	
# 214	300	
# 217	50	
# 218	250	
		(1,350)
Corrected balance		$7,300
Book balance		$7,450
Less: Preauthorized withdrawal		(140)
Service charge		(10)
Corrected balance		$7,300

Exhibit 6A-2 also shows that Quick wrote nine checks during April. However, checks 211, 214, 217, and 218 do not appear on the bank statement. Accordingly, these outstanding checks are subtracted from the bank balance.

Quick's bank statement (refer to Exhibit 6A-1) contains two entries that do not appear in the accounting records: the preauthorized withdrawal and the service charge. The book balance should be reduced by these amounts. Also note that when Quick receives the bank statement and discovers the preauthorized withdrawal and the service charge, the accounting records should be adjusted accordingly.

At this point in the reconciliation, the book balance and the bank balance have been adjusted and show the same corrected balance. This indicates that the reconciliation is complete.

One final point must be made about the Quick Company illustration. All the reconciling items for the April 30 reconciliation arose during the month of April. This is not always the case. For example, Quick could have written a check in March that did not clear the bank by the end of April. This check would be outstanding at the end of April and would need to appear on the April 30 reconciliation. In general, items from the immediately preceding reconciliation should be reviewed to ascertain if they should be carried forward to the current month's reconciliation.

KEY TERMS

SUMMARY OF LEARNING OBJECTIVE

Prepare a bank reconciliation.
A bank reconciliation explains why a firm's bank statement balance differs from its book balance. Differences arise for three general reasons: (1) transactions were recorded in the accounting records but not the bank statement; (2) transactions were recorded on the bank statement but not the accounting records; and (3) errors.

Bank Statement Reconciliation

6A-1 Theraux Corporation received its bank statement for the month ended October 31, 1999. Contained in the bank statement were the following items:

	Check #	$ Amount
Checks cleared:	1140	$100
	1156	400
	1159	250
	1161	500
	1162	183
	1163	175
	1165	194

	Date	$ Amount
Deposits cleared:	10/3/99	$1,250
	10/5/99	480
	10/16/99	1,595
	10/25/99	942
	10/28/99	2,106

Other Items:

(NSF) from J. Strauss	$ 275
Bank charges	80
Note receivable collected	640
Interest on note receivable	15
Beginning bank balance	5,300
Ending bank balance	10,171

Theraux's check register showed the following during October:

	Check #	$ Amount
Checks written:	1140	$100
	1155	65
	1156	400
	1157	320
	1158	82
	1159	520
	1160	125
	1161	500
	1162	183
	1163	175
	1164	104
	1165	194
	1166	220

	Date	$ Amount
Deposits:	10/3	1,250
	10/5	480
	10/12	1,190
	10/16	1,595
	10/20	1,800
	10/25	942
	10/28	2,106
	10/31	745

Other Items:

- Outstanding check from September's bank reconciliation: #1142 for $195.
- Beginning checking balance: $5,105
- Ending checking balance: $12,225

Required

a. Prepare a bank reconciliation for October, 1999. (Be aware of transposition errors.)

b. What adjustment to the accounting equation is necessary for October?

c h a p t e r 7

Noncurrent Assets

LEARNING OBJECTIVES

1 Identify three major types of noncurrent assets: (1) property, plant, and equipment; (2) intangible assets; and (3) natural resources.
2. Explain how to account for the acquisition of these assets.
3. Describe the procedures for depreciation, amortization, and depletion.
4. List the factors affecting managers' selection of a depreciation method.
5. Determine which postacquisition expenditures should be expensed and which should be capitalized.
6. Explain the accounting issues associated with asset write-downs and disposals.
7. Interpret financial statement disclosures about noncurrent assets.

INTRODUCTION

Recall from the previous chapter that current assets will be converted into cash or used in operations within a year or the firm's operating cycle, whichever is longer. **Noncurrent assets** are not expected to be fully consumed within that period; thus, they are long-lived assets.

This chapter examines three noncurrent assets: 1) property, plant and equipment, 2) intangible assets, and 3) natural resources.

PROPERTY, PLANT, AND EQUIPMENT

Property, plant and equipment (PPE) are tangible, long-lived assets used by a firm. Tangible assets derive value from their physical substance. These assets include land, land improvements (such as parking lots and roads), office buildings, office equipment, manufacturing facilities (factories), and factory equipment. These assets are sometimes referred to as **fixed assets.**

Initial Valuation

Property, plant, and equipment are initially valued at their historical cost, which includes all costs incurred to acquire an asset, place it in its desired location, and make it operational. Costs include invoice amounts (less any discounts), sales taxes, transportation charges, installation costs, costs of trial runs to adjust equipment, and costs to refurbish equipment purchased in a used condition.

As an example, assume that a machine was purchased at an invoice price of $5,000. The sales tax was 7% and transportation charges were $145. The machine required a concrete base, which cost $80 for materials and $120 for labor. The machine's total cost is calculated as follows:

Invoice cost	$5,000
Sales tax ($5,000 × .07)	350
Transportation	145
Concrete base ($80 + $120)	200
Total cost	$5,695

To record the purchase, increase the asset machine and decrease the asset cash.

ASSETS		=	LIABILITIES	+	SHAREHOLDERS' EQUITY
Cash	Machine				
− $5,695	+ $5,695				

Initially valuing property, plant, and equipment at historical cost is quite reasonable. Because a firm's managers have paid this amount, they certainly expect at least this level of benefit; otherwise, the asset would not have been acquired. Moreover, historical cost is an objective valuation basis, meaning it can easily be verified by examining invoices and canceled checks.

Sometimes, however, the proper accounting for asset acquisition and development is not obvious. Let's examine Chambers Development, Inc., a business that develops landfill sites for waste disposal. In developing its sites, Chambers incurs public relations and legal costs, as well as costs to pay its executives who work on various projects. Conceptually, two accounting alternatives are possible for these costs. One option is to expense them immediately. The analysis involves a decrease in cash and a decrease in shareholders' equity via an expense.

ASSETS	=	LIABILITIES	+	SHAREHOLDERS' EQUITY
Cash				Retained earnings
− $xxx				− $xxx (various expenses)

Because net income and shareholders' equity are reduced, this approach is quite conservative.

The second option views these expenditures as part of the cost of the asset, "landfill sites." Accordingly, these costs are **capitalized;** that is, the asset, landfill sites, is increased as these costs are incurred. The analysis decreases cash and increases landfill sites. Note that this is a much less conservative, perhaps even an aggressive, approach.

ASSETS		=	LIABILITIES	+	SHAREHOLDERS' EQUITY
Cash	Landfill sites				
− $xxx	+ $xxx				

GAAP requires that costs be capitalized only when they reflect future economic benefits. Thus, one must ask, how closely tied are these expenditures to future economic benefits? At one time, Chambers capitalized these costs. Subsequently, however, the business began expensing those costs and restated prior years' financial statements to reflect the more conservative accounting alternative. Such accounting issues can have serious consequences, and Chambers' accounting practices were the subject of an SEC probe and a criminal investigation by the U.S. Attorney General's Office.

WHAT WOULD YOU DO?

As chief accountant for the Craig Manufacturing Company (CMC), you oversee all accounting functions. Both you and Mr. Craig are very concerned about this year's financial statements. CMC will probably violate its loan covenant dealing with the debt to assets ratio. CMC's loan agreement specifies that CMC must maintain a ratio of .4 or lower. Failure to do so will result in a renegotiation of the loan's terms. Interest rates have risen since the loan was obtained, and there is every reason to believe that the bank would require a higher interest rate. This additional cash drain could force CMC to lay off up to 100 workers.

CMC, like most corporations, has an accounting policy regarding the capitalization of fixed assets. All fixed assets costing $100 or more are capitalized and depreciated. Fixed assets costing less than $100 are expensed immediately. The **materiality principle** justifies CMC's policy. This principle states that items that are sufficiently small in dollar value need not be treated in strict accordance with GAAP. Most accountants feel that the clerical costs of capitalizing modest expenditures, developing depreciation schedules, and making annual depreciation adjustments outweigh the benefits of small increases in the precision of the financial statements.

Mr. Craig has just suggested that CMC change its capitalization policy. He wants CMC to capitalize all fixed asset acquisitions. Mr. Craig states that this policy is not forbidden by the materiality principle and that more accurate financial statements would result.

Why do you think that Mr. Craig really wants to change this policy? What are the ethical implications of a policy change?

Depreciation

Many fixed assets have extended but limited lives. Because these assets help generate revenues throughout their useful lives, their costs must be reflected as expenses during that time. **Depreciation** is the process of allocating the cost of a fixed asset as an expense in the years when the asset helps generate revenue. Depreciation is an application of the matching principle. Because land has an unlimited life, it is not depreciated.

GAAP permits the use of any depreciation method that is systematic and rational. Methods differ in the *timing* of expense recognition during an asset's life, yet over the course of an asset's entire life, total depreciation expense will be the same under all methods. Three commonly used methods are illustrated here: straight-line, sum-of-the-years' digits, and declining-balance.

Straight-Line Method The **straight-line (SL) method** allocates an equal amount of depreciation expense to each year in an asset's life. This method is based on the rationale that each year benefits equally from the asset's services.

To illustrate, assume that a machine has a cost of $4,900, an economic life of five years, and an estimated residual value of $400. **Residual value (**or **salvage value)** is the amount the firm expects to receive from selling the asset at the end of its useful economic life.

Useful economic lives and residual values are estimates. Both are affected by the physical deterioration an asset is expected to undergo and by technological obsolescence. The latter effect is well illustrated by computers. Computers can physically perform their tasks for extended periods of time (perhaps a decade or more), but due to rapid advances in the computer industry, computers frequently become outdated. This affects both the length of time a firm expects to use a computer (its economic life) and the estimated residual value when the computer is taken out of service.

Annual straight-line depreciation expense is calculated by first subtracting the residual value from the cost. This difference is the **depreciable basis.** Next divide the depreciable basis by the number of years in the asset's estimated useful life:

$$\text{Annual depreciation expense} = \frac{\text{Historical cost} - \text{Residual value}}{\text{Number of years}}$$

$$= \frac{\$4{,}900 - \$400}{5 \text{ years}}$$

$$= \$900 \text{ per year}$$

To record depreciation expense, the asset is decreased and shareholders' equity is decreased by an expense. Although Chapter 2, "The Basic Concepts of Financial Accounting," suggested that the asset account should be decreased, actual practice uses a contra-asset account called **accumulated depreciation.**

ASSETS		=	LIABILITIES	+	SHAREHOLDERS' EQUITY
Equipment	Accumulated depreciation				Retained earnings
Bal. $4,900					
	– $900				– $900 (depreciation expense)

On the balance sheet, accumulated depreciation is deducted from the cost of property, plant, and equipment, and the difference, called the **book value** (or property, plant, and equipment, net), is included in total assets. After the preceding analysis, for example, the book value is $4,000:

Historical cost	$4,900
Less accumulated depreciation	– 900
Book value	$4,000

Depreciation expense, accumulated depreciation, and book value over the five years can be summarized as follows:

Date	Depreciation Expense	Accumulated Depreciation	Book Value
At acquisition	$ 0	$ 0	$4,900
End of year 1	900	900	4,000
End of year 2	900	1,800	3,100
End of year 3	900	2,700	2,200
End of year 4	900	3,600	1,300
End of year 5	900	4,500	400

Sum-of-the-Years'-Digits Method The **sum-of-the-years'-digits (SYD) method** is one of several accelerated methods. Such methods result in relatively large depreciation charges in the early years of an asset's life. This pattern can be justified by the notion that some assets are more efficient in the earlier years of their life and therefore render greater services. In other words, they help generate more revenue. To properly match costs with revenues, expenses should be larger in those early years.

SYD annual depreciation expense is calculated by multiplying an asset's depreciable basis by a fraction that varies from year to year. The denominator is always the sum of the years' digits in the useful life of the asset. For an asset with a five-year life, the denominator would be 5 + 4 + 3 + 2 + 1 = 15. The sum of the years' digits can be computed with the following formula:

$$\text{Sum of the years' digits} = \frac{N \times (N + 1)}{2}$$

in which N equals the number of years in the asset's life. For an asset with a five-year life, the computation is

$$\text{Sum of the years' digits} = \frac{5 \times (5 + 1)}{2} = 15$$

The fraction's numerator is the number of years remaining in the asset's useful life at the beginning of the year for which depreciation is being calculated. Therefore, depreciation expense for years 1 and 2 would be $1,500 and $1,200, respectively.

	Year 1	Year 2
Depreciation expense	$= \$4{,}500 \times \frac{5}{15} = \$1{,}500$	$\$4{,}500 \times \frac{4}{15} = \$1{,}200$

Under the sum-of-the-years' digits method, depreciation expense declines each year. At the end of the fifth year, the entire depreciable basis of $4,500 will be depreciated.

Date	Depreciation Expense	Accumulated Depreciation	Book Value
At acquisition	$ 0	$ 0	$4,900
End of year 1	1,500	1,500	3,400
End of year 2	1,200	2,700	2,200
End of year 3	900	3,600	1,300
End of year 4	600	4,200	700
End of year 5	300	4,500	400

To make sure you understand this concept, verify the calculation of year 5's depreciation expense of $300.

Declining-Balance Methods **Declining-balance (DB) methods** also result in accelerated depreciation charges. Annual depreciation expense is calculated by multiplying an asset's book value (cost minus accumulated depreciation) at the beginning of the year by a percentage. The percentage equals a multiple of the straight-line *rate*. Frequently used multiples are 200% and 150%. Residual values are not used in the initial determination of declining-balance depreciation rates or depreciation expense.

Because the asset in our illustration has a five-year life, the straight-line rate is 20% (1/5 = 20%). Using a multiple of 200% (200% = 2.0) results in a declining-balance rate of 40% (20% × 2.0). A multiple of 200% is referred to as the **double-declining-**

balance method (DDB). Depreciation charges for the first two years are $1,960 and $1,176, respectively:

Depreciation expense year 1 = (Cost − Accumulated Depreciation) × .4
= ($4,900 − $0) × .4
= $1,960

Depreciation expense year 2 = (Cost − Accumulated Depreciation) × .4
= ($4,900 − $1,960) × .4
= $1,176

A depreciation schedule for the five years is:

Date	Depreciation Expense	Accumulated Depreciation	Book Value
At acquisition	$ 0	$ 0	$4,900
End of year 1	1,960	1,960	2,940
End of year 2	1,176	3,136	1,764
End of year 3	706	3,842	1,058
End of year 4	423	4,265	635
End of year 5	235	4,500	400

To be sure that you understand declining-balance depreciation, verify the calculation of year 3's depreciation expense of $706.

Depreciation expense in the fifth year is not calculated in the typical way. The conventional calculation multiplies the book value at the end of year 4 ($635) by 40%. This yields an expense of $254. However, that expense would result in total accumulated depreciation of $4,519 ($4,265 + $254) and a book value of $381. Because an asset should not be depreciated to an amount below its residual value, depreciation in year 5 is limited to $235 (the amount that would leave a book value of $400).

Residual value is not utilized in the original determination of declining-balance depreciation because the computations themselves include an implicit residual value. By setting depreciation expense equal to a percentage of book value, a book value will always remain. Thus, there is no need to consider residual value explicitly until the end of an asset's depreciation schedule; residual value must then be considered so that an asset's book value is not depreciated below its residual value.

Exhibit 7-1 summarizes the results of the three depreciation methods discussed in this section.

Tax Depreciation Tax law requires firms to use the Modified Accelerated Cost Recovery System (MACRS). This system specifies the useful lives to be assigned to different types of assets and also indicates the depreciation method to be used. For example, cars are assigned a five-year life and double-declining-balance depreciation is required. Therefore, cars are depreciated at a 40% declining-balance rate. As another example, land improvements, such as sidewalks and fences, are assigned a 15-year life and a 150% declining-balance rate is used. Sidewalks and fences would then be depreciated at a 10% rate (1/15 × 150% = 10%).

The details of tax depreciation and financial reporting depreciation differ because their objectives differ. Financial reporting is designed to provide useful information for financial statement readers. Therefore, utilizing reasonable estimates of useful lives, for

EXHIBIT 7-1 Summary of Depreciation Methods

Assumptions
Cost $4,900
Residual value $ 400
Estimated life 5 years

Summary

End of Year	SL Deprec. Expense	SL Accum. Deprec.	SL Book Value	SYD Deprec. Expense	SYD Accum. Deprec.	SYD Book Value	DDB Deprec. Expense	DDB Accum. Deprec.	DDB Book Value
0	$ 0	$ 0	$4,900	$ 0	$ 0	$4,900	$ 0	$ 0	$4,900
1	900	900	4,000	1,500	1,500	3,400	1,960	1,960	2,940
2	900	1,800	3,100	1,200	2,700	2,200	1,176	3,136	1,764
3	900	2,700	2,200	900	3,600	1,300	706	3,842	1,058
4	900	3,600	1,300	600	4,200	700	423	4,265	635
5	900	4,500	400	300	4,500	400	235*	4,500	400

*Assets should not be depreciated below their residual value.
NOTE: Total depreciation expense over the five years combined is the same under all methods. The methods differ only in the timing of depreciation charges. Also note that because total depreciation expense is the same across the five years, total net income over the five years will also be the same.

example, is desirable. In contrast, one purpose of our tax laws is to spur economic growth. Using extremely short estimated lives and highly accelerated methods provides firms with tax benefits more quickly. As a consequence, firms are more inclined to acquire fixed assets, helping to fulfill the objective of economic growth.

Selection of Depreciation Method Several factors influence managers' selection of a depreciation method for financial reporting. Managers might wish to provide financial statement readers with useful information. This would prompt them to select a depreciation method that best reflects the pattern of benefit usage. For example, if an asset is uniformly productive throughout its life, the straight-line method would be chosen.

Additionally, however, some economic issues may influence their decisions. If managers' compensation is tied to reported accounting earnings, managers are likely to prefer the straight-line method because it initially results in lower depreciation charges and higher reported income. Lending agreements may also play a role. For example, some agreements require the firm to keep its debt to assets ratio below a specified value. This ratio contains total assets in the denominator. Because recorded asset values decline more quickly under accelerated depreciation methods, managers can reduce the likelihood of violating such agreements by selecting the straight-line method.

Firms do not generally use the same depreciation method for both financial reporting and tax purposes. MACRS is required for tax purposes but is not always acceptable for financial reporting. This is partially due to the permissive nature of MACRS. For example, under MACRS, cars are given a five-year life and a zero residual value. These may not be realistic assumptions for many firms and might yield misleading financial statements. Also, as mentioned earlier, firms frequently wish to report the lower depreciation expense associated with the straight-line method on their financial statements. In fact, as Exhibit 7-2 shows, the vast majority of publicly held companies uses the straight-line method for financial reporting.

EXHIBIT 7-2 Selection of Depreciation Methods

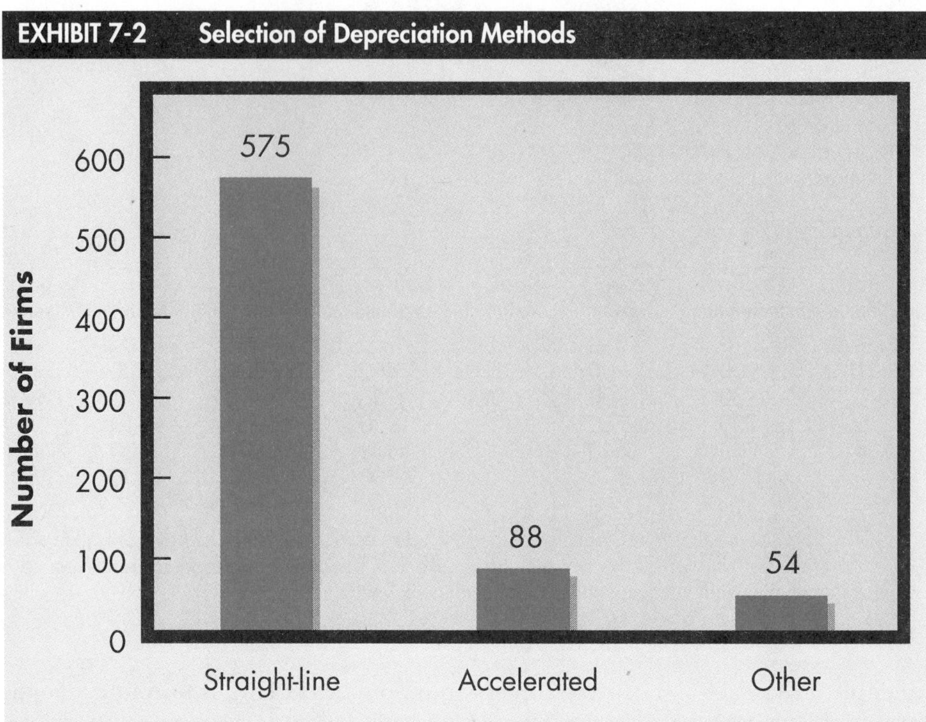

SOURCE: Accounting Trends and Techniques, 1997.

Some Misconceptions About Depreciation Two misconceptions frequently arise regarding depreciation. First, some people believe that depreciation is a valuation procedure. That is, they believe the book value that results from depreciation reflects an asset's market value. It does not. Book value results from the application of a rather mechanical depreciation method. No attempt is made to estimate the current market value of an asset by surveying recent transactions.

Second, depreciation expense is alleged to be a source of cash. This misconception is due to the format of the statement of cash flows. Recall that under the indirect approach, depreciation expense is added to net income in calculating cash provided by operating activities. Depreciation expense is added, not because it is a source of cash, but because (1) it was previously subtracted in determining net income and (2) it does not involve a cash outflow. Be especially careful not to fall into this "cash flow trap." Depreciation, by itself, does not generate cash.

Expenditures After Acquisition

Firms often make expenditures during a fixed asset's life. Frequently, the expenditures are for routine repairs and maintenance. Because these expenditures merely maintain the economic benefit already contained in the asset, they do not enhance the asset's value. Accordingly, these expenditures are immediately expensed. Usually, cash is decreased and shareholders' equity is decreased by an expense.

Some expenditures, however, do enhance an asset's value. For example, Northwest Airlines renovated 40 of its DC-9 twin jets. The renovations included engine modifications to reduce jet noise, new seats, and new carpeting. These changes extended each jet's life by 15 years. Other expenditures can expand an asset or make it more efficient and productive. As another example, a personal computer's hard drive can be replaced with a larger one, and new chips can be installed that enable the computer to perform tasks more quickly. Because all of these expenditures increase an asset's value, they should be capitalized. In other words, the asset's recorded value should be increased. Note that a change in an asset's book value or remaining estimated life will necessitate a change in the periodic depreciation charge.

Disposals

Firms frequently sell fixed assets when needs change or when assets age or become obsolete due to technological advances. To illustrate the accounting for a disposal, assume that the machine described in the previous section was depreciated for two years, using the straight-line method. At that point, the machine's book value is $3,100 ($4,900 − $1,800). Also assume that the asset was sold at the beginning of year 3 for $2,500. Because an asset with a book value of $3,100 was sold for $2,500, the firm incurred a $600 loss. The analysis increases cash by $2,500, reduces the asset machine by $4,900, eliminates accumulated depreciation of $1,800, and decreases shareholders' equity via a $600 loss.

	ASSETS			= LIABILITIES +	SHAREHOLDERS' EQUITY
	Cash	Machine	Accumulated depreciation		Retained earnings
Beginning Balance		$4,900	−$1,800		
	+$2,500	−$4,900	+$1,800		−$600 (loss on sale)
Ending Balance		$ 0	$ 0		

Gains and losses on sales of property, plant, and equipment are included in the income statement. If material, they are separately disclosed; otherwise, they are combined with other items. These gains and losses must be interpreted carefully. First, note that the loss just illustrated is associated with a cash *inflow*. Therefore, the firm's overall cash position has improved, even though a loss is reported on the income statement.

Second, gains and losses on fixed asset disposals do not necessarily reflect good or poor managerial performance in the year of the disposal. They may be more a function of poorly estimated depreciation charges. Finally, managers have considerable discretion over the timing of these transactions. Therefore, whenever gains or losses appear on the income statement, the reader must always assess the possible reasons behind such gains or losses.

Write-Downs

As discussed earlier, most firms value property, plant, and equipment at depreciated historical cost. However, when a fixed asset's utility drops below its book value, the asset should be written down. The purpose of this principle is to avoid overstating asset values. A fixed asset's value to a firm can decline for a variety of reasons. Firms in the computer and electronics industry must have state-of-the-art facilities, for instance; the PPE of these firms are particularly susceptible to loss in value due to technological obsolescence. Other facilities can lose value if the firm terminates the production of certain inventory items and the facilities are of little use for other purposes.

To illustrate the accounting for a write-down, consider General Motors Corporation (GM). GM wrote down assets by $6.4 billion in 1997. The analysis of this write-down is:

ASSETS	=	LIABILITIES	+	SHAREHOLDERS' EQUITY
Fixed assets – $6.4 billion				Retained earnings – $6.4 billion (loss on write-down)

Most analysts applaud the conservative nature of write-downs; however, their implementation involves significant ambiguities. For example, GAAP requires a write-down when the estimated future cash flows from using an asset are less than the asset's book value.[1] Estimating cash flows is a difficult task and involves numerous judgments. Because of this, managers enjoy a great deal of discretion and are accordingly provided with a tool for earnings manipulation. When it is in their best interest, managers can often successfully argue with their auditors to delay a write-down. Alternatively, managers sometimes engage in a *big bath,* which was discussed in Chapter 4, "The Income Statement." Recall that a big bath involves recording large charges to income in a single year. Managers do this to relieve future years' income of these charges and to pave the way for reporting improved financial performance.

Financial Statement Presentation

Most balance sheets contain only one line item for property, plant, and equipment. This line shows the book value of all fixed assets. Notes to the financial statements contain more detailed information.

Exhibit 7-3 contains a partial balance sheet for OshKosh B'Gosh, Inc. (OB), which contains the conventional one-line presentation. Exhibit 7-3 also contains excerpts from OB's notes. Note 1 indicates that OB uses straight-line depreciation and also discloses OB's estimates of its assets' useful lives. By comparing these estimates to industry norms, analysts can ascertain if a firm is overstating its earnings by selecting useful life estimates that are unduly long. Such estimates understate depreciation expense and overstate net income.

A breakdown of OB's property, plant, and equipment is provided in Exhibit 7-3. It discloses the cost of the major types of fixed assets as well as accumulated depreciation. Notice that the differences between cost and accumulated depreciation agrees with the amounts appearing on the balance sheet.

Analysis

The analysis of property, plant, and equipment deals with two issues. First, is PPE effectively utilized? Second, what is the age of the assets? That is, is the firm replacing its productive capacity in a timely manner?

[1]In cases where a write-down is indicated, the asset should be written down to the present value of its cash flows. Present value techniques are discussed in Appendix C.

EXHIBIT 7-3 Partial Balance Sheet and Related Notes

OshKosh B'Gosh, Inc.
Selected Financial Statement Information
(dollars in thousands)

	December 31	
	1997	**1996**
Property, plant and equipment, net	$32,955	$41,782

Related Notes

Note 1. Property, plant and equipment

Property, plant, and equipment are carried at cost or at management's estimate of fair market value if considered impaired under the provisions of Statement of Financial Accounting Standards (SFAS) No. 121. Depreciation and amortization for financial reporting purposes is calculated using the straight line method based on the following useful lives:

	Years
Land improvements	10 to 15
Buildings	10 to 40
Leasehold improvements	5 to 10
Machinery and equipment	3 to 10

Note 4. Property, plant and equipment

A summary of property, plant and equipment follows:

	December 31	
	1997	**1996**
Land and improvements	$ 3,667	$ 3,910
Buildings	15,035	17,999
Leasehold improvements	14,036	15,231
Machinery and equipment	27,630	30,607
Construction in progress	1,814	—
Total	62,192	67,747
Less: Accumulated depreciation and amortization	29,237	25,965
Property, plant and equipment, net	$32,955	$41,782

Utilization Utilization is measured by **fixed asset turnover.** To calculate fixed asset turnover, divide sales by the average book value of property, plant, and equipment. In 1997, OB's sales were $395,196,000. Recall that book value equals historical cost less accumulated depreciation; it is also referred to as PPE − net. The average is calculated by adding beginning and ending PPE − net and dividing by two.

Fixed asset turnover reflects the number of sales dollars generated by a $1 investment in PPE. OB's 1997 fixed asset turnover was 10.6:

$$
\begin{aligned}
\text{Fixed asset turnover} &= \frac{\text{Net sales}}{\text{Average PPE} - \text{net}} \\
&= \frac{\text{Net sales}}{(\text{Beginning} + \text{Ending PPE} - \text{net})/2} \\
&= \frac{\$395{,}196}{(\$32{,}955 + \$41{,}782)/2} \\
&= 10.6
\end{aligned}
$$

Firms generally prefer a higher turnover. A low fixed asset turnover might suggest that property, plant, and equipment is being underutilized and that the firm might have excess capacity. On the other hand, a firm might elect the strategy of relying heavily on new, efficient, and costly equipment in the hope of reducing labor and other costs. This would reduce turnover and increase depreciation expense, but other cost savings will be realized. The extent to which a firm relies on leased assets can also affect turnover. Because some leased assets might not appear on balance sheets, firms using leased assets might have a smaller denominator and a correspondingly higher turnover.

Some additional factors might also affect fixed asset turnover. Accelerated depreciation methods reduce PPE − net more quickly than straight-line depreciation and result in a higher turnover ratio. Price changes and the maturity of a firm might also affect fixed asset turnover. As an example, let's assume that fixed asset prices are increasing over time. New entrants into an industry will be forced to acquire their productive capacity at higher costs than firms that are already established. New entrants, therefore, would have a higher PPE − net and a lower turnover. In summary, although fixed asset turnover is intended to measure asset utilization, other factors such as those just described can also affect it.

Exhibit 7-4 summarizes selected ratios for OB, Garan Inc. (one of OB's competitors in the apparel industry), and, as a point of contrast, Birmingham Steel Corp. OB's fixed asset turnover is nearly identical to that of its industry rival, Garan, suggesting that OB and Garan are equally successful in generating sales dollars from their investment in PPE. Also notice from Exhibit 7-4 that the steel industry has a relatively low fixed asset turnover. This is because the steel industry is capital intensive. Greater amounts of property, plant, and equipment are needed to manufacture steel than to produce clothing.

Percentage of PPE Depreciated (Age) Financial statements contain information about the original cost of property, plant, and equipment, as well as the depreciation that has been taken since the assets' acquisition. This permits an assessment of the relative age of a firm's assets. The calculation involves dividing accumulated depreciation by PPE − gross. PPE − gross is simply the assets' historical cost. Older assets have larger proportions of PPE − gross that have already been depreciated. OB's ratio for 1997 is 47%:

$$\text{Percentage of PPE depreciated} = \frac{\text{Accumulated depreciation}}{\text{PPE} - \text{gross}} = \frac{\$29{,}237}{\$62{,}192} = 47\%$$

EXHIBIT 7-4 Selected Ratios

OshKosh B'Gosh Inc.
Selected Ratios and Inter-firm Comparisons

	OB	Garan Inc.	Birmingham Steel Corp.
Fixed asset turnover	10.6	10.8	1.5
Percentage of PPE depreciated	47%	58%	19%

This is considerably below Garan's percentage that appears in Exhibit 7-4 and suggests that OB replaces its equipment more quickly than its competitor. That is, OB might have depreciated a lower percentage of its total property, plant, and equipment because it recently acquired fixed assets that have not yet generated much depreciation. Another interpretation might be that OB is a relatively young entrant into the apparel industry; an examination of OB's history, however, indicates that this is not the case.

Evaluation of the Accounting for Property, Plant, and Equipment GAAP requires the use of depreciated historical cost. As previously mentioned, this valuation does not reflect current market value. Accordingly, care must be taken when using this information. Lending institutions, for example, sometimes require loan applicants to pledge assets as collateral. In evaluating the adequacy of the pledged assets, historical cost is not particularly relevant; the loan officer is more interested in current market value.

Although the financial statements of U.S. companies do not disclose the market value of fixed assets, a few countries do permit the use of market value. Exhibit 7-5 contains a note from the annual report of an Australian company. The note shows that Monroe revalued its land, building, and improvements in 2001. In this particular case, market value significantly exceeds historical cost. Because such differences can

EXHIBIT 7-5 Australian Firms Write Up Fixed Assets

Monroe Limited
Property, Plant and Equipment Note

	2001	2000
Note 14—Property, Plant, and Equipment		
Freehold land		
At cost	$ 412	$ 3,182
At independent valuation 2001[a]	11,173	—
	11,585	3,182
Buildings and improvements		
At cost	526	2,973
Accumulated depreciation	(73)	(217)
	453	2,756
At independent valuation 2001[a]	9,691	—
	10,144	2,756
Leasehold improvements, at cost	136	106
Accumulated amortisation	(28)	(1)
	108	105
Plant and equipment, at cost	4,091	1,956
Accumulated depreciation	(543)	(356)
	3,548	1,600
Plant and equipment under lease	722	1,021
Accumulated amortisation	(247)	(249)
	475	772
Capital works in progress, at cost	—	7,801
	$25,860	$16,216

a) The stud property (including fixed improvements), the winery, and vineyards were independently valued by Murdoch International Property Consultants Pty. Limited in June, 2001.

dramatically affect a number of ratios, care must be taken when comparing the financial statements of firms from different countries.

INTANGIBLE ASSETS

Intangible assets are long-lived assets whose values do not depend on their physical substance. Rather, their value is based on the legal rights they convey. Various intangible assets are described in this section.

Patents, granted by the federal government, convey the exclusive right to use a product or process for a period of 20 years. Patents are intended to promote innovation by ensuring that the firm that discovers and applies new knowledge reaps the benefits of its efforts.

Copyrights, also granted by the federal government, convey the exclusive right to use artistic or literary works for a period of 70 years beyond the author's death. Common examples of works that can be copyrighted include books, songs, and movies. The economic life of a copyright may be considerably shorter than its legal life.

Trademarks are words, symbols, or other distinctive elements used to identify a particular firm's products. You are probably familiar with Kleenex tissue. Kleenex is a registered trademark of the Kimberly-Clark Corporation. McDonald's Golden Arches and MGM's Lion are well-known symbols established and protected by their corporations as trademarks. Trademarks have unlimited legal lives, but their economic lives may be limited.

Franchises and licenses are rights to market a particular product or service or to engage in a particular activity. For example, Pizza Hut sells franchises to various individuals and businesses. A franchise permits the holder to operate a Pizza Hut restaurant at a specified location. This right has economic value to the holder and would be reflected as an asset. As another example, some pharmaceutical companies acquire the right to sell the products of other companies. This right also has value and would be shown as an asset (see the following discussion on research and development costs).

For accounting purposes, the intangible asset **goodwill** can only arise in one situation: acquiring an ongoing business. In many such acquisitions, the purchase price exceeds the total fair value of the separately identifiable assets. The higher purchase price reflects the willingness of the buyer to pay for loyal customers, trained workers, and the like, which many ongoing businesses possess. Goodwill equals the excess of the purchase price over the total fair value of all specifically identifiable assets acquired. As an illustration, Storage Technology Corporation (StorageTek) acquired Edata Scandinavia AB for $75,000,000 and recorded $44,700,000 of goodwill. In other words, more than half of the purchase price was recorded as goodwill.

Acquisition

Intangible assets acquired from others are initially recorded at their historical cost. For example, if a company acquires a patent for $300,000, cash would decrease and patents would increase by $300,000.

ASSETS		=	LIABILITIES	+	SHAREHOLDERS' EQUITY
Cash	Patents				
−$300,0000	+$300,000				

Because the patent has already been developed, future economic benefits seem probable and recording an asset is proper.

As another illustration, StorageTek's purchase of Edata is recorded as follows (in thousands):

ASSETS			=	LIABILITIES	+	SHAREHOLDERS' EQUITY
Cash	Various assets	Goodwill				
−$75,000	+$30,300	+$44,700				

Intangible assets can also be developed internally. In most cases, costs incurred to develop separately identifiable intangible assets are capitalized. Costs incurred to protect these assets (such as legal costs incurred to protect intangible assets from infringement) can also be capitalized. Nike's trademarks, such as its swoosh, have a balance sheet value of $221 million and Nike considers its trademarks to be its "most valuable assets." However, Nike's balance sheet shows total assets of $5.4 billion. How can trademarks be Nike's most valuable asset yet represent such a small percentage of its total assets? The answer, of course, is that balance sheets show many assets at their historical cost, which may understate their economic value.

Research and Development Costs Many firms internally develop new products, as opposed to purchasing patents from others. Because large expenditures can be made without the assurance of ultimate success, this strategy is more risky. Substantial uncertainty exists regarding future economic benefits and, because of this, GAAP requires that all research and development costs be expensed immediately. **Research and development costs** are those incurred to generate new knowledge or to translate knowledge into a new product or process. Most countries follow the practice of immediately expensing these costs.

The divergence in the accounting rules for externally acquired versus internally developed patents can reduce the inter-firm comparability of financial statements, particularly in research-intensive industries such as pharmaceuticals. As shown in Exhibit 7-6, Roberts Pharmaceutical Corporation's intangible asset, property rights acquired (from others), increased from $204,611,000 in 1996 to $217,919,000 in 1997. Roberts' strategy is to acquire already-established pharmaceutical products from other companies. These rights are obtained in one of two ways: (1) the direct purchase of a patent from the holder or (2) a licensing agreement with the holder of the patent. The acquisition cost of those rights is capitalized as assets.

In contrast, Merck, Inc., internally develops its pharmaceutical products. Accordingly, the nearly $1.8 billion Merck spent to develop new products in 1997 was expensed immediately, even though some of those products proved successful and resulted in patents. As this situation illustrates, the economic value of patents (and other intangible assets) can be significantly different from the value assigned for accounting purposes.

Special accounting rules exist for software development costs. For a given project, these costs are expensed until *technological feasibility* is demonstrated, and costs incurred after that point are capitalized. To some extent, these rules are inconsistent with the general procedures for research and development. Exhibit 7-7 contains a note from StorageTek's financial statements that describes StorageTek's accounting for software development costs.

EXHIBIT 7-6 Intangible Assets

Roberts Pharmaceutical Corporation
Excerpts from Financial Statement Notes

Note 1 (partial)
Intangible assets are stated at cost less accumulated amortization. Amortization is determined using the straight-line method over the estimated useful lives of the related assets that are estimated to range from 10 to 40 years.

Note 4 (partial) Intangible Assets

Intangible assets consist of the following (dollars in thousands):

	December 31	
	1996	**1997**
Product rights acquired	$204,611	$217,919
Less: Accumulated amortization	21,032	27,195
	$183,579	$190,724

EXHIBIT 7-7 Software Development Costs

Storage Technology Corporation
Excerpt from Financial Statement Notes

Capitalized Software Costs
StorageTek capitalized costs associated with acquiring and developing software products to be marketed to customers of $616,000 in 1997, $510,000 in 1996, and $25,463,000 in 1995. Other assets as shown on the Consolidated Balance Sheet include unamortized software costs of $13,907,000 as of December 26, 1997, and $33,988,000 as of December 27, 1996. Amortization expense is recognized over the estimated useful lives of the related products, generally four years. Amortization expense and write-offs associated with capitalized software costs were $20,697,000 in 1997, $20,556,000 in 1996, and $26,627,000 in 1995. The company evaluates the realizability of the carrying value of the capitalized software based on estimates of the associated future revenue.

Amortization

Like many fixed assets, intangible assets have limited useful lives. Accordingly, the cost of these assets must be allocated as an expense to the years when they help generate revenue. With fixed assets, this expense was labeled "depreciation." **Amortization expense** is the term used for intangible assets. It is usually calculated on a straight-line basis and the maximum amortization period is 40 years.

Suppose, for example, the patent acquired above for $300,000 was estimated to have a six-year life. Amortization expense in the amount of $50,000 ($300,000/6) would be recorded each year.

ASSETS	=	LIABILITIES	+	SHAREHOLDERS' EQUITY
Patents – $50,000				Retained earnings – $50,000 (amoritization expense)

Unlike fixed assets, no contra asset account is used and the asset account patents is reduced directly. Reality Check 7-1 addresses the issues of capitalization and amortization.

NATURAL RESOURCES

Natural resources are assets such as mines containing gold, silver, copper, or other minerals; wells containing oil or gas; and timberlands. Natural resources (also called **wasting assets**) are important assets of firms in the extractive industries.

Initial Valuation

Natural resources acquired from others are valued at their historical cost, but many firms self-explore and develop natural resource sites. The accounting for this type of

REALITY CHECK 7-1

As described in Exhibit 7-7, StorageTek capitalizes certain software development costs. Because firms outside of the computer industry expense all their research and development costs, StorageTek's financial statements may not be comparable to those of firms in other industries. In 1997, StorageTek reported the following results (dollars in thousands):

Income before taxes	$316,117
Provision for income taxes	84,300
Net income	$231,817

Required

Based on the information contained in Exhibit 7-7, recalculate StorageTek's net income to reflect the immediate expensing of all software development costs.

Solution

	(dollars in thousands)
Income before taxes as reported	$316,117
Less: Costs capitalized	(616)
Plus: Amortization of previously capitalized costs	20,697
Income before taxes, adjusted	336,198
Provision for income taxes*	(90,773)
Income, adjusted	$245,425

Because StorageTek has capitalized less software development costs in recent years, the amortization of prior years' capitalized costs exceeds the capitalized value of the current year's costs. The net result is that adjusted income actually exceeds reported income.

*Using StorageTek's approximate effective tax rate $= \frac{\$84,300}{\$316,117} = .27$

Provision for income taxes $= \$336,198 \times .27 = \$90,773$

REALITY CHECK 7-2

Newmont Mining Corporation
Excerpt from Financial Statement Notes

Mineral exploration costs are expensed as incurred. When it has been determined that a mineral property can be economically developed, the costs incurred to develop such property are capitalized, including costs to further delineate the ore body and remove overburden to initially expose the ore body. Such costs, and estimated future development costs, are amortized using a units-of-production method over the estimated life of the ore body. Ongoing development expenditures to maintain production are generally charged to operations as incurred.

Significant payments related to the acquisition of exploration interests are also capitalized. If a mineable ore body is discovered, such costs are amortized using a units-of-production method. If no mineable ore body is discovered, such costs are expensed in the period in which it is determined the property has no future economic value.

Required

Does Newmont use the full cost or the successful efforts method? Why?

Solution

Newmont uses the successful efforts method, indicated by two aspects:

1. Exploration costs are expensed as incurred. No costs are capitalized until it is probable that a property has valuable reserves.
2. Costs incurred to acquire exploration interests are capitalized. If no reserves are found, however, the costs are expensed immediately.

situation is somewhat controversial. The issue involves the treatment of exploration costs associated with unsuccessful sites.

One approach, the **full cost method,** capitalizes the exploration costs of both successful and unsuccessful sites as an asset. This approach recognizes that a firm cannot expect success every time it attempts to locate valuable resources. Accordingly, the expenditures associated with both successful and unsuccessful sites are viewed as costs incurred to obtain successful sites.

The **successful efforts method** immediately expenses the cost of unsuccessful sites. Only the costs directly associated with locating and developing successful sites are capitalized. Because assets are recorded at lower amounts and expenses are recognized more quickly, successful efforts is the more conservative method. Reality Check 7-2 describes how the Newmont Mining Corporation accounts for its exploration costs.

GAAP permits the use of either method. Large firms such as Exxon tend to use successful efforts, while small firms tend to use full cost because higher net income and larger asset values make them appear more profitable in the short term. The higher net income and larger asset values under the full cost method also reduce the likelihood of violating loan covenants based on accounting ratios. Large, established firms are in much less danger of violating loan covenants. They select the conservative successful efforts method because the lower reported net income helps reduce the political costs of the very visible oil industry. That is, lower net income numbers help the oil industry to argue that it is not unduly profiting at the public's expense.

Depletion

Depletion is quite similar to depreciation and amortization. As with all long-lived assets, natural resources help generate revenue over their useful lives. Accordingly, the cost of those resources must be matched as an expense to that revenue.

As an illustration, assume that an oil well was acquired for $255,000. The analysis increases the asset oil well and decreases cash.

ASSETS		=	LIABILITIES	+	SHAREHOLDERS' EQUITY
Cash	Oil well				
– $255,000	+ $255,000				

Further assume that the well is estimated to contain 45,000 barrels of oil, and that the property can probably be sold for $30,000 after all the oil is extracted. Depletion is calculated on a per-unit basis. Subtract the residual value from the historical cost and then divide by the estimated number of barrels in the well:

$$\text{Depletion per barrel} = \frac{\text{Historical cost} - \text{Residual value}}{\text{Estimated number of barrels}}$$

$$= \frac{\$255{,}000 - \$30{,}000}{45{,}000} = \$5$$

The depletion charge per barrel is $5. If during the first year of operation 8,000 barrels were extracted and sold, the depletion charge would be $40,000 ($5 × 8,000). The analysis would decrease the recorded value of the oil well; shareholders' equity would be reduced via depletion expense.

ASSETS	=	LIABILITIES	+	SHAREHOLDERS' EQUITY
Oil well				Retained earnings
– $40,000				– $40,000 (depletion expense)

KEY TERMS

Accumulated depreciation 268
Amortization expense 280
Book value 268
Capitalize 266
Copyrights 278
Declining-balance methods (DB) 269
Depletion 281
Depreciable basis 267
Depreciation 267
Double-declining-balance method (DDB) 269
Fixed assets 265
Fixed asset turnover 275
Franchises and licenses 278
Full cost method 281
Goodwill 278
Intangible assets 278
Materiality principle 269
Natural resources 281
Noncurrent assets 265
Patents 278
Percentage of PPE depreciated (age) 276
Property, plant, and equipment 265
Research and development costs 279
Residual value 267
Salvage value 267
Straight-line method (SL) 267
Successful efforts method 281
Sum-of-the-years'-digits method (SYD) 268
Trademarks 278
Wasting assets 281

SUMMARY OF LEARNING OBJECTIVES

1. **Identify three major types of noncurrent assets: (1) property, plant, and equipment, (2) intangible assets, and (3) natural resources.**
Property, plant, and equipment (fixed assets) are tangible, long-lived assets. These assets consist of land, land improvements, buildings, factories, furniture, and equipment. Intangible assets have no physical substance. Rather, their value derives from the legal rights they convey to firms. Intangible assets include patents, copyrights, and franchises. Natural resources are important assets to firms in the extractive industries. They include oil and gas wells, timberlands, and mines containing gold, copper, and other minerals.
2. **Explain how to account for the acquisition of these assets.**
All fixed assets and the intangible assets acquired from others are initially valued at their historical cost. The accounting for intangible assets developed internally is more problematic. Given that intangible assets have no physical substance, it is sometimes difficult to verify that expenditures made to develop them really reflect future economic benefits. Because of this, the FASB provides specific guidance in certain situations. For example, all research and development expenditures must be expensed immediately.

   Natural resources acquired from others are recorded at their historical cost. Two methods are available to account for natural resources obtained through self-exploration: the full cost method and the successful efforts method. The successful efforts method is the more conservative one because assets are valued at lower amounts and expenses are recognized more quickly.
3. **Describe the procedures for depreciation, amortization, and depletion.**
Many fixed assets have limited useful lives and help generate revenue during only those years. Accordingly, the matching principle requires that these assets (except land) be depreciated. That is, the cost of fixed assets must be allocated as an expense over their useful lives. Managers are also free to choose from a number of generally accepted depreciation methods. Because intangible assets have limited lives, they are amortized. This is a procedure very similar to depreciation. Amortization is usually calculated on a straight-line basis over a maximum period of 40 years. Natural resources are subject to depletion charges because they are consumed over their useful lives. Depletion charges are calculated on a per-unit (ton, barrel, and so on) basis.
4. **List the factors affecting managers' selection of a depreciation method.**
Managers might want to provide financial statement users with useful information. If so, they would select the depreciation method that best reflects the expiration of benefits contained in the firm's assets. Because the choice of depreciation method affects reported net income, some managers might be motivated to select the straight-line method, which initially results in the lowest depreciation expense and the highest net income. This tends to increase managers' bonuses and decrease the chances of violating loan covenants.
5. **Determine which postacquisition expenditures should be expensed and which should be capitalized.**
Expenditures that extend an asset's life, enlarge the asset, or make the asset more efficient are capitalized. Expenditures that merely maintain the asset or the asset's productivity are expensed.

6. **Explain the accounting issues associated with asset write-downs and disposals.**
Asset write-downs are needed when an asset's utility falls below its book value, and the associated loss appears on the income statement. Asset disposals often give rise to gains and losses that do not necessarily reflect the performance of management in the year in which the gain or loss is recorded. Rather, they more frequently reflect faulty estimates used in previous depreciation calculations. Because managers can influence the timing (and perhaps the amount) of gains and losses recognized from write-downs and disposals, these items must be carefully evaluated.
7. **Interpret financial statement disclosures about noncurrent assets.**
Analyses of noncurrent assets provide insights into how effectively these assets are being used; firms naturally want to generate as many sales as possible with a given fixed asset base. A firm's success in doing this is measured by fixed asset turnover. Financial statements also provide information about assets' ages. This is measured by the percentage of PPE depreciated. Firms with older assets will find it difficult to compete with firms that have newer, more efficient assets.

QUESTIONS

7-1 Define the following terms related to non-current assets:
   a. Depreciation expense
   b. Intangibles
   c. Amortization
   d. Straight-line method versus sum-of-the-years'-digits method
   e. Wasting assets
   f. Depletion

7-2 Discuss the differences between depreciation and amortization.

7-3 Identify key differences between property, plant, and equipment (PPE) and intangible assets.

7-4 How are current assets different from noncurrent assets?

7-5 Current assets, such as inventory, are not depreciated. Why should noncurrent assets be depreciated, amortized, or depleted?

7-6 Discuss the differences between the full cost method and the successful efforts methods when accounting for natural resources. Why might large firms prefer one method and small firms the other?

7-7 Discuss the term *accumulated depreciation.* How does this differ from depreciation expense? Why is accumulated depreciation treated as a contra asset? Why is this often called a "negative" asset?

7-8 Under what circumstances could the sum-of-the-years'-digits depreciation method produce the same pattern of total annual expenses as would the straight-line method?

7-9 Discuss two different types of noncurrent assets that may be found on a typical balance sheet.

7-10 Discuss three different types of intangible assets, indicating what types of firms might hold such assets.

7-11 Why do accountants write off, or reduce, a noncurrent asset? Why might such write-offs be confusing? How could these possibly confusing effects be reduced? How does a "big bath" relate to such write-offs?

7-12 Refute the assertion that "*depreciation is a source of cash.*"

7-13 Refute the assertion that "*balance sheets reflect 'true' values (market values) of noncurrent assets.*"

7-14 When depreciation expense is shown in a firm's financial statements, how and why is it often shown as a source of cash? How does depreciation expense affect cash flows?

7-15 When accumulated depreciation is shown on a balance sheet, how do changes in accumulated depreciation affect cash flows? What events result in changes to accumulated depreciation? Which have an effect on cash flows?

7-16 Identify the only transactions involving noncurrent assets that have an effect on cash flows.

7-17 How does depletion of natural resources affect cash flows? When does cash change as a result of transactions involving natural resources?

7-18 How does amortization of an intangible asset affect cash flows? When does cash change as a result of transactions involving intangibles?

7-19 Discuss the following proposition: Intangible assets have no substance; therefore, they have no value and should not be shown on the firm's balance sheet.

7-20 Discuss the following proposition: Intangible assets reflect so much uncertainty that they should not be shown on the firm's balance sheet.

7-21 Discuss the following proposition: Intangible assets may last one year, or they may last indefinitely; therefore, no one can determine the proper amortization schedule until the asset is exhausted or retired.

7-22 Identify key differences between three depreciation methods: straight-line, sum-of-the-years'-digits, and declining-balance.

7-23 Why would a firm choose one depreciation method over another?

7-24 Discuss the following proposition: GAAP should only include one depreciation method: options give managers too much flexibility and too many opportunities to manipulate net income.

7-25 Discuss the following proposition: GAAP should permit managers the flexibility to choose from among several depreciation methods; each firm is unique and may require the flexibility to match its depreciation method to its own unique circumstances.

EXERCISES

Classifying and Capitalizing Costs

7-26 Identify the following costs that could be capitalized on the firm's balance sheet. Identify costs that should be included in property, plant, and equipment (PPE).

a. New windshield wiper blades on the company's truck
b. New sidewalks in front of the firm's factory
c. Freight expenses for new equipment installed in the factory
d. Installation costs for the new equipment
e. Realtor's fees associated with land purchase
f. Minor engine repair on the truck
g. Engine replacement on the truck
h. Razing or demolishing a building on newly acquired land
i. Design costs for a new building

Classifying and Capitalizing R&D Costs

7-27 Firm A purchased a patent from another firm at a cost of $1 million. Firm B spent the same amount in developing a patent through its own internal research and development (R&D) efforts.

Required

a. Describe the accounting treatment for each firm. Show the balance sheet and income statement effects for each firm.
b. Why might a firm prefer one method over the other?

Calculating Property, Plant, and Equipment Cost

7-28 A firm purchased machinery on account with an invoice price of $15,000. The terms of payment were 2/10, net 30. In addition, transportation of $250, installation of $420, and sales tax of $1,000 were paid in cash. While installing the machinery, an employee's negligence caused $150 worth of damage to the machine, which was repaired and the repair bill paid in cash.

Required

a. Calculate the total cost of the machinery.
b. How should managers view the damage to the equipment?

Calculating Property, Plant, and Equipment Cost

7-29 A firm purchased land for $150,000. Broker commissions of $3,000 and other closing costs of $1,800 were paid in acquiring the land. An old building that was on the land was demolished. The demolition costs were $4,500, but some of the demolished building scrap parts were sold for $2,200. In addition, there were delinquent real estate taxes of $800 owing on the land, which the firm had to pay to acquire the land.

Required

a. Calculate the total cost of the land.
b. Provide several reasons for not recording the land purchase at its nominal price of $150,000.

Calculating Depletion Expense

7-30 A firm purchased an oil well costing $2,600,000, which is expected to produce five million barrels of oil. The well can probably be sold for $100,000 after all the oil is extracted. If 500,000 barrels of oil were extracted and sold this year, what is the depletion expense?

Income Statement Effects of Capitalizing Installation Costs

7-31 A firm acquired a machine for $150,000 and spent $50,000 to install it. The machine has a five-year life and a zero residual value. The firm is considering the possible effects on net income if it chooses to capitalize or expense the installation costs. Calculate the effect on net income each year if the firm uses straight-line depreciation.

PROBLEMS

Three Methods of Calculating Depreciation Expense

7-32 A firm purchased computer-aided drafting and machining equipment at the beginning of the year for $420,000. The machine has an expected useful life of six years and a $38,000 residual value.

Required

a. Calculate the annual depreciation expense for the first four years of the equipment's life using the straight-line method.
b. Calculate the annual depreciation expense for the first four years of the equipment's life using the double-declining-balance method.
c. Calculate the annual depreciation expense for the first four years of the equipment's life, using the sum-of-the-years'-digits method.
d. Comment on the differences in your results. Which method would managers prefer if they are trying to maximize their net income? Which method is preferred if the objective is to minimize income taxes? Why?
e. Using double-declining-balance depreciation, calculate depreciation expense through the sixth year. What adjustment to depreciation should be made in the sixth year?

Transaction Analysis: Disposal of Fixed Assets

7-33 A firm acquired a $650,000 fixed asset that has a four-year life and a residual value of $50,000. Show the effects on the balance sheet equation of the asset's disposal at the end of the fourth year, assuming the following separate circumstances:

a. The asset is sold for its estimated residual value.
b. The asset is sold for $75,000.
c. The asset is sold for $35,000.
d. The asset is scrapped (junked) and disposal costs are $10,000.

Transaction Analysis: Sum-of-the-Years'-Digits Depreciation

7-34 A firm acquired a $24,000 truck that has a three-year life and an estimated residual value of $6,000. Using the balance sheet equation, record the truck's purchase and depreciation using sum-of-the-years'-digits depreciation. Show the effects in each year, and be sure to include separate columns for accumulated depreciation and retained earnings in your equation.

Transaction Analysis: Double-Declining-Balance Depreciation

7-35 A firm acquired a $20,000 computer, along with $14,000 of related ancillary equipment that can only be used on this machine. The computer and the related equipment have an estimated life of five years and a residual value of $2,000.

Required

a. Using the balance sheet equation, record the computer's purchase and depreciation using the double-declining-balance method. Show the effects in each year, and be sure to include separate columns for accumulated depreciation and retained earnings in your equation.
b. Show the effects on the balance sheet equation of disposing of the computer and the related equipment under each of the following separate circumstances:

i. At the end of the fifth year, sold for $2,000.
ii. At the end of the fifth year, sold for $6,000.
iii. At the end of the fourth year, sold for $8,000.

Financial Statement Effects: Recognizing Patents

7-36 A firm acquired a patent for $125,000 and expected its economic useful life to be 15 years.

Required

a. What useful life should be used to amortize the patent?
b. Show the balance sheet effects of holding the patent for three years.
c. What if the firm had to defend its patent in a lawsuit at the beginning of year 4? Assume that the firm spent $5,000 on legal fees and lost the lawsuit.

Financial Statement Effects: Depletion

7-37 A firm spent $1,500,000 for an oil well that is expected to produce 3,000,000 barrels of oil. During the first year, no oil is extracted. During the second year, 1,000,000 barrels are extracted and sold.

Required

a. Show the effects on the balance sheet equation of the oil well acquisition and depletion during these two years.
b. Discuss the impact on both the income statement and the balance sheet during each year.

Financial Statement Effects: Depletion

7-38 A firm acquired a $4.5 million gold mine that is expected to yield 500,000 ounces of gold. During each of the first two years, 100,000 ounces of gold are mined and sold.

Required

a. Show the effects on the balance sheet equation from the mine acquisition and depletion for each of these two years.
b. Discuss the impact on the income statement and balance sheet at acquisition and at the end of each year.
c. What would the depletion be during each of the first two years if the firm estimated it would cost $200,000 to clean up the mine at the end of its productive life? (Note that the mine has a negative residual value.)
d. Assume that the mine is sold for $5 million at the end of the second year. Show the effects on the firm's income statement and the balance sheet.
e. Assume that the mine is fully exhausted and declared worthless at the end of the third year. Show the effects on the firm's income statement and the balance sheet.

Balance Sheet Effects of Alternative Depreciation Methods

7-39 A firm purchased a computer-controlled drill press at the beginning of 2000 for $360,000. The drill press has an expected useful life of 10 years and a $40,000 residual value. Assume that the firm begins the year prior to the purchase of the drill press with the following balance sheet totals:

Plant and equipment	$3,500,000
Less: Accumulated depreciation	(1,235,000)
Plant and equipment, net	$2,265,000

Required

a. Determine the ending balances in each of these balance sheet accounts, after including the annual straight-line depreciation for the first three years of the drill press's life. Ignore depreciation on the existing plant and equipment.
b. Determine the ending balances in each of these accounts, after including the annual double-declining-balance depreciation for the first three years of the drill press's life. Ignore depreciation on the existing plant and equipment.
c. Calculate the effects on net income if the firm used double-declining-balance depreciation, instead of straight-line depreciation. Calculate these differences for each of the first three years for the drill press and for the same three years combined. Ignore depreciation on the existing plant and equipment.
d. Comment on the net income differences. Do they seem significant each year or in total?
e. After the firm has owned the drill press for 10 years, what effects will any of these depreciation methods have on the firm's net income? Why?
f. Using double-declining-balance depreciation, calculate depreciation expense through the tenth year. What adjustment to depreciation is necessary in the tenth year?

Calculating Depreciation Expense Using The Double Declining Balance Method

7-40 A firm purchased computer-aided drafting and machining (CAD-CAM) equipment at the beginning of 1998 for $420,000. The machine has an expected useful life of six years and a $38,000 residual value. Assume that the firm begins the year (before purchasing the CAD-CAM equipment) with the following balance sheet totals:

Plant and equipment	$6,250,000
Less: Accumulated depreciation	(1,145,000)
Plant and equipment, net	$5,105,000

Required

a. Calculate the ending balances in each of these accounts after including the annual double-declining-balance depreciation for the first four years of the equipment's life. Ignore depreciation on the existing plant and equipment.
b. After the firm has owned the CAD-CAM machine for six years, what effects would the use of straight-line depreciation versus double-declining-balance depreciation have on the firm's net income? Why?

Two Methods of Calculating Depreciation Expense

7-41 A firm purchased a computer-controlled drill press for $480,000 at the beginning of 2000. The drill press has an expected useful life of 10 years and zero residual value. Assume that the firm begins the year with the following balance sheet accounts, ignoring depreciation on the existing plant and equipment:

Cash and other assets	$8,115,000
Plant and equipment	$3,500,000
Less: Accumulated depreciation	(1,040,000)
Plant and equipment, net	$2,460,000
Liabilities	$1,000,000
Shareholders' equity	$9,575,000

Required

a. Show the effects of the drill press purchase on the firm's balance sheet equation. Assume that the firm borrowed money to purchase the drill press.
b. Show the effects of straight-line depreciation on the balance sheet equation for the first two years of the drill press's life.
c. Show the effects of double-declining-balance depreciation on the balance sheet equation for the first two years of the drill press's life.
d. Comment on these differences. Is the firm's balance sheet stronger under either method? Why?

Gain or Loss on Disposal of Fixed Assets

7-42 Swen and Jerry are twins who each own an ice cream company. Four years ago, they each purchased an ice cream mixer. Each mixer was identical in all respects, including the cost of $35,000. Each had an estimated useful life of five years and an estimated residual value of $5,000.

The only difference between the two mixers was in the depreciation method chosen. Swen chose the straight-line method, whereas Jerry chose the double-declining-balance method.

Because of the intense competition in the ice cream business and the resulting rapid changes in technology and mixing methods, Swen and Jerry each decided to replace their mixers on the same day at the end of the fourth year. They sold their old mixers to twins Haskin and Dobbins for exactly the same price, $10,000.

Later, at a family reunion, Swen mentioned that he had sold his mixer at a loss of $1,000. Jerry, while smiling under his beard, said that he had done better than that, and that Swen should check with his accountant because Jerry had realized a gain on the sale of his mixer.

Required

Explain how Swen could have had a loss on the sale of the same mixer on which Jerry had a gain. Show the relevant calculations that will convince Swen and Jerry of the accuracy of your analysis.

Gain or Loss on Disposal of Fixed Assets

7-43 Warhol Enterprises purchased a spray painter at the beginning of 1999 at a cost of $150,000. Warhol estimated that the spray painter would last five years and have a residual value of $30,000. The company decided to use straight-line depreciation. Two years later, at the end of 2000, Warhol sold the spray painter for $100,000.

Required

a. Calculate the book value of the spray painter at the end of 1999 and the end of 2000, prior to its sale.
b. Calculate the gain or loss on the sale of the spray painter.
c. Calculate the income statement effect, assuming that Warhol decided to give the spray painter to a charitable foundation.

Ethics

Gain or Loss on Disposal of Fixed Assets

7-44 Johns Inc. purchased a canvas stretcher at a cost of $16,000 at the beginning of 1999. Johns estimated that the canvas stretcher would last four years and have no residual value. Johns decided to use straight-line depreciation. Three years later, at the end of 2001, Johns sold the canvas stretcher for $10,000.

Required

a. Calculate the book value of the canvas stretcher at the end of 1999 and the end of 2001, prior to its sale.
b. Calculate the gain or loss on the sale of the canvas stretcher.
c. Calculate the income statement effects, assuming that Johns decided to give the canvas stretcher to a charitable foundation.
d. Calculate the gain or loss on the sale of the canvas stretcher, if Johns had originally decided to use the sum-of-the-years'-digits depreciation method.
e. Assume that Johns originally thought that the stretcher would have only a three-year life, but that its residual value would be $10,000. In other words, Johns made perfect predictions in 1999 about the life and value of the canvas stretcher at the end of 2001. Compute the gain or loss and compare it with your answer in part d.
f. Assume an alternate scenario for the donation of the canvas stretcher to a charitable foundation. What if, through this gift, Johns would realize significant tax benefits, especially by claiming that the market value of the canvas stretcher was actually $50,000? This high value could presumably be justified because of its collectible value, having been used by such a popular artist. Comment on the ethical implications of the disposal decision and of the valuation decision.

Property, Plant, and Equipment Ratio Analysis

7-45 The following financial statement information is from BRN, Inc. BRN is a global company specializing in high-tech components for the automotive, space, and computer industries.

Property, plant, and equipment on the basis of cost (in millions)	**1999**	**1998**
Land	$ 104	$ 104
Buildings	1,527	1,461
Machinery and equipment	3,925	3,555
	5,556	5,120
Less: Accumulated depreciation	3,067	2,793
Total property, plant, and equipment	2,489	2,327
Other Information		
Sales revenue	$9,087	$7,948

Required

a. Comment on the changes in the property, plant, and equipment accounts.
b. Calculate fixed asset turnover (1999 only) and the percentage of PPE depreciated (both years).
c. Comment on these results. Identify any managerial implications associated with these results.

Amortization of Intangibles

7-46 Bishop Corporation had the following intangible assets on December 31, 1999:

1. A patent was acquired from another company on January 1, 1999, for $25,000. The patent had been registered with the U.S. Patent Office on January 1, 1993. Assume that the legal life is the useful life.
2. On April 2, 1999, the company was successful in obtaining a patent. The legal fees paid to an outside law firm were $8,400. The development costs paid to engineers who were employees of Bishop were $75,000. The patent's estimated useful life is its legal life.
3. On July 1, 1999, Bishop acquired all the assets net of the liabilities of Fargo Company. The identifiable net assets' market values at the time of purchase totaled $100,000. Bishop acknowledged the superior earnings and loyal customer following of Fargo Company. Therefore, Bishop and Fargo agreed on a total purchase price of $145,000. Any goodwill arising from the purchase is to be amortized over 40 years.
4. On December 31, 1999, Bishop paid a consulting firm $17,000 to develop a trademark. In addition, legal fees paid in connection with the trademark were $3,000. Assume a useful life of 20 years.

Required

a. Determine the amortization expense for 1999.
b. Determine the book value of each of the intangible assets listed above.

Interpreting Financial Statements: Fixed Assets

7-47 Refer to Reebok's financial statements in Appendix E. Review the balance sheet to determine how and where fixed assets and the associated accumulated depreciation were reported.

Required

a. Read Notes 1 and 4. Identify and discuss any unusual terms. Trace any numerical disclosures of fixed asset costs in the notes to corresponding disclosures in the financial statements.
b. Determine whether Reebok has any unusual fixed assets. If so, discuss how they might be interpreted by financial analysts. Discuss how Reebok's managers might view such assets.
c. Identify Reebok's accumulated depreciation balances at the end of each year. If these items are not disclosed, what effects will this have on your analysis of the financial statements?
d. Calculate the following ratios for Reebok:
   - Fixed asset turnover
   - Percentage of PPE depreciated
e. Based on your answers above, how effectively is Reebok managing its long-term assets?

Interpreting Financial Statements: Fixed Assets

7-48 Refer to Wendy's financial statements in Appendix D. Review the balance sheet to determine how and where fixed assets and the associated accumulated depreciation were reported.

Required

a. Read all notes concerning fixed assets. Identify and discuss any unusual terms. Trace numerical disclosures of fixed asset costs in the notes to corresponding disclosures in the financial statements.
b. Determine whether Wendy's has any unusual fixed assets. If so, discuss how they might be interpreted by financial analysts. Discuss how Wendy's managers might view such assets.
c. Identify Wendy's accumulated depreciation balances at the end of each year. If these items are not disclosed, what effects will this have on your analysis of the financial statements?
d. Calculate the following ratios for Wendy's:
   - Fixed asset turnover
   - Percentage of PPE depreciated
e. Based on your answers above, how effectively is Wendy's managing its long-term assets?

Interpreting Financial Statements: Disposal of Fixed Assets

7-49 Refer to Wendy's financial statements in Appendix D. Review the financial statements to determine how and where any disposals of fixed assets were reported. Also identify how and where any gains or losses on disposals of fixed assets were reported.

Required

a. Were the gains or losses on disposals of fixed assets clearly reported?
b. How much of Wendy's income before income taxes can be attributed to the disposal of fixed assets?
c. Refer to the statement of cash flows. How much cash was received from restaurant dispositions? How much cash was spent on capital expenditures?

Financial Statement Effects: Amortizing Intangible Assets

Critical Thinking

7-50 Assume that you are the manager of a small firm that has an intangible asset valued at $10 million. You believe that the firm's earnings prospects are quite favorable during the next five years. You also learn that you have a choice in selecting the amortization period for this intangible, which can range from five years to 40 years in length.

Required

a. Choose an amortization period of either five or 40 years, and defend your choice.
b. Suppose that the firm's earnings prospects for the next five years are very unfavorable. In fact, you discover that the amortization period of five years for this intangible will certainly result in a net loss (negative net income) over the next five years. Again choose an amortization period of either five or 40 years and defend your choice.
c. Discuss any other viable options. What option might be preferable? Why?

Critical Thinking

Conceptual Discussion: Recognizing Gain or Loss on Disposal

7-51 Discuss the concept of recognizing a gain or loss at the time an asset is sold. Is such a gain or loss a function of good management, or is it a function of improper estimates of residual values? Why do you think that such gains or losses should be shown on the income statement? How do they affect your evaluation of the current year's net income?

Critical Thinking

Conceptual Discussion: Choosing a Depreciation Method

7-52 A firm acquired a $26,000 computer, including software, with an estimated useful life of four years and an estimated residual value of $6,000. The firm's financial vice president (CFO) is trying to choose between using straight-line depreciation and double-declining-balance depreciation. It is rumored that the computer will be obsolete at the end of the second year. She also believes that the firm will have relatively high profits during the next two years.

Required

a. Provide advice to the CFO regarding your recommendation about the preferred depreciation method.

b. Calculate the effects on the balance sheet equation for the first two years, using each depreciation method. Be sure to include separate accounts for accumulated depreciation and retained earnings in your balance sheet equation.

c. Assume that the computer is sold on the first day of the third year for $4,000 because it is obsolete and no longer useful for any purpose in this firm.
   i. Calculate the effect on net income from the computer's disposal, using each depreciation method.
   ii. Assuming that these experiences are typical for most computers, what advice would you now give the CFO regarding depreciation methods that should be used for computers?
   iii. Under what circumstances might the controller still want to use straight-line depreciation for computer equipment?

Critical Thinking

Graphing Depreciation Cost Flows

7-53 Draw a freehand graph with dollars on the vertical axis and time (years) on the horizontal axis, showing the pattern of depreciation expenses that would be expected under each of the following depreciation methods:

a. Straight-line depreciation
b. Double-declining-balance depreciation
c. Sum-of-the-years'-digits depreciation

Critical Thinking

Financial Statement Effects: Land Ownership

7-54 Answer the following questions:

a. How would land owned by a manufacturer be shown on its balance sheet?

b. Would land owned by a real estate investment company perhaps have a different purpose than land occupied by a factory? Contrast the balance sheet presentation of land as a fixed asset and as some other type of asset.

c. Create a numerical example showing two ways a firm may report land on its balance sheet, depending on the proposed use of the land. How much discretion do you suppose that managers might have in making this choice?

Critical Thinking

Conceptual Discussion: Recognizing Estimated Residual Value

7-55 Estimating an asset's residual value incorporates significant uncertainties into the financial statements. Discuss the proposition that residual values should be ignored when an asset is depreciated.

Critical Thinking

Conceptual Discussion: Recognizing Asset Write-Downs

7-56 Discuss the concept of write-downs, that is, writing down the value of noncurrent assets on the firm's balance sheet. Why do write-downs provide managers with flexibility to manipulate earnings?

Critical Thinking

Conceptual Discussion: Recognizing Asset Write-Downs

7-57 Defend the statement that write-downs are an essential part of the conservative nature of accounting. Defend the notion that write-downs should be permitted whenever the firm or its accountants believe that an asset's value has been permanently impaired.

Critical Thinking

Conceptual Discussion: Recognizing Asset Write-Ups

7-58 Asset write-ups are permitted in Australia. That is, when managers of an Australian firm believe that an asset's market value has increased, they are permitted to increase the asset's reported value on the balance sheet. Defend or refute asset write-ups.

Integration of Concepts

Comprehensive Analysis: Fixed Assets

7-59 Pfizzel Inc. reported the following information in its property, plant, and equipment note to the 1999 financial statements (dollars in millions):

	1999	1998	1997
Land	$ 85.2	$ 81.8	$ 71.7
Buildings	1,218.6	1,093.8	953.9
Machinery and equipment	2,108.4	1,897.8	1,706.9
Furniture, fixtures, and other	940.2	812.8	698.3
Construction in progress	640.5	414.5	385.6
Total PPE	4,992.9	4,300.7	3,816.4
Less accumulated depreciation	1,919.7	1,668.2	1,511.3
Book value PPE	$3,073.2	$2,632.5	$2,305.1

Required

Part I

a. Identify and describe each term in this note.
b. During which year(s) did Pfizzel acquire substantial fixed assets? How can you tell?
c. During which year(s) did Pfizzel sell some fixed assets? How can you tell?
d. Did Pfizzel's construction change markedly during these three years? What evidence supports your conclusion?
e. Calculate the percentage of PPE depreciated for each year. Discuss the meaning and implications of your results.

(Continued)

Part II

Given the following additional information from Pfizzel's 1999 annual report (dollars in millions):

	1999	1998	1997
Net sales	$8,281.3	$7,477.7	$7,230.2
Income from operations	1,972.5	913.3	1,553.9

f. Calculate fixed asset turnover for 1999 and 1998.

g. Evaluate and discuss your results.

Part III

h. If you now learn that the average fixed asset turnover is 1.4 for firms similar to Pfizzel, reevaluate and discuss your earlier results.

Part IV

Pfizzel Inc. reported the following summary of significant accounting policies in its 1999 annual report:

Property, plant, and equipment are recorded at cost. Significant improvements are capitalized. In general, the straight-line method of depreciation is used for financial reporting purposes and accelerated methods are used for U.S. and certain foreign tax reporting purposes.

i. Discuss each part of this note, indicating how it relates to the concepts described in this chapter.

j. Identify and discuss areas where managers have some discretion to choose between alternative accounting policies or methods.

k. Similarly, identify areas where substantial judgment and subjectivity may be used.

l. What opportunities may Pfizzel use to adjust or to manipulate net income? Are they significant? Why?

Integration of Concepts

Comprehensive Analysis: Fixed Assets

7-60 Spelling Entertainment, which produces films and videos and other entertainment media, lists the following items in its 1994 annual report (dollars in thousands):

	1994	1993	1992	1991
Property, plant, and equipment net	$ 16,161	$ 4,770	$ 4,834	$ 6,331
Other assets	19,678	4,562	6,512	13,879
Net assets held for disposition	0	0	0	16,475
Intangibles, net of accumulated amortization of $17,671, $10,527, $6,713 and $2,626	400,751	1,549,983	159,291	154,946
Revenues	$599,839	$ 274,899	$257,546	$122,748
Operating income	50,743	39,727	25,315	13,987

Required

Part I

a. Describe each of Spelling's non-current assets.

b. Identify any unusual trends or unusual terms.

c. Calculate fixed asset turnover for 1993 and 1994. Use property, plant, and equipment, net.

(Continued)

Part II

d. How does Spelling seem to be managing its fixed assets? What evidence supports your conclusion?

e. Why are intangibles Spelling's largest noncurrent asset? What problems might this create, especially if these intangibles represent copyrights and trademarks that are no longer fashionable?

Part III

f. What additional information is needed before you can calculate Spelling's percentage of PPE depreciated?

g. Where might you find such information?

h. Upon carefully reading the notes to Spelling's 1994 financial statements, you do not find the requisite information. What would you do next to find this information?

Part IV

Further review of Spelling's notes reveals the following additional information about its asset disposal strategy or the effects thereof.

Net assets (liabilities) held for disposition consisted of the following at December 31, (dollars in thousands):

	1994	1993	1992	1991
Receivables, net	$ 608	$ 2,714	$ 7,445	$40,282
Investments	0	0	0	2,600
Property, plant, and equipment, net	3,161	4,467	4,572	23,050
Other assets	0	0	247	5,280
Accounts payable and other accruals	(1,749)	(1,780)	(4,023)	(16,681)
Notes payable	0	0	0	(19,500)
Other liabilities	0	0	(1,090)	(4,707)
	$ 2,020	$ 5,401	$ 7,151	$30,324
Less allowance for estimated estimated losses on disposal of segment	(20,368)	(29,621)	(15,058)	(13,849)
	$(18,348)	$(24,220)	$(7,907)	$16,475

i. Describe each item in the above note. Note that only one of the above subtotals was reported in Spelling's balance sheet (see above, Part I). Where were the other subtotals reported? Why?

j. Discuss the implications of this note. What does this note imply about the valuations of Spelling's other assets? Why?

k. How have Spelling's perceptions regarding its asset disposal activities changed over the years? Why?

l. Would an external analyst view Spelling's note as optimistic or worse? Why?

m. If Spelling completes its disposition program in 1995, what is the likely effect on 1995's net income? Why?

Integration of Concepts

Comprehensive Analysis: Noncurrent and Intangible Assets

7-61 Boudreaux Group is an international biochemical and pharmaceutical firm, headquartered in Switzerland. Its 1999 annual report includes the following (Swiss francs in millions):

	1999	1998	1997
Property, plant, and equipment, net	FF 7,010	FF 6,319	FF 5,815
Intangible assets	1,895	2,050	2,200
Other long-term assets	1,583	1,313	1,064
Total long-term assets	FF 10,488	FF 9,682	FF 9,079
Sales	FF 13,576	FF 12,702	FF 11,840
Gross profit	8,145	7,139	6,295
Gross (original) cost PPE	13,077	11,950	10,905

Intangible assets

Intangible assets comprise acquired intellectual property (including patents, technology, and know-how), trademarks, licenses, and other similarly identified rights. They are recorded at their acquisition cost and are amortized over the lower of their legal or estimated economic lives up to a maximum of 10 years. Costs associated with internally developed intangible assets are expensed as incurred.

Required

a. Describe each of Boudreaux's disclosures related to noncurrent assets.
b. For 1998 and 1999, calculate the fixed asset turnover.
c. For 1998 and 1999, calculate the percentage of PPE depreciated.
d. Discuss and interpret the results of these ratio computations.
e. With regard to intangibles, how has Boudreaux constrained some of the discretion and subjectivity that it might have had otherwise?
f. What impact does the term *know-how* have on your analysis of Boudreaux's noncurrent assets?

Critical Thinking

Financial Statement Interpretation: R&D Costs

7-62 Beaubox, one of Europe's leading packaging manufacturers, is headquartered in Paris. Its 1997 annual report contains the following note.

Research and Development Expenditure

Such expenditure is charged to the profit and loss account in the year in which it is incurred. Tangible assets related to research and development are depreciated over the expected useful lives of the assets.

Required

a. Discuss the meaning and possible interpretation of this note.
b. Rewrite this note to clarify its meaning.
c. Does this treatment of R&D seem consistent with U.S. GAAP? In what ways?

Critical Thinking

Financial Statement Interpretation: Depreciation and Depletion

7-63 Inco Limited, headquartered in Toronto, is one of the world's premier mining and metals companies. Its 1994 annual report contains the following note:

Depreciation and Depletion
Depreciation is calculated using the straight-line method and, for the nickel operations in Indonesia, the units-of-production method, based on the estimated economic lives of property, plant, and equipment. Such lives are generally limited to a maximum of 20 years and are subject to annual review. Depletion is calculated by a method that allocates mine development costs ratably to the tons of ore mined.

Upon further study, you learn that the units-of-production depreciation method is very similar to the methods described in this chapter to determine depletion allowances.

Required

a. Identify and discuss each unusual term in this note.
b. Why would a company want to use more than one depreciation method?
c. Does the 20-year limitation on useful lives result in more conservative, or less conservative, measures of net income? What other information would you need to better assess this issue?
d. What choices does Inco Limited have during its annual review of useful lives? What would be the most likely balance sheet and income statement effects of such a review? Why?

Integration of Concepts

Financial Statement Interpretation: Cash Flow Effects

7-64 Sigma Designs is a diversified graphic systems corporation. Its statement of cash flows is summarized as follows:

Sigma Designs, Inc.
Statement of Cash Flows
For the Years Ended January 31, 1995 and 1994

	1995	1994
	(Dollars in thousands)	
Cash Flows from Operating Activities		
Net loss	$(8,773)	$(29,546)
Adjustments to reconcile net loss to net cash provided by operating activities (summary of all net adjustments)	(110)	15,885
Net cash provided by (used for) operating activities	(8,883)	(13,661)
Cash Flows from Investing Activities		
Purchases of marketable securities	(25,350)	(22,542)
Sales of marketable securities	22,296	33,355
Equipment additions	(721)	(612)
Software development costs (capitalized)	(1,255)	(494)
Other asset transactions	0	183
Net cash provided (used for) investing activities	(5,030)	9,890
Cash Flows from Financing Activities		
Common stock sold	13,201	493
Repayment of long-term obligations	1,710	0
Other financing transactions	(1,925)	0
Net cash provided (used for) financing activities	12,986	493
Decrease in cash and equivalents	$ (927)	$ (3,278)

Required

a. What does the category of cash flows shown as "Software development costs (capitalized)" represent? Who has received these cash payments?
b. Do these "Software development costs" payments seem material, relative to the size of Sigma Designs? How would your views change if the cash payment was $3,000,000 each year?

Critical Thinking

Conceptual Discussion: Loss of Fixed Assets

7-65 Becky's Courier Service is a one-person, one-bicycle operation. Becky's only capital equipment is a highly specialized, custom-designed mountain bike that can be used throughout the urban jungle.

Required

a. Assume that Becky's mountain bike broke, what accounting recognition should be given to this tragedy?
b. How would your answer change if the bike had been stolen? Why?
c. Assume that Becky's mountain bike was destroyed in a fire while chained in a bike rack at a client's site. The client's insurance company provided Becky with a check for the replacement cost of the bicycle, which was twice its original price. What accounting recognition should be given to this event?

Ethics

Capitalizing or Expensing Decisions

7-66 The president of your company clearly wants to report as large a net income number as possible. Part of your responsibility as the controller is to determine if certain expenditures should be expensed or capitalized. Knowing the president's wishes, which of the following expenditures would you capitalize? Support each choice with proper accounting reasons and ethical behavior.

a. Painting costs (part of the factory and office building are painted each year)
b. Costs to repair cracks in the parking lot
c. Cost of tree pruning on corporate grounds
d. Cost to produce brochures that will be given to prospective customers next year
e. Costs to replace an engine in a company truck

Critical Thinking

Income Statements Effects of Amortizing Intangibles

7-67 The following income statements for SOS Staffing Services, Inc. were extracted from the SEC's EDGAR database (see next page).

SOS Staffing Services, Inc.
Consolidated Statements of Income
Fiscal Years Ended December 28, 1997, December 29, 1996 and December 31, 1995

	Fiscal Year (52 Weeks) Ended		
	1997	1996	1995
SERVICE REVENUES	$ 209,250,847	$ 136,163,973	$ 87,532,903
DIRECT COST OF SERVICES	162,539,859	108,589,322	69,353,212
Gross profit	46,710,988	27,574,651	18,179,691
OPERATING EXPENSES:			
Selling, general and administrative	32,867,550	20,397,240	13,826,034
Intangibles and amortization	1,492,637	470,119	32,566
Total operating expenses	34,360,187	20,867,359	13,858,600
INCOME FROM OPERATIONS	12,350,801	6,707,292	4,321,091
OTHER INCOME (EXPENSE):			
Interest expense	(368,145)	(301,207)	(145,646)
Interest income	497,661	90,793	109,684
Other, net	145,386	13,695	120,604
Total, net	274,902	(196,719)	84,642
INCOME BEFORE PROVISION FOR INCOME TAXES	12,625,703	6,510,573	4,405,733
PROVISION FOR INCOME TAXES (including pro forma for 1995)	(5,099,476)	(2,481,413)	(1,728,653)
NET INCOME	$ 7,526,277	$ 4,029,160	$ 2,677,080
NET INCOME PER COMMON SHARE:			
Basic	$ 0.78	$ 0.59	$ 0.54
Diluted	$ 0.77	$ 0.59	$ 0.43
WEIGHTED AVERAGE COMMON SHARES:			
Basic	9,654,204	6,780,400	4,984,616
Diluted	9,780,505	6,838,479	6,229,021

Required

a. Conduct a horizontal and vertical analysis of SOS's income statements for all three years.
b. Identify any unusual terms, along with any unusual trends in SOS's income statements.
c. Identify the most likely reasons for such trends.
d. What business events resulted in SOS's huge increase in "Intangibles and amortization"?
e. Write a short memo to a prospective investor, evaluating SOS's future prospects.

Inter-Company Analysis of Noncurrent Assets

Integration of Concepts

7-68 The following data for Pfizer and Eli Lilly have been excerpted from the SEC's EDGAR database:

Pfizer (excerpts from balance sheet and income statement)	1997	1996	1995
Pfizer Inc. and Subsidiary Companies			
Long-term loans and investments	1,340	1,163	545
Property, plant and equipment, less accumulated depreciation	4,137	3,850	3,473
Goodwill, less accumulated amortization: 1997--$152; 1996--$115; 1995--$79	1,294	1,424	1,243
Other assets, deferred taxes and deferred charges	1,745	1,762	1,316
Total assets	$15,336	$14,667	$12,729

(millions, except per share data)	1997	1996	1995
Net sales	$12,188	$11,306	$10,021
Alliance revenue	316	--	--
Total revenues	12,504	11,306	10,021

NOTES TO CONSOLIDATED FINANCIAL STATEMENTS

1 Significant Accounting Policies

A -- Consolidation and Basis of Presentation

The consolidated financial statements include the parent company and all significant subsidiaries, including those operating outside the U.S. Balance sheet amounts for the foreign operations are as of November 30 of each year and income statement amounts are for the full year periods ending on the same date. All significant transactions among our businesses have been eliminated.

In preparing the financial statements, management must use some estimates and assumptions that may affect reported amounts and disclosures. Estimates are used when accounting for long-term contracts, depreciation, amortization, employee benefits and asset valuation allowances. We are also subject to risks and uncertainties that may cause actual results to differ from estimated results, such as changes in the health care environment, competition, foreign exchange and legislation. "Forward-Looking Information and Factors That May Affect Future Results" beginning on page 36, discusses these and other uncertainties.

D -- Long-Lived Assets

Long-lived assets include:

- property, plant and equipment--These assets are recorded at original cost and the cost of any significant improvements after purchase is added. We depreciate the cost evenly over the assets' useful lives. For tax purposes, accelerated depreciation methods are used as allowed by tax laws.
- goodwill--Goodwill represents the difference between the purchase price of acquired businesses and the fair value of their net assets when accounted for by the purchase method of accounting. We amortize goodwill evenly over periods not exceeding 40 years.
- other intangible assets--Other intangible assets are included in "Other assets, deferred taxes and deferred charges" in the Balance Sheet. We amortize these assets evenly over their estimated useful lives.

We review long-lived assets for impairment when events or changes in business conditions indicate that their full carrying value may not be recovered. We consider assets to be impaired and write them down to fair value if expected associated cash flows are less than the carrying amounts. Fair value is the present value of the expected associated cash flows.

4 Business Alliances

We have entered into agreements related to two new pharmaceutical products developed by other companies:

- Lipitor, a cholesterol-lowering medication, developed by the Parke-Davis Research Division of Warner-Lambert Company
- Aricept, a medication to treat symptoms of Alzheimer's disease, developed by Eisai Co., Ltd.

Under copromotion agreements, these products are marketed and copromoted with alliance partners. We provide funds, staff and other resources to sell, market, promote and further develop these medications. In the Statement of Income, "Alliance revenue" represents revenues earned under the copromotion agreements (a percentage of net sales adjusted, in some cases, for certain specific costs). "Selling, informational and administrative expenses" in the Statement of Income include other expenses for selling, marketing and further developing these products.

5 Financial Instruments

Most of our financial instruments are recorded in the Balance Sheet. Several "derivative" financial instruments are "off-balance-sheet" items.

A -- Investments in Debt and Equity Securities
Information about our investments follows:

(millions of dollars)	1997	1996	1995
Amortized cost and fair value of held-to-maturity debt securities:*			
Corporate debt	$ 626	$ 602	$ 682
Certificates of deposit	655	657	350
Municipals	56	29	222
Other	104	81	186
Total held-to-maturity debt securities	1,441	1,369	1,440
Cost and fair value of available-for-sale debt securities	686	636	--
Cost of available-for-sale equity securities	81	81	68
Gross unrealized gains	106	73	50
Gross unrealized losses	(4)	(8)	(8)
Fair value of available-for-sale equity securities	183	146	110
Total investments	$2,310	$2,151	$1,550

*Gross unrealized gains and losses are immaterial.

These investments are in the following captions in the Balance Sheet:

(millions of dollars)	1997	1996	1995
Cash and cash equivalents	$ 636	$ 640	$ 153
Short-term investments	712	487	1,109
Long-term loans and investments	962	1,024	288
Total investments	$2,310	$2,151	$1,550

The contractual maturities of the held-to-maturity and available-for-sale debt securities as of December 31, 1997 were as follows:

(millions of dollars)	Years				
	Within 1	Over 1 to 5	Over 5 to 10	Over 10	Total
Held-to-maturity debt securities:					
Corporate debt	$ 567	$ 54	$ 4	$ 1	$ 626
Certificates of deposit	646	9	--	--	655
Municipals	56	--	--	--	56
Other	79	--	15	10	104
Available-for-sale debt securities:					
Certificates of deposit	--	256	189	--	445
Corporate debt	--	91	150	--	241
Total debt securities	$1,348	$410	$358	$11	2,127
Available-for-sale equity securities					183
Total investments					$2,310

E -- Fair Value

The following methods and assumptions were used to estimate the fair value of derivative and other financial instruments at the balance sheet date:

- short-term financial instruments (cash equivalents, accounts receivable and payable, forward-exchange contracts, short-term investments and borrowings)--cost approximates fair value because of the short maturity period
- loans--cost approximates fair value because of the short interest reset period
- long-term investments, long-term debt, forward-exchange contracts and purchased currency options--fair value is based on market or dealer quotes
- interest rate and currency swap agreements--fair value is based on estimated cost to terminate the agreements (taking into account broker quotes, current interest rates and the counterparties' creditworthiness)

The differences between fair and carrying values were not material at December 31, 1997, 1996 or 1995.

Note 6: Property, Plant and Equipment

The major categories of property, plant and equipment follow:

(millions of dollars)	1997	1996	1995
Land	$ 142	$ 119	$ 95
Buildings	1,682	1,597	1,406
Machinery and equipment	2,719	2,511	2,345
Furniture, fixtures and other	1,385	1,291	1,100
Construction in progress	530	487	517
	6,458	6,005	5,463
Less: accumulated depreciation	2,321	2,155	1,990
Total property, plant and equipment	$4,137	$3,850	$3,473

Management's Report

The Company's management has designed a system of internal control to safeguard its assets, ensure that transactions are properly authorized and provide reasonable assurance, at reasonable cost, as to the integrity, objectivity and reliability of financial information. Even an effective internal control system, regardless of how well designed, has inherent limitations and, therefore, can provide only reasonable assurance with respect to financial statement preparation. The system is built on a business ethics policy that requires all employees to maintain the highest ethical standards in conducting Company affairs. The system of internal control includes careful selection, training and development of financial managers, an organizational structure that segregates responsibilities and a communications program which ensures that Company policies and procedures are well understood throughout the organization. The Company also has an extensive program of internal audits, with prompt follow-up, including reviews of separate Company operations and functions around the world.

Eli Lilly (excerpts from balance sheet and income statement)

Consolidated Balance Sheets
ELI LILLY AND COMPANY AND SUBSIDIARIES
(Dollars in millions)

Other Assets		
Prepaid retirement	579.1	512.9
Investments (Note 6)	465.6	443.5
Goodwill and other intangibles, net of allowances for amortization of $119.3 (1997) and $311.0 (1996) (Note 2)	1,550.5	4,028.2
Sundry	559.8	1,124.3
	3,155.0	6,108.9
Property and Equipment (Note 1)	4,101.7	4,307.0
Total Assets	$12,577.4	$14,307.2

Consolidated Statements of Income
ELI LILLY AND COMPANY AND SUBSIDIARIES
(Dollars in millions, except per-share data)

Year Ended December 31	1997	1996	1995
Net sales....................................	$8,517.6	$7,346.6	$6,763.8

Notes to Consolidated Financial Statements
ELI LILLY AND COMPANY AND SUBSIDIARIES
(Dollars in millions, except per-share data)

Note 1: Summary of Significant Accounting Policies (excertped)

Basis of Presentation: The accounts of all wholly owned and majority-owned subsidiaries are included in the consolidated financial statements. All intercompany balances and transactions have been eliminated. The preparation of financial statements in conformity with generally accepted accounting principles requires management to make estimates and assumptions that affect the reported amounts of assets, liabilities, revenues, expenses and related disclosures at the date of the financial statements and during the reporting period. Actual results could differ from those estimates.

Investments: All short-term debt securities are classified as held-to-maturity because the company has the positive intent and ability to hold the securities to maturity. Held-to-maturity securities are stated at amortized cost, adjusted for amortization of premiums and accretion of discounts to maturity. Substantially all long-term debt and marketable equity securities are classified as available-for-sale at December 31, 1997. Available-for-sale securities are carried at fair value, with the unrealized gains and losses, net of tax, reported in a separate component of shareholders' equity. The company owns no investments that are considered to be trading securities.

Intangible Assets: Intangible assets arising from acquisitions and research alliances are amortized over their estimated useful lives, ranging from five to 40 years, using the straight-line method. Impairments are recognized in operating results if impairment indicators are present and the fair value of the related assets is less than their carrying amounts.

Property and Equipment: Property and equipment is stated on the basis of cost. Provisions for depreciation of buildings and equipment are computed generally by the straight-line method at rates based on their estimated useful lives. At December 31, property and equipment consisted of the following:

	1997	1996
Land	$ 130.6	$ 143.9
Buildings	2,057.1	2,103.5
Equipment	4,373.8	4,247.0
Construction in progress	473.4	602.0
	7,034.9	7,096.4
Less allowances for depreciation	2,933.2	2,789.4
	$4,101.7	$4,307.0

Depreciation expense related to continuing operations for 1997, 1996 and 1995 was $397.5 million, $394.9 million and $371.4 million, respectively. Approximately $20.4 million, $35.8 million and $38.3 million of interest costs were capitalized as part of property and equipment in 1997, 1996 and 1995, respectively. Total rental expense for all leases related to continuing operations, including contingent rentals (not material), amounted to approximately $126.1 million for 1997, $119.6 million for 1996 and $106.8 million for 1995. Capital leases included in property and equipment in the consolidated balance sheets and future minimum rental commitments are not material. However, the company entered into capital lease obligations aggregating $8.8 million in 1997 and $27.4 million in 1996.

Note 2: Asset Impairment

In November 1994, the company purchased PCS Health Systems, Inc. (PCS), McKesson Corporation's pharmaceutical-benefits-management business, for approximately $4.1 billion. Substantially all the purchase price was allocated to goodwill.

Subsequently, pursuant to SFAS No. 121, "Accounting for the Impairment of Long-Lived Assets and for Long-Lived Assets to Be Disposed Of," the company evaluated the recoverability of the long-lived assets, including intangibles, of its PCS health-care-management businesses. While revenues and profits are growing and new capabilities are being developed at PCS, the rapidly changing, competitive and highly regulated environment in which PCS operates has prevented the company from significantly increasing PCS' operating profits from levels that existed prior to the acquisition. In addition, since the acquisition, the health-care-industry trend toward highly managed care has been slower than originally expected and the possibility of selling a portion of PCS' equity to a strategic partner has not been realized. In the second quarter of 1997, concurrent with PCS' annual planning process, the company determined that PCS' estimated future undiscounted cash flows were below the carrying value of PCS' long-lived assets. Accordingly, during the second quarter of 1997, the company adjusted the carrying value of PCS' long-lived assets, primarily goodwill, to their estimated fair value of approximately $1.5 billion, resulting in a noncash impairment loss of approximately $2.4 billion ($2.21 per share). The estimated fair value was based on anticipated future cash flows discounted at a rate commensurate with the risk involved.

Note 3: Restructuring and Special Charges

In both 1993 and 1992, the company announced major actions designed to enhance the company's competitiveness in the changing health care environment, reduce expenses and improve efficiencies. During 1997 and 1996, the company continued to take steps to complete these actions.

Significant components of these charges and their status at December 31, 1996 and 1997, respectively, are summarized as follows:

	Original Charges	1996	1997
1993			
Work force reductions......................	$ 534.5	$ 24.7	$ -
Manufacturing consolidations and other closings........................	204.3	91.8	48.1
Pharmaceutical streamlining.................	35.3	-	-
Asset write-downs, legal accruals and other........................	258.5	4.4	4.8
Total - continuing operations............	$1,032.6	$120.9	$ 52.9
1992			
Global manufacturing strategy.............	$ 218.9	$ 59.1	$ 38.6
Legal, environmental, asbestos abatement and other.....................	185.5	61.3	54.0
Total - continuing operations............	$ 404.4	$120.4	$ 92.6

The 1993 restructuring actions consisted primarily of early-retirement and other severance programs associated with work force reductions as well as streamlining core pharmaceutical operations. In addition, restructuring actions in both 1993 and 1992 have resulted or will result in a consolidation of certain manufacturing operations and changes in the nature and/or location of certain manufacturing operations. Asset write-downs reflected changes in pharmaceutical markets. Special charges were established for patent and product liability matters in both 1993 and 1992.

Note 6: Financial Instruments

Risk-Management Instruments and Off-Balance-Sheet Risk

Financial instruments that potentially subject the company to credit risk consist principally of trade receivables and interest-bearing investments. Wholesale distributors of life-sciences products and managed care organizations account for a substantial portion of trade receivables; collateral is generally not required. The risk associated with this concentration is limited due to the company's ongoing credit review procedures. The company places substantially all its interest-bearing investments with major financial institutions, in U.S.

Government securities or with top-rated corporate issuers. In accordance with documented corporate policies, the company limits the amount of credit exposure to any one financial institution.

Fair Value of Financial Instruments

A summary of the company's outstanding financial instruments at December 31 follows. As summarized, "cost" relates to investments while "carrying amount" relates to long-term debt.

	1997		1996	
	Cost/Carrying Amount	Fair Value	Cost/Carrying Amount	Fair Value
Short-term investments:				
Debt securities..........	$ 77.1	$ 76.9	$ 141.4	$ 144.5
Noncurrent investments:				
Marketable equity.........	77.7	86.0	72.0	91.4
Debt securities...........	93.0	93.3	56.9	57.0
Nonmarketable equity......	34.2	33.7	20.3	19.0
Long-term debt................	2,266.4	2,426.5	2,465.5	2,511.6

The company determines fair values based on quoted market values where available or discounted cash flow analyses (principally long-term debt). The fair values of nonmarketable equity securities, which represent either equity investments in start-up technology companies or partnerships that invest in start-up technology companies, are estimated based on the fair value information provided by these ventures. The fair value and carrying amount of risk-management instruments were not material at December 31, 1997 or 1996.

At December 31, 1997 and 1996, the gross unrealized holding gains on available-for-sale securities were $19.1 million and $27.5 million, respectively, and the gross unrealized holding losses were $13.8 million and $9.4 million, respectively. Substantially all these gains and losses are associated with the marketable equity securities. The proceeds from sales of available-for-sale securities totaled $39.7 million and $102.1 million in 1997 and 1996, respectively. Realized gains and losses were $6.6 million and $25.3 million, respectively, in 1997. Purchases of available-for-sale securities were not significant in 1997 and 1996. The net adjustment to unrealized gains and losses on available-for-sale securities reduced shareholders' equity by $7.7 million and $39.0 million in 1997 and 1996, respectively.

The company is a limited partner in certain affordable housing investments that generate benefits in the form of tax credits. The determination of fair value of these investments is not practicable. The carrying value of such investments was $253.2 million and $276.3 million as of December 31, 1997 and 1996, respectively.

Responsibility for Financial Statements

The company maintains internal accounting control systems that are designed to provide reasonable assurance that assets are safeguarded, that transactions are executed in accordance with management's authorization and are properly recorded, and that accounting records are adequate for preparation of financial statements and other financial information. The design, monitoring and revision of internal accounting control systems involve, among other things, management's judgments with respect to the relative cost and expected benefits of specific control measures. A staff of internal auditors regularly monitors, on a worldwide basis, the adequacy and effectiveness of internal accounting controls.

In addition to the system of internal accounting controls, the company maintains guidelines of company policy emphasizing proper overall business conduct, possible conflicts of interest, compliance with laws and confidentiality of proprietary information. The guidelines are reviewed on a periodic basis with employees worldwide.

Required

a. Describe each of Pfizer's and Lilly's noncurrent assets.
b. Identify any unusual trends or unusual items. Use the notes to gain further insight on each item in the financial statement excerpts.
c. Calculate fixed asset turnover for each year.
d. How does each company seem to be managing its fixed assets? What evidence supports your conclusion?
e. Discuss the implications of each note. How does each note change your opinions about the valuations of each company's noncurrent assets?
f. What is the impact of Lilly's special charges?
g. Would an external analyst view Lilly's or Pfizer's notes as optimistic or worse? Why?
h. Discuss the managerial implications of each company's disclosures related to its noncurrent assets.
i. Review each company's management report. Identify any unusual items. How does the information in this report change any of your earlier opinions?

Internet

Evaluating Fixed Assets

7-69 Locate the most recent set of financial statements for the computer manufacturers listed below. You may use either the 10-K available at EDGAR **(www.sec.gov/edaux/searches.htm)** or the annual report available at the company page on the Web.

Corporation	Home Page Location
Compaq	**www.compaq.com** (under "Contents")
Gateway	**www.gw2k.com** (under "Tell Me About Gateway")
IBM	**www.ibm.com/ibm/**
Dell	**www.dell.com**

Required

a. What is the total value of the property, plant, and equipment owned by each corporation? What percentage of total assets do they represent?
b. What is the composition of the property, plant, and equipment account (in other words, what percentage is land and so on)? What is the method of depreciation used for each fixed asset class?
c. Calculate the fixed asset turnover and the percentage of PPE depreciated for each company.
d. Compare and evaluate each company's results.
e. Identify whether any of these companies experienced sudden changes in fixed asset composition or depreciation method. Discuss any such changes.

Evaluating Intangible Assets

7-70 For each of the following companies, locate the most recent 10-K available using the EDGAR database **(www.sec.gov/edaux/searches.htm):** Walt Disney Corp., Schering Plough, Oncogene Science, *Chicago Tribune,* John Wiley & Co., RJR Nabisco, and Macromedia Inc.

Required

a. Identify a unique intangible asset owned by each company.
b. For each intangible asset, identify (1) its value in both dollars and as a percentage of total assets and (2) the method of amortization used. (*Hint:* You will find useful and relevant information in the Notes to the Financial Statements.)
c. Compare and contrast the different types of intangible assets reported by each company.
d. Identify any instances where one of these firms tried to "manage" its earnings by changing its method of amortizing intangible assets.

Evaluating Noncurrent Assets

7-71 Companies in different industries naturally use different assets in daily operations. The differences are reflected in both type and amount of long-term tangible assets. Locate, from 10-Ks on file with EDGAR **(www.gov.sec/edaux/searches.htm),** the latest balance sheet and Notes to the Financial Statements for the following companies:

- Ameritech (telecommunications)
- Bank One (banking)
- Boeing (airplane manufacturing)
- Dole (food products)
- Southwest Airlines (air transportation)

Required

a. Before looking at the 10-Ks, list the types of long-term tangible assets that would normally be included on each company's balance sheet.
b. Identify the primary long-term tangible assets for each company and determine the percent of total assets it represents.
c. Comment on any observed differences across these various industries.

chapter

8 Accounts Payable, Commitments, Contingencies, and Risks

LEARNING OBJECTIVES

1. Recognize the types of current liabilities reported on the balance sheets of most business firms.
2. Understand the types of business transactions and events that create current liabilities.
3. Appreciate how liability reporting often depends on estimates and judgments.
4. Be alert to a variety of other potential liabilities and risks that are not presently reported in the balance sheet.

INTRODUCTION

Chapters 6, "Current Assets," and 7, "Noncurrent Assets," discussed accounting and reporting for assets. Our focus now shifts to the sources of the funds that are invested in assets. The balance sheet equation indicates that the firm's economic resources or assets are obtained from two sources: creditors and investors.

ASSETS = LIABILITIES + SHAREHOLDERS' EQUITY

This chapter and Chapter 9, "Noncurrent Liabilities," examine liability accounting and reporting issues. Chapter 10, "Shareholders' Equity," discusses shareholders' equity.

Liabilities or "borrowed capital" constitute a major source of funds for business firms. In fact, the average corporation relies on debt for more than half the funds it has invested in assets. The extent to which firms rely on debt financing depends upon the relative costs of issuing debt or equity securities. These relative costs differ across industries, and consequently the typical percentages of debt financing also vary across industries. In some industries (such as public utilities and financial institutions), debt financing can exceed 90 percent of total assets. Financial statement users pay careful attention to the sources of financing because the success of a firm depends as much on the effective management of its liabilities and shareholders' equity as it does on the efficient utilization of its assets. The firm's liability management also affects the risks and the returns available to the firm's creditors and shareholders.

TYPES OF CURRENT LIABILITIES

Exhibit 8-1 shows the current liabilities section of a recent balance sheet for Ersatz International Corporation, a firm doing business in the electronics, aerospace, and automotive components industries. The items and amounts shown in the exhibit are typical of those reported by business firms. The next section discusses the accounting and reporting issues associated with each major current liability shown on Ersatz International's balance sheet.

EXHIBIT 8-1 Current Liabilities

Ersatz International Corporation
Current Liabilities at September 30, 2000
(Dollars in millions)

Current Liabilities	
Accounts payable–trade	$ 859.8
Short-term debt	166.4
Accrued compensation and benefits	710.1
Current portion of long-term debt	7.4
Advance payments from customers	362.7
Accrued product warranties	165.6
Accrued income taxes	94.1
Accrued restructuring costs	62.1
Other	562.7
Total current liabilities	$2,990.9

Current liabilities are short-term obligations that usually must be paid from current assets within a year. These liabilities are a critical link in the operating cycles of most firms. In the course of day-to-day operations, firms incur short-term obligations to suppliers, employees, and other entities. The cash received from sales of goods and services to customers is then used to pay these obligations as they are due.

Current liabilities can be of several types: (1) obligations to pay cash to other entities, such as accounts payable, notes payable, and accrued liabilities; (2) obligations to provide other entities with goods or services for which payment has already been received, such as revenues received in advance; and (3) obligations to honor product warranties (guarantees). Examples of each are discussed next.

Accounts Payable

The largest single item listed among Ersatz's current liabilities is accounts payable-trade. Accounts payable represent debts that the firm incurs in purchasing inventories and supplies, as well as amounts that the firm owes for other services used in its operations, such as rentals, utilities, insurance, and so on. Most business transactions with suppliers involve short-term credit, for which payments are due within a designated period, such as 30 or 60 days. To illustrate, assume that a firm purchased inventory for $100,000 to be paid within 30 days. The purchase of inventory would increase inventory and accounts payable.

At the date of purchase:

ASSETS	=	LIABILITIES	+	SHAREHOLDERS' EQUITY
Inventory		Accounts payable		
+$100,000		+$100,000		

The $100,000 payment to the supplier would decrease cash and eliminate the accounts payable.

At the date of payment:

ASSETS	=	LIABILITIES	+	SHAREHOLDERS' EQUITY
Cash		Accounts payable		
+$100,000		+$100,000		

Discounts

Suppliers frequently offer discounts for early payment and the discount rates are usually high enough to induce customers to pay promptly. If the buyer intends to pay within the discount period, then the inventory is usually recorded at its cost, net of the discount. In the preceding example, if the supplier offered a 2% discount for early payment and the purchaser intends to pay within the discount period, then the inventory would be recorded initially at a cost of $98,000 ($100,000 invoice price, minus a $2,000 discount).

At the date of purchase:

ASSETS	=	LIABILITIES	+	SHAREHOLDERS' EQUITY
Inventory		Accounts payable		
+$98,000		+$98,000		

If the account subsequently is paid *after* the discount period has expired, then the purchaser would incur an interest expense of $2,000 ($100,000 − $98,000).

At the date of payment:

ASSETS	=	LIABILITIES	+	SHAREHOLDERS' EQUITY
Cash		Accounts payable		Retained earnings
−$100,000		−$98,000		−$2,000 (interest expense)

In times of low liquidity, some managers are tempted to "stretch out" their payments to suppliers and thereby forgo the available purchase discounts. Such a tactic represents a very high cost of borrowing and should be avoided. For example, recall from Chapter 6 that discount terms of 2/10, net 30 imply an annual interest rate of about 36%. Firms can usually borrow from other sources at rates much lower than this. Consequently, most firms pay their accounts within the discount period and rely instead on other, less costly sources of borrowed capital.

Reality Check 8-1 evaluates a major firm's changes in the amounts of accounts payable between two consecutive balance sheet dates.

Notes Payable

Ersatz's current liabilities include $166.4 million of short-term debt, which consists mainly of notes payable to financial institutions. Business firms frequently borrow funds from banks or other lenders by signing a formal **note payable** with a fixed repayment date, and notes payable may be either interest-bearing or discounted. To illustrate the accounting for an interest-bearing note, assume that a firm borrows $200,000 from a bank to be repaid in six months at an interest rate of 12% per year. Interest rates are usually stated on a yearly basis, even if the loan is for a shorter time period. This transaction increases cash and notes payable by $200,000.

At the date of borrowing:

ASSETS	=	LIABILITIES	+	SHAREHOLDERS' EQUITY
Cash		Notes payable		
+$200,000		+$200,000		

REALITY CHECK 8-1

The fiscal 1996 report of Apple Computer, Inc. shows the following current liabilities:

	(Dollars in millions) 1996	1995
Current liabilities:		
Notes payable to banks	$ 186	$ 461
Accounts payable	791	1,165
Accrued liabilities	675	422
Other current liabilities	351	277
Total current liabilities	$2,003	$2,325

Required:

Provide some plausible reasons for the substantial decline in Apple's accounts payable between 1995 and 1996.

Solution

The substantial decline in Apple's accounts payable could be due to several factors. First, Apple's production levels may have declined during 1996. If so, the firm may have reduced its purchases of goods and services from suppliers. Alternatively, Apple may have decided to pay its accounts payable in a shorter time period in order to take better advantage of supplier cash discounts. It is also possible that the firm's suppliers have become more reluctant to extend trade credit to Apple due to changes in the market for Apple's products.

Recall that the principal amount (*P*), the interest rate (*r*), and the time period (*t*) of the loan are used to determine the interest expense (*I*) in the following way:

$$\begin{aligned} \text{Interest} &= \text{Principal} \times \text{Rate} \times \text{Time} \\ &= P \times r \times t \\ &= \$200{,}000 \times 12\% \times 1/2 \text{ year} = \$12{,}000 \end{aligned}$$

When the note is repaid with interest, cash is reduced by $212,000, the notes payable balance is eliminated, and the firm incurs interest expense of $12,000.

At the date of payment:

ASSETS	=	LIABILITIES	+	SHAREHOLDERS' EQUITY
Cash		Notes payable		Retained earnings
− $212,000		− $200,000		− $12,000 (interest expense)

To illustrate the accounting for a discounted note, assume that the firm signs a note promising to pay the bank $200,000 in six months. The bank discounts the note by deducting the interest charge in advance. Assuming the interest rate is 12%, the bank deducts interest of $12,000 ($200,000 × 12% × .5 (half year) = $12,000) in advance. The amount paid to the borrower upon signing the note is then $188,000 ($200,000 − $12,000 = $188,000). This transaction increases cash and notes payable by $188,000.

At the date of borrowing:

ASSETS	=	LIABILITIES	+	SHAREHOLDERS' EQUITY
Cash		Notess payable		
+ $188,000		+ $188,000		

When the note is repaid, cash is reduced by $200,000 (the face amount of the note), the note payable balance is eliminated, and the firm incurs interest expense of $12,000.

At the date of payment:

ASSETS	=	LIABILITIES	+	SHAREHOLDERS' EQUITY
Cash		Notes payable		Retained earnings
− $200,000		− $188,000		− $12,000 (interest expense)

Note in this case that the note was discounted at a nominal rate of 12%. The actual rate of interest is greater than 12%, however, because the firm only received $188,000 from the lender and paid $12,000 in interest expense for six months. The interest expense is thus 6.38% ($12,000/$188,000 = 6.38%) for six months, or 12.76% per year (2 × 6.38% = 12.76%).

Accrued Compensation and Benefits

Ersatz International's current liabilities listed in Exhibit 8-1 include $710.1 million in accrued compensation and benefits. **Accrued liabilities** represent expenses that have been incurred prior to the balance sheet date but have not been paid nor included with liabilities as of the balance sheet date. An adjustment must be made to recognize the expense and the related obligation at the balance sheet date.

Ersatz's accrued compensation benefits consist primarily of (1) wages and salaries earned, though unpaid, at the balance sheet date and (2) vacation and holiday pay. To illustrate an adjustment to recognize accrued wages and salaries, assume that Ersatz has a weekly payroll of $400 million, and that Ersatz's balance sheet date of September 30, 2000, falls on a Tuesday. In such a situation, Ersatz's employees have earned two days' pay, or $160 million (2 days / 5 days = 40%; $400 million weekly payroll × 40% = $160 million) as of the balance sheet date. If so, it is necessary for Ersatz to accrue the expense and liability as of September 30, 2000:

ASSETS	=	LIABILITIES	+	SHAREHOLDERS' EQUITY
		Accrued compensation +$160 million		Retained earnings −$160 million (compensation expense)

As a result, $160 million of compensation expense would be recognized in 2000, and the current liabilities reported at September 30, 2000, would include an accrued liability for this amount. When the weekly payroll ($400 million) is paid to the employees on October 3, 2000, the following balance sheet effects occur:

ASSETS	=	LIABILITIES	+	SHAREHOLDERS' EQUITY
Cash −$400 million		Accrued compensation −$160 million		Retained earnings −$240 million (compensation expense)

Note that this accrual of compensation expense is used to achieve the objective of matching costs and benefits that was discussed earlier (especially in Chapter 2, "The Basic Concepts of Financial Accounting," and Chapter 4, "The Income Statement"). The total compensation expense of $400 million has been appropriately divided between the fiscal years ending on September 30 of 2000 and 2001 in proportion to the benefits obtained each year.

To illustrate the accrual of vacation benefits, assume that Ersatz's employees earn vacation benefits evenly over the period July 1 through June 30, and the firm incurs total vacation expenses each year of $2 billion. In this case, at the balance sheet date of September 30, 2000, Ersatz's employees would have earned three months (July, August, and September) of vacation benefits, or $500 million (3 months / 12 months = 25%;

$2 billion annual expense × 25% = $500 million). For this reason, Ersatz's 2000 income statement would include an expense and the balance sheet at September 30, 2000, would include a current liability for accrued employee benefits of $500 million.

Current Maturities of Long-Term Debt

A variety of long-term borrowing arrangements will be discussed in Chapter 9, "Noncurrent Liabilities," but for the present, bear in mind that as time goes by long-term debts become short-term debts. For this reason, the current liabilities of many firms include the portion of long-term debt that matures within the coming year. Note in Exhibit 8-1 that Ersatz International reports $7.4 million among its current liabilities, described as the current portion of long-term debt. On the balance sheets of previous years, this amount was included in Ersatz's long-term debts because it was not due within a year of the balance sheet date. During 2000, however, the amount was reclassified from long-term debt to a current liability. This amount is a claim against the company's current assets in the coming year.

Accrued Income Taxes

Ersatz's current liabilities shown in Exhibit 8-1 include accrued income taxes in the amount of $94.1 million. Business corporations are taxable entities and must file tax returns with the federal and state governments. In fiscal 2000, Ersatz reported income before taxes of $904.1 million, and was assessed $343.4 million in income taxes. Of this amount, $94.1 million remains unpaid at September 30, 2000. The remaining $249.3 million ($343.4 million tax expense less $94.1 million remaining tax liability) was paid before the balance sheet date.

Accrued Restructuring Costs

Ersatz's current liabilities shown in Exhibit 8-1 include $62.1 million in accrued restructuring costs. During the difficult economic climate of the early 1990s, many major corporations decided to restructure, or to downsize and refocus their operations. Corporate downsizing often entails the retraining, layoff, or termination of many employees, and the associated costs to the firms may be substantial. Corporations that refocus their operations may discontinue various lines of business, often at considerable losses, and the process of restructuring a firm may take several years.

When a firm decides to restructure, the total estimated costs of restructuring are expensed in the current year. For example, Ersatz embarked on a restructuring program in fiscal 1998 and in that year reported an expense and an accrual of restructuring costs of $271.5 million.

During fiscal 1998:

ASSETS	=	LIABILITIES	+	SHAREHOLDERS' EQUITY
		Accrued restructuring costs +$271.5 million		Retained earnings −$271.5 million

During fiscal 1999 and 2000, the firm made expenditures of $209.4 million in its attempts to downsize and refocus operations.

During fiscal 1999 and 2000:

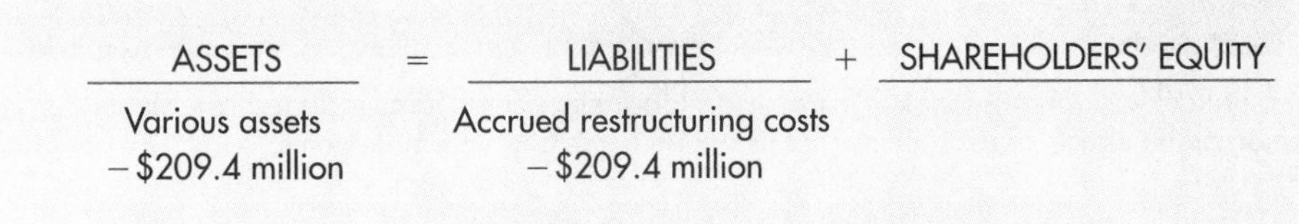

ASSETS	=	LIABILITIES	+	SHAREHOLDERS' EQUITY
Various assets − $209.4 million		Accrued restructuring costs − $209.4 million		

As a result, the remaining obligation for restructuring costs is $62.1 million ($271.5 − $209.4 = $62.1) at the end of fiscal 2000. Bear in mind that this amount is based on estimates made in 1998 when the restructuring program was undertaken. If the actual restructuring costs incurred (in the future) differ from this estimated amount, Ersatz will need to make adjustments to income reported in future periods.

Accounting for restructuring costs is a controversial issue in financial reporting because the dollar amounts are often material and require difficult estimates of costs to be incurred over several years in the future. Moreover, in many cases, the costs are related to actions that are planned by management in future periods, rather than being based on completed agreements or transactions. Some investors and analysts suggest that current accounting practices in reporting restructuring costs give managers too much discretion in shaping the numbers that will appear on the present and future income statements. Reality Check 8-2 shows footnote disclosures of restructuring charges reported by a major corporation.

Advance Payments from Customers

In many industries, customers pay in advance for goods and services to be provided at future dates. Education, transportation, magazine publishing, advertising, and construction are all examples of industries where advance customer payments are often required. The current liabilities of Ersatz International at the end of 2000, for instance, include an obligation of $362.7 million, described as advance payments from customers.

To illustrate the accounting for such advance customer payments, assume that during 2000 Ersatz received $800 million as advance payments from customers. Assume also that $437.3 million of this amount is earned by September 30, 2000, and the remainder is earned in the following fiscal year; these events are recognized in each year.

In 2000, on receiving the customers' deposits, the entire $800 million is unearned, and the company has an obligation to perform future services.

Upon receipt of customer deposits:

ASSETS	=	LIABILITIES	+	SHAREHOLDERS' EQUITY
Cash + $800 million		Advance payments from customers + $800 million		

REALITY CHECK 8-2

The fiscal 1997 annual report of Rockwell International Company, a global electronics firm, included a footnote containing the following explanation of the effects of restructuring costs on the firm's financial statements:

> During 1996, the Company recorded restructuring charges of $76 million ($47 million after-tax, or 22 cents per share). The restructuring charges relate to a decision to exit non-strategic product lines of continuing operations as well as the costs associated with staff reductions in the Automation and Avionics & Communications businesses.
>
> The provision includes asset impairments of $51 million, severance and other employee costs of $9 million, and contractual commitments and other costs of $16 million. These actions were substantially completed by the end of 1997.

Required

a. Why do firms accrue restructuring costs before such costs are actually incurred? Do such costs satisfy the definition of liabilities that was presented in Chapter 3, "The Balance Sheet"?
b. Based on the footnote information, Rockwell has recognized restructuring costs of $76 million in 1996 and no significant additional charges in 1997. How will these charges affect the amounts of income reported by the firm in future years? How would these charges influence your comparison of the firm's profit trend between 1996 and 1997?

Solution

a. Firms accrue restructuring costs because it has become apparent to management that the related assets have become less beneficial to the firm. Conservatism in financial accounting requires that such impairments in value be recognized currently. Because the decision to restructure operations is made in the current period, all the estimated associated expenses are recognized in the current period. It can be argued that such costs meet the definition of current liabilities because (1) the firm is presently obliged to make the future transfers, (2) the obligation is unavoidable, and (3) the event causing the liability has already occurred.
b. Because these costs have already been recognized as expenses by Rockwell in 1996, they will not result in expenses in future periods. Income in future years will be higher as a result. The income reported in 1996 is lower by the after-tax amount of the restructuring costs recorded in that year, and income reported in 1997 and subsequent years will be higher. Analysts may find it useful to adjust the reported income numbers to reflect earnings before the impact of the restructuring charges is taken into account.

Because $437.3 million of the payments has been earned by the end of fiscal 2000, this amount is recognized as revenue in 2000.

ASSETS	=	LIABILITIES	+	SHAREHOLDERS' EQUITY
		Advanced payments from customers		Retained earnings
		−$437.3 million		+$437.3 million (revenue)

Because $800 million was received in advance from customers and $437.3 million has been earned during 2000, the balance sheet at September 30, 2000, would show a remaining obligation of $362.7 million. When these amounts are earned in the following year, the remaining obligation will be eliminated, and revenues of $362.7 million will be recognized.

As revenues are earned in 2001:

ASSETS	=	LIABILITIES	+	SHAREHOLDERS' EQUITY
		Advanced payments from customers −$362.7 million		Retained earnings +$362.7 million (revenue)

Notice in this case that although Ersatz's balance sheet at the end of 2000 reports a $362.7 million obligation for advance payments, this does not represent a dollar amount that the company must pay to outside entities. Rather, it represents resources that Ersatz has received from customers but has not yet earned. Ersatz must earn these payments in future periods, and the resulting revenues (together with any related expenses) will be recognized in these future periods. If Ersatz does not fulfill this obligation, the advances would be returnable and then would be a liability payable in cash. Reality Check 8-3 shows how a major airline reports obligations to provide transportation services to its customers, for which payment has been received in advance.

Obligations for Warranties

It is common business practice for companies to stand behind the quality of their products by offering assurances of repairs, replacements, and/or refunds in the event of product failures or customer dissatisfaction. The eventual costs of such **obligations for warranties** cannot be known with certainty at the date of sale, although most companies can make reasonable estimates; these costs are associated with current sales revenues. For revenues and expenses to be properly matched, the future costs of warranties and guarantees associated with the current period revenues must be estimated and recorded in the current period. Also, the related obligations must be reported on the balance sheet.

As an example, Ersatz International provides warranties on many of its sales. Exhibit 8-1 shows that Ersatz reports among its current liabilities an obligation for product warranties in the amount of $165.6 million. This implies that Ersatz's managers estimate that the company will eventually make expenditures of about $165.6 million related to merchandise sold prior to the balance sheet date. If we assume that the entire obligation relates to 2000 sales and no costs have yet been incurred for warranties on 2000 sales, the company must have recognized the following event in 2000:

ASSETS	=	LIABILITIES	+	SHAREHOLDERS' EQUITY
		Warranty obligation +$165.6 million		Retained earnings −$165.6 million (warranty expense)

In subsequent years, the firm will spend cash or use other resources to perform warranty repairs. As the warranty repairs occur in subsequent periods, the liability will be eliminated.

REALITY CHECK 8-3

Delta Air Lines is one of the world's largest airlines and provides scheduled passenger service, air freight, mail, and other related aviation services. Delta's current liabilities at the end of fiscal 1997 include over $1.4 billion in obligations for air traffic liabilities and a frequent flyer program. Accompanying footnotes provide the following explanations:

```
FREQUENT FLYER PROGRAM - The Company accrues the estimated incremental cost of
providing free travel awards earned under its SkyMiles(R) frequent flyer program
when free travel award levels are achieved.

PASSENGER AND CARGO REVENUES - Passenger ticket sales are recorded as air traffic
liability in the company's consolidated balance sheets. Passenger and cargo
revenues are recognized when the transportation is provided, reducing the air
traffic liability.
```

Required

a. Contrast the ways that Delta measures its air traffic and frequent flyer liabilities. Attempt to justify the differences in the two measurements.
b. In what way does Delta's air traffic liability differ from accounts payable included in current liabilities? In what ways are the two items similar?

Solution

a. Delta measures its air traffic liability based on the value of the unused tickets. In contrast, Delta's frequent flyer liability is measured at the estimated incremental cost of providing travel. As a result, Delta reports revenues, costs, and operating profits when the air traffic liability is satisfied.

   It is difficult to justify the different methods used in measuring these two obligations. Both represent liabilities to provide future air travel service. Airline company managements prefer measuring frequent flyer obligations at incremental cost because this results in a lower reported obligation than would measurements based on the value of frequent flyer awards.

b. Delta's air traffic liability obligates the firm to provide passenger services in the future. Assuming that Delta operates at a profit, the cost of satisfying the liability will be less than the reported amount of the liability. Accounts payable, on the other hand, are recorded at the actual amounts that are expected to be paid to creditors.

   The two items are similar in the sense that both items obligate Delta to disburse current assets or to provide services in the near-term future (in other words, within the longer of a year or operating cycle).

In subsequent periods:

ASSETS	=	LIABILITIES	+	SHAREHOLDERS' EQUITY
Cash (or other resources) −$165.6 million		Warranty obligation −$165.6 million		

Note that no additional expenses are recognized at these points because the warranty expenses were matched against sales in 2000. Of course, the cost to be incurred for product warranties cannot be known for certain in the period of sale. For this reason, Ersatz must rely on its past experience and on information from other firms engaged in similar activities to make a reasonable estimate of its obligations for warranties. If the amounts of warranty expenses and obligations are potentially significant to users of Ersatz's financial statements, the firm's auditors will carefully evaluate the assumptions used to estimate this obligation.

COMMITMENTS, CONTINGENCIES, AND RISKS

Most financial statements include a footnote captioned "commitments and contingencies." The purpose of this note is to alert financial statement users to the fact that a variety of actual and potential future claims exist that do not meet the FASB's criteria for recognition as liabilities at the balance sheet date. Yet these claims may be important to users in assessing the firm's debt position.

Commitments are agreements with suppliers, customers, employers, or other entities that are not yet completed transactions and consequently have not been recognized in the accounts. If such agreements are significant, they should be disclosed in the notes to the financial statements. **Contingencies** are existing conditions whose resulting gains and losses are currently uncertain, but will be resolved by the occurrence of future events. Commitments and contingencies may be referenced in either the current or the noncurrent liability sections, depending on when they are likely to require payment, or they may only be disclosed in the notes.

Exhibit 8-2 includes portions of the note discussing commitments and contingencies included in the 1997 annual report of Intel Corporation, and the first portion of the exhibit illustrates a commitment. The company has signed a variety of contracts related to its future operations, yet because these contracts are not yet executed, they are not valued in the financial statements.

The second portion of Exhibit 8-2 illustrates Intel Corporation's significant contingent obligations. Similar obligations are faced by many firms in the chemical, petroleum refining, nuclear power, and special metals fabrication industries. Pursuant to environmental laws, this obligation is the requirement to control potentially hazardous emissions and correct the effects of past disposals of toxic wastes. Although Intel's managers are currently unable to put a "price tag" on the ultimate amount of the liability, the dollar magnitude is potentially substantial.

OTHER OFF-BALANCE SHEET RISKS

Most business entities are exposed to a wide variety of market risks. These can include changes in the future costs of acquiring materials and supplies, changes in the market values of financial assets and liabilities, effects on future revenues and expenses of swings in foreign exchange rates, potential effects of defaults on accounts receivable from major customers, and many other risks. In some cases, managers insulate themselves from some of these risks by using risk management strategies. Detailed footnote disclosures are required in order to alert readers to various risks that a firm might have, and the actions (if any) that management is taking to insulate the firm from potential losses.

Exhibit 8-3 shows portions of such disclosures included in Delta Air Lines' 1997 financial report. Many of the terms in the exhibit are probably not familiar to you, and detailed discussions of these items are beyond the scope of this book. Yet it is instructive to review the exhibit as a reminder that each firm faces a somewhat unique set of exposures that are not measured and reported in the body of the financial statements. Nonetheless, these risks can be quite important to analysts in assessing the credit-worthiness of the firm.

EXHIBIT 8-2 Commitments and Contingencies

Intel Corporation
Selected Portions of Footnotes to 1997 Financial Statements

Commitments

In October 1997, the Company and Digital Equipment Corporation announced that they have agreed to establish a broad-based business relationship. The agreement includes sale of Digital's semiconductor manufacturing operations to Intel for approximately $700 million, a 10-year patent cross-license, supply of both Intel and Alpha microprocessors by Intel to Digital, development by Digital of future systems based on Intel's 64-bit microprocessors, and termination of litigation between the companies as described below (see "Contingencies"). This agreement is also subject to U.S. government review. The transactions in the agreement are not expected to have a material adverse effect on the Company's financial condition or ongoing results of operations in any reporting period.

Contingencies

Intel has been named to the California and U.S. Superfund lists for three of its sites and has completed, along with two other companies, a Remedial Investigation/Feasibility study with the U.S. Environmental Protection Agency (EPA) to evaluate the groundwater in areas adjacent to one of its former sites. The EPA has issued a Record of Decision with respect to a groundwater cleanup plan at that site, including expected costs to complete. Under the California and U.S. Superfund statutes, liability for cleanup of this site and the adjacent area is joint and several. The Company, however, has reached agreement with those same two companies that significantly limits the Company's liabilities under the proposed cleanup plan. Also, the Company has completed extensive studies at its other sites and is engaged in cleanup at several of these sites. In the opinion of management, including internal counsel, the potential losses to the Company in excess of amounts already accrued arising out of these matters will not have a material adverse effect on the Company's financial position or overall trends in results of operations, even if joint and several liability were to be assessed.

EXHIBIT 8-3 Other Off Balance-Sheet Risks

Delta Air Lines
Selected Portions of Footnotes to 1997 Financial Statements

OFF-BALANCE SHEET FINANCIAL INSTRUMENTS: RISKS AND FAIR VALUES - FUEL PRICE RISK MANAGEMENT - Under its fuel hedging program, the Company can enter into certain contracts with counterparties, not to exceed one year in duration, to manage the Company's exposure to jet fuel price volatility. Gains and losses from fuel hedging transactions are recognized as a component of fuel expense when the underlying fuel being hedged is used. Any premiums paid for entering hedging contracts are recorded as a prepaid expense and amortized to fuel expense over the respective contract periods. On June 30, 1997, Delta had contracted for approximately 441 million gallons of its projected fiscal 1998 fuel requirements. At June 30, 1997, the fair value of option contracts used for purchases of jet fuel at fixed average prices was immaterial. The Company will be exposed to fuel hedging transaction losses in the event of non-performance by counterparties, but management does not expect any counterparty to fail to meet its obligations.

FOREIGN EXCHANGE RISK MANAGEMENT - The Company has entered into certain foreign exchange forward contracts, all with maturities of less than two months, in order to manage risks associated with foreign currency exchange rate and interest rate volatility. The aggregate face amount of such contracts was approximately $29 million at June 30, 1997. Gains and losses resulting from foreign exchange forward contracts are recognized as a component of miscellaneous income (expense), offsetting the foreign currency gains and losses resulting from translation of the Company's assets and liabilities denominated in foreign currencies.

CREDIT RISKS - To manage credit risk associated with its fuel price risk and foreign exchange risk management programs, the Company selects counterparties based on their credit ratings. It also limits its exposure to any one counterparty under defined guidelines and monitors the market position of the program and its relative market position with each counterparty.

CONCENTRATION OF CREDIT RISK - Delta's accounts receivable are generated primarily from airline ticket and cargo services sales to individuals and various commercial enterprises that are economically and geographically dispersed, and the accounts receivable are generally short-term in duration. Accordingly, Delta does not believe it is subject to any significant concentration of credit risk.

KEY TERMS

SUMMARY OF LEARNING OBJECTIVES

1. **Recognize the types of current liabilities that are reported on the balance sheets of most business firms.**
Current liabilities belong to one of three broad categories: (1) obligations to pay cash to other entities at specific dates, such as accounts payable, notes payable, and accrued liabilities; (2) obligations to provide goods or services for which payment has been received in advance; and (3) estimated costs to be incurred that are associated with revenues recorded in earlier periods, such as warranty obligations. Each of these three categories of current liabilities shows a common characteristic: Each obligates the firm to use current assets within the coming year or operating cycle.
2. **Understand the types of business transactions and events that create current liabilities.**
Most businesses purchase inventories, supplies, and services using short-term credit or accounts payable. Firms also frequently borrow operating funds through short-term loans or notes payable. At the end of an accounting period, firms usually require accruals to recognize expenses and current obligations for expenses, such as wages and salaries, income taxes, and other items. In addition, firms often guarantee their products and services and must report obligations for the estimated costs of warranties of past sales.
3. **Appreciate how liability reporting often depends on estimates and judgments.**
The matching concept that underlies the measurement of income requires that all costs associated with current revenues be recognized in the current period. In some cases (such as product warranties orrestructuring costs), the actual expenditures will be made in future years, and the dollar amounts to be incurred are not known with certainty. For this reason, currently reported expenses and liabilities are the results of estimates, based on past experience, industry norms, and professional judgments.
4. **Be alert to a variety of other potential liabilities and risks that are not presently reported in the balance sheet.**
A variety of actual and potential future claims against the firm's assets do not meet the FASB's requirements for recognition in the body of the financial statements, yet they may be important in assessing the firm's risks and debt position. Information about such commitments, contingencies, and risks is contained in the notes to the financial statements.

QUESTIONS

8-1 Define a liability. What is the difference between liabilities and other equities?

8-2 If liabilities represent amounts owed to others, why is judgment needed in determining the amount of some liabilities? Identify several cases where the accountant must use judgment because the amount of the liability cannot be readily determined from a bill or other document.

8-3 a. Identify three different types of liabilities.
b. Indicate how they are created, and how they are then reduced or eliminated. What does it mean to reduce a liability?
c. How else might you describe a reduction of a liability?
d. What generally happens when a liability "matures" or reaches its maturity date?

8-4 Why do firms want to have liabilities? Could a firm operate without liabilities? Who would be advantaged or disadvantaged if there were no opportunities for a firm to incur liabilities? Under what circumstances might a firm be unable to obtain credit and incur a liability?

8-5 a. Discuss the differences between current and long-term liabilities.
b. Identify three types of each.
c. Indicate how such current liabilities reduce a firm's need for cash.
d. Discuss how noncurrent liabilities are used as a source of capital.

8-6 a. Describe how three different types of current liabilities might be established.
b. What, or who, restricts the growth of current liabilities?
c. How might current liabilities be abused or misused?
d. Why are current maturities of long term debt shown as part of current liabilities?

8-7 Describe four separate items that are typically included in the current liability section of the balance sheet.

8-8 Evaluate the following statement: "The success of a firm depends as much on the effective management of its liabilities and shareholders' equity as it does on the efficient utilization of its assets."

8-9 Explain why most business firms pay their accounts payable within the discount period. As a manager, in what circumstance might you decide to pay after the discount period has expired?

8-10 Discuss the similarities and differences between notes payable and accounts payable.

8-11 Explain why the matching concept that guides the measurement of periodic net income often entails the reporting of accrued liabilities on the balance sheet.

8-12 How do restructuring costs originate? Should costs associated with restructuring activities that will be undertaken in future years be reported as liabilities? Why?

8-13 Various current liabilities reported in the balance sheet require that managers make estimates and assumptions concerning future events. Identify several such liabilities. If some of these estimates and assumptions are subsequently found to be incorrect, how should this be reflected in the financial statements? Discuss.

8-14 Indicate which, if any, of the following items would be reported as a current liability:
a. Advance payments from customers for services to be performed at future dates.
b. Agreements signed with suppliers to purchase inventory at future dates.
c. Agreements signed with customers to deliver completed products at future dates.
d. Advanced payment to suppliers for inventory to be shipped at future dates.
e. Accrued wages for work already performed by employees.
f. Accrued vacation and holiday benefits earned by employees.

8-15 Explain your agreement or disagreement with the inclusion of the following items among a firm's current liabilities:
a. Estimated future expenditures to provide warranty repairs on items sold prior to the balance sheet date.
b. Estimated future expenditures for legal costs to be incurred in defending the firm from product liability suits filed before the balance sheet date.
c. Accrued restructuring costs due to a plant closure.
d. Contingent liability resulting from environmental damages caused by illegal dumping of hazardous waste materials.

8-16 Explain why each of the following items should (or should not) be reported as liabilities in the financial statements:

a. Estimated future repair and maintenance costs for equipment owned by the firm at the balance sheet date.
b. Estimated employee retraining costs related to a plant closing that management has planned to implement subsequent to the balance sheet date.
c. Potential effects of defaults on accounts receivable owed by the firm's largest customer.
d. An airline's obligations to redeem $5 billion of unused frequent flyer miles, for which the passengers can claim free or discounted tickets.

8-17 A firm has sold one million units of a product that has a one-year warranty. Management estimates that about 5% of the units will require repairs, and the costs per repair will average about $12. What dollar amount of liability would you recognize in this case?

8-18 To reduce insurance costs, a firm insures its sales automobile fleet with a $1,000 deductible per vehicle (in other words, the insurance company only reimburses losses in excess of $1,000 per accident). The firm insures 800 vehicles and estimates that about 50 of these will incur substantial collision damages in the coming year. What liability dollar amount (if any) would you recognize in the firm's current balance sheet?

8-19 At the balance sheet date, an airline's passengers have accumulated 20 million frequent flyer miles, which could be exchanged for about 1,000 "free" domestic round-trip tickets. Similar tickets are sold at an average price of $600, and the company incurs an incremental cost of about $200 for each passenger carried. Management believes that about 75% of these tickets will ultimately be issued. What dollar amount of liability would you recognize in this case?

8-20 Deltoid Health Club has received $2.5 million in prepaid annual membership fees from its members and estimates that its cost of providing services to these customers over the coming year will be $1.6 million. How much of a liability should Deltoid report in its financial statements?

8-21 Manuel's Transmission Shoppe, Inc., is comparing prices from two potential suppliers for a similar component part. The first supplier quotes a price of $100, with payment in cash on delivery. The second supplier quotes a price of $105, with full payment due in 60 days. The second supplier also offers a 4% discount for payment within 30 days. Discuss how Manuel should evaluate these competing price quotations. Determine the amount of the liability that would be recorded if the purchase were made from the second supplier.

8-22 Bob's Steakhouse can either pay its suppliers within 30 days at a 1% discount or pay the full amount due in 60 days. The firm can also borrow from banks by signing short-term notes payable at an interest rate of 10% per year. Pat Forebode, the firm's treasurer, advises that the firm pay all its bills in full in 60 days, thereby taking full advantage of "interest-free" supplier accounts payable. Evaluate Pat's proposal. Identify where the liabilities associated with each proposal would be shown on the financial statements.

8-23 Compare and contrast the terms *contingencies* and *commitments*. Could a particular firm disclose one and not the other? Why?

8-24 Discuss the fact that many companies disclose many details about contingencies and commitments, but fail, or refuse, to put any dollar valuation on them.

8-25 Choose the best response to the following **multiple choice** questions:

1. All of the following are current liabilities except:
   a. Unearned revenue
   b. Accrued liabilities
   c. Prepaid insurance
   d. Current maturities of long-term debt
2. Jason Company received $5,000 from customers in advance. The company recorded this receipt to cash and to sales revenue. What effect does this incorrect entry have on the company's financial position?
   a. Assets are overstated; liabilities are understated; stockholders' equity is overstated.
   b. No effect on assets; liabilities are understated; stockholders' equity is overstated.
   c. Assets are understated; liabilities are understated; stockholders' equity is overstated.
   d. No effect on assets, liabilities, or stockholders' equity.
3. At December 31, Daniels Chocolate Company owes $200,000 under a 20-year mortgage to Interstate Industrial Bank. Approximately $11,000 of principal is due and payable the next year. How should the liability be reported on the December 31 balance sheet?
   a. All of the $200,000 should be reported as a long-term liability and nothing reported as a current liability.
   b. All of the $189,000 should be reported as a long-term liability and $11,000 as a current liability.
   c. All $200,000 should be reported as a current liability.
   d. Of the $200,000, only report $189,000 as a long-term liability and nothing as a current liability.

EXERCISES

Transaction Analysis: Inventory and Accounts Payable

8-26 Use the accounting equation to show the effects of each of the following transactions on the firm's balance sheet:

1. Purchased $250,000 of inventory on account.
2. Paid creditors $125,000 on account.
3. Purchased $200,000 of inventory on account at a 2% discount.
4. Paid creditors the amount due from transaction 3.
5. Purchased $300,000 of inventory, half for cash, half on account.
6. Paid creditors the amount due from transaction 5.
7. Purchased $400,000 of inventory all at a 3% discount, half on account, half for cash.

Transaction Analysis: Inventory and Accounts payable

8-27 Use the accounting equation to record the effects of each of the following transactions on the firm's balance sheet (create separate columns for cash, inventory, and accounts payable):

1. Purchased $350,000 of inventory on account, terms 2/10, net 30. The firm records the inventory net of the discount.
2. Paid the creditors in transaction 1 within the discount period.

3. Purchased $300,000 of inventory on account, terms 3/15, net 45. The firm records the inventory net of the discount.
4. Purchased $400,000 of inventory, no terms, half for cash and half on account.
5. Paid creditors the amount due from transaction 4.
6. Paid the creditors in transaction 3 *after* the discount period.

Transaction Analysis: Inventory and Current Liabilities

8-28 Use a balance sheet equation to analyze the effects of the following transactions on Jack's Shoe Company:

1. Jack's Shoe Company acquired 300 pairs of shoes and is billed $18,000. Jack's has not yet paid for the shoes.
2. Jack's Shoe Company made a partial payment of $6,000.
3. Jack's Shoe Company returned 10 pairs of shoes with a note requesting a credit of $610 to its account.
4. Jack's paid the balance due on its account.
5. Assume that Jack's Shoe Company is offered a 10% discount for prompt payment of all due amounts. Jack's intends to take advantage of all discounts, and all payments are made within the discount period. Show how the previous transactions would be recorded, using the balance sheet equation and assuming that the 10% discount is properly taken at the end of the appropriate discount period.

Transaction Analysis: Notes Payable and Interest

8-29 Use the accounting equation to show the effects of each of the following transactions on the firm's balance sheet:

1. Borrowed $20,000 cash from First Bank and signed an interest-bearing 120-day note (12% annual interest rate) on October 1.
2. On November 1, borrowed cash from Interwest Bank. Signed a note with a face value of $18,000 and a maturity of 90 days. The bank discounted the note at a 10% annual interest rate and issued the net proceeds to the firm.
3. At December 31 (year-end), record the following adjustments:
   - Accrued interest on the note in transaction 1.
   - Interest incurred on the note in transaction 2.
4. Paid the note in transaction 1 plus interest at maturity.
5. Paid the note in transaction 2 at maturity.

Transaction Analysis: Unearned Revenue and Interest

8-30 Use the accounting equation to show the effects of each of the following transactions on the firm's balance sheet:

1. Received subscription orders and cash of $360,000, representing 160,000 magazines.
2. Mailed 30,000 magazines (ignore any inventory effects).
3. Borrowed $100,000 at 6% annual interest for one year.
4. Mailed 30,000 magazines (ignore any inventory effects).
5. Mailed 70,000 magazines (ignore any inventory effects).
6. Accrued interest on the loan for six months. (Set up an interest payable account.)
7. Accrued interest on the loan for the following six months.

8. Repaid the loan, plus accrued interest.
9. Discuss the implications and meaning of the remaining subscriptions. Where will they appear on the firm's balance sheet? What aspects of these subscriptions will most concern the firm's managers?

Transaction Analysis: Notes and Interest

8-31 Use the accounting equation to analyze the effects of the following transactions on Town Floral, Inc.:

1. Acquired 2,000 floral bouquets at a billed cost of $15 per bouquet. Terms of payment are 2/10, n/30. Town Floral records purchases, net of the discount.
2. Signed a 120-day note for $15,000. The bank discounted the note at an annual rate of 10% and deposited the proceeds in Town Floral's bank account.
3. Borrowed $18,000 from the president's rich uncle at 10% annual interest. The company made no entry for the interest.
4. Paid the bills to the suppliers of the bouquets after the discount period had lapsed.
5. Paid six months interest to the president's rich uncle.
6. Recorded interest incurred for 90 of the 120 days on the note described in transaction 2.

Transaction Analysis: Warranties and Interest

8-32 Set up column headings as necessary (including a Warranty Payable column) and use the accounting equation to record the effects of each of the following transactions on the firm's balance sheet:

1. Accrued warranties estimated at $1,200,000 on December 31, 2000. (Set up a Warranty Payable column.)
2. Paid warranty claims costing $1,300,000 in cash during 2001.
3. Borrowed $10,000,000 at 9% annual interest for 240 days on September 30, 2001. Assume 360 days in a year.
4. Sold goods costing $12,000,000 for $25,000,000 cash during 2001.
5. Accrued interest on the loan on December 31, 2001. (Set up an interest payable column in your worksheet.)
6. Management estimated that the warranties obligation at December 31, 2001 (based on past sales and warranty claims) should be $1,500,000. Why was there a negative balance in the Warranty Payable column before your adjustment?
7. Repaid the loan, plus interest at the maturity date.

Transaction Analysis: Warranties

8-33 Use the accounting equation to show the effects of each of the following transactions on the firm's balance sheet:

1. Accrued estimated warranties of $3,375,000.
2. Paid warranty claims of $1,500,000.
3. Designed a new warranty plan that provided "full" coverage or a refund of the purchase price (for two years after the purchase date).
4. Paid warranty claims of $500,000.
5. Received a registered letter from Ralph Nadar inquiring about the meaning of "full" coverage.
6. Paid additional warranty claims costing $1,250,000.
7. Advertised the new warranty plan.

8. Decided that the estimated warranty costs were too low and increased them by $1,000,000.
9. Paid additional warranty claims of $300,000.
10. Discuss the meaning of the unexpired warranty obligation. Where do such obligations appear on the firm's balance sheet? What might the firm do if it expects warranty claims to continue at the same rate for another year?

Transaction Analysis: Loans and Interest

8-34 Jill's Slipper Shop took out a short-term bank loan of $32,000 to pay for merchandise. This bank loan carried a simple interest rate of 12% per year.

Required

a. Use the balance sheet equation to show the effect of this bank loan on Jill's financial statements.
b. Show the effect of using the loan proceeds to pay for merchandise inventory.
c. Show the effects of the interest expense at the end of the first and second months on the balance sheet equation, assuming that the loan has not yet been repaid.
d. Assume that the loan is repaid at the end of the third month. Show the effects of the loan repayment and the interest for three months on the balance sheet equation.

Transaction Analysis: Subscriptions

8-35 Maggie's Millinery Magazine (MMM) is very popular among the jet set, which rely on Maggie's exotic hats and other fine apparel for every film premiere and Academy Award ceremony. MMM is only available by subscription at an annual rate of $360 for 12 monthly issues. Show the effects of the following events, using the balance sheet equation:

1. MMM receives orders for 10 annual subscriptions with full payment enclosed.
2. MMM sends six issues to each of these subscribers during the current year. Ignore inventory effects.
3. These subscribers have all failed to win an Oscar so they cancel their subscriptions after the first six months, and MMM sends them a refund for the remaining issues.

Transaction Analysis: Subscriptions

8-36 MMM has many satisfied subscribers who have now realized their objectives of fame, fortune, and glory. Show the effects of the following transactions on MMM's balance sheet:

1. As a result of its popularity, MMM receives subscription renewals of $36 million, for 1997, at the end of 1996.
2. During the first quarter of 1997, MMM receives additional subscriptions of $55 million, all for 1997.
3. At the end of the first quarter of 1997, MMM decides to prepare quarterly financial statements. What is the financial statement effect of transactions 1 and 2?
4. What will be the effects on the financial statements at the end of 1997?
5. What would have been the effect on MMM's financial statements if you had not properly recorded the 1997 subscriptions?

6. How could MMM mislead itself or others by not properly recording subscriptions in the appropriate time period?

Contingencies

8-37 How should the following contingencies be treated in the annual report of Akronite Corporation on December 31, 1997?

a. The corporation is presently being sued for patent infringement. The damages are estimated to be $12 million and Akronite's attorneys feel this will probably be the amount required to be paid. However, the court date is set for June of the following year.

b. The corporation is being sued by the federal government for environmental pollution. The damages alleged by the federal government will probably be assessed against the corporation, yet no estimate has been determined at this point.

c. The corporation is suing another corporation for various patent infringements. The court date is scheduled for March 1998. The lawsuit total is $15 million, and it is almost a sure thing that Akronite will prevail and collect $15 million.

PROBLEMS

Transaction Analysis: Warranties and Interest

8-38 Set up the following accounts and balances at December 31, 2000, in an accounting equation:

Cash	$ 5,000,000
Inventory	10,000,000
Warranty obligation	2,250,000
Notes payable	0
Interest payable	0
Common stock	500,000
Retained earnings	12,250,000

Required

1. Show the effects of each of the following transactions on the firm's balance sheet:
   a. Borrowed $150,000,000 cash on June 1, 2001, and signed a nine-month note at an 8% annual interest rate.
   b. During 2001, sold goods during 2001 costing $8,000,000 for $18,000,000 cash.
   c. Paid warranty claims of $1,600,000 during 2001.
   d. Accrued interest on the note at December 31, 2001.
2. Discuss the meaning of the remaining warranty obligation. Discuss the underlying business reasons for offering warranties. What might the firm do if it expects warranty claims to continue at the same rate for another year?
3. What is the maturity date of the note? Assuming no additional interest has been accrued since December 31, 2001, what is the effect on the firm's balance sheet when the note is paid (including all the accrued interest)?

Transaction Analysis: Inventory and Current Liabilities

8-39 Use the balance sheet equation to analyze the effects of the following transactions:

1. Jill's Slipper Shop was formed with an original investment of $100,000 in exchange for common stock.
2. Jill's signed a 12-month rental agreement for its retail shop. Jill's pays a deposit of $2,000, along with the first month's rent of $2,000.
3. Jill's ordered and received merchandise for resale on account at an invoice cost of $32,000.
4. Jill's returned $1,800 worth of merchandise because it has been water-stained in transit.
5. Jill's paid the balance of its liability for the merchandise.
6. Jill's two employees worked in the shop for the first month, but Jill's cannot pay them until the end of the next month. Each employee earns a salary of $2,000 and commissions of $1,200. Ignore any payroll taxes or other employer obligations that may normally be recorded in conjunction with payroll transactions.
7. What effect does not paying the employees have on Jill's balance sheet? What effect is it likely to have on the employees? Which is more significant?
8. What is the long-term effect of not paying employees? What are the possible long-term effects of not paying suppliers? In other words, if Jill's continues to defer its employees' salaries and commissions, and if Jill's fails to pay for its merchandise, what will happen to the shop?

Integration of Concepts

Transaction Analysis: Comprehensive Problem

8-40 In its first year, Sam's Subway Emporium engaged in the following transactions. Indicate the effects of each transaction on Sam's balance sheet by using the balance sheet equation. Total your worksheet at the end of the first year and prepare a simple balance sheet.

1. Sam's was formed with a cash investment of $50,000 in exchange for common stock.
2. Sam's purchased a lunch cart for $10,000 cash.
3. Sam's ordered food and other supplies at a cost of $13,500, not yet received.
4. Sam's received the food and supplies, but intended to pay later.
5. Sam's felt quite generous and gave its employees an advance on their first week's wages of $2,500.
6. Sam's then got a bit nervous about whether it could pay its employees and suppliers in subsequent months, so a bank loan of $100,000 was acquired at an annual interest rate of 10%.
7. Sam's failed to pay for its first month's food and other supplies; the supplier billed Sam's a 20% late fee.
8. Sam's paid the employee's salaries of $67,500 during the year and also recognized the wages that were paid in advance as expenses.
9. Assume that an entire year has passed and Sam's has made no payments on the loan or the supplier's bill. The late fee is assessed quarterly (four times each year) if the account is not paid. Accrue interest on the loan and use an interest payable account for both the late fees and the interest on the loan.
10. On the first day of the next year, will Sam's be able to repay the loan? If so, show the effects of the loan repayment.

Changes in Various Current Liabilities

8-41 The Distraught Novelty Co. reports the following current liabilities in its balance sheet on December 31, 2000:

Accounts payable to suppliers	$2,500,000
Revenues received in advance	920,000
Income taxes payable	480,000
Warranty obligations	650,000
Total current liabilities	$4,550,000

The firm's current liabilities changed during 2001 for the following reasons:

1. Additional credit purchases from suppliers totaled $10,300,000, and cash payments to suppliers totaled $9,800,000.
2. Revenues received in advance were fully earned during 2001. The associated expenses, paid in cash, were $570,000.
3. The firm recognized $1,500,000 in income tax expense during 2001 and made total tax payments of $1,350,000.
4. For merchandise sold prior to 2001, warranty services costing a total of $575,000 were performed during 2001, that fully satisfied all the outstanding warranties. The company estimates that its warranty obligation for this year's sales is approximately $700,000 at December 31, 2001.

Required

a. Determine how each of the described events affects the firm's balance sheet in 2001.

b. Determine the composition of Distraught's current liabilities on December 31, 2001.

Transactions Affecting Various Current Liabilities

8-42 Antic Evenings, a local catering service, had the following transactions during December 2000:

1. Purchased decorative paper products on credit for $75,000 to be paid in full in 60 days.
2. On December 20, purchased cutlery and chinaware on credit for $120,000, at terms of 2/30, net 90 (a 2% discount is allowed if the bill is paid within 30 days). The company intends to pay this bill prior to January 18, 2001.
3. Received a property tax bill for $12,000, covering the period December 1, 2000 to November 30, 2001.
4. Received a deposit of $5,000 for catering services to be performed in February 2001.

Required

Show how each of the described transactions would affect Antic Evening's balance sheet equation.

Revenues Received in Advance and Warranty Obligations

8-43 Road Scholars offers a program of study leading to its E.Z. MBA degree. Classes are offered during commuting hours in a leased car traveling from suburban areas to urban business centers. The firm has received $400,000 in tuition payments for classes to be taught during the Fall 1999 and Spring 2000 semesters. The fall semester lasts from October through January, and the spring semester lasts from March through June.

Required

a. On the basis of the information given, determine the amounts of tuition revenue to be recognized in the firm's income statements during 1999 and 2000, and any liability for revenues received in advance to be reported in the balance sheet on December 31, 1999.

b. Upon further inquiry, you have learned that the firm offers students three basic core-level courses during the fall semester, and two more advanced courses during the spring semester. How, if at all, does this information affect your answers to part a?

c. To attract additional students, Road Scholars is offering students a rebate of half their tuition if their salaries have not increased by at least 50% within five years after completing their degrees. How would such a guarantee affect your answers to part a?

Ethics

Warranty Obligations: Adequacy and Revisions of Estimates

8-44 Tenuous Products provides a two-year warranty for repairs and services of its products. The firm has been operating for four years, and each year's warranty expense has been estimated at 5% of product sales. A summary of warranty expenses and actual warranty costs is provided below.

Year	Product Sales	Warranty Expense (5% of sales)	Warranty Expenditures
1	$ 10,000,000	$ 500,000	$ 120,000
2	30,000,000	1,500,000	840,000
3	60,000,000	3,000,000	2,160,000
4	90,000,000	4,500,000	3,960,000
	$190,000,000	$9,500,000	$7,080,000

Required

a. Determine the Estimated Warranty Obligations balance to be reported on the balance sheet at the end of each year. Does the assumption that warranty expenses will average about 5% of sales appear to be justified?

b. Tim Plistic, general manager of Tenuous Products, makes the following observation upon seeing your response to part a: "Clearly we are too conservative in estimating our warranty expenses. Every year we are estimating greater expenses than we are actually incurring, and this creates an ever-increasing overstatement of our warranty obligations." Comment on this inference.

c. After further inquiry among the factory service personnel, you learn that products sold in a given year are likely to require about 20% of their warranty repairs in the year of sale, and the remaining 80% of their repairs in the year after the sale. How does this information affect your assessment of the adequacy of Tenuous Products' reported liability for warranty expenses as of the end of the fourth year?

d. Based on your analysis in part c, what is your estimate of the amount of warranty expense that should be reported in Tenuous Products' income statement during the fourth year?

(Continued)

e. Assume that no changes are made to the warranty expenses that are shown above (the four-year total expense remains at $9,500,000). If sales in the fifth year are $70,000,000, what will be the year-end balance in the Estimated Warranty Obligation account? In this case, what financial reporting action do you recommend?

Critical Thinking

Identifying Transactions from Worksheet Entries

8-45 The following worksheet entries were retrieved from a water-logged worksheet stored in a flooded basement. Identify the transaction to which the worksheet entry refers. Discuss the underlying business reason supporting each transaction.

	Assets	Notes Pay.	Sal. Pay.	Warr. Oblig.	Adv, Cust. Payments	Shareholders' Equity
a.	100,000	100,000				
b.			25,500			– 25,500
c.				150,000		–150,000
d.	80,000				80,000	
e.	–50,000	–50,000				
f.	–22,000			–22,000		
g.					–30,000	30,000 (Revenue)
h.	–55,000	–50,000				– 5,000
i.	195,000	195,000				
j.	–200,000	–195,000				– 5000

Critical Thinking

Restructuring Charges

8-46 The annual report of the Jolly Gold Giant, an international food processing and food service firm, included a liability for accrued restructuring costs of $179.3 million. Footnotes contain the following explanation:

> In 1999, restructuring charges of $88.3 million on a pre-tax basis were reflected in operating income to facilitate the consolidation of functions, staff reductions, organizational reform, and plant modernization and closures.
>
> In 2000, restructuring charges of $192.3 million on a pre-tax basis were reflected in operating income. The major components of the restructuring plan related to employee severance and relocation costs ($99 million) and facilities consolidation and closure costs ($73 million). Upon completion of all the projects in 2002, the total headcount reduction will be achieved.

Required

a. Why do firms accrue restructuring costs before such costs are actually incurred? Do such costs satisfy the definition of liabilities that was presented in Chapter 3, "The Balance Sheet," of this text?

b. Based on the footnote information, Jolly Gold Giant has recognized restructuring costs of $280.6 million ($88.3 in 1999 plus $192.3 in 2000 equals $280.6). How will these charges affect the amounts of income reported by the firm in future years? How would these charges influence your comparison of the firm's profit trend beyond 2000?

Commitments and Contingencies

8-47 Refer to the Wendy's financial statements in Appendix D. Review the balance sheet to determine how and where commitments and contingencies were reported.

Required

a. Read Note 10. Identify and discuss any unusual terms. Trace any numerical disclosures of commitments and contingencies in the notes to corresponding disclosures in the financial statements.
b. Discuss the underlying business reasons that may be justifying the recognition of these contingencies and commitments. How might these contingencies and commitments be viewed by financial analysts? Discuss how Wendy's managers might view them.
c. Scan the remainder of Wendy's notes to see if any additional business risks might justify additional disclosures. Do you notice any evidence of off-balance-sheet risks? If so, describe them and discuss the underlying business reasons supporting their use.
d. Discuss any other unusual concerns regarding Wendy's business risks. What other related information might an external analyst require? Would a creditor prefer additional disclosures in these areas? Why?

Current Liabilities: Interpreting Financial Statements

8-48 Refer to Wendy's financial statements in Appendix D. Review the balance sheet to determine how and where current liabilities are reported.

Required

a. Read Note 3. Identify and discuss any unusual terms. Trace any numerical disclosures of current liabilities in this note, or other related notes, to corresponding disclosures in the financial statements.
b. Determine whether Wendy's has any unusual current liabilities. If so, discuss how financial analysts might interpret them. Discuss how Wendy's managers might view such liabilities.
c. Discuss how accrued expenses for salaries and wages are related to accounts payable. In your opinion, should they be disclosed separately? Why?
d. Discuss any other unusual concerns regarding Wendy's current liabilities. What other related information might an external analyst require? Would analysts prefer additional information? Why?
e. Comment on the apparent stability and lack of change in Wendy's current liabilities. Why do you think Wendy's exhibits such stability in this area?

Current Liabilities: Interpreting Financial Statements

8-49 Refer to Reebok's financial statements in Appendix E. Review the balance sheet to determine how and where current liabilities were reported.

Required

a. Read Note 6. Identify and discuss any unusual terms. Trace any numerical disclosures of current liabilities in the notes to corresponding disclosures in the financial statements.
b. Determine whether Reebok has any unusual current liabilities. If so, discuss how financial analysts might interpret them. Discuss how Reebok's managers might view such liabilities.
c. Discuss how accounts payable are related to accrued expenses. In your opinion, should they be disclosed together? Why?
d. Discuss how income taxes payable are related to notes payable. In your opinion, should they be disclosed separately? Why?
e. Discuss any other unusual concerns regarding Reebok's current liabilities. What other related information might an external analyst prefer?

Contingencies

8-50 Refer to Reebok's financial statements in Appendix E. Review the balance sheet to determine how and where contingencies were reported.

Required

a. Read Note 17. Identify and discuss any unusual terms. Trace any numerical disclosures of contingencies in the notes to corresponding disclosures in the financial statements. Why aren't contingencies mentioned on Reebok's balance sheet?

b. Determine whether Reebok has any unusual commitments or contingencies. If so, discuss how financial analysts might interpret them. Discuss how Reebok's managers might view such liabilities.

c. Discuss any other unusual concerns regarding Reebok's business risks. What other related information might an external analyst prefer?

Disclosures of Commitments and Contingencies

Critical Thinking

8-51 Review the following notes provided by an oil company in its annual report and identify any unusual terms. Compare and contrast its commitments and contingencies. Also identify the types of business risks faced by such an oil company.

Note 18 – Commitments (Excerpted)

The company also has certain long-term fixed or minimum commitments under agreements negotiated to assist suppliers in obtaining financing for facilities. In addition, the company has contractual commitments to certain companies in which it has equity interests to pay minimum shipping and processing charges or advance funds that can be applied against future charges. Payments and future commitments under all these arrangements are not material in aggregate.

Note 18 – Contingencies (Excerpted)

The company is subject to loss contingencies pursuant to environmental laws and regulations that in the future may require the company to correct or ameliorate the effects of prior disposal or release of chemical or petroleum substances on the environment. Such contingencies may exist for various sites including but not limited to superfund sites, operating refineries, closed refineries, oil fields, service stations, terminals, and land development areas. The amount of such future costs is indeterminable due to such factors as

- the unknown magnitude of possible contamination,
- the unknown timing and extent of the corrective actions that may be required,
- the determination of the company's liability in proportion to other responsible parties, and
- the extent to which such costs are recoverable from insurance.

Interpreting Contingency Disclosures

8-52 The following excerpts from their notes on commitments and contingencies were reported by three different companies:

PolyGram N.V.

PolyGram has extensive international operations and is subject to a number of legal proceedings incidental to these operations. PolyGram does not expect that the outcome of these current proceedings will have a material adverse effect upon the financial condition of the company either individually or in the aggregate.

Oncogene Science, Inc.

Oncogene has received several letters from other companies and universities advising them that various products and research being conducted by Oncogene may be infringing on existing patents of such entities. These matters are presently under review by management and outside counsel for Oncogene. Where valid patents of other parties are found by Oncogene to be in place, management will consider entering into licensing arrangements with the universities and/or other companies, or discontinuing the sale or use of any infringing products. Management believes that the ultimate outcome of these matters will not have a material adverse effect on the financial position of the company.

Sigma Designs, Inc.

This company pays royalties for the right to sell certain products under various license agreements. During fiscal 1995, 1994, and 1993, Sigma Designs incurred royalty expenses of $508,040, $181,405, and $275,000, respectively.

On January 31, 1995, the company had letters of credit outstanding in the amount of $941,000, maturing at various dates up to June 1996.

Sigma Designs also sponsors a 401(k) savings plan in which most employees are eligible to participate. The company is not obligated to make contributions to the plan and no contributions have been made by the company.

Required

a. Compare and contrast these three notes.

b. Do you believe that companies should be more specific or more general in such notes? Why?

c. Which of these companies do you think faces the greatest risk, based only on the information presented herein? Why?

Financial Statement Effects: Warranty Recognition

8-53 The following summary data (thousands of dollars) are available for Hilary's Lo-Tech Health Care Concern:

	2000	2001
Total liabilities	$ 3,500	$ 4,600
Warranty obligations (unrecorded)	750	850
Stockholders' equity	10,000	12,000
Total assets	13,500	16,600

Required

a. Compute the debt to total assets ratio for each year, assuming no recognition of warranty obligations.

b. Compute the debt to total assets ratio for each year, assuming warranty obligations have been recorded.

c. Compute the debt to total assets ratio for each year, assuming warranty obligations have been underestimated and a more realistic estimate would require that they be quadrupled.

d. Explain why total assets have not changed under either of the changes suggested in parts b and c.

e. Identify the effects on the income statement (that is, on warranty expenses) of each of the changes suggested in parts b and c.

f. Why do you think managers might want to underestimate warranty liabilities? Discuss both balance sheet and income effects. Discuss the business reasons underlying Hilary's treatment of its warranty obligations.

Critical Thinking

Financial Statement Effects: Warranty Costs

8-54 Engineering Group, Inc., is a major British international engineering firm with the following liabilities shown on its 1999 balance sheet (shown in millions of pounds):

Loans and other borrowings	392.0
Other creditors	31.0
Provisions for liabilities and charges	130.5

Required

a. Where should warranty obligations, if any, be included in these accounts?
b. A note to the financial statements, titled "Provisions for Liabilities and Charges," disclosed the following items:

Recognition of post-retirement benefits	32.9
Exchange rate adjustments	15.2
New subsidiaries (reorganization costs)	71.4
Profit and loss account	11.0
Total	130.5

Where are warranty obligations, if any, included in these accounts?
c. Why doesn't Engineering Group make any more explicit mention of warranty obligations?
d. Use the accounting equation to record the following warranty obligations of an engineering consulting firm:
   i. Estimated warranty expenses of 10% for the prior year's billings of $50 million.
   ii. Warranty claim of $1.5 million for bridge repairs.
   iii. Payment of bridge warranty claim totaling $1.6 million.

Liabilities: Interpreting Financial Statements

8-55 Cabot Corporation is principally involved in the manufacture of carbon black and other specialty chemicals. Its 1994 financial statements have an accrued liability for environmental proceedings related to cleanup as a result of divesting businesses worth $44,000,000.

Required

a. Why is this liability included on Cabot Corporation's balance sheet?
b. Under what circumstances will these costs be paid? Is it likely that they will be paid on a certain date in the future? Why not?
c. If not, should this liability be shown at its expected future cost, or at the present value of its expected future cost? Why? (Hint: Use the appendix to answer this part.)

Critical Thinking

Liabilities: Interpreting Financial Statements

8-56 Tyler Corporation is a diversified company that provides goods and services through three major operating subsidiaries: (1) a retailer of auto parts and supplies; (2) a marketer of products for fund-raising programs in schools; and (3) a manufacturer of cast iron pipe and fittings for waterworks applications. Its 1994 financial statements include the following current liabilities on the next page.

	1994	1993
Accounts payable	$20,083,000	$11,675,000
Accrued customer discounts	4,204,000	4,055,000
Accrued insurance	4,181,000	4,780,000
Accrued wages and commissions	5,133,000	1,736,000
Income tax	967,000	1,250,000
Other accrued liabilities	16,991,000	12,408,000
	$51,559,000	$35,904,000

Required

a. Describe each of the liabilities shown on Tyler's balance sheet. Describe the business purpose of each liability.

b. Why is Tyler accruing customer discounts?

c. Tyler's total current assets were $102,878,000 and $75,395,000 for 1994 and 1993, respectively. Included in these amounts are inventories, prepaid, and deferred taxes totaling $61,761,000 and $39,424,000 for 1994 and 1993, respectively. Calculate current and quick ratios and comment on your results.

d. At the end of 1994, Tyler accrued an estimated contingent liability of $3,953,000 for environmental contamination. This amount is included in other accrued liabilities. As an investor, is this disclosure adequate on the balance sheet? Why haven't they separately disclosed this obligation? What concerns would an investor have and what other information would an investor want to see?

Liabilities: Interpreting Financial Statements

Critical Thinking

8-57 Oncogene Science, Inc., is a biopharmaceutical company involved in developing innovative products for the diagnosis and treatment of cancer, cardiovascular disease, and a number of other important human illnesses. Its proprietary core technologies include oncogenes, tumor suppressor genes, and gene transcription. Its 1994 financial statements include the following current liabilities and no other liabilities:

	1994	1993
Accounts payable and accrued expenses	$2,522,171	$2,202,060
Unearned revenue, current portion	457,384	258,000
Total current liabilities	$2,979,555	$2,460,060

Required

a. Describe each of the liabilities shown on Oncogene's balance sheet. Describe the business purpose of each liability.

b. Why did Oncogene report unearned revenues? Why only the current portion?

c. How would a lender or an investor evaluate Oncogene's liability disclosures? Are there any missing categories of information for which additional disclosures are preferred?

d. Why might these liabilities, which are relatively immaterial in amount, reflect high risks for an investor or lender?

Critical Thinking

Liabilities: Interpreting Financial Statements

8-58 Polygram is an international entertainment company, which has published such hits as Billy Ray Cyrus' *Achy Breaky Heart*. Polygram is headquartered in Amsterdam. It lists the following current liabilities in a note to its 1994 annual report (stated in millions of Netherlands guilders):

	1993	1994
Payables to banks	25	155
Short-term notes	459	749
Accounts payable to trade creditors	665	798
Accounts payable to other companies	41	20
Income taxes payable	106	139
Dividend payable (to shareholders)	135	153
Other accrued expenses	1,931	2,167
Total	3,362	4,181

Required

a. Identify and describe each of Polygram's current liabilities. Describe the business purpose of each liability.
b. Identify and discuss any unusual trends in its current liabilities.
c. Given that Polygram's total assets and net sales increased by only about 5%, how does that affect your evaluation of its current liabilities?
d. Assume that most of the other accrued expenses are comprised of accrued license fees. Why would such a firm have almost half its current liabilities in accrued license fees? Discuss the timing associated with the payments of such fees, as compared to Polygram's debts to banks or to trade creditors?

Ethics

Financial Statement Effects of Warranty Recognition

8-59 Hiram's Hi-Tech Industries assembles specialized electronic interfaces that are used in hand-held computers and communications devices (PDAs). Hiram's has had significant warranty claims on its interfaces and is wondering what liability recognition would be appropriate for 2000. Hiram's 1998 statements showed a warranty liability of $12 million, which was totally exhausted by the end of 1999. Hiram's sales doubled during 1999, while its quality enhancement efforts had little effect. In fact, Hiram's president privately admits that quality may have significantly declined since 1998. The president also wonders whether Hiram's should shorten its typical two-year warranty period.

Hiram's controller is arguing for the recognition of warranty obligations of $12 million because that amount appeared to be adequate for the prior year. Hiram's auditors are arguing for a liability recognition of $30 million on the grounds that $12 million is not adequate for the prior year and that, with an increase in sales, more warranty claims are likely.

Hiram's balance sheet equation, without any liability recognition, is as follows:

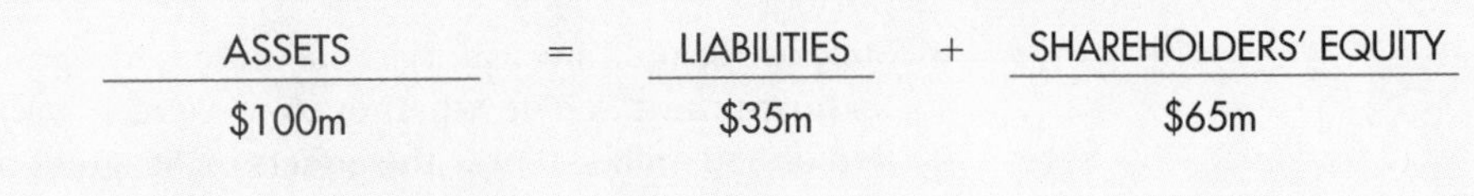

ASSETS	=	LIABILITIES	+	SHAREHOLDERS' EQUITY
$100m		$35m		$65m

Required

a. Indicate the effect of the controller's recommendation on the balance sheet equation.
b. Indicate the effect of the auditor's recommendation on the balance sheet equation.
c. Calculate the debt to total assets ratio under each recommendation.
d. How do you think an external user of these financial statements will view the differences between a 35% debt to assets ratio and the ratios that you calculated in part c?
e. Now assume that the actual warranty costs in 2000 were $25 million. Show the effects on the balance sheet equation under both the controller's recommendation and the auditor's recommendation. How has matching been affected by following the controller's recommendation?
f. Although the controller has obviously underestimated these warranty claims, do you feel that the auditor has conversely overestimated the warranty claims? Why?
g. What other recommendations regarding quality and warranty issues might you make to Hiram's Hi-Tech Industries?
h. Why might managers want to underestimate warranty liabilities? Discuss both balance sheet and income effects. Discuss the business reasons underlying Hiram's treatment of its warranty obligations.

Warranty Costs

8-60 Seagull Designs does not report any warranty costs in its income statement, nor does it report any warranty obligations in its balance sheet. Seagull reports only the following four types of costs and expenses in its income statement:

- Costs of sales
- Sales and marketing
- Research and development
- General and administrative

Its sales decreased significantly from 1998 to 1999, at which point they stabilized through 2000. Its balance sheet equation is summarized below:

ASSETS	=	LIABILITIES	+	SHAREHOLDERS' EQUITY
$44M		$6M		$38M

Required

a. Assuming Seagull offers warranties to its clients, where are its warranty costs reported on the income statement? Why might they not be separately reported?
b. Suppose Seagull's warranty costs increased significantly from 1998 to 2000. Its board must decide whether to recognize warranty obligations of $5 million or $10 million. Show the effects on Seagull's balance sheet equation (dollars in millions) at the end of 2000 under each of these proposals.

(Continued)

c. Calculate the effects of each proposal on Seagull's debt to total assets ratio.
d. Assume that Seagull's CEO estimated, and had strong evidence, that warranty costs would be $10 million. Prepare a one-paragraph memo that justifies the CEO's recommendations for recognizing warranty obligations of $10 million. In what way is this treatment the most conservative possible?
e. Assume that Seagull's controller is very liberal and wants to recognize no additional warranty costs. Write a one-paragraph memo justifying this position.
f. Which position (part d or e) would you approve or support? Why? Discuss the ethical implications of each choice.

Identifying Current Liabilities

8-61 Locate the most recent set of financial statements for the regional telecommunications companies listed below. You may use either the 10-K available at EDGAR **(www.sec.gov/edaux/searches.htm)** or the annual report available at the company's homepage. The annual report is usually located in the Investor Information section.

Corporation	Home Page Location
Ameritech	**www.ameritech.com**
U S West	**www.uswest.com**
Bell Atlantic	**www.bell-atl.com**
Pacific Bell	**www.pacbell.com**

Required

a. Identify or compute the following for each corporation:
   i. Total current liabilities and current liabilities as a percentage of total liabilities
   ii. Composition of current liabilities
   iii. Income tax payable and income tax payable as a percent of current liabilities
b. Compare and contrast each company's results.
c. Identify any significant consequences of these results; that is, how might investors or creditors react to these results?

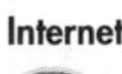

Evaluating Current Liabilities

8-62 Locate the most recent set of financial statements for the companies listed below. Use the 10-K available on the SEC's EDGAR database **(www.sec.gov/edaux/searches.htm)** or the annual report available on the company's home page. The annual report is usually located in the Investor Information section.

Corporation	Home Page Location
Dell Computers	**www.dell.com**
Ben & Jerry's	**www.benjerry.com**
Lewis Galoob Toys	**www.galoob.com**

Required

a. For each company, what is the percentage of accrued liabilities to current liabilities?
b. List any unusual accrued liabilities. Explain what these items represent, given the main business of each company.
c. How might investors or creditors react to each of these liability issues?

Internet

Current Liabilities: Linkage to Revenue Recognition

8-63 Locate the 10-K filing for the following companies from EDGAR **(www.sec.gov/edaux/searches.htm).** Read the Notes to the Financial Statements sections where the following current liabilities are explained:

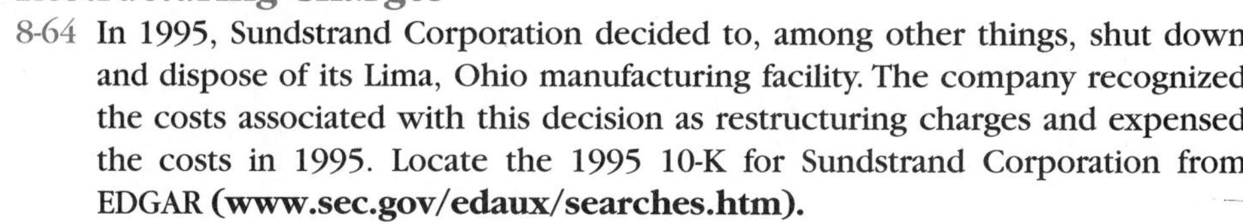

Corporation	Current Liability
Novell	Deferred revenue
Browning-Ferris	Deferred revenue
Reader's Digest	Unearned revenue
FHP International	Unearned premium, medical claims payable

Required

a. Describe the nature of the liability that each of the above terms represents.

b. Why has revenue recognition been deferred for each of the above cases?

c. How might investors or creditors react to these various revenue recognition policies?

Internet

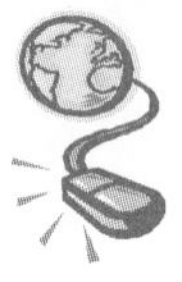

Restructuring Charges

8-64 In 1995, Sundstrand Corporation decided to, among other things, shut down and dispose of its Lima, Ohio manufacturing facility. The company recognized the costs associated with this decision as restructuring charges and expensed the costs in 1995. Locate the 1995 10-K for Sundstrand Corporation from EDGAR **(www.sec.gov/edaux/searches.htm).**

Required

a. Read the income statement and identify the total amount of the restructuring charge shown on the 1995 income statement. Also calculate its impact as a percentage of net income.

b. Based on the information provided in the Notes to the Financial Statements, determine why the charge was taken and what it includes. When did the company plan to complete shutdown and disposition of the Lima facility?

c. Refer to the balance sheet and determine the amount of the restructuring charge that has been accrued as a current liability. What percentage of current liabilities does this represent? Based on the time frame for the shutdown and disposition of the Lima facility, is it reasonable to classify the accrued restructuring costs as a current liability?

d. In each case, discuss the underlying business reasons or transactions supporting the restructuring or reorganization.

Internet

Contingencies

8-65 Locate the most recent set of financial statements for the companies listed below. You may use either the 10-K available at EDGAR **(www.sec.gov/edaux/searches.htm)** or the annual report available at the company's home page. The annual report is usually located in the Investor Information section.

Corporation	Home Page Location
Owens Corning	**www.owens-corning.com**
Rohm & Haas	**www.rohmhaas.com**
Utilicorp	**www.utilicorp.com**
Eli Lilly	**www.lilly.com**

The Notes to the Financial Statements contain a section on contingencies.

Required

a. Describe at least one contingency faced by each company.
b. How has each corporation accrued its loss contingency, or is it only mentioned in the Notes to the Financial Statements? If it is only mentioned in the notes, is a dollar amount disclosed? Discuss these alternative disclosures.
c. If a dollar amount for contingent liabilities is available, calculate the percentage of shareholders' equity it represents for each company. In your opinion, is this a significant amount?
d. In each case, discuss the underlying business reasons supporting the need for disclosing a contingency or a commitment.

chapter

Noncurrent Liabilities

LEARNING OBJECTIVES

1. Recognize the types of noncurrent obligations that are reported by business firms.
2. Comprehend features of long-term borrowing contracts, such as notes and bonds payable.
3. Determine periodic interest expense and the valuation of noncurrent obligations in financial reports.
4. Appreciate why income is measured differently for income tax and financial reporting purposes.
5. Understand why the tax basis and the financial reporting basis of assets and liabilities may differ.
6. Interpret financial statement measurements of income tax expense and deferred income tax liability.

INTRODUCTION

Noncurrent liabilities represent obligations of the firm that generally are due more than one year after the balance sheet date. The major portion of noncurrent liabilities consists of notes and bonds payable. In addition, deferred income tax payments are an important component of liabilities for many companies. Each of these types of liabilities is discussed in the following sections. Note that this chapter relies on the present value concepts developed in Appendix C.

Other types of noncurrent liabilities that are included in financial reports are more controversial in nature. The acceptable methods of accounting and reporting for these controversial items have changed substantially in recent years and continue to evolve. For this reason, Chapter 12, "Additional Issues in Liability Reporting," is devoted to a discussion of controversial areas in liability reporting including accounting for leases, pensions, and post-employment benefits.

LONG-TERM NOTES PAYABLE

Firms often borrow money by signing notes payable to banks or other lending institutions. Such notes can either be interest-bearing or discounted notes. This section describes the essential features of both types.

Interest-Bearing Notes

One way a firm borrows funds is by signing an **interest-bearing note.** A bank or other lender will loan the face amount, or principal, of the note for a specified period. The borrower will then pay interest periodically and repay the principal when the note becomes due (or at its **maturity date**). If Random Enterprises, Inc., for example, borrows $10 million at the beginning of 2000 for two years at a market interest rate of 12% per year, the financial statements would reflect the following events.

Upon receipt of the loan proceeds at the beginning of 2000, cash and long-term notes payable are each increased by $10 million:

ASSETS	=	LIABILITIES	+	SHAREHOLDERS' EQUITY
Cash +$10 million		Long-term notes payable +$10 million		

In *each* of the years 2000 and 2001, as the periodic interest payments are made, cash is decreased by $1.2 million ($10 million × 12% = $1.2 million) and interest expense is recognized.

ASSETS	=	LIABILITIES	+	SHAREHOLDERS' EQUITY
Cash −$1.2 million				Retained earnings −$1.2 million (interest expense)

When the loan is repaid at maturity at the end of 2001, cash and long-term notes payable are each decreased by $10 million:

ASSETS	=	LIABILITIES	+	SHAREHOLDERS' EQUITY
Cash −$10 million		Long-term notes payable −$10 million		

The net result of these three transactions is that $10 million cash has been borrowed, and later $12.4 million was repaid. The firm has incurred interest expense of $1.2 million each year, or a total interest expense of $2.4 million, for the privilege of using the $10 million for two years.

Discounted Notes

In the previous example, Random Enterprises borrowed $10 million by signing an interest-bearing note. Suppose that the note did not require periodic payments of interest. Instead, assume that Random Enterprises signs a note on January 1, 2000, promising to pay the lender $10 million in two years, and will not make periodic interest payments. In this case, the lender will be unwilling to provide Random the full

$10 million face value of the note. No one is willing to loan money without interest and all long-term financing arrangements involve interest, even if it is not separately identified and paid periodically.

If a prospective lender instead invested some smaller amount (as yet to be determined) for two years to earn 12%, that initial investment would grow to $10 million by the end of 2001. How much would a lender be willing to loan in return for Random's noninterest-bearing note? To answer this question, we must discount the note. Random Enterprises will receive only the present value of the note (see Appendix C), computed at the current lending rate of 12%. The present value of the note is $7,970,000, computed as follows:

$$\begin{aligned} P &= A \times PVF_n^i \\ &= \$10 \text{ million} \times PVF_{2\text{ years}}^{12\%} \\ &= \$10 \text{ million} \times (.797) \text{ (from Exhibit C} - 2) \\ &= \$7{,}970{,}000 \end{aligned}$$

In other words, if the prospective lender instead deposited $7,970,000 at the beginning of 2000 in a bank account for two years to earn 12% per year, the initial deposit would grow to $10 million by the end of 2001. For this reason, lenders would be unwilling to loan more than $7,970,000 for Random Enterprise's note. As a result, Random Enterprises must issue the note at a discount of $2,030,000 ($10,000,000 − $7,970,000).

The discount on Random's note payable represents the interest that is associated with this transaction. It should be recognized as interest expense by Random Enterprises over the two-year term of the note. The discount also represents interest income to the lender over the same period. In each year, the amount of interest to be recognized is 12% of the value of the note at the start of the year. The yearly amounts of interest are calculated as follows:

Amount received from lender, January 1, 2000	$ 7,970,000
Interest during 2000 ($7,970,000 × .12)	956,400
Loan balance, December 31, 2000	$ 8,926,400
Interest during 2001 ($8,926,400 × .12)	1,073,600*
Loan balance, December 31, 2001	$10,000,000

*Rounded

Notice that the amount of interest expense increases between 2000 and 2001. This occurs because Random Enterprises makes no interest payment to the lender in 2000. As a result, the amount of the loan increases to include the unpaid interest. In other words, the lender is earning compound interest (interest on interest) in 2001. These events would affect Random Enterprise's financial statements in the following manner.

The receipt of cash from the lender at the beginning of 2000 in exchange for Random's note payable will increase cash and noncurrent liabilities:

ASSETS	=	LIABILITIES	+	SHAREHOLDERS' EQUITY
Cash + $7,970,000		Long-term notes payable + $7,970,000		

Interest expense during 2000 and 2001 will decrease retained earnings and increase the reported value of noncurrent liabilities:

ASSETS	=	LIABILITIES	+	SHAREHOLDERS' EQUITY
		Long-term notes payable +$956,400		Retained earnings −$956,400 (interest expense)

On January 1, 2001, the carrying value of the note is $8,926,400 ($7,970,000 + $956,400). In 2001, interest is again added to the loan balance:

ASSETS	=	LIABILITIES	+	SHAREHOLDERS' EQUITY
		Long-term notes payable +$1,073,600		Retained earnings −$1,073,600 (interest expense)

On December 31, 2001 (the maturity date of the note), the carrying value of the note has been increased to $10,000,000 ($8,926,400 + $1,073,600). This amount is eliminated, and the lender is paid cash of $10 million.

ASSETS	=	LIABILITIES	+	SHAREHOLDERS' EQUITY
Cash −$10 million		Long-term notes payable −$10 million		

The net result of these transactions is that slightly less than $8 million has been borrowed and used by Random Enterprises for two years, and interest expense of slightly more than $2 million has been incurred for the privilege of using the $8 million for two years. In the end, Random has repaid $10 million, which included both principal and interest.

BONDS PAYABLE

Bonds payable represents a major source of borrowed capital for U.S. firms. **Bonds** are notes, sold to individual investors as well as to financial institutions. For a variety of reasons, managers may prefer to issue bonds to investors rather than borrowing directly from financial institutions. Bond financing can also offer advantages in terms of the availability and cost of borrowing and the managers' subsequent flexibility in making business decisions. For example, the amount that financial institutions are willing to loan to a single firm may be limited because the lender aims to diversify its risks by loaning smaller amounts to many different borrowers. The sale of bonds, on the other hand, enables the borrower to obtain access to much larger amounts of loanable funds from large institutional investors and also from thousands of individual investors.

In addition, for some firms, bond financing may be less expensive. The interest rates that prevail in the bond market can be less than the rate available from financial institutions. Finally, bond financing may also offer managers greater flexibility in the future. A direct lending agreement often imposes various restrictions on managers' investing and financing activities until the loan is repaid. As examples, a lending agreement can restrict the firm's dividend payments or limit the amounts that the firm can borrow from other lenders until the debt is repaid. Although bond issuances can also entail similar restrictions, they can be less onerous than the restrictions imposed by financial institutions.

A bond is also a contract that is sold to investors. Bonds obligate the borrower (the issuing corporation) to make periodic interest payments, usually every six months, and to pay the principal or face value of the bond at a specified maturity date. Prior to issuing bonds, managers meet with financial advisers to decide on the maturity value and other terms of the bond contract, as well as to predict the market interest rate at which the bonds can be sold. The predicted interest rate usually becomes the **coupon rate** (also called the face rate or nominal rate) that is contained in the bond contract. This rate, in conjunction with the face value, determines the cash interest to be paid periodically to bondholders.

The **market rate** of interest cannot be known with certainty until the date on which the bonds are sold. Market interest rates are the "cost of money" and are determined by the forces of supply and demand in the financial markets. The federal government, through the actions of the Federal Reserve, also influences interest rates. Because the market rate constantly changes, and the coupon rate is fixed when the bonds are printed, it is rare that the bond coupon rate will coincide exactly with the market interest rate when the bonds are sold. The following sections illustrate the issuance and reporting for bonds when the market interest rate in turn equals, exceeds, or falls below the coupon rate of interest.

Issuance of Bonds at Par

If the coupon rate of a bond coincides with the market rate of interest when the bonds are actually sold to investors, then the bonds will sell at **par value** or face value. The price at which a bond is trading is usually quoted as a percentage of the bond's par value, so that a bond that sells at par has a price of 100. To illustrate the sale of bonds at par, assume Marley Company issues bonds on January 1, 2000, with a principal amount of $100 million, to be repaid in 10 years and a 12% coupon rate of interest payable semiannually. The bond contract obligates Marley to make the following payments:

Principal: $100,000,000 due in 10 years (after 20 six-month periods),

Interest: $6,000,000 due at the end of each six-month period, for 10 years ($100,000,000 × 12% × 6/12 = $6,000,000).

Because the market rate and the coupon rate of interest are the same, the bonds sell at their face value of $100 million. The quoted annual interest rate of 12% is actually 6% each six-month period because the bonds pay interest each six months. When interest is paid each six months, the interest rate is said to be compounded semiannually. To use the present value tables, bonds with a 12% semiannual interest coupon are regarded as outstanding for a number of six-month periods (20 in this case), and the interest rate is 6% per period. In general, when interest is compounded *n* times each year, the periodic interest rate is ***i/n***, and the number of periods is ***n* × *years*.** In the present case, the periodic interest rate is 6% (*i/n* or 12%/2 = 6%), and the number of periods is 20 (*n* × years or 2 × 10 = 20).

The following events would be reported in the financial statements over the life of the bond. On January 1, 2000, Marley Company receives $100 million in cash, and bonds payable are recorded in this amount:

ASSETS	=	LIABILITIES	+	SHAREHOLDERS' EQUITY
Cash +$100 million		Bonds payable +$100 million		

Each six months for 10 years, Marley Company recognizes interest expense and pays $6 million to the bondholders each June 30 and December 31 from 2000 through 2009:

ASSETS	=	LIABILITIES	+	SHAREHOLDERS' EQUITY
Cash – $6 million				Retained earnings – $6 million (interest expense)

On the maturity date, December 31, 2009, Marley Company pays $100 million in bond principal and retires the bonds:

ASSETS	=	LIABILITIES	+	SHAREHOLDERS' EQUITY
Cash – $100 million		Bonds payable – $100 million		

To recap, Marley Company received $100 million from investors when the bonds were issued and paid a total of $220 million to bondholders over the life of the bond issue. The total interest expense was, therefore, $120 million ($220 million in payments minus $100 million in receipts), and the interest expense each year was $12 million (2 × $6 million).

Sale or Issuance of Bonds at a Discount

In cases where the coupon rate of interest differs from the market rate on the date that bonds are sold, the present value of the bond issue will not equal the face amount of the bond. Consider, for example, an investor buying a bond when the *coupon rate is below the market rate of interest.* Because the coupon rate does not provide the investor with a rate of return equal to that available on other similar investments, the investor will buy the bonds only if they are sold at a **discount** from the par or face value. Bear in mind that the bond contract represents a fixed series of cash payments to bondholders. The present value of any fixed series of cash payments depends on the discount rate, which in this case is the market rate of interest.

To illustrate the accounting for bonds sold at a discount, assume that the Marley Company bonds described earlier were sold on January 1, 2000, and that the market rate of interest was 16% (compounded semiannually) on that date. Investors will discount the bonds' cash flows at the current market rate of interest. Because the coupon rate is only 12%, the bonds will sell at a discount. Note, however, that the interest coupon payments will still be $6 million because that is the amount stated in the bond contract. The present value is computed as follows.

Principal, due in 20 six-month periods at 8% (half the 16% annual rate):

Amount	×	Present value factor (Exhibit C-2) $n = 20$, $i = 8\%$		
$100,000,000	×	0.215	=	$21,500,000

Interest payments, due each six months for 20 periods:

		(Exhibit C-3) $n = 20$, $i = 8\%$		
$6,000,000	×	9.818	=	58,908,000
		Total present value		$80,408,000

Consequently, the bonds will sell at $80,408,000 ($100 million face value, minus $19,592,000 discount), i.e., at a price of $80.408. If prospective bondholders were to deposit $80,408,000 in an account earning interest at 16% compounded semiannually, they would be able to withdraw $6 million each six months and $100 million at the end of 10 years. For this reason, bond investors would be unwilling to pay more than $80,408,000 for the Marley Company bonds.

Upon issuing the bonds, Marley Company's cash and bonds payable (net of the bond discount) will increase by $80,408,000:

ASSETS	=	LIABILITIES	+	SHAREHOLDERS' EQUITY
Cash		Bonds payable		
+$80,408,000		+$80,408,000		

In effect, the discount represents additional interest paid to bondholders. This compensates for the fact that the coupon interest payments are lower than those provided by competing investments. The total interest expense is determined as follows:

Total explicit interest payments	$120,000,000
Add: Bond discount	19,592,000
Total interest expense	$139,592,000

The amount of this interest expense to be recognized each interest period (an interest period is six months in this example) is based on the reported value of the bonds at the start of the interest period and the market rate of interest when the bonds were issued. Because Marley Company's bonds were sold on January 1, 2000, when the market rate of interest was 16% compounded semiannually, or 8% each six-month period, the interest expense during 2000, 2001, and 2009 would be determined as shown in Exhibit 9-1.

Whenever the periodic interest expense differs from the periodic cash payments to the bondholders, the reported value of the bonds will be adjusted for the difference. This adjustment is termed **amortization.** In Exhibit 9-1, note that the interest expense recorded in each period exceeds the cash interest ($6,000,000) that is paid to the bondholders. Because the actual interest expense incurred each period is greater than the amount that is paid currently to the bondholders, the reported value of the bonds (bonds payable minus discount) increases each period. In fact, as shown in Exhibit 9-1, the reported value of the bonds will increase to exactly $100,000,000, the principal amount of the bonds, by the date that the bond issue matures (at the end of the year 2009). In other words, the discount on the bonds will be completely amortized by that date, so the bonds will be reported at their face value of $100 million. The interest expense and bond coupon payment for the first six months in 2000 would be recorded in the following way:

ASSETS	=	LIABILITIES	+	SHAREHOLDERS' EQUITY
Cash – $6,000,000		Bonds payable + $432,640		Retained earnings – $6,432,640 (interest expense)

EXHIBIT 9-1 Calculation of Interest Expense

Marley Company
Calculation of Interest Expense
Bonds Sold at a Discount

Six-month Period Beginning	(1) Reported Value of Bonds, Beginning	(2) Interest Expense (1) × 8%	(3) Interest Payment	(4) Increase in Reported Value (2) – (3)	(5) Reported Value of Bonds End of Period (1) + (4)
Jan. 1, 2000	$80,408,000	$ 6,432,640	$6,000,000	$ 432,640	$ 80,840,640
July 1, 2000	80,840,640	6,467,251	6,000,000	467,251	81,307,891
Total expense, 2000		$12,899,891			
Jan. 1, 2001	81,307,891	$ 6,504,631	6,000,000	504,631	81,812,522
July 1, 2001	81,812,522	6,545,000	6,000,000	545,000	82,357,523
Total expense, 2001		$13,049,631			
.	.	.	.	.	.
Jan. 1, 2009	96,433,440	$ 7,714,674	6,000,000	1,714,674	98,148,114
July 1, 2009	98,148,114	7,851,886	6,000,000	1,851,886	100,000,000
Total expense, 2009		$15,566,560			

NOTE: The reported value of the bonds increases each period because the interest expense exceeds the amount paid to the bondholders, which increases the company's obligation to the bondholders. At the maturity date of the bonds, the reported value will equal the principal (face) amount of $100 million.

As you can see, because the cash payment required by the coupon rate of interest is less than the actual interest expense for the period, the amount of the liability must be increased for the difference. During the first interest period (January 1 to June 30, 2000), $432,640 of the bond discount has been amortized.

Sale or Issuance of Bonds at a Premium

Suppose the market rate of interest on January 1, 2000, when the Marley Company bonds were sold, is *below* the coupon rate of 12%. In this case, investors would find the bonds to be quite attractive because *the coupon rate is higher than the market interest rate* available on other investments of equivalent risk. As a result, the market price of Marley's bonds increases. The bonds are issued at a **premium,** in other words, at an amount greater than the principal amount of $100 million. For example, if the market interest rate is 8% when the bonds are issued, investors will be willing to pay $127,140,000, a price of 127.14, determined as follows.

Principal, due in 20 six-month periods at 4% (half the 8% annual rate):

Amount	×	Present value factor (Exhibit C-2) $n = 20$, $i = 4\%$		
$100,000,000	×	0.456	=	$45,600,000

Interest payments, due each six months for 20 periods:

		(Exhibit C-3) $n = 20$, $i = 4\%$		
$6,000,000	×	13.590	=	81,540,000
		Total present value		$127,140,000

Consequently, the bonds will sell at $127,140,000 ($100,000,000 face value + $27,140,000 premium). The total interest expense over the life of the bonds is determined as follows:

Total explicit interest payments	$120,000,000
Less: Bond premium	– 27,140,000
Total interest expense	$ 92,860,000

The amount of interest expense to be recognized each interest period (each six months in this example) is based on the reported value of the bonds at the start of the interest period. Exhibit 9-2 shows how the interest expense during 2000, 2001, and 2009 would be determined.

The amount of this interest expense to be recognized in each period would be determined as before; the reported value of the bonds at the start of each interest period would be multiplied by the market rate of interest when the bonds were issued. The logic of this calculation is the same as that shown in Exhibit 9-1 for the case of bonds sold at a discount. The total interest expense incurred by Marley Company over the life of bonds sold at a premium will be less than the total interest coupons paid. In effect, the premium represents a reduction in interest paid to the bondholders, to compensate for the fact that the coupon rate is too high.

Early Retirement of Bonds

After bonds are sold to investors, they are often subsequently traded (bought and sold) among investors. The market value of bonds that are traded among investors varies

EXHIBIT 9-2 Calculation of Interest Expense

Marley Company
Calculation of Interest Expense
Bonds Sold at a Premium

Six-month Period Beginning	(1) Reported Value of Bonds, Beginning	(2) Interest Expense (1) × 4%	(3) Interest Payment	(4) Decrease in Reported Value (3) − (2)	(5) Reported Value of Bonds End of Period (1) − (4)
Jan. 1, 2000	$127,140,000	$ 5,085,600	$6,000,000	$ 914,400	$126,225,600
July 1, 2000	126,225,600	5,049,024	6,000,000	950,976	125,274,624
Total expense, 2000		$10,134,624			
Jan. 1, 2001	125,274,624	$ 5,010,985	6,000,000	989,015	124,285,609
July 1, 2001	124,285,609	4,971,424	6,000,000	1,028,576	123,257,033
Total expense, 2001		$ 9,982,409			
.	.	.	.	.	.
.	.	.	.	.	.
.	.	.	.	.	.
Jan. 1, 2009	103,772,411	$ 4,150,896	6,000,000	1,849,104	101,923,307
July 1, 2009	101,923,307	4,076,693	6,000,000	1,923,307	100,000,000
Total expense, 2009		$ 8,227,589			

NOTE: The reported value of the bonds decreases each period because the amount paid to the bondholders exceeds the interest expense, which decreases the company's obligation to the bondholders. On the maturity date of the bonds, the reported value will equal the principal (face) amount of $100 million.

from day to day as prevailing interest rates rise and fall. This occurs because the bond contract specifies a set of cash payments to be made to bondholders, and the present value of a given set of future cash flows changes whenever there is a change in the rates used to make the present value calculations. For example, market interest rates on corporate bonds fell dramatically in the 1990s and as a result the value of existing bonds increased substantially. If monetary authorities begin to tighten money and increase interest rates in subsequent years, the market value of existing bonds will again decline.

Fluctuations in the market prices of outstanding bonds do not result in additional cash inflows and outflows for the issuing company. Consistent with the historical cost principle, the reported value of bonds in the financial statements of the issuing company is *not* revised to reflect changes in market interest rates and market prices of the outstanding bonds. For this reason, changes in market rates of interest may motivate firms to buy back their outstanding bonds prior to their scheduled maturity dates. If market rates of interest have changed subsequent to the issuance of the bonds, then the current market prices of the bonds may differ substantially from values shown on the books of the issuing firm. If the firm does repurchase its own bonds, any difference between the reported value and the repurchase price must be recognized as an extraordinary gain or loss by the issuer when the transaction is completed.

To illustrate this point, assume that Marley Company issued bonds at par early in 2000, and that interest rates have risen subsequently. When interest rates rise, the market values of outstanding bonds decline because the remaining cash payments (principal and interest coupons) are discounted by lenders at higher rates. If we assume that Marley repurchases bonds with a $100 million reported value at a market value of $85 million, the firm would report a gain of $15 million:

Reported value of bonds payable	$100,000,000
Cost to repurchase bonds payable	– 85,000,000
Gain on repurchase of bonds	$ 15,000,000

This transaction would be recognized in Marley's financial statements in the following way:

ASSETS	=	LIABILITIES	+	SHAREHOLDERS' EQUITY
Cash		Bonds payable		Retained earnings
– $85,000,000		– $100,000,000		+ $15,000,000 (gain)

The financial reporting of such gains or losses upon early retirement of bonds has been a matter of sharp debate. Managers argue that in cases where bonds are retired at less than their reported values, there is an economic gain to the firm; liabilities have been eliminated for less than their reported values and net assets have been increased. Analysts and accounting policy makers, on the other hand, observe that managers are able to decide whether and when to repurchase outstanding bonds, and for this reason have considerable control over the time periods in which the resulting gains or losses are recognized. Reality Check 9-1 shows the composition of long-term debt for a major company that has debt issued at a variety of different interest rates.

Managers can use bond repurchases as a means of "smoothing" fluctuations in income. For example, in periods of poor operating performance, managers can improve reported income merely by repurchasing outstanding bonds with market values below their reported values. Moreover, firms that retire bonds early often issue additional bonds in order to replace the retired debt. This practice has the appearance of "paper shuffling" because the firm's debt position is essentially unchanged, but substantial gains have been included in income. Also, because firms must issue new debt at higher interest rates in order to retire older debt bearing lower interest rates, future periods will report higher interest expenses and lower net income.

In response to this issue, the FASB requires that material gains and losses from the early retirement of debt be reported as extraordinary items on the income statement. Recall from our discussion of the income statement in Chapter 4, "The Income Statement," that extraordinary gains and losses are reported in a separate section of the income statement, separate from the calculation of the firm's income from ongoing or recurring operations. This separation is useful to financial statement users who want to assess the firm's ability to generate profit from its ongoing operations in future periods.

Other Aspects of Borrowing Agreements

In addition to specifying payments of principal and interest, borrowing agreements **(indentures)** can include a variety of other provisions that are important to users of financial statements. These provisions are added to make the debt issues more attractive to prospective lenders. Common provisions include restrictive covenants, collateral, and convertibility. Each of these features is described briefly in this section.

REALITY CHECK 9-1

Kerr McGee Corporation, a global energy and chemical company, includes the following information in a footnote describing the long-term debt reported in its 1997 financial statements:

Long-term debt (Partial)	(Dollars in millions)
7.125% Debentures due October 15, 2027 (7.01% effective rate)	$ 150
7% Debentures due November 1, 2011, net of unamortized debt discount of $108 million in 1997 and $111 million in 1996 (14.25% effective rate)	142
8-1/2% Sinking fund debentures due June 1, 2006	22
Notes payable -	
6.625% Notes due October 15, 2007 (6.54% effective rate)	150
Other	90

Required

a. Why do the interest rates differ among the various debt issues reported by Kerr McGee?
b. Why is the information concerning the due dates of Kerr McGee's debt useful to the analyst?
c. Note that the coupon rates and effective interest rates differ for several of Kerr McGee's debt issues. Based on the information provided above, which of these issues was sold at a discount? Which was sold at a premium?
d. Assume that the market rate of interest on similar debt is 10 percent at the balance sheet date (December 31, 1997). If so, would the market values of the first two issues listed above be greater or less than their book values? Explain.
e. Based on your answer to part d, if Kerr McGee's management wished to report a gain on early debt retirement, which of the issues would be retired?

Solution

a. The primary reason that interest rates differ among debt issues is that interest rates prevailing in financial markets change over time. Consequently, some debt is issued when interest rates in general are relatively high, and other debt is issued when interest rates in general are relatively low.

In addition, interest rates may differ because of the features of individual debt issues. For example, Kerr McGee's sinking fund debentures have a relatively low interest rate (8 1/2%). A sinking fund debenture requires that the company makes periodic payments to a fund that is earmarked to repay the debt at maturity. This feature is usually attractive to investors, so lenders are willing to accept a lower rate of interest.

b. The information about the maturity dates of Kerr McGee's outstanding debt is useful to the analyst in predicting the firm's future cash flows. The company must generate sufficient cash to retire the debt from operating cash flows and/or from additional borrowings and shareholders' investments.
c. The effective interest rate on the debentures due October 15, 2027 is 7.01%, which is below the coupon rate of 7.125%, implying that this issue was sold at a premium. Conversely, the effective interest rate on the debentures due November 1, 2011, is 14.25%, which is above the coupon rate of 7%, implying that this issue was sold at a discount.
d. A market rate of interest of 10% would exceed the 7.01% effective rate of the issue due October 15, 2027, so this issue would have a market price that is below its book value. Conversely, a market rate of interest of 10% would be less than the 14.25% effective rate of the issue due November 1, 2011, so this issue would have a market price that is above its book value.
e. In order to report a gain, management would retire the issue due October 15, 2027. The reported gain would be the difference between the book value and the (lower) market value of the issue.

Restrictive Covenants

Borrowers may agree to various restrictions on management's ability to invest, pay dividends, incur additional debt, or take other actions that can affect the firm's ability to meet its repayment obligations. Such **restrictive covenants** are often based on accounting measurements of assets, liabilities, and/or income. Violation of these restrictions constitutes technical default on the debt and may allow lenders to increase interest rates or impose other penalties on the borrower.

Exhibit 9-3 shows a portion of the footnote disclosures included in Ethyl Corporation's 1997 financial statements, describing restrictive covenants related to the company's long-term debt. These agreements require Ethyl to maintain certain financial ratios at specified levels.

The existence and the nature of restrictive covenants are an important concern to analysts of financial reports. Restrictions that are based directly on accounting measurements, such as working capital (current assets minus current liabilities) and net worth (total assets minus total liabilities, which we have already described as net assets), can affect the choice of accounting methods in use by the firm.

To illustrate, recall that in periods of rising costs the FIFO method of inventory costing results in higher reported profits and inventory valuations than does LIFO. Also, the straight-line method of depreciating plant and equipment results in lower depreciation charges and higher asset valuations than do accelerated methods of depreciation. Consequently, managers who face restrictive covenants that are based on asset values, income, or net worth would be more likely to choose FIFO rather than LIFO costing for inventories, despite possibly paying higher taxes. They would also probably choose straight-line rather than accelerated depreciation methods for long-lived assets.

Debt covenant restrictions can be affected by changes in GAAP, such as new statements of the FASB. For instance, if a firm is approaching the minimum limits of working capital or net worth specified in its lending agreements, then management is likely to favor accounting standards that increase reported asset valuations and net worth. Management is also likely to oppose prospective new accounting standards that would make violations of these restrictions more likely. Some debt contracts provide for exceptions or adjustments to the restrictions if there are subsequent changes in GAAP. Another example of restrictive covenants on long-term borrowings is provided in Reality Check 9-2.

EXHIBIT 9-3 Sample of Footnote Disclosures of Restrictive Convenants

Ethyl Corporation
1997 Annual Report

Note 10-Long-term debt (Partial)

The Company has an unsecured Amended and Restated Competitive Advance, Revolving Credit Facility, and Term Loan Agreement with a group of banks that permit it to borrow up to $750 million. The credit facility permits borrowing for the next five years at various interest rate options. The facility contains a number of covenants, representations, and events of default typical of a credit facility agreement of this size and nature, including financial covenants relating to consolidated debt (as defined) including: (i) maximum consolidated leverage or indebtedness to earnings of 3.5 to 1.0, (ii) minimum consolidated earnings to fixed charges coverage of 1.25 to 1.0 and (iii) minimum consolidated net worth (defined as a percentage of shareholders' equity after the effects of the repurchase of about 35 million shares on October 2, 1997, plus 50% of future net income). The Company was in compliance with such covenants at December 31, 1997.

REALITY CHECK 9-2

The following information concerning restrictive covenants has been adapted from footnotes to the 1996 financial statements of Nuclear Metals, Inc., a metallurgical technology firm:

The Industrial Revenue Bonds (IRBs) outstanding consist of two note issues. The interest rates on these notes range from 66.5% to 70% of the bank's prime interest rate. These notes are secured by property, plant, and equipment. The IRBs contain restrictive covenants including, among others, a requirement to maintain minimum working capital, consolidated net worth, and a minimum current ratio

The following amounts appear on the year-end balance sheet:

Current assets	$18,633,000
Total assets	35,118,000
Current liabilities	9,384,000
Total liabilities	10,878,000

Required

a. Assume for purposes of illustration that Nuclear Metals, Inc.'s restrictive covenants require minimum working capital of $7,000,000, consolidated net worth of not less than $20,000,000, and current assets greater than 150% of current liabilities. Would the firm be in compliance with these covenants at the end of 1996?
b. By how much might the firm's current assets decrease and still not violate the working capital restriction? (Assume that current liabilities remain constant.)
c. By how much might the firm's current assets decrease and still not violate the current ratio constraint? (Assume that current liabilities remain constant.)
d. Why might lenders restrict both the current ratio and the dollar amount of working capital in restrictive covenants?

Solution

a. Evaluation of compliance with restrictive covenants:

Minimum working capital of $7,000,000:

Current assets	$18,633,000
Less: Current liabilities	−9,384,000
Working capital	$ 9,249,000

Therefore, the firm complies with the minimum working capital restriction.

Current ratio of 150% (or 1.5):

$$\text{Current ratio} = \frac{\text{Current assets}}{\text{Current liabilities}}$$

$$198.5\% \text{ (or 1,985)} = \$18{,}633{,}000/\$9{,}384{,}000$$

Therefore, the firm complies with the current ratio restriction.

Net worth of $20,000,000:

Net worth = Total assets less total liabilities
$24,240,000 = $35,118,000 − $10,878,000

Therefore, the firm complies with the net worth restriction.

b. The firm's current assets might decrease up to $2,249,000 before violating the working capital restriction:

Actual working capital (see calculation in part a)	$9,249,000
Working capital restriction	−7,000,000
Excess over restriction	$2,249,000

c. The firm's current assets might decrease to $4,557,000 before violating the current ratio restriction:

Actual current assets	$18,633,000
Current liabilities × 150% ($9,384,000 × 1.5)	−14,076,000
Difference	$ 4,557,000

d. Lenders may restrict *both* the current ratio and the dollar amount of working capital for the following reason. Long-term borrowings extend over many years and during that time the firm's operating level may change substantially. For lower levels of output, the firm may have relatively small amounts of current assets and liabilities, and a high current ratio would not provide much protection for long-term lenders. In this case, the dollar amount of working capital is an important feature. At higher levels of output, when current assets and liabilities are relatively large, a high current ratio offers stronger protection to the long-term creditors.

Collateral

Debt agreements sometimes require that specific assets of the firm be pledged as security in the event of default by the borrower. These assets are termed **collateral.** Mortgages on office buildings, plant, and equipment are frequent examples, especially in transportation industries such as airlines, railroads, and trucking companies. On the other hand, lenders are sometimes reluctant to accept as collateral a business asset that has limited resale value or alternative use. In these cases, the lender may require that a sinking fund be established to secure the debt. The sinking fund is segregated cash and/or other liquid temporary investments, usually administered by an independent trustee or financial institution and pledged as collateral to retire a specific bond or note.

Convertibility

An attractive feature to many investors is the right to exchange debt instruments for other securities, usually common stock of the borrowing firm. **Convertible bonds** give the bondholder the option to exchange bonds for a predetermined number of shares of stock. If the stock price subsequently increases above the value of the bonds, the bondholders will likely convert their holdings to stock. Conversely, if the stock price remains below the value of the debt, the bondholders will continue to collect interest and will receive the bond principal at maturity. Convertible debt is described in more detail in Chapter 10, "Shareholders' Equity," which discusses shareholders' equity.

FINANCIAL REPORTING FOR INCOME TAXES

Corporations measure income for financial reporting and income tax purposes, and the objectives of these measurements differ. Income measures for financial reporting purposes should help financial analysts to assess the firm's future ability to generate cash. Income measures for income tax purposes, on the other hand, must comply with the relevant provisions of the Internal Revenue Service (IRS) tax code. IRS regulations reflect the objectives of government fiscal policy, rather than the objectives of financial analysis and reporting.

Book and Tax Differences

Because of these differing objectives, revenue and expense measurements that are used to determine taxable income may differ from those used in financial reporting. Accountants in these cases distinguish between book and tax measurements in that book measurements are used for financial reporting purposes, while tax measurements must comply with income tax laws.

In most cases, differences between book and tax measurements are **temporary** in nature. In order to stimulate purchases of property, plant, and equipment, for example, the U.S. government allows firms to depreciate such assets quickly for tax purposes. Firms can thereby reduce their income taxes in the earlier years after purchasing such assets. This accelerated depreciation usually exceeds the amount of depreciation expense that is used for financial accounting measurements of income. In later years, however, the situation is reversed. Financial statements continue to report depreciation expense, although the asset is already fully depreciated for tax purposes.

Accounting standards for reporting income tax expenses and liabilities reflect a basic premise: all events that affect the tax impact of temporary differences should be recognized currently in the financial statements. Broadly, two types of events can affect these expected tax impacts: (1) a change in the amount of temporary differences between the book and the tax bases of a firm's assets (or liabilities) and (2) a change in tax rates that will apply to those temporary differences.

To illustrate the measurement of income tax expenses and liabilities, consider the information provided in Exhibit 9-4 about the financial statement and income tax accounting used by Dorian Company to account for its plant and equipment. As shown in Exhibit 9-4, Dorian uses the straight-line method of depreciation for financial reporting purposes and an accelerated method of depreciation for income tax purposes. As a result, the financial statement carrying value, or book basis, of these assets is $700 million at December 31, 2000, and the tax basis of these assets is $300 million. The book and tax bases of Dorian's plant and equipment differ by $400 million:

Book basis of plant and equipment	$700 million
Tax basis of plant and equipment	300 million
Difference	$400 million

Deferred Tax Liability Because temporary differences such as those resulting from accelerated tax depreciation only allow a firm to postpone its tax payments to later years, the postponed taxes will be paid eventually. For this reason, accounting standards require that firms recognize a liability for such future income taxes.

EXHIBIT 9-4 Depreciation for Book and Tax Purposes

Dorian Company
Depreciation of Plant and Equipment for Book and Tax Purposes, 2001

	Book	Tax
On December 31, 2000:	**Book**	**Tax**
Plant and equipment, original cost	$900 million	$900 million
Accumulated depreciation	200 million[a]	600 million[b]
Basis	$700 million	$300 million
During 2001:		
Income tax rate	35%	35%
Income before depreciation	$250 million	$250 million
Depreciation	60 million	150 million
Pre-tax income	$190 million	$100 million
On December 31, 2001:	**Book**	**Tax**
Plant and equipment, original cost	$900 million	$900 million
Accumulated depreciation	260 million	750 million
Basis	$640 million	$150 million
Income tax actually payable for 2001:		
Income before depreciation	$250 million	
Tax depreciation	− 150 million	
Taxable income	100 million	
Income tax rate	× 35%	
Tax actually payable	$ 35 million	

(a) Straight-line depreciation is used for financial reporting.
(b) Accelerated depreciation is used for tax reporting.

The liability for future income taxes is referred to as a deferred income tax liability. The measurement of a firm's deferred income tax liability is obtained by multiplying the difference between the asset's book and tax bases by the appropriate income tax rate.

Dorian Company's income tax rate is expected to be 35% over the relevant future. Consequently, Dorian's deferred tax liability at December 31, 2000, is $140 million, computed as follows:

Excess of book over tax basis of plant and equipment	$400 million
Income tax rate	× 35%
Deferred tax liability, December 31, 2000	$140 million

Income tax expense reported in the financial statements is computed in the following manner:

Income tax actually payable		$XXX
Increase (decrease) in deferred tax liability	+(−)	YYY
Total income tax expense		$ZZZ

To illustrate, refer again to Exhibit 9-4, which shows that during 2001 Dorian's tax depreciation exceeds the book depreciation of the plant and equipment by $90 million ($150 million − $60 million). As a result, the difference between the tax and book bases of these assets has increased by $90 million, and the amount of the deferred tax liability has increased by $31.5 million, computed as follows:

Book basis of plant and equipment, December 31, 2001	$ 640 million
Less: Tax basis of plant and equipment, December 31, 2001	−150 million
Difference at December 31, 2001	490 million
Income tax rate	× 35%
Deferred tax liability, December 31, 2001	$171.5 million
Less: Deferred tax liability, December 31, 2000	−140.0 million
Increase in deferred tax liability during 2001	$ 31.5 million

Dorian's 2001 income tax expense is the sum of the amount actually payable, $35 million (shown in Exhibit 9-4), and the increase in the deferred tax liability during 2001 computed above:

Income tax payable (Exhibit 9-5)	$35.0 million
Plus: Increase in deferred tax liability	31.5 million
Total income tax expense	$66.5 million

This tax expense would affect Dorian's financial statements in the following manner:

ASSETS	=	LIABILITIES	+	SHAREHOLDERS' EQUITY
Cash		Deferred taxes		Retained earnings
− $35 million		+ $31.5 million		− $66.5 million (income tax expense)

Note that the income tax expense of $66.5 million is equal to 35% of Dorian's reported pre-tax income of $190 million. This relationship occurs because our example assumes that tax rates remain stable at 35%. On the other hand, the percentage relationship of the income tax actually payable, $35 million, to Dorian's pre-tax income is just 18.4% ($35 million / $190 million). If this amount were to be reported as income tax expense on the income statement, investors might be misled about Dorian's true tax burden. For this reason, deferred tax accounting appears to provide a better matching of expenses on the income statement, at least when tax rates are expected to be stable over time. Reality Check 9-3 illustrates the relationships between income tax expenses, tax payments, and effective tax rates for a large U.S. firm.

Historically, tax rates in the U.S. have been relatively stable. In the third quarter of 1993, however, a new deficit-reduction law raised the corporate tax rate from 34 to 35%. This apparently minor adjustment in tax rates required that firms revalue their deferred tax liabilities upward by about 2.9% (1% rate increase/34% old rate). Because accounting standards require this adjustment to be included in the calculation of tax expense for the quarter in which the new tax law is signed, many firms experienced a considerable drop in the forecast for third-quarter profits. As examples, International

REALITY CHECK 9-3

The Aluminum Company of America (Alcoa) includes the following information in its 1997 Financial Report:

	(Dollars in millions)
Income before income taxes	$1,601.7
Provision (expense) for income tax	528.7
Income taxes paid currently	445.5
Deferred tax liabilities related to depreciating assets at December 31,1997	840.4

Required

Based solely on the information provided above

a. Determine Alcoa's effective income tax rate during 1997.
b. Determine the percentage relation between Alcoa's actual tax payments and income before taxes during 1997.
c. Provide a likely reason for the difference between the percentages determined in parts a and b above.
d. Assume that Alcoa's statutory tax rate is 35 percent. What would you estimate as the difference between the tax basis and the book basis of Alcoa's depreciable assets at the end of 1997?

Solution

a. Alcoa's effective tax rate during 1997 is the percentage relation of the provision for income tax ($528.7 million) to income before income tax ($1,601.7 million), or 33% ($528.7/$1,601.7).
b. Alcoa's tax payments of $445.5 million are 27.8 percent of income before taxes ($445.5/$1,601.7).
c. A likely reason for the fact that Alcoa's effective tax rate exceeds the percentage of income actually paid in income taxes during 1997 is that Alcoa's taxable income is below the amount of income recognized in Alcoa's financial statements. This may be due to timing differences in recognizing revenues (such as lower revenues recognized for tax purposes) or in recognizing expenses (such as higher expenses recognized for tax purposes).
d. If Alcoa's statutory tax rate is 35%, the differences between the tax and book bases of the depreciating assets may be estimated as follows:

Deferred tax liabilities related to depreciation	$ 840.4
Tax rate of 35%	÷ 35%
Difference in tax basis and book basis of depreciable assets	$2,401.1

Paper's profit forecast fell by 50.8%, and Georgia Pacific's forecasted profits were revised to a forecasted loss.

Other Aspects of Income Tax Reporting

The foregoing discussion of income tax reporting has emphasized the issue of accelerated depreciation. This focus is appropriate because the predominant portion of temporary differences between the book and the tax bases of U.S. firms' corporate assets is due to differences in tax and book depreciation.

Tax and book income measurements differ, however, for many other reasons. For example, revenue and expense measurements in areas such as leasing, warranties, debt refinancing, exchanges of assets, and various other areas are treated differently for tax and book purposes. In some cases, the differences result in postponements of taxable income (as with accelerated depreciation). In other cases, however, the different treatments result in earlier recognition of taxable income. As a result, some firms may report deferred tax assets, rather than deferred tax liabilities. Exhibit 9-5 shows the reasons why the tax and book bases of various assets and liabilities differ

EXHIBIT 9-5 Composition of Deferred Tax Assets and Liabilities

Ethyl Corporation
Footnote disclosures of deferred tax items

(Adapted from the 1997 annual report)

	(In Thousands) 1997
Deferred tax assets:	
Environmental reserves	$15,708
Intercompany profit in inventories	10,467
Loss on impairment of non-operating assets	6,358
Undistributed earnings of foreign subsidiaries	4,744
Future employee benefits	4,268
Other	7,425
Gross deferred tax assets	48,970
Valuation allowance	-
Net deferred tax assets	48,970
Deferred tax liabilities:	
Depreciation	41,056
Future employee benefits	20,056
Long-term contingent note payable	18,169
Deferred tax liabilities	92,744
Net deferred tax liabilities	$43,774

for a major U.S. firm. Although further discussion of these other types of temporary differences is too specialized for this text, the basic framework that was used in calculating tax differences due to differences in depreciation methods applies in many other areas.

In addition to timing differences that give rise to deferred tax assets and liabilities, there are various other reasons why the percentage relation between a firm's reported pre-tax income and its income tax expense may differ from the federal statutory corporate tax rate, which is currently 35 percent. For this reason, firms are required to disclose the causes of any significant differences between the statutory and the **effective tax rate** in the footnotes to the financial statements. The effective tax rate is the reported income tax expense as a percentage of reported income before tax. Exhibit 9-6 provides an example of such a disclosure. Note that for a given firm, effective tax rates can be either above or below the federal statutory rate. Some differences between these rates may be relatively stable over time (such as state and local taxes), and other causes may vary in their effects over time (such as settlements and adjustments of prior years' taxes).

Deferred Taxes and the Liability Concept

Present financial reporting standards emphasize that deferred tax obligations are liabilities. In some respects, however, the manner in which deferred tax obligations are classified and measured is inconsistent with liability reporting.

Generally, business liabilities are classified as current or noncurrent based on the length of time to repayment. Deferred tax obligations, in contrast, are classified based on the current versus noncurrent classification of the related asset. Depreciating assets are classified as noncurrent assets, for example, and the related deferred tax obligations are also classified as noncurrent for this reason. Accounting literature does not provide any compelling reason for this practice.

EXHIBIT 9-6 Reconcilation of Statutory and Effective Tax Rates

Ethyl Corporation
Footnote disclosures of income tax rates
(Adapted from the 1997 annual report)

The significant differences between the U.S. federal statutory rate and the effective income tax rate are as follows:

	% of Income Before Income Taxes	
	1997	1996
Federal statutory rate	35.0%	35.0%
State taxes, net of federal tax benefit	2.0	1.8
Favorable tax settlements and adjustments	(3.5)	-
Other items, net	(4.0)	(0.6)
Effective income tax rate	29.5%	36.2%

Generally, long-term obligations are reported at their present values; in other words, the future payments are discounted to the present at an appropriate rate of interest. Deferred tax obligations are not discounted, however, even in cases where the temporary differences are not expected to reverse for many years. Consequently, managers and investment analysts often argue that the amounts reported as deferred tax obligations are substantial overstatements of these liabilities' economic value.

KEY TERMS

SUMMARY OF LEARNING OBJECTIVES

1. **Recognize the types of noncurrent obligations that are reported by business firms.**
   The major portion of long-term debt that is reported on corporate balance sheets consists of notes and bonds payable. Many corporations also report substantial obligations for deferred income taxes.
2. **Comprehend the features of long-term borrowing contracts, such as notes and bonds payable.**
   Notes payable represents direct borrowings by the firm from banks or other lenders. The note is a formal contract to repay a specific amount at a definite future date. Most notes require interest payments periodically over the life of the loan. Some notes do not entail periodic interest payments and instead are sold at a discount to compensate lenders for the use of their funds.
   Bonds payable constitutes a major form of borrowed capital for business corporations. They are contracts that obligate the issuing corporation to make periodic interest payments and to repay the principal at a specified maturity date. Bonds are sold to investors and are actively traded among investors subsequent to their issuance. The amount that the issuing firm receives for its bonds depends on the relationship between the coupon or face rate of interest and the market rate of interest when the bonds are issued. Bonds will sell at par (face) value if the coupon and market rates are equal; they will sell at a discount if the market interest rate exceeds the coupon rate or at a premium if the coupon rate exceeds the market rate.
3. **Determine periodic interest expense and the value of noncurrent obligations in financial reports.**
   Firms use compound interest calculations to determine the periodic interest expense and balance sheet valuation of bonds payable. Fluctuations in the market prices of bonds payable that occur subsequent to their issuance are not reflected in the financial statements. If firms retire bonds early, or before the maturity date, any difference between the carrying value and the cost to retire the bonds is reported as an extraordinary gain or loss.
4. **Appreciate why income is measured differently for income tax and financial reporting purposes.**
   Income measurement for tax purposes must comply with income tax laws, and income measurement for financial reporting purposes must comply with current accounting standards. Because these two income measures serve different purposes, the resulting pre-tax book (financial reporting) income and tax (tax return) income will differ.
5. **Understand why the tax basis and the financial reporting basis of assets and liabilities may differ.**
   Differences between book and tax income imply differences in the book and tax bases (or carrying values) of the related assets. These differences are usually tem-

porary in nature because total taxable income over the entire useful life of an asset will usually be the same for tax and book purposes. In other words, timing differences may allow a firm to postpone tax payments to future years, but not to avoid the tax payments. Consequently, firms must recognize an obligation for deferred (postponed) taxes.

6. **Interpret financial statement measurements of income tax expense and deferred income tax liability.**
Income tax expense reported in the financial statements is computed by adding income tax payable and any change in the total amount of deferred tax liability:

Income tax actually payable		$XXX
Increase (decrease) in deferred tax liability	+(−)	YYY
Total income tax expense		$ZZZ

Deferred tax obligations are reported in the balance sheet as part of a firm's total debt. Unlike other long-term obligations, however, they are not shown at their present values and therefore may reflect an overstatement of a firm's liabilities.

QUESTIONS

9-1 Define long-term or noncurrent liabilities. What are the differences between current and noncurrent liabilities?

9-2 Identify some of the reasons why a firm may prefer to have both current and some noncurrent liabilities.

9-3 If a firm has noncurrent liabilities with a fixed interest rate, what will happen to the firm's liabilities when market interest rates increase? Decrease? Although interest rates on a firm's financial instruments may be fixed, actual current market interest rates can vary on a daily basis. Why don't accountants value liabilities using current market rates?

9-4 Under what circumstances would managers prefer fixed interest rates and when might they prefer to have variable interest rates on their noncurrent liabilities? Discuss several choices that managers might make in these circumstances. What are the financial statement consequences of these choices? Under what circumstances do managers have the opportunity to adjust the valuation of their liabilities to reflect market conditions?

9-5 Describe the major differences between a bond discount and a bond premium. Discuss the distinctions between coupon (or nominal) interest rates and market interest rates at the bond issuance date.

9-6 If a long-term bond is issued at a discount, both the carrying value of the bond and the recognized interest expense will increase in each successive period during which the bond is outstanding. Explain why this occurs.

9-7 If a long-term bond is issued at a premium, both the carrying value of the bond and the recognized interest expense will decrease in each successive period during which the bond is outstanding. Explain why this occurs.

9-8 Evaluate the following statement: "When a firm issues bonds at a discount, in effect the firm is paying the lender some of the bond interest expense in advance. The difference between the bond principal and the amount paid to the issuer should be reported on the balance sheet as prepaid interest expense and be listed as an asset."

9-9 Identify several reasons why managers may prefer to issue long-term bonds to a number of investors, rather than borrow directly from a few financial institutions.

9-10 Discuss why lenders include various restrictive covenants in a lending agreement. Provide several examples of restrictive covenants.

9-11 Assume that a firm has several long-term bonds outstanding at different interest rates. Explain the relationship between bond coupon rates and current market interest rates that would cause the bonds to sell at par, below par, and above par value.

9-12 Discuss the purposes of income measurement for financial reporting. Then discuss why income taxes are included in a firm's financial statements as an expense *and* as a liability.

9-13 Most firms keep at least two "sets of books," in the sense that a given transaction can be interpreted differently for "book" (financial reporting) and "tax" (income tax calculations) purposes. Is this ethical? Discuss.

9-14 Suppose the U.S. Congress decides to stimulate business investment in new plant and equipment by providing a reduction in income taxes equal to 10% of the costs of eligible new investments. If a firm acquires $100 million in new plant and equipment and consequently receives a $10 million dollar reduction in income taxes, should the $10 million be interpreted (a) as income, (b) as a reduction in the cost of the acquired assets, or (c) in some other manner? Discuss.

9-15 Explain the nature of *temporary* differences between book and tax measurements of assets and liabilities. Why is this concept important for financial reporting of income tax expense? Why is it important for reporting a firm's liabilities?

9-16 Whether a firm uses straight-line or accelerated depreciation in accounting for a long-lived depreciable asset, the total amount of depreciation expense over the entire service life of the asset will be the same. If so, why is the choice among these depreciation methods for financial statement purposes important? Why is the timing of depreciation expense on a firm's tax return important?

9-17 Discuss the meaning of a deferred income tax liability. At minimum, address the following points:

a. Why does a deferral exist?
b. Do these obligations satisfy the definition of liabilities that was provided in Chapter 3, "The Balance Sheet"?
c. How (if at all) would the carrying value of these liabilities be affected by changes in income tax rates?
d. How (if at all) would the carrying value of these liabilities be affected by changes in interest rates?

9-18 Provide a reply to the following: *"If a firm does not earn taxable income in future periods, then it will not pay taxes. For this reason, it makes no sense to report deferred tax liabilities. These amounts will only be payable if the firm earns future taxable income, and that is an event that has not yet happened. Financial accounting is supposed to be historical in nature. Deferred tax accounting does not fit into the historical cost framework."*

9-19 Evaluate the following proposal: *"If an asset is fully depreciated for income tax purposes, it is less valuable than an asset that has a substantial undepreciated cost for tax purposes. This implies that the valuation of assets on the balance sheet should be adjusted as their tax bases are reduced."*

9-20 Comment on the following observation: *"Mammoth Company is not paying its fair share of the national budget. The firm reported income before taxes of $4 billion in 1994, and paid only $40 million in income taxes. That is only 1% of its income. Even the middle class pay more tax than that. I suppose it's le-*

gal, but it's sure not ethical. That company's management should be removed from office."

9-21 Assume U.S. nominal or maximum income tax rates are increased from 35 to 40%. How would this increase affect a firm that presently reports a deferred tax liability of $700 million? Specifically, how would the firm's net income be affected in the period when the rate increase is enacted, and how would the carrying value of the deferred tax liability be changed? Do you agree with these financial statement effects? Discuss.

9-22 Current financial accounting standards do not permit the discounting of deferred tax obligations, even in cases where the deferred obligations will not be paid for many years. Evaluate this practice. At minimum, address the following points:

a. Is it consistent to discount some long-term debt (such as bonds payable), and not other long-term liabilities (such as tax deferrals), and then add these amounts together in order to measure total liabilities? Why?

b. If deferred tax obligations are to be discounted, what rate should be used—a current market interest rate or some other rate? On the other hand, support the view that tax deferrals are essentially an "interest-free" loan from the government and therefore they should be discounted at a zero interest rate.

c. If deferred tax obligations are to be discounted, and interest rates in general subsequently rise, how (if at all) would the carrying values of the deferred tax obligations be adjusted?

9-23 If a firm has noncurrent liabilities with floating (variable) interest rates, what will happen to a valuation of the firm's liabilities when the market rate of interest increases? Decreases? Why is there more consistency in this case than in the case of fixed interest rates?

EXERCISES

Long-term Debt: Interpreting Financial Statements

9-24 Cabot Cove's annual report contained a note on long-term debt. A partial list of the long-term debt follows, exclusive of current maturities (dollars in thousands):

	2000	1999
Notes due 2001, 9.875%	$150,000	$150,000
Notes due 2002-2022, 8.07%	105,000	105,000
Overseas Private Investment Corp. due 2002, floating rate 6.5%	15,000	—
Industrial revenue bonds, due 2001-2014, 9.35%-14%	5,000	6,000

Required

a. Comment on why Cabot might have long-term debt with such different interest rates and different maturities.

b. Based on current interest rates, which of these liabilities will sell above (or below) par values? Why?

c. Discuss how managers might use an aggressive debt retirement strategy to increase or decrease net income.

Interpreting Liability Disclosures

9-25 Yellow-Jacket Company, which manufactures imaging and health products for commercial and medical customers, included the following information in a note describing its long-term debt:

Long-term debt (partial)	
Issue:	(Dollars in Millions)
10.05% notes due 1999	$ 350
7 7/8% notes due 2001	135
8.55% notes due 2000	200
6 3/8% convertible debentures due 2001	278
Zero-coupon convertible debentures due 2011 ($3,680 face value)	1,127

Required

a. Why do the interest rates differ among the various debt issues reported by Yellow-Jacket?
b. Why is information on these due dates useful to a financial analyst?
c. Assume that the prevailing market interest rate is 8.25% at the balance sheet date, and that each of the first four issues listed was initially issued at par (face) value. Which of these liabilities will have a current market value above par? Which issues would have a market value below par value?
d. If Yellow-Jacket's managers or board of directors wished to report a gain on early debt retirement. Which of these liabilities (see part c) will be retired first? Why?
e. Why would lenders be willing to invest in zero-coupon bonds (bonds that do not pay periodic interest)?

Restrictive Covenants on Debt

9-26 Nuclear Indentures, a firm specializing in providing debt financing to high-tech firms, provided the following information concerning restrictive covenants in its notes to the financial statements:

> All long-term obligations contain restrictive covenants including, among others, a requirement to maintain minimum working capital of $17,000,000, consolidated net worth . . . of not less than $25,000,000 and current assets greater than 200% of current liabilities.

The following amounts appear on the year-end balance sheet (millions of dollars):

Current assets	$41.3
Total assets	$65.1
Current liabilities	$ 8.2
Total liabilities	$22.0

Required

a. Is Nuclear Indentures in compliance with its restrictive covenants?
b. By how much might the firm's current assets decrease and still not violate the working capital restriction? (Assume current liabilities remain constant.)
c. By how much might the firm's current assets decrease and still not violate the current ratio constraint? (Assume current liabilities remain constant.)
d. Why might a firm's borrowing agreements restrict both the dollar amount of working capital *and* the current ratio?

Interpreting Liability Disclosures

9-27 Consider the following notes from the annual report of Jocko Enterprises. Interpret any unusual terms. How are lines of credit and long-term debt used by Jocko's managers? Explain how these notes indicate restrictions on managerial decisions. Alternatively, how do such liabilities create flexibility for managers?

Note 7 – Line of Credit (Partial)
To be able to draw under the line, or if borrowings are outstanding, the agreement with the bank requires Jocko to maintain certain minimum levels of cash, cash equivalents, and/or certain marketable securities, working capital, and net worth. As of June 30, 1999, Jocko was in compliance with all the requirements. The agreement also provides that, except for borrowings represented by the 8.75% Convertible Subordinated Debentures due May 14, 2014 (the "debentures," see Note 8), additional institutional borrowings cannot exceed $2,000,000 and seller or assumed financing of future acquisitions, if any, cannot exceed $5,000,000.

Note 8 – Long-Term Debt (Partial)
The debentures were issued under an indenture containing a number of restrictive covenants. These include restrictions on mergers and sales of assets and the creation of liens on assets; limitations on payments of cash dividends and purchases of Jocko's common stock (see Note 9); and the use of the debenture proceeds by Jocko and its subsidiaries, which are reserved for the acquisition of other businesses, and, pending such acquisition, certain short-term investments.

Bond Terms

Writing

9-28 Write a short memo describing the key features of long-term bonds. Include at least the following terms in your memo: par or face value, collateral, restrictive covenants, coupon rate, maturity date, and semiannual compounding.

Long-Term Debt: Interpreting Financial Statements

9-29 Refer to Wendy's financial statements in Appendix D. Review the balance sheet to determine how and where long-term liabilities are reported.

Required

a. Read Note 3 "Term Debt." Identify and discuss any unusual terms. Trace numerical disclosures of long-term liabilities in the notes to corresponding disclosures in the financial statements.
b. Discuss any other unusual concerns regarding Wendy's long-term liabilities. What other related information might an external analyst prefer?

Long-Term Debt: Interpreting Financial Statements

9-30 Refer to Reebok's financial statements in Appendix E. Review the balance sheet to determine how and when long-term liabilities are reported.

Required

a. Read Note 8 "Long Term Debt." Identify and discuss any unusual terms. Trace numerical disclosures of long-term liabilities in the notes to corresponding disclosures in the financial statements.
b. Discuss any other unusual concerns regarding Reebok's long-term liabilities. What other related information might an external analyst prefer?
c. Note 8 contains a list of various debt issues, maturity dates, and interest rates. Comment on why Reebok might have long-term debt issues with such different interest rates and different maturities.

(Continued)

d. Based on current interest rates, which of these do you think would sell above or below par values at today's rates? Why?
e. Discuss how managers might use an aggressive debt retirement strategy to increase or decrease net income.

Transaction Analysis: Noninterest-Bearing Notes

9-31 On June 1, 1999, the Brewer Company signed a $450,000, four-year note, discounted at 16% (compounded rate) payable to First Bank. The note matures May 30, 2003.

Required

Use the balance sheet equation to record the following transactions:
a. Cash proceeds received by Brewer Company.
b. Interest for each of the four years.
c. The final payment on the note.

Issuing Noninterest-Bearing Notes

9-32 Calculate the financial statement effects at the date of issue for each of the following discounted notes (also, refer to Chapter 8, "Accounts Payable, Commitments, Contingencies, and Risks"):
a. $10,000,000 note for one year at a 10% market interest rate.
b. $20,000,000 note for three years at a 12% market interest rate.
c. $5,000,000 note for 10 years at a 10% market interest rate.
d. What amount of cash is necessary to repay these notes at maturity, assuming no other changes during the term of the notes? (*Hint*: No further calculations are necessary to answer this part.)

Transaction Analysis: Issuing Bonds

9-33 Use the balance sheet equation to analyze the effects of issuing the following long-term bonds. Assume semiannual compounding and a coupon rate of 8%. Set up separate columns as necessary. Use a separate cash column.
a. $10,000,000 bonds for one year at a market interest rate of 8%.
b. $20,000,000 bonds for three years at a market interest rate of 12%.
c. $5,000,000 bonds for 10 years at a market interest rate of 4%.

Transaction Analysis: Issuing Bonds

9-34 Use the balance sheet equation to analyze the effects of issuing the following long-term bonds. Assume a market interest rate of 12% and semiannual compounding. Set up separate columns as necessary.
a. $10,000,000 bonds for one year at a coupon interest rate of 10%.
b. $20,000,000 bonds for three years at a coupon interest rate of 12%.
c. $5,000,000 bonds for 10 years at a coupon interest rate of 10%.
d. Discuss why some of these bonds were issued at a premium or a discount.

Transaction Analysis: Issuing Bonds

9-35 Use the balance sheet equation to analyze the effects of issuing the following long-term bonds. Assume a market interest rate of 8% and semiannual compounding. Set up separate columns as necessary. Use a separate cash column.
a. $10,000,000 bonds for one year at a coupon interest rate of 10%.
b. $20,000,000 bonds for three years at a coupon interest rate of 12%.

c. $5,000,000 bonds for 10 years at a coupon interest rate of 10%.
d. Discuss why each of these bonds was issued at a premium or discount.

Transaction Analysis: Bond Principal and Interest

9-36 Use the balance sheet equation to analyze the financial statement effects of the following transactions involving long-term bonds. Assume semiannual compounding. Set up separate columns as necessary. Use a separate cash column.

a. Issue $10,000,000 of five-year bonds carrying a coupon interest rate of 8% (paid semiannually). The market rate of interest at the time of issuance for similar bonds was 4%.
b. Record interest due and paid after the first six months.
c. Record interest due and paid at the end of the first year.
d. Record interest due and paid during each six-month period during the second year.
e. How much cash will be paid at maturity (at the end of the fifth year)?
f. Show the effects of the bond repayment on the financial statements at the end of the fifth year.(Ignore any amortization of premium or discount in the last year.)
g. Discuss why these bonds were issued and recorded at a premium or discount.

Transaction Analysis: Bond Principal and Interest

9-37 Use the balance sheet equation to analyze the financial statement effects of the following transactions involving long-term bonds. Assume semiannual compounding. Set up separate columns as necessary and use a separate cash column.

a. Issue $20,000,000 of five-year bonds carrying a coupon interest rate of 8%, payable semiannually. The market rate of interest at the time of issuance for similar bonds was 12%.
b. Record interest paid after the first six months.
c. Record interest due and paid at the end of the first year.
d. Record interest due and paid during each six-month period during the second year.
e. How much cash will be paid at the end of the fifth year?
f. Show the effects of the bond repayment on the financial statements at the end of the fifth year.
g. Discuss why these bonds were issued and recorded at a premium or discount.

PROBLEMS

Calculating Gain or Loss on Bond Retirement

9-38 Assume that a firm has bonds outstanding with a principal amount of $100 million, a carrying value of $105 million, and a current market value of $112 million. What gain or loss would the firm report if the bonds were to be retired at current market values (ignoring transactions costs)? Do you consider this to be a "real" gain or loss? Explain.

Transaction Analysis: Long-Term Notes Payable

9-39 Use the balance sheet equation to analyze the effects of the following transactions involving noncurrent liabilities. Set up separate columns as necessary for each liability. Use a separate column for cash.

1. A firm signed a long-term note for $5 million for three years at an interest rate of 8% and received $5 million in cash.
2. The first interest payment was paid at the end of the first year.
3. The interest payment at the end of the second year was due, but wasn't paid.
4. The note was paid at the end of the third year, including the accrued interest from year 2. Show the effects of each interest payment and the repayment separately. Assume that interest on any unpaid balances *compounds*; in other words, interest accrues on the unpaid interest carried over from year 2.

Transaction Analysis: Notes Payable and Simple Interest

9-40 Use the balance sheet equation to analyze the effects of the following transactions involving noncurrent liabilities. Set up separate accounts for each liability and use a separate column for cash.

1. Sally Shrimpton wanted to expand her pottery business, but had a negative cash flow. She borrowed $150,000 from her local bank and signed a note upon receipt of the cash.
2. Sally purchased a new kiln for $50,000 cash.
3. Sally purchased clay, paint, and other supplies for $20,000 cash.
4. Sally was paid a bonus of $25,000. She needed the cash to remodel her kitchen.
5. Interest for the first six months is due at an annual rate of 15%.
6. Sally paid the interest due.
7. Interest for the second six months is due.
8. Interest for the third six-months is due.
9. Sally paid the interest for both six-month periods and made partial payment of $50,000 on the loan.
10. Interest for the fourth six-month period is due.
11. Interest for the final year (two six-month periods) is due.
12. Sally fully paid the note, along with all accumulated interest.

Issue Bonds, Calculate Interest, and Amortize Premium or Discount

9-41 Zany Sam's issued $600,000 of six-year, 8% bonds at a time when the market demanded a yield of 12% (on similar bonds). The bonds were issued on January 1, requiring interest payments on each subsequent June 30 and December 31 until maturity.

Required

a. Compute the issue price and determine the amount of any premium or discount at the issue date.

b. Using the balance sheet equation, show the effects of issuing the bonds on the financial statements.

c. Prepare a table showing the amortization of the discount or premium at each of the first four semiannual periods.

(Continued)

d. Under normal circumstances, how much cash will be paid at each interest date?
e. Determine the carrying value two years after the date of issue. (*Reminder*: The carrying value or book value of the bonds equals the face amount of the bonds plus the premium, or minus the discount.)

Issue Bonds, Calculate Interest, and Amortize Premium or Discount

9-42 Dagwood's issued $800,000 of 10-year, 8% bonds at a time when the market demanded a yield of 4% (on similar bonds). The bonds were issued on January 1, requiring interest payments on each subsequent June 30 and December 31 until maturity.

Required

a. Compute the issue price and determine the amount of any premium or discount at the issue date.
b. Show the effects of the bond issue on the financial statements, using the balance sheet equation.
c. Prepare a table showing the amortization of the discount or premium for each of the first four semiannual periods.
d. Under normal circumstances, how much cash will be paid at each interest date?
e. Determine the book value (face amount, plus premium or minus discount) two years after the date of issue.
f. Assume the bonds can be retired at 102 (102% of par value), two years after issue. Show the effects of this early retirement on the financial statements.
g. Why would a firm want to retire bonds early? Why would a firm pay more than book value to retire bonds early?

Transaction Analysis: Noninterest-Bearing Notes

9-43 Sally Shrimpton's pottery business was quite successful and needed to expand further. However, she wanted to avoid paying periodic interest payments to the bank. She saw an ad for discounted notes and decided they were preferable, compared to an interest-bearing note. Show the effects of each of the following transactions on the balance sheet equation. Set up separate columns as necessary and use a separate cash column.

1. Sally signed a discounted, three-year, $200,000 note (see Chapter 8) and received the proceeds. When she got home and read the fine print on the note, she found that the note doesn't require periodic interest payments as intended. She also found, however, that the note includes a 12% interest rate. She was convinced that the bank made a mistake. On her next bank statement, she was surprised and shocked that her account didn't show a deposit of $200,000 into her account on the day she signed the note; in fact, the deposit was much less. Calculate the loan proceeds and determine the effects of the loan on the firm's balance sheet equation.
2. Because Sally now understands that interest is included in all notes, whether she makes any periodic interest payments, record interest expense for the first year.
3. Record interest expense for each of the next two years.

4. Record the final payment on the note.
5. What payment would Sally have been required to make if she had repaid the note at the end of the second year? Why wouldn't she pay the entire $200,000 if she repaid the note at the end of the second year?

Interpreting Financial Statements: Ratio Calculations

9-44 Oncogene Science, Inc., reported no long-term debt in its 1994 financial statements. The equity section of its balance sheet can be summarized as:

	1994	1993
Total current liabilities	$ 2,979,555	$ 2,460,060
Total long-term liabilities	405,031	109,875
Total stockholders' equity	38,656,314	45,044,603
Total liabilities and equity	$42,040,900	$47,614,538

Required

a. Calculate Oncogene's debt and equity composition ratios (vertical analysis) using the capital composition ratios first introduced in Chapter 3.
b. Using only the information shown above, what does this evidence say, pro and con, about Oncogene's ability to meet its liabilities? Would this suggest a high or low likelihood of bankruptcy? Why?
c. What other information would you need to assess the firm's liquidity? Its default risk?

Interpreting Financial Statements: Ratio Calculations

9-45 Sigma Designs repaid much of its long-term debt between January 31, 1994 and January 31, 1995. Its liabilities and stockholders' equity at January 31 were as follows (dollars in thousands):

	1995	1994
Total current liabilities	$13,564	$ 8,622
Total long-term liabilities	1,102	1,518
Total shareholders' equity	18,721	16,499
Total liabilities and equity	$33,387	$26,639

Required

a. Calculate Sigma Designs' debt and equity composition ratios (vertical analysis).
b. Using only the information shown above, what does this evidence say, pro and con, about Sigma Designs' ability to meet its liabilities? Would this suggest a high or low likelihood of bankruptcy? Why?
c. What other information would be helpful in assessing the firm's liquidity? Its default risk?

Integration of Concepts

Interpreting Financial Statements

9-46 Contrast the debt management strategies of Oncogene Science and Sigma Designs (see data in the preceding two assignments). Which company seems to be the most conservative in managing its liabilities? Why? Is there anything unusual about changes in their stockholders' equity accounts that might make them somewhat noncomparable?

Interpreting Financial Statements: Ratio Calculations

9-47 Pfizer, Inc. reported these subtotals in its 1997 annual report (dollars in millions):

	1997	1996	1995
Total current liabilities	$ 5,305	$ 5,640	$ 5,187
Total liabilities	7,403	7,713	7,223
Total shareholders' equity	7,933	6,954	5,506
Total liabilities and equity	$15,336	$14,667	$12,729

Required

a. Calculate the debt and equity composition ratios (vertical analysis) for Pfizer for each year. (*Hint*: you must calculate the amount of any long-term liabilities.)
b. Which factors indicate that Pfizer is a very stable company, especially with respect to its management of debt and equity? Would a more stable company generally have high or low risk of default? Why?
c. What other information should be examined before concluding that Pfizer is a stable company with low default risk?

Interpreting Financial Statements: Ratio Calculations

9-48 Exabyte Corporation reported the following subtotals in its 1994 annual report, in thousands of dollars, for the years ending December 31, 1994 and January 1, 1994 (note that these dates still represent two consecutive fiscal years):

	December 31 1994	January 1 1994
Total current liabilities	$ 45,621	$ 38,318
Long-term obligations	237	454
Total stockholders' equity	196,907	158,535
Total liabilities and equity	$242,765	$197,307

Required

a. Calculate Exabyte's debt and equity composition ratios (vertical analysis).
b. Which factors indicate that Exabyte has a low risk of default on its long-term debt?
c. What is Exabyte's apparent debt management strategy?
d. Which other indicators might be used to assess Exabyte's risk of default?
e. Can the most recent year be compared with the fiscal year ended January 1, 1994? Why would a company change its year-end by a few days? What other information would be helpful in assessing these issues?

Interpreting Financial Statements

Integration of Concepts

9-49 Compare and contrast the 1995 composition ratios for Exabyte and Pfizer (see the preceding two assignments). Which company seems to be the most conservative in managing its liabilities? Why? Which company seems to have the higher default risk? Why? Does the relative difference in size of these two companies have an impact on your relative assessments? Why?

Issuing Bonds: Premium or Discount

9-50 Maggie Markel's Moving Emporium needs to acquire additional capital in order to purchase new trucks and warehouse storage space, and to conduct a national advertising campaign. Maggie has heard of bonds and thinks that her friends and relatives would buy them if they were especially attractive. Although bonds issued by similar moving companies are currently yielding about 8% compounded semiannually, she decided to be kind to her friends and relatives and offer an interest rate of 10% compounded semiannually on the bonds. Maggie has never heard of premiums or discounts on bonds and intends to sell the bonds at their face amount (par).

Required

a. How many $1,000 bonds must Maggie issue *at par* in order to raise $1,000,000?
b. Write a memo to Maggie explaining the possible effects and consequences of selling $1,000,000 of 10% bonds at par when similar bonds yield 8%.
c. If Maggie sells the bonds at their market value, including an appropriate premium or discount, how much would Maggie receive for the $1,000,000 bonds? (Assume five-year bonds.) How realistic is this assumption? Why?
d. Write a short memo summarizing your recommendations to Maggie about issuing these bonds.
e. Now assume that bonds similar to those issued by Maggie Markel's Moving Emporium are very risky and require an interest rate of 12% compounded semiannually (6% each six months) before they can be sold to anyone, even to Maggie's friends and relatives. Recalculate the issue price and any discount or premium.

Interpreting Financial Statements: Long-Term Liabilities

9-51 Hansel, Inc., is an international company specializing in debt collection with a range of complementary credit management services. It is headquartered in Amsterdam and aims to maintain and enhance its position as Europe's leading force in debt collection. Its 1999 financial statements list bank loans of £17,000,000 (£ = pounds sterling) with the following related note:

BANK LOANS

The company has entered into a syndicated loan facility of £25,400,000 of which £20,000,000 has been used as of December 31, 1999 (December 31, 1998: £13,000,000). £17,000,000 has been classified as long-term (1998: £13,000,000). The facility expires on December 16, 2001. The interest is calculated at 1.5% over LIBOR. A fee of 0.5% p.a. over the non-utilized part of the facility is payable. There are no additional costs on an early redemption.

Required

a. Explain each of the unusual terms or provisions described in this footnote. Note that "LIBOR" is the "London Inter-Bank Offer Rate" and that "p.a." means "per annum" or annually.
b. Calculate the annual fee on the unused portion of this credit arrangement, assuming the above balances were all outstanding during 1999.
c. Assuming no changes in monetary amounts, will these liabilities be shown as a current liability at the end of 2000? What must happen for them to remain as a long-term liability?

(Continued)

d. What amount must be included as the long-term liability on the balance sheet at the end of 1999? Why?
e. From the perspective of management, what else would you like to know about these long-term debts that is not shown in the financial statements?
f. For an investor evaluating a large international company, are these significant and unusual long-term debts?
g. How does the accounting disclosure of these long-term debts compare to the treatment of 30-year bonds discussed in this chapter?

Interpreting Financial Statements: Ratio Calculations

Integration of Concepts

9-52 The following balance sheets for Eli Lilly and Company and Pfizer, Inc., were extracted from the SEC's EDGAR database:

Consolidated Balance Sheets
ELI LILLY AND COMPANY AND SUBSIDIARIES
(Dollars in millions)

December 31	1997	1996
Assets		
Current Assets		
Cash and cash equivalents	$ 1,947.5	$ 813.7
Short-term investments	77.1	141.4
Accounts receivable, net of allowances of $53.3 (1997) and $82.4 (1996)	1,544.3	1,474.6
Other receivables	338.9	262.5
Inventories (Note 1)	900.7	881.4
Deferred income taxes (Note 12)	325.7	145.2
Prepaid expenses	186.5	172.5
Total current assets	5,320.7	3,891.3
Other Assets		
Prepaid retirement (Note 13)	579.1	512.9
Investments (Note 6)	465.6	443.5
Goodwill and other intangibles, net of allowances for amortization of $119.3 (1997) and $311.0 (1996) (Note 2)	1,550.5	4,028.2
Sundry	559.8	1,124.3
	3,155.0	6,108.9
Property and Equipment (Note 1)	4,101.7	4,307.0
	$12,577.4	$14,307.2

Consolidated Balance Sheets
ELI LILLY AND COMPANY AND SUBSIDIARIES
(Dollars in millions)

December 31	1997	1996
Liabilities and Shareholders' Equity		
Current Liabilities		
Short-term borrowings (Note 7)	$ 227.6	$ 1,212.9
Accounts payable	985.5	829.3
Employee compensation	456.6	388.4
Dividends payable	221.7	198.8
Income taxes payable (Note 12)	1,188.0	691.8
Other liabilities	1,112.2	901.0
Total current liabilities	4,191.6	4,222.2
Other Liabilities		
Long-term debt (Note 7)	2,326.1	2,516.5
Deferred income taxes (Note 12)	215.5	376.0
Retiree medical benefit obligation (Note 13)	118.3	136.4
Other noncurrent liabilities	920.3	956.0
	3,580.2	3,984.9
Commitments and contingencies (Note 14)	--	--
Minority interest in subsidiary (Note 10)	160.0	--
Shareholders' Equity (Notes 8 and 9)		
Common stock-no par value		
Authorized shares: 1,600,000,000		
Issued shares: 1,111,521,927	694.7	355.6
Additional paid-in capital	--	67.4
Retained earnings	4,483.1	7,207.3
Deferred costs-ESOP	(155.7)	(176.9)
Currency translation adjustments	(267.0)	(57.4)
	4,755.1	7,396.0
Less cost of common stock in treasury:		
1997 -- 1,000,000 shares		
1996 -- 16,079,323 shares	109.5	1,295.9
	4,645.6	6,100.1
	$12,577.4	$14,307.2

PFIZER INC AND SUBSIDIARY COMPANIES
December 31

CONSOLIDATED BALANCE SHEET

(millions, except per share data)	1997	1996	1995
Assets			
Current Assets			
Cash and cash equivalents	$ 877	$1,150	$ 403
Short-term investments	712	487	1,109
Accounts receivable, less allowance for doubtful accounts:			
1997--$51; 1996--$58; 1995-$61	2,527	2,252	2,024
Short-term loans	115	354	289
Inventories			
Finished goods	677	617	564
Work in process	852	695	579
Raw materials and supplies	244	277	241
Total inventories	1,773	1,589	1,384
Prepaid expenses, taxes and other assets	816	636	943
Total current assets	6,820	6,468	6,152
Long-term loans and investments	1,340	1,163	545
Property, plant & equipment, less accumulated depr.	4,137	3,850	3,473
Goodwill, less accumulated amortization:			
1997—$152; 1996—$115; 1995—$79	1,294	1,424	1,243
Other assets, deferred taxes and deferred charges	1,745	1,762	1,316
Total assets	$15,336	$14,667	$12,729
Liabilities and Shareholders' Equity			
Current Liabilities			
Short-term borrowings, incl. current portion LTD	$ 2,255	$ 2,235	$ 2,036
Accounts payable	765	913	715
Income taxes payable	785	892	822
Accrued compensation and related items	477	436	421
Other current liabilities	1,023	1,164	1,193
Total current liabilities	5,305	5,640	5,187
Long-term debt	729	687	833
Post-retirement benefit obligation (excl. pension plans)	394	412	426
Deferred taxes on income	156	253	166
Other noncurrent liabilities	819	721	611
Total liabilities	7,403	7,713	7,223

	1997	1996	1995
Total liabilities (from page 385)	7,403	7,713	7,223
Shareholders' Equity Preferred stock, without par value; 12 shares authorized, none issued -- --Common stock, $.05 par value; 3,000 shares authorized;			
issued: 1997--1,388; 1996--1,378; 1995--1,371	69	69	69
Additional paid-in capital	3,239	1,693	1,200
Retained earnings	9,349	8,017	6,859
Currency translation adjustment and other	(85)	145	163
Employee benefit trusts	(2,646)	(1,488)	(1,170)
Treasury stock, at cost: 1997--94; 1996--87; 1995--96	(1,993)	(1,482)	(1,615)
Total shareholders' equity	7,933	6,954	5,506
Total liabilities and shareholders' equity	$15,336	$14,667	$12,729

Required

a. Calculate the debt and equity composition ratios (vertical analysis) of each company for 1997 and 1996.
b. Which company has a lower risk of default on its long-term debt?
c. What is each company's apparent debt management strategy?
d. What other indicators might be used to assess each company's risk of default?
e. Concentrate specifically on each company's noncurrent liabilities. What items are similar for both companies? Different? Explain any unusual terms. What other information would you like to examine before fully answering all these questions?
f. Compare and contrast the 1997 and 1996 composition ratios for Eli Lilly and Pfizer. Which company seems to be the most conservative in managing its liabilities? Why? Does the relative difference in size of these two companies have an impact on your evaluation of each company's liabilities? Why?

Integration of Concepts

Comprehensive Financial Statement Analysis

9-53 Using a library or other information sources, obtain financial statements or summaries of financial information for one set of three companies in the same industry:

1. IBM	StorageTek	Compaq
2. UAL (United Airlines)	American Airlines (AMR)	Delta Air Lines
3. General Motors	Ford Motor Company	Chrysler

Required (for each company)

a. Examine the liability section of each company's balance sheet. Calculate the relevant subtotals for current liabilities, noncurrent liabilities, and shareholders' equity.
b. Identify any unusual trends and terms.
c. Read the relevant notes and identify any major measurement and valuation issues.
d. Calculate the debt and equity composition ratios.
e. Assess the relative changes in debt and equity for each year. Also identify the relative default and any other risks in these statements.

(Continued)

f. Calculate liquidity ratios for each company and evaluate your results.
g. Calculate profitability ratios and evaluate the results.
h. Identify any factors that may inhibit the comparability of these companies. Also compile any other information that is needed to make a better inter-company comparison.

Effects of Changing Debt Strategies

Critical Thinking

9-54 ALZA Corporation develops, manufactures, and markets therapeutic products that incorporate drugs into advanced dosage forms designed to provide controlled, predetermined rates of drug release for extended time periods. ALZA may be best known for its Nicoderm nicotine transdermal system. It reported the following liabilities in its 1994 and 1993 balance sheet:

Liabilities	1994	1993
	(Dollars in thousands)	
Short-term debt	$ —	$249,520
Accounts payable	20,006	11,678
Accrued liabilities	18,773	17,415
Deferred revenue	16,340	6,698
Current portion of long-term debt	869	867
Total current liabilities	$ 55,988	$286,178
5¼% zero coupon convertible subordinated debentures	$344,593	$ —
Other long-term liabilities	41,192	28,969
Total long-term liabilities	$385,785	$ 28,969

Required

a. Identify and describe any unfamiliar terms in ALZA's balance sheet (excerpts).
b. What strategic decision did ALZA implement in 1994? How do you know this?
c. Describe how this decision will affect ALZA's current ratio. How are its capital composition ratios affected?
d. Should ALZA's investors or creditors be unduly concerned about the decision of part b? Why?
e. ALZA's net income for 1994 and 1993, respectively, was $58,120,000 and $45,612,000. The "fine print" at the bottom of the financial highlights indicated that ALZA's 1993 net income includes "a $3.8 million ($.05 per share) extraordinary charge relating to the redemption of ALZA's 5¼% zero-coupon convertible subordinated debentures." How does this new information change your conclusions regarding ALZA's decision (see part b)?
f. How would your conclusions differ if ALZA's net income had only been $5 million each year?

Evaluating Liabilities: Restrictive Covenants

Critical Thinking

9-55 Tall Tree Timber, Inc., issued $10 million in long-term bonds that contained the following restrictive covenants:

- Current ratio must exceed 2.0.
- Return on assets must exceed 2%.
- Net income ratio must exceed 2%.
- Debt composition ratio must be less than 60%.

Tall Tree Timber's most recent financial results (dollars in millions) follow:

Current assets	$ 40	Current liabilities	$ 10
Property, plant, and equipment	55	Long-term debt	9
Other assets	10	Stockholders' equity	86
Total assets	$105	Total liabilities and stockholders' equity	$105
Net revenues	$600	Income tax rate	20%
Net income	$ 30	Interest expense	$ 5

Required

a. Compute the appropriate ratios described in the loan covenants and evaluate whether they have been met. Use ending total assets for average total assets.

b. Suppose the auditors find that revenues have been overstated by $38 million, thereby reducing revenues and reducing net income by $28 million net of tax. This new calculation will reduce stockholders' equity and current assets by $28 million. Recalculate the appropriate ratios and test whether the loan covenants have been met.

c. Alternatively, suppose Tall Tree changes its depletion allowance calculations (of natural trees). This new calculation will reduce stockholders' equity (net income) and property, plant, and equipment by $50 million. Again, recalculate the appropriate ratios and test whether the loan covenants have been met.

d. Alternatively, suppose Tall Tree Timber decides to switch from FIFO to LIFO and that such a switch will reduce current assets and stockholders' equity (net income) by $30 million. Again, recalculate the appropriate ratios and test whether the loan covenants have been met.

e. Which of the above scenarios would cause the greatest concern to bondholders? Would any of these likely result in default proceedings to redeem or "call" the bonds? Why?

Ethics

Calculating Bond Premium (or Discount) and Refinancing

9-56 Tall Tree Timber issued $10 million in bonds with a nominal interest rate of 8%, at a time when the market rate for similar bonds was 4%. The bonds have a four-year maturity and pay interest semiannually.

Required

a. Calculate the premium or discount on the issue date. Indicate how the bonds would be shown on Tall Tree Timber's balance sheet on the date of issue.

b. Calculate the interest expense and the cash outflows that would occur at the end of each semiannual period.

c. Tall Tree Timber anticipates refinancing the bonds at the end of the second year, in other words, after four semiannual periods have expired. To do so, it would issue $10 million of new 5% bonds at par. The firm has sufficient operating resources to pay for any other redemption costs, including the call premium of 2% over par.

   i. Calculate the cash flows associated with refinancing or refunding the old bonds. Also calculate the gain or loss to be recognized.

   ii. Evaluate whether the proposed refunding is advantageous for the firm's shareholders? Why?

d. Discuss the advantages and disadvantages of a GAAP requirement that all long-term debt must be shown at its current market value, rather than at its market value only on the issue date.

Internet

Analyzing Long-Term Debt and Calculating Appropriate Ratios

9-57 Retrieve the most recent 10-K filings for Kmart, Wal-Mart, Gillette, and Mem Co. from the EDGAR archives **(www.sec.gov/edaux/searches.htm).** Examine the long-term debt section of the Notes to the Financial Statements:

Required

a. Calculate the ratio of long-term debt to total assets for each company for the last two years. Comment on any changes that you observe.

b. Analyze the long-term debt for each company, using the following format:

Term to Maturity	**Interest Rates (Range)**
Due within one year	
Due in two years	
Due in three years	
Due in four years	
Due in five years and beyond	

c. Compare Kmart to Wal-Mart. Which company obtained better terms from its lenders? Why?

d. Compare Gillette to Mem. Which company obtained better terms from its lenders? Why?

Retirement of Long-term Debt

9-58 Many corporations retire part of their long-term debt prematurely (prior to maturity). Two such corporations are Kodak and Scotts Co. For each company, locate the 10-K filing for fiscal 1994 from the EDGAR archives **(www.sec.gov./edaux/searches.htm).**

Required

For each company determine:

a. Cash outflow for the debt retired

b. Face value of the debt retired and its associated stated interest rate

c. Impact of the retirement on the income statement

d. Long-term debt-to-total assets ratio for 1993 and 1994 (What impact did the retirement have on this ratio?)

e. Net income as a percentage of sales for 1993 and 1994 (What impact did the retirement have on this ratio?)

Deferred Taxes: Interpreting Financial Statements

9-59 Refer to Wendy's financial statements in Appendix D. Review the balance sheet to determine how and where deferred taxes were reported.

Required

a. Read Note 6, "Income Taxes." Identify and discuss any unusual terms. Also trace disclosures of deferred taxes in the notes to corresponding disclosures in the financial statements.

b. Determine whether Wendy's has a net long-term deferred tax liability. If it is not a liability, determine what it is and how Wendy's managers might view the income tax carryforward.

c. Identify the years where Wendy's income taxes paid (shown at the bottom of the cash flow statement) as a percentage of income before tax was close to the statutory rate. Identify the years where Wendy's paid less. Did it ever pay more than the overall statutory rate?

d. Discuss any other unusual concerns regarding Wendy's deferred taxes. What other related information might an external analyst prefer?

Deferred Taxes: Interpreting Financial Statements

9-60 Refer to Reebok's financial statements in Appendix E. Review the balance sheet to determine how and where deferred taxes were reported.

Required

a. Read Notes 1 and 14. Identify and discuss any unusual terms. Also trace disclosures of deferred taxes in the notes to corresponding disclosures in the financial statements.
b. Determine whether Reebok has a deferred tax liability. If it is not a liability, determine what it is and how Reebok's managers might view its deferred income taxes.
c. Identify the years where Reebok's income taxes paid (shown at the bottom of the cash flow statement) as a percentage of income before taxes was close to the statutory rate. Also identify any years where Reebok paid less. Did it ever pay more than the overall statutory rate?
d. Discuss any other unusual concerns regarding Reebok's deferred taxes. What other related information might an external analyst prefer?

Income Tax Expense, Tax Payable, and Deferred Tax Liability: Change in Tax Rates

9-61 Selected information from the income statements and tax returns of Buchanan Trading Co. are provided below for 1999 and 2000, the firm's first two years of operations (dollars in millions):

	Selected Income Statement Items	
	1999	**2000**
Income before depreciation and taxes	$1000	$1100
Depreciation expense	400	450
Pre-tax income	600	650
Income tax expense (35%)	210	227.5

	Selected Tax Items	
	1999	**2000**
Income before depreciation and taxes	$1000	$1100
Depreciation expense	700	800
Taxable income	300	300
Income tax payable (35%)	105	105

Required

Determine the following amounts:

a. Difference between the tax basis and book basis of Buchanan's assets at the end of each year.
b. Deferred tax liabilities at the end of each year.
c. In the year 2001, Buchanan Trading Company reported $800 million of depreciation in its income statement and $600 million of depreciation on its tax return. The firm's income before depreciation and income taxes was $950 million. Enacted income tax rates applicable to firms such as Buchanan were increased to 45% effective at the beginning of the year 2001. Based on this new information, determine Buchanan's income tax expense and net income after tax reported on its income statement for the year 2001. Calculate the deferred tax liability reported on its balance sheet at December 31, 2001.

Tax Expense, Tax Payable, Deferred Tax Liability, and Stable Tax Rate

9-62 Wilbur Mills, Inc., began operations in 1999. The firm recognized $12 million of depreciation expense on its income statement and reported $20 million as depreciation on its tax return for 1999. The 1999 income statement shows pre-tax income of $10 million with an income tax rate of 40%.

Required

Determine the following amounts for 1999:

a. Income tax expense.
b. Income tax payable.
c. Difference between the book and tax bases of Wilbur Mills' assets at year-end.
d. Deferred tax liability at year-end.

Tax Expense, Tax Payable, and Deferred Tax Liability: Changing Tax Rate

9-63 During 2000, Wilbur Mills, Inc., recognized an additional $12 million of depreciation expense on its income statement and reported $16 million as depreciation on its tax return. During 2000, the statutory income tax rate was reduced from 40 to 35%, effective at the beginning of 2000. Pre-tax income was $14 million.

Required

Determine the following amounts for 2000:

a. Income tax expense.
b. Income tax payable.
c. Difference between the book and tax bases of Wilbur Mills' assets at year-end.
d. Deferred tax liability at year-end.
e. Percentage relationship between pre-tax income and income tax expense reported in the income statement.

Tax Expense, Tax Payable, and Deferred Tax Liability: Effects of Tax Rate Changes

9-64 Rosty Co. began operations in 2000. The firm recognized $30 million of depreciation expense on its income statement and reported $50 million as depreciation on its 2000 tax return. The firm's income was taxed at 30%, and pre-tax income was $25 million.

Required

Determine the following:

a. Tax liability.
b. Deferred tax liability at the end of the year.
c. Difference between the book and tax bases of Rosty's assets at the end of the year.
d. Income tax expense.
e. During 2001, Rosty Co. recognized an additional $30 million of depreciation expense on its income statement and reported $40 million as depreciation on its tax return. During 2001, the statutory income tax rate applicable to firms such as Rosty Co. increased from 30 to 40%. Pre-tax income in 2001 was $12 million. Determine the following amounts:

(Continued)

i. Difference between the book and tax bases of Rosty's assets at the end of 2001.
ii. Deferred tax liability at the end of 2001.
iii. Tax liability for 2001.
iv. Income tax expense for 2001.
v. Percentage relationship between pre-tax income and income tax expense reported in the 2001 income statement.

Financial Statement Effects of Deferred Taxes

9-65 Gottlieb Enterprises is concerned about its balance sheet disclosures of deferred tax liabilities. Gottlieb's preliminary balance sheet at the end of 2000 is summarized as:

Current assets	$ 400,000	Current liabilities	$ 250,000
Fixed assets, net	1,400,000	Long-term debt	500,000
		Shareholders' equity	1,050,000
Total assets	$1,800,000	Total liabilities and shareholders' equity	$1,800,000

Gottlieb's tax return shows that the net book value of its fixed assets for tax purposes is only $900,000.

Required

a. Based on the above information, compute Gottlieb's deferred tax liability at the end of 2000, assuming a 38% average tax rate.
b. Assume that Gottlieb has already calculated a deferred tax liability of $250,000 at the beginning of 2000 and has included it erroneously in shareholders' equity. Calculate the change in Gottlieb's deferred tax liability.
c. Based on your answer in part b, indicate how Gottlieb's income tax expense must have been affected by these tax deferrals.
d. Prepare Gottlieb's corrected balance sheet at the end of 2000.
e. Discuss why it is important for a firm to disclose its deferred tax liabilities. To illustrate this importance, compare Gottlieb's balance sheet shown earlier with the corrected balance sheet from part d.

Financial Statement Effects of Deferred Taxes

9-66 Tyler Corporation's statement of operations is summarized below (dollars in thousands):

	2000	1999	1998
Net sales	$357,850	$282,403	$286,206
Costs and expenses:			
Cost of sales	256,195	221,024	223,826
Selling, general, and administrative expense	103,402	57,972	55,667
Interest expense, net	3,820	487	608
Total costs and expenses	363,417	279,483	280,101
Income (loss) before income tax (benefit)	(5,567)	2,920	6,105
Income tax (benefit)			
Current	(859)	2,649	4,051
Deferred	(7)	(1,067)	(1,181)
	(866)	1,582	2,870
Income (loss) before cumulative changes	(4,701)	1,338	3,235
Cumulative effect of changes in accounting principles		(3,601)	
Net income (loss)	$ (4,701)	$ (2,263)	$ 3,235

Required

1. Explain the item "Income tax (benefit)." How can income tax be positive? That is, how can income tax be deducted from income before tax in 1998 and 1999, and added in 2000?
2. Calculate the following ratios for 2000 and 1999:
   a. Operating income.
   b. Net income.
   c. ROE. Assume that average stockholders for 2000 and 1999 are $114,000 and $117,000 (dollars in thousands). *Note*: You may want to take out non-recurring items before calculating the ratios.
3. Evaluate Tyler's performance during 1999 and 2000.

Deferred Taxes

9-67 The following information was reported by Pfizer, Inc., in its 1997 Financial Report:

	(Dollars in millions)
Income before income taxes	$3,088
Provision (expense) for income tax	865
Income taxes paid currently	856
Deferred tax liabilities related to depreciating assets:	
December 31,1996	253
December 31,1997	156

Required

Based on the information provided above,

a. Determine Pfizer's effective income tax rate during 1997.
b. Determine the percentage relation between Pfizer's actual tax payments and income before taxes during 1997.
c. Provide a likely reason for the difference between the percentages determined in parts a and b above.
d. Assume that Pfizer's statutory tax rate is 32%. What would you estimate as the difference between the tax basis and the book basis of Pfizer's depreciable assets at the end of 1996? at the end of 1997? What does this change during 1997 imply about the relative amounts of depreciation expense in Pfizer's tax return and financial statements in 1997?

Interpreting Deferred Taxes

Critical Thinking

9-68 Sigma Designs' statement of operations is summarized below (dollars in thousands):

	1995	1994	1993
Net sales	$43,700	$ 34,989	$27,058
Costs and expenses:			
Cost of sales	36,980	27,538	23,045
Restructuring charges	(517)	13,654	0
Sales and marketing	9,022	9,448	7,476
Research and development	4,349	11,988	5,043
General and administrative	3,521	2,718	1,951
Total cost and expenses	53,355	65,346	37,515
Income (loss) from operations	(9,655)	(30,357)	(10,457)
Interest income—net	336	699	1,207
Other net	546	(39)	(67)
Income (loss) before income taxes	(8,773)	(29,697)	(9,317)
Provision (credit) for income taxes	—	(151)	(2,151)
Net income (loss)	$(8,773)	$(29,546)	$(7,166)

Required

a. Explain the item "Provision (credit) for income taxes." How can income taxes be positive? That is, how can income taxes be added to income?
b. How does this new interpretation about deferred taxes (see part a) affect your evaluation of Sigma Design's profitability? Calculate relevant income statement ratios using both "bottom line" net income and any other income figures that you deem relevant. Be sure to calculate the net income ratio on an after-tax basis. Calculate any other appropriate ratios and evaluate Sigma Design's performance for 1995. Assume interest expense is $200 (dollars in thousands).

Interpreting Deferred Taxes

Critical Thinking

9-69 Waco Rubber Co. disclosed the following items in its 1999 financial statements:

	1999	1998
Current assets		
Deferred income tax benefit	$1,894,550	$4,139,205
Current liabilities		
Deferred income taxes payable	—	236,543

Required

a. Discuss the nature of each of these deferred tax items. How should an analyst use these data?
b. Upon further examination of Waco's notes to its financial statements, you find the following additional disclosures:

> On December 31, 1999, the Company had NOL [non-operating loss] carryforwards for federal income tax and financial reporting purposes of approximately $15,000,000 and $34,000,000, respectively, available to offset future taxable income. These carryforwards will expire at various dates between 2003 and 2000. Using a portion of both the federal income tax carryforward and the financial reporting loss is restricted, based upon the purchase price of two subsidiaries of the company.

Based on this new information, reconsider the two items shown in Waco's balance sheet. Why might they be so different? How much future benefit might really occur?

c. Upon further examination of Waco notes to its financial statements, you find no further disclosures or explanations of the above items shown on its balance sheet. In fact, the company only disclosed details relating to $338,000 of deferred tax provisions in 1999 and to $839,000 of deferred tax provisions (benefits) in 1998. What other information would you find helpful in order to analyze and interpret Waco's financial statements?

c h a p t e r

10

Shareholders' Equity

LEARNING OBJECTIVES

1. Understand why large business firms prefer to organize as corporations.
2. Comprehend the types of transactions and events that affect the components of shareholders' equity.
3. Interpret shareholders' equity ratios that are helpful in analyzing financial statements.

INTRODUCTION

Corporations are the dominant form of business organization in advanced industrial nations such as the United States. Although they only represent about 25 percent of business firms, they generate about 80 percent of business revenues. A corporation is an entity that is owned by its shareholders and raises **equity capital** by selling shares of stock to investors. Equity capital is an ownership interest in the corporation and each share of stock represents a fractional interest in the issuing firm. It's important to note that equity capital is *not* a liability to be repaid at a future date.

Most major corporations' stock is traded (bought and sold) on major security exchanges, such as the New York and American Stock Exchanges. For business managers, a primary advantage of the corporate form of organization is the capability to raise large amounts of cash by selling shares of stock to many different individuals and institutions (such as mutual funds, insurance companies, and pension plans), rather than relying on the investments of a few owners and lenders.

Stockholders expect to earn returns on their investments in the form of **dividends** and **capital gains.** Dividends are distributions of assets, usually cash, that the corporation elects to make periodically to its stockholders. Capital gains (or losses) result from increases (or decreases) in the market price of stocks over the period during which an investor holds them. Neither the payment of dividends nor the appreciation in stock prices is guaranteed to the equity investor. Instead, the capability of a corporation to generate cash through profitable operations determines its capability to pay dividends and also influences the market price of its stock.

A corporation comes into existence when its **charter** is approved by the state in which it chooses to locate and incorporate. State laws vary, so consequently many features of corporations depend on the state in which a firm incorporates. Among other things, the charter indicates the corporation's business purpose and authorizes the firm to issue one or more types of ownership shares. The most basic type of ownership share is **common stock.** Common shareholders are the true **residual owners** of a corporation. After all other claims against a firm's assets have been satisfied, the common shareholders own what remains. This view of shareholders' equity is apparent when we write the basic balance sheet equation in the following way:

$$\text{SHAREHOLDERS' EQUITY} = \text{ASSETS} - \text{LIABILITIES}$$

This expression shows that the value of shareholders' equity reported on a firm's balance sheet is determined by the valuation of its assets and liabilities. Recall that financial accounting reports use historical costs rather than current market prices in evaluating the firm's assets and liabilities. For this reason, the reported value of shareholders' equity does not attempt to measure the market value of the firm's outstanding shares of stock.

Shareholders' equity comes primarily from two sources: **invested (paid-in) capital** and **retained earnings.** Invested capital is the amount received by the corporation after the sale of its stock to investors. Note that invested capital usually includes two components: **par value** and **additional paid-in capital.** For our purposes, we will concentrate on the sum of these parts, not on the individual components. Retained earnings are the amount of prior earnings that the firm has reinvested in the business, that is, the portion that has not been paid to shareholders as dividends. Exhibit 10–1 shows the shareholders' equity section from the 1997 balance sheet of E. I. Du Pont de Nemours and Company (Du Pont). Note that Du Pont's total shareholders' equity at the end of 1997 was $11,270 (in millions of dollars). Of that amount, $8,574 was received from the sale of stock to investors, $4,389 represented past earnings that were reinvested in the firm's operations, and $1,693 represented reductions in shareholders' equity from various other sources. For most profitable firms, retained earnings represents the major part of shareholders' equity.

The description of DuPont's common stock in Exhibit 10–1 distinguishes between the number of common shares that are **authorized** and **issued.** Authorized shares are those that the firm is permitted to issue according to its corporate charter.

EXHIBIT 10-1 Shareholders' Equity Components

Du Pont Company
1997 Annual Report
Shareholders' Equity (partial)
(Dollars in Millions)

	December 31, 1997	**December 31, 1996**
Shareholders' equity:		
Preferred stock	$ 237	$ 237
Common stock: $0.30 par value; 1,800,000,000 shares authorized; 1,152,762,128 shares and 1,158,085,450 shares issued and outstanding	346	347
Additional paid-in capital	7,991	6,676
Reinvested earnings	4,389	4,931
Other items (net)	(1,693)	(1,598)
Total shareholders' equity	$11,270	$10,593

Some of the issued shares may have been repurchased and held as treasury stock, as is explained later in the chapter.

Exhibit 10–1 also shows that Du Pont's common stock has been assigned a par value of $0.30 per share, and the total par value of the outstanding shares is reported separately on the balance sheet. Although for legal purposes the shares of most firms have a designated par or stated value, this value is usually a minor amount compared to the actual market price of the stock. For example, although Du Pont's common stock has a par value of just $0.30 per share, the stock has a market price per share of about $62 at the end of 1997.

BASIC TRANSACTIONS AFFECTING STOCKHOLDERS' EQUITY

Three basic transactions account for most of the changes that occur in shareholders' equity:

1. Sale of stock to investors
2. Recognition of periodic net income or loss
3. Declaration of cash dividends to shareholders

Each of these transactions is examined in this section. Other less frequent types of transactions are discussed in a subsequent section.

Sale of Stock to Investors

Suppose that Du Pont's management decides to issue an additional 10 million shares of stock to investors, and the market price is $70 per share of stock. In this case, Du Pont would receive a total of $700 million ($70 × 10 million shares) from investors. In this example, note that we are ignoring any transactions costs, such as fees and commissions incurred by the issuing firm. The transaction would increase cash and invested capital by $700 million. The invested capital would consist of $3 million in par value (10 million shares × $0.30 par value per share), and $697 million in capital invested in excess of par value ($700 million total invested minus $3 million recorded as par value).

ASSETS	=	LIABILITIES	+	SHAREHOLDERS' EQUITY	
Cash				Par value	Additional paid-in capital
+$700 million				+3 million	+$697 million

Managers would immediately put these funds to work to earn returns for the shareholders, such as by investing in additional plant and equipment. In other words, the transaction to issue shares of stock is immediately followed by many other transactions in which the money is used for some corporate purpose.

In some instances, noncash items can be received when stock is issued to investors. Examples include noncash assets, such as property or intangible assets, and services, such as work from a company's attorneys.

Recognition of Periodic Net Income or Loss

Business firms must periodically determine the amount of net income (or loss) from their activities. Net income (loss) represents an increase (or decrease) in a firm's shareholder equity, or net assets, due to its revenues, expenses, gains, and losses during the period. For example, Du Pont earned $2,405 million of net income during 1997 and paid $1,401 million as dividends. In addition, other items reduced Du Pont's retained earnings by $1,546. Note the amounts of Du Pont's retained earnings shown in Exhibit 10–1 at the beginning and the end of 1997. These amounts (millions of dollars) are related in the following way:

Retained earnings, December 31, 1996	$ 4,931
Add: Net income during 1997	+ **2,405**
Less: Dividends declared during 1997	− **1,401**
Other changes(net)	− 1,546
Retained earnings, December 31, 1997	$ 4,389

Declaration and Payment of Cash Dividends

Du Pont paid dividends of $1,401 million to its shareholders in 1997. On the date of declaration, the dividend became a liability because Du Pont obligated itself to make the dividend payment. On that date, retained earnings were decreased and liabilities were increased by $1,401 million:

ASSETS	=	LIABILITIES	+	SHAREHOLDERS' EQUITY
		Dividends payable +$1,401 million		Retained earnings −$1,401 million

Management also specified a **date of record,** and the dividend was paid to investors who owned the shares on that specific date. Subsequently, the stock was considered *ex dividend*, which means that subsequent purchasers were not entitled to receive the previously declared dividend. On the **date of payment,** Du Pont's cash and dividends payable (liability) were reduced by $1,401 million:

ASSETS	=	LIABILITIES	+	SHAREHOLDERS' EQUITY
Cash −$1,401 million		Dividends payable −$1,401 million		

Observe that the change in retained earnings over a period is due primarily to the difference between a firm's net income and dividends during the period. The ending balance in retained earnings reflects the total net income of the firm in all past periods, less the total amount of dividends to shareholders, plus or minus the effects of any other adjustments.

ADDITIONAL TRANSACTIONS AFFECTING STOCKHOLDERS' EQUITY

In addition to the three basic transactions discussed in the last section, a variety of other, less frequent occurrences may affect the reported amount and composition of shareholders' equity. This section examines several of these additional types of transactions and events.

Stock Dividends

On occasion, firms distribute additional shares of stock to shareholders in proportion to the number of shares presently owned. If a firm declares a one percent **stock dividend,** for example, this means that existing shareholders will receive additional shares equal to one percent of their present holdings. In this case, a shareholder with 100 shares would receive an additional share (1% × 100 shares) as a stock dividend.

Stock dividends reduce retained earnings in an amount equal to the value of the stock that is distributed. As an example, assume that the Flotsam Company has 10 million common shares issued and outstanding and declares a two percent stock dividend when the market price of its stock is $45 per share. The firm will distribute an additional 200,000 shares (2% × 10 million shares = 200,000 shares), and the total value of the dividend is $9 million ($45 × 200,000 shares = $9 million). Retained earnings will decrease, and paid-in capital will increase, by $9 million. The number of shares outstanding will also increase by two percent.

ASSETS	=	LIABILITIES	+	SHAREHOLDERS' EQUITY	
Cash				Paid-in capital	Retained earnings
				+ $9 million	− $9 million

Notice that this transaction does not affect the firm's assets and liabilities, and therefore does not affect total shareholders' equity. The *composition* of shareholders' equity is affected, however. The transaction decreases retained earnings and creates an off-setting increase in paid-in capital.

As a stockholder of 100 shares of Flotsam Company, would you be better off as a result of the stock dividend? Although it is true that you have received two additional shares of stock, your proportionate interest in Flotsam remains unchanged. Moreover, because the company's assets and liabilities are unchanged, the stock dividend has no direct effect on Flotsam's operating capability. In fact, the market price of each share of stock could decline just enough to leave the total value of your investment unchanged (100 shares × old price = 102 shares × new price).

Surprisingly, stock dividends do appear to benefit existing shareholders. The market price per share of existing shares usually does not decline sufficiently to offset the effect of issuing additional shares. Some analysts suggest that this otherwise puzzling result may be due to the use of stock dividends as a "signal to the market" by managers that the firm expects higher profits and cash flows in the future. Managers may be reluctant to make public forecasts about future earnings increases, however, and may instead prefer to communicate their favorable expectations by less direct actions such as stock dividends.

Stock Splits

Stock splits are distinct from stock dividends and involve an exchange of multiple shares of stock for existing outstanding shares. In a two-for-one stock split, for example, each "old" share held by existing shareholders can be exchanged for two "new" shares. Unlike stock dividends, stock splits usually do not entail a reduction in retained earnings nor an increase in paid-in capital. In fact, stock splits usually do not change any of the elements in the financial statements. Only the description of the firm's stock is amended to reflect the new number of shares authorized, issued, and outstanding.

Managers may split a firm's stock when they believe that the price per share has risen beyond the range that is attractive to smaller investors. Therefore, splitting the shares is expected to reduce the share price and increase demand. Similar to stock dividends, stock splits also seem to be interpreted by investors as favorable signals by management about future operating performance. Stock splits usually result in an increase in the total market value of the firm's outstanding shares because the price per share typically does not decline sufficiently to offset the increase in the number of shares. For example, a two-for-one stock split usually does not cut the price per share in half.

Reality Check 10–1 shows how a stock split is reported by one major corporation.

Treasury Stock

Firms sometimes repurchase their own outstanding shares and hold them for future use. Such repurchased shares are termed **treasury stock** and are no longer outstanding, although they continue to be labeled as "issued."

A variety of motives lead managers to acquire treasury stock. For example, managers may consider the stock to be undervalued in the stock market and to be a "good buy" that can be resold later at a higher price. Also, treasury stock purchases can be preferable to dividend payments as a way of reducing a firm's shareholders' equity. Note that this use of treasury stock depends on income tax features that are beyond the scope of this text. In addition, treasury stock purchases can enable managers to "buy out" certain groups of shareholders in order to re-align votes on future issues of corporate policy. Treasury stock can also be distributed to employees under an employee stock option plan.

The acquisition of treasury stock reduces both cash and shareholders' equity.

REALITY CHECK 10-1

A footnote to the 1997 financial statements of Du Pont Company includes the following information:

The company's common stock was split two-for-one effective May 15, 1997; all per-share data and common stock information have been restated to reflect this split.

Required

a. Why does Du Pont give retroactive recognition to the stock split in all related financial statement references?
b. Why do you suppose Du Pont's management decided to split the company's stock?
c. As an existing Du Pont shareholder, would you be pleased by management's decision to split your stock? Explain.

Solution

a. Du Pont gives retroactive recognition to the stock split in order to aid analysts in making comparisons with prior years. For example, if net income is unchanged from the prior year and the number of shares is *not* retroactively adjusted, the earnings per share would appear to decrease by 50 percent.
b. The company may have split the stock in order to reduce the per-share price, thereby making the stock more accessible for smaller investors. Alternatively, management may use stock splits as an indirect way to signal investors that management expects higher per share earnings and dividends in the future.
c. Generally, existing shareholders benefit from stock splits. Although each shareholder's fractional interest in Du Pont is not changed by the stock split, the total value of existing shares usually increases around the date of such announcements. The increase in stock prices may reflect investor expectations of higher future cash flows.

In this sense, treasury stock acquisitions are the opposite of a shareholder investment. The cost of treasury shares is usually subtracted from total shareholders' equity. For this reason, the purchase price of treasury stock is a **contra-equity account.**

To illustrate the reporting of treasury stock, Exhibit 10–2 shows the shareholders' equity portion of Handy Corporation's balance sheet at the end of 2001. As of that date, Handy has paid $6,722,000 to acquire its treasury stock. This amount is subtracted when computing Handy's total shareholders' equity. We can infer that the treasury stock purchase has the following effect on Handy's balance sheet:

Suppose that Handy sold the treasury stock at a greater amount, say $10 million,

ASSETS	=	LIABILITIES	+	SHAREHOLDERS' EQUITY
Cash – $6,722,000				Treasury Stock – $6,722,000*

*Although treasury stock has been increased by $6,722,000, this represents a decrease in shareholders' equity because treasury stock is a contra-equity account. Also note that the common stock account has not changed because the repurchased stock has not been retired. It is being held for future use.

EXHIBIT 10-2 Treasury Stock Reporting

Handy Corporation
2001 Annual Report
Treasury Stock Reporting
(Dollars in Thousands)

	December 31, 2001	December 31, 2000
Shareholders' equity:		
Common stock: $.01 par value, 50,000 shares authorized, 21,309,277 shares issued	$ 213	$ 213
Capital surplus	48,587	49,109
Retained earnings	68,220	72,921
	117,020	122,243
Less 1,450,178 treasury shares in 2001 and 1,011,046 treasury shares in 2000, at cost	6,722	4,279
Total shareholders' equity	$110,298	$117,964

at a future date. Generally accepted accounting principles (GAAP) do not allow the recognition of gains or losses due to transactions in a firm's own stock. Consequently, Handy's cash increases by $10 million, the treasury stock is eliminated, and paid-in capital increases by the difference of $3,278,000 ($10,000,000 – 6,722,000).

ASSETS	=	LIABILITIES	+	SHAREHOLDERS' EQUITY	
Cash				Invested capital	Treasury Stock
+$10,000,000				+3,278,000	+$6,722,000*

*Although treasury stock has been decreased, this represents an increase in shareholders' equity because treasury stock is a contra-equity account.

Employee Stock Options

Stock options are rights to purchase a firm's stock at a specific price at some designated period in the future. Although stock options are sometimes sold directly to investors, they are usually granted as part of the compensation paid to key executives and other employees. Stock options, as a means of compensation, offer several distinct benefits to firms and employees. Because the value of stock options depends on the future market price of the firm's stock, option holders are highly motivated to improve the performance of the firm. Actions that benefit the firm's stockholders also directly benefit the option holders. As a result, managers and other employees who hold stock options have the same objective as company shareholders: to make the firm's equity securities more valuable. In addition, although option holders gain if the price of the optioned stock subsequently rises, they avoid the "downside risk" of loss if the stock price declines. If the stock price is below the option price, the option simply will not be exercised.

A more arguable advantage of stock options from the firm's point of view is the manner in which options are currently handled in financial statements. Current accounting rules allow firms to choose between two different ways of reporting the cost of employee stock options, based either on intrinsic values or fair values of the options at the date of grant. The **intrinsic value** method measures the compensation cost of stock options as the excess of the stock's market price over the option price at the date of the grant. Because most employee options are granted at or above market value, firms that elect this method do not recognize any compensation expense associated with the options. Under the alternative **fair value** method, compensation expense is measured at the grant date based on the estimated fair market value of the award. Fair values of options must be estimated based on a theoretical model and various assumptions. Estimated stock option values and related compensation expenses can vary significantly, depending on the assumptions used and the model selected.

To illustrate how stock options for employees are treated when the issuing firm employs the intrinsic value method, assume that Jetsom Inc. issued options to its employees to purchase one million shares of its common stock in 2001 at an option price of $10 per share, equal to the market price at the date of the grant. Subsequently, in 2005, assume that all the options were exercised when Jetsom's market price per share had risen to $90.

For financial statement purposes, Jetsom records no compensation expense in 2001 when the options are granted. In 2005, when the options are exercised, Jetsom records the cash proceeds of $10 million ($10 × 1 million shares) as an issuance of common stock for cash.

ASSETS	=	LIABILITIES	+	SHAREHOLDERS' EQUITY
Cash				Invested Capital
+$10 million				+$10 million

Although this method of accounting for stock options is presently followed by U.S. firms, opponents of current practice argue that in situations like the Jetsom case the granting of stock options in 2001 should entail the recognition of compensation expense. The grantees were given valuable rights that might otherwise have been sold to other investors. Moreover, in 2005, Jetsom's optioned shares had a market value of $90 million, yet these options had been issued to the option holders for only $10 million in cash. In retrospect, granting the options in 2001 seems to have cost Jetsom $80 million ($90 million market value less $10 million proceeds). Consequently, some accountants believe that reported compensation expense is understated and reported net income is overstated.

The value of employee stock options is often substantial in specific industries. In high-technology companies that rely heavily on stock options to attract and retain talented employees, it is estimated that stock-option-related compensation expenses, if measured using fair values, reduce net income anywhere from 10 to 100 percent ("Options' Effect On Earnings Sparks Debate," *WSJ*, May 13, 1998). For this reason, companies that elect not to recognize compensation expense using the fair value method must show net income and earnings per share in a footnote to the financial statements as if the fair value method had been used. Reality Check 10–2 shows a portion of such a footnote for a major technology company.

Preferred Stock

In addition to common stock, firms often issue **preferred stock,** which has a priority claim over common stock with respect to dividends. In addition, if the firm should liquidate its assets and cease to exist, preferred shareholders' claims would be satisfied before any assets were distributed to the common stockholders.

The description of preferred stock in corporate financial reports discloses the special features of the stock issue. To illustrate, Exhibit 10–3 shows the description of Sequel Corporation's preferred stock contained in its 2001 annual report. Sequel's preferred shares have an annual dividend of $5 per share. Analysts would also note that Sequel's preferred shares are cumulative and convertible. **Cumulative** indicates that if the firm does not declare a dividend in any year, the amount accumulates and must be paid before any dividends are paid to common stockholders. If Sequel did not pay dividends for three years, for example, then a cumulative dividend of $15 per share ($5 × 3 years) must be paid to preferred shareholders before dividends are paid to common shareholders.

Convertible preferred shares can be exchanged for common shares at the preferred shareholders' option. To illustrate, each share of Sequel's preferred stock is converted into 1.322 shares of common stock. Presently, 797,000 shares of preferred stock have been issued. If the entire issue were to be converted to common stock, then Sequel would issue 1,053,634 common shares (797,000 preferred shares × 1.322 exchange ratio) and would retire the preferred stock. In this case, the preferred stock component of shareholders' equity is eliminated and transferred to common stock. Note that the conversion of preferred stock does not change total shareholders' equity. Assets and liabilities are also unaffected. The number of common shares outstanding increases, however, and the preferred stock's dividend requirement is eliminated.

Convertible Debt

Firms that borrow by issuing bonds frequently include a conversion privilege in the bond contract. **Convertible bonds** allow the bondholder to exchange the bonds for a specified number of shares of stock. As an example, let's assume that in 2001 the

REALITY CHECK 10-2

Digital Equipment Corporation, a leading developer and producer of computer hardware and software, reports the following information in its 1997 financial statements:

Stock options granted during 1997: 3,750,800 shares at an average exercise price of $36.30 per share.
Stock options exercised during 1997: 647,222 shares at an average exercise price of $21.01 per share.

Net income (loss) applicable to common shareholders, as reported in the income statement:

	1997	1996
Total	$105,375,000	$(147,312,000)
Per common share	$ .68	$ (.97)

Net income (loss) applicable to common shareholders if stock options granted during the year were valued at fair value:

	1997	1996
Total	$36,198,000	$(188,040,000)
Per common share	$ .23	$ (1.24)

Required

a. By how much does the market value of the shares after the exercise of the stock options during 1997 differ from the exercise proceeds received by the company? Would this difference affect your assessment of Digital's compensation expense for 1997?

b. Digital uses the intrinsic value method to account for the cost of employee stock-based compensation. As a result, Digital did not recognize any expenses related to these stock options in 1997. How much would the compensation expense have differed in each year if the firm used the fair value method to measure this compensation expense?

Solution

a. The market value of the shares issued by Digital after the exercise of options during 1997 was $23,494,158 (647,222 shares × $36.30 per share). The exercise proceeds received by the company was $13,598,134 (647,222 shares × $21.01 per share). The difference between these amounts is $9,896,024 ($23,494,158 − $13,598,134). This difference represents the additional economic value of Digital's shares above the amounts received from the option holders. Some analysts suggest that this additional value should be regarded as compensation cost.

b. The differences in compensation costs can be determined by comparing the net income amounts reported in the income statements and the amounts in the footnotes. In 1997 the compensation expense would be higher by $69,177,000 ($105,375,000 − 36,198,000), and in 1996 the compensation expense would be higher by $40,728,000 ($188,040,000 − $147,312,000). Note that in both years the additional expenses related to the stock options are substantially higher than the amount computed.

EXHIBIT 10-3 Reporting of Preferred Stock

Sequel Corporation
2001 Annual Report
Footnote Disclosures of Preferred Stock (Partial)

Capital Stock
The Company's capital stock consists of Class A and Class B common stock, and $5.00 cumulative convertible preferred stock.

Each share of $5.00 cumulative convertible preferred stock is convertible into 1.322 shares of Class A common stock. On December 31, 2001, 4,543,636 shares of Sequel Class A common stock were reserved for conversion of preferred and Class B common stock and stock options. On December 31, 2001, 5,724 Class B common shares were reserved for stock options. The preferred stock is redeemable, at the option of the Company, at $100 per share.

Aloha Company's long-term debt included $150 million principal in convertible bonds payable, exchangeable for common stock at $15 per share at any time before the year 2002. If all the bondholders elected to convert to common stock, Aloha would then issue 10 million shares of common stock ($150 million bond principal ÷ $15 conversion price). Aloha's bonds payable would be reduced, and paid-in capital would be increased by $150 million:

ASSETS	=	LIABILITIES	+	SHAREHOLDERS' EQUITY
		Bonds Payable − $150 million		Paid-in Capital + $150 million

Note that the conversion of debt to common stock reduces the firm's liabilities and increases shareholders' equity. The number of common shares outstanding is increased, and the periodic interest expense is eliminated.

Convertible bonds such as those issued by Aloha are **hybrid securities.** A hybrid security is neither clearly debt nor clearly equity. Instead, it combines certain features of both types of securities. In the case of convertible bonds, the bondholder is in one sense a lender and owns the firm's promise to make future interest and principal payments. In another sense, the holder of a convertible bond holds an option to acquire a specified number of common shares at a fixed price at any time over the life of the bond issue. In fact, investors in convertible bonds are willing to pay for this combination of debt and equity features. Convertible bonds generally are issued at higher prices (in other words, at lower interest rates) than nonconvertible debt.

The proper way to account for hybrid securities is a matter of debate. Present accounting standards reflect the view that convertible debt is to be reported as debt until it is actually converted and as equity thereafter. No recognition is given in the financial statements to the likelihood that conversion will actually occur, or to the relative values to investors of the hybrid security's debt and equity features.

Opponents of present practice argue that it is misleading to ignore the hybrid nature of convertible securities. In the case of debt, they argue that the issue price should be apportioned between the amount the investor is paying for the debt features and the additional amount being paid for the conversion privilege. Ignoring these separate elements, they contend, causes the financial statements to overvalue the firm's reported liabilities, undervalue its shareholders' equity, and understate periodic interest expense. To address these and related issues, the FASB is pursuing a comprehensive financial instruments project. The project aims to identify the component claims that are bundled in hybrid financial assets and liabilities and to develop appropriate methods of valuation for these components.

EARNINGS PER SHARE

Perhaps the most widely cited number in corporate financial reports is **earnings per share (EPS).** EPS focuses on the common stock and indicates the portion of total company income that is applicable to a single share of common stock. The reporting of EPS depends upon whether the firm has a **simple** or a **complex capital structure.** A simple capital structure includes no "potential" common equity securities other than common stock outstanding. A complex capital structure includes, in addition to common stock, other securities or agreements that represent potential issues of common stock. Examples of potential issues of common stock include outstanding stock options as well as convertible bonds and convertible preferred stocks. Firms with a simple capital structure report a measure of **basic EPS**, and firms with a complex capital structure report measures of basic and **diluted EPS**. The calculations of basic and diluted EPS are explained and illustrated below.

Basic EPS

Basic EPS is computed by dividing income available to the common stockholders by the average number of shares outstanding:

$$\text{EPS} = \frac{\text{Net income available for common shareholders}}{\text{Average number of common shares outstanding}}$$

For example, Starbright Company reported net income of $99 million in 2001 and had 45 million shares of common stock outstanding throughout the entire year. Starbright's 2001 EPS is $2.20, calculated as follows:

$$\begin{aligned} \text{EPS} &= \frac{\$99 \text{ million}}{45 \text{ million shares}} \\ &= \$2.20 \end{aligned}$$

Basic EPS Calculations with Changes in Shares Outstanding It is unusual for a large firm's **outstanding shares** to remain constant throughout the year. Additional stock transactions cause the number of shares to vary over the year. In these cases, the denominator in the EPS calculation is the **weighted average** of the common shares outstanding during the year. To illustrate, assume that Starbright reported net income of $118 million during 2001 and that the firm's common shares changed as shown in Exhibit 10–4.

To calculate Starbright's EPS for 2001, we need first to determine the firm's weighted average shares outstanding during the year. The calculation appears in Exhibit 10–5 and shows that each level of outstanding shares is weighted by the fraction of the year that it stayed constant.

EXHIBIT 10-4 Common Shares Outstanding

Starbright Company
Common Shares Outstanding During 2001

Outstanding shares, January 1, 2001	45 million
Add: Additional shares issued May 1, 2001	+15 million
Balance, May 1, 2001	60 million
Less: Treasury shares purchased July 1, 2001	−10 million
Balance, July 1, 2001	50 million
Add: Additional shares issued October 1, 2001	+16 million
Outstanding shares, December 31, 2001	66 million

EXHIBIT 10-5 Weighted Average Common Shares

Starbright Company
Weighted Average Common Shares During 2001

Period	Length	Fraction of a year	×	Shares Outstanding	=	Shares
January 1–April 30, 2001	4 months	4/12	×	45 million	=	15.0 million
May 1–June 30, 2001	2 months	2/12	×	60 million	=	10.0 million
July 1–Sept 30, 2001	3 months	3/12	×	50 million	=	12.5 million
October 1–Dec 31, 2001	3 months	3/12	×	66 million	=	16.5 million
Totals	12 months					54.0 million

Exhibit 10–5 shows that Starbright's average shares outstanding in 2001 was 54 million. Accordingly, the firm's EPS in 2001 was

$$\text{EPS} = \frac{\text{Net income, \$118 million}}{\text{Weighted average shares, 54 million}}$$

$$= \text{\$2.19 per share}$$

Basic EPS Calculations with Preferred Stock Outstanding When a firm has both preferred and common stock outstanding, the preferred stock's share of net income must be subtracted in order to determine the basic EPS of the common stock. This is required because dividends must be paid to preferred shareholders before any earnings are available to common shareholders. Cumulative preferred stock always must be allocated its portion of net income. Noncumulative preferred stock is assigned a portion of income only in years when the firm actually declares a preferred stock dividend.

To illustrate, assume that Avalon Company reports net income of $120 million in 2001 and has both preferred and common stock outstanding. Pertinent details about the stock issues appear in Exhibit 10–6.

EXHIBIT 10-6 Stock Issue Details

Avalon Company
Descriptions of Preferred and Common Stock
Outstanding During 2001

Preferred stock, cumulative annual dividend of $10 per share, two million shares outstanding throughout all of 2001.
Common stock, 40 million shares outstanding throughout 2001.

Avalon's income available for common stock is determined as follows:

Net income, 2001	$120 million
Less: Income applicable to preferred shares ($10 per share × 2 million shares)	− 20 million
Income applicable to common shares	$100 million

Consequently, the basic EPS of the common stock is $2.50 ($100 million of income ÷ 40 million common shares outstanding).

Diluted EPS

Diluted EPS considers the effects on EPS of all the potential common shares that were outstanding during the year. If inclusion of these shares in the EPS calculation reduces the amount of EPS, then these potential common shares are **dilutive** and will be included in the calculation of diluted EPS. Otherwise, they are **anti-dilutive** and will be omitted from the calculation of diluted EPS. Including dilutive potential common shares in the EPS calculation may require adjustments to the numerator and the denominator of the basic EPS calculation. We will illustrate these adjustments for convertible preferred stock.

Recall from our earlier discussion that the dividends declared or accumulated during the period on preferred stock must be subtracted from net income in order to obtain the income applicable to the common shares. If the convertible preferred stock had been converted at the start of the period, however, the preferred dividends would not be subtracted from net income, and the denominator of the EPS calculation would include the additional shares that were issued on conversion. To illustrate, assume that Groucho company has a basic EPS of $5.00 per share, computed as shown in Exhibit 10–7.

Inclusion of the potential common shares associated with the convertible preferred stock in the EPS calculation would result in a diluted EPS of $ 4.80, as follows:

$$\text{Diluted EPS} = \frac{\text{Net Income}}{\text{Common shares outstanding} + \text{shares issuable upon conversion of preferred stock}}$$

$$= \frac{\$48 \text{ million}}{9 \text{ million shares} + 1 \text{ million shares}}$$

$$= \$4.80 \text{ per share}$$

In this case, Groucho would report on the face of the 2001 income statement a basic EPS of $5.00 and a diluted EPS of $4.80. Reality Check 10–3 shows the calculation of basic and dilutive EPS for a firm with potential common shares related to convertible preferred stock in its capital structure.

EXHIBIT 10-7 Basic EPS Calculation

Groucho Company
Basic EPS Calculation During 2001

Preferred stock, cumulative annual dividend of $3 per share, one million shares outstanding throughout 2001, convertible to onemillion shares of common stock.
Common stock, nine million shares outstanding throughout 2001.

Net income during 2001:	$48 million
Less: Preferred dividend	$ 3 million
Income applicable to Common stock	$45 million

Basic EPS: $5.00 ($45 million ÷ 9 million shares)

REALITY CHECK 10-3

Bethlehem Steel Corporation, a major steel fabricator, reports the following amounts of basic and diluted EPS in its 1997 financial statements:

	Basic EPS	Diluted EPS
Net income	$ 280,700,000	$ 280,700,000
Less: Preferred dividends	(41,600,000)	(22,500,000)
Net income applicable to common stock	$ 239,100,000	$ 258,200,000
Average shares outstanding	÷112,439,000	÷127,040,000
EPS	$ 2.13	$ 2.03

Required:

a. Explain why the amounts of preferred dividends that are subtracted in order to determine net income applicable to the common shares differ between the basic and diluted EPS calculations. Why are some preferred dividends included in the diluted EPS calculation?
b. Determine the total number of potential common shares and the total preferred dividends that are associated with Bethlehem's dilutive convertible preferred stock.
c. Based on your answer to b, determine the preferred stock dividend per potential common share, and explain why this relation causes these preferred shares to be dilutive.
d. Explain why you would consider either basic or diluted EPS to be a more useful measure of Bethlehem's per share earnings.

Solution

a. The calculation of basic EPS requires the subtraction of all preferred stock dividends. In computing diluted EPS, the dividends on dilutive preferred stock are added back because the related potential common shares are treated as if outstanding during the period; in other words the potential common shares are added to the denominator. Some of Bethlehem's preferred dividends remain in the calculation of diluted EPS, either because those preferred shares are not convertible to common stock, or because the EPS effects would be anti-dilutive (EPS would be higher if these shares were converted).
b. The numbers of potential common shares and the dividends on dilutive preferred stock can be determined by comparing the amounts used in computing basic and diluted EPS. The potential common shares are 14,601,000 (127,040,000 – 112,439,000), and the preferred dividend is $19,100,000 ($41,600,000 – $22,500,000).
c. The preferred stock dividend per potential common share for the dilutive preferred stock is $1.308 per share. Note that this amount is below the firm's basic EPS of $2.13. For this reason, the inclusion of these shares in the EPS calculation reduces the measured EPS.
d. Whether basic or diluted, EPS is more useful depending in part on the likelihood that the preferred shares will be converted to common shares. This in turn depends on many factors, including the future profitability of the company.

ANALYSIS BASED ON SHAREHOLDERS' EQUITY

The starting point in any analysis of a corporation's borrowed and equity capital is a careful reading of the descriptions provided in the body of the financial statements and the accompanying footnotes. As you have seen in this chapter, terms such as *convertible, cumulative, preferred,* and many others are critical in understanding the relative rights and priorities of the debt and equity claims on corporate assets.

The number and type of financial ratios that are based on shareholders' equity are constrained only by the imagination of the analyst. New ratios are continually being developed and tested by the "gurus of the day" quoted in the business press. This section discusses three ratios that seem to have stood the test of time: the financial leverage ratio, the market-to-book value ratio, and the price-to-earnings ratio.

The Financial Leverage Ratio

A basic decision faced by financial managers is the extent to which a firm should rely on borrowed capital. Shakespeare's adage "neither a borrower nor a lender be" is poor business advice. It is beneficial for most corporations to rely on debt to some extent, because the interest expense on debt is tax deductible, while dividends paid to stockholders are not. The degree of reliance on debt, or **financial leverage,** is measured as the ratio of debt to assets:

$$\text{Financial leverage} = \frac{\text{Total liabilities}}{\text{Total assets}}$$

Exhibit 10–8 shows financial leverage ratio calculations for two firms, based on financial reports for 1997. Wendy's International's debt is equal to about 39 percent of its total assets. This reflects Wendy's reliance mainly on the retention of its earnings to finance its growth. Seacoast Banking Corporation provides a dramatic contrast; borrowed capital is equal to more than 91 percent of its total assets. This reflects the fact that Seacoast Banking is engaged in the banking industry. Banks accept deposits from customers and report substantial liabilities for future withdrawals.

The lesson to be learned in comparing Wendy's and Seacoast Banking in Exhibit 10–8 is that comparisons of financial leverage ratios across companies in different industries must be undertaken with caution. To some extent, differences in financial leverage reflect management's willingness (or reluctance) to rely on borrowed capital. To a large extent, however, financial leverage is determined by industry characteristics and practices.

Financial leverage ratios are widely used by analysts to assess the risks of debt and equity securities. Firms with debt percentages that are substantially above their industry averages tend to have a higher likelihood of default on debt payments. As a result, high financial leverage is associated with lower bond quality ratings and therefore higher borrowing (interest) costs. Equity investments have also been found to be riskier

EXHIBIT 10-8 Financial Leverage Ratio Calculations

Financial Leverage Ratios
Two Firms Measured on December 31, 1997
(Dollars in Thousands)

Wendy's International Corporation	
(Restaurants)	
Debt	$ 757,446
Equity	1,184,234
Total assets (debt plus equity)	$1,941,680
Financial leverage ratio: $757,446 ÷ $1,941,680 = .390	
Seacoast Banking Corporation	
(Banking)	
Debt	$ 861,973
Equity	81,064
Total assets (debt plus equity)	$ 943,037
Financial leverage ratio: $861,973 ÷ $943,037 = .914	

for firms with high financial leverages. The share prices of highly leveraged firms tend to be more volatile than the share prices of firms with lower financial leverage.

Market-to-Book Value Ratio

Analysts often compare the market value of a firm's outstanding common stock to the reported value (book value) of common shareholders' equity. For example, at the end of 1997, Kerr-McGee Corporation had 47,686,000 shares of stock outstanding, and the market price per share was about $63. Kerr-McGee reported total shareholders' equity at $1,440,000,000, or $30.20 book value per share ($1,440,000,000 total shareholders' equity ÷ 47,686,000 shares outstanding). Accordingly, Kerr-McGee's market-to-book value ratio is computed as follows:

$$\text{Market-to-book value ratio} = \frac{\text{Market price per share}}{\text{Book value per share}}$$

$$= \frac{\$63}{\$30.20}$$

$$= 2.1$$

Why would investors be willing to buy Kerr-McGee's stock at over two times its underlying book value? The answer rests on the fact that the current market price of Kerr-McGee's stock depends on the future cash flows (dividends and resale price) that stockholders expect. In this sense, market price measures the **economic value** of Kerr-McGee's stock. The book value of Kerr-McGee's stock, on the other hand, reflects the methods used to identify and measure Kerr-McGee's assets and liabilities. Accounting measurements are based largely on historical costs and do not purport to reflect contemporary expectations about future cash flows. Despite its popularity, the market-to-book value ratio appears to be comparing apples to oranges.

Price-to-Earnings Ratio

The ratio of a stock's market price per share to its EPS is termed its price-to-earnings (P/E) ratio. Investors often use P/E ratios as a basis for attempting to detect over- or under-valued securities. Analysts often suggest that firms with low P/E ratios may be undervalued, while firms with high P/E ratios are likely to be overvalued. Kerr-McGee's market price per share at the end of 1997 was $63, and its 1997 EPS was reported at $4.04. The resulting P/E ratio is:

$$P/E = \frac{\text{Price per share}}{\text{EPS}}$$

$$= \frac{\$63}{\$4.04}$$

$$= 15.6$$

This result indicates that Kerr-McGee's stock was selling at a price that is 15.6 times its earnings per share.

P/E ratios are often used to assess growth, risk, and earnings quality. How would we expect Kerr-McGee's P/E ratio to compare to those of other firms? To answer this question, we must consider the effects of growth, risk, and earnings quality on inter-firm comparisons of P/E ratios.

Growth and the P/E Ratio P/E ratios vary directly with expected future growth rates in earnings. If investors expect a firm's future earnings to grow rapidly, then the current earnings understate the future earning power of the firm. Stock price, on the other hand, reflects investor expectations of future earnings and cash flows. Consequently, the ratio of prices to earnings will be relatively high for firms with high expected rates of earnings growth.

Risk and the P/E Ratio It is well established among investors that riskier investments require higher returns. Lenders require higher interest payments from borrowers with lower credit ratings, and equity investors demand greater returns and therefore pay lower prices for the stocks of risky firms. For this reason, high-risk firms are expected to have lower-than-average P/E multiples, and low-risk firms are expected to exhibit higher-than-average P/E multiples.

Earnings Quality and the P/E Ratio **Earnings quality** refers to the sustainability of currently reported earnings in future periods. Firms that use conservative methods of income measurement (LIFO inventory costing and accelerated depreciation and amortization) are more likely to be viewed as having higher earnings quality than firms that use more liberal income measurement methods. The securities market is likely to place a higher share price on firms with quality earnings. In other words, P/E multiples should vary directly with firms' earnings quality. The market price is based on the *expectations* of investors about a company's future performance.

SUMMARY OF LEARNING OBJECTIVES

1. **Understand why large business firms prefer to organize as corporations.** Major business firms prefer to organize as corporations. The capability of a corporation to sell its ownership shares to a large number of individual and institutional investors allows the firm to invest in large-scale operations. The basic ownership shares in a corporation are referred to as common stock, which represents a residual interest in the assets of the firm. Some corporations also issue preferred stock, which has priority over common stock in receiving dividends and other distributions of assets.
2. **Comprehend the types of transactions and events that affect the components of shareholders' equity.**
   Corporate shareholders' equity arises from both the sale of ownership shares and the retention of profits in the business. Most changes that occur in shareholders' equity arise from three basic transactions:
   a. Issuance of stock to investors, which increases paid-in capital.
   b. Recognition of periodic income (loss), which increases (decreases) retained earnings.
   c. Declaration of cash dividends, which decreases retained earnings.
   Other events that affect shareholders' equity include the following:
   d. Stock dividends, which are distributions of additional shares to investors. These dividends decrease retained earnings and increase paid-in capital, but they have no effect on total shareholders' equity or total assets.
   e. Stock splits, an occurrence when each "old" share of a stock is exchanged for multiple "new" shares. These exchanges do not change any of the components of shareholders' equity.
   f. Purchase of treasury shares, the cost of which is subtracted from shareholders' equity, and the subsequent resale of treasury shares.
   g. Issuance of stock options, which are the rights to purchase the firm's stock at a specified price over a designated future period.
   h. Conversion of securities, such as bonds payable or preferred stock, that allows the holder to exchange the securities for a predetermined number of common shares.
3. **Interpret shareholders' equity ratios that are helpful in analyzing financial statements.**
   Shareholders' equity is used extensively in ratio analysis of financial statements. Four widely employed measures are the following:

$$\text{Earnings per share} = \frac{\text{Net income}}{\text{Weighted average number of common shares outstanding}}$$

$$\text{Debt-to-assets or financial leverage ratio} = \frac{\text{Total debt}}{\text{Total assets}}$$

$$\text{Market-to-book value ratio} = \frac{\text{Market price per share}}{\text{Book value per share}}$$

$$\text{Price-to-earnings ratio} = \frac{\text{Market price per share}}{\text{EPS}}$$

KEY TERMS

Additional paid-in-capital 396
Anti-dilutive 408
Authorized shares 396
Basic EPS 406
Capital gains 395
Charter 395
Common stock 396
Complex capital structure 405
Contra-equity account 401
Convertible bonds 405
Convertible preferred shares 403
Cumulative preferred stock 403
Date of declaration 398
Date of payment 398
Date of record 398
Diluted EPS 406
Dilutive 408
Dividends 395
Earnings per share (EPS) 405
Earnings quality 412
Economic value 411
Equity capital 395
Fair Value 402
Financial leverage ratio 410
Hybrid securities 405
Intrinsic value 402
Invested capital 396
Issued shares 396
Market-to-book value ratio 411
Outstanding shares 406
Paid-in capital 396
Par value 396
Preferred stock 404
Price-to-earnings (P/E) ratio 411
Residual owners 396
Retained earnings 396
Simple capital structure 405
Stock dividend 399
Stock option 402
Stock split 399
Treasury stock 400
Weighted average 406

The proper interpretation of each of these ratios requires that you be familiar with the conventions and limitations of historical-cost-based financial accounting methods.

QUESTIONS

10-1 Describe the differences between shareholders' equity and liabilities.

10-2 Identify three components of shareholders' equity and describe each component.

10-3 Describe how dividends decrease shareholders' equity. Under what circumstances will dividends *not* reduce shareholders' equity?

10-4 Write a short memo explaining why large firms prefer to organize as corporations.

10-5 Describe why a firm's owners might prefer a corporate structure, rather than a partnership.

10-6 Under what circumstances might a partnership want to shift *immediately* to a corporate structure?

10-7 Describe the differences between common and preferred stock.

10-8 Describe why a firm's financial statements do not reflect the market value of the firm's shares of common and preferred stock.

10-9 Describe the differences between an equity or ownership interest in a corporation as compared to a creditor interest. What different rights does each have?

10-10 Distinguish between dividends and other benefits that an investor gets by owning shares in a corporation. Why would an investor prefer a $100 noncash benefit, rather than a $100 cash dividend? Under what circumstances would an investor prefer the $100 in cash?

10-11 Describe why retained earnings is not cash. Why can't shareholders withdraw their portion of shareholders' equity as cash?

10-12 Describe why shareholders' equity can be referred to as a residual interest in a corporation.

10-13 Distinguish between invested capital and retained earnings. What are the sources of each? Describe how each can be reduced.

10-14 With regard to common stock, distinguish among authorized, issued, and outstanding shares. Why would a firm never have more outstanding shares than authorized and issued shares?

10-15 Under what circumstances does a firm receive cash when it issues stock? Under what circumstances might it not receive cash?

10-16 Identify and describe the differences between a stock dividend and a stock split.

10-17 With regard to common stock, describe the concept of treasury stock. Describe why this is shown in a contra-equity account.

10-18 Distinguish between outstanding common stock and treasury stock. Why would a firm want to have treasury stock?

10-19 Describe the concept of employee stock options. Why might a firm want to issue stock options?

10-20 What are cumulative dividends as compared to noncumulative dividends?

10-21 Identify and describe the differences between convertible preferred stock and convertible bonds.

10-22 Why might a firm want to issue hybrid securities, such as convertible bonds or preferred stock with special preference rights?

10-23 a. Describe how earnings per share (EPS) is computed.
b. Why is EPS such an important ratio?
c. Describe what EPS represents. Describe what it does *not* represent.

10-24 Describe why the market-to-book value ratio is analogous to comparing apples to oranges. Why have analysts found this ratio to be useful?

10-25 Explain why price-to-earnings ratios may differ among firms. Describe why investors might prefer to buy a stock that has a relatively high price-to-earnings ratio? Why might some investors prefer low price-to-earnings ratios? Discuss.

10-26 Assume that a firm uses relatively conservative methods of accounting (LIFO inventory costing and/or accelerated depreciation methods). Describe how this would affect your interpretation of the following measures: EPS, financial leverage ratio, and price-to-earnings ratio.

EXERCISES

Transaction Analysis: Shareholders' Equity

10-27 Davidson Corp. has the following transactions. Use the balance sheet equation to analyze the financial statement effects of these transactions. Set up the following columns: cash, patent, preferred stock, capital in excess of par, common stock, and treasury stock.

1. Issued five million shares of $2.00 par value preferred stock at a price of $10.00.
2. Issued five million shares of no-par common stock at a price of $20.00.
3. Purchased 100,000 shares of its own common stock as treasury stock at a market price of $35.00.
4. Issued 200,000 shares of no-par common stock in exchange for patent rights. The stock has a market price of $40.00.

Transaction Analysis: Shareholders' Equity

10-28 DWN Corporation began operations in 2000. Calculate the balances in each component of shareholders' equity at the end of 1998, after recognizing the following transactions:

1. Issue one million shares of $5.00 par value common stock at a price of $15.00.
2. Earn net income of $450,000.
3. Declare and pay dividends of $200,000.
4. Purchase 10,000 shares of its common stock as treasury stock at $25.00.
5. Sell 5,000 shares of treasury stock for $30.00.

Transaction Analysis: Shareholders' Equity

10-29 SKN Corporation began operations in 1999. Calculate the balances in each component of shareholders' equity at the end of 1999, after recognizing the following transactions:

1. Issue two million shares of $10.00 par value common stock at a price of $25.00.
2. Incur high R&D costs and show a net loss on its 1996 income statement of $1,500,000.00.
3. Issue four million shares of $25.00 preferred stock at a price of $30.00.

Transaction Analysis: Shareholders' Equity

10-30 RMN Corp. had a variety of shareholders' equity transactions in 2000. It had the following balances in Shareholders' Equity accounts and Cash and other assets accounts at the beginning of 2000:

Cash and other assets	$78,000,000
Common stock, $1.00 par value	5,000,000
Capital in excess of par	25,000,000
Retained earnings	50,000,000
Treasury stock (40,000 shares)	(2,000,000)

RMN had the following transactions that affected shareholders' equity during 2000:

1. Issue five million shares of no-par preferred stock at a price of $4.00.
2. Sell the treasury stock for $4,500,000.00.
3. Earn net income of $35,000,000.00.
4. Declare and pay dividends of $10,000,000.00.
5. Employee stock options were granted with the purchase of 100,000 shares of common stock. The market price is currently $7 per share. The exercise price is $7 per share.
6. The stock options were exercised and the company issued the 100,000 shares. The current market price is $8 per share.

Required:

Record these transactions in each of the components of shareholders' equity and in Cash and other assets. Use the balance sheet equation to calculate the ending balance in each account.

Earnings Per Share Calculations

10-31 Calculate earnings per share (EPS), given the following information:

- Net income, $255,000,000
- Authorized common stock, 50,000,000 shares
- Common stock, 25,000,000 shares outstanding all year
- Bonds payable, $50,000,000

Earnings Per Share Calculations

10-32 Calculate EPS, given the following information:

- Net loss, $20,000,000
- Common stock, 2,000,000 shares outstanding all year
- Preferred stock, 2,000,000 shares authorized, but none issued

Earnings Per Share Calculations

10-33 Calculate EPS, given the following information:

- Net income, $345,000,000
- Authorized common stock, 20,000,000 shares, $1.00 par value
- Weighted average number of shares outstanding, 11,455,678
- Dividends paid, $35,000,000

Earnings Per Share Calculations

10-34 Calculate EPS, given the following information:

- Net income, $65,100,000
- Common stock outstanding, 3,100,000 shares
- Preferred stock outstanding, 1,000,000 shares
- Dividends paid on preferred stock, $5,000,000
- Bonds payable, $40,000,000
- Retained earnings (ending balance), $45,679,000

Comprehensive Exercise: Stockholders' Equity

10-35 Swan and Duboner Corporation has the following stockholders' equity on December 31, 1999:

Six percent preferred stock: $100 par value, 20,000 shares authorized, 5,000 shares issued and outstanding	$ 500,000
Common stock: $5 par value, 1,000,000 shares authorized, 250,000 shares issued	1,250,000
Additional paid-in capital	1,740,000
Total contributed capital	$3,490,000
Retained earnings	850,000
Total stockholders' equity	$4,340,000

The corporation had the following transactions during 2000:

1. *February 1:* Declared a dividend of $6 per share on the preferred stock, and $0.50 per share on the common stock.
2. *February 10:* The board of directors established this as the record date.
3. *February 25:* The dividends were paid.
4. *March 31:* A two-for-one stock split on the common stock was declared and issued.
5. *April 30:* The corporation bought back 100,000 shares of its common stock for $6 per share. These shares will be reissued in the future.
6. *June 30:* Employee stock options were granted for 10,000 shares. The current market price is $5.50 per share. The exercise price is $6.00 per share.
7. *August 15:* The corporation sold 20,000 shares of its treasury stock for $7.00 per share.
8. *October 31:* Employees exercised their stock options. The current market price is $7.50 per share.
9. *December 31:* The net income for the year is $600,000.

Required

a. Set up an accounting equation and record the above transactions.
b. Calculate EPS, assuming a weighted average of 380,000 common shares outstanding.
c. Why do companies, in general, declare and issue a stock split?

Transaction Analysis: Shareholders' Equity

10-36 Record the effects of the following transactions, using the balance sheet equation and Cash and other assets. Calculate the ending balance in Retained Earnings.

1. The beginning balance in retained earnings is $2,590,000; common stock, $1.00 par value, is $2,000,000; and Cash and other assets is $4,590,000.

2. Earn net income of $3,560,000.
3. Declare and pay dividends of $2,000,000.
4. Issue four million shares of common stock, par value, $1.00 at a price of $4.00.
5. Issue stock dividends in the amount of $3,000,000 representing 1,000,000 shares.

Earnings Per Share Calculations

10-37 Calculate earnings per share (EPS), given the following information:

- Net income, $63,000,000
- Common stock outstanding, 3,000,000 shares
- Bonds payable, $35,000,000
- Retained earnings (ending balance), $42,300,000

Earnings Per Share Calculations

10-38 Calculate EPS, given the following information:

- Common stock outstanding, 4,000,000 shares
- Net income, $55,000,000
- Bonds payable, $33,000,000
- Retained earnings (ending balance), $44,000,400
- Preferred shares outstanding, 1,000,000, $10.00 par value
- Preferred dividends, $2,000,000

Transaction Analysis: Shareholders' Equity

10-39 Use the balance sheet equation to calculate the ending balances in each of the following accounts, given the beginning balances and various transactions during the year.

Beginning Balances	
Cash	$ 25,000,000
Other assets	100,000,000
Convertible bonds payable	20,000,000
Convertible preferred stock, $10 par value	30,000,000
Common stock, $10 par value	40,000,000
Retained earnings	35,000,000

Transactions

1. Convert half of the convertible bonds payable to common stock at a conversion price of $40.00 per share.
2. Convert all the convertible preferred stock to common stock at 1.5 shares of preferred stock for each share of common stock (conversion ratio).
3. Purchase 500,000 shares of its own common stock as treasury stock at a market price of $12.50.
4. Earn net income of $17,500,000.
5. Pay dividends of $5,000,000.
6. Issue one million shares of common stock at the market price of $15.00 per share in exchange for a parcel of land priced at $20,000,000.

PROBLEMS

Critical Thinking

Comprehensive Dividend Problem: Stockholders' Equity

10-40 Macintosh Browning Corporation has the following stockholders' equity at December 31, 1999:

Seven percent cumulative preferred stock: $120 par, 50,000 shares authorized, 20,000 shares issued and outstanding	$2,400,000
Common stock: $10 par, 500,000,000 shares authorized, 300,000 shares issued	3,000,000
Additional paid-in capital	900,000
Total contributed capital	6,300,000
Retained earnings	1,200,000
Treasury stock (74,000 shares of common stock)	(1,110,000)
Total stockholders' equity	$6,390,000

Required

a. Why did Macintosh issue preferred stock? What does the seven percent cumulative term indicate?

b. Assume that the board of directors has not declared a dividend in the past three years (the preferred stock was outstanding during these years). What is the amount of dividends outstanding for the previous three years on these cumulative shares?

c. Why might Macintosh prefer preferred stock rather than additional debt?

d. If the board declared and paid dividends to the preferred and common shareholders during the year, show the effects (use + and − and ignore $ amounts) on stockholders' equity on the date of declaration, date of record, and date of payment.

Comprehensive Problem: Stockholders' Equity

10-41 LP&G Corporation has the following stockholders' equity at December 31, 1999:

Common stock: $20 par, authorized 700,000 shares, issued 200,000 shares	$ 4,000,000
Additional paid-in capital	3,200,000
Total contributed capital	7,200,000
Retained earnings	5,400,000
Total stockholders' equity	$12,600,000

During 2000, the following transactions occurred:

1. *January 31:* A two-for-one common stock split was declared by the board of directors. The shares were issued and the market price was $110 per share.
2. *March 15:* The corporation repurchased 50,000 shares of its common stock as treasury stock at $54 per share.
3. *May 31:* The board of directors declared a $2 cash dividend per share.
4. *June 10:* This is the date of record that the board of directors established.
5. *June 20:* The dividends were paid.
6. *August 30:* The corporation granted employee stock options of 20,000 shares. The market price was $54 per share. The exercise price is $54 per share.
7. *October 15:* The corporation sold 30,000 shares of its treasury stock for $55 per share.
8. *November 25:* Employee stock options were exercised. The market price was $56 per share.

Required

a. Set up an accounting equation and record the above transactions.
b. Why did the corporation issue a two-for-for stock split?
c. Why would a company issue a stock dividend instead of cash? What impact does a stock dividend have on overall stockholders' equity?

Critical Thinking

Conceptual Discussion: Preferred Stock

10-42 The H. Houdini Company's capital structure includes $10,000,000 of long-term debt at an average rate of 12%. The capital structure also includes $3,000,000 of (cumulative) preferred stock, with stated dividends of five percent and $6,000,000 of common stock. It has no retained earnings.

Required

a. How does the preferred stock affect the risk and potential returns of the long-term debt and the common stock?
b. In what ways might preferred stock be considered debt? How might it be viewed as equity?

Critical Thinking

Financial Statement Impact: Debt Versus Equity

10-43 The Open Sesame Company has assets of $300,000,000, long-term debts of $100,000,000, common stock of $100,000,000, and retained earnings of $100,000,000. Most of the long-term debt consists of convertible debt carrying fairly high interest rates that are about five points above the current prevailing market. Open Sesame wants to issue $100,000,000 of new debt at current market rates. It will then "call," or retire, the existing convertible debt, using the money from the new debt. Because its share prices have also increased 40% over the past several years, Open Sesame is also considering raising additional funds by issuing new shares of common stock. Funds from the common stock issue would then be used to refinance the debt.

Required

a. If Open Sesame issued new debt, what would be the impact on its balance sheet? On its income statement?
b. If Open Sesame issued new common stock, what would be the impact on its balance sheet? What assumption is crucial to answering this question?
c. What other considerations might drive Open Sesame's decision about this possible refinancing of its long-term debt?
d. How might the current creditors be affected if Open Sesame tries to "call," or retire, its convertible debt? How might they feel? What actions might they take immediately after hearing about the call?

Critical Thinking

Financial Statement Impact: Debt Versus Equity

10-44 Smith Smyth, Inc., has the following capital structure:

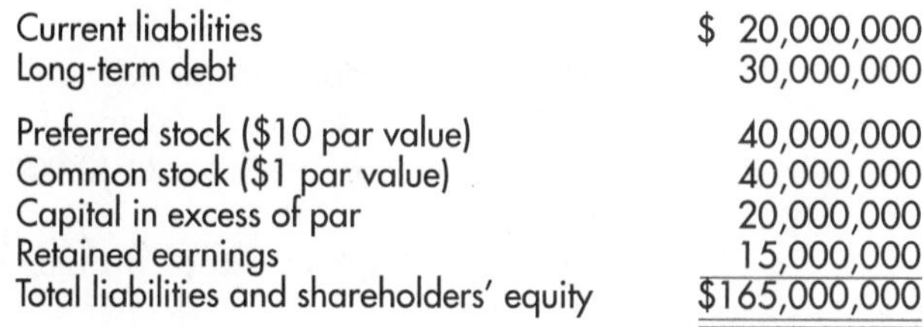

Current liabilities	$ 20,000,000
Long-term debt	30,000,000
Preferred stock ($10 par value)	40,000,000
Common stock ($1 par value)	40,000,000
Capital in excess of par	20,000,000
Retained earnings	15,000,000
Total liabilities and shareholders' equity	$165,000,000

Required

a. Determine the impact on Smyth's capital structure if it issues an additional long-term debt of $20,000,000. In other words, show what Smyth's capital structure will be with the new debt.

b. Determine the impact on Smyth's capital structure if it converts half the long-term debt, including that issued in part a, to common stock at a conversion price of $10.

c. Determine the impact on Smyth's capital structure if it converts all its preferred stock to common stock. The conversion ratio is 2.5 shares of common stock for each share of preferred stock.

d. Determine the impact on Smyth's capital structure if it purchases 5,000,000 shares for its common stock at a market price of $12 per share.

e. Determine the impact on Smyth's capital structure if it suffers losses of $10,000,000 in the next fiscal year.

f. Reconstruct the right side of the balance sheet, reflecting all the above changes, as if they occurred simultaneously. (*Hint:* Set up an accounting equation and record all the transactions.)

Financial Statement Impact: Debt Versus Equity

10-45 Bitsy Betsy, Inc. has the following capital structure:

Current liabilities	$ 35,000,000
Long-term debt	35,000,000
Preferred stock (no par)	45,000,000
Common stock (no par)	45,000,000
Retained earnings	10,000,000
Total liabilities and shareholders' equity	$170,000,000

Required

a. Calculate Betsy's capital structure after issuing $25 million of new debt.

b. Recalculate Betsy's capital structure after converting half the long-term debt, including that issued in part a, to common stock.

c. Recalculate Betsy's capital structure after converting all its preferred stock to common stock.

d. Recalculate Betsy's capital structure after suffering losses of $10 million in the next fiscal year.

Effects on Financial Statements and Ratios

10-46 A list of business transactions and events follows:

1. Sale of common stock to investors
2. Sale of preferred stock to investors
3. Declaration of a cash dividend to common shareholders
4. Purchase of treasury stock
5. Sale of treasury stock
6. Issuance of options to employees, which will become exercisable in two years
7. Announcement of a two-for-one stock split

Required

Indicate how each of these items affects the following financial statement items or ratios:

a. Total assets
b. Liabilities
c. Shareholders' equity
d. Retained earnings
e. Earnings per share
f. Financial leverage (debt divided by total assets)

Comparing Financial Ratios of Two Firms Using Differing Accounting Methods

10-47 Two firms provided the following information at the end of 1999 (dollars in millions):

	Adam Co.	Zachary Co.
Total assets	$ 105	$ 210
Total liabilities	$ 70	$ 120
Shareholders' equity	$ 35	$ 90
Net income during 1999	$ 15	$ 25
Shares outstanding during 1999	1 million	1.2 million
Market price per share	$ 125.00	$ 150.00

Required

a. Based on the information above, determine the following items for each firm:
   - Earnings per share
   - Price-to-earnings ratio
   - Financial leverage ratio
b. Adam used LIFO inventory costing and accelerated depreciation of plant and equipment costs, while Zachary used FIFO costing and straight-line depreciation. If Adam had been using the same inventory costing and depreciation methods as Zachary, then Adam's net income during 1998 would have been higher by $20 million, and the carrying value of Adam's total assets would have been higher by $85 million. Based on this information, recompute the three ratios above as if Adam and Zachary used the same accounting methods for inventory and depreciation.
c. Describe your overall conclusions regarding the two firms.

Stock Options as Executive Compensation

10-48 Late in 1999, Natalie Attired, a recent MBA graduate, signed a four-year employment contract with Generic Co. that provides her with an annual salary of $90,000. In addition, at the start of each year, 2000 through 2003, Natalie received options to purchase 3,000 shares of Generic's common stock at the market price when the options were received. These options are exercisable for four years from the date of receipt. Assume the following information related to these options:

Year	Market Price per Share, Beginning of Year	Options Exercised During the Year
2000	$ 50	None
2001	$ 80	4000*
2002	$130	2000**
2003	$ 90	None

*3,000 options at $50.
**2,000 options at $80.

Required

a. Determine the total compensation expense to Natalie that would be reported by Generic in each year from 2000 through 2003.
b. Determine the total economic benefit that Natalie has received (salary plus value of stockholding and options) from Generic over the three-year period.
c. Comment on any difference between the results in parts a and b.

Critical Thinking

No-Par Shares

10-49 Why might a firm prefer to issue shares with no par value (zero stated value)?

Critical Thinking

Research Project: Stock-Based Compensation

10-50 Conduct a research study on stock-based compensation. Write a memo describing how stock-based compensation should be reflected or disclosed on a company's financial statements.

Critical Thinking

Interpreting Financial Statements: Shareholders' Equity

10-51 Refer to Wendy's financial statements in Appendix D. Review the balance sheet to determine how and where shareholders' equity has been reported.

Required

a. Read the Consolidated Statement of Shareholders' Equity. Identify and discuss any unusual terms.
b. Determine whether Wendy's has any unusual types of shareholders' equity. If so, discuss how they might be interpreted by financial analysts. Discuss how Wendy's managers might view such equity items.
c. Discuss how preferred stock is related to common stock. In your opinion, should they be disclosed separately? Why? Determine why Wendy's shows preferred stock on its balance sheet and at zero amounts.
d. Discuss several reasons why Wendy's has treasury stock.
e. Discuss any other unusual concerns regarding Wendy's shareholders' equity. What other related information might an external analyst require or prefer?

Interpreting Financial Statements: Equity Ratio Calculations

10-52 Refer to Wendy's financial statements in Appendix D. Review the financial statements to determine how and where shareholders' equity has been reported.

Required

a. Calculate Wendy's financial leverage ratio for each year. Discuss the results.
b. Based on the notes, is there any other way to calculate the leverage ratio? If so, do so by taking a more liberal (or more conservative) approach to reclassifying any convertible securities. Contrast these results. *Note:* Refer to Note 4 pertaining to convertible debentures (bonds).

(Continued)

c. Calculate the market-to-book value ratio. If market prices are not disclosed somewhere in the annual report, use other resources to determine the market price at the end of each fiscal year. Discuss the results.
d. Calculate the price-to-earnings ratio, using the market price determined above and basic earnings-per-share information. Discuss the results.
e. Discuss any other unusual concerns regarding Wendy's shareholders' equity. What other related information might an external analyst prefer?

Interpreting Financial Statements: Shareholders' Equity

Critical Thinking

10-53 Refer to Reebok's financial statements in Appendix E. Review the balance sheet to determine how and where shareholders' equity has been reported.

Required

a. Read the Consolidated Statement of Stockholders' Equity. Identify and discuss any unusual terms. Trace any numerical disclosures of shareholders' equity in the notes to corresponding disclosures in the balance sheet.
b. Determine whether Reebok has any unusual types of shareholders' equity. If so, discuss how they might be interpreted by financial analysts. Discuss how Reebok's managers might view such equity items.
c. Discuss how paid-in capital is related to common stock. Should they be disclosed separately? Why?
d. Determine why Reebok had the same amount of "shares in treasury" each year. How many shares of common stock are outstanding?
e. Evaluate the decrease in "unearned compensation." Why is this item shown as part of shareholders' equity? Is this account, or the increase, significant? Why?
f. Discuss any other unusual concerns regarding Reebok's shareholders' equity. What other related information might an external analyst require or prefer?

Interpreting Financial Statements: Equity Ratio Calculations

10-54 Refer to Reebok's financial statements in Appendix E. Review the financial statements to determine how and where shareholders' equity has been reported.

Required

a. Calculate the financial leverage ratio for each year. Interpret your results.
b. Based on the notes, is there any other possible way in which the leverage ratio can be calculated? If so, do so by taking a more liberal (or more conservative) approach to reclassifying any convertible securities. Contrast these results with your earlier results.
c. Calculate the market-to-book value ratio. If market prices are not disclosed somewhere in the annual report, go to your library to determine the market price at the end of each fiscal year. Discuss your results.
d. Calculate the price-to-earnings ratio, using the market price determined above. Discuss your results.
e. Discuss any other unusual concerns regarding Reebok's shareholders' equity. What other related information might an external analyst require or prefer?

Critical Thinking

"Hybrid" Stock Splits

10-55 A footnote to the 1999 financial statements of General Dynamite, Inc., a major producer of explosive weapons, armored vehicles, and other weapons systems, includes the following information:

> Stock split: On March 4, 2000, the company's board of directors authorized a two-for-one stock split in the form of a 100 percent stock dividend to be distributed on April 11 to shareholders of record on March 21. Shareholders' equity has been restated to give retroactive recognition to the stock split for all periods presented by reclassifying the par value of the additional shares arising from the split from retained earnings to common stock. In addition, all references in the financial statements to the number of shares, per share amounts, stock option data, and market prices of the company's common stock have been restated.

Required

a. Explain why the accounting treatment described by General Dynamite is not typical of either a stock split or a stock dividend.
b. Why did General Dynamite give retroactive recognition to the stock split in all related financial statement references?
c. Why did General Dynamite's management decide to split the company's stock?
d. Would an existing General Dynamite shareholder be pleased by management's decision to split the stock? Explain.

Valuation of Stock Options

Critical Thinking

10-56 Crown Resources, Inc., an international producer of cardboard packaging, reports the following information in its 1999 financial statements:

Stock issued under stock option and employee savings plans:	1,415,711 shares
Resulting changes in shareholders' equity:	
Paid-in capital increase	$23,600,000
Treasury stock decrease	7,000,000
Total increase in shareholders' equity	$30,600,000

The market price of Crown's common stock averaged about $40 per share during 1999.

Required

a. What was the average amount of proceeds per share that Crown received for the stock issued in 1999 under its stock option and employee savings plans?
b. What was the aggregate market value of the shares issued by Crown during 1999 under these plans?
c. Discuss the difference between the aggregate market value and the aggregate proceeds received by Crown for the stock issued in 1999. Is this interpretation consistent with the accounting treatment? Explain.

Critical Thinking

Interpreting Notes Related to Shareholders' Equity

10-57 Gap, Inc. provided the following notes (excerpts) in its 1997 financial statements:

Note F: Employee Benefit
And Incentive Stock Compensation Plans
Retirement Plans

The company has a qualified defined contribution retirement plan, called GapShare, which is available to employees who meet certain age and service requirements. This plan permits employees to make contributions up to the maximum limits allowable under the Internal Revenue Code. Under the plan, the company matches all or a portion of the employee's contributions under a predetermined formula. The company's contributions vest over a seven-year period. Company contributions to the retirement plan in 1997, 1996, and 1995 were $12,907,000, $11,427,000, and $9,839,000, respectively.

A nonqualified executive deferred compensation plan was established on January 1, 1994 and a nonqualified executive capital accumulation plan was established on April 1, 1994. Both plans allow eligible employees to defer compensation up to a maximum amount defined in each plan. The company does not match employees' contributions.

A deferred compensation plan was established on August 26, 1997 for nonemployee members of the board of directors. Under this plan, board members can elect to defer receipt on a pre-tax basis of eligible compensation received for serving as nonemployee directors. In exchange for compensation deferred, board members are granted discounted stock options to purchase shares of the company's common stock. All options are fully exercisable upon the date granted and expire seven years after the date or one year after retirement from the board, if earlier. The company can issue up to 300,000 shares under the plan.

Incentive Stock Compensation Plans

The 1996 Stock Option and Award plan (the "Plan") was established on March 26, 1996. The board authorized 41,485,041 shares for issuance under the Plan, which includes shares available under the Management Incentive Restricted Stock plan (MIRSP) and an earlier stock option plan established in 1981, both of which were superseded by the Plan. The Plan empowers the Compensation and Stock Option Committee of the board of directors to award compensation primarily in the form of nonqualified stock options or restricted stock to key employees. Stock options generally expire 10 years from the grant date or one year after the date of retirement, if earlier. Stock options generally vest over a three-year period, with shares becoming exercisable in full on the third anniversary of the grant date. Nonqualified stock options are generally issued at fair market value but can be issued at prices less than the fair market value at the date of grant or at other prices as determined by the committee. Total compensation cost for those stock options issued at less than fair market value under the Plan and for the restricted shares issued under MIRSP was $17,170,000, $22,248,000, and $23,743,000 in 1997, 1996, and 1995, respectively.

Employee Stock Purchase Plan

The company has an Employee Stock Purchase plan under which all eligible employees can purchase common stock at 85 percent of the lowest closing price of the company's common stock on the grant date or the purchase date on the New York Stock Exchange Composite Transactions Index. Employees pay for their stock purchases through payroll deductions at a rate equal to any whole percentage from one percent to 15 percent. There were 645,625 shares issued under the plan during fiscal 1997, 599,495 during 1996, and 578,301 during 1995. All shares were acquired from reissued treasury stock. At January 31, 1998, there were 4,176,579 shares reserved for future subscriptions.

Note G: Shareholders' Equity And Stock Options

Common and Preferred Stock

The company is authorized to issue 60,000,000 shares of Class B common stock, which is convertible into shares of common stock on a share-for-share basis; transfer of the shares is restricted. In addition, the holders of the Class B common stock have six votes per share on most matters and are entitled to a lower cash dividend. No Class B shares have been issued.

The board of directors is authorized to issue 30,000,000 shares of one or more series of preferred stock and to establish at the time of issuance the issue price, dividend rate, redemption price, liquidation value, conversion features, and such other terms and conditions of each series (including voting rights) as the board deems appropriate, without further action on the part of the shareholders. No preferred shares have been issued.

In October 1996, the board of directors approved a share-buyback program under which the company can repurchase up to 45,000,000 shares of its outstanding stock in the open market over a three-year period. As of January 31, 1998, 28,184,650 shares were repurchased for $743,805,000 under this program.

Stock Options

Under the company's Stock Option plans, nonqualified options to purchase common stock are granted to officers, directors, and key employees at exercise prices equal to the fair market value of the stock at the date of grant or at other prices as determined by the Compensation and Stock Option Committee of the board of directors.

Stock option activity for all employee benefit plans is as follows:

	Shares	Weighted-Average Exercise Price
Balance on January 28, 1995	11,619,816	$10.18
Granted	14,226,600	11.94
Exercised	(1,491,558)	6.48
Canceled	(894,222)	12.27
Balance on February 3, 1996	23,460,636	$11.41
Granted	9,364,110	20.60
Exercised	(2,386,761)	8.30
Canceled	(1,198,608)	14.85
Balance on February 1, 1997	29,239,377	$14.46
Granted	11,392,531	21.62
Exercised	(2,849,034)	10.65
Canceled	(2,559,295)	16.01
Balance on January 31, 1998	35,223,579	$16.97

Outstanding options on January 31, 1998 have expiration dates ranging from March 20, 1998 to January 29, 2008 and represent grants to 2,347 key employees.

On January 31, 1998, the company reserved 60,083,011 shares of its common stock, including 14,996 treasury shares, for the exercise of stock options. There were 24,859,432 and 32,745,096 shares available for options on January 31, 1998 and February 1, 1997, respectively. Options for 4,299,847 and 4,373,222 shares were exercisable as of January 31, 1998 and February 1, 1997, respectively, and had a weighted-average exercise price of $11.66 and $9.01 for those respective periods.

The company accounts for its Stock Option and Award plans in accordance with APB Opinion No. 25, under which no compensation cost has been recognized for stock option awards granted at fair market value. Had compensation cost for the company's stock-based compensation plans been determined based on the fair value at the grant dates for awards under those plans in accordance with the provisions of SFAS No. 123, Accounting for Stock-Based Compensation, the company's net earnings and earnings per share would have been reduced to the pro forma amounts indicated below. The effects of applying SFAS No. 123 in this pro forma disclosure are not indicative of future amounts. SFAS No. 123 does not apply to awards prior to fiscal year 1995. Additional awards in future years are anticipated.

	Fifty-two Weeks Ended Jan. 31, 1998	Fifty-two Weeks Ended Feb. 1, 1997	Fifty-three Weeks Ended Feb. 3, 1996
Net earnings ($000)			
As reported	$533,901	$452,859	$354,039
Pro forma	507,966	437,232	348,977
Earnings per share			
As reported-basic	$ 1.35	$ 1.09	$ .85
Pro forma-basic	1.28	1.05	.84
As reported-diluted	1.30	1.06	.83
Pro forma-diluted	1.24	1.02	.82

Note H: Earnings Per Share

Under SFAS No. 128, the company provides a dual presentation of EPS on a basic and diluted basis. The company's granting of certain stock options and restricted stock resulted in a potential dilution of basic EPS. The following summarizes the effects of the assumed issuance of dilutive securities on weighted-average shares for basic EPS.

	Fifty-two Weeks Ended Jan. 31, 1998	Fifty-two Weeks Ended Feb. 1, 1997	Fifty-three Weeks Ended Feb. 3, 1996
Weighted-average number of shares—basic	396,179,975	417,146,631	417,718,397
Incremental shares from assumed issuance of:			
Stock options	10,037,700	5,597,219	1,939,485
Restricted stock	3,983,083	4,523,370	8,094,633
Weighted-average number of shares—diluted	410,200,758	427,267,220	427,752,515

The number of incremental shares from the assumed issuance of stock options and restricted stock is calculated applying the treasury stock method.

Excluded from the above computation of weighted-average shares for diluted EPS were options to purchase 440,063 shares of common stock during fiscal 1997, 5,084,978 during 1996 and 3,087,269 during 1995. Issuance of these securities would have resulted in an antidilutive effect on EPS.

Required

a. Review the notes provided by Gap, Inc. Identify any unusual terms.
b. Identify reasons why Gap provided these stock options.
c. Describe each major transaction involving stockholders' equity. Use the accounting equation to show the effects of each transaction.
d. Comment on the effects of each major transaction. How would an investor evaluate each of these transactions? List some reasons why managers would support them.

Interpreting Financial Statements: Shareholders' Equity

10-58 Vicorp Restaurants, Inc., headquartered in Denver, operates or franchises 408 midscale restaurants, primarily under the names Bakers Square and Village Inn. Its 1994 balance sheet included the following shareholders' equity section (in thousands):

	1994	1993	1992
Common stock: $0.05 par value, 20,000,000 shares authorized, 9,509,426, 9,911,536, and 10,189,066 issued	$ 476	$ 496	$ 509
Additional paid-in capital	91,544	98,338	105,701
Retained earnings	42,846	49,484	32,960
Treasury stock, at cost (0,0, and 212,851 shares)	0	0	(3,725)
Total shareholders' equity	$134,866	$148,318	$135,445

Required

a. Explain each item in the shareholders' equity section of Vicorp's balance sheet.

b. Why is there such a large discrepancy between the amounts assigned to common stock versus the additional paid-in capital?

c. Assuming zero dividends, did Vicorp have positive or negative net income in 1993? in 1994? Why?

d. How many shares of its own common stock did Vicorp purchase in 1992? At what price? Assume that Vicorp did not sell any additional shares in 1992.

e. Could Vicorp issue 10,000,000 shares of common stock to quickly raise additional funds? In which years?

f. Calculate the amount of dividends paid by Vicorp, if any, in 1993 and 1994. For this purpose, assume that Vicorp's net income was $16,524,000 in 1993, and it had a net loss of $6,638,000 in 1994.

Interpreting Financial Statements: Earnings per Share

10-59 Pierre's, headquartered in Paris, reports the following note to its 1999 financial statements:

Share Capital: The share capital comprises fully paid shares with a nominal value of 1 FRF [French franc]. Shares at the beginning of the year and changes in the number of shares are as follows:

	1999	1998
On January 1	75,452,501	74,442,637
In lieu of cash (stock) dividends	—	725,402
Exercise of stock options	112,095	140,550
Conversion of bonds	745	3,324
Exercise of staff (employee) options	—	25,733
On December 31	75,565,341	75,337,646

Information relevant to the earnings per share calculations is as follows:

Average outstanding	75,422,540	75,122,483
Profit attributed to shareholder (FRF)	965,000,000	841,000,000

Required

a. Explain each item in Pierre's note.
b. What differences might exist between stock options and staff options?
c. Why does the average number of shares outstanding differ from the balances on January 1 and December 31?
d. Calculate Pierre's earnings per share (EPS).

Interpreting Financial Statements: Shareholders' Equity

10-60 Exabyte Corporation reported the following information in its 1994 balance sheet (dollars in thousands and shares in thousands as well):

	1994	1993
Preferred stock: $0.001 par value; 14,000 shares authorized, no shares issued and outstanding	—	—
Common stock: $0.001 par value, 50,000 shares authorized; 21,657 and 21,190 shares issued	22	21
Capital in excess of par value	57,208	51,242
Treasury stock, at cost, 15 and 15 shares	(9)	(9)
Retained earnings	139,686	107,281
Total stockholders' equity	$196,907	$158,535
Total assets	$242,765	$197,307
Common and common equivalent shares	21,965	21,399
Net income	$ 32,405	$ 16,182

Required

a. Explain each of Exabyte's stockholders' equity items.
b. What significance is there to the equality of par values for both the preferred and common stock?
c. How many shares of stock were actually owned by the public at the end of each year?
d. Why does Exabyte disclose preferred stock, even though no shares have been issued?
e. Why does the number of shares listed as "Common and common equivalent shares" differ from the number of shares outstanding?
f. Using the information on treasury stock, determine the price paid for treasury shares. Should it concern an investor that this price is so much higher than the shares' par value?
g. Calculate Exabyte's earnings per share (EPS).
h. On the basis of the above information, calculate Exabyte's ROE ratios. Evaluate the results.
i. If Exabyte paid no dividends in 1994, would that be of concern to an investor?

Cash Flow Impact on Shareholders' Equity

10-61 Sigma Designs is a high-tech software development company specializing in imaging and multimedia computer applications. Sigma Designs' statement of cash flows is presented below:

Sigma Designs, Inc.
Statement of Cash Flows
For the Years ended January 31, 1995 and 1994
(Dollars in thousands)

	1995	1994
Cash flows from operating activities		
Net loss	$(8,773)	$(29,546)
Adjustments to reconcile net loss to net cash provided by operating activities (summary of all adjustments, net)	(110)	15,885
Net cash provided by (used for) operating activities	(8,883)	(13,661)
Cash flows from investing activities		
Purchases of marketable securities	(25,350)	(22,542)
Sales of marketable securities	22,296	33,355
Equipment additions	(721)	(612)
Software development costs (capitalized)	(1,255)	(494)
Other asset transactions	0	183
Net cash provided (used for) investing activities	(5,030)	9,890
Cash flows from financing activities		
Common stock sold	13,201	493
Repayment of long-term obligations	1,710	0
Other financing transactions	(1,925)	0
Net cash provided (used for) financing activities	12,986	493
Decrease in cash and equivalents	$ (927)	$ (3,278)

Required

a. If the majority of payments included in the caption "Other financing transactions" in 1995 was made for repurchasing common stock owned by officers and their family members, how would this new information affect an investor's views of Sigma Designs?

b. Under what circumstances would a banker loan money to Sigma Designs? Why or why not?

c. How would these conclusions change if the repurchases of stock were $100,000?

d. If Sigma planned to repurchase shares for $2,000,000 and needed to sell more shares or borrow to accomplish this objective, how would this information affect an investor's views of Sigma Designs?

Interpreting Financial Statements: Shareholders' Equity

10-62 Consider Sigma Designs' balance sheets for 1995 and 1994 (dollars in thousands). Sigma Designs is a high-tech software development company specializing in imaging and multimedia computer applications.

	1995	1994
Assets		
Cash and equivalents	$ 881	$ 1,808
Marketable securities	7,349	3,514
Accounts receivable, net of allowances	11,958	7,246
Inventories	9,736	10,602
Prepaid expenses and other	1,086	569
Total current assets	31,010	23,739
Equipment, net	1,343	1,200
Other assets	1,034	1,700
Total assets	$33,387	$26,639
Liabilities and Shareholders' Equity		
Current Liabilities		
Bank lines of credit	$ 1,710	$ 0
Accounts payable	9,333	4,207
Accrued salary and benefits	1,748	2,313
Other accrued liabilities	773	2,102
Total current liabilities	13,564	8,622
Long-term liabilities	1,102	1,518
Shareholders' Equity		
Common stock	38,820	27,544
Retained earnings (Deficit)	(20,099)	(11,045)
Shareholders' equity	18,721	16,499
Total liabilities and shareholders' equity	$33,387	$26,639

Required

a. Concentrate on the equity section of the balance sheet. What major changes have occurred in this section? What may have caused these changes?

b. Because Sigma had a net loss each year, its return on equity (ROE) ratios were negative each year. What aspects of Sigma's shareholders' equity would concern investors? Why?

Critical Thinking

International Comparisons: Shareholders' Equity

10-63 BF Group, a British company, reported the following components of shareholders' equity in its 1999 balance sheet (the relative size of each account balance is also shown):

- Called- up share capital (large balance)
- Share premium account (small balance)
- Capital reserve (large balance)
- Profit and loss account (small balance, but much larger than the current year's net income

Required

a. Compare and contrast each of these terms with corresponding terms typically shown on a U.S. firm's balance sheet.

b. Why do you suppose that a British firm would show both a reserve account and a profit and loss account?

Critical Thinking

Comprehensive Problem

10-64 The Nothing But Cheese (NBC) Company is a small but successful family-owned business that specializes in family photography in wholesome circumstances. The company conducts still and video photography of individuals and families in settings that can best be described as "heartwarming." NBC's photographic techniques are unique, incorporating several patented photographic equipment innovations and improvements. The company fully expects to dominate its market niche within the region in the foreseeable future.

The firm has been in existence for over 40 years and has had a long-term philosophy of "no debt" and "family control." Currently 5,000 shares of $1 par value common stock are outstanding, all of which are held by family members. NBC's shareholders' equity section of its December 31, 1996 balance sheet contained the following data:

Common stock: $1 par value, 100,000 shares authorized, 5,000 shares issued	$ 5,000
Additional paid-in capital in excess of par value	595,000
Retained earnings	9,898,000
Total shareholders' equity	$10,498,000

Sophia Fuji, NBC's current president, has found three alternative ways of raising additional capital that would be used for both current operating purposes and an expansion to neighboring regions.

- *Alternative 1:* Issue 40,000 shares of six percent, $100 par value cumulative preferred stock to a local but very wealthy investor. Each share could be converted to four shares of common stock anytime after the year 2000.
- *Alternative 2:* Borrow $4,000,000 from a local bank at 10 percent with a maturity date at the end of the year 2000.
- *Alternative 3:* Transform NBC immediately into a public company by issuing 500,000 shares of common stock at an estimated price of $8 per share. Of course, any member of the Fuji family could purchase stock on the open market at the issue date or at any later date.

Required

a. Has NBC been successful in the past? Has it been profitable? What information is needed to answer these questions?

b. How can it obtain cash for expansion or operating purposes if none of these options is successful? In other words, what other options could Sophia also pursue?

c. Show the effects on the shareholders' equity section of NBC's balance sheet from each of the three alternatives identified earlier by Sophia.

d. Noting that interest is deductible for tax purposes, while dividends are not, evaluate the advantages and disadvantages of each of the three options. Show the effects on net income of each option.

e. Write a short memo from Sophia to her relatives, recommending one of the three options, while at the same time criticizing the other two options.

f. One of Sophia's more vocal and complaining relatives responds to your memo and suggests that each of the three options is too expensive and threatens the loss of family control. He suggests that the family members must invest the additional $4,000,000 through purchase of additional shares. Because Sophia has already been told that other Fuji family members will not consider this option, write a short but tactful memo from Sophia to the dissenting family, indicating why your recommendation above (part e) is still preferable.

Critical Thinking

Conceptual Discussion: Exchanges of Debt or Equity

10-65 Many U.S. firms have completed exchanges or swaps of stock for debt. Collectively, such swaps often retire more debt than the value of the stock that is exchanged. In other words, the face value of the debt often exceeds the market value of the stock that is exchanged. Typical swaps might include:

- Convertible preferred stock for common stock
- Debt for convertible preferred stock
- Convertible debt for common stock
- Debt for cash and common stock

Required

a. What do you suppose are the incentives or motivations for such swaps? Why would an investor or owner give up something with a historical cost higher than its current market value?
b. What is the effect of such swaps on a firm's balance sheet?

Ethics

Debt Disguised as Equity

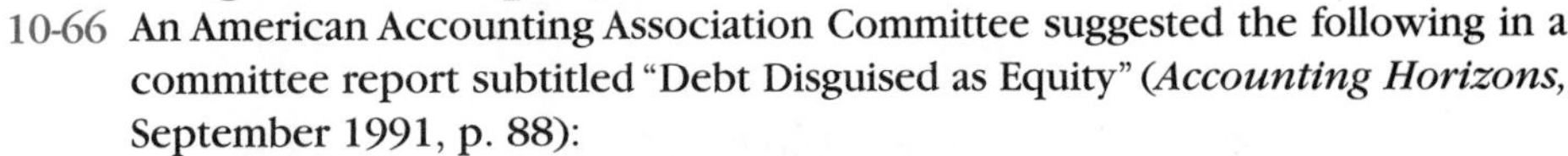

10-66 An American Accounting Association Committee suggested the following in a committee report subtitled "Debt Disguised as Equity" (*Accounting Horizons,* September 1991, p. 88):

> . . . If [debt can be made to look like equity] while at the same time retaining the tax-deductibility of the interest on the debt, so much the better. Complex schemes have been thought up to secure these ends, and even relatively simple steps may be taken to disguise a liability as equity. . . . One proposal that the FASB is exploring is to get rid of the distinction altogether.

Required

a. Identify two ways in which a firm might disguise or transform its debt into equity.
b. Identify two reasons why a firm might want to disguise its debt as equity. List two reasons why a firm might not want to do this.
c. Discuss the ethical implications of disguising debt as equity.
d. Who do you think should set rules to control a firm's choices regarding the disclosure of debt and equity? Why?
e. What recommendations would you propose to solve these issues?

Critical Thinking

Research Project: Shareholders' Equity

10-67 Locate recent annual reports for three companies in the same industry. If such reports are not conveniently available, use a business reference service, such as *Moody's, Standard & Poor's, Compustat,* or the SEC's EDGAR database to obtain the following information:

- Company name and industry designation
- Preferred stock (number of shares outstanding and dollar amount)
- Common stock (number of shares outstanding and dollar amount)
- Retained earnings
- Total shareholders' equity
- Total current liabilities
- Total long-term liabilities
- Total assets
- Earnings per share
- Market price (year-end or representative price)

Required

a. For each company, compute the financial leverage ratios.
b. For each company, prepare a vertical analysis (percentage composition) of its balance sheet.
c. For each company, compute the price-to-earnings ratio and the market-to-book value ratio.
d. Write a short memo comparing and contrasting the financial structure and risks associated with the three companies.

Critical Thinking

Interpreting Financial Statements: Shareholders' Equity

10-68 DUD Computer is a private company. DUD's major product lines are CAD/CAM computer vision design systems, midrange computers, and computer services. DUD had $1.26 billion in debt at the end of 2000, its losses were more than half a billion dollars, and its net worth (retained earnings) was a negative $674.9 million. It will be in default on its loan covenants if it fails to secure new financing by the end of 2002. Its summary financial trends were:

	2000	1999
Revenue (in billions)	$1.44	$1.55
Net (loss) (in millions)	($562.8)*	($172.8)
Loss per share	($ 9.02)	($ 3.21)

*Includes nonrecurring charges of $352.2 million.

Required

a. A business editor claimed that "DUD is in peril with too much debt." On what basis was this comment made?
b. Construct a scenario with high debt levels where such a comment would be premature.
c. Using the data given above, calculate the net loss and loss per share after *excluding* the nonrecurring charges.
d. The company's president and CEO suggested that DUD had a positive cash flow and would have been profitable if it weren't for huge debt payments and write-downs. Critique the president's conclusions. Is it possible for a company with such huge losses to have positive cash flows? Why? Is it also possible for a company's debt payments to affect its net income? Why?

Ethics

Financial Statement Impact: Earnings Per Share

10-69 Premier Anesthesia is a high-tech health services provider that transformed itself from a private company to a public company in 1992. At the end of 1992, its price-to-earnings ratio was 45.0, based on *estimated* 1992 earnings. Its quarterly earnings for the first and second quarter of 1992 were, respectively, three cents and six cents a share. Curiously, its year-to-date EPS at the end of the second quarter of 1992 was 11 cents per share (*WSJ,* December 8, 1992, p. C1). The company's market price more than doubled during the last half of 1992 (from less than $6.00 per share to more than $14.00 per share).

Required

a. Comment on the discrepancy between the reported earnings-per-share data.
b. Comment on Premier Anesthesia's spectacular share prices relative to its earnings.

Additional Data

A reporter, Mr. Craig Torres, reported that "much of Premier's interest earnings come from high interest loans to a group of clinics" owned and controlled by Premier's chairman and largest stockholder (*WSJ,* December 8, 1992, p. C1). These loans carried interest rates ranging from 12 to 24 percent. Premier also booked management fees from the clinics as operating income. Mr. Torres suggested that "Premier's earnings come not from the hospital world, but from collecting interest income." The article was headlined as "Premier Anesthesia's Earnings Are Bloated by Interest Income" and "Premier Anesthesia's Earnings Get a Big Boost from Large Injection of Loan-Interest Income." Approximately 42 percent of the firm's earnings were derived from these related-party loans.

a. Find one to two articles (using the library or Internet) on "related-party" issues. Summarize the key issues as they reflect financial reporting and ethics.
b. Describe how a company can earn interest income from another company, particularly one that it controls. Comment on the ethical issues of such loans and the reporting of such income, particularly given the market's response to Premier Anesthesia's earnings. Also comment on the interest rates, given that the prime rate during this period was around six percent.

Additional Data

Mr. Torres also reported that no buyer had been found for the clinics, so the loans were essentially "bridge" financing until Premier Anesthesia could acquire the clinics. He reported that "Some analysts suspect Premier is deliberately delaying the deal's closing to keep collecting interest income, and thus to avoid losing an important source of earnings in its first year as a public company" (*WSJ,* December 8, 1991, p. C2).

a. Reassess your conclusions about the sources of Premier's earnings and about the ethics of its earnings management tactics.
b. What might you recommend in similar circumstances? Why?

Transfer of Cash to Related Companies

10-70 Philip Morris was the founder and chairman of Lollipops, Inc. until his death in 1998. The company's performance had been sharply declining during the 1990s. Because Morris owned the majority of the shares in the company, he was very concerned about the resultant decline in the share prices and market value of Lollipops. To protect his investments, he secretly funneled $300,000,000 from other companies that he owned into purchases of additional Lollipops shares. These new shares were used by the other companies as collateral for bank loans, for financing the purchase of the shares, and for supporting the operations of the other companies. After his death, this series of stock purchases and bank loans was revealed in the financial press, and Lollipops' shares plummeted in value!

Required

a. In what ways were these transactions unethical?
b. How might Lollipops have survived this calamity?

Research Project: Corporate Restructuring

10-71 Scan the recent financial press, such as *Business Week, Forbes,* or the *Wall Street Journal,* to identify a company that has recently changed its capital structure. Read one or two recent articles on this company and write a short summary of the restructuring, addressed as a memo to your instructor. In your memo, include the company's stated reasons for the restructuring as well as any other reasons that you might consider relevant and rational. To the extent possible, show how the company's capital structure appeared before and after the restructuring.

Critical Thinking

Research Project: Changes in Capital Structure

10-72 Choose one of the companies whose financial statements appear in Appendixes D or E. Obtain the company's most recent financial statement, or get its balance sheet on the Internet. Find one or two recent articles that describe the company's changes in its capital structure.

Required

a. Compare the company's capital structure as of the original financial statements (in the appropriate appendix) to the company's most recent capital structure.
b. Document or identify any possible reasons for changes in the company's capital structure.
c. Identify any problems in the firm's original capital structure or in its most recent capital structure. What might the firm's managers do to resolve these problems?
d. Identify any inconsistencies in the firm's behavior. That is, were its actions consistent with the problems that you identified? Discuss these inconsistencies, particularly from the viewpoint of an external analyst who has to make predictions about the future success of the company.

Critical Thinking

Research Project: Changes in Capital Structure

10-73 Choose an industry. Identify the three largest firms in that industry. Obtain their most recent financial statements or summaries thereof. Obtain one or two recent articles on this industry or on the three selected firms.

Required

a. Discuss the similarities and differences in the three firms' capital structures.
b. Discuss how these firms might be changing their capital structure, especially in response to industry or market factors.
c. Discuss how the firms' capital structures might reflect problems or opportunities in this industry.
d. Identify any inconsistencies in the firms' management of their capital structures. That is, discuss how each firm's capital structure is responsive to both its particular circumstances and to industry and market factors. Discuss how the firm might be acting consistently and rationally relative to these factors. Discuss any inconsistencies, particularly from the viewpoint of an external analyst who has to make predictions about the future success of the company.

Critical Thinking

Understanding Disclosures in Notes

10-74 Pfizer, Inc. provided the following information in the notes to its 1997 financial statements:

12 Common Stock

We effected a two-for-one split of our common stock in the form of a 100 percent stock dividend in both 1997 and 1995. Both splits followed votes by shareholders to increase the number of authorized common shares. All share and per share information in this report reflects both splits.

The board of directors authorized us to repurchase up to $2 billion of our outstanding common stock through September 1998. In 1997, we repurchased approximately 11.4 million shares at an average price of $51 per share and approximately .6 million shares in 1996 at an average price of $44 per share.

13 Preferred Stock Purchase Rights

Preferred Stock Purchase Rights granted in 1987 expired in October 1997. Those rights were replaced by new Preferred Stock Purchase Rights that have a scheduled term through October 2007, although that may be extended or redeemed. One right was issued for each share of common stock issued by our company. These rights are not exercisable unless certain change-in-control events transpire, such as a person acquiring or obtaining the right to acquire beneficial ownership of 15 percent or more of our outstanding common stock or an announcement of a tender offer for at least 30 percent of that stock. The rights are evidenced by corresponding common stock certificates and automatically trade with the common stock unless an event transpires that makes them exercisable. If the rights become exercisable, separate certificates evidencing the rights will be distributed and each right will entitle the holder to purchase from our company a new series of preferred stock at a defined price. The preferred stock, in addition to preferred dividend and liquidation rights, will entitle the holder to vote with the company's common stock.

The rights are redeemable by us at a fixed price until 10 days, or longer as determined by the board, after certain defined events, or at any time prior to the expiration of the rights.

We have reserved 3.0 million preferred shares to be issued pursuant to these rights. No such shares have yet been issued. At the present time, the rights have no dilutive effect on the earnings per common share calculation.

Required

a. Review Pfizer's notes. Identify any unusual terms.
b. Reconstruct each of the transactions described by Pfizer. Use the accounting equation to summarize these transactions.
c. Indicate how each of these transactions may affect Pfizer's (a) EPS and (b) ROE.
d. Discuss the possible impact of Pfizer's stock repurchasing plan.
e. Discuss the implications of Pfizer's unissued preferred shares.
f. Identify whether Pfizer's disclosures are favorable or unfavorable for existing shareholders. Are they advantageous for future shareholders? Why?

Critical Thinking

Understanding Disclosures in Notes

10-75 Eli Lilly and Company provided the following information in the notes (excerpts) to its 1997 financial statements:

Note 8: Stock Plans

Stock options and performance awards have been granted to officers and other executive and key employees. Stock options are granted at exercise prices equal to the fair market value of the company's stock at the dates of grant. Generally, options vest 100 percent after three years from the grant date and have a term of 10 years.

In October 1995, the company issued its second grant under the GlobalShares program. Essentially all employees were given an option to buy 400 shares of the company's common stock at a price equal to the fair market value of the company's stock at the date of grant. Options to purchase approximately 10.3 million shares were granted as part of the program. Individual grants generally become exercisable on or after the third anniversary of the grant date and have a term of 10 years.

The company has elected to follow Accounting Principles Board Opinion (APB) No. 25, "Accounting for Stock Issued to Employees" and related interpretations in accounting for its stock options. Under APB No. 25, because the exercise price of the company's employee stock options equals the market price of the underlying stock on the date of grant, no compensation expense is recognized. Total compensation expense for stock-based awards reflected in income on a pretax basis was $242.1 million, $164.2 million, and $93.1 million in 1997, 1996, and 1995, respectively. However, SFAS No. 123, "Accounting for Stock-Based Compensation," requires presentation of pro forma information as if the company had accounted for its employee stock options granted subsequent to December 31, 1994, under the fair value method of that statement. For purposes of pro forma disclosure, the estimated fair value of the options is amortized to expense over the vesting period. Under the fair value method, the company's net income (loss) and earnings (loss) per share would have been as follows:

	1997	1996	1995
Net income (loss)	$(424.2)	$1,496.5	$2,285.3
Earnings (loss) per share—diluted	$ (0.39)	$ 1.34	$ 1.98

Because SFAS No. 123 is applicable only to options granted subsequent to December 31, 1994, and the options have a three-year vesting period, the pro forma effect will not be fully reflected until 1998.

Note 9: Shareholders' Equity

On September 15, 1997, the company's board of directors declared a two-for-one stock split to be effected in the form of a 100 percent stock dividend payable to shareholders of record at the close of business on September 24, 1997. The outstanding and weighted-average number of shares of common stock and per-share data in these financial statements have been adjusted to reflect the impact of the stock split for all periods presented. The company now has 1,111,521,927 issued shares of common stock without par value, including 554,331,485 shares issued October 15, 1997, as a result of the stock split. Treasury shares held by the company were not split.

The company has an Employee Stock Ownership Plan (ESOP) as a funding vehicle for the existing employee savings plan. The ESOP used the proceeds of a loan from the company to purchase shares of common stock from the treasury. In 1991, the ESOP issued $200 million of third-party debt, repayment of which was guaranteed by the company (see Note 7). The proceeds were used to purchase shares of the company's common stock on the open market. Shares of common stock held by the ESOP will be allocated to participating employees annually through 2006 as part of the company's savings plan contribution. The fair value of shares allocated each period is recognized as compensation expense.

Under the terms of the company's Shareholder Rights plan, all shareholders of common stock received for each share owned a preferred stock purchase right entitling them to purchase from the company one four-hundredth of a share of Series A Participating Preferred Stock at an exercise price of $40.63. The rights are not exercisable until after the date on which the company's right to redeem has expired. The company may redeem the rights for $.00125 per right up to and including the tenth business day after the date of a public announcement that a person (the "Acquiring Person") has acquired ownership of stock having 20 percent or more of the company's general voting power (the "Stock Acquisition Date").

The plan provides that, if the company is acquired in a business combination transaction at any time after a stock acquisition date, generally each holder of a right will be entitled to purchase at the exercise price a number of the acquiring company's shares having a market value of twice the exercise price. The plan also provides that, in the event of certain other business combinations, certain self-dealing transactions or the acquisition by a person of stock having 25 percent or more of the company's general voting power, generally each holder of a right will be entitled to purchase at the exercise price a number of shares of the company's common stock having a market value of twice the exercise price. Any rights beneficially owned by an acquiring person shall not be entitled to the benefit of the adjustments with respect to the number of shares described above. The rights will expire on July 28, 1998 unless redeemed earlier by the company.

Required

a Review Lilly's notes. Identify any unusual terms.

b. Reconstruct each of the transactions described by Lilly. Use the accounting equation to summarize these transactions.

c. Indicate how each of these transactions may affect Lilly's (a) EPS and (b) ROE.

d. Discuss the possible impact of Lilly's preferred rights issue.

e. Discuss the implications of Lilly's stock option plan.

f. Identify whether Lilly's disclosures are favorable or unfavorable for existing shareholders. Are they advantageous for future shareholders? Why?

Identifying Shareholders' Equity Information

10-76 Clorox and Lubrizol repurchased some common stock in 1995. Locate their 10-K filings for 1995 from the EDGAR archives **(www.sec.gov/edaux/searches.htm).**

Required

a. For each company, list the number of shares of common stock authorized, issued, and outstanding. Does either company hold any treasury stock?
b. How many shares of common stock did each of these companies repurchase in 1995? What was the cash outflow for shares repurchased?
c. What was the impact of the repurchase program on shareholders' equity?

Internet

Searching for Information: Shareholders' Equity

10-77 Quicken.com's home page **(www.quicken.com)** contains information on several hundred corporations. In addition to links to corporate home pages or financial information, it also provides current and historical stock price data (as well as other market-related data). Access the market-related data for Hewlett-Packard, Bell Atlantic, and Oracle.

Required

a. Which stock exchange is each company listed on, and what is its ticker symbol?
b. Identify the most recent stock price and price-to-earnings ratio for each company.
c. Examine the latest set of financial statements for each company from either the corporate home page or EDGAR **(www.sec.gov/edaux/searches.htm).** What is the EPS and book value per share for each company?
d. For each company, compute the market-to-book value ratio and the price-to-earnings ratio (based on the annual EPS identified in part c). Based on these two ratios, which company do you believe has the highest growth expectations as per the market?

Internet

Stock Prices & Shareholders' Equity

10-78 Access Quicken.com's home page **(www.quicken.com),** which provides links to corporate pages and market-related data. The menu contains two options for charts.

Required

a. Set the time horizon so that it will capture enough price history to include the stock prices for Applied Materials on October 12, 1995. Your chart should show a marked price drop for that month. What were the share prices before and after the drop?
b. Use the EDGAR archives **(www.sec.gov/edaux/searches.htm)** to locate the 10-K filings for Applied Materials for fiscal 1994 and 1995. Examine the shareholders' equity section of the consolidated balance sheet for each year. Determine the par value of the common stock and the number of shares of common stock issued and outstanding for each year. Note your observations and check the Notes section for any explanations.
c. Is the stock price reaction consistent with the information provided in the financial statements?

chapter 11

A Framework for Financial Statement Analysis

LEARNING OBJECTIVES

1. Understand why financial statements are analyzed.
2. Know where to obtain financial information.
3. Determine when financial information is comparable and alternatively, learn how to enhance the comparability of financial information that may appear to be noncomparable.
4. Identify, calculate, use, and interpret appropriate ratios.
5. Identify limitations of financial statement analyses.

INTRODUCTION

Accountants produce financial information in the form of financial statements and many different excerpts from annual financial reports have been shown earlier in this book. In this chapter, we link many of the ratios and analytical concepts that have been previously introduced. The purpose of this chapter is to show how a comprehensive financial statement analysis can be conducted. To accomplish this purpose, we will use the entire set of financial statements from Wendy's International, Inc., which is one of the United States' largest restaurant chains, with more than 4,000 company- and franchise-operated restaurants.

In order for financial information to be useful, it must be interpreted. A comprehensive set of ratios in an organized framework enhances the usefulness and interpretability of financial statements and eases the communication of financial information between firms and users.

USERS OF FINANCIAL STATEMENTS

Users of financial statements can be found in many sectors of the economy. Typical users include a firm's owners, creditors, managers, employees, customers, and suppliers. Users of financial statements include those who already have an economic link to the firm as well as those who may want to have a future economic relationship.

Most users have, or intend to have, a transactional relationship with the firm and some users may be able to obtain information directly from the firm. For example, a potential creditor can request that a credit application be prepared according to its own specifications. Potential customers or potential suppliers may also request special information as they see fit. Most users, however, will use the annual financial statements as well as quarterly and other interim reports.

Each of these users may have different objectives while analyzing financial statements:

- *Investors* use financial statement information to help decide whether to increase or decrease their ownership interests in the firm. These decisions are based on projections of investment risks and returns. Financial ratios are widely used in making these projections.
- *Managers* use financial statement information in many different ways, but one of the most important is in setting goals. Managerial goals can be stated in terms of increasing various profitability ratios. Goals can be stated in terms of maintaining or increasing the firm's liquidity, or they can be stated in terms of changing the capital structure in favor of more debt or more equity.
- *Customers* often use annual financial statements to evaluate the firm's stability and its capability to deliver on a timely basis the quantity and quality of goods or services that may be purchased.
- *Potential suppliers and creditors* often are most interested in whether the firm can pay its bills.
- *Other users* of financial statements have a more distant relationship with the firm. These users include government regulators in areas such as securities trading, taxation, environmental protection, occupational health and safety, insurance and other financial markets, and foreign trade. Other interactions could occur with employee trade unions or other community groups. Finally, various economic and public policy analysts might review a firm's financial statements in their quest to create or improve legislation affecting many broad areas of commerce and social welfare. Any of these groups might want to explore how the firm has affected various components of society.

SOURCES OF FINANCIAL INFORMATION

In addition to the basic business financial statements and disclosures that we have described in earlier chapters, other kinds of financial information are available to financial analysts that can be used in combination with financial statements. Most regulatory agencies, for example, require firms to prepare special-purpose regulatory reports, such as tax returns or environmental impact statements. The SEC also requires special reports each year and each quarter. The SEC's annual report is called a Form 10-K, which is discussed more thoroughly in Chapter 14. The Form 10-K is an expanded version of the firm's annual report, which can frequently be used to clarify issues of concern or ambiguity in the annual report.

In addition to annual reports filed with the SEC, public companies must also file quarterly reports, which are less detailed than the annual reports. Furthermore, whenever major events require public disclosure, public firms are also required to file special reports with the SEC, designed to provide immediate information to any interested party. Events that must be reported include replacement of the firm's auditor, a major acquisition or disposition of a business segment, or any major news announcement.

Other sources of public information that are more readily available include various business periodicals such as the *Wall Street Journal, Business Week, Forbes, Fortune, Barron's,* or various newsletters that specialize in certain industries or locales. Even your local newspaper will often have a business section on either a weekly or daily basis.

Investment advisory services also publish summary information about specific firms and industries. Some of the more well known of these include *Standard & Poors, Moody's, Value Line, Dun & Bradstreet's,* and *Robert Morris and Associates.* Such services provide condensed information from company annual reports. This information is usually prepared in a standardized format. The process of "homogenizing" the information from the annual report, however, may obscure some of the important insights that could have been obtained from the report itself. One advantage of these services is that they provide interpretations of the financial results and their opinions regarding the future prospects of the companies.

The major source of financial information we are concerned with is the firm's **annual report.** A major portion of the 1997 annual report of Wendy's is included in Appendix D and will be referenced throughout our discussion. Such reports usually contain the following elements (see Appendix D for examples of each):

1. Management discussion and analysis (MDA), which is a narrative report providing a qualitative description of the year's highlights. This section may also include a letter from the CEO.
2. Independent accountant's report (auditor's report), which is usually presented as an unqualified opinion or as some version of a qualified opinion regarding the financial statements (see Chapter 14, "Additional Dimensions of Financial Accounting"). Annual reports generally include the management's statement of responsibility for the information contained in the financial statements.
3. Primary financial statements, which include the balance sheet, the income statement, and the statement of cash flows.
4. Secondary financial statements, which may include the statement of shareholders' equity, other reconciliations related to the cash flow statement, and other disclosures regarding the primary financial statements.
5. Notes to the financial statements, which include a variety of supplementary disclosures such as quarterly data, business segment information, and trend information in the form of five- or 10-year comparisons of selected financial data or key ratios.

This information in the annual report provides the basis for much of the analysis conducted by users of financial statements. Little formal analysis can be applied to the qualitative statements contained in the discussion sections and in the notes, but the qualitative and narrative discussions can provide much insight into many of the relationships that are revealed by the ratio calculations. Both the quantitative and qualitative information must be reviewed by the conscientious analyst.

Later in this chapter, we provide a framework for reviewing this information in order to assess the firm's past performance and its future potential. For the remainder of the chapter, we focus exclusively on analyzing financial statements from the perspective of an equity investor. Although many of the same ratios are used by creditors and other financial statement users identified earlier, we will take an *investor focus* as we develop and illustrate our framework.

BASIS OF COMPARISON

One of the analyst's first decisions is to identify the basis of comparison. That is, what data will be used to compare and evaluate the target firm? It's also important to note that financial data do not exist in a vacuum. Analyzing financial statements from one firm for a single year is like reporting only part of a football score (14)! Therefore, financial statement analysis is often concerned with comparing the current year's results with other related results. The choices include

1. The prior year(s) results
2. Another similar firm in the same industry
3. Another firm in which the analyst may invest
4. All firms in the same industry and/or industry averages
5. Benchmarks or targets that have been previously established, such as lending or investing criteria

The analyst must determine that one of these choices is a comparable and useful reference with which to compare the target firm. Usually, the prior year or years are a good reference point with which to begin. Any statements that include the effects of a major financial restructuring or merger would generally be noncomparable. In other words, before comparing a firm's results with the prior year, the analyst must examine both sets of statements and notes to determine whether a significant unusual event occurred.

If significant unusual events have occurred that would distort comparisons, then the financial statements may need to be restated or rearranged to make them more comparable. Restatements may be necessary in the following situations:

- Mergers or major acquisitions
- Discontinued operations or major dispositions
- Changes in accounting principles or estimates
- Extraordinary items (on the income statement)
- Changes in account classifications
- Changes in reporting periods (such as fiscal periods)
- Shifts in industry structure or classification
- Any other unusual or nonrecurring event

It is beyond the scope of this text to illustrate all of these possible restatements, but several examples are given in the case discussion later in this chapter. The primary guideline is that "more comparability is better." Financial information from firms might be comparable if the firms

- operate in the same country,
- follow similar accounting practices,
- are of similar size (revenues and/or assets),
- produce similar products or services, and
- have a similar capital structure.

Although other important dimensions of comparability may be available, size, capital structure, and product mix are the most important for our purposes. The analyst must decide whether differences in these areas are material or whether they might have an impact on the final conclusions. Comparability is a subjective and qualitative issue that can never be quantified by a numerical index.

Thus far, we have identified four major steps that must be accomplished before starting to calculate financial statement ratios:

1. Identify the purpose and objectives of the analysis.
2. Review the financial statements, notes, and audit opinion to identify any unusual events or characteristics and become familiar with the nature of the firm's operations.
3. Determine whether any restatements due to mergers, discontinued operations, and so on, are necessary to enhance the comparability of the firm's financial statements.
4. Determine whether the firm's size, capital structure, and product mix are sufficiently comparable (between firms or time periods) to proceed with the ratio calculations.

FINANCIAL STATEMENT ANALYSIS RATIOS AND FRAMEWORK

The next major step is to conduct horizontal and vertical analyses of the financial statements. Usually this analysis begins with the income statement, including all its major revenue and expense items. A horizontal analysis focuses on year-to-year changes or growth for each major element in the income statement. Common-size financial statements, a tool employed in a vertical analysis, examine the percentage composition of the income statement. Percentages are calculated on the basis of net revenues, where each item on the income statement is separately analyzed.

Horizontal and vertical analyses of the major subtotals in the balance sheet and in the cash flow statement should also be conducted. The results of these analyses will focus attention on areas of significant change. Such analyses do not provide complete answers. Rather, they indicate areas of concern that require further investigation. Therefore, step 5 in our framework is

5. Conduct horizontal and vertical analyses of each financial statement. Identify any unusual trends.

Categories of Financial Ratios

Analysts find it useful to classify ratios into broad groupings, based on the characteristics that particular ratios are intended to measure. In this section, we discuss ratios under four major headings that are widely employed by analysts: liquidity, profitability, capital structure, and investor ratios.

Liquidity Ratios **Liquidity ratios** indicate the short-term solvency of the firm. They also indicate how effectively the firm is managing its working capital. Exhibit 11-1 shows the formulas used in computing a representative set of liquidity ratios. Each of these ratios has been described earlier in the text, as indicated by the chapter references in the exhibit. The **current ratio** and **quick ratio** are measures of solvency. Other measures of cash availability can also be used to indicate how long the firm could operate using only its current cash balances. A limitation of these ratios is that they do not reflect the availability of short-term credit. Many firms operate with decreasing levels of liquidity as they rely more heavily on "lines of credit" that can be used, or repaid, on a daily basis. Humana, Inc. (a health care insurance and hospital company), for example, reported zero cash on its balance sheet for three years (1990–1992)! In many cases, high current or quick ratios indicate mismanagement or wasteful investment in working capital. Some firms may just have too much liquidity because excess cash might be more effectively used by either paying off liabilities, paying dividends to shareholders, or buying treasury shares.

EXHIBIT 11-1 Summary of Liquidity Ratios

Current ratio	=	$\frac{\text{Current Assets}}{\text{Current Liabilities}}$ (Chapter 3)
Quick ratio	=	$\frac{\text{Cash + Cash Equivalents + Accounts Receivable}}{\text{Current Liabilities}}$ (Chapter 3)
Average sales per day	=	$\frac{\text{Sales Revenue}}{365}$ (Chapter 6)
Collection period	=	$\frac{\text{Accounts Receivable}}{\text{Average Sales Per Day}}$ (Chapter 6)
Cost of goods sold per day	=	$\frac{\text{Cost of Goods Sold}}{365}$ (Chapter 6)
Number of days' sales in ending inventory (NDS)	=	$\frac{\text{Ending Inventory}}{\text{Cost of Goods Sold Per day}}$ (Chapter 6)

The **number of days in inventory** indicates how quickly the firm is "turning" its inventory. Comparative industry statistics can often be used to evaluate the days in inventory. Certainly, comparisons with the prior periods will indicate whether the turnover has increased or decreased, and changes in product mix will dramatically affect the inventory ratios.

Step 6 in our framework encompasses liquidity ratios

6. Calculate the basic liquidity ratios. In cases where liquidity seems to be too high or too low, conduct further analyses as necessary.

Profitability Ratios **Profitability ratios** are the second major focus of analysis for any investor. Without profits, there will be no return to the investor or no one will want to invest. The primary profitability ratios are defined in Exhibit 11–2; they reference the earlier chapters in which they were initially discussed.

The **gross profit percentage** is the first source of profitability for a manufacturing or merchandising firm. The data for the gross profit margin are found in the first sections of the income statement. These data indicate the level of profits earned from buying and reselling goods. A decreasing gross profit percentage may indicate decreased sales prices, higher costs of production, or a shift from high-profit to low-profit products.

The **operating income ratio** is the second indicator of profitability because it includes all the other normal and recurring operating costs. Increasing or stable levels of operating income indicate sustainability of the firm's profits. Decreasing operating income ratios usually indicate a need for the firm to examine its production efficiency, its marketing strategies, and its control of administrative costs.

EXHIBIT 11-2 Summary of Profitability Ratios

$$\text{Gross Profit Percentage} = \frac{\text{Gross Profit}}{\text{Net Sales Revenue}}$$
(Chapter 6)

$$\text{Operating Income Percentage} = \frac{\text{Operating Income}}{\text{Net Sales Revenue}}$$
(Chapter 4)

$$\text{Return on Equity} = \frac{\text{Net Income}}{\text{Average Shareholders' Equity}}$$
(Chapter 4)

$$\text{Return on Assets} = \frac{\text{Net Income} + (\text{Interest Expense} \times [1 - \text{Tax Rate}])}{\text{Average Total Assets}}$$
(Chapter 4)

$$\text{Cash Return on Assets} = \frac{\text{Cash Flow from Operating Activities} + \text{Interest Paid}}{\text{Average Total Assets}}$$
(Chapter 5)

$$\text{Quality of Income} = \frac{\text{Cash Flow from Operating Activities}}{\text{Net Income}}$$
(Chapter 5)

The most important profitability ratio from an investor's viewpoint is the **return on equity (ROE) ratio.** It is often called ROI, return on investment ratio, because it indicates the annual rate of return to the firm's investors or owners. Return on equity represents the residual return that is available to owners after deducting all other financing costs.

The **return on assets (ROA) ratio** indicates the rate of return on the firm's assets. It can be used to compare rates of return with alternative investments that could be undertaken. Just as in the adjusted net income percentage described earlier, ROA adjusts for the effects of debt financing by removing the after-tax effects of interest expense. It can also be used to compare profitability across firms and over different time periods.

Some analysts may prefer to analyze the firm's profitability and financial returns in terms of cash and not in terms of accrual-based net income. The **cash return on assets ratio** should be compared with the corresponding profitability ratios based on net income and ROA. Results that appear to be inconsistent should be examined carefully. These ratios look at financial returns to the firm in terms of cash, not in terms of accrual-based net income. As such, the cash-based profitability ratios are often viewed as more objective by analysts.

The final profitability ratio, **quality of income,** is a direct comparison between cash flows from operating activities (CFOA) and net income (NI). The analyst must examine trends within the same company to determine that CFOA is not decreasing relative to NI. Therefore, step 7 in our financial statement analysis framework follows.

7. Calculate profitability ratios based on net income and on cash flows from operating activities. Evaluate trends in profitability and compare the appropriate NI and CFOA ratios for consistency. Compare profitability ratios across similar companies and against industry averages.

Capital Structure **Capital structure** analysis assesses the firm's strategies for financing its assets and indicates the relative amounts of debt and equity capital. The analyst evaluates how those sources change and how they compare with other firms in the same industry. The analyst then tries to gain insight into the firm's decisions about capital sources in order to predict future capital financing decisions. An investor would surely like to know whether the firm is likely to issue new debts or sell additional shares of stock. Identifying shifts in capital structure over time may indicate how the firm will make future decisions about sources of capital. The major ways to examine capital structure are summarized in Exhibit 11-3.

The **percentage composition analysis** is the starting point for any analysis of capital structure. It describes the relative amounts of capital obtained from each major source of financing. The analyst can examine the percentage composition results to note changes from the prior year as well as compare percentage composition ratios with similar firms and with industry averages.

EXHIBIT 11-3 Summary of Capital Structure Ratios

Percentage Composition	=	The results of the vertical analysis of right side of the balance sheet, such that the sum of all sources of capital must be 100%: (Chapter 3)
		$\frac{\text{Current Liabilities}}{\text{Total Liabilities and Shareholders' Equity}}$
		$\frac{\text{Long-term Debt}}{\text{Total Liabilities and Shareholders' Equity}}$
		$\frac{\text{Deferred Taxes + Other Similar Liabilities}}{\text{Total Liabilities and Shareholders' Equity}}$
		$\frac{\text{Shareholders' Equity}}{\text{Total Liabilities and Shareholders' Equity}}$
Financial Leverage (also called Debt to Assets)	=	$\frac{\text{Total Liabilities}}{\text{Total Assets}}$ (Chapters 3, 10)
Times Interest Earned	=	$\frac{\text{Earnings Before Interest and Taxes (EBIT)}}{\text{Interest Expense}}$ (Chapter 4)

Note that the **financial leverage ratio** is simply a variation on percentage composition analysis. All liabilities are added and are then divided by total assets (which, by definition, must equal total liabilities and shareholders' equity). It is not always clear whether to include deferred taxes and other similar liabilities, however. In many cases, the analyst will find that this category of liabilities may be a dominant source of capital because of recent changes in accounting rules regarding deferred taxes.

The other capital structure ratio is also informative about the financing strategies that the firm has chosen. The **times interest earned ratio** is an indicator of relative risk. The lower the times interest earned, the higher the risk of bankruptcy or other default. Times interest earned indicates the "cushion" or margin of safety that the firm enjoys in meeting its interest expenses. A ratio close to 100 percent indicates that the firm is barely covering its interest expenses. Any slight decrease in earnings would then result in an inability to cover the interest expenses. As usual, trends in this ratio should be monitored. Therefore, step 8 in our financial statement analysis framework is

8. Evaluate the firm's capital structure with special emphasis on trends in the percentage composition ratios.

Investor Ratios **Investor ratios** were introduced in Chapter 10, "Shareholders' Equity." These ratios all relate to an external dimension of ownership interest. Most indicate how the firm is performing with regard to the market value of its shares. A listing of investor ratios appears in Exhibit 11–4.

The **earnings-per-share (EPS) ratio** indicates the net income earned by each share of outstanding stock. It is most often used by investors as a primary comparison of performance and profitability across different companies. However, we believe that it is overemphasized. It should not be used in isolation outside the context of other dimensions of financial performance. Furthermore, it should be used in conjunction only with EPSs from prior years and/or with EPSs from other comparable firms.

The **market-to-book value ratio** indicates the relationship between the market's valuation of the firm and the book values shown in the firm's financial statements. It is often used by investors to select targets of opportunity where the market is thought to undervalue a particular firm. It can also be used to influence an investor's decision to sell shares in a firm when the market may overvalue the firm's assets. On the other hand, a high market-to-book value ratio may reflect the fact that

EXHIBIT 11-4 Summary of Investor Ratios

$$\text{Earnings Per Share} = \frac{\text{Net Income}}{\text{Weighted Average Number of Shares Outstanding}}$$

(Chapter 10)

$$\text{Market-to-Book Value} = \frac{\text{Market Price Per Share}}{\text{Book Value Per Share}}$$

(Chapter 10)

$$\text{Price-to-Earnings (P/E)} = \frac{\text{Market Price Per Share}}{\text{Earnings Per Share}}$$

(Chapter 10)

financial accounting may undervalue the firm's recorded assets; many valuable economic resources of the firm may not even appear on the balance sheet.

The **price-to-earnings (P/E) ratio** indicates the relationship between market prices and earnings and is widely used to compare firms. Investors often establish guidelines, or cutoffs, such that they only purchase shares with a P/E of less than 30. In any event, the P/E ratio indicates the interaction between stock market prices and the income statement. As such, it is a convenient and widely accessible way to compare alternative investment opportunities.

Finally, step 9 in our financial statement analysis framework is

9. Examine the firm's market performance, using EPS, P/E, and market-to-book value ratios.

Final Steps

After assembling this myriad of ratios, the astute analyst must ask a series of questions, such as so what? what's missing? how do we predict the future?

Obviously, there are no easy recipes in this area. The analyst must look for inconsistencies and ambiguities that are evidenced in peculiar trends or unusual ratio results. Many ratios merely provide clues that require the analyst to look further at the notes to determine events and accounting treatments that are the cause of the numbers in the financial statements. The thoughtful analyst will always go back and forth between the numerical calculations and the underlying information in the notes while trying to decipher reality. Therefore, the last step is

10. Examine any inconsistencies in the ratio results and review the notes for further clarification. Then recalculate the ratios based on new insight and information obtained from the notes. Finally, try to estimate how the firm's liquidity, profitability, capital structure, and investor performance may change in the future.

Financial Statement Analysis Framework

In summary, our entire financial statement analysis framework is

1. Identify the purpose and objectives of the analysis. Who is the user and what decisions are to be made after the analysis?
2. Review the financial statements, notes, and audit opinions to identify any unusual events or characteristics.
3. Determine whether any restatements due to mergers, discontinued operations, accounting changes, or other factors are necessary to enhance the comparability of the statements.
4. Determine whether the firm's size, capital structure, and product mix are appropriate to proceed with the ratio calculations.
5. Conduct horizontal and vertical analyses of each financial statement. Identify any unusual trends.
6. Calculate the basic liquidity ratios. In cases where liquidity seems to be too high, or too low, conduct further analyses as necessary.
7. Calculate profitability ratios based on net income and on CFOA. Evaluate trends in profitability and compare the appropriate NI and CFO ratios for consistency. Then compare profitability ratios across similar companies and against industry averages.

8. Evaluate the firm's capital structure with special emphasis on trends in the percentage composition ratios.
9. Examine the firm's market performance using EPS, P/E, and market-to-book value ratios.
10. Examine any inconsistencies in the ratio results. Review the notes for further clarification. Recalculate the ratios based on new insight and information obtained from the notes. Try to estimate how the firm's liquidity, profitability, capital structure, and investor performance may change in the future.

FINANCIAL STATEMENT ANALYSIS, WENDY'S INTERNATIONAL, INC.

In this section, we apply our financial statement analysis framework to Wendy's International, Inc. We chose the Wendy's statements because they are representative of how most large companies present their financial data and because their statements include a variety of interesting but typical complications, where we can concentrate as much on the sources of information as on the numerical calculations. We have taken an investor focus to this analysis, concentrating on information that might be useful to someone contemplating purchasing shares of Wendy's common stock.

Initial Review of Wendy's International, Inc.

The independent auditor's report by Coopers & Lybrand (now Pricewaterhouse-Coopers) is a fairly typical, unqualified opinion (see Appendix D). Note that the fiscal year ended on different dates in 1997 and 1996. It is somewhat unusual to have a different fiscal year-end each year; however, in an industry that is open and available for business each day, the number of days in each fiscal period may be significant. Because Wendy's financial statements are based on 52 weeks in both 1997 and 1996, each year includes the same number of weekdays and weekends.

Although some unique events occurred during each year, the statements have sufficient detail to permit comparison across the 1997 and 1996 fiscal years. Note that all the dollar amounts, except the per-share amounts, are stated in thousands of dollars. As you have already seen, this type of rounding is quite typical in financial reporting. Such rounding will make no significant difference in the ratio results.

Horizontal and Vertical Analyses of Wendy's International, Inc. Income Statements

Horizontal and vertical analyses of Wendy's income statements for fiscal 1997 and 1996 appear in Exhibits 11–5 and 11–6, respectively. The horizontal analysis for Wendy's income statement, Exhibit 11–5, indicates that net sales grew about 7.4 percent in fiscal 1997, while expenses grew in a greater proportion than net sales (10.7 percent versus 7.4 percent). The more interesting comparison relates to net earnings, which decreased 16.3 percent in 1997.

Normally earnings grow faster than sales because at least some of the firm's expenses, such as depreciation and administrative costs, do not vary directly with sales from year to year. Yet the comparisons in Exhibit 11–5 indicate that Wendy's income has declined while revenues have increased. Note that Wendy's general and administrative expenses increased more than 76 percent during 1997, and that this single factor accounts for the decline in income during the year. The vertical analysis of Wendy's

EXHIBIT 11-5 Horizontal Analysis of An Income Statement

Wendy's International, Inc.
Income Statement: Horizontal Analysis
Fifty-Two Weeks Ended December 28, 1997, and December 29, 1996
(In Thousands, Except Per-Share Data)

	1997	Percent Change	1996
Revenues			
Retail sales	$1,651,689	+5.4%	$1,566,888
Franchise revenues	385,641	+16.7	330,256
	2,037,330	+7.4	1,897,144
Costs and expenses			
Cost of sales	1,026,026	+5.1	976,666
Company restaurant and other operating costs	452,709	+ 4.3	434,114
General, administrative, and other expenses	239,882	+76.7	135,778
Depreciation and amortization of property and equipment	95,638	+7.5	88,957
Interest, net	3,604	−47.1	6,812
	1,817,859	+10.7	1,642,327
Income before income taxes	219,471	−13.9	254,817
Income taxes	(88,972)	−10.0	(98,869)
Net income	$ 130,499	−16.3%	$ 155,948
Basic EPS	$ .99	−19.5	$ 1.23
Diluted EPS	$ .97	−18.5	$ 1.19
Dividends per share	$ .24		$ .24
Basic shares	131,595		126,461
Diluted shares	140,738		133,684

EXHIBIT 11-6 Vertical Analysis of An Income Statement

Wendy's International, Inc.
Income Statement: Vertical Analysis
Fifty-Two Weeks Ended December 28, 1997, and December 29, 1996
(In Thousands, Except Per-Share Data)

	1997 Dollars	Percentage	1996 Dollars	Percentage
Revenues				
Retail sales	$1,651,689	81.0%	$1,566,888	82.6%
Franchise revenues	385,641	18.9	330,256	17.4
	2,037,330	100.0	1,897,144	100.0
Costs and expenses				
Cost of sales	1,026,026	50.4	976,666	51.5
Company restaurant and other operating costs	452,709	22.24	434,114	22.9
General, administrative and other expenses	239,882	11.8	135,778	7.2
Depreciation and amortization of property and equipment	95,638	4.7	88,957	4.7
Interest, net	3,604	.2	6,812	.4
	1,817,859	89.2	1,642,327	86.6
Income before income taxes	219,471	10.7	254,817	13.4
Income taxes	(88,972)	4.4	(98,869)	5.2
Net income	$ 130,499	6.4%	$ 155,948	8.2%

income statement in Exhibit 11–6 reinforces the observation that, except for the general and administrative expenses, all the other categories of operating expenses had a stable or declining relation to sales, indicative of effective cost control and increasingly efficient operations. Because of the material and unexpected change in the general and administrative expenses, the analyst would refer to the footnotes and other financial disclosures to determine the reasons for this change. The entire financial report of Wendy's for 1997 is included as Appendix D, and cases at the end of this chapter will enable you to explore this issue further.

Horizontal and Vertical Analyses of Wendy's International, Inc. Balance Sheets

Analysts generally expect that a firm's working capital balances will increase in amounts that are proportional to the change in revenues during the period. This is because most components of working capital are directly affected by the firm's operating level. On the other hand, changes in noncurrent assets and liabilities are more sporadic in nature and result from episodic events such as capital spending and issuances of debt and equity securities. The horizontal analysis of Wendy's balance sheet, shown in Exhibit 11–7, indicates an overall increase in current assets of 13.2 percent and an increase in total assets of 9.0 percent. Although several individual items on the balance sheet show large percentage changes, the dollar amounts of the changes are relatively minor. The percentage changes are large because the amounts of these items in the base year, 1996, are rather small. Overall, the percentage changes shown in Exhibit 11–7 appear reasonable and consistent with the changes noted in the income statement.

The vertical analysis of Wendy's balance sheet in Exhibit 11–8 shows that the composition of the assets and the overall mix of liabilities and shareholder's equity have remained very stable over the year. The firm appears to be very liquid, with over 12 percent of its assets in cash and cash equivalents. Also the major portion of the firm's financing is from shareholders' investments and the retention of earnings, rather than from borrowing.

One interesting component of Wendy's capital structure is mandatorily redeemable preferred stock, which accounts for over 10 percent of Wendy's capital in both years. Although these securities are technically stock, they are in economic substance more similar to debt than to shareholders' equity because Wendy's is obligated to buy back these shares at a predetermined date and price in the future. For this reason, accounting standards require that such securities be classified with debt on the balance sheet, and analysts will regard these securities as debt in assessing the firm's capital structure.

Liquidity Analysis of Wendy's International, Inc.

Wendy's liquidity ratios for each fiscal year are calculated in Exhibit 11–9 and provide the following insights. Wendy's current ratio and quick ratio have increased slightly during the year, although the composition and dollar amounts of the current assets and liabilities have remained relatively stable over the year. The collection period of the accounts receivable has increased slightly from 10.2 to 11.9 days, and the number of days' sales in inventory has decreased from 14.2 days to 12.6 days. Given the nature of Wendy's business, customer receivables and inventories are very minor components of the balance sheet, so these changes are not very consequential. On the whole, Wendy's liquidity ratios have increased. An analyst must consider these liquidity improvements in the context of profitability and other ratios.

EXHIBIT 11-7 Horizontal Analysis of the Balance Sheet

Wendy's International, Inc.
Balance Sheet: Horizontal Analysis
December 28, 1997, and December 29, 1996
(Dollars in thousands)

	December 28 1997	Percent Change 1996 to 1997	December 29 1996
Assets			
Current assets			
Cash and cash equivalents	$ 234,262	+6.9%	$ 218,956
Accounts receivable, net	66,755	+25.4	53,250
Notes receivable, net	13,897	+26.3	11,003
Deferred income taxes	31,007	+96.7	15,760
Inventories and other	35,633	−6.2	37,994
	381,554	+13.2	336,963
Property and equipment, net	1,265,500	+4.8	1,207,944
Notes receivable, net	178,681	+50.1	118,994
Goodwill, net	51,346	−.1	51,636
Deferred income taxes	15,117	+16.8	12,938
Other assets	49,482	−6.6	52,959
	$1,941,680	+9.0%	$1,781,434
Liabilities and shareholders' equity			
Current liabilities			
Accounts payable	$ 107,157	−1.4	$108,629
Accrued expenses	98,306	+6.3	92,454
Current portion of long-term obligations	7,151	+7.0	6,681
	212,614	+2.3	207,764
Long-term obligations			
Term debt	205,872	+4.2	197,622
Capital leases	43,891	−.7	44,206
	249,763	+3.3	241,828
Deferred income taxes	81,017	+28.7	62,956
Other long-term liabilities	14,052	+16.0	12,114
Mandatorily redeemable preferred stock	200,000	0.0	200,000
Shareholders' equity			
Preferred stock, authorized: 250,000 shares			
Common stock: $0.10 stated value, authorized: 200,000,000 shares			
Issued: 115,946,000 and 113,148,000 shares, respectively	11,595	+2.5	11,315
Capital in excess of stated value	353,327	+13.0	312,570
Retained earnings	839,215	+13.4	740,311
Translation adjustments and other	(18,191)	+218.5	(5712)
Treasury stock at cost: 129,000 shares	(1,712)	—	(1,712)
	1,184,234	+12.1	1,056,772
	$1,941,680	+9.0%	$1,781,434

EXHIBIT 11-8 Vertical Analysis of the Balance Sheet

Wendy's International, Inc.
Balance Sheet: Vertical Analysis
December 28, 1997, and December 29, 1996
(Dollars in thousands)

	December 28, 1997		December 29,1996	
	Dollars	%	Dollars	%
Assets				
Current assets				
Cash and cash equivalents	$ 234,262	12.1%	$ 218,956	12.3%
Accounts receivable, net	66,755	3.4	53,250	3.0
Notes receivable, net	13,897	.7	11,003	.6
Deferred income taxes	31,007	1.6	15,760	.9
Inventories and other	35,633	1.8	37,994	2.1
	381,554	19.6	336,963	18.9
Property and equipment, net	1,265,500	65.3	1,207,944	67.8
Notes receivable, net	178,681	9.2	118,994	6.7
Goodwill, net	51,346	2.6	51,636	2.9
Deferred income taxes	15,117	.8	12,938	.7
Other assets	49,482	2.5	52,959	3.0
	$1,941,680	100.0%	$1,781,434	100.0%
Liabilities and shareholders' equity				
Current liabilities				
Accounts payable	$ 107,157	5.5%	$ 108,629	6.1%
Accrued expenses	98,306	5.1	92,454	5.2
Current portion of long-term obligations	7,151	.4	6,681	.4
	212,614	11.0	207,764	11.7
Long-term obligations				
Term debt	205,872	10.6	197,622	11.1
Capital leases	43,891	2.3	44,206	2.5
	249,763	12.9	241,828	13.6
Deferred income taxes	81,017	4.2	62,956	3.5
Other long-term liabilities	14,052	.7	12,114	.6
Mandatorily redeemable preferred stock	200,000	10.3	200,000	11.2
Total liabilities	757,446	39.1	724,662	40.6
Shareholders' equity				
Preferred stock, authorized: 250,000 shares				
Common stock: $0.10 stated value, authorized: 200,000,000 shares				
Issued: 115,946,000 and 113,148,000 shares, respectively	11,595	.6	11,315	.6
Capital in excess of stated value	353,327	18.2	312,570	17.5
Retained earnings	839,215	43.2	740,311	41.7
Translation adjustments and other	(18,191)	(.9)	(5,712)	(.3)
Treasury stock at cost: 129,000 shares	(1,712)	(.2)	(1,712)	(.1)
Total stockholder's equity	1,184,234	60.9	1,056,772	59.4
	$1,941,680	100.0%	$1,781,434	100.0%

EXHIBIT 11-9 Liquidity Analysis

Wendy's International, Inc.
Liquidity Ratios, 1997 and 1996
(Dollars in thousands)

Ratio		Formula		1997	1996
Current ratio	=	Current assets / Current liabilities	=	\$381,554 / \$212,614	\$336,963 / \$207,764
			=	1.79	1.62
Quick ratio	=	Cash and equivalents, and accounts receivable / Current liabilities	=	\$234,262 + 66,755 / \$212,614	\$218,956 + 53,250 / \$207,764
			=	1.42	1.31
Average sales per day	=	Sales revenue / Days in the year*	=	\$2,037,330 / 364	\$1,897,144 / 364
			=	\$5,597	\$5,212
Collection period**	=	Accounts receivable / Average sales per day	=	\$66,755 / \$5,597	\$53,250 / \$5,212
			=	11.9 days	10.2 days
Cost of goods sold per day	=	Cost of goods sold / Days in the year*	=	\$1,026,026 / 364	\$976,666 / 364
			=	\$2,819	\$2,683
Number of days' sales in ending inventory	=	Ending inventory / Cost of goods sold per day	=	\$35,633 / \$2,819	\$37,994 / \$2,683
			=	12.6 days	14.2 days

*The number of days in the reporting years is 364 days (52 weeks × 7 days = 364).

**Because gross receivables are used in this ratio, the balances in the Allowance for uncollectible accounts usually must be added to the net accounts receivable. Because this adjustment is not material for Wendy's, we have used net accounts receivable in the calculation.

Profitability Analysis of Wendy's International, Inc.

Wendy's profitability ratios are calculated in Exhibit 11–10. The operating income ratio indicates a decline in profitability. Return on equity and return on assets have both decreased as a result. These trends in profitability ratios must be interpreted cautiously, however, until the analyst obtains a better understanding of the reasons for the unusual increase in general and administrative expenses that was noted earlier.

On the other hand, the cash-based profitability ratios indicate positive trends. The statement of cash flows (see Appendix D) shows that operating cash flows increased from \$189,928,000 in 1996 to \$223,402,000 in 1997. Wendy's cash return on assets increased from 12.4 percent to 13.0 percent. Its quality of income also increased from 122 percent to 171 percent.

These results dictate that the investor look more closely at the sources of cash flow from operations to determine whether they are likely to continue at these same

EXHIBIT 11-10 Profitability Analysis

Wendy's International, Inc.
Profitability Ratios, 1997 and 1996
(Dollars in Thousands)*

Ratio		Formula		1995	1994
Operating income percentage	=	Operating income / Sales revenue	=	$219,471 / $2,037,330	$254,817 / $1,897,144
			=	10.8%	13.4%
Return on equity	=	Net income / Shareholders' equity	=	$130,499 / $1,185,946	$155,948 / $1,058,484
			=	11.0%	14.7%
Return on assets	=	Net income + [Interest expense × (1 – tax rate)]** / Total assets	=	$132,842 / $1,941,680	$160,376 / $1,781,434
			=	6.8%	9.0%
Cash return on assets	=	Cash flow from operating activities + Interest paid / Total assets	=	$223,402 + 29,126 / $1,941,680	$189,928 + 30,556 / $1,781,434
			=	13.0%	12.4%
Quality of income	=	Cash flow from operating activities / Net income	=	$223,402 / $130,499	$189,928 / $155,998
			=	171%	122%

*For convenience we have used end-of-year balance sheet amounts in these ratio calculations. If the balance sheet amounts fluctuate markedly during the year, analysts would instead use averages rather than year-end amounts.
**Calculated using Wendy's federal statutory tax rate of 35 percent. In 1997, the numerator is $132,842 ($130,499 + $3,604 × (1 – .35)), and in 1996 the numerator is $160,376 ($155,948 + $6,812 × (1 – 35)).

levels. As we indicated earlier, most investors prefer cash flows to net income, if they have to make a choice. Wendy's exhibits a decline in profitability, based on net earnings and accrual-based calculations. On the other hand, the cash flow-based ratios seem strong. The investor must decide on which set of profitability ratios to rely most heavily.

Capital Structure Analysis of Wendy's International, Inc.

Wendy's capital structure can be described by the ratios in Exhibit 11–11. The vertical analysis of Wendy's liability and shareholders' equity indicates a modest decline in the percentage of long-term debt. Deferred taxes and other similar liabilities were minor portions of total debt in both years. Shareholders' equity increased in percentage terms, reflecting the decreases shown in long-term liabilities. Wendy's times interest earned increased from 38.4 to 61.9, indicating a healthy margin of safety. On the whole, after considering the decrease in debt and associated interest expenses, Wendy's capital structure analysis does not indicate any major concerns.

EXHIBIT 11-11 Capital Structure Analysis

Wendy's International, Inc.
Capital Structure Ratios, 1997 and 1996
(Dollars in thousands)

Composition analysis: Percentage of total financing provided by each type of debt and shareholders's equity.

	1997 Amount	%	1996 Amount	%
Total assets (equals total liabilities and shareholders' equity)	$1,941,680	100.0	$1,781,434	100.0
Financed by:				
Current liabilities	$ 212,614	11.0%	$ 207,764	11.7%
Long-term debt + capital leases	249,763	12.9	241,828	13.6
Deferred taxes and other debts	95,069	4.9	75,070	4.1
Mandatorily redeemable preferred stock	200,000	10.3	200,000	11.2
Total liabilities	757,446	39.1	724,662	40.6
Shareholders' equity	1,184,234	60.9	1,056,772	59.4
	$1,941,680	100.0%	$1,781,434	100.0%

Additional Ratio Analysis:

Ratio	Formula		1997	1996
Financial leverage	$\frac{\text{Total liabilities}}{\text{Total assets}}$	=	39.1% (above)	40.6% (above)
Times interest earned	$\frac{\text{Earnings before interest and taxes}}{\text{Interest expense}}$	=	$\frac{\$223,075}{\$3,604}$	$\frac{\$261,629}{\$6,812}$
		=	61.9 times	38.4 times

Investor Ratios, Wendy's International, Inc.

Wendy's investor ratios are calculated in Exhibit 11–12. Based on the ratios shown, it appears that the market is reassured by Wendy's performance in 1997. Its market-to-book value ratio has remained steady. Further evaluations based on trends should also be conducted. The P/E ratio has increased substantially from 17.5 to 23.6. To some extent, this increase in the P/E ratio may reflect the market's view that Wendy's 1997 earnings are lower than "normal," perhaps due to a temporary increase in general and administrative expenses as noted earlier. In any event, the analyst would need to separate out the effects of economy-wide influences on P/E ratios (such as changes in interest rates or other factors causing changes in the overall market prices of equity securities) in order to interpret this change in Wendy's P/E ratio.

Summary, Wendy's International, Inc.

Our analysis of Wendy's financial statements are cautiously positive. The primary weak indicator is in the area of profitability (based on accrual-based earnings), and this re-

EXHIBIT 11-12 Investor Analysis

Wendy's International, Inc.
Investor Ratios, 1997 and 1996

Ratio	Formula		1997	1996
Earnings per share	Provided directly on the income statement (Exhibit 11–5)			
Basic			$ .99	$ 1.23
Diluted			$ .97	$ 1.19
Market-to-book value*	Market price per share / Book value per share	=	$22.88 / $10.21	$20.88 / $ 9.34
		=	2.24	2.24
Price-to-earnings*	Market price per share / Earnings per share	=	$22.88 / $ .97	$20.88 / $ 1.19
		=	23.6	17.5

*We have used the fiscal year-end market price per share, and computed book value per share using the number of shares shown on the balance sheet.
*Based on diluted EPS.

sult may be due to transitory effects that may not persist in the future. There were significant positive trends in liquidity, and stability in investor ratios. Further examination of supplementary information, as well as subsequent quarterly results for 1998 and 1999, could be used to support or challenge these conclusions.

LIMITATIONS OF FINANCIAL STATEMENT ANALYSIS

Financial statement analysis is limited on several dimensions. GAAP, and its underlying accounting conventions and measurement rules and principles, present some limits. Managers often have the ability to select favorable accounting methods. They can make choices as to the timing for reporting favorable or unfavorable results. A close reading of the notes can indicate where some of these choices have had an impact on the financial ratios, yet many of these managerial choices will not be revealed to external users of financial statements. Investors, in particular, must rely on independent accountants' assessments of the suitability of management's accounting choices.

A second major limitation of financial statement analysis concerns the "What's missing?" factor. Many major factors affecting profitability and survival of the firm are just not included in accrual accounting, nor in the financial statements. Examples of such omissions include changes in the firm's market share, changes in customer relations or preferences, changes in the firm's labor productivity, other changes in its human resources or human resource management systems, innovations or structural changes in technology, changes in the environment, changes in legislation or public policy, changes in competitors, or changes in substitute products or services. Sometimes these factors are discussed in the narrative sections of the annual report. They are often mentioned in the CEO's letter. Wendy's Management Review section (see Appendix D) alludes to some of these qualitative factors.

A third concern in financial statement analysis is that "real" events are often hard to distinguish from the effects of alternative accounting methods or principles. By focusing more on cash flows, the investor or other analyst can identify cases where financial reports based on accrual accounting may diverge from the cash flows or inadequately reflect other pertinent economic events.

A fourth and final limitation of financial statement analysis concerns predictability. The past may not be a reliable indicator of the future. Stable trends may be reversed tomorrow! Financial statements are just one of the important inputs that the investor must use as a basis for investing decisions. Further study of finance and accounting will give you additional tools on which to rely. Appendix B of this text gives you some ideas on how you might pursue your study of these important topics.

SUMMARY OF LEARNING OBJECTIVES

1. **Understand why financial statements are analyzed.**
   Investors comprise the primary audience of financial reporting. Financial analysts use financial accounting reports in order to assess the potential risks and returns from investing in debt and equity securities.
2. **Know where to obtain financial information.**
   Although financial statement analysis begins with the set of financial statements included in published financial reports, analysts gather additional information from a variety of sources, including the financial sections of major newspapers, specialized business periodicals, reports of changes in governmental fiscal and monetary policies, conferences and addresses by business leaders, and many other sources.
3. **Determine when financial information is comparable and alternatively learn how to enhance the comparability of financial information that may appear to be noncomparable.**
   The analyst must determine that a comparable and useful reference is available with which to compare the target firm. Usually, the prior year or years are a good reference point with which to begin. Before comparing a firm's results with the prior year, the analyst must examine both sets of statements and notes to determine whether an unusual event occurred. If significant unusual events have occurred that would distort comparisons, then the financial statements for any of these years may need to be restated or rearranged to make them more comparable. The primary guideline is "more comparability is better." Financial information is more comparable between two firms if they
   - operate in the same country,
   - follow similar accounting practices,
   - are of similar size (revenues and/or assets),
   - produce similar products or services, and
   - have a similar capital structure.
4. **Identify, calculate, use, and interpret appropriate ratios.**
   We have operationalized this objective by developing a general framework that can be used to conduct a comprehensive financial statement analysis. Financial analysis relies on both qualitative and quantitative analyses, and cannot be reduced to a simple set of recipes. The techniques summarized in this chapter merely provide a point of departure for the analyst in assessing the investment worth of a given firm.

KEY TERMS

Annual Report 495
Capital structure 450
Cash return on assets ratio 449
Current ratio 447
Earnings-per-share (EPS) ratio 451
Financial leverage ratio 451
Horizontal analysis 447
Gross profit percentage 448
Investor ratios 457
Liquidity ratios 447
Market-to-book value ratio 451
Number of days in inventory 448
Operating income ratio 448
Percentage composition analysis 450
Price-to-earnings (P/E) ratio 452
Profitability ratios 448
Quality of income ratio 449
Quick ratio 447
Return on assets (ROA) ratio 449
Return on equity (ROE) ratio 449
Times interest earned ratio 451
Vertical analysis 447

A summary of our financial statement analysis framework follows:

a. Identify the purpose and objectives of the analysis.
b. Review the financial statements, accompanying notes, management letters, and other commentary, and the report of the independent auditor. Be alert to any unusual events that may affect your interpretations of the numerical items in the financial statements.
c. Determine whether any adjustments are needed to make the financial statements comparable to those of the previous year, or to financial statements of other, supposedly similar firms. Be especially aware of mergers, discontinued operations, changes in methods of accounting, or major shifts in product mix.
d. Conduct horizontal and vertical analyses of each financial statement. The horizontal analysis will aid you in discussing major changes in financial statement items compared to previous periods. The vertical analysis will help you focus on variations in the composition of the firm's assets, and the relative proportions of its debt and equity financing. A vertical analysis will also help you focus on causes of variation in net income.
e. Organize your ratio calculations under the broad headings of liquidity, profitability, capital structure, and investor performance. Compute the standard financial ratios in each of these categories.
f. Compare the financial ratios to prior years and to industry norms. If the firm's ratios depart from its past history or prevailing norms, attempt to explain these departures by reviewing other supplementary disclosures in the financial statements. Remember that there are often excellent reasons why a firm will differ from its competitors and may alter its policies over time. These steps have been illustrated using Wendy's financial statements.

5. **Identify limitations of financial statement analyses.**
A variety of judgments are used to decide how to calculate a given financial ratio. Rarely do the line items that are reported in the financial statements fit neatly into a standard formula. Often the results of the ratio calculations provide more questions than answers. The most useful product of ratio analysis may well be the list of intelligent questions that result.

QUESTIONS

11-1 Discuss the basic goals of financial statement analysis. Indicate those goals with which you agree or disagree. Identify any additional goals that may be added.

11-2 Identify several users of financial statement analysis. Discuss the differences between users who have regular interaction with the firm versus those who may have less frequent interactions.

11-3 Identify and describe several sources of financial information for publicly traded U.S. companies.

11-4 Discuss why it is so important that financial information be comparable before conducting analysis and computing ratios.

11-5 Discuss several ways that comparability between firms can be enhanced.

11-6 Discuss several aspects of non-comparability that the analyst cannot overcome.

11-7 Identify several bases of comparability that might be established before attempting to compare ratio results.

11-8 Identify the major elements of financial statements that form the basis for an investor's analysis.

11-9 Describe several situations that may require restatement of the financial statements prior to conducting ratio calculations.

11-10 Describe the benefits of conducting horizontal and vertical analyses.

11-11 Why must both cash and accounts receivable be analyzed as part of a liquidity analysis?

11-12 Why must both cash flows and net income be analyzed as part of a profitability analysis?

11-13 Describe the similarities between the collection period and the number of days' sales in ending inventory.

11-14 Describe the relationship between return on equity (ROE) and cash return to shareholders.

11-15 Describe the relationship between return on assets (ROA) and cash return on assets.

11-16 Describe the relationship between quality of sales and accounts receivable as a percent of sales.

11-17 Discuss the differences between cash flow from operating activities (CFOA) and cash collections from customers.

11-18 Compare and contrast the quality of the income ratio with dimensions of income quality.

11-19 Discuss why a tax adjustment is necessary as part of return on assets (ROA).

11-20 Discuss the relationship between financial leverage and percentage composition.

11-21 Under what circumstances might the percentage composition ratios *not* sum to 100 percent?

11-22 Describe why the percentage composition ratios might have three or four components. Why might they have less than three components? Why might they have more than four such components?

11-23 Describe the relationships between cash interest coverage and times interest earned.

11-24 Why would a lender not be too concerned about market-to-book value and price-to-earnings (P/E) ratios? Why would a creditor or banker be more concerned?

11-25 Why would a lender and an investor be equally concerned with earnings per share (EPS)?

11-26 Under what conditions might the financial leverage ratio be confusing and less useful than the percentage composition ratios?

11-27 Discuss why the "What's missing?" question is so crucial during all phases of financial statement analysis.

11-28 Describe several limitations of financial statement analysis. What can be done to minimize these limitations?

Critical Thinking

11-29 Describe several possible choices of accounting methods that managers may make in an effort to manipulate or influence reported earnings. What can the analyst do to combat these earnings manipulation possibilities?

Critical Thinking

11-30 Describe how managers can affect the timing of earnings recognition. What can the analyst do to combat these earnings manipulation possibilities?

Critical Thinking

11-31 Describe how managers may make biased estimates that will cause net income to be overstated or understated. What can the analyst do to combat these earnings manipulation possibilities?

PROBLEMS

Comprehensive Financial Statement Analysis

11-32 Dairy King, LTD., reported the following results for 1999 (dollars in millions):

	1999	1998
Revenues:		
Net sales	$268.8	$241.6
Service fees	54.2	51.6
Franchise sales (fees)	8.6	7.6
Property management	8.1	9.0
Other	1.1	1.3
	340.8	311.1
Costs and expenses:		
Cost of sales	242.4	217.2
Property management expenses	7.6	8.4
Selling, general, and administrative	40.5	37.5
Interest expense (income)	(1.6)	(1.4)
	288.9	261.7
Income before income taxes	51.9	49.4
Income taxes	20.5	19.5
Net income	$ 31.4	$ 29.9
Earnings per common share	$ 1.30	$ 1.19

Dairy King's Consolidated Balance Sheet is shown below:

	1999	1998
Assets		
Current assets:		
Cash and cash equivalents	$ 31.8	$ 21.2
Marketable securities	7.0	10.0
Notes receivable, net	7.4	3.4
Accounts receivable, net	25.1	23.2
Inventories	5.4	4.6
Prepaid expenses	2.4	1.1
Miscellaneous	1.2	1.5
Total current assets	80.3	65.0
Other assets:		
Notes receivable, net	14.4	21.4
Miscellaneous	1.3	1.6
Total other assets	15.7	23.0
Other revenue-producing assets:		
Franchise rights, net	87.8	83.8
Rental properties, net	2.9	3.2
Total other assets	90.7	87.0
Property, plant, and equipment,		
Net	9.8	9.3
Total assets	$196.5	$184.3

Liabilities and Stockholders' Equity	1999	1998
Current liabilities:		
Drafts and accounts payable	$ 17.1	$ 16.8
Committed advertising	1.1	2.1
Other liabilities	7.5	6.8
Income taxes payable	.4	1.1
Current maturities (L-T debt)	.4	1.8
Total current liabilities	26.5	28.6
Deferred franchise income	.4	.3
Deferred income taxes	15.0	15.0
Long-term debt	23.3	23.7
Contingencies and commitments (Note 4)		
Total liabilities	65.2	67.6
Stockholders' equity:		
Class A common stock	.1	.1
Class B common stock	.1	.1
Paid-in capital	4.1	4.0
Retained earnings	129.2	114.4
Equity adjustments	(2.2)	(1.9)
Total stockholders' equity	131.3	116.7
Total liabilities and shareholders' equity	$196.5	$184.3

Dairy King's cash flow statement is summarized as follows (dollars in millions):

	1999	1998
Net cash provided by operating activities	$33.8	$35.0
Net cash provided by (used in) investing activities	(4.6)	(17.3)
Net cash used in financing activities	(18.5)	(27.5)
Net (decrease) increase in cash	$10.7	($ 9.8)
Cash payments for income taxes	$21.1	$18.8
Cash payments for interest	$ 1.9	$ 2.5

Required

a. Identify any unusual terms in Dairy King's financial statements.
b. Prepare a horizontal analysis of Dairy King's income statement.
c. Prepare a vertical analysis of Dairy King's income statement.
d. Calculate the appropriate liquidity ratios from Dairy King's balance sheet.
e. Conduct a profitability analysis.
f. Prepare a capital structure analysis.
g. Write a short memo summarizing your conclusions. Indicate why Dairy King might be facing financial threats or opportunities. Also indicate any additional data necessary to refine your analyses or conclusions.

Introductory Problem and Data Set

11-33 General Cinema Companies, Inc., reported the following results for 1994 as summarized below (dollars in thousands except for per-share amount):

Years Ended October 31	1994	1993
Revenues	$452,563	$495,031
Costs applicable to revenues	188,616	214,653
Selling, general and administrative expenses	241,435	260,128
Corporate expenses	5,646	1,900
Operating earnings (loss)	16,866	18,350
Investment income	1,640	96
Interest expense	(648)	(605)
Other income (expense), net	5,188	(600)
Earnings (loss) before income taxes, and cumulative effect of accounting change	23,046	17,241
Income tax expense	9,449	6,738
Net earnings (loss)	$ 13,597	$ 10,503
Amounts applicable to common shareholders:		
Earnings per share	$ 1.73	NA

General Cinema's consolidated balance sheet is summarized below (dollars in thousands):

October 31	1994	1993
Assets		
Current assets:		
Cash and equivalents	$ 85,021	$ 7,790
Deferred income taxes	2,090	0
Other current assets	5,722	2,622
Total current assets	92,833	10,412
Property and equipment:		
Land, buildings, and improvements	32,411	38,675
Equipment and fixtures	130,016	131,710
Leasehold improvements	151,442	159,289
	313,869	329,674
Less accumulated depreciation and amortization	136,174	130,349
Total property and equipment, net	177,695	199,325
Other assets:		
Other	26,130	798
Total assets	$296,658	$210,535

October 31	1994	1993
Liabilities		
Current liabilities:		
Current maturities of long-term liabilities	$ 722	$ 637
Trade payables	39,065	34,028
Other current liabilities	59,972	53,956
Total current liabilities	99,759	88,621
Long-term liabilities:		
Capital lease obligations	4,179	4,756
Other long-term liabilities	28,016	27,551
Total long-term liabilities	32,195	32,307
Deferred income taxes	15,181	17,376
Commitments and contingencies	—	—
Total liabilities	147,135	138,304
Shareholders' Equity		
Common stock: $0.01 par value; authorized 25,000; issued and outstanding 7,802, 0	78	—
Paid-in capital	135,848	—
Retained earnings	13,597	—
Investment by Harcourt General	—	72,231
Total shareholders' equity	149,523	72,231
Total liabilities and equity	$296,658	$210,535

General Cinema's cash flow statement is summarized below (dollars in thousands):

Year ended October 31	1994	1993
Net cash provided by operations	$28,512	$53,849
Net cash used by investment activities	(14,949)	(16,322)
Net cash (used) provided by financing transactions	63,668	(35,288)
Net increase (decrease) in cash during the year	$77,231	$ 2,239
Supplemental schedule of cash flow information		
Cash paid for interest	$ 610	$ 720
Cash paid for income taxes	$13,100	$ 9,500

Required

a. Identify any unusual terms in General Cinema's summarized financial statements.
b. Prepare a horizontal analysis of General Cinema's income statement.
c. Prepare a vertical analysis of General Cinema's income statement.
d. Calculate the appropriate liquidity ratios.
e. Conduct a profitability analysis.
f. Conduct a capital structure analysis. Discuss why General Cinema reported no EPS in 1993.
g. With regard to your analysis of General Cinema Companies, Inc., write a short memo summarizing your conclusions. Indicate why the company might be facing financial threats or opportunities. Also indicate if additional data is necessary to refine your analyses or conclusions.

Critical Thinking

Comprehensive Financial Statement Analysis

11-34 Electronic Fab Technology (EFT) is a leader in information technology. EFT reported the following results for 2000, as summarized below (dollars in thousands):

Year Ended December 31	**2000**	**1999**
Net sales	$52,541,842	$29,816,626
Cost of goods sold	47,123,066	25,688,263
Gross profit	5,418,776	4,128,363
Selling, general and administrative	2,395,164	1,842,442
Operating income	3,023,612	2,285,921
Other income (expense):		
Interest expense	(175,400)	(236,917)
Interest income	78,933	0
Other, net	31,187	(11,723)
Total other income (expense)	(65,280)	(248,640)
Income before income taxes	2,958,332	2,037,281
Income tax expense	1,041,415	736,612
Net income	$ 1,916,917	$ 1,300,669
Weighted average shares outstanding	3,626,845	2,483,000

EFT reported the following consolidated balance sheets, as summarized below (dollars in thousands):

December 31	2000	1999
Assets		
Current assets:		
Cash and cash equivalents	$ 153,483	$ 43,879
Accounts receivable, net	3,858,523	2,480,421
Inventories	7,479,374	4,639,969
Income taxes receivable	64,655	0
Deferred income taxes	85,847	85,490
Prepaids and others	49,467	49,165
Total current assets	11,691,349	7,298,924
Property and equipment, net:		
Land	662,098	161,903
Buildings	4,779,049	1,589,865
Machinery and equipment	8,395,468	3,763,995
Furniture and fixtures	1,043,098	328,555
	14,879,713	5,844,318
Less accumulated depreciation	3,162,155	2,188,893
Property plant and equipment	11,717,558	3,655,425
Other assets:		
Cash surrender value of life insurance	36,248	41,750
Other assets	33,929	176,067
	70,177	217,817
Total assets	$23,479,084	$11,172,166

December 31	2000	1999
Liabilities and Shareholders' Equity		
Current liabilities:		
Notes payable	$ —	$ 300,000
Current portion of long-term debt	170,000	244,433
Accounts payable	3,606,645	3,273,461
Income taxes payable	—	611,790
Accrued compensation	813,788	326,869
Other accrued expenses	356,598	138,827
Total current liabilities	4,947,031	4,895,380
Long-term debt, net of current portion	3,230,000	2,539,337
Deferred income taxes	312,660	190,918
Commitments and contingencies	—	—
	8,489,691	7,625,635
Shareholders' equity:		
Preferred stock: $0.01 par value, authorized 5,000,000 shares	—	—
Common stock; $0.01 par value, authorized 45,000,000 shares, issued 3,891,000 and 2,368,500 shares	38,911	23,685
Additional paid-in capital	10,016,035	505,316
Retained earnings	4,934,447	3,017,530
Total shareholders' equity	14,989,393	3,546,531
Total liabilities and shareholders' equity	$23,479,084	$11,172,166

EFT's consolidated statements of cash flow disclosed the following summary information:

December 31	2000	1999
Net cash provided by operating activities	$ (697,000)	$814,000
Net cash used in investing activities	(9,035,000)	(870,000)
Net cash used in financing activities	9,842,000	59,000
Net increase (decrease) in cash	$ 110,000	$ 3,000
Cash paid for:		
Income taxes (refund)	$1,596,475	$ (16,591)
Interest	$ 175,400	$236,917

Required

a. Identify any unusual terms in EFT's summarized financial statements.
b. Prepare a horizontal analysis of EFT's income statement.
c. Prepare a vertical analysis of EFT's income statement.
d. Calculate the appropriate liquidity ratios.
e. Conduct a profitability analysis.
f. Conduct a capital structure analysis.
g. Write a short memo summarizing your conclusions. Indicate why EFT might be facing financial threats or opportunities. Also indicate what additional data you might need to refine your analyses or conclusions.

Applying the Financial Statement Analysis 10-Step Framework

11-35 Conduct a comprehensive financial analysis of Reebok International's financial statements (see Appendix E).

Required:

a. Review Reebok International's financial statements (see Appendix E) to determine whether any unusual or noteworthy events may limit the scope or comparability of financial statement analysis. Review Ernst & Young's audit report. Determine whether any restatements might be necessary and whether any barriers would restrict the comparability of Reebok's performance. In other words, conduct the first four steps in the financial statement analysis framework.
b. Prepare horizontal and vertical analyses of Reebok's income statement for 1997 and 1996 (step 5 of our financial statement analysis framework).
c. Conduct an analysis of Reebok's liquidity for 1997 and 1996 (step 6 of our financial statement analysis framework).
d. Conduct an analysis of Reebok's profitability for 1997 and 1996 (step 7 of our financial statement analysis framework).
e. Analyze Reebok's capital structure for 1997 and 1996 (step 8 of our financial statement analysis framework).
f. Calculate Reebok's investor ratios for 1997 and 1996 (step 9 of our financial statement analysis framework).

(Continued)

g. Review your results from the previous six problems, state your overall conclusions regarding Reebok's performance in 1997 and 1996, and then determine whether your results are consistent (step 10 of the financial statement analysis framework). Recalculate, as necessary, any ratios that could be restated based on new information found in the notes. Identify any additional information that you may require before making an investment in Reebok.

Applying the Financial Statement Analysis Framework: Reviewing the Notes

11-36 Review Wendy's financial statements in Appendix D to determine whether any unusual or noteworthy events may limit the scope or comparability of financial statement analysis. Review the audit report and determine whether any restatements might be necessary. Also determine whether any barriers would restrict the comparability of Wendy's performance. In other words, conduct the first four steps of the financial statement analysis framework.

Integration of Concepts

Reviewing the Results of Financial Statement Analysis Framework

11-37 This assignment is based on the computations and exhibits shown earlier that are based on Wendy's financial statements. In each case, refer to the relevant exhibits and review the results.

Required

a. Review the horizontal and vertical analyses of Wendy's income statement for 1997 and 1996 (step 5 of the financial statement analysis framework).
b. Review the results of Wendy's liquidity analysis for 1997 and 1996 (step 6 of the financial statement analysis framework).
c. Review the results of Wendy's profitability analysis for 1997 and 1996 (step 7 of the financial statement analysis framework.
d. Review the results of Wendy's capital structure analysis for 1997 and 1996 (step 8 of the financial statement analysis framework).
e. Review Wendy's investor ratios for 1997 and 1996 (step 9 of the financial statement analysis framework).
f. Conduct step 10 of the financial analysis framework, as may be necessary. Recalculate, as necessary, any ratios that could be restated based on new information found in the notes.
g. On the basis of these results, evaluate the various dimensions of Wendy's performance in 1997 and 1996. How do any restatements in the previous step change your conclusions about Wendy's profitability? Identify any additional information needed before making an investment in Wendy's.

Critical Thinking

Financial Statement Analysis: Comparison of Two Companies

11-38 Financial statements for two companies, The Gap and Intimate Brands, are presented below. Although the notes were omitted, a statement from each company's auditor is included. Both companies are in the retail apparel industry.

Independent Auditors' Report
To the Shareholders and Board of Directors of The Gap, Inc.:

We have audited the accompanying consolidated balance sheets of The Gap, Inc. and subsidiaries as of January 31, 1998 and February 1, 1997, and the related consolidated statements of earnings, shareholders' equity, and cash flows for each of the three fiscal years in the period ended January 31, 1998. These financial statements are the responsibility of the Company's management. Our responsibility is to express an opinion on these financial statements based on our audits.

We conducted our audits in accordance with generally accepted auditing standards. These standards require that we plan and perform the audits to obtain reasonable assurance about whether the consolidated financial statements are free from material misstatement. An audit includes examining, on a test basis, evidence supporting the amounts and disclosures in the financial statements. An audit also includes assessing the accounting principles used and significant estimates made by management, as well as evaluating the overall financial statement presentation. We believe that our audits provide a reasonable basis for our opinion.

In our opinion, such consolidated financial statements present fairly, in all material respects, the financial position of the company and its subsidiaries as of January 31, 1998 and February 1, 1997, and the results of their operations and their cash flows for each of the three fiscal years in the period ended January 31, 1998 in conformity with generally accepted accounting principles.

Deloitte & Touche LLP San Francisco, California February 27, 1998

1997 Annual Report

Gap Inc.

Consolidated Statements of Earnings

($000 except share and per share amounts)	Fifty-two Weeks Ended January 31, 1998	Fifty-two Weeks Ended February 1, 1997	Fifty-three Weeks Ended February 3, 1996
Net sales	$ 6,507,825	$ 5,284,381	$ 4,395,253
Costs and expenses			
Cost of goods sold and occupancy expenses	4,021,541	3,285,166	2,821,455
Operating expenses	1,635,017	1,270,138	1,004,396
Net interest income	(2,975)	(19,450)	(15,797)
Earnings before income taxes	854,242	748,527	585,199
Income taxes	320,341	295,668	231,160
Net earnings	$ 533,901	$ 452,859	$ 354,039

Weighted-average number of shares-basic	396,179,975	417,146,631	417,718,397
Weighted-average number of shares-diluted	410,200,758	427,267,220	427,752,515
Earnings per share-basic	$ 1.35	$ 1.09	$ .85
Earnings per share-diluted	1.30	1.06	.83

Gap Inc.
Consolidated Balance Sheets

($000)

	January 31, 1998	February 1, 1997
Assets		
Current Assets		
Cash and equivalents	$ 913,169	$ 485,644
Short-term investments	-	135,632
Merchandise inventory	733,174	578,765
Prepaid expenses and other current assets	184,604	129,214
Total current assets	1,830,947	1,329,255
Property and Equipment		
Leasehold improvements	846,791	736,608
Furniture and equipment	1,236,450	960,516
Land and buildings	154,136	99,969
Construction-in-progress	66,582	101,520
	2,303,959	1,898,613
Accumulated depreciation and amortization	(938,713)	(762,893)
Property and equipment, net	1,365,246	1,135,720
Long-term investments	-	36,138
Lease rights and other assets	141,309	125,814
Total assets	$ 3,337,502	$2,626,927

Liabilities and Shareholders' Equity		
Current Liabilities		
Notes payable	$ 84,794	$ 40,050
Accounts payable	416,976	351,754
Accrued expenses	389,412	282,494
Income taxes payable	83,597	91,806
Deferred lease credits and other current liabilities	16,769	8,792
Total current liabilities	991,548	774,896
Long-Term Liabilities		
Long-term debt	496,044	-
Deferred lease credits and other liabilities	265,924	197,561
Total long-term liabilities	761,968	197,561
Shareholders' Equity		
Common stock $.05 par value		
Authorized 500,000,000 shares; issued 439,922,841 and 476,796,135 shares; outstanding 393,133,028 and 411,775,997 shares	21,996	23,840
Additional paid-in capital	317,674	434,104
Retained earnings	2,392,750	1,938,352
Foreign currency translation adjustments	(15,230)	(5,187)
Deferred compensation	(38,167)	(47,838)
Treasury stock, at cost	(1,095,037)	(688,801)
Total shareholders' equity	1,583,986	1,654,470
Total liabilities and shareholders' equity	$ 3,337,502	$2,626,927

Gap Inc.
Consolidated Statements of Cash Flows

($000)	Fifty-two Weeks Ended January 31, 1998	Fifty-two Weeks Ended February 1, 1997	Fifty-three Weeks Ended February 3, 1996
Cash Flows from Operating Activities			
Net earnings	$ 533,901	$ 452,859	$ 354,039
Adjustments to reconcile net earnings to net cash provided by operating activities:			
Depreciation and amortization(a)	269,706	214,905	197,440
Tax benefit from exercise of stock options by employees and from vesting of restricted stock	23,682	47,348	11,444
Deferred income taxes	(13,706)	(28,897)	(2,477)
Change in operating assets and liabilities:			
Merchandise inventory	(156,091)	(93,800)	(113,021)
Prepaid expenses and other	(44,736)	(16,355)	(15,278)
Accounts payable	63,532	88,532	1,183
Accrued expenses	107,365	87,974	9,427
Income taxes payable	(8,214)	25,706	24,806
Deferred lease credits and other long-term liabilities	69,212	56,681	21,524
Net cash provided by operating activities	844,651	834,953	489,087
Cash Flows from Investing Activities			
Net maturity (purchase) of short-term investments	174,709	(11,774)	116,134
Net purchase of long-term investments	(2,939)	(40,120)	(30,370)
Net purchase of property and equipment	(465,843)	(371,833)	(302,260)
Acquisition of lease rights and other assets	(19,779)	(12,206)	(6,623)
Net cash used for investing activities	(313,852)	(435,933)	(223,119)
Cash Flows from Financing Activities			
Net increase in notes payable	44,462	18,445	20,787
Net issuance of long-term debt	495,890	-	-
Issuance of common stock	30,653	37,053	17,096
Net purchase of treasury stock	(593,142)	(466,741)	(71,314)
Cash dividends paid	(79,503)	(83,854)	(66,993)
Net cash used for financing activities	(101,640)	(495,097)	(100,424)
Effect of exchange rate changes on cash	(1,634)	2,155	(465)
Net increase (decrease) in cash and equivalents	427,525	(93,922)	165,079
Cash and equivalents at beginning of year	485,644	579,566	414,487
Cash and equivalents at end of year	$ 913,169	$ 485,644	$ 579,566

See Notes to Consolidated Financial Statements.
(a) Includes amortization of restricted stock, discounted stock options, and discount on long-term debt.

Intimate Brands, Inc.

Consolidated Statements of Income

(Thousands except per share amounts)

	1997	1996	1995
NET SALES	$ 3,617,856	$ 2,997,340	$ 2,516,555
Costs of Goods Sold, Occupancy and Buying Costs	(2,257,824)	(1,942,295)	(1,695,627)
GROSS INCOME	1,360,032	1,055,045	820,928
General, Administrative and Store Operating Expenses	(787,780)	(584,903)	(434,632)
Special and Nonrecurring Charge	(67,600)	(12,000)	-
OPERATING INCOME	504,652	458,142	386,296
Interest Expense	(30,326)	(32,544)	(49,536)
Other Income, Net	8,610	4,612	3,299
INCOME BEFORE INCOME TAXES	482,936	430,210	340,059
Provision for Income Taxes	194,000	172,000	136,000
NET INCOME	$ 288,936	$ 258,210	$ 204,059
DILUTED AND BASIC NET INCOME PER SHARE:	$ 1.14	$ 1.02	$ 0.92

Intimate Brands, Inc.
CONSOLIDATED BALANCE SHEETS

(Thousands)

ASSETS	JANUARY 31, 1998	February 1, 1997
CURRENT ASSETS:		
Cash and Equivalents	$ 308,720	$ 135,111
Accounts Receivable	34,639	18,750
Inventories	417,703	434,800
Intercompany Receivable	12,457	60
Other	102,540	68,255
TOTAL CURRENT ASSETS	876,059	656,976
PROPERTY AND EQUIPMENT, NET	392,504	395,647
OTHER ASSETS	79,137	82,539
TOTAL ASSETS	$ 1,347,700	$ 1,135,162
LIABILITIES AND SHAREHOLDERS' EQUITY		
CURRENT LIABILITIES:		
Accounts Payable	$ 94,498	$ 88,896
Accrued Expenses	224,380	136,598
Income Taxes	94,058	98,187
TOTAL CURRENT LIABILITIES	412,936	323,681
LONG-TERM DEBT	350,000	350,000
DEFERRED INCOME TAXES	13,068	50,935
OTHER LONG-TERM LIABILITIES	10,901	8,493
SHAREHOLDERS' EQUITY:		
Common Stock	2,527	2,527
Paid-In Capital	674,620	675,240
Retained Earnings (Deficit)	(114,465)	(272,071)
	562,682	405,696
Less: Treasury Stock, at Cost	(1,887)	(3,643)
TOTAL SHAREHOLDERS' EQUITY	560,795	402,053
TOTAL LIABILITIES AND SHAREHOLDERS' EQUITY	$ 1,347,700	$ 1,135,162

Intimate Brands, Inc.
Consolidated Statements of Cash Flows

(Thousands)

	1997	1996	1995
CASH FLOWS FROM OPERATING ACTIVITIES			
Net Income	$ 288,936	$ 258,210	$ 204,059
IMPACT OF OTHER OPERATING ACTIVITIES ON CASH FLOWS			
Depreciation and Amortization	106,197	85,573	75,686
Special and Nonrecurring Charge, Net of Income Taxes	40,600	7,200	-
CHANGE IN ASSETS AND LIABILITIES			
Inventories	7,097	(75,954)	(63,374)
Accounts Payable and Accrued Expenses	55,785	53,510	33,459
Income Taxes	(14,996)	3,664	92,808
Other Assets and Liabilities	(43,144)	5,461	(18,730)
NET CASH PROVIDED BY OPERATING ACTIVITIES	440,475	337,664	323,908
INVESTING ACTIVITIES			
Capital Expenditures	(124,275)	(123,630)	(128,229)
FINANCING ACTIVITIES			
Proceeds from Short-Term Borrowings	-	-	250,000
Repayment of Short-Term Borrowings	-	-	(800,000)
Proceeds from Sale of Common Stock	-	-	677,948
Dividends Paid	(131,330)	(121,270)	(280,324)
Purchase of Treasury Stock	-	(3,986)	-
Decrease (Increase) in Intercompany Receivable	(12,397)	34,076	(34,136)
Stock Options and Other	1,136	162	(5,941)
NET CASH USED FOR FINANCING ACTIVITIES	(142,591)	(91,018)	(192,453)
NET INCREASE IN CASH AND EQUIVALENTS	173,609	123,016	3,226
Cash and Equivalents, Beginning of Year 135,111	12,095	8,869	
CASH AND EQUIVALENTS, END OF YEAR	$ 308,720	$ 135,111	$ 12,095

```
In 1995, non-cash financing activities included the transfer of equity to debt of $550
million of short-term intercompany borrowings and $350 million of long-term
intercompany debts.

The accompanying notes are an integral part of these Consolidated Financial
Statements.

COOPERS & LYBRAND LLPL.L.P.

                         CONSENT OF INDEPENDENT ACCOUNTANTS

We consent to the incorporation by reference in the registration statement of Intimate
Brands, Inc. on Form S-8, Registration Nos. 333-1960, 333-04921, 333-04923, and 333-
10215 of our report dated February 20, 1998, on our audits of the consolidated
financial statements of Intimate Brands, Inc. and subsidiaries as of January 31, 1998,
and February 1, 1997, and for the fiscal years ended January 31, 1998, February 1,
1997, and February 3, 1996, which are included in this Annual Report on Form 10-K.

COOPERS & LYBRAND LLP      Columbus, Ohio             April 28, 1998
```

Required

a. Conduct a complete analysis of each company's financial statements using the financial statement analysis framework (to the extent possible given the available data).
b. Review the statements provided by each firm's auditor. In what ways are they comparable? Non-comparable? In the case of Intimate Brands, where could a more complete audit report be obtained? Indicate whether you can rely on the information supplied by the auditors. Why?
c. Prepare a memo to an investor who is contemplating an equity investment of $100,000 in one of these two firms. Make a firm recommendation as to whether such an equity investment in either firm can be supported by your analysis.

Critical Thinking

Financial Statement Analysis: Comparison of Two Companies

11-39 Financial statements for two companies, Eli Lilly and Pfizer, have been presented in a variety of earlier assignments in Chapters 5, 6, 7, and 9. Use these financial statements to complete the following requirements:

Required

a. Conduct a complete analysis of each company's financial statements using the financial statement analysis framework (to the extent possible given the available data).
b. Prepare a memo to an investor who is contemplating an equity investment of $100,000 in one of these two firms. Make a firm recommendation as to whether such an equity investment in either firm can be supported by your analysis.

Critical Thinking

Research Project: Interviewing a User

11-40 Interview a local stockbroker or financial analyst to determine what financial ratios he/she finds most useful.

Critical Thinking

Research Project: User Interviews and Industry Comparisons

11-41 Select three large firms in the food service industry. Use your library or Internet sources to obtain balance sheet and profitability ratios for each of those three firms. Review these ratios with reference to the ratios described in this text. Compare the ratios that are computed in a manner consistent with the approaches taken in this text to Wendy's ratio results as shown in this chapter.

Critical Thinking

Research Project: Interviewing a User

11-42 Interview a local stockbroker or financial analyst and discuss the differences between liquidity and profitability ratios. Identify the three most important ratios used by this professional in each area and describe why they are important.

Critical Thinking

Research Project: Interviewing a User

11-43 Interview a local stockbroker or financial analyst and discuss the differences between the debt-to-equity ratio and financial leverage (debt/assets). At the same time, discuss the percentage composition ratios and determine whether he/she would find them more helpful than debt-to-equity (or similar) ratios.

Writing

Research Project: Comparing Two Companies in the Same Industry

11-44 Obtain financial statements from two companies in the same industry. From the Internet or a local business library, obtain appropriate operating statistics and ratios for this industry. Conduct a comprehensive financial statement analysis of each company. Compare each company to the industry averages and to each other. Write a short report describing the positive and negative aspects of each firm with respect to its past performance, relative to each other and its industry.

Writing

Research Project: Financial Statement Analysis and Interviewing Company Managers

11-45 Obtain financial statements from a local company. Conduct a comprehensive financial statement analysis of this company using the financial statement analysis framework. After completing your analysis, conduct an interview with a financial manager (such as a CFO) and a general manager (such as a CEO or operating vice president). Use your ratio results and initial conclusions as a basis for learning more about the company's performance. After your interview(s), write a report describing your conclusions regarding the company's performance. Indicate why you would or would not invest in this company.

Critical Thinking

Research Project: Apply Financial Statement Analysis to Nonprofit Organization

11-46 Review the financial statement ratios in this chapter and consider which might apply to a nonprofit organization. Write a short report indicating why each of these ratios would (or would not) apply to a nonprofit organization.

Research Project: Financial Statement Analysis Applied to a Nonprofit Organization

11-47 Obtain the audited financial statements of a local nonprofit organization. Apply our financial statement analysis framework, as appropriate, to this organization. Write a short report describing your conclusions regarding this organization's performance and indicate why you would, or would not, make a contribution to this organization.

Research Project: Comparing Two Companies in the Same Industry and Evaluating a Possible Merger Strategy

11-48 Obtain the financial statements from two companies in the same industry and conduct a comprehensive financial statement analysis of each company. Then consider a scenario under which the largest of these two companies would consider acquiring or merging with the smaller company. Write a short report evaluating the advantages and disadvantages of this hypothetical merger or acquisition.

Financial Statement Analysis: Notes

11-49 Refer to the following excerpts from Fiddler Capital Management Incorporated's 1999 financial statements. You have been provided with the independent auditor's report, financial statements, and Notes 1 and 2.

Independent Auditors' Report

Board of Directors
Fiddler Capital Management Inc.
Edina, Minnesota

We have audited the accompanying statement of financial condition of Fiddler Capital Management Inc. (the Company), wholly owned by HHS Companies, Inc., as of September 30, 1999. This financial statement is the responsibility of the Company's management. Our responsibility is to express an opinion on this financial statement based on our audit.

We conducted our audit in accordance with generally accepted auditing standards. Those standards require that we plan and perform the audit to obtain reasonable assurance about whether the statement of financial condition is free of material misstatement. An audit includes examining, on a test basis, evidence supporting the amounts and disclosures in the financial statement. An audit also includes assessing the accounting principles used and significant estimates made by management, as well as evaluating the overall financial statement presentation. We believe that our audit of the statement of financial condition provides a reasonable basis for our opinion.

In our opinion, such financial statement presents fairly, in all material respects, the financial position of Fiddler Capital Management Inc. as of September 30 1999, in conformity with generally accepted accounting principles.

Touch, Rose, & Thorne March 1, 2000

FIDDLER CAPITAL MANAGEMENT INCORPORATED
(wholly owned by HHS Companies Inc.)
STATEMENT OF FINANCIAL CONDITION
September 30, 1999 (Dollars in thousands)

ASSETS:	
Cash	$ 5,100
Advisory fees receivable (Note 3)	5,567
Expense reimbursements receivable	1,076
Net receivable from Parent and Affiliate	12,851
Prepaid expenses	135
Furniture and equipment at cost	
(net of 1,041,000 accumulated depreciation)	1,577
Other assets	288
	$26,594
LIABILITIES AND STOCKHOLDERS' EQUITY	
LIABILITIES:	
Employee compensation and related benefits payable (Note 5)	$ 8,347
Accounts payable and accrued expenses	1,618
Total liabilities	9,965
STOCKHOLDERS' EQUITY:	
Common stock, $1 par value; 10,000 shares authorized, issued, and outstanding	10
Additional paid-in capital	2,239
Retained earnings	14,380
Total stockholders' equity	16,629
	$26,594

See notes to statement of financial condition.

NOTES TO STATEMENT OF FINANCIAL CONDITION
September 30, 1999

1. Summary of Significant Accounting Practices

Fiddler Capital Management Inc. (the Company) is a wholly owned subsidiary of HHS Companies Inc. (the Parent) and is an investment advisor registered under the Investment Advisors Act of 1940. The Company furnishes investment advice to profit sharing and pension plans, financial institutions, corporate funds, management investment companies, and individuals. As of September 30, 1999, the Company managed over $14 billion of assets with approximately $118 million managed by a foreign sub-advisor and $848 million managed by two affiliates.

The Company is charged various expenses, including rent, by the Parent based on specifically identified charges and other cost allocations. The effect of these charges on retained earnings is not necessarily indicative of the costs that would have been incurred had the Company operated independently.

Depreciation of furniture and equipment is provided using accelerated methods over estimated useful lives of five or seven years.

The Company files consolidated federal and state income tax returns with its Parent and affiliates. Payments are made to the Parent for income taxes computed on pretax book income using the consolidated effective tax rate under

Accounting Principles Board Opinion No. 11. The Company adopted the provisions of Financial Accounting Standards Board Statement No. 109, *Accounting for Income Taxes,* in fiscal year 1997. Adoption of the statement did not have a material impact on the financial condition of the Company.

2. Canadian Accounting Principles

The financial statements have been prepared in accordance with accounting principles generally accepted in the United States which, in the case of the Company, conform in all material respects with those in Canada.

Required

a. Identify what is missing in these excerpts. What items would you normally expect to find in an annual report that Fiddler omitted? Comment on why Fiddler may have chosen to omit these items.
b. Review Note 1 and discuss each item in your own words.
c. Write a short memo responding to Note 2, describing the ways that you agree and disagree with the assertions in Note 2, regarding generally accepted accounting principles in the United States. Ignore the reference to Canadian accounting principles.

Writing

Research Project: New Ratios

11-50 Use a business library or the Internet to identify two recent articles that discuss financial statement analysis.

Required

a. Compare and contrast the ratios presented in this text with those in the articles you selected.
b. Discuss the advantages and disadvantages of any new ratios that were described in these articles. If these articles consistently support several ratios, focus your attention on the new ratios.
c. Apply these new ratios from part b to Wendy's. Compare the results of using these new ratios with the results obtained using the ratios described in this text.

Writing

Research Project: New Cash Flow-Based Ratios

11-51 Use a business library or the Internet to identify several recent articles discussing cash flow-based ratios that can be used in financial statement analysis.

Required

a. Compare and contrast the cash flow-based ratios presented in this text with those in the articles you selected.
b. Discuss the advantages and disadvantages of any new cash flow-based ratios that are described in these articles. If these articles consistently support several new cash flow-based ratios, focus your attention on these new ratios.
c. Apply these new ratios from part b to an analysis of Wendy's (see Appendix D). Compare the results of using these new cash flow-based ratios with the results obtained using the ratios described in this text.

Research Project: Ratio Analysis of a Service Firm

11-52 Review the financial statement ratios in this chapter and consider which might apply to a service organization, such as a law firm or an accounting firm. Write a short report indicating why each of your selected ratios would apply to a service firm.

Writing

Research Project: Ratio Analysis of Service Firm

11-53 Obtain the audited financial statements of a local service firm. Apply the financial analysis framework, as appropriate, to this firm. Write a short report describing your conclusions regarding this firm's performance. Indicate why you would or would not be concerned about the long-term success of this firm.

Internet

Comprehensive Financial Statement Analysis

11-54 Access the EDGAR archives **(www.sec.gov/edaux/searches.htm)** to locate the latest available 10-K filings for Kmart and Wal-Mart. Scroll down to the Summary of Key Financial Information and calculate the following ratios for the most recent two years. *Hint:* Some data must be obtained from the consolidated financial statements:

a. *Liquidity ratios:* current ratio, quick ratio, average sales per day, collection period, number of days' sales in ending inventory, and cost of sales per day.
b. *Profitability ratios:* gross profit percentage, operating income percentage, net income percentage, return on equity, and return on assets.
c. *Capital structure ratios:* debt to assets, capital composition analysis, and times interest earned.
d. *Earnings-per-share, market-to-book value, and price-to-earnings ratio* for the most recent year only: Use **http://quotes.galt.com** for the latest market price of each stock.
e. In your opinion, which company is doing a better job of managing its business? Which company has better growth prospects?

Internet

Analyzing Management's Disclosures

11-55 Locate the latest available 10-K filing **(www.sec.gov/edaux/searches)** of Diebold, Inc., an Ohio-based manufacturer of automated teller machines or use the company's home page **(www.diebold.com).** Scroll down to the Management Analysis of Results of Operations where vertical and horizontal analyses of the results have been included and answer the following questions:

Required

a. Describe the products and services in which the company deals. Which item (products or services) is growing at the fastest rate? Which item constitutes the largest percentage of sales revenue?
b. For both products and services, how has the cost of sales as a percentage of revenue changed during the last year? Do products or services have a higher gross margin percentage in the most recent year?
c. Have operating and sales expenses been increasing as a percentage of sales?
d. What is the operating income percentage (of net sales) for each of the three years? Comment on the causes of the year-to-year changes.

chapter

12

Additional Issues in Liability Reporting

This chapter consists of two parts, each of which can be read independently. Part I deals with financial reporting of lease obligations.

PART I LEARNING OBJECTIVES

1. Distinguish between leases that are ordinary rentals, and those that are in substance a purchase of assets.
2. Understand how leases impact the measurement of financial position and operating performance.

Part II discusses financial reporting of obligations for retirement benefit plans, mainly pensions and medical benefits.

PART II LEARNING OBJECTIVES

3. Know the difference between defined contribution and defined benefit pension plans.
4. Appreciate the impact of pension and non-pension postretirement benefit liabilities on reported financial position and operating results.
5. Understand the key assumptions necessary to measure postretirement obligations and expenses.

INTRODUCTION TO PART I: FINANCIAL REPORTING OF LEASE OBLIGATIONS

Business firms obtain the right to use property, plant, and equipment by means of either a purchase or a lease. A **lease** is an agreement between an owner (or **lessor**) and a renter (or **lessee**) that conveys the right to use the leased property for a designated future period (typically several years). The lessee makes periodic payments, usually of the same dollar amount each time, over the term of the lease. Leases can be relatively short term, such as three or four years, or can extend over the entire economic life of the leased asset.

Leasing is an increasingly popular way of obtaining business assets. In fact, leasing is one of the fastest growing industries in the United States. In recent years, leasing has accounted for more than one-third of all new equipment investment in this country. The U.S. Department of Commerce projects that leasing will grow more quickly than other types of asset acquisition throughout the next decade.

BENEFITS OF LEASING

From a lessee's perspective, there are many potential advantages to leasing, rather than purchasing, an asset. Some of these advantages are based on sound economic incentives, and others are based on the methods used to report leases in financial statements.

Leases offer financial flexibility beyond that available with other borrowing arrangements. For example, loan agreements sometimes impose considerable restrictions on borrowers. These restrictions may concern key financial ratios, profitability requirements, dividend payments, and other financial actions. Lease agreements, on the other hand, do not generally give the lessor the power to impose such restrictions. Instead, the lessor's claim is secured by the leased asset.

Leasing can also reduce the lessee's risks of equipment obsolescence. A lessor can have less risk than a lessee if the asset has a well-developed secondary market so that the lessor can resell or re-lease the used equipment. The economic life of an asset depends on its uses; national airlines, for example, cannot use outdated airplanes, but many regional carriers regularly use them for short-haul flights. Consequently, new passenger airplanes are usually first leased to major airlines, and after the initial leasing period, they are then leased to regional carriers. Leases can reduce financial risk as well. Unlike some forms of debt financing that carry variable interest rates, lease payments normally are uniform each month or year. This feature insulates the lessee from the effects of interest rate increases. On the other hand, the lessee does not benefit if interest rates decline.

ANALYZING LEASES

To provide a framework for discussing the financial statement effects of leasing, we first consider the case in which a firm borrows in order to purchase a long-lived asset. Exhibit 12-1 provides pertinent information about a jet aircraft to be acquired by the Exec Perk Company.

The company finances the purchase by installment debt and will make a series of $2 million repayments at the end of each of the next six years. This payment pattern is an ordinary annuity, which can be evaluated using present value methods.

EXHIBIT 12-1 Purchase of a Long-Lived Asset

Exec Perk Company
Information Regarding Installment Purchase of an Asset

Asset to be purchased:	Jet aircraft
Estimated useful life:	Six years
Benefit pattern:	Straight-line
Residual value:	Zero
Method of financing:	Installment debt
Annual payments (end of year):	$2 million
Borrowing rate:	12%

Present value	=	Periodic loan payment	×	Annuity present value factor, six periods at 12%
	=	\$2 million	×	4.111 (Exhibit C-3; i = 12%, n = six periods)
	=	\$8,222,000		

Because the present value of the loan payments is \$8,222,000, this is a suitable measure of the aircraft's cost to Exec Perk Company. Upon purchasing the aircraft, Exec Perk would increase both its noncurrent assets and noncurrent liabilities by \$8,222,000.

ASSETS	=	LIABILITIES	+	SHAREHOLDERS' EQUITY
Equipment +\$8,222,000		Installment debt +\$8,222,000		

Over the six-year estimated useful life of the aircraft, the cost will be systematically expensed. Assuming a straight-line benefit pattern, the annual depreciation expense is \$1,370,333 (\$8,222,000 cost ÷ 6 years).

ASSETS	=	LIABILITIES	+	SHAREHOLDERS' EQUITY
Equipment, net of accumulated depreciation −\$1,370,333				Retained earnings −\$1,370,333 (depreciation expense)

In addition, Exec Perk has borrowed the money (\$8,222,000) from the seller in order to purchase the asset at an interest rate of 12 percent. For this reason, the firm must also recognize an interest expense of \$986,640 (\$8,222,000 × 12 percent = \$986,640) during the first year of the loan.

ASSETS	=	LIABILITIES	+	SHAREHOLDERS' EQUITY
		Installment debt +\$986,640		Retained earnings −\$986,640 (Interest expense)

Exec Perk will also make the first installment payment at the end of the year:

ASSETS	=	LIABILITIES	+	SHAREHOLDERS' EQUITY
Cash		Installment debt		
– $2,000,000		– $2,000,000		

As a result of these events, Exec Perk has recognized total aircraft-related expenses of $2,356,973:

Depreciation expense	$1,370,333
Interest expense	986,640
Total expense	$2,356,973

In each of the remaining five years, Exec Perk would continue to record a depreciation expense of $1,370,333 and an interest expense computed at 12 percent of the installment debt's carrying value. Because the debt is being repaid in installments, the interest expense would be smaller in each successive year.

In summary, the installment purchase of the aircraft has affected Exec Perk's financial statements in the following ways: long-term assets and long-term debt have increased to reflect the cost of the asset and the firm's obligation to make installment payments. Also, the income statement includes both depreciation expense and the interest expense on the amount borrowed.

CAPITAL AND OPERATING LEASES

If a firm decides to lease an asset, the impact on the financial statements depends on how the lease is classified according to rules established by the FASB. Accountants must classify leases as either capital leases or operating leases. A **capital lease** is interpreted as if it is essentially a purchase of an asset, financed by debt to be repaid in installments. Consequently, a capital lease affects the financial statements the same way an installment purchase would. It increases the amounts of reported long-term assets and long-term debts, as shown earlier. An **operating lease,** on the other hand, is interpreted as an ordinary rental, where the asset is merely used by the lessee. Operating leases do not entail increases in reported long-term assets and debt. Instead, the lease payments are merely reported as a rent expense.

A lease is classified as a capital lease if it meets one or more of the following criteria:

1. The lease transfers ownership of the property to the lessee by the end of the lease.
2. The lease gives the lessee an option to purchase the leased asset at a bargain price.
3. The lease term is equal to 75 percent or more of the estimated economic life of the leased property.
4. The present value of the lease payments is 90 percent or more of the fair value of the property at the inception of the lease.

Note that any of these criteria recognize that ownership rights have, in substance, been transferred from the lessor to the lessee. Only if a lease meets *none* of these four criteria will it be classified as an operating lease.

EXHIBIT 12-2 Prospective Lease Information

Rapid Dispatch Company
Information Regarding Prospective Lease Agreement

Property to be leased	Mainframe computer
Lessor's fair value of property	$9 million
Economic life of property	10 years
Annual lease payment (due at the end of each year)	$2 million
Term of lease	Six years
Lessee's incremental borrowing rate	12%
Renewal or purchase options	None
Ownership transfer to lessee	No

To show the accounting treatment of capital leases, consider Exhibit 12-2, describing Rapid Dispatch's prospective lease of a mainframe computer. Note that the first three criteria for a capital lease are not met in this case. The lease does not transfer ownership (first criterion) and there is no bargain purchase option (second criterion). The lease term of six years is less than 75 percent of the estimated economic life (75% of 10 years = 7.5 years) of the leased property (third criterion).

To evaluate the fourth criterion, that the present value of the lease payments must equal or exceed 90 percent of the leased property's fair value, the lease payments must be discounted using the lessee's borrowing rate (assumed at 12 percent). Note that the lease obligates Rapid Dispatch to make payments of $2 million to the lessor at the end of each year for six years. This lease payment pattern is an ordinary annuity, which can be evaluated using present value methods:

Present value	=	Periodic lease payment	×	Annuity present value factor, six periods at 12%
	=	$2 million	×	4.111 (Exhibit C-3; i = 12%, n = six periods)
	=	$8,222,000		

Because the present value of the lease payments is $8,222,000 and the fair value of the property at the inception of the lease is $9 million (see Exhibit 12-2), we can see that the present value of the lease payments exceeds the 90 percent test ($8,222,000 ÷ $9,000,000 = 91.3%). Consequently, Rapid Dispatch must capitalize the lease. Capitalization will increase both the firm's noncurrent assets and noncurrent liabilities by $8,222,000 when the lease is signed.

ASSETS	=	LIABILITIES	+	SHAREHOLDERS' EQUITY
Leased assets +$8,222,000		Lease obligation +$8,222,000		

Over the six-year term of the lease, the asset cost will be systematically expensed. Because the lease is an intangible asset, the term *amortization* is used, rather than depreciation. Assuming a straight-line benefit pattern, the annual lease amortization expense is $1,370,333 ($8,222,000 cost ÷ 6 years):

ASSETS	=	LIABILITIES	+	SHAREHOLDERS' EQUITY
Leased Assets – $1,370,333				Retained earnings – $1,370,333 (amortization expense)

In addition, Rapid Dispatch has in effect borrowed the money ($8,222,000) needed to purchase the asset from the lessor at an interest rate of 12 percent. For this reason, the firm must also recognize an interest expense of $986,640 ($8,222,000 × 12 percent). Rapid Dispatch will also make the first $2 million lease payment at year-end.

ASSETS	=	LIABILITIES	+	SHAREHOLDERS' EQUITY
Cash		Lease obligation		Retained earnings
		+ $986,640		– $986,640
– $2,000,000		– $2,000,000		(interest expense)

As a result of these events, Rapid Dispatch has recognized total lease-related expenses during the first year of $2,356,973:

Amortization expense	$1,370,333
Interest expense	986,640
Total expense	$2,356,973

The reported value of the lease obligation at year-end, after the first lease payment, is $7,208,640:

Lease obligation, beginning of the year	$8,222,000
Add: Interest expense	986,640
Less: Lease payment	(2,000,000)
Lease obligation, end of the year	$7,208,640

The reported value of the leased assets at the end of this first year is $6,851,667 ($8,222,000 original cost less $1,370,333 amortization).

If Rapid Dispatch's lease contract had qualified as an operating lease, then no asset or liability would have been recognized at the inception of the lease. Instead, each year the firm would recognize a rental expense of $2,000,000, paid in cash to the lessor at year-end.

ASSETS	=	LIABILITIES	+	SHAREHOLDERS' EQUITY
Cash – $2,000,000				Retained earnings – $2,000,000 (rental expense)

Exhibit 12-3 contrasts the impact of capital versus operating lease treatments on Rapid Dispatch's balance sheet and income statement over the life of the lease. Note the following:

1. Capital and operating leases both result in a total expense of $12 million over the entire term of the lease because this is the total amount to be paid to the lessor ($2 million × 6 years = $12 million).
2. Under a capital lease, the total yearly expense (amortization plus interest) is higher in the earlier years and lower in the later years. This occurs because the interest expense declines as the lease debt is partially repaid in installments. In contrast, the operating lease shows a constant annual expense of $2 million.
3. The capital lease is reported as a leased asset on the balance sheet. The asset is systematically amortized over the lease term. A lease obligation, to be repaid in installments, is also reported as a liability. In contrast, the operating lease treatment reports neither an asset nor a liability.

EXHIBIT 12-3 Capital versus Operating Lease Treatments

Rapid Dispatch Company

Comparison of Capital and Operating Leases Effects on

Selected Financial Statement Items

Capital Lease Effects:

	Balance Sheet		Income Statement, Year Ended				
Date	Leased Assets	Lease Obligation	Amortization Expense	+	Interest Expense	=	Total
Inception (Jan. 1)	$8,222,000	$8,222,000					
December 31,							
year 1	6,851,667	7,208,640	$1,370,333	+	$ 986,640	=	$ 2,356,973
year 2	5,481,334	6,073,677	1,370,333	+	865,037	=	2,235,611
year 3	4,111,001	4,802,518	1,370,333	+	728,841	=	2,099,429
year 4	2,740,668	3,378,820	1,370,333	+	576,302	=	1,946,904
year 5	1,370,335	1,784,278	1,370,333	+	405,458	=	1,776,076
year 6	-0-	-0-	1,370,335*	+	215,722*	=	1,584,777
	Totals		$8,222,000	+	$3,778,000	=	$12,000,000

Operating Lease Effects:

Balance Sheet		Income Statement	
Leased Assets	Lease Obligation	Rental Expense, each year	$2,000,000 × 6 years
-0-	-0-	Total over 6 years	$12,000,000

*Differs due to rounding.

IMPACT OF LEASES ON RATIO RELATIONSHIPS

The differences in the financial reporting of capital and operating leases may have a major impact on financial ratios for firms with many leases. Recall that capital leases result in higher asset values and greater amounts of debt than do operating leases. Also, capital leases initially result in lower incomes (because total lease expenses are higher in the earlier years of the lease). Consequently, ratios that use net income, total assets, or debt in their calculations will be affected. As examples, return on assets, the debt-to-assets ratio, and earnings per share will all appear less favorable in the earlier years under capital leases because capital leases must be shown as both an asset and a liability.

Operating leases, on the other hand, are accounted for as rentals, so that neither the leased property nor the liability for future lease payments is shown on the balance sheet. For this reason, operating leases are often referred to as "off-balance-sheet" financing. Accounting standards, however, require that footnotes to the financial statements include substantial disclosures about operating leases. Financial analysts, if they desire, can use this supplementary information to recast the balance sheet as if the operating leases are treated similarly to capital leases. Reality Check 12-1 illustrates how financial analysts can use supplementary information regarding operating leases in evaluating a firm's indebtedness.

INTRODUCTION TO PART II: POSTRETIREMENT BENEFIT OBLIGATIONS

Most medium- and larger-sized business firms provide retired employees with pensions and other postretirement benefits, mainly medical insurance coverage. The costs

REALITY CHECK 12-1

Delta Air Lines is one of the largest airlines in the world. It provides scheduled passenger service, airfreight, mail, and other related aviation services. Selected balance sheet information from Delta's 1997 annual report is given here along with Note 8 to the financial statements, describing Delta's lease obligations.

Like most airlines, Delta leases the major portion of its assets. Most of these leases are structured to meet the FASB's criteria for operating leases. Accounting standards require that the minimum annual rental commitments under both capital and operating leases be disclosed for the ensuing five years and in the aggregate for later years.

Delta Air Lines, Inc.
Selected Financial Information, 1997 Annual Report
(Dollars in Millions)

Balance sheet	
Current assets	$ 2,867
Property and equipment	6,109
Other assets	3,765
Total	$12,741
Current liabilities	$ 4,083
Noncurrent liabilities and other credits	5,651
Total liabilities	9,734
Common stockholders' equity	3,007
Total	$12,741
Net income	$ 854

(Continued)

REALITY CHECK 12-1

Delta Air Lines, Inc.
Footnote Disclosures of Lease Obligations
1997 Annual Report

Note 8. Lease Obligations:

The Company leases certain aircraft, airport terminal and maintenance facilities, ticket offices, and other property and equipment. Rent expense is generally recorded on a straight-line basis over the lease term. Amounts charged to rental expense for operating leases were $0.9 billion in fiscal 1997 and fiscal 1996 and $1.1 billion in fiscal 1995.

At June 30, 1997, the Company's minimum rental commitments under capital leases and noncancelable operating leases with initial or remaining terms of more than one year were as follows:

Years Ending June 30	Capital Leases	Operating Leases
	(In Millions)	
1998	$101	$ 860
1999	100	860
2000	68	840
2001	57	830
2002	57	850
After 2002	118	9,780
Total minimum lease payments	501	$14,020
Less: Amounts representing interest	117	
Present value of future minimum capital lease payments	384	
Less: Current obligations under capital leases	62	
Long-term capital lease obligations	$ 322	

SOURCE: Delta Air Lines, Inc., *1997 Annual Report.*

Required

a. Assume that for purposes of financial analysis, you wish to treat Delta's operating leases as if they were capital leases. Develop an approximation of the capitalized value of Delta's leases, based on the information provided in Note 8.

b. Show how your approximation of the capitalized values of Delta's operating leases would affect your measurements of total assets, total liabilities, property and equipment, the ratio of liabilities to assets, the ratio of property, plant, and equipment to assets, net income, and the ratio of net income to total assets.

Solution

a. The present values of Delta's capital leases are included in the asset and liability totals reported in its balance sheet (and in our summary balance sheet information). If financial analysts also desire to incorporate Delta's operating leases as if they were capital leases, it is necessary first to discount the future minimum lease payments at Delta's

(Continued)

REALITY CHECK 12-1

borrowing rate. The borrowing rate is not disclosed in the financial statements, however. If it may be assumed that Delta's capital and operating leases have relatively similar cash flow patterns, then an approximate present value for the operating leases may be computed as follows:

	(millions of dollars):
Present value of capital lease payments (Note 8)	$384
Total minimum capital lease payments (Note 8)	$501
Percentage of present value to total payments:	

$$\frac{\$384}{\$501} = 76.6\%$$

Total minimum operating lease payments	$14,020
Percentage of present value to total payments (above)	×76.6%
Estimated present value of operating lease payments	$10,739

b. This approximation indicates that capitalization of the operating leases would increase Delta's reported property, plant, and equipment, as well as debt, by about $10.7 billion. Selected financial statement relationships would be affected by capitalizing leases as follows:

Delta Air Lines, Inc.
Selected Financial Ratios Before and After
Capitalization of Operating Leases
(Dollars in millions)

	Before Capitalization (See Reality Check 12-1)	**After Capitalization**[a]	**Percent Change**
Total assets	$12,741	$23,441	+84%
Total liabilities	$ 9,734	$20,434	+110%
Property and equipment	$ 6,109	$16,809	+175%
Liabilities/assets	76.4%	87.3%	
Property and equipment/assets	47.9%	71.7%	
Net income	$ 854	$ 854[b]	
Net income divided by total assets	6.7%	3.6%[b]	−46%[b]

[a]The amounts after capitalization are determined by adding $10.7 billion to debt and property, plant, and equipment, based on the approximate present value of the operating lease commitments computed earlier.

[b]For convenience, we assume that net income is the same before and after capitalization. Lease expense is generally higher in the earlier years for capital leases. Although the income effect is not readily calculable given the information in Delta's financial report, Delta's reported net income would likely have decreased if the operating leases had been capitalized.

As shown in the preceding calculations, the capitalization of Delta's operating leases would increase the reported amount of total assets, liabilities, and property and equipment by 84 percent, 110 percent, and 175 percent, respectively.

of these postretirement benefits are a component of employee expenses incurred during the **service lives** of the retirees, which are the working years prior to retirement. For this reason, the periodic expenses and obligations for postretirement benefits must be estimated to measure the operating performance and financial position of the employer firms.

Standards for the measurement and reporting of postretirement expenses and obligations have tightened considerably during the past decade. Separate standards govern reporting for pensions and reporting for other (nonpension) postemployment benefits. The following sections describe and contrast the financial reporting standards for both types of retiree benefits.

PENSION EXPENSES AND OBLIGATIONS

Pension plans are either defined contribution plans or defined benefit plans. A **defined contribution pension plan** specifies the periodic amount, usually a percentage of an employee's current salary that the firm must contribute to a pension fund. The employee's retirement benefit depends on how well the pension fund invests the contributions that it has received. In any event, the employer's only obligation is to make the agreed-on contributions to the plan. In effect, the employee bears all the risks and rewards of the investment performance of the pension fund. The financial reporting effects of defined contribution plans are straightforward and noncontroversial.

Defined benefit pension plans, in contrast, specify the benefits that employees will receive at retirement. The employer makes periodic contributions to a pension fund in order to set aside funds to pay these benefits. Income tax rules and other government regulations influence the amounts of these periodic contributions.

Because defined benefit plans specify the dollar amounts of the pensions to be paid to retirees, the employer assumes all the risks and rewards associated with the pension fund investments. For instance, if pension fund assets are insufficient to pay the agreed-on benefits, then the employer must make additional payments. On the other hand, if the pension fund's assets exceed the amounts required for benefits, the employer can reduce its contributions and in some cases can even withdraw the excess funds from the pension fund.

Defined benefit pension plans have proven to be especially popular in U.S. industries that have strong labor union representation. Unions usually favor labor agreements that offer security and low risk to their members. Managers in these industries also have tended to favor labor contracts that postpone the cash impact of labor costs. Defined benefit plans, therefore, are prevalent in the automobile, chemical, machinery, steel, paper, and transportation industries. Among firms with less labor union representation, the current trend has been away from defined benefit plans to defined contribution plans.

Exhibit 12-4 shows the relationships among the employer, the pension plan, and the retirees in a typical defined benefit pension plan. The employer makes contribu-

EXHIBIT 12-4 Defined Benefit Pension Plans

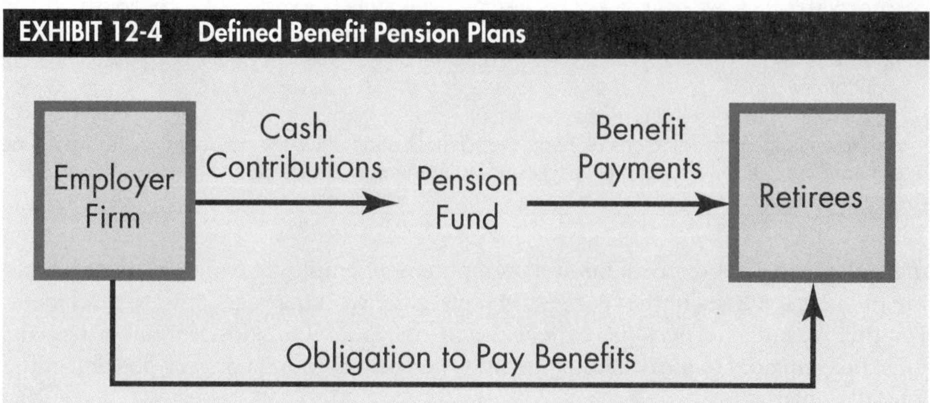

tions to the pension fund, and the pension fund ultimately makes payments to retirees as specified in the employer's labor agreements. Unlike a defined contribution plan, however, the employer's pension obligation is to pay the benefits promised by the pension plan. In substance, the employer has an obligation to the beneficiaries, and the pension fund itself is just an intermediary.

BASIC ACCOUNTING FOR PENSIONS

To illustrate financial reporting for a defined benefit pension plan, refer to Exhibits 12-5 and 12-6, which contain portions of the pension footnote disclosures from Bethlehem Steel's annual report for 1997. Bethlehem Steel's pension benefits are based both on the employees' years of service and highest earnings levels in the years preceding

EXHIBIT 12-5 Pension Liability Footnote Disclosures

Bethlehem Steel Corporation
Pension Liability Footnote Disclosures
(Adapted from the 1997 Annual Report)

POSTRETIREMENT PENSION BENEFITS
We have noncontributory defined benefit pension plans that provide benefits for substantially all our employees. Defined benefits are based on years of service and the five highest consecutive years of pensionable earnings during the last 10 years prior to retirement or a minimum amount based on years of service. We fund annually the amount required under ERISA minimum funding standards plus additional amounts as appropriate.

The following sets forth the plans' actuarial assumptions used and funded status at our valuation date of November 30 together with amounts recognized in our consolidated balance sheets:

(Dollars in millions)	1997	1996
Assumptions:		
Discount rate	7.375%	7.75%
Average rate of compensation increase	3.10%	3.10%
Actuarial present value of benefit obligations:		
Vested benefit obligation	$ 5,030	$ 4,910
Accumulated benefit obligation	5,185	5,075
Projected benefit obligation	5,495	5,325
Plan assets at fair value:		
Fixed income securities	1,552	1,656
Equity securities	3,102	2,381
Cash and marketable securities	276	178
Total plan assets	$ 4,930	$ 4,215
Projected benefit obligation in excess of plan assets	565	1,110
Various adjustments (net)	(125)	(240)
Pension liability at December 31	$ 440	$ 870

EXHIBIT 12-6 Pension Expense Footnote Disclosures

Bethlehem Steel Corporation
Pension Expense Recognized in Consolidated Income Statement
(Adapted from the 1997 Annual Report)

The assumptions used in each year and the components of our annual pension cost follow:

(Dollars in millions)	1997	1996	1995
Assumptions:			
Return on plan assets	9.00%	8.75%	10.00%
Discount rate	7.75%	7.25%	9.00%
Pension cost:			
Service cost – benefits earned during the period	$ 48	$ 59	$ 45
Interest on projected benefit obligation	395	372	402
Return on plan assets	(375)	(329)	(317)
Other items (net)	87	90	80
Total cost	$ 155	$ 192	$ 210

retirement. Special attention should be given to the measurements of pension obligations and annual pension cost. Both items are discussed in the following sections.

Measurement of Benefit Obligations

Exhibit 12-5 explains the measurement of Bethlehem Steel's pension obligations. Because pension benefits will be paid in future years, it is necessary to estimate the future payments and discount these to present values using an appropriate rate of interest. Bethlehem Steel uses a discount rate of 7.375 percent to measure its pension obligations.

The choice of a discount rate is crucial in evaluating pension obligations because minor variations in discount rates cause large variations in present values. Analysts often use the following rule of thumb: A one percent variation in the assumed discount rate causes about a 20 percent variation in the valuation of pension obligations.

Observe that Bethlehem Steel reports three present value measurements. The **vested benefit obligation** indicates amounts to which employees have irrevocable rights, even if they leave the firm prior to retirement. The **accumulated benefit obligation** shows the amount of pension benefits that employees have earned to date, based on current salary levels. The **projected benefit obligation** measures the amount of pension benefits that employees have earned to date, based on the expected future salary levels that will determine these pension benefits.

Bethlehem Steel's disclosures indicate that 97 percent of the company's benefits were vested at the end of 1997 ($5,030 vested benefit ÷ $5,185 accumulated benefit = 97 percent). The inclusion of expected future salary levels in the calculation increases the pension obligation by only six percent ($5,495 projected benefit ÷ $5,185 accumulated benefit = 106 percent). These relationships reflect the fact that Bethlehem Steel has a stable and mature workforce.

Exhibit 12-5 also shows that the total market value of Bethlehem Steel's pension plan assets was $4.93 billion at the end of 1997. This amount is less than the pension liability and indicates that Bethlehem Steel's pension plan was underfunded at that date. Accounting standards require that Bethlehem Steel report the unfunded liability in the balance sheet. The liability is measured as shown in Exhibit 12-5, and as a result Bethlehem Steel reported a pension liability of almost $440 million dollars at the end of 1997.

Measurement of Pension Expenses

Exhibit 12-6 shows the components of the pension expense reported in Bethlehem Steel's income statement, defined as follows:

- **Service cost,** also called the "normal cost," is the value of future pension benefits that employees have earned during the current year.
- **Interest cost** is the interest on the projected benefit obligation for the year. Recall that the projected benefit obligation is a present value, the discounted value of future payments. Each year this present value increases because the payment date is closer.
- **Return on plan assets** is a reduction in pension expense for the return that is expected on the plan's assets. This component is based on anticipated, not actual, return so that pension costs are not severely influenced by variations in investment values.
- **Other items (net)** includes the systematic amortization of liabilities existing when present pension reporting standards were adopted, the obligations resulting from subsequent changes in pension benefits, the revisions in various assumptions underlying the pension valuation, and other factors.

EVALUATION OF PENSION REPORTING

Pension reporting continues to be an area of controversy in financial accounting. The basic issues center on (1) the assumptions used in measuring pension obligations and expenses, (2) the appropriate definition of pension obligations, and (3) whether pension funds are entities distinct from the employer firms.

Assumptions

A myriad of actuarial and economic assumptions underlie the estimation of pension obligations. **Actuarial assumptions** (employee turnover, service lives, longevity, and so on) are fairly standardized and noncontroversial. The major controversies concern **economic assumptions,** particularly the assumed interest rate used to discount future pension benefits, and the anticipated rate of return on pension plan assets.

Employers are required to re-evaluate all potentially material assumptions when they perform annual measurements of pension and other postretirement benefit obligations. Many corporations have needed to re-assess the adequacy of the assumed discount rates as a result of the declines in interest rates on high-quality bonds that occurred during the 1990s. Using lower interest rates to measure these obligations increases their present values, but on the other hand, related assumptions may also need to be revised because they are based on the same set of expectations about future economic conditions. For example, lower long-term interest rates are usually associated with lower rates of expected inflation, and this may suggest that the assumed rates of salary progression and health-care-cost trend rates should be revised downwards also.

If so, these changes reduce the related liabilities. Consequently, the effects of interest rate changes may create revisions of several related assumptions that have offsetting (positive and negative) effects on pension and other postretirement obligations.

Measurements of Pension Obligations

Exhibit 12-5 shows three separate measures of Bethlehem Steel's pension obligation vested, accumulated, and projected benefit obligations. Managers and analysts often disagree about which of these best represents the firm's pension obligation. Managers sometimes assert that vested benefits are the best measure of the obligation, because this is the amount that must be paid to employees, even if the firm discontinues its operations immediately. Bear in mind, however, that financial statements reflect a "going concern" assumption, unless the firm is actually expected to liquidate in the near-term future. Alternatively, some firms argue that the accumulated benefit amount is a suitable measure, because it assumes continuity of the firm but does not incorporate salary increases that have yet to occur.

Finally, analysts frequently argue that the projected benefit obligation is most realistic, because it is based on expected pension payments (assuming normal rates of salary increase). Moreover, analysts argue that the accumulated benefit measurement is not meaningful because future salary increases are ignored in estimating future pension payments. Future inflation is reflected in the discount rates used to compute present values.

Present accounting standards do not aim to resolve these disputes. In fact, as discussed earlier, balance sheet disclosures of minimum pension obligations use the accumulated benefits measure, whereas income measures are based on the projected benefits measure. Accounting standards reflect a compromise that incorporates two types of pension obligations, along with extensive supplementary disclosures.

Pension Fund as a Distinct Entity

The pension fund is merely an intermediary between the employer and the pension beneficiary, as depicted in Exhibit 12-4. The employer is ultimately liable for all pension benefits and bears all of the risks associated with the pension fund's investments. Consequently, many analysts do not regard the pension fund as an entity distinct from the employer firm and suggest that pension plan assets and obligations should be included (consolidated) with those of the employer for financial reporting purposes.

The consolidation of the employer firm and its pension plan would dramatically alter the financial statements of most industrial firms. For example, Bethlehem Steel's pension plan had $4.9 billion in assets and $5.5 billion in obligations at the end of 1997. Bethlehem Steel itself had about $4.8 billion in assets (exclusive of pension amounts) at that date and only $1.2 billion in shareholders' equity. In this case, inclusion of the pension fund assets and obligations on Bethlehem Steel's balance sheet would almost double the apparent size of the company and more than double its reported debt financing.

OTHER POSTRETIREMENT EXPENSES AND OBLIGATIONS

Approximately one-third of all U.S. workers are covered by employer medical plans that continue the employee's coverage after retirement. The costs of retiree medical benefits are substantial and are expected to continue to increase as people live longer. Inflation and improvements in medical technology will also likely contribute to rising health costs.

Until 1993, the predominant way of reporting these nonpension postretirement benefits was on a **pay-as-you-go** basis, in which expenses were reported on a cash basis and no obligations were recognized for future payments. Current accounting standards, however, require that firms report their obligations to provide future benefits and accrue the expenses during the years that employees provide service (*SFAS No. 106,* "Employers' Accounting for Postretirement Benefits Other Than Pensions," December, 1990). For most affected firms, conversion to an accrual basis increased the amount of expenses currently recognized for medical benefits by two to three times (200 to 300 percent). As a result, adoption of the new standard in 1993 reduced profits at the 100 largest U.S. corporations by about 33 percent. Moreover, recognition of the related obligations reduced shareholders' equity an average of 20 percent. At General Motors Corporation, for example, the reduction in shareholders' equity exceeded 80 percent ("Retiree Benefits to Take Bigger Bite of Profits," *The Wall Street Journal,* September 1, 1993).

Illustration of Nonpension Postretirement Benefit Disclosures

Exhibits 12-7 and 12-8 contain excerpts of Bethlehem Steel's other postretirement benefit disclosures and will serve as a basis for our discussion. Observe that the overall format and content of these disclosures parallels that shown earlier for pension benefits (refer to Exhibits 12-5 and 12-6). The analyst would focus on the measurement of the firm's obligation and the determination of the annual expense. Exhibit 12-7 shows that Bethlehem Steel reports a liability of $1.9 billion for nonpension postretirement benefits at the end of 1997. This amount represents the difference between the present value of these benefits ($2.06 billion) and the plan assets at fair value ($120 million).

Although this measurement is similar to the measurement of pension obligations shown earlier (refer to Exhibit 12-5), there are two notable differences. First, the **accumulated postretirement benefit obligation** measures the present value of the future benefits that employees and retirees have earned to date. The calculation incorporates future medical cost changes, based on an assumed average health care trend rate. This contrasts sharply with the calculation of the minimum pension liability, which ignores expected future price changes. The future price of medical inflation is admittedly hard to predict, and Bethlehem Steel also provides the analyst with an estimate of the sensitivity of the measurements to a one percent increase in the assumed rate.

Second, the fair values of the plan assets are minor, relative to the accumulated benefit obligation. Few firms fund any of their nonpension retirement benefits. There are no regulatory funding requirements or income tax advantages to motivate early funding, and most firms opt instead to simply pay the medical and life insurance premiums when they become due.

Measurement of Nonpension Postretirement Benefit Expense

The cost components shown in Exhibit 12-8 for the nonpension expenses follow the same format as those for pension costs (refer to Exhibit 12-6). The service cost represents the amount of the accumulated benefit obligation that was earned by employees over the current year. The interest cost is the beginning of the year obligation multiplied by the discount rate. For firms like Bethlehem Steel, with mature employee groups, interest cost is the largest component of the net expense because the benefit obligation is so large. Because the benefits are not substantially funded, the return on plan assets provides only a minor offset to the other cost components.

EXHIBIT 12-7 Nonpension PostRetirement Expenses

Bethlehem Steel Corporation
Postretirement Benefits Other Than Pensions
Obligations and Expenses Recognized in Financial Statements
(1997 Annual Report)

POSTRETIREMENTS BENEFIT OBLIGATION:
In addition to providing pension benefits, we currently provide health care and life insurance benefits for most retirees and their dependents. The following sets forth our plans' actuarial assumptions used and funded status at our valuation date of November 30, together with the amounts recognized in our consolidated balance sheets:

(Dollars in millions)	1997	1996
Assumptions:		
Discount rate	7.375%	7.75%
Trend rate		
- beginning next year	6.00%	7.00%
- ending year 2000	4.60%	4.60%
Accumulated postretirement benefit obligation:		
Retirees	$ 1,760	$ 1,705
Fully eligible active plan participants	155	145
Other active plan participants	140	150
Total	2,055	2,000
Plan assets at fair value:		
Fixed income securities	120	130
Accumulated postretirement benefit obligation in excess of plan assets	1,935	1,870

A comparison of the financial statement effects of pension and nonpension benefits for Bethlehem Steel indicates that both types of postretirement benefits have significant effects on the firm's financial position and operating results. Although the total obligations for pensions are much greater than those for nonpension benefits, the pension benefits are substantially funded, while the nonpension benefits are not. As a result, the unfunded obligations are notably higher for the nonpension benefits (about $565 million for pension benefits and over $1.9 billion for nonpension benefits) at the end of 1997. Similarly, the firm's expenses in 1997 were approximately the same for pension and nonpension benefits, because pension costs were substantially offset by investment returns on the pension fund assets.

Bethlehem Steel's postretirement disclosures reflect the reporting standards that were in effect through 1997. Early in 1998, the FASB significantly expanded these reporting requirements (*SFAS No. 132*, "Employers' Disclosures About Pensions and Other Postretirement Benefits"). The additional reporting requirements include a complete reconcilation of the beginning and ending balances of the benefit obligations, as

EXHIBIT 12-8 Postretirement Benefits Expense Footnote Disclosures

Bethlehem Steel Corporation
Postretirement Benefit Expense Recognized in Consolidated Income Statement
(Adapted from the 1997 Annual Report)

POSTRETIREMENT BENEFITS EXPENSE:
The assumptions used in each year and the components of our postretirement benefit cost follow:

(Dollars in millions)	1997	1996	1995
Assumptions:			
Return on plan assets	9.00%	8.75%	10.00%
Discount rate	7.75%	7.25%	9.00%
Trend rate			
- beginning current year	7.00%	8.00%	9.00%
- ending year 2000	4.60%	4.60%	4.60%
Postretirement benefit cost:			
Service cost	$ 7	$ 10	$ 7
Interest on accumulated postretirement benefit obligation	148	140	148
Return on plan assets	(11)	(12)	(12)
Other (net)	6	8	-
Total cost	$ 150	$ 146	$ 143

A one-percentage-point increase or decrease in the assumed health care trend rate would increase or decrease the accumulated postretirement benefit obligation by about $150 million and 1997 expense by about $10 million.

SOURCE: Excerpts from Note I to Bethlehem Steel Corporation's *1997 Annual Report.*

well as a reconciliation of the changes in the plan assets' fair values. These expanded disclosures respond to numerous requests by investor analysts that additional information about the magnitudes and composition of these important assets, obligations, and expenses be mandated.

Because standards for the measurement and reporting of postretirement benefits in financial statements have changed considerably in recent years, financial analysts must reconsider the usefulness of conventional financial ratio calculations in light of these new employee benefits, measurements, and disclosures. No simple recipes exist for modifying the typical ratios. The informed user of financial reports must be aware that financial statement analysis is more art than science, and that much of the information that is pertinent to a decision may not appear in the body of the financial statements. Recognition of these new financial reporting standards may require a modification of analysts' traditional rules of thumb regarding trends and changes in a firm's performance.

Reality Check 12-2 contrasts the disclosures related to pensions and nonpension postemployment benefits for a large U.S. corporation.

REALITY CHECK 12-2

PPG Industries, Inc. is a major supplier of coatings, flat and speciality glass, and special chemicals. The following information has been abstracted from the notes to PPG's 1997 financial statements:

	Pension Benefits		Other Postretirement Benefits	
	1997	1996	1997	1996
	(Dollars in Millions)		(Dollars in Millions)	
Funded status of benefit plans:				
Plan assets at market value	$ 2,308	$2,006	$ —	$ —
Accumulated benefit obligation	1,857	1,704	704	676
Projected benefit obligation	2,023	1,859	—	—
Components of annual expense:				
Service cost	36	36	7	7
Interest cost	134	124	48	43
Return on assets	(212)	(189)	—	—
Other	17	30	6	4
Total cost	$ (25)	$ 1	$ 61	$ 54
Underlying assumptions:				
Discount rate	7.0%	7.5%	7.0%	7.5%
Expected return on plan assets	10.9%	10.9%	—	—
Future compensation increases	4.6%	4.6%	—	—
Health care cost trend	—	—	7.0%	7.3%

Required

a. Do you consider PPG's pension benefits and other postemployment benefits to be overfunded or underfunded at the end of 1993? Explain.
b. Distinguish between the "accumulated benefit obligation" amounts reported for each type of plan.
c. With respect to the components of the annual costs, why is interest expense included? Why does the return on plan assets appear as a negative component?
d. The disclosure of assumptions reveals two changes between 1997 and 1996: (1) the discount rate has been decreased from 7.5 percent to 7.0 percent, and (2) the health care cost trend rate has been changed from 7.3 percent to 7.0 percent. Explain how each of these changes would affect your comparisons of postemployment liabilities and costs between 1997 and 1996.

Solution

a. *Pension plans:* PPG's plan assets at market value exceed the accumulated benefit obligation by $451 million ($2,308 million less $1,857 million), and PPG's plan assets exceed the projected benefit obligation by $285 million ($2,308 million less $2,023 million). By either measure, PPG's plans are fully funded at the end of 1997. The projected benefit obligation, which includes projected rates of compensation increases, is a more meaningful definition of the pension obligation.
   Other (nonpension) plans: PPG's accumulated benefit obligation is $704 million, which is entirely unfunded at the end of 1997.
   All plans combined: In the aggregate, PPG's postretirement plans appear to be underfunded by $419 million ($704 unfunded nonpension benefits less $285 overfunded pension benefits).
b. The "accumulated benefit obligation" has a different interpretation for pension obligations than for other postretirement obligations. For pension obligations, the accumulated benefit obligation assumes that present salary levels continue through the employee retirement dates; in other words, future rates

(Continued)

REALITY CHECK 12-2

of compensation increases are ignored. For nonpension obligations, on the other hand, future rates of medical cost inflation are formally incorporated in the calculation of the accumulated benefit obligations. The financial statement analyst must be alert to the different meanings of "accumulated benefits."

c. Interest expense is a component of the annual cost of postretirement benefits because the obligations are reported at present value; the expected future benefit payments are discounted at an appropriate interest rate. As time passes, the present value of future payments increases. This increase in the value of a liability is due to interest expense.

The return on plan assets represents amounts that have been earned on the invested plan assets. Increases in the value of the plan's investments reduce the amount of the unfunded pension obligation. For this reason, these returns constitute income (or a reduction in expense) related to pensions.

d. *Discount rate:* Expected future benefit payments are discounted to determine the present value of the pension obligation. Reductions in the discount rate increase the present value of the pension obligation.

Health care cost trend rate: A decrease in this rate reduces the firm's estimated future payments for medical benefits and thereby reduces the firm's obligation.

SUMMARY OF LEARNING OBJECTIVES

1. **Distinguish between leases that are ordinary rentals and those that are in substance a purchase of assets.**
A lease is an agreement between an owner (or lessor) and a renter (or lessee) that conveys the right to use the leased property for a designated future period. Accountants classify leases as either capital leases or operating leases. A capital lease is interpreted as essentially a purchase of the leased asset, while an operating lease is reported on the same basis as an ordinary rental.

   Accounting standards provide a set of explicit criteria to identify capital leases. Essentially, a capital lease transfers the potential risks and rewards of ownership to the lessee. A capital lease is reported as an asset financed by installment debt.

2. **Understand how leases impact the measurement of financial position and operating performance.**
Capital leases affect the balance sheet and income statement in the same manner as an installment purchase of the asset would. Noncurrent assets and lease obligations are reported based on the present value of the series of lease payments. The annual expense (lease amortization expense and interest expense) is relatively higher in the earlier years and declines as the lease obligation is reduced over time. By contrast, operating leases are reported as ordinary rentals. Neither assets nor liabilities are recognized in the balance sheet when the lease is signed. The annual expense is generally equal to the annual lease payments.

   Extensive disclosures in the Notes to Financial Statements are provided for all long-term leases, both capital and operating, indicating the amount and timing of future minimum lease payments. Financial statement analysts must use these "off-balance-sheet" amounts in order to aid in assessments of liquidity and solvency of lessee firms.

KEY TERMS

3. **Know the difference between defined contribution and defined benefit pension plans.**
   Pension plans are either defined contribution or defined benefit plans. Defined contribution plans specify the employer's required payments to the pension fund and do not present any special reporting issues. Defined benefit plans, on the other hand, specify the future pension payments to which an employee will be entitled. Both types of plans require that the employer make periodic payments to a pension fund, but under a defined benefit plan the employer assumes all of the risks associated with pension fund investments.
4. **Appreciate the impact of pension and non-pension postretirement benefit liabilities on reported financial position and operating results.**
   Firms with defined benefit plans must report on the balance sheet a minimum liability equal to the difference between pension obligations and the value of pension fund assets. Pension expense reported on the income statement consists mainly of current service costs plus interest on the pension obligation minus returns expected to be earned on the pension fund's assets.
5. **Understand the key assumptions necessary to measure postretirement obligations and expenses.**
   Measurements of pension obligations and expenses are based on a variety of assumptions, including assumptions about future earnings of pension fund investments and future salary increases of covered employees. The critical assumptions are disclosed in footnotes to the financial statements. Financial analysts must be alert to variations in assumptions used by different firms to measure pension obligations and expenses.

   Standards for the financial reporting of nonpension postretirement benefits have been adopted recently and are similar to the standards used for reporting pensions. The future trend of medical costs must be considered in predicting future benefits. Such costs are difficult to predict due to changes in medical technology, medical cost inflation, changing standards of medical care, the potential impact of a national health plan, and other factors. For this reason, the liabilities and expenses associated with nonpension retiree benefits are difficult to measure. Financial analysts must be creative as well as cautious when incorporating these measurements in financial ratio analysis.

QUESTIONS

12-1 Discuss several reasons why a firm's managers might choose to lease rather than purchase operating assets (such as buildings and equipment).

12-2 Describe the key features that are normally found in a long-term lease agreement.

12-3 Distinguish between capital leases and operating leases as the terms are used in financial reporting. Is the distinction meaningful? Discuss.

12-4 Which criteria are used in deciding whether a given lease agreement constitutes a capital lease or an operating lease? Do these criteria make economic sense? Discuss.

12-5 Contrast the effects that capital leases and operating leases have on the following financial statement elements and relationships. Discuss how each of these effects might influence a manager's decision about how to design a lease contract.

a. Total assets
b. Total liabilities
c. Net income, earlier years
d. Net income, later years
e. Ratio of debt to total assets
f. Ratio of operating income to total assets

12-6 Assume that a given lease contract qualifies as a capital lease.
a. How would the lease be reported in the balance sheet as an asset?
b. How would this dollar amount change over successive balance sheets?
c. How would the lease be reported in the balance sheet as a lease obligation?
d. How would the amount of the obligation change over successive balance sheets? Would the balance sheet amounts reported as leased assets and lease obligations ever be the same? Explain.

12-7 Explain why the total annual expenses associated with capital leases are higher in the earlier years, and lower in the later years, of the lease term. Why is it necessary that the total expense over the entire life of the lease be the same for capital and operating leases?

12-8 Evaluate the following statement: *Capitalizing a lease creates a fictitious asset. The lessee does not own the leased asset, because the lessor retains title and will repossess the asset at the end of the lease term. A lease is simply a rental, and this is true regardless of the length of the lease term.*

12-9 Respond to the following statements: *Firms have many different types of contracts that obligate them to make a series of cash payments at dates well into the future. For example, CEOs and other top managers often have multiyear contracts that guarantee substantial salaries even if the manager is terminated. Should the cash payments specified in these contracts also be capitalized? Would it make sense to put managers on the balance sheet as intangible assets? If not, why do we make an exception for leases?*

12-10 Notes to financial statements cover disclosures about operating leases, including minimum rental commitments, disclosed by year for the ensuing five years, and in the aggregate for later years. How should a financial analyst use this supplementary (note) information when evaluating a firm's total debt? If you consider operating leases to be components of a firm's total debt, should the related amounts be reported in the body of the financial statements? Discuss.

12-11 For a capital lease, the amounts that are initially recorded as leased assets and lease obligations depend on the interest rate used to discount the lease payments. In addition, the discount rate also affects the periodic amounts of expense reported for capital leases.
a. Assume that a manager wishes to report relatively small amounts of leased assets and obligations. Would she prefer a low or a high discount rate? Explain.
b. Assume that a manager wishes to report relatively larger amounts of income in the earlier years of a lease. Would she prefer a low or a high discount rate? Explain.
c. Assume that a manager wishes to report a relatively high ratio of income to assets in the earlier years of a lease. Would she prefer a low or a high discount rate? Explain.

12-12 What types of postretirement benefits are usually provided to employees by larger-sized business firms?

12-13 Why do firms provide postretirement benefits to employees?

12-14 When should the costs of postretirement benefits be reported as expenses on the income statement?

12-15 Distinguish between defined contribution and defined benefit pension plans. Which arrangement is riskier for the employee? Which is riskier for the employer? Explain.

12-16 A typical defined benefit pension plan involves three entities: the employer firm, the pension plan, and the covered employee. Describe the relationships among these three entities.

12-17 Firms with defined benefit pension plans report three separate liability amounts in the notes to the financial statements. These are the obligations for vested benefits, accumulated benefits, and projected benefits.
a. Describe how these amounts differ.
b. Identify which of these amounts best measures the employer's liability as of the balance sheet date. Explain the reasons for your choice.

12-18 Accounting standards require that firms report their unfunded pension liabilities on the balance sheet. Describe what is meant by an unfunded pension liability. Explain why such an amount should (or should not) be included on the balance sheet.

12-19 Pension expense includes three main components: service cost, interest cost, and a reduction in expense for the return on plan assets. Explain how each of these amounts is determined.

12-20 Distinguish between the actuarial assumptions and the economic assumptions that underlie the measurement of pension liabilities and expenses. Which of these types of assumptions is more controversial? Why?

12-21 Present accounting standards report only the amount of unfunded pension obligations on the balance sheet. Gross pension assets and liabilities are not reported on the financial statements. This practice is based on the premise that the pension fund is an entity distinct from the employer firm.
a. Identify arguments in support of this premise and against it.
b. If the pension fund is not a distinct entity, how should pension assets and liabilities be reported in the financial statements?
c. Which key financial statement elements and ratios would be likely to change dramatically, if the pension fund were consolidated with (added to) the employer firm's financial statements?

12-22 Many firms provide their employees with other, nonpension postretirement benefits, primarily medical plans. Outline the similarities and differences in accounting for pensions and nonpension postretirement benefits with respect to:
a. Liability measurement
b. Balance sheet reporting
c. Expense recognition

EXERCISES

Installment Purchase

12-23 Determine the first year's financial statement impact of the following purchase terms:
- Annual payments, at year-end, $15,000
- Five-year useful life and note term

- 10 percent borrowing rate
- Straight-line benefit pattern
- Zero residual value
- Installment purchase

Operating or Capital Lease

12-24 Determine the first year's financial statement impact of the following lease terms:

- Annual payments, at year-end, $15,000
- Five-year useful life
- 10 percent borrowing rate
- Straight-line benefit pattern
- Zero residual value
- Five-year lease term
- Lessor's fair value of property, $60,000

Lease Versus Purchase

12-25 Consider the following terms:

- Annual payments, end of each year, $40,000
- 10-year useful life
- 10 percent borrowing rate
- Straight-line benefit pattern
- Zero residual value
- Lease purchase
- Initial deposit upon signing agreement, $20,000, refundable upon satisfying all purchase terms
- Five-year lease terms
- Lessor's fair value of property, $170,000

Required

a. What lease terms should be changed to insure this purchase would be reported as a capital lease?

b. Using the accounting equation, show the first year's financial statement impact of your revised terms, and compare it to the financial statement impact of the original terms.

Lease Versus Purchase

12-26 Consider the following terms:

- Annual payments, end of each year, $30,000
- 12-year useful life
- Eight percent borrowing rate
- Straight-line benefit pattern
- Zero residual value
- Lease purchase
- Initial fees paid upon signing agreement, $20,000
- Eight-year lease term
- Lessor's fair value of property, $220,000

Required

a. What lease terms should be changed to insure this purchase is reported as a capital lease?
b. Using the accounting equation, show the first year's financial statement impact of your revised terms, and compare it to the financial statement impact of the original terms.

PROBLEMS

Capital Versus Operating Lease

12-27 Schott Sausages, in trying to lease a sausage machine, is concerned about whether the machine will be reported as a capital or operating lease. Consider the following facts in your deliberations:

- Annual lease payment required, $30,000
- Term of lease and useful life of machine, five years
- Discount rate, 10 percent

Required

a. Should the sausage machine be reported as a capital or operating lease? Why?
b. Calculate the annual expense for the first two years associated with a capital lease, using straight-line depreciation and zero residual value. Show the impact of this lease on the accounting equation.
c. Why are the capital lease costs higher than the operating lease costs in part b?

Capital Versus Operating Lease

12-28 Hannah Steel Corporation signed a five-year lease agreement on January 2, 2000, for the lease of equipment. The annual lease payment required at the end of each year is $4,000. The useful life of the equipment is five years and the fair market value is $18,000.

Required

a. Assume that Hannah's (the lessee) incremental borrowing rate is eight percent. Calculate the present value of the lease payments.
b. Is this a capital lease or an operating lease?
c. If the lease payments are $4,000 per year, totaling $20,000, why isn't $20,000 the present value of the lease?
d. Show the impact of this lease on Hannah's balance sheet. (*Hint:* Use the accounting equation)
e. Advise Hannah on the advantages and disadvantages of a capital versus an operating lease.

Evaluation of Liabilities: Potential Creditor Viewpoint

12-29 L'alpane is a transportation company headquartered in Paris. Its 1999 annual report includes the following liabilities (all in French francs):

	1998	1999
Payables to:		
Affiliated companies	38,642,541	8,325,461
Third parties	5,162,034	3,705,679
Accrued expenses and provisions	22,655,420	37,042,469
Total liabilities	66,459,995	49,073,609

Required

a. Describe each of L'alpane's liabilities.

b. All other things being equal, is L'alpane more or less liquid at the end of 1999? Why?

c. How would L'alpane's lenders react to the firm's handling of its liabilities? Why?

d. How would a creditor who had *leased an airplane* to L'alpane, whose account is 60 days past due, react to L'alpane's management of its liabilities? Why?

e. Relative to many other large companies, does L'alpane owe much money to external parties? What evidence supports this position? Given a natural and long-standing aversion to debt by many French companies, does L'alpane's balance sheet suggest that this firm also avoids debt? Why or why not?

Ratio Effects: Lease Versus Purchase

12-30 Consider the following summary financial statements at the beginning of the period:

Current assets	$ 40,000	Current liabilities	$ 15,000
Other assets	110,000	Other liabilities	113,150
		Capital stock	10,000
		Retained earnings	11,850
Total	$150,000	Total	$150,000

Net income during the period (exclusive of the lease) was $35,000. Also assume the company entered into a lease with the following terms:

- Annual payments, end of each year, $30,000
- 12-year useful life
- Eight percent borrowing rate
- Straight-line benefit pattern
- Zero residual value
- Six-year lease term
- Lessor's fair value of property, $240,000

Required

Use *beginning* balance sheet data to calculate the following requirements:

a. Calculate the return on equity (ROE) ratio at year-end and the financial leverage ratio for this company, assuming that this new asset is reported on the financial statements as a capital lease.

b. Calculate the return on equity (ROE) ratio and the financial leverage ratio for this company, assuming that this new asset is reported on the financial statements as an operating lease.

c. Discuss the relative impact of acquiring this asset under an operating lease versus a capital lease on these financial statements. Show the effects of each option, using the accounting equation.

Ratio Effects: Lease Versus Purchase

12-31 Consider the following summary financial statements at the beginning of the period:

Current assets	$1,050,000	Current liabilities	$ 650,000
Other assets	2,450,000	Other liabilities	1,500,000
		Capital stock	100,000
		Retained earnings	1,250,000
Total	$3,500,000	Total	$3,500,000

Net income during the period (exclusive of the lease) was $250,000. Also consider the following lease terms:

- Annual payments, at year-end, $25,000
- Ten-year useful life
- Twelve percent borrowing rate
- Straight-line benefit pattern
- Zero residual value
- Lease purchase
- Eight-year lease term
- Lessor's fair value of property, $225,000

Required

Use *beginning* balance sheet data to calculate the following requirements:

a. Calculate the ROE ratio and the financial leverage ratio for this company, assuming that this new asset is reported on the financial statements as a capital lease.

b. Calculate the ROE ratio and the financial leverage ratio for this company, assuming that this new asset is reported on the financial statements as an operating lease.

c. Discuss the relative impact of acquiring this asset under an operating lease versus a capital lease on these financial statements. Demonstrate these effects using the accounting equation.

Interpreting Financial Statements: Leases

Critical Thinking

12-32 Review Wendy's financial statements in Appendix D.

Required

a. Read Note 5. Identify any unfamiliar or unusual terms. Match the terms presented in this chapter to the terms used by Wendy's.

b. Do the firm's capital leases (the firm is the lessee) have any significant effect on its balance sheet? How?

c. Do the firm's operating leases (the firm is the lessee) have any significant effect on its balance sheet? How?

d. What proportion of the firm's total assets were financed by capital leases?

e. What other impact might leases have on the long-term success or failure of this firm?

Interpreting Financial Statements: Leases

Critical Thinking

12-33 Review Reebok's financial statements in Appendix E.

Required

a. Read Note 7. Identify any unfamiliar or unusual terms and match the terms presented in this chapter to the terms used by Reebok.
b. Does the firm have any capital leases?
c. Do the firm's operating leases have any significant effect on its balance sheet? How?
d. What other impact might leases have on the long-term success or failure of this firm?

Interpreting Lease Disclosures

12-34 Triangle Air Lines is one of the largest airlines in the world. It provides scheduled passenger service, airfreight, mail, and other related aviation services. Selected balance sheet information from Triangle's 1999 annual report is given here, along with Note 4 to the financial statements, describing Triangle's lease obligations.

Like most airlines, Triangle leases the major portion of its assets. Most of these leases are structured to meet the FASB's criteria for operating leases. Accounting standards require that the minimum annual rental commitments under both capital and operating leases be disclosed for the ensuing five years and in the aggregate for later years.

Triangle Air Lines, Inc.
Selected Financial Information, 1999 Annual Report
(Dollars in Thousands)

Balance sheet	
Current assets	$ 1,698,444
Property and equipment	7,093,312
Other assets	1,369,818
Total	$10,161,574
Current liabilities	$ 3,542,814
Noncurrent liabilities and other credits	4,724,692
Total liabilities	8,267,506
Common stockholders' equity	1,894,068
Total	$10,161,574
Net loss	$ 506,318

Triangle Air Lines, Inc.
Footnote Disclosures of Lease Obligations
1999 Annual Report

Note 4. Lease Obligations:

The company leases certain aircraft, airport terminal and maintenance facilities, ticket offices, and other property and equipment under agreements with terms of more than one year. Rent expense is generally recorded on a straight-line basis over the lease term. Amounts charged to rental expense for operating leases were $997,326,000 in fiscal 1999; $668,848,000 in 1998; and $545,542,000 in fiscal 1997.

On June 30, 1999, the Company's minimum rental commitments under capital leases and noncancelable operating leases with initial or remaining terms of more than one year were as follows on the next page.

Years Ending June 30	Capital Leases	Operating Leases
	(Dollars in Thousands)	
1999	$ 19,708	$ 906,698
2000	20,565	896,793
2001	18,323	880,980
2002	18,274	894,651
2003	17,530	901,514
After 2004	72,842	12,851,687
Total minimum lease payments	167,242	$17,332,323
Less: Amounts representing interest	47,423	
Present value of future minimum capital lease payments	119,819	
Less: Current obligations under capital leases	10,321	
Long-term capital lease obligations	$109,498	

Special facility revenue bonds have been issued by certain municipalities and airport authorities to build or improve airport terminal and maintenance facilities that are leased under operating leases by Triangle. Under these lease agreements, the Company is required to make rental payments sufficient to pay principal and interest on the bonds as they become due. On June 30, 1999, Triangle guaranteed $679,505,000 principal amount of such bonds.

Note 4 on lease obligations shows that Triangle's existing operating leases require total minimum lease payments exceeding $17 billion dollars in future years. These operating lease obligations are more than 100 times the company's capital lease obligations of $167.2 million.

Required

a. Assume that for purposes of financial analysis, you wish to treat Triangle's operating leases as if they were capital leases. Develop an approximation of the capitalized value of Triangle's leases, based on the information provided in Note 4.
b. Show how this approximation of the capitalized values of Triangle's operating leases would affect measurements of total assets, total liabilities, property and equipment, ratio of liabilities to assets, ratio of property, plant, and equipment to assets, and net income.

Leases

Critical Thinking

12-35 The following note was provided by Adolph Coors Company in its 1997 annual report:

NOTE 3:
Leases

The Company leases certain office facilities and operating equipment under cancelable and non-cancelable agreements accounted for as operating leases. On December 28, 1997, the minimum aggregate rental commitment under all non-cancelable leases was (in thousands): 1998, $5,403; 1999, $4,578; 2000, $3,124; 2001, $2,353; and $15,021 for years thereafter. Total rent expense was (in thousands) $13,870, $11,680, and $10,376 for years 1997, 1996, and 1995, respectively.

Required

a. Coors' total liabilities in 1997 and 1996, respectively, were $675,515,000 and $647,049,000. Based on the information in Note 3, does it seem that the leases were a material component of these liabilities? If not, did the choice to capitalize or expense the lease payments have any material effect on Coors' debt/asset ratios? Liquidity ratios? Asset turnover ratios?

b. Coors' net income in 1997 and 1996, respectively, was $82,260,000 and $43,425,000. Again, based on the information in Note 3, was the rent expense a material component of net income? If so, did the choice of capitalizing or expensing the leases have a significant effect on Coors' EPS? Return on Sales? ROE?

c. Discuss the differing effects of capitalized leases on balance sheet ratios, as compared to profitability ratios.

Leases

Critical Thinking

12-36 Whole Foods Market, Inc. reported the following information about leases in its 1997 annual report:

Whole Foods Market, Inc. and Subsidiaries
Notes to Consolidated Financial Statements

(8) Leases
The Company and its subsidiaries are committed under certain capital leases for rental of equipment and certain operating leases for rental of facilities and equipment. These leases expire or become subject to renewal at various dates from 1998 to 2028. The rental expense charged to operations under operating leases for fiscal years 1997, 1996, and 1995 totaled approximately $29,153,000, $24,683,000, and $19,303,000, respectively. Minimum rental commitments required by all noncancelable leases are approximately as follows (in thousands):

	Capital	Operating
1998	$ 788	$ 30,817
1999	275	35,252
2000	302	35,473
2001	10	35,512
2002	0	35,205
Future years	0	$335,356
	1,375	
Less amounts representing interest	179	
	1,196	
Less current installments	695	
	$ 501	

Minimum rentals for operating leases do not include certain amounts of contingent rentals that may become due under the provisions of leases for retail space. These agreements provide that minimum rentals can be increased based on a percent of annual sales from the retail space. During fiscal 1997, 1996, and 1995, the Company paid contingent rentals of approximately $1,200,000, $981,000, and $587,000, respectively. Certain officers of the Company own approximately 13.4 percent of a business that leases facilities from the Company under a 20-year lease that commenced in fiscal 1995. The Company's rental income from this lease totaled approximately $582,000 in fiscal years 1997 and 1996 and $96,000 in fiscal year 1995.

Required

a. For the purposes of financial analysis, it may be necessary to treat Whole Food's operating leases as if they were capital leases. Develop an approximate capitalized value of Whole Food's lease based on the information provided in Note 8.
b. Show how this amount will affect the results of various ratio calculations, including the debt to assets ratio, the net income ratio, ROA, and ROE.
c. Compare and contrast Whole Foods' disclosure of its leases with the disclosures provided by Coors' (see Problem 12-35). Which company provides more information? More useful information? What factors might have resulted in these differences in lease disclosures?

Writing

Capital Versus Operating Lease

12-37 Movie Madness, Inc., sells and rents movies, video games, and VCRs. The company wanted to lease some video editing equipment in order to expand its market. They are also considering signing either an operating lease for the video editing equipment or a lease that meets one of the four criteria of a capital lease. What advice would you give the company? Write a short memo to the company's president.

Internet

Leases

12-38 Access the EDGAR archives **(www.sec.gov/edaux/searches.htm)** and locate the most recent 10-K filings for US Air Group and Southwest Airlines. Both these companies rely extensively on the use of leased assets.

Required

a. For each company, determine the total minimum lease payments for operating leases and capital leases, and the present value of the future minimum capital lease payments.
b. Calculate the percentage of the minimum lease payments' present values for capital leases to the total minimum lease payments.
c. Estimate the present value of the operating lease payments for each company.
d. For each company, calculate the debt-to-assets ratios before including operating leases and the debt-to-assets ratios after including operating leases. Note your observations. Which company shows the most significant shift in the debt-to-assets ratio?

Critical Thinking

Pension Plan Disclosures

12-39 Spelling Entertainment Group (SEI), specializing in film and video entertainment, reported the following liabilities on its 1993 balance sheet:

- Accounts payable, accrued expenses, and other liabilities
- Accrued participation expense
- Deferred revenue
- Bank and other debts
- Income taxes
- Net liabilities related to discontinued operations

Required

a. Describe each of these liabilities and the economic events from which they were derived.
b. Identify whether any of these liabilities pertain to pension and/or postretirement expenses. Why might a company not have such liabilities?

SEI also reported the following:

Benefit Plans: The Company maintained two defined contribution employee retirement plans that covered substantially all nonunion employees of SEI. Contributions by SEI were discretionary or set by formula . . . Expenses under the various employee retirement plans were $463,000, $586,000, and $355,000 for the years ended . . . A significant number of the Company's production employees are covered by union-sponsored, collectively bargained, multi-employer pension plans. The Company contributed approximately $4,259,000, $3,714,000, and $1,383,000 for the years ended . . . The Company does not have any postretirement or postemployment benefits.

Required

c. Explain Spelling's various pension plans.
d. Why doesn't Spelling report any pension or postretirement liabilities on its balance sheet? Explain why this might or might not be justified.

Pension Plan Disclosures

Critical Thinking

12-40 Public Service Company of Colorado, a major supplier of natural gas and electricity in Colorado, included the following amounts in its 1993 balance sheet (dollars in thousands):

	1993	1992
Deferred Charges		
Employees' postretirement benefits, other than pensions (Note 10)	$ 25,855	—
Pension benefits (Note 10)	23,149	$ 15,629
Noncurrent Liabilities		
Defueling and decommissioning liability (Note 2)	140,008	140,008
Employees' postretirement benefits, other than pensions (Note 10)	42,878	43,078

Part I

Required

a. Describe each of the items excerpted from Public Service's balance sheet.
b. Why did Public Service show $25,855,000 of deferred charges for employees' postretirement benefits in 1993, but none in 1992?
c. Why do you suppose that Public Service's liability for defueling and decommissioning did not change during 1993?
d. Why did Public Service's deferred charges for pension benefits increase significantly in 1993?

Part II

Public Service Company of Colorado also included Note 10 in its annual report, as shown in the following excerpt:

Notes To Consolidated Financial Statements

Public Service Company of Colorado and Subsidiaries

10. Employee Benefits

Pensions

The company and its subsidiaries (excluding Natural Fuels) maintain a non-contributory defined benefit pension plan covering substantially all employees. During 1993, the Board of Directors of the Company approved amendments that: 1) eliminated the minimum age of 21 for receiving credited service, 2) provided for an automatic increase in monthly payments to a retired plan member in the event the member's spouse or other contingent annuitant dies prior to the member, and 3) provided for Average Final Compensation to be based on the highest average of three consecutive year's compensation. These plan changes increased the projected benefit obligation by $24.6 million.

The company and its subsidiaries' funding policy is to contribute annually, at a minimum, the amount necessary to satisfy the Internal Revenue Service (IRS) funding standards.

The net pension expense in 1993, 1992 and 1991 was comprised of:

	(Thousands of Dollars)		
	1993	1992	1991
Service cost	**$15,868**	$14,788	$12,196
Interest cost on projected benefit obligation	**38,106**	35,695	33,322
Return on plan assets	**(52,369)**	(34,317)	(79,467)
Amortization of net transition asset at adoption of Statement of Financial Accounting Standards No. 87	**(3,674)**	(3,674)	(3,673)
Other items	**8,219**	(6,317)	39,807
Net pension expense	**$ 6,150**	$ 6,175	$ 2,185

Significant assumptions used in determining net periodic pension cost were:

	1993	**1992**	**1991**
Discount rate	**8.2%**	8.2%	8.9%
Expected long-term increase in compensation level	**5.5%**	5.5%	5.5%
Expected weighted average long-term rate of return on assets	**11%**	11%	11%

Variances between actual experience and assumptions for costs and returns on assets are amortized over the average remaining service lives of employees in the plan.

A comparison of the actuarially computed benefit obligations and plan assets on December 1, 1993 and 1992, is presented in the following table. Plan assets are stated at fair value and are comprised primarily of corporate debt and equity securities, a real estate fund and government securities held either directly or in commingled funds.

	(Thousands of Dollars) 1993	1992
Actuarial present value of benefit obligations:		
Vested	**$392,623**	$336,632
Nonvested	**39,343**	29,800
	431,966	366,432
Effect of projected future salary increases	**128,294**	110,776
Projected benefit obligation for service rendered to date	**560,260**	477,208
Plan assets at fair value	**(523,548)**	(483,941)
Projected benefit obligation (in excess of) less than plan assets	**(36,712)**	6,733
Unrecognized net less	**58,252**	34,763
Prior service cost not yet recognized in net periodic pension cost	**34,673**	10,870
Unrecognized net transition asset at January 1, 1986, being recognized over 17 years	**(33,064)**	(36,737)
Prepaid pension asset	**$ 23,149**	$ 15,629

Significant assumptions used in determining the benefit obligations were

	1993	1992
Discount rate	**7.5%**	8.2%
Expected long-term increase in compensation level	**5.0%**	5.5%

On January 25, 1994, the Board of Directors approved an amendment to the Plan that offers an incentive for early retirement for employees age 55 with 20 years of service as well as a Severance Enhancement Program (SEP) option for these same eligible employees. The Plan amendment and the SEP are effective for the period February 4, 1994 to April 1, 1994. The Plan amendment generally provides for the following retirement enhancements: a) unreduced early retirement benefits, b) three years of additional credited service, and c) a supplement of either a one-time payment equal to $400 for each full year of service to be paid from general corporate funds or a $250 social security supplement each month up to age 62 to be paid by the Plan.

The SEP provides for: a) a one-time severance ranging from $20,000 to $90,000, depending on an employee's organization level, b) a continuous years of service bonus (up to 30 years), and c) a cash benefit of $10,000.

Eligible employees can elect to participate in either program. The total cost of the programs is estimated to range between $25 to $32 million. The Company intends to amortize such cost to expense over a period not to exceed approximately five years in accordance with anticipated regulatory treatment of such costs.

Postretirement benefits other than pensions

The Company and its subsidiaries provide certain health care and life insurance benefits for retired employees. A significant portion of the employees become eligible for these benefits if they reach either early or normal retirement age while working for the Company or its subsidiaries. Historically, the Company has recorded the cost of these benefits on a pay-as-you-go basis, consistent with the regulatory treatment. Effective January 1, 1993, the Company and its subsidiaries adopted Statement of Financial Accounting Standards No. 106, "Employers' Accouting for Postretirement Benefits Other Than Pensions" (SFAS 106), which requires the accrual, during the years that an employee renders the service to the Company, of the expected cost of providing postretirement benefits other than pensions to the employee and the employee's beneficiaries and covered dependents. The additional other postretirement employee benefits (OPEB) costs of 1993 resulting from this new accounting standard, which exceed amounts being recovered through rates, have been deferred for future recovery.

During 1991, the CPUC approved a rate Settlement Agreement (see Note 8) and the Fort St. Vrain Supplmental Settlement Agreement (see Note 2), both of which addressed the accounting and regulatory treatment of the costs of postretirement benefits other than pensions. The rate Settlement Agreement stipulated that the Company would continue to recover such costs as paid until the date new rates are effective. The Fort St. Vrain Supplemental Settlement Agreement stipulated that on the effective date of new rates (December 1, 1993) the Company would be allowed to recover the costs of postretirement benefits other than pensions as accrued in accordance with the provisions of SFAS 106, modified as follows:

- The actuarial calculation of such liabilities would include a return on assets that reflects monthly contributions net of benefit payments throughout the year;
- the attribution period would reflect each employee's expected retirement date rather than the full eligibility date;
- a 40-year levelized principal and interest amortization will be used for the transition obligation; and
- the accounting and regulatory treatment for life insurance benefits would remain on an as-paid basis.

Pursuant to the Fort St. Vrain Supplemental Settlement Agreement, the Company anticipated that any difference in expense resulting from the CPUC prescribed approach and the expense required by SFAS 106 would be reflected as a regulatory asset in the consolidated balance sheet and would be recovered from customers over future periods.

In January 1993, however, the Emerging Issues Task Force (EITF) provided guidance as to what additional criteria or evidence is needed for a rate-regulated enterprise to recognize a regulatory asset equal to the amount of OPEB costs for which rate recovery has been deferred. Generally, a utility must determine if it is probable that future rates will allow for the recovery of this OPEB regulatory asset. In addition, no later than approximately five years from the date of adoption, rates must include full SFAS 106 costs and the recovery of the regulatory asset established during the deferral period must be accomplished within approximately 20 years. The EITF's conclusions do not include the CPUC approach prescribed in the Fort St. Vrain Supplemental Settlement Agreement.

As a result, and under the provisions of the Fort St. Vrain Supplemental Settlement Agreement, the parties to this agreement have initiated discussions and negotiations focused on resolving this issue to the mutual acceptance of all parties without disrupting the overall agreement. These discussions are continuing, and the Company believes it is probable that the matter will ultimately be resolved in a manner that will comply with the conclusions reached by the EITF relative to the recognition of OPEB regulatory assets for which rate recovery has been deferred. Should the currently approved methodology not be modified to conform with the EITF consensus, the Company would be required to record as an expense the difference between the amounts allowed in rates and that required by SFAS 106.

Effective December 1, 1993, the Company began recovering such costs based on the level of expense determined in accordance with the CPUC approach in the Fort St. Vrain Supplemental Settlement Agreement (approximately $18 million on an annual basis for retail jurisdiction). During 1993, the Company deferred $25.9 million of SFAS 106 costs for future recovery. The Company plans to file a FERC rate case in 1994 that will include a request for approval to recover all wholesale jurisdiction SFAS 106 costs. Effective January 1, 1993, Cheyenne began recovering SFAS 106 costs as approved by the WPSC. The Company and Cheyenne intend to fund this plan based on the amounts reflected in cost-of-service, consistent with the rate orders.

The OPEB expense on a pay-as-you-go basis was $9.1 million and $8 million for 1992 and 1991, respectively.

The net periodic postretirement benefit costs in 1993 under SFAS 106 was comprised of

	(Thousands of Dollars) 1993
Service cost	$ 4,943
Interest cost on projected benefit obligation	20,828
Return on plan assets	(164)
Amortization of net transition obligation on January 1, 1993, assuming a 20-year amortization period	12,710
Net postretirement benefit cost required by SFAS 106	38,317
1993 OPEB expense recognized in accordance with current regulations	(12,462)
Regulatory asset on December 1, 1993	$25,855

The funded status of the plan on December 1, 1993 and January 1, 1993 is as follows:

	(Thousands of Dollars) December 31, 1993	January 1, 1993
Accumulated postretirement benefit obligation:		
Retirees and eligible beneficiaries	$ 86,718	$ 79,692
Other fully eligible plan participants	95,103	95,262
Other active plan participants	98,342	79,238
Total	280,163	254,192
Plan assets at fair value	(476)	—
Accumulated benefit obligation in excess of plan assets	279,687	254,192
Unrecognized net loss	(10,059)	—
Unrecognized transition obligation	(241,483)	(254,192)
Accrued postretirement benefit obligation	$ 28,145	$ —

Significant assumptions used in determining the accumulated postretirement benefit obligation were

	December 31, 1993	January 1, 1993
Discount rate	7.5%	8.2%
Ultimate health care cost trend rate	5.3%	6.0%
Expected long-term increase in compensation level	5.0%	5.5%

The assumed healthcare cost trend rate for 1993 is 12 percent, decreasing to 5.3 percent in 0.5 percent annual increments. A one percent increase in the assumed health care cost trend will increase the estimated total accumulated benefit obligation by $37.7 million and will also increase the service and interest cost components of net periodic postretirement benefit costs by $5.2 million.

Postemployment benefits

In November 1992, the Financial Accounting Standards Board issued Statement of Financial Accounting Standards No. 112 "Employers' Accounting for Postemployment Benefits" (SFAS 112), which establishes the accounting standards for employers who provide benefits to former or inactive employees after employment but before retirement (postemployment benefits). This statement became effective January 1, 1994 and the Company has estimated its benefit obligation to be approximately $32 million, assuming a 7.5 percent discount rate. The Company believes it is probable that it will receive CPUC approval to recover these costs in future rates; therefore, the application of the new standard will not have a material impact on the Company's financial position or results of operations as a regulatory asset, and a corresponding liability will be established on the consolidated balance sheet.

Required

e. Read Note 10 and identify any questions you may have regarding the interpretation or clarification of unusual terms in this note. See your instructor or an accounting dictionary regarding such terms.
f. With reference to Part I, trace each item from Public Service's balance sheet to Note 10 (ignore the defueling and decommissioning liability, Note 2).
g. After studying Note 10, reconsider your answer to part b regarding why Public Service reported more than $25 million of deferred postretirement benefits in 1993 and none in 1992.
h. After studying Note 10, describe why Public Service's deferred pension benefits increased significantly in 1993.
i. With reference to the first paragraph in Note 10, describe why Public Service's balance sheet does not show any "projected benefit obligation," and why it does not show the increase of $24.6 million in its projected benefit obligation.
j. Describe in your own words the implications of the very last paragraph in Note 10.
k. In Note 10, what does OPEB mean? What is its significance?

(Continued)

l. A short paragraph toward the end of Note 10 discusses the OPEB expense on a pay-as-you-go basis. Discuss the implication of this paragraph, and why this information might be relevant to analysts and employees.

m. Public Service Company's total assets at the end of 1993 and 1992, respectively, were \$4,057,600,000 and \$3,759,583,000. Furthermore, Public Service Company's net income in each year, respectively, was \$157,360,000 and \$136,623,000. Given the variety and multitude of information about Public Service Company's employee benefit costs in Note 10 and in the balance sheet excerpts (see Part I), how important are the related assets and liabilities? How much impact do they have on the overall evaluation of the company? In other words, how significant, or material, are these items? Does their significance justify the more than three pages of detailed information in Note 10? Why?

Interpreting Financial Statements: Retirement Benefits

12-41 Review Wendy's financial statements in Appendix D.

Required

a. Read Note 11. Identify any unfamiliar or unusual terms. Match the terms presented in this chapter to the terms used by Wendy's.

b. Determine the firm's total obligations for pension benefits.

c. Determine the amount of the firm's unfunded obligations for pension benefits.

d. Determine the firm's expense for pension benefits and nonpension benefits.

e. Does the firm disclose any types of obligations that are not included in the financial statements? If so, evaluate the significance of these potential obligations to the extent possible using the information in the financial statements. Why were these potential obligations not included as liabilities?

Critical Thinking

Interpreting Financial Statements: Retirement Benefits

12-42 Review Reebok's financial statements in Appendix E.

Required

a. Scan the notes and the rest of the financial statement for information pertaining to Reebok's retirement benefits. Identify any unfamiliar or unusual terms. Match the terms presented in this chapter to the terms used by Reebok.

b. Why does Reebok have no pension liability?

c. What was the expense recorded for retirement plans?

d. What reasons would support Reebok's failure to have a defined benefit plan?

Critical Thinking

Postretirement Benefits

12-43 Adolph Coors Company included the following two notes in its 1997 annual report as follows on the next page.

NOTE 7:
Employee Retirement Plans

The Company maintains several defined benefit pension plans for the majority of its employees. Benefits are based on years of service and average base compensation levels over a period of years. Plan assets consist primarily of equity, interest-bearing investments, and real estate. The Company's funding policy is to contribute annually not less than the ERISA minimum funding standards, nor more than the maximum amount that can be deducted for federal income tax purposes. The total expense of all these plans was $14.1 million in 1997, $24.8 million in 1996, and $22.7 million in 1995. These amounts include the Company's matching for the savings and investment (thrift) plan of $5.8 million in 1997 and $5.7 million each for 1996 and 1995. The decrease in 1997 pension expense versus 1996 was caused primarily by an improvement in the funded position of the Coors Retirement Plan and an increase in the discount rate (settlement rate) used to compute the 1997 pension cost of 7.75 percent from the rate used for 1996 pension cost of 7.25 percent. The increase in 1996 pension expense versus 1995 was caused primarily by a decrease in the 1996 discount rate (settlement rate) to 7.25 percent from the 1995 rate of 8.5 percent.

Note that the settlement rates shown in the table on the following page were selected for use at the end of each of the years shown. Actuaries calculate pension expense annually based on data available at the beginning of each year that include the settlement rate selected and disclosed at the end of the previous year.

	For the years ended		
	December 28, 1997	December 29, 1996 (In thousands)	December 31, 1995
Service cost-benefits earned during the year	$11,234	$12,729	$ 9,858
Interest cost on projected benefit obligations	32,730	31,162	29,285
Actual gain on plan assets	(75,242)	(65,504)	(69,346)
Net amortization and deferral	39,539	40,691	47,005
Net pension cost	$ 8,261	$19,078	$16,802

The funded status of the pension plans and amounts recognized in the accompanying balance sheets are as follows:

	As of	
	December 28, 1997 (In thousands)	December 29, 1996
Actuarial present value of accumulated plan benefits, including vested benefits of $368,288 in 1997 and $332,444 in 1996	$385,989	$350,506

Projected benefit obligations for services rendered to date	$465,229	$422,516
Plan assets available for benefits	465,494	394,206
Plan assets (more than) less than projected benefit obligations	(265)	28,310
Unrecognized net gain	21,560	2,359
Prior service cost not yet recognized	(16,577)	(18,851)
Unrecognized net assets being recognized over 15 years	4,110	5,800
Net accrued pension liability	$ 8,828	$ 17,618

(Note: These accrued pension liabilities were not separately shown on Coors' balance sheet. Based on the following note, we presume that they were included as part of "Long-term postretirement benefits.")

Significant assumptions used in determining the valuation of the projected benefit obligations as of the end of 1997, 1996 and 1995 were:

	1997	1996	1995
Settlement rate	7.75%	7.25%	7.25%
Increase in compensation levels	4.50%	5.00%	5.00%
Rate of return on plan assets	10.25%	10.25%	9.75%

NOTE 8:
Non-Pension Postretirement Benefits

The Company has postretirement plans that provide medical benefits and life insurance for retirees and eligible dependents. The plans are not funded.

The obligation under these plans was determined by the application of the medical and life insurance plans' terms together with relevant actuarial assumptions and healthcare cost trend rates ranging ratably from 9.0 percent in 1997 to 4.5 percent in the year 2007. The effect of an annual one percent increase in trend rates would increase the accumulated postretirement benefit obligation by approximately $3.5 million and $3.2 million in 1997 and 1996, respectively. The effect of a one percent increase in trend rates also would have increased the ongoing annual cost by $0.5 million and $0.6 million in 1997 and 1996, respectively. The discount rate used in determining the accumulated postretirement benefit obligation was 7.75 percent and 7.25 percent on December 28, 1997, and December 29, 1996, respectively.

Net periodic postretirement benefit cost included the following:

	For the years ended December 28, 1997	December 29, 1996	December 31, 1995
		(In thousands)	
Service cost-benefits attributed to service during the period	$1,408	$2,065	$2,281
Interest cost on accumulated postretirement benefit obligation	4,775	5,082	6,426
Amortization of net (gain)	(353)	(310)	(560)
Net periodic postretirement benefit cost	$5,830	$6,837	$8,147

Effective November 29, 1995, changes were made to postretirement life insurance and medical benefits that resulted in a curtailment gain of $3.3 million and $18.6 million in 1996 and 1995, respectively. The 1996 decrease in plan expense resulted principally from the curtailment of these benefits. The 1997 decrease in expense was a result of an increase in the discount rate used to 7.75 percent in 1997 from 7.25 percent in 1996.

The status of the postretirement benefit plan was as follows:

	As of December 28, 1997	December 29, 1996
	(In thousands)	
Retirees	$43,087	$39,780
Fully eligible active plan participants	5,411	5,014
Other active plan participants	19,418	17,883
Accumulated postretirement obligation	67,916	62,677
Unrecognized net gain	7,188	8,452
Unrecognized prior service cost	434	2,209
Accrued postretirement benefit obligation	75,538	73,338
Less current portion	(3,630)	(3,565)
Long-term postretirement benefit	$71,908	$69,773

(Note: These amounts were shown as part of Coors' long-term liabilities.)

Required

a. Are Coors' retirement plans, as shown in Note 7, over- or underfunded at the end of 1997? Explain.

b. Are Coors' non-pension postretirement benefits, as shown in Note 8, over- or underfunded at the end of 1997? Explain.

c. Distinguish between the "net accrued pension liability" and the "long-term postretirement benefit" amounts reported in each Note.

d. With respect to "service cost," why are interest costs included? Why is the "actual gain on plan assets" deducted from service costs?

e. Examine the assumptions disclosed at the end of Note 7. Why do some of these assumptions change in 1996 and 1997? Do these changes seem material? What impact will each change have on the reported liabilities? Explain.

Postretirement Benefits

12-44 Mercury, Inc. designs, develops, and markets human and animal health products and specialty chemicals. The following information has been abstracted from the notes to Mercury's 2000 financial statements:

	Pension Benefits		Other Postretirement Benefits	
	2000	1999	2000	1999
	(Dollars in Millions)		(Dollars in Millions)	
Funded status of benefit plans:				
Plan assets at market value	$1,329.6	$1,411.8	$310.2	$ 30.4
Accumulated benefit obligation	1,364.3	1,193.9	979.6	758.4
Projected benefit obligation	1,834.2	1,573.2	—	—
Components of annual expense:				
Service cost	97.4	86.4	31.0	31.2
Interest cost	135.7	123.7	69.2	62.9
Actual return on assets	(61.5)	(94.1)	(22.4)	(1.8)
Other	(74.6)	(34.7)	2.1	(1.9)
Total cost	$ 97.0	$ 81.3	$ 79.9	$ 90.4
Underlying assumptions:				
Discount rate	7.5%	9.0%	7.5%	9.0%
Expected return on plan assets	10.0%	10.0%	10.0%	10.0%
Future compensation increases	5.0%	6.0%	—	—
Healthcare cost trend	—	—	12.0%	13.0%

Required

a. Do you consider Mercury's pension benefits and other postemployment benefits to be overfunded or underfunded at the end of 2000? Explain.

b. Distinguish between the "accumulated benefit obligation" amounts reported for each type of plan.

c. With respect to the components of the annual costs, why is interest expense included? Why does the return on plan assets appear as a negative component?

d. The disclosure of assumptions reveals three changes between 2000 and 1999: (1) the discount rate has been decreased from 9 percent to 7.5 percent, (2) the rate of future compensation increases has been revised from 6 percent to 5 percent, and (3) the health care cost trend rate has been changed from 13 percent to 12 percent. Explain how each of these changes would affect your comparisons of postemployment liabilities and costs between 2000 and 1999.

Postretirement Benefits

12-45 Bethany Iron, Inc.'s 2000 annual report provided the following information regarding postretirement benefits:

Bethany Iron, Inc.
Pension Liability Recognized in Consolidated Balance Sheet
(2000 Annual Report)

We have noncontributory defined benefit pension plans that provide benefits for substantially all employees. Defined benefits are based on years of service and the five highest consecutive years of pensionable earnings during the last 10 years prior to retirement or a minimum amount based on years of service. We fund annually the amount required under ERISA minimum funding standards plus additional amounts as appropriate.

The following table sets forth the plan's actuarial assumptions used and funded status at year-end together with amounts recognized in our consolidated balance sheets:

	December 31	
	2000	1999
	(Dollars in Millions)	
Assumptions:		
Discount rate	8.50%	8.50%
Average rate of compensation increase	4.4%	4.5%
Actuarial present value of benefit obligations:		
Vested benefit obligation	$4,357.9	$4,324.4
Accumulated benefit obligation	**4,490.1**	**4,457.2**
Projected benefit obligation	4,822.7	4,769.6
Plan assets at fair value:		
Fixed income securities	1,979.8	2,090.3
Equity securities	1,006.0	1,187.1
Cash and marketable securities	315.6	214.9
Total plan assets	3,301.4	3,492.3
Projected benefit obligation in excess of plan assets	1,521.3	1,277.3
Unrecognized net gain	(58.3)	87.8
Remaining unrecognized net obligation resulting from adoption of Statement No. 87	(339.0)	(378.0)
Unrecognized prior service cost from plan amendments	(174.9)	(194.2)
Adjustment required to recognize minimum liability, intangible asset	239.6	172.0
Balance sheet liability	$1,188.7	$964.9

Bethany Iron, Inc.
Pension Expense Recognized in Consolidated Income Statement
(2000 Annual Report)

The assumptions used in each year and the components of our annual pension cost are as follows:

	1999	2000
	(Dollars in Millions)	
Assumptions:		
Return on plan assets	9.50%	10.25%
Discount rate	8.50%	9.25%
Defined benefit plans:		
Service cost, benefits earned during the period	$ 45.0	$ 45.6
Interest on projected benefit obligation	394.2	386.6
Return on plan assets	(312.2)	(317.2)
Other items (net)	63.4	71.7
Total cost	$190.4	$186.7

Bethany Iron, Inc.
Postretirement Benefits Other Than Pension
Obligations and Expenses Recognized in Financial Statements
(2000 Annual Report)

1. Postretirement Benefits Other Than Pensions

In addition to providing pension benefits, we currently provide healthcare and life insurance benefits for most retirees and their dependents. We continue to fund healthcare benefits through various third-party administrators based on claims incurred. Therefore, the adoption of this statement has no effect on our cash flow. Life insurance benefits have been funded on an actuarial basis, which amounted to $7.9 million in 2000.

Information regarding our plan's actuarial assumptions, funded status, liability, and transition obligation follows:

	December 31, 2000 (Dollars in Millions)
Accumulated postretirement benefit obligation:	
Retirees	$1,413.7
Fully eligible active plan participants	105.1
Other active plan participants	176.2
Total	1,695.0
Plan assets at fair value:	
Fixed income securities	159.6
Accumulated postretirement benefit obligation in excess of plan assets	1,535.4
Unrecognized net gain	4.5
Balance sheet liability	$1,539.9

The components of our postretirement benefit cost follow:

	2000 (Dollars in Millions)
Service cost	$ 9.0
Interest on accumulated postretirement benefit obligation	139.0
Return on plan assets—actual	(18.4)
—deferred	4.5
Multi-employer plans	7.1
Total cost	$141.2

The assumed weighted average healthcare trend rate used to calculate the accumulated postretirement benefit obligation and 2000 expense was 6.5 percent, which will decline gradually until it reaches an ultimate average rate of 4.5 percent in the year 2004. A one percent increase in the assumed healthcare trend rate would increase the accumulated postretirement benefit obligation by $147 million and 2000 expense by $14 million. The discount rate used in calculating the obligation and 2000 expense was 6.5 percent, and the assumed earnings on plan assets was 7.5 percent.

Required

a. Do you consider Bethany's pension benefits and other postemployment benefits to be overfunded or underfunded at the end of 2000? Explain.
b. Distinguish between the "accumulated benefit obligation" amounts reported for each type of plan.
c. With respect to the components of the annual costs, why is interest expense included? Why does the return on plan assets-actual appear as a negative component?
d. The disclosure of assumptions reveals some changes including (1) changes in healthcare trend ratios, (2) changes in the discount rate, and (3) changes in the postretirement benefit obligation and expense. Explain how each of these changes would affect your evaluation of postemployment liabilities and costs for 2000.

Internet

Postretirement Benefits

12-46 Access the EDGAR archives **(www.sec.gov/edaux/searches.htm)** and locate the most recent 10-K filing by Kmart. Information about Kmart's pension plan can be found in the Notes to the Financial Statements.

Required

a. What are the total pension assets and liabilities?
b. What is the funding status of the pension plan?
c. What discount rate and average rate of return have been adopted by the company?
d. Identify total assets and total debt as reported on the balance sheet and calculate the debt-to-assets ratio. Then, including all retirement plan-related assets and liabilities, recalculate the values of total assets, total liabilities, and the debt-to-assets ratio. What do you observe?
e. Now examine the latest 10-K for Wal-Mart (available at EDGAR). Should you make the same adjustments for Wal-Mart that you made for Kmart? State your reasons.

chapter 13

Reporting Issues for Affiliated and International Companies

This chapter consists of two parts, each of which can be read independently.

PART I LEARNING OBJECTIVES

1. Understand the reasons for reporting consolidated financial statements.
2. Appreciate how affiliated firms construct and report their consolidated financial statements.

PART II LEARNING OBJECTIVES

3. Understand how foreign exchange rate fluctuations affect the financial reporting of transactions conducted in foreign currencies.
4. Determine how financial statements prepared initially in foreign currencies are translated to U.S. dollars.
5. Appreciate the wide diversity of international accounting practices.

INTRODUCTION TO PART I: FINANCIAL REPORTING FOR AFFILIATED FIRMS

Most large firms grow by a combination of internal and external expansion. **Internal expansion** occurs as firms invest in new plant and equipment, research, and other productive assets in order to serve growing markets or to extend the scope of their operations into new products and markets. **External expansion** occurs as firms take over, or merge with, other existing firms. The first part of this chapter discusses the reasons why corporate takeovers may be preferable to internal expansion. Financial reporting for affiliated firms is also explained as of the date of acquisition and for subsequent periods.

MOTIVATIONS FOR BUSINESS COMBINATIONS

Business firms often expand by taking over existing corporations. Such actions, known as **business combinations** can be more attractive than direct investments in new plant and equipment for several reasons. The buyer firm, for example, may believe that external expansion is less costly than purchasing new assets and competing for customers in new markets. Also, the acquired firm may offer other advantages, such as a stable and reliable network of suppliers, a seasoned workforce, and proven methods of production and distribution. As a consequence, expansion by combination may avoid many of the uncertainties and start-up costs encountered under internal expansion.

When existing firms are combined, it can enable them to eliminate duplicate facilities or yield economies of scale in production, distribution, marketing, finance, and/or general corporate administration. A buyer company may believe that the acquired firm's assets are poorly managed and that more profits could be earned by improving its asset management. A purchaser may also feel that new management may introduce operating efficiencies that yield higher profits.

Business combinations also can permit a firm to diversify quickly. A buyer firm in a declining industry may attempt to redeploy its resources into other products and markets. As cigarette smoking has declined among informed adults, for example, many larger tobacco firms have diversified by acquiring firms in other industries. Many firms may attempt, through business combinations, to diversify their risks related to cyclical or seasonal demands.

A major factor in recent business combinations is the rapid pace of technological change in communications, which has created links between industries that were previously considered to be unrelated. The "information superhighway" has inspired combinations of firms in areas as disparate as cable television, telecommunications, banking, cinema, and catalog retail sales. The ongoing information revolution promises to redefine the boundaries among industries and provide impetus to many additional unconventional business combinations.

FORMS OF BUSINESS COMBINATIONS

Business combinations occur in a variety of different ways. In a **merger,** a buyer firm acquires either the stock or the assets and liabilities of an investee firm. The investee is then dissolved and no longer exists as a separate corporation. Alternatively, firms can combine by **consolidation.** In a consolidation, a new corporation is created to acquire the stock or the net assets of two or more existing companies. The original companies then cease to exist as separate corporations. Finally, a business combination can occur as an **acquisition.** In an acquisition, a buyer firm acquires more than 50 percent of an investee firm's voting stock and thereby controls the investee. The buyer firm is referred to as the **parent company,** and the acquired firm continues to exist and operate as a **subsidiary** of the parent company.

Acquisitions comprise a major portion of the business combinations that occur among larger corporations. This type of business combination offers several advantages over mergers and consolidations. Because the parent may obtain effective control of a subsidiary without the need to acquire 100 percent of the seller's shares, the required investment by the parent may be reduced substantially. Also, because the subsidiary continues to exist as a legally separate entity, the parent has only limited liability for the debts of the subsidiary. In addition, it is relatively easy for the parent to increase or decrease its investment at future dates by purchasing or selling the subsidiary's shares.

A parent company and the other firms that it influences or controls are referred to as **affiliated companies**. The remainder of the discussion in this part of the chapter will explain financial reporting for affiliated companies.

FINANCIAL REPORTING FOR CONTROLLING INTERESTS IN AFFILIATED FIRMS

When one firm acquires the stock of another firm, the value of the resources (cash, shares of stock, or debt) paid by the parent is used to measure the historical cost of the parent's investment. Because the parent's investment exceeds 50 percent of the affiliate's voting shares, the parent is assumed to control the affiliate. Subsequent accounting and reporting for the affiliated firm are based on the historical cost concepts that were explained in earlier chapters

In some circumstances, firms combine by an exchange of voting stock. These combinations are interpreted as a "uniting of ownership interests," rather than a purchase of one firm by another. The accounting treatment for such exchanges is termed a **pooling of interests.** Illustrating pooling is beyond the scope of this text.

Accounting for the Acquisition of a Subsidiary Firm

To illustrate a typical acquisition, refer to Exhibit 13-1, which shows the preacquisition balance sheets and other pertinent information for Pepper Company and Shaker Inc., on January 1, 2001. On that date, Pepper Company paid a total of $400 million ($100 million in cash and $300 million in common stock) to acquire all of Shaker's outstanding shares from the existing shareholders.

Note that Shaker's balance sheet at the date of combination shows net assets (and therefore shareholders' equity) of $310 million. Pepper's willingness to pay $400 mil-

Exhibit 13-1 Preacquisition Balance Sheets

Pepper Company and Shaker Inc.
Preacquisition Balance Sheets and Other Information, on January 1, 2001
(Dollars in Millions)

Pepper Company
Balance Sheet at January 1, 2001

Current assets:		Current liabilities	$ 420
Cash	$ 150		
Other current assets	520	Long-term debt	540
Total	670	Total liabilities	960
Noncurrent assets			
Property, plant, and equipment, (net)	1,230	Shareholders' equity:	
		Invested capital	280
Other	450	Retained earnings	1,110
Total	1,680	Total equity	1,390
Total assets	$2,350	Total liabilities and equity	$2,350

Shaker, Inc.
Balance Sheet at January 1, 2001

Current assets:		Current liabilities	$ 50
Cash	$ 20		
Other current assets	1,260	Long-term debt	1,280
Total	1,280	Total liabilities	1,330
Noncurrent assets			
Property, plant, and equipment,		Shareholders' equity	
(net)	320	Invested capital	150
Other	40	Retained earnings	160
Total	360	Total equity	310
Total assets	$1,640	Total liabilities and equity	$1,640

NOTE: An independent appraisal of Shaker Inc.'s assets and liabilities on January 1, 2001, indicates that book values and fair market values are equal, except that Shaker has $90 million of internally generated goodwill that does not appear on the balance sheet.

lion indicates that the carrying value of Shaker's net assets at the combination date is less than the economic value of those net assets by at least $90 million ($400 million – $310 million). Indeed, the note to Exhibit 13-1 reveals that the firm has $90 million of internally generated goodwill that does not appear on the balance sheet.

The acquisition of Shaker's stock increases Pepper's investment in affiliated companies by $400 million; cash decreases by $100 million, and invested capital increases by $300 million. Pepper's net assets increase by $300 million.

ASSETS		=	LIABILITIES	+	SHAREHOLDERS' EQUITY
Cash	Investments in affiliates				Invested capital
–100 million	+400 million				+300 million

Shaker's balance sheet is unaffected by the acquisition. Because Pepper Company bought Shaker's shares directly from existing shareholders, Shaker was not a party to the transaction. Shaker Company has neither received any resources nor issued any additional shares of stock.

Reality Check 13-1 illustrates the effect of acquiring a subsidiary company at a cost in excess of the acquired net assets' fair value.

Financial Reporting Subsequent to the Acquisition

Because Pepper Company has effective control of Shaker through ownership of all their voting shares, generally accepted accounting practices require that Pepper Company's financial statements be prepared on a consolidated basis. **Consolidated financial statements** report the combined financial position, cash flows, and operating results for all firms that are under the parent company's control. Consolidation looks beyond the fact that affiliated firms are distinct legal entities and focuses on the fact that they constitute a single economic entity. Consolidation is mainly a process of adding together the financial statement elements of the parent and its controlled subsidiaries with certain necessary adjustments that will be described later.

A consolidation of Pepper Company and Shaker Inc. at the acquisition date would entail only the preparation of a consolidated balance sheet because no combined operations or cash flows have yet occurred at that date. Exhibit 13-2 shows the consolidation process. Note the following:

1. The balance sheet of each firm is listed side by side in a vertical format to facilitate adding the elements across each row.
2. A firm does not report an investment in its own shares as an asset on the balance sheet. Therefore, the balance of the investment account that appears on the separate (unconsolidated) balance sheet of the parent company must be eliminated because the investee firm is included in the consolidated entity.
3. Shaker's shareholders' equity must be eliminated because, from a consolidated point of view, its stock is not outstanding. All of Shaker's stock is held by Pepper, and none is held by outside investors.
4. Shaker's net assets are revalued in the process of consolidation in order to reflect their appraised values at the acquisition date. Recall that Pepper Company paid $400 million to acquire Shaker's shareholders' equity, which has a carrying value

REALITY CHECK 13-1

The Du Pont Company, one of the world's largest chemical companies, provides the following information about a business combination that occurred during 1997 (edited; dollars in millions):

Protein Technologies International was purchased on December 1, 1997. PTI is a global supplier of soy proteins and applied technology to the food and paper processing industries. Du Pont common stock shares totaling 22,500,000, with a fair value of $1,297, were issued in this transaction. In addition, related costs of $4 were incurred. For accounting purposes, the acquisition has been treated as a purchase. Based on preliminary estimates that are subject to revision, the purchase price has been allocated as follows: cash, $47; other current assets, $158; noncurrent assets, $897; and liabilities assumed, $301, including $188 of debt.

Required

a. Based on the above information, show how Du Pont's balance sheet was affected by the acquisition of Protein Technologies. (Assume that Protein Technologies continues in existence as a legally distinct company.)
b. Determine the excess of Du Pont's purchase price over the fair value of Protein Technologies' net assets (in other words, the goodwill) implicit in the Protein Technologies acquisition.
c. Why do you suppose that Du pont was willing to pay a substantial premium over the net assets' fair value in order to acquire protein technologies?
d. Assume that Du Pont prepares a consolidated balance sheet immediately following the acquisition of protein technologies. Show how the balance sheet of Du Pont would differ before and after consolidation.

Solution

a. The total value of the consideration (cash plus common stock) paid by Du Pont is $1,301 million, which would affect Du Pont's balance sheet as follows on the acquisition date:

ASSETS		=	LIABILITIES	+	SHAREHOLDERS' EQUITY
Cash – $4 million	Investment in PTI + $1,301 million				Common stock + $1,297 million

b. The goodwill implicit in the acquisition price is computed as follows (dollars in millions):

Cost of investment in PTI (see above)		$1,301
Fair value of net assets:		
Fair value of assets acquired	$1,102	
Less: Fair value of liabilities assumed	(301)	
Net		–801
Excess of cost over fair value of net assets (goodwill)		$ 500

c. Du Pont's managers believe that the value of the future cash flows to be earned from the PTI acquisition justify the substantial acquisition premium. The economic values of many firms exceed the fair values of their identifiable net assets. This is especially true for firms such as PTI that have substantial investments in research and development, highly skilled employees, and a well-developed customer base.
d. Du Pont's balance sheet would be adjusted in order to be consolidated with PTI at the acquisition date. The entire investment account would be eliminated and PTI 's assets and liabilities would be added to Du Pont's assets and liabilities, and the goodwill would be recognized on the consolidated balance sheet.

ASSETS		=	LIABILITIES	+	SHAREHOLDERS' EQUITY
Investment in PTI:	– $1,301 million		+ $301 million		
Other assets:	+ $1,102 million				
Goodwill:	+ $ 500 million				

of $310. The $90 million difference is attributed to goodwill. From a consolidated perspective, Shaker's net assets are $90 million higher than they are from the perspective of Shaker as a separate company. Pepper incurred this additional cost by buying Shaker's shares at an amount in excess of book value.

As a result of these consolidating adjustments, the consolidated balance sheet of Pepper Company, shown on the right side of Exhibit 13-2, shows consolidated assets of $3.98 billion and consolidated liabilities of $2.29 billion. Both of these amounts are greater than those shown on Pepper's separate balance sheet. The shareholders' equity of Pepper, $1.69 billion, is the same before and after consolidation, however, because the shareholders' equity of the subsidiary has been eliminated in the consolidation process.

A further complication can occur whenever the parent does not own 100 percent of the subsidiary's stock. Because Pepper Company owns 100 percent of Shaker Inc., the subsidiary's entire shareholders' equity is eliminated. In cases where a parent achieves control by acquiring less than 100 percent of a subsidiary's stock, the book value of the remaining outstanding shares of the subsidiary will appear on the consolidated financial statements with the label **minority interest in consolidated**

EXHIBIT 13-2 Consolidation Process

Pepper Company and Shaker Inc.
Consolidation at the Acquisition Date,
January 1, 2001
(Dollars in Millions)

	Pepper Company[a]	Shaker, Inc.	Adjustments	Consolidated
Current assets				
Cash	$ 50	$ 20		$ 70
Other current assets	520	1,260		1,780
Total current assets	570	1,280		1,850
Noncurrent assets				
Property, plant, and equipment (net)	1,230	320		1,550
Investment in Shaker Inc.	400	—	−400[b]	—
Goodwill	—	—	+90[b]	90
Other	450	40		490
Total noncurrent assets	2,080	360		2,130
Total assets	$2,650	$1,640		$3,980
Current liabilities	$ 420	$ 50		$470
Long-term debt	540	1,280		1,820
Total liabilities	960	1,330		2,290
Shareholders' equity				
Invested capital	580	150	−150[b]	580
Retained earnings	1,110	160	−160[b]	1,110
Total shareholder's equity	1,690	310		1,690
Total liabilities and equity	$2,650	$1,640		$3,980

[a]Pepper Company's balance sheet differs from Exhibit 13-1 because cash was reduced by $100 million and invested capital was increased by $300 million in order to acquire the investment in Shaker Inc. for $400 million.
[b]Pepper's investment in Shaker is eliminated, as well as Shaker's shareholders' equity. The difference of $90 million ($400 less $310 million) results in a revaluation of goodwill (+90 million).

subsidiaries. This term often appears either as another category of shareholders' equity or as a separate item between liabilities and shareholders' equity.

Equity Method of Accounting for Affiliate Subsequent to the Acquisition Date

After the acquisition date, a parent company will often account for its investment in affiliated firms, using the **equity method of accounting.** The equity method requires that Pepper recognize its share of Shaker's subsequent reported income (or loss). Moreover, any dividends paid by Shaker to Pepper will be considered as a reduction of Pepper's investment cost. Because Pepper recognizes Shaker's income as it is earned, Pepper cannot also count Shaker's dividend payments as additional income. To do so would be "double-counting."

To illustrate the equity method, assume that Shaker Inc. earned $12 million in 2001 and paid dividends of $6 million. All the dividends are paid to Pepper, which owns all of Shaker's stock. Pepper Company would recognize Shaker's income as an increase in the carrying value of the investment and as income of $12 million:

ASSETS	=	LIABILITIES	+	SHAREHOLDERS' EQUITY
Investment in subsidiary +$12 million				Retained earnings +$12 million (Income from investments)

Upon receipt of the dividend, Pepper Company would increase cash and reduce the investment balance by $6 million:

ASSETS		=	LIABILITIES	+	SHAREHOLDERS' EQUITY
Cash	Investment in Subsidiary				
+$6 million	−$6 million				

Recall that Pepper Company paid an amount that was $90 million in excess of the book value of Shaker's shareholders' equity at the acquisition date. This amount was attributed to goodwill. This asset is being used in Shaker's operations, and from Pepper Company's point of view, the additional asset cost must be recognized as an expense over the useful life of the asset. In other words, Pepper's income from its investment in Shaker is less than the $12 million recorded earlier. If we assume that goodwill has a useful life of 18 years, the annual amortization expense for goodwill is $5 million ($90 million cost ÷ 18 years of useful life). This additional annual expense of $5 million must be recognized by Pepper Company. Accordingly, each year the carrying value of the investment is reduced by $5 million, and income from the subsidiary is reduced by the same amount. The net result is that the investment carrying value increased by $1 million in the first year ($12 million income less $6 million dividends and $5 million goodwill amortization).

ASSETS	=	LIABILITIES	+	SHAREHOLDERS' EQUITY
Investment in subsidiary − $5 million				Retained earnings − $5 million (Income from investments)

Other Types of Consolidation Adjustments

The consolidation of Pepper Company and its subsidiary Shaker Inc. requires relatively few adjustments because we assume that the operations of both firms are completely independent. In many cases, however, numerous transactions take place between affiliated firms, and these transactions require further adjustments as part of the consolidation process. Consider, for example, a parent firm that has acquired controlling ownership of a major supplier. After the acquisition, the firms would certainly continue their existing business relationship and, as a result, the subsequent consolidated financial statements of the parent firm would require the following types of adjustments:

1. The accounts payable of the parent would include amounts owed to the subsidiary. Correspondingly, the accounts receivable of the subsidiary would include amounts due from the parent. These **intercompany receivables and payables** would be eliminated in consolidation. It makes no sense to report amounts owed to and from oneself on a consolidated balance sheet.
2. The sales among companies included in a consolidation do not constitute sales to outside entities. As a result, unless these **intercompany sales** are eliminated in preparing the consolidation, both consolidated sales and cost of goods sold would be overstated in the financial statements.
3. The inventories reported by the parent would very likely include items purchased from the subsidiary at a profit to the subsidiary. From a consolidated point of view, however, these inventories have not been sold to outside entities at the balance sheet date. As a result, these **unrealized inventory profits** would be removed from the carrying value of the inventory and from the subsidiary's income in the process of consolidation.

Various other transactions between affiliated firms occur frequently and must be adjusted appropriately in preparing a set of consolidated financial statements. Bear in mind that a set of legally distinct companies is consolidated as a single economic or reporting entity. As a result, financial statement elements, such as receivables, payables, revenues, and expenses, must involve transactions only with other, outside entities.

FINANCIAL RATIOS AND CONSOLIDATED FINANCIAL STATEMENTS

Consolidated financial statements are prepared primarily to serve investors and financial analysts. A useful starting point in the analysis of financial statements is the calculation of a set of key financial ratios. Note that many of these ratios were first introduced in earlier chapters and were summarized in Chapter 11, "A Framework for Financial Statement Analysis." This section illustrates how the consolidation of affiliated companies affects selected financial statement ratios.

As seen earlier, some financial statement elements change dramatically as a result of consolidating subsidiary firms, while other items are unaffected. To illustrate the effects of consolidation on selected financial ratios, Exhibit 13-3 repeats the financial statements of Pepper Company before and after consolidation, as developed earlier in the chapter. Exhibit 13-3 also shows the calculation of two widely used financial ratios.

EXHIBIT 13-3 Financial Ratios

Selected Financial Ratios Before and After Consolidation
Pepper Company and Shaker Inc.
on January 1, 2001
(Dollars in Millions)

	Pepper Company, Unconsolidated (from Exhibit 13-1)	Pepper Company, Consolidated (from Exhibit 13-1)
Current assets	$ 570	$1,850
Noncurrent assets	2,080	2,130
Total assets	$2,650	$3,980
Current liabilities	$420	$470
Long-term debt	540	1,820
Total liabilities	960	2,290
Shareholders' equity	1,690	1,690
Total liabilities and equity	$2,650	$3,980
Net income during 2001:	$30 million	

Ratio	Unconsolidated	Consolidated
Debt-to-assets	$960/$2,650	$2,290/$3,980
	= 36.2%	= 57.5%
Current ratio	$570/$420 = 1.36	$1,850/$470 = 3.94

Note the following:

1. Pepper's debt-to-assets ratio increased markedly from 36.2 to 57.5 percent as a result of consolidation. This ratio increases whenever a consolidated subsidiary has debt financing.
2. In Pepper Company's case, the current ratio increased from 1.36 to 3.94 percent as a result of consolidation. This occurs because Shaker Inc., the subsidiary, has a higher current ratio than the parent company.

These illustrative ratio calculations show that many of the ratios used by analysts will differ before and after consolidation. Analysts must be careful when examining ratio trends that cover periods when new subsidiaries are being consolidated (or when subsidiaries are being sold or divested).

EVALUATION OF CONSOLIDATION ACCOUNTING

Financial accounting standards require the reporting of consolidated financial statements, based on a presumption that investor analysts need to evaluate the total set of economic resources that are controlled by the parent company, as well as the total liabilities and other claims against those resources. Correspondingly, the consolidated income statement measures the total revenues and expenses attributed to these economic resources and claims.

The FASB has initiated a comprehensive reexamination of the principles and assumptions that underlie consolidated financial statements. Two key issues are (1) developing a meaningful measure of "control" for purposes of including an investee in the consolidation and (2) the extent to which consolidation may in some cases impair rather than enhance the usefulness of financial statements.

With respect to the issue of control, it is unclear that owning a majority of an investee's outstanding shares is a necessary means of establishing control. For example, a substantial portion of the outstanding shares in widely held companies is not voted at stockholders' meetings. Smaller investors with minor shareholdings may lack the incentive to study the issues and participate in the governance of a corporation. As a consequence, a parent company owning much less than 50 percent of an affiliate's outstanding stock can still regularly cast a majority of the votes on matters of company policy. The issue of control is further muddied by the existence of convertible securities (such as convertible bonds and preferred stock, discussed in Chapter 10, "Shareholders' Equity"). If the holders of such securities can convert their holdings to voting common stock at any time, then the ownership percentages in an investee can shift dramatically on short notice.

The usefulness of consolidated financial statements has also been questioned on grounds that aggregations of information cause a loss of information. Some analysts and company managers argue that, because consolidation often entails adding together financial statements from companies of diverse industries, the resulting totals are very difficult to interpret. For example, most automotive companies and other durable goods manufacturers have subsidiary companies that extend consumer credit to the parent company customers. It has been a long-standing practice for the parent firms to exclude finance subsidiaries from their consolidations, which is defended on the grounds that analysts would be misled by an aggregation of manufacturing and financial companies. Subsequently, the FASB issued a standard that requires the consolidation of all majority-owned subsidiaries (see *SFAS No. 92,* "Consolidation of All Majority-Owned Subsidiaries," October, 1987).

INTRODUCTION TO PART II: INTERNATIONAL ASPECTS OF FINANCIAL REPORTING

Business activities are increasingly international. As tariff barriers dissolve through regional trade arrangements, such as the North American Free Trade Agreement (NAFTA) and the European Union (EU), domestic business firms rely more extensively on international trade both for sources of supply and as markets for their products. The political and economic reshaping of Eastern Europe and the still embryonic modernization of China ensure that international trade will be a substantial and rapidly growing component in the business affairs of domestic firms.

As foreign suppliers and customers become more essential to business activities, companies frequently establish or acquire subsidiary companies that operate in foreign nations. To report financial statements on a consolidated basis to U.S. investors, the foreign operations of those affiliates need to be translated into U.S. dollars. Because most foreign currency exchange rates fluctuate over time, a variety of issues arise in the preparation of dollar-denominated financial reports.

This part of the chapter discusses three related aspects of financial reporting for firms engaged in international business:

1. the reporting of transactions between foreign and domestic firms, when the transactions are valued on the basis of the foreign currency;
2. the method used in translating the financial statements of foreign affiliates that have been prepared in other currencies into U.S. dollars; and
3. the diversity of accounting practices that exist among nations and the emerging efforts to achieve international harmonization of accounting practices.

FOREIGN CURRENCY TRANSACTIONS

If a U.S. company either buys from or sells to a foreign company, the firms must specify the currency that will be used to settle the resulting accounts receivable or payable. **Foreign currency transactions** create receivables or payables that must be settled in a foreign currency. These balances are said to be **denominated** in the foreign currency.

When a U.S. firm collects an account receivable that is paid in a foreign currency, it then converts the foreign currency to dollars. Conversely, in order for a U.S. firm to make payment of an account that is payable in a foreign currency, it must first convert U.S. dollars into the foreign currency. In either case, the U.S. firm must buy or sell foreign currency at the current **foreign exchange rate** between the U.S. dollar and the foreign currency. The foreign exchange rate specifies the number of U.S. dollars needed to obtain one unit of a specific foreign currency. Note that **direct rates** for foreign exchange quote the number of U.S. dollars required for one unit of a foreign currency. **Indirect rates** indicate the number of foreign currency units required for one U.S. dollar. The discussion in this chapter uses *only* direct quotations.

As a basis for discussion, hypothetical foreign exchange rates between the U.S. dollar ($) and the British pound (£) for various dates are provided in Exhibit 13-4. These rates show the number of U.S. dollars required to buy one British pound at the dates indicated. If we assume the rate is 1.40 on April 1, 2001, then U.S. $1.40 is needed to buy one British pound.

The information in Exhibit 13-4 includes **spot rates** and **forward rates.** A spot rate is the rate of exchange for the immediate delivery of foreign currencies. A forward rate is the rate of exchange for the future delivery of foreign currencies, and the

EXHIBIT 13-4 Hypothetical Foreign Exchange Rates

Foreign Exchange Rates Between the U.S. Dollar ($) and the British Pound (£), Spot and Forward Rates

Date			$/£
April 1, 2001	Spot rate:		1.40
	Forward rate:	30 days	1.395
		60 days	1.38
		90 days	1.37
May 30, 2001	Spot rate:		1.30

market in which foreign currencies are bought and sold for future delivery is referred to as a **currency forward market.** Exhibit 13-4 indicates that the 60-day forward exchange rate of dollars to pounds is 1.38. If a U.S. firm needs British pounds in 60 days, it could contract today with a foreign exchange broker to buy pounds 60 days hence at a price of U.S. $1.38 per pound. Alternatively, the firm could simply wait and buy the pounds in 60 days at the prevailing spot rate on that date.

Firms frequently contract to buy or sell foreign currencies in the forward market in order to protect against the risks of foreign exchange rate fluctuations. The exchange rates between most pairs of currencies change frequently in response to the forces of supply and demand. As the number of U.S. dollars that is needed to buy a unit of foreign currency increases (or decreases), that foreign currency is said to strengthen (or weaken) against the dollar. As a result, if a U.S. firm has a foreign currency-denominated receivable or payable, then the dollar value of the account will vary as foreign currency exchange rates fluctuate.

The existence of forward markets for the foreign currencies of most major U.S. trading partners allows managers to **hedge,** or protect against the risks of exchange rate fluctuations. To illustrate, assume that on April 1, 2001, the Reagan Company, a U.S. firm, sells merchandise to Thatcher, Ltd., a British firm. The sales agreement specifies that Thatcher will make a payment of £150,000 to Reagan in 60 days, on May 30, 2001. Sales are recorded using the spot rate on the date of sale, rather than the forward rate for the date of anticipated collection. Because the spot rate of exchange at the transaction date, April 1, 2001, is 1.40 (see Exhibit 13-4), Reagan would record the account receivable and sale at $210,000 ($1.40 × 150,000).

ASSETS	=	LIABILITIES	+	SHAREHOLDERS' EQUITY
Accounts receivable				Retained earnings
+$210,000				+$210,000
				(Sales revenue)

Exhibit 13-4 shows that the spot rate of exchange on May 30, 2001, when the receivable balance is paid by Thatcher, Ltd., has fallen to 1.30. This indicates that the U.S. dollar has strengthened against the British pound and it requires fewer dollars to buy British pounds. Conversely, because the Reagan Company has a pound-denominated account receivable, the dollar value of the receivable has declined to $195,000 ($1.30 × £150,000). Reagan's collection of the receivable would increase cash by $195,000, but the entire receivable must be eliminated, so an exchange rate loss would be recognized for $15,000 ($210,000 − $195,000).

ASSETS		=	LIABILITIES	+	SHAREHOLDERS' EQUITY
Cash	Accounts receivable				Retained earnings
+$195,000	−$210,000				−$15,000
					(Foreign currency loss)

In this example, the Reagan Company was exposed to the risk of exchange rate fluctuations over the 60-day collection period. The firm held an accounts receivable denominated in a foreign currency and incurred a loss because that foreign currency weakened against the dollar. Consequently, the dollar value of the receivable declined. Reagan could instead have chosen to protect itself against rate fluctuations at the date of sale by contracting on April 1 with a foreign exchange broker to sell 150,000 British pounds in 60 days at the 60-day forward exchange rate of 1.38.

Upon signing such a **hedging contract,** the Reagan Company would recognize an account receivable from the currency broker for $207,000 ($1.38 forward rate × 150,000) in dollars to be received in 60 days. Reagan would also recognize an account payable to the broker for $210,000 ($1.40 spot rate × 150,000), to be paid in British pounds in 60 days, and a hedging expense of $3,000 ($210,000 account payable less $207,000 account receivable).

ASSETS	=	LIABILITIES	+	SHAREHOLDERS' EQUITY
Accounts receivable + $207,000		Accounts payable + $210,000		Retained earnings − $3,000 (hedging expense)

In effect, Reagan would have paid $3,000 to protect itself from exposure to foreign currency rate fluctuations over the collection term of the account receivable. They would have an account receivable from Thatcher, Ltd. in British pounds that is offset by a liability to the foreign exchange broker that also is denominated in British pounds.

When the spot rate of exchange subsequently falls from $1.40 on April 1 to $1.30 on May 30, the Reagan Company would revalue downward by $15,000 the pound-denominated receivables and payables. Because the $15,000 loss on the account receivable is exactly offset by the $15,000 gain on the account payable, no net gain or loss results.

ASSETS	=	LIABILITIES	+	SHAREHOLDERS' EQUITY
Accounts receivable − $15,000		Accounts payable − $15,000		

In summary, when a U.S. firm contracts either to receive or to pay future accounts that are denominated in foreign currencies, there is an attendant risk of gains or losses from fluctuations in foreign exchange rates. Usually, firms are able to insulate themselves from risk by hedging, which is accomplished by entering into contracts with foreign exchange brokers to buy or sell foreign currencies at future dates.

The example in this section has shown how a firm would hedge a foreign currency account receivable by contracting to sell foreign currency in the future. Firms with foreign currency accounts payable, however, would hedge in the opposite fashion. They would hedge by contracting to buy foreign currency in the future. In either case, the objective is the same: to have offsetting receivables and payables in the foreign currency. Besides hedging foreign currency-denominated accounts receivable or payable, firms often hedge commitments to engage in future transactions. These can include purchase commitments, sales agreements, employment contracts, and so on.

Hedging one's exposure to foreign exchange rate fluctuations is similar in concept to the payment of an insurance premium in order to avoid risk. Firms engaged in international trade may have significant amounts of foreign currency-denominated financial assets and liabilities. If these are left unhedged, gains and losses caused by changes in exchange rates might account for a substantial portion of periodic profits and losses. Rather than speculate on the future strength or weakness of the dollar, most managers of industrial trading firms hedge to avoid exposure to exchange rate fluctuations. Reality Check 13-2 describes how one firm hedges its exposures to foreign exchange rate fluctuations.

REALITY CHECK 13-2

General Motors Company is a major automotive producer. The company included the following disclosures related to the management of its foreign exchange exposures in its 1997 financial statements (edited):

"GM is an international corporation with operations in over 50 countries and has foreign currency exposures at these operations related to buying, selling, and financing in currencies other than the local currency. The magnitude of these exposures significantly varies over time depending on the strength of local automotive markets and sourcing decisions.

GM enters agreements in order to manage certain foreign exchange exposures in accordance with established policy guidelines. These agreements primarily hedge cash flows such as debt, firm commitments, and anticipated transactions involving vehicles, components, fixed assets, and subsidiary dividends. GM uses foreign exchange forward contracts as well as purchased and written foreign exchange options. Foreign exchange forward contracts are legal agreements between two parties to purchase or sell a foreign currency for a price specified on the contract date with delivery and settlement in the future."

Required

a. The Note discussion indicates that the firm attempts to hedge debt, firm commitments, and anticipated transactions. Commitments and anticipated transactions are not formally recognized in the body of the financial statements, however. Discuss the advisability of hedging events that have not yet been recorded for financial statement purposes.
b. Provide an example of both a commitment and an anticipated transaction that exposes a firm to foreign currency risk. In each case, describe how the risk might be hedged.

Solution

a. In attempting to insulate the firm from changes in foreign exchange rates, managers need not be bound by the completed transaction convention in financial accounting. Commitments are firm agreements to engage in future transactions at specific amounts of foreign currency and, if unhedged, represent exposure in an economic sense. Anticipated transactions, on the other hand, represent intentions rather than firm agreements, and in many cases these anticipated transactions eventually may not occur. For this reason, it is arguable whether they represent economic exposures to future exchange rate changes.
b. An example of a foreign currency commitment is a future purchase agreement made to a supplier, to be paid in a specified amount of foreign currency. An example of an anticipated transaction would be budgeted sales to customers abroad, with the sales proceeds to be received in foreign currencies. Regarding the purchase commitment, if future exchange rates change, the cost of the inventory and the liability to the supplier will both be changed in terms of U.S. dollars. The commitment could be hedged by selling the foreign currency for future delivery (by creating an offsetting account receivable denominated in the foreign currency). Regarding the future sales transactions, it is not easily known whether the terms or the equivalent dollar amounts of those sales will be changed as a consequence of future changes in foreign exchange rates. Because future sales represent expected future receipts of a foreign currency, the selling firm might hedge by contracting for a future sale of the foreign currency. It would be difficult to determine whether the foreign currency risks had been fully hedged, however, because the actual future sales amounts are not presently known.

TRANSLATION OF FOREIGN CURRENCY FINANCIAL STATEMENTS

Foreign subsidiaries of U.S. firms usually prepare their financial statements in the currencies in which they transact their business, which is referred to as their **functional currency.** The U.S. parent firm prepares its financial reports in U.S. dollars and, as a consequence, the financial statements of the foreign subsidiaries must be translated into U.S. dollars in order to be consolidated with those of the parent company.

To illustrate the process of translating foreign currency financial statements, consider the balance sheets and income statements of Perot, Inc., a subsidiary of a U.S. company, at the end of 2001, as shown in Exhibit 13-5. Perot, Inc., operates in Taiwan and prepares its financial statements in New Taiwan dollars, or NT$. Because Perot,

EXHIBIT 13-5 Translation of Foreign Currency Financial Statements

Perot, Inc.
Summary Income Statement and Balance Sheet
Year Ended December 31, 2001

(All Currencies in Millions)

Income Statement, Year Ended December 31, 2001

Account	NT$	Translation Rate	US$
Revenues	5,000	.04[a]	200.0
Expenses	(4,200)	.04[a]	(168.0)
Net income	800		32.0

Balance Sheet, December 31, 2001

Account	NT$	Translation Rate	US$
Assets	8,500	.038[b]	323.0
Liabilities	4,600	.038[b]	174.8
Invested capital	2,500	.050[c]	125.0
Retained earnings	1,400	—	60.8
Translation adjustment	—	—	(37.6)
Total	8,500		323.0

Analysis of Retained Earnings Changes During 2001

Account	NT$	Translation Rate	US$
Beginning balance	900	—[d]	40.5
Net income	800	—[e]	32.0
Dividends	(300)	.039[f]	(11.7)
Ending balance	1,400		60.8

NOTES: [a]Average exchange rate during 2001.
[b]Current (spot) rate on December 31, 2001
[c]Historical rate when capital stock was issued.
[d]Beginning balance in U.S. dollars is obtained from the translated balance sheet on January 1, 2001.
[e]See translated income statement above.
[f]Historical rate when dividends were declared.

Inc., is a subsidiary of a U.S. company, its financial statements must be translated into U.S. dollars prior to consolidation with those of the U.S. parent.

Foreign exchange rates between U.S. and New Taiwan dollars must be used to translate the various elements of Perot's financial statements into U.S. dollars. Accounting standards require the use of different rates for different financial statement elements. The FASB specifies the following rates for translation (*SFAS No. 52,* "Foreign Currency Translation"):

- The **average exchange rate** during the reporting period is used to translate income statement items. Average rates are appropriate when operating activities have been level throughout the year, and changes in exchange rates have occurred evenly throughout the year. Exhibit 13-5 shows that the average rate during 2001 was $0.04. Thus, it required US$0.04 to buy one NT dollar.
- The current exchange rate (the spot rate at the balance sheet date) is used to translate asset and liability items. Exhibit 13-5 shows that the current exchange rate was US$0.038 on December 31, 2001.
- Various **historical exchange rates** are used to translate the balances of invested capital, beginning retained earnings, and dividends. Exhibit 13-5 shows that the exchange rate when Perot's stock was issued was $.05, and the rate when dividends were declared in 2001 was US$0.039. The balance of Perot's retained earnings, translated into U.S. dollars, was $40.5 million at the beginning of 2001.

The ending balance in retained earnings is not translated directly from Perot Inc.'s foreign currency balance sheet. Instead, it is computed in the following manner:

	millions of US$
Retained earnings, beginning balance (January 1, 2001)	$40.5
Add: Translated amount of net income (Exhibit 13-5)	32.0
Less: Translated amount of dividends (Exhibit 13-5)	(11.7)
Retained earnings, ending balance (December 31, 2001)	$60.8

Note in Exhibit 13-5 that the translated balance sheet for Perot, Inc. requires a **translation adjustment** in order to remain in balance. This adjustment is required because not all balance sheet elements are translated at the same exchange rate. In Perot's case, the translated amounts of total assets are less than the translated amounts of total liabilities and shareholders' equity (exclusive of the translation adjustment) by $37.6 million. For this reason, $37.6 million must be subtracted from shareholders' equity to restore the balance.

The interpretation of this translation adjustment is a matter of continuing controversy. The FASB suggests the following interpretation: When a foreign subsidiary of a U.S. firm has assets in excess of its liabilities, this is similar to a partially unhedged investment in a foreign currency. If a foreign currency strengthens (or weakens) against the U.S. dollar, then this unhedged investment gives rise to an unrealized gain (or loss). In Perot's case, the foreign currency (NT$) has weakened against the U.S. dollar, and the translation adjustment can be interpreted as an unrealized loss. Because the parent company intends to maintain its investment in Perot, Inc. over the foreseeable future, and because foreign currency exchange rates are likely to continue to fluctuate, it would be premature to recognize such unrealized gains or losses in income.

Some analysts question the view that a firm's net asset position should be viewed as an unhedged foreign currency investment. Instead, they argue that investments in nonmonetary items, such as inventories, property, plant, equipment, and other assets, should be accounted for based on the historical cost concept that underlies the parent company's financial statements. Translation of asset costs at current exchange rates causes the U.S. dollar book values of the assets to change whenever the translation rate fluctuates. For this reason, the translated book values do not represent historical costs. In a partial recognition of this problem, the FASB has established a special set of "remeasurement" rules for foreign currency financial statements in high-inflation countries.

Many analysts who otherwise accept the FASB's interpretation of the net assets reported in foreign currency financial statements object to the exclusion of gains or losses from net income. These critics suggest that financial accountants have no special expertise in identifying temporary versus permanent changes in currency exchange rates. If current exchange rates are determined in a well-functioning foreign exchange market based on the trading activities of informed investors, these analysts argue that the gains or losses that result from unhedged net assets or liabilities should be reported as part of net income when they occur.

INTERNATIONAL VARIATIONS IN ACCOUNTING STANDARDS

Diversity pervades the world community. Variations in language, custom, cuisine, and architecture, as well as in business, political, and social organizations, give truth to the adage that "travel is broadening." Although tour books routinely ignore the fact, accounting standards also vary among nations. International diversity in accounting standards complicates the task for investor analysts when attempting to evaluate risks and returns based on comparable financial information. Moreover, disparate accounting standards and disclosure requirements impede the capability of firms to raise debt and equity capital across national boundaries.

The accounting standards that have developed in a given nation or region reflect to some extent the unique characteristics of the society and business community in which they have evolved. Accordingly, as business firms become more international in their activities, and as investors aim for greater international diversification of their investments, it becomes essential to understand the differences in accounting standards that exist among nations.

UNDERLYING CAUSES OF ACCOUNTING DIVERSITY

Differences in accounting standards originate mainly from differences in the objectives of financial reporting across nations. In turn, different objectives exist for financial reporting due to the differing characteristics of legal systems, the financial structure of business firms, the relation between financial and tax accounting, and other factors.

Legal System Influences

The legal system of a nation influences the extent to which accounting standards establish general, flexible guides for reporting practices, as opposed to providing a complete set of detailed, rigid rules with minimal scope for professional judgment by reporting firms. Countries such as the United States and the United Kingdom, for example, have legal systems that rely on statutes, which are then interpreted by the courts in a flexible manner to deal with the unique circumstances in individual cases. Other nations, such as France and Germany, have legal systems in which laws are designed to cover virtually all possible circumstances.

Corresponding to these differing legal systems, accounting rules in France and Germany tend to be very detailed and explicit, leaving no scope for judgment.

Accounting disputes are resolved by "looking up" the correct solution in the applicable rule books. By contrast, and with some notable exceptions, U.S. and British accounting standards tend to establish broad frameworks and allow considerable room for interpretations and assumptions in individual cases.

Financial Structure Influences

The financial structure of a firm refers to the sources from which its investment capital is obtained. In the United States and the United Kingdom, a major portion of financing is obtained by the sale of equity shares on security exchanges. These securities are typically held by diverse individuals and institutions that rely on published financial reports for investment-relevant information. For this reason, the focus of financial accounting standards is on the decision-making usefulness of published financial reports.

In many other nations, including Germany and Japan, corporate financing is obtained primarily from direct borrowings and from sales of equity securities to banks and other financial institutions. In these cases, the lenders and investors are able to demand relevant and timely financial information directly from the firm. Because major lenders and investors do not depend on public financial reports, accounting standards for public financial reports are determined by factors other than investor information, such as conformity with the tax rules or the information needs of government economic planners.

Taxation Influences

In countries such as Germany, Italy, France, and Japan, there is a very close correspondence between financial reporting standards and the rules used to determine taxable income. In these nations, there is no distinction made between the possibly different measurements needed for purposes of government fiscal policy and the information needs of investors. Revenues and expenses must be recognized for tax purposes in the same periods in which they are reported to investors. Not surprisingly, accounting standards in these countries tend to be very conservative relative to U.S. standards. For example, price-to-earnings multiples (the ratio of market price per share to earnings per share) are much higher in Germany and Japan than in the United States. This comparison suggests that investors consider German and Japanese earnings numbers to be of higher quality (more conservative) than reported earnings of U.S. firms.

INTERNATIONAL DIFFERENCES IN SELECTED ACCOUNTING PRACTICES

This section considers five specific areas of accounting practice: accounting for goodwill in business acquisitions, consolidation policy, accounting for leases, pension reporting, and departures from historical cost in valuing assets. In each case, U.S. standards are compared to those in several major industrial nations.

Goodwill

As discussed in the first part of this chapter, goodwill arises in a business acquisition when the buyer pays an amount that exceeds the fair value of the identifiable net assets of the seller. The amount assigned to goodwill often accounts for a major portion of the purchase price. For U.S. firms, reported earnings subsequent to the acquisition must be reduced by systematic amortization of the amount attributed to goodwill.

In several European nations, including Germany, the Netherlands, and Italy, goodwill can be charged immediately to shareholders' equity. As a result, the asset (goodwill) does not appear on the balance sheet, and subsequent earnings are not reduced by goodwill amortization. Managers of U.S. firms often claim that this difference in accounting standards causes an "uneven playing field," because their European counterparts can report higher profits subsequent to business combinations.

Until late in 1998, almost all British companies wrote off goodwill to shareholders' equity immediately on acquisition. During this same period, U.K. firms often outbid U.S. companies for acquisition targets because the goodwill that was immediately written-off would not reduce future earnings. Recently, however, U.K. standards were changed to require that companies capitalize purchased goodwill and amortize it against future earnings over periods of up to 20 years.

Consolidations

Firms in the United States are required to consolidate all majority-owned subsidiaries. Except for Australia, most major industrial nations do not require the consolidation of **nonhomogeneous subsidiaries,** which are those whose major operating activities take place in industries that differ from those of the parent company. U.S. automobile manufacturers, for example, are required to consolidate their financing subsidiaries, even though the activities are quite distinct from those of the parent companies. American managers argue that a substantial portion of the assets and debt controlled by foreign parent companies can easily be hidden on the books of unconsolidated, controlled subsidiaries. As a consequence, financial ratio calculations that are based on published financial statements can appear to be less favorable for U.S. firms.

Leases

As discussed in Chapter 12, "Additional Issues in Liability Reporting," U.S. accounting standards require that long-term leases be **capitalized,** or recorded as assets and liabilities based on present value measurements when the lessee acquires both the risks and the rewards of ownership. Although many advanced industrial nations have similar standards, the criteria they use to identify a capital lease are considerably more flexible than those in the United States. As a result, most leases are interpreted as operating leases, in other words, as ordinary rentals of assets, rather than capital leases. In Japan, most leases are designed as operating leases in order to minimize taxes. In Italy, *all* leases are reported as operating leases. Therefore, lease disclosures are not comparable between firms in these countries.

Pensions

The defined benefit type of pension plan that has been widely adopted by U.S. firms, as discussed in Chapter 12, is relatively less important in other nations. In many countries, government-sponsored pension arrangements are more prominent than are company-sponsored plans, and most of the latter are defined contribution plans. Even in cases where defined benefit plans do exist, only the U.S. requires an annual evaluation of the discount rate that is used to estimate the value of the pension liability. This annual evaluation has in recent years caused the amounts of unfunded pension liabilities, and also the reported pension expense, to be more volatile for mature U.S. firms. Moreover, U.S. standards require much greater detail in the footnote disclosures of pension assumptions, funding status, cost components, and other items.

Asset Valuations

American accounting standards generally require that assets be valued at historical cost. Exceptions to this are the lower of cost or market (LCM) rules, which are applied to the most current assets and the fair market value rules for investments in marketable securities. In contrast, U.K. companies may choose to revalue tangible and intangible noncurrent assets at the current replacement cost. Alternatively, tangible noncurrent assets can be valued at current market values. France allows current cost revaluations of tangible assets, but not intangibles. Because of extremely high inflation rates, South American countries require that the historical costs of most noncurrent assets be adjusted by a purchasing power index to reflect inflation.

INTERNATIONAL HARMONIZATION OF ACCOUNTING STANDARDS

Recent years have seen a burgeoning demand by foreign firms for debt and equity capital, which has been obtained by selling securities in other nations. This demand is partly attributable to the wave of **privatization** in Eastern and Western Europe and in South America. Privatization is the act of selling government-owned or controlled enterprises to private investors, and the resultant demands for investment capital often exceed what is available in the local economies.

The demand for access to investment capital in other nations is also due in part to international differences in the cost of capital. For example, because of a rigorous and comprehensive set of financial reporting standards and well-regulated securities markets, the cost of investment capital in U.S. financial markets is generally lower than that in other Western nations. It can be quite costly, however, for foreign companies that initially prepare financial statements in their domestic currencies and apply domestic accounting standards to expand and recast their financial reports in a manner that allows them to list their shares on foreign stock exchanges. As an example, in 1993, Daimler-Benz AG, a German automaker, decided to list its shares on the New York Stock Exchange. To comply with U.S. financial reporting standards, the company incurred expenses that were estimated to exceed $500 million ("Foreign Firms Raise More and More Money in the U.S. Markets," *The Wall Street Journal,* October 5, 1993).

The considerable amount of expense incurred by firms in preparing financial reports to comply with multiple sets of accounting standards, as well as the difficulties encountered by investor analysts in evaluating investment opportunities across national boundaries, has given impetus to efforts for creating international accounting standards. This would require that financial statements worldwide conform to a single set of accounting standards.

To promote harmonization of accounting standards throughout the world business community, the International Accounting Standards Committee (IASC) was formed in 1973. This committee is a joint effort, initially undertaken by professional accounting groups in 10 Western nations (including the AICPA in the United States). The IASC issues accounting pronouncements, termed International Accounting Standards (IAS). To date, more than 36 such standards have been issued. Exhibit 13-6 contains a statement by IASC of the reasons why international accounting standards are desirable.

The effectiveness of the IASC as a force for international harmonization is limited by several factors. First, the committee has no power to enforce its standards. Recall that in the United States, the authority of the FASB is backed by the endorsement of the SEC, and firms must follow FASB pronouncements in order to list and sell securities. No similar authority exists to give credibility to IASC standards.

A second reason why IASC standards have failed to achieve harmonization is the fact that the standards themselves usually fail to create a single method of accounting. Instead, most standards enumerate and endorse a variety of accounting methods that

EXHIBIT 13-6 Purposes of International Accounting Standards

The Need for International Accounting Standards

At present, financial reports prepared for shareholders and other users involve principles and procedures that can vary widely from country to country, and sometimes even within a country. Accounting reports, therefore, can lack comparability. This is highly unsatisfactory because

- it can cause preparation costs for financial reports that are much higher than necessary. A multinational company may have to prepare different reports on its operations for use in different countries; and
- businesses will want to have a uniform system for assessing financial performance in their operations in different countries. They will also want their external reports to be consistent with internal assessments of performance. These two objectives are not achievable if accounting standards vary from country to country.

Investment analysts and other users of financial reports incur extra costs of analysis when the reports are prepared according to different standards in different countries. They may be confused in their interpretation of the reports. Effective competition among the capital markets of the world may be impaired and companies may have to bear higher costs of capital because of the difficulties involved in financial analysis. The credibility of accounting suffers. Accounting reports will significantly lose credibility if a company reports different profit numbers in different countries for given transactions.

International Accounting Standards are also of great usefulness for developing countries or other countries which do not have a national standard setting body or do not have the resources to undertake the full process of preparing accounting standards. The preparation of accounting standards involves considerable cost and, quite apart from the advantages of uniformity, it would not be economic for each country to have a separate process.

The magnitude of cross-border financing transactions, securities trading, and direct foreign investment is enormous, often in smaller as well as larger countries. The need of a single set of rules by which assets, liabilities, and income are recognized and measured is urgent.

SOURCE: International Accounting Standards Committee (IASC) internet web site, *www.iasc.org.uk*

are used by member nations. Only in this manner has the IASC been able to achieve the consensus needed to issue its standards and no agreement exists among IASC members regarding the set of accounting standards that is "best" for the international financial market. For example, there is wide acknowledgment that U.S. accounting standards require more elaborate and comprehensive disclosures than do the standards in other nations. Yet accounting groups in other nations argue that "more is not necessarily better." Financial reporting in the United States might be unduly complicated and expensive, thereby putting extra burdens on preparers and users alike.

It is questionable whether any international group, whatever its composition, will be able to achieve worldwide harmonization of accounting standards. Throughout the earlier chapters of this book we have considered many of the FASB standards that govern financial reporting in the United States. As you have seen, such standards are the result of a political process that attempts to balance the economic impact of accounting rules across a variety of different constituencies, and similar processes exist in other nations. Accordingly, existing accounting standards can vary from those in the United States because a different political consensus has been achieved in those nations. It may be naive to believe that the FASB, or its counterpart groups in other countries, will modify their standards purely in the interest of international harmonization.

THE CHANGING INTERNATIONAL ECONOMIC CLIMATE

Financial reporting does not exist in a vacuum, and major international developments, both planned and unplanned, will inevitably affect the form and content of financial statements. Changes in international monetary arrangements, capital markets, governmental fiscal policies, and business risks will ultimately impact the types of information that investors require from financial reports. Two major changes in the recent international environment include the adoption of a supra-national currency by several major European nations and the economic upheavals experienced by a number of Asian nations.

A Supra-National Currency

In the early 1990s, the European Union (EU) agreed to introduce a single European currency in an effort to create a European Monetary Union. The *euro*, which was introduced in early 1999, will coexist with existing national currencies for three years. After that time, the national currencies of EU members will no longer be legal tender. The expected advantages of this single currency include the elimination of risks due to foreign currency fluctuations, savings in transactions costs with a resulting stimulation of trade and investment, and the potential of lower inflation and interest rates for some member nations. A single currency, however, implies a coordination of the monetary policies of the member countries. Because monetary policy is very closely tied to fiscal (taxation and government spending) policy, this also implies an evolving similarity across nations in terms of political and social policies.

The introduction of the euro will have various direct and indirect effects on accounting. Financial reports will be prepared in the common currency across all member nations, and historical data will be recast in terms of the new currency. During the transition process, firms may require that transactions be recorded in parallel currencies (that is, the euro and the domestic currency). Firms' pricing policies, wage levels, tax regulations, and overall business strategies may all be impacted by the introduction of the euro.

The introduction of a common European currency might even displace the U.S. dollar as the world's leading currency. Governments, firms, and individuals may reconsider the present prominence of the U.S. dollar as the currency in which to keep reserves and issue debt. Potentially strong shifts in international capital flows could change costs of capital (and the values of publicly traded debt and equity securities) in ways that are difficult to predict.

The Asian Crisis

During the past few years, many Asian economies have experienced significant economic upheaval, which has led to precipitous declines in the trading value of stocks and bonds and the failures of many banks, industrial corporations, and other entities. As the U.S. dollar has strengthened against most Asian currencies, the price of imports from other nations has declined in the U.S., while the cost of U.S. exports of goods and services has increased to customers in other nations.

The ultimate impact of the Asian crisis on U.S. firms and on their financial reports is presently unknown. Major factors that are affecting firms doing business in Asia are currency devaluation and political instability in the region, as well as declining share prices leading to higher costs of local financing. The stronger U.S. dollar makes it harder for U.S. firms to market their now relatively more expensive products and services abroad, while at the same time it increases the degree of domestic competition from now relatively less expensive imports. In addition, the financial statements of many firms may require substantial write-downs of asset values. As Asian market values have tumbled, the market values of debt and equity securities carried on the balance sheets of many U.S. firms have fallen well below their carrying values. Moreover, even the recorded values of investments in long-lived tangible assets in Asian countries may need to be reduced. Managers also may need to expand their disclosures of significant risks and uncertainties to assure that they adequately communicate the increased business, financial, and political risks in their international activities.

SUMMARY OF LEARNING OBJECTIVES

1. **Understand the reasons for reporting consolidated financial statements.** Business firms often expand by taking over existing firms. Most takeovers occur as acquisitions, in which a buyer firm acquires a majority of the voting shares of a seller firm. The buyer is thereafter referred to as the parent company, and the seller as a subsidiary company. Both firms continue to exist as legally distinct corporations. Because they are under common control, their financial statements must be consolidated for financial reporting purposes.
2. **Appreciate how affiliated firms construct and report their consolidated financial statements.**
Consolidation requires adding together the assets, liabilities, revenues, and expenses of the parent and subsidiary firms. A variety of consolidation adjustments must be made to reflect the fact that both firms are now a single economic entity. The following adjustments characterize most consolidations:
   a. The balance of the parent's investment account in the subsidiary must be eliminated because, from a consolidated perspective, the subsidiary is not a distinct economic entity. The subsidiary's shareholders' equity also must be eliminated because its shares are not held outside the consolidated entity.
   b. The subsidiary's individual assets and liabilities may require revaluation in the process of consolidation in order to reflect differences between the parent's cost of acquisition and their carrying values at the acquisition date. In subsequent periods, these revaluations may require adjustments to the revenues and expenses used in computing consolidated income.
   c. Intercompany borrowing and lending might result in accounts receivable and payable on the balance sheets of a parent and its consolidated subsidiaries. If so, these amounts must be eliminated.
   d. Revenues and expenses reported on the consolidated income statement must reflect only transactions with outside entities, which are firms that are not included in the consolidation. Similarly, the carrying values of assets must exclude any unrealized profits for assets that have been transferred among the affiliated firms.
3. **Understand how foreign exchange fluctuations affect the financial reporting of transactions conducted in foreign currencies.**
Companies engaged in international trade often have accounts receivable or accounts payable that are denominated in foreign currencies. Fluctuations in foreign currency exchange rates affect the dollar value of such receivables and payables, resulting in gains or losses.

   The existence of forward markets for foreign currencies allows managers to hedge and thereby protect against the risks of exchange rate fluctuations. Firms with foreign currency receivables may contract to sell foreign currency in the future, and firms with foreign currency payables may contract to buy foreign currency in the future. In either case, the firm's goal is to have offsetting amounts of

KEY TERMS

Acquisition 532
Affiliated Companies 532
Average exchange rate 546
Business combination 531
Capitalize 549
Consolidated financial statements 534
Consolidation 532
Currency forward market 542
Current exchange rate 542
Denominated 541
Direct rates 541
Equity method of accounting 537
External expansion 531
Foreign currency transactions 541
Foreign exchange rate 541
Forward rate 541
Functional currency 545
Hedge 542
Hedging contract 543
Historical exchange rates 546
Indirect rates 541
Intercompany receivables and payables 538
Intercompany sales 532
Internal expansion 531
Merger 532
Minority interest in consolidated subsidiaries 536
Nonhomogeneous subsidiaries 549
Parent company 532
Pooling of interests 533
Privatization 550
Spot rate 541
Subsidiary 532
Translation adjustment 546
Unrealized inventory profits 538

receivables and payables denominated in a given foreign currency.

4. **Determine how financial statements prepared initially in foreign currencies are translated to U.S. dollars.**
Foreign subsidiaries of U.S. firms usually prepare their financial statements in the currencies in which they transact their business. For financial reporting purposes, these foreign currency financial statements must be translated into U.S. dollars in order to be consolidated with the U.S. parent.
Generally, an average exchange rate for the period is used to translate the income statement; the current exchange rate on the balance sheet date is used to translate assets and liabilities, and historical exchange rates are used to translate most components of shareholders' equity. As a consequence of using a variety of exchange rates, the balance sheet requires a translation adjustment in order to balance. Currently, accounting standards do not recognize changes in this translation adjustment as gains or losses in the income statement. Instead, the adjustment is reported as a separate component of shareholders' equity.
5. **Appreciate the wide diversity of international accounting practices.**
Many different sets of accounting standards coexist in the world economy. In any given nation, local accounting standards are influenced by the unique characteristics of the society and business community. Because international diversity in accounting standards complicates the task of investment analysis and impedes the international flow of capital, there is widespread interest in the establishment of uniform worldwide accounting standards. Such efforts have had only limited success to date, however. There is no consensus internationally that any existing set of national standards would be best for all nations.

QUESTIONS

13-1 Distinguish between business growth through internal and external expansion. Discuss several reasons why a firm might seek to expand externally, rather than internally.

13-2 Explain how a firm might attempt to diversify risks by combining with other business firms.

13-3 Business combinations usually occur in the form of mergers, consolidations, or acquisitions. How do each of these types of combinations differ?

13-4 What advantages might a business acquisition offer as opposed to a merger or a consolidation?

13-5 Evaluate the following statements: *Accounting for goodwill makes no sense. If a firm generates goodwill internally, the costs are written off as expenses, and no related asset appears on the balance sheet. If, on the other hand, a firm purchases goodwill by acquiring another firm, the amount paid for goodwill is reported as an asset. How is an analyst supposed to make comparisons given these rules? Wouldn't it be more sensible to make all firms write off goodwill immediately?*

13-6 Suppose that Psycho Company buys all of Somatic Inc.'s outstanding shares directly from Somatic's existing shareholders. Describe how Somatic's balance sheet would be affected by the acquisition.

13-7 Describe what is meant by consolidated financial statements. In what circumstances should a parent company's financial statements be prepared on a consolidated basis?

13-8 Consolidation is mainly a process of adding together the financial statement elements of a parent and its controlled subsidiaries with certain necessary adjustments. Discuss why the following items may require adjustments in preparing a consolidated balance sheet:

a. Investment in a subsidiary (on the parent's balance sheet)
b. Shareholders' equity (on the subsidiary's balance sheet)
c. Accounts receivable
d. Accounts payable
e. Inventory
f. Goodwill
g. Property, plant, and equipment

13-9 Discuss why the following items may require adjustments when preparing a consolidated income statement:

a. Income from a subsidiary (on the parent's income statement)
b. Sales
c. Cost of goods sold
d. Depreciation and amortization expenses

13-10 Which of the following items would differ on a firm's financial statements before and after consolidation of its subsidiaries? Explain your answers.

a. Total assets
b. Total liabilities
c. Shareholders' equity
d. Sales
e. Expenses
f. Net income

13-11 Indicate how each of the following financial ratios changes after a consolidation of a parent firm and its subsidiaries:

a. Debt-to-total assets ratio
b. Net income-to-shareholders' equity ratio
c. Net income-to-total assets ratio
d. Net income-to-sales ratio
e. Current ratio

13-12 Respond to the following remarks: *I just read in the financial pages that Whale company owns 60 percent of Minnow Inc.'s shares. Whale Company includes all of Minnow's assets and liabilities and all of Minnow's revenues and expenses in its consolidated financial statements. It seems to me that this is a misrepresentation. If Whale owns 60 percent of Minnow, then it should only reflect 60 percent of Minnow in its financial statements.*

13-13 Is it necessary for one firm to own more than 50 percent of the voting stock of another firm in order to exert control over the investee firm? If not, how should control be defined for purposes of deciding on the preparation of consolidated financial statements?

13-14 It is sometimes argued that consolidation may result in a loss of information and may produce aggregations in the financial statements that are difficult to interpret. Do you agree or disagree? In what areas, other than consolidations, are accounting numbers too aggregated to serve investment analysts? Discuss.

13-15 Describe what is meant by a foreign currency transaction.

13-16 Which of the following events is a foreign currency transaction from the point of view of the U.S. firm?

a. A U.S. firm purchases inventory from a British firm, with payment to be made in British pounds.
b. A U.S. firm sells to an Italian firm, with payment to be made in U.S. dollars.
c. A U.S. firm purchases from a Taiwanese firm, with payment to be made in Japanese yen.

13-17 Explain whether a U.S. firm would experience a gain or a loss related to its unhedged accounts receivable or payable in each of the following cases:
a. A U.S. firm has accounts receivable in British pounds, and the pound strengthens relative to the U.S. dollar.
b. A U.S. firm has accounts payable in Mexican pesos, and the peso weakens relative to the U.S. dollar.
c. A U.S. firm has accounts receivable in French francs, and the franc weakens relative to the U.S. dollar.
d. A U.S. firm has accounts payable in Canadian dollars, and the Canadian dollar strengthens relative to the U.S. dollar.

13-18 Explain what is meant by a hedge of a foreign currency-denominated account receivable or payable.

13-19 Assume that a U.S. firm has an account receivable in Swiss francs, with payment due in 90 days, and wishes to hedge its exposure to currency rate fluctuations. Explain the actions the U.S. firm would take to accomplish such a hedge. Describe how the U.S. firm's financial statements would be affected if the Swiss franc strengthened relative to the U.S. dollar before the account receivable was collected.

13-20 Distinguish between spot rates and forward rates of foreign currency exchange. Which rate would a U.S. firm use in order to report its balance sheet accounts receivable in foreign currencies?

13-21 Explain why the financial statements of U.S. firms' foreign subsidiaries must be translated to U.S. dollars in order to prepare consolidated financial statements.

13-22 The balance sheets of foreign firms, prepared in their local currencies, must be in balance (assets equal liabilities plus shareholders' equity). Yet when such balance sheets are translated to U.S. dollars, they usually require a "translation adjustment" in order to balance. Explain why this is so.

13-23 Identify the exchange rate (current, historical, or average) that would be used to translate each of the following elements of a foreign subsidiary's financial statements to U.S. dollars:
a. Accounts receivable
b. Property, plant, and equipment
c. Total liabilities
d. Paid-in capital
e. Sales
f. Net income
g. Dividends

13-24 Assume that a foreign subsidiary of a U.S. firm acquired a parcel of land in 1998, and that each year thereafter the functional currency of the foreign subsidiary continues to weaken against the U.S. dollar. Describe how the carrying value of the land would change on successive translated balance sheets of the foreign subsidiary. Is the result sensible? What remedy could be suggested?

13-25 Describe the main factors that cause differences in accounting standards across nations.

13-26 Is worldwide harmonization of accounting standards a desirable objective? If so, prepare a memo indicating how such accounting standards should be developed and enforced. If *not*, prepare a memo identifying the major reasons why the costs of standardization outweigh its benefits.

13-27 Explain how the legal system of a nation can influence the types of accounting standards that are established.

13-28 Explain how the prevailing financial structure of business firms can affect the types of financial reports that are published.

13-29 Describe how taxation rules can influence the types of financial accounting standards that are developed. How might this influence differ in nations where there is no difference between income measurements for investor and taxation purposes?

13-30 Identify several areas of accounting practice where there are substantial differences among nations. In each case, defend what you consider to be the superior practice.

EXERCISES

Purchased Goodwill

13-31 The following excerpt is from the acquisitions note contained in Tyler Corporation's 1994 annual report:

> On January 7, 1994, the company completed the purchase of Institutional Financing Services, Inc. (IFS) . . . IFS was acquired for approximately $50,000,000 and the assumption of seasonal working capital debt of $12,800,000. The purchase price and expenses associated with the acquisition exceeded the fair value of IFS's net assets by approximately $40,854,000, which has been assigned to goodwill.

Required

a. Why did Tyler Corporation pay over $40 million more than the fair value of IFS's net assets?
b. If Tyler amortizes goodwill over 40 years, what would be the impact on the income statement for the annual amortization?

Consolidation

13-32 Goliath Corporation purchased all of Masonry Corporation's outstanding stock on January 1, 1999, for $6,000,000. The purchase price was paid as follows: Goliath Corporation issued 40,000 shares of its own common stock, par $1, with a market price of $102/share, and cash paid of $1,920,000. The acquisition was accounted for as a purchase. Therefore, Masonry's income statement has been included with Goliath's since the acquisition date. The estimated fair value and carrying value of the assets purchased and the liabilities assumed totaled $7,600,000 and $2,100,000. The excess of the purchase price over the fair value of the assets is being amortized over 40 years on a straight-line basis.

Required

a. Use the balance sheet equation to show how Goliath's financial statements will be affected by its acquisition of Masonry. (Assume that Masonry continues as a separate corporation.)
b. Determine any goodwill inherent in this acquisition.
c. Why did Goliath pay more than the fair value of Masonry's net assets?

Consolidation and Goodwill

13-33 On January 1, 1999, Maplegrove Deli, Inc. purchased all of the outstanding stock of Bizno's Sub Shops, Inc. for $4,500,000. Maplegrove paid $2,000,000 cash and issued 25,000 shares of its common stock, no par value, currently selling for $100 per share. The estimated fair value and carrying value of Bizno's assets (purchased by Maplegrove) and liabilities (assumed by Maplegrove) approximated $6,200,000 and $1,920,000 respectively. The excess of the purchase price over the fair value of the assets is being amortized over 40 years on a straight-line basis. During 1999, Bizno's earned a net income of $3,400,000 and paid dividends of $230,000.

Required

a. Use the balance sheet equation to show how Maplegrove's financial statements are affected at the date of acquisition.
b. How is Maplegrove affected by Bizno's net income and dividends?
c. How much goodwill should Maplegrove amortize? Show the effect on Maplegrove's balance sheet equation.
d. What is the net amount Maplegrove earned from owning Bizno's during the year?

PROBLEMS

Critical Thinking

Consolidation: Adjustment to the Income Statement

13-34 Presented below are condensed income statements for the MHL Company and its wholly owned subsidiary, PTE Inc., for the year ended December 31, 2000 (dollars in millions). MHL acquired its ownership of PTE in 1989.

	MHL Company	PTE Inc.
Sales	$260	$180
Cost of sales	(110)	(75)
Other operating expenses	(145)	(85)
Net income*	5	20

*MHL has not recognized any income during 2000 related to its ownership of PTE's shares.

Required

Explain how each of the following items would affect your preparation of a consolidated income statement for MHL and PTE:

a. During 2000, PTE made sales to MHL totaling $40 million.
b. At the end of 2000, MHL's inventory includes $10 million for items purchased from PTE. The cost of these sales incurred by PTE was $4.5 million.
c. At the beginning of 2000, none of MHL's inventory consisted of goods purchased from PTE.
d. Prepare a consolidated income statement for MHL Company for the year 1998.

Critical Thinking

Consolidation: Adjustments to the Balance Sheet

13-35 Presented below are condensed balance sheets for the ASAP Company and its wholly owned subsidiary, BYOB Inc., at December 31, 1999 (dollars in millions):

	ASAP Company	BYOB Inc.
Current assets	$ 30	$ 55
Noncurrent assets	210	95
Total	$240	$150
Liabilities	$110	$ 85
Shareholders' equity	130	65
Total	$240	$150

Required

Explain how each of the following items would affect your preparation of a consolidated balance sheet for ASAP and BYOB:

a. The noncurrent assets of ASAP include its investment in BYOB at a value of $65 million.

b. The current assets of BYOB include an account receivable from ASAP of $9 million.

c. The noncurrent assets of BYOB include land purchased from ASAP for $25 million. The cost of the land to ASAP was $7 million.

d. Prepare a consolidated balance sheet for ASAP Company on December 31, 1999.

Consolidation of Balance Sheets

13-36 Selected items from the unconsolidated financial statements of Tipton Financial Services, Inc., and its wholly owned subsidiary are provided below. Tipton accounts for its investment in Smartcom, Inc., using the equity method. Its investment cost is equal to Smartcom's net asset book value (shareholders' equity).

	Tipton (Dollars in thousands)	Smartcom
Total assets (including the investment)	$ 420,000	$210,000
Total liabilities	230,000	190,000
Total shareholders' equity	190,000	20,000
Sales	1,200,000	575,000
Interest expense	40,000	30,000
Net income	24,000	100

Required

a. Combine the two unconsolidated companies' financial statements and show the *consolidated* financial statements of Tipton, similar to Exhibit 13-2. Remember to eliminate Tipton's investment against Smartcom's shareholders' equity.

b. Calculate the following ratios for Tipton *before* and *after* consolidation:

- Debt-to-total assets ratio
- Return on shareholders' equity ratio (use ending shareholders' equity to approximate the average)

c. Comment on any differences in these ratios before and after consolidation.

Statement of Consolidation Policy

13-37 Cabot Corporation, a producer of specialty chemicals and materials, reported the following accounting policies for intercorporate investments:

Principles of Consolidation: The Consolidated Financial Statements include the accounts of Cabot Corporation and majority-owned and controlled domestic and foreign subsidiaries. Investments in majority-owned affiliates where control is temporary and investments in 20 to 50 percent-owned affiliates are accounted for on the equity method. All significant intercompany transactions have been eliminated.

Required

a. Cabot noted only "majority-owned and controlled" subsidiaries are included in the consolidation. Is it possible that majority ownership (greater than 50 percent) in a subsidiary would not constitute control? Discuss.
b. Why are subsidiaries that are less than 100 percent-owned included in the consolidation?
c. Cabot used the equity method to account for investments in 20- to 50 percent-owned affiliates. Explain how consolidation of these affiliates would affect Cabot's reported total assets, total liabilities, shareholders' equity, and net income.
d. Cabot stated that all significant intercompany transactions were eliminated. Provide several examples of intercompany transactions that require elimination in order to consolidate affiliated firms.

Effects of Consolidation on Selected Accounts and Ratios

13-38 Selected items from the unconsolidated financial statements of Mammoth Motors Company and its wholly owned subsidiary, Chattel Credit Corp., are provided below. Mammoth uses the equity method to account for its investment in Chattel, and the investment cost is equal to Chattel's book value of shareholders' equity.

	Mammoth Motors Co.	Chattel Credit Corp.
	(Dollars in millions)	
Total assets (including investments)	$29,000	$18,500
Total liabilities	15,500	17,700
Total shareholders' equity	13,500	800
Sales	54,000	10,200
Interest expense	4,000	—
Net income	3,000	1,100
Income tax rate	35%	30%

Required

a. Determine how the following items would be valued in Mammoth Motors' consolidated financial statements:
   - Total assets
   - Total liabilities
   - Shareholders' equity
   - Sales
   - Net income
b. Contrast the following financial ratios of Mammoth Motors before and after consolidation with Chattel Credit:
   - Debt-to-total assets ratio
   - Return on assets ratio
   - Return on shareholders' equity ratio
   - Operating income ratio
   - Asset turnover ratio

Interpreting Financial Statements: Affiliated Firms

13-39 Review Reebok's financial statements in Appendix E.

Required

a. Read Notes 1 and 12. Identify any unfamiliar or unusual terms. Match the terms presented in this chapter to the terms used by Reebok.
b. Determine whether Reebok's relationships with its subsidiaries seem to have a significant effect on the firm's liquidity, profitability, capital structure, or other important dimensions of the firm's performance.
c. Does the firm use the equity method of accounting for its ownership of affiliated companies? How does the firm's choice of method affect its results? To the extent possible, characterize the method used as being either conservative, aggressive, or in-between in terms of its impact on net income.

Allocation of Acquisition Cost in a Purchase

13-40 Ronco, Inc. purchased all of the outstanding voting stock of Nanco, Ltd. on January 1, 1999, at a cost of $750 million paid in cash. On the acquisition date, Nanco had the following assets and liabilities (dollars in millions):

	Book Value	Fair Market Value
Cash	$ 55	$ 55
Other assets	820	950
Liabilities	430	364

Required

a. Explain why the fair market values of Nanco's identifiable assets and liabilities may differ from their book or carrying values at the acquisition date.
b. Determine the excess of Ronco's investment cost over the book value of Nanco's net assets.
c. Determine the excess of Ronco's investment cost over the fair market value of Nanco's net assets.
d. Is goodwill implicit in the investment cost incurred by Ronco? If so, what amount would be reported as goodwill in Ronco's consolidated balance sheet on January 1, 1999?

Preparation of Consolidated Balance Sheet at Acquisition Date

13-41 On January 1, 1999, Tipper Company purchased all of Albert Inc.'s outstanding stock. The post-combination balance sheets of both firms are listed below (dollars in millions):

	Tipper Company	Albert Inc.
Cash	$ 20	$ 5
Accounts receivable	120	65
Other assets	950	330
Investment in Albert, Inc.	410	—
Total assets	$1500	$400
Liabilities	$650	160
Shareholders' equity	850	240
Total liabilities and shareholders' equity	$1500	$400

Additional information:

1. On the date of acquisition, Albert Inc.'s other assets had a fair market value of $380 million. All other components of net assets had fair market values approximately equal to book values.
2. Albert's accounts receivable include $25 million that is due from Tipper Company.

Required

a. Assume that Tipper Company will report a consolidated balance sheet on January 1, 1999. Indicate how each of the following items would be valued in the consolidated statement:

- Accounts receivable
- Other assets
- Investment in Albert Inc.
- Goodwill
- Liabilities
- Shareholders' equity

Critical Thinking

Valuation and Amortization of Goodwill

13-42 a. In the takeover battle between Viacom and QVC over Paramount, the potential cost of acquiring Paramount varied between $8 and $11.5 billion. How do you suppose a potential buyer (Viacom) would determine how much to pay in order to acquire another firm (Paramount)? To what extent would the assets and liabilities reported in Paramount's balance sheet influence the amounts offered for Paramount's ownership shares?

b. Assume that Viacom purchases Paramount for $11 billion and that the recorded value of Paramount's net assets at that date is $6.5 billion. For purposes of subsequent financial reports, how would Viacom account for the difference of $4.5 billion ($11 billion − $6.5 billion)? How would this difference affect the balance sheets and the income statements of Viacom in subsequent years?

Internet

Business Acquisitions

13-43 Access the EDGAR archives **(www.sec.gov/edaux/searches.htm)** and locate the 8-K report filed by Disney Enterprises Inc. (formerly Walt Disney Co.) on February 9, 1996. This report was filed on the successful acquisition of a communications corporation. Examine the 8-K report and answer the following questions based on *scenario 1:*

a. Which company did Disney acquire?

b. What were the separate revenue and operating incomes for each company prior to the acquisition (for the year ended September 30, 1995)? Refer to the Pro Forma Combined Condensed Statement of Income and identify the revenue and operating income for the same period had the companies been combined.

c. Separately calculate the operating income percentage and net income percentage (of net sales) for each company and for the combined company. What are your observations?

d. What were the total assets and total liabilities of each company? Compare it to the combined company. What do you observe?

Foreign Currency Transactions

13-44 In each of the following examples, determine the gain or loss resulting from foreign exchange transactions. All exchange rates are shown as the number of U.S. dollars required to obtain one unit of foreign currency.

a. Bancroft Company purchases supplies and records an account payable of 100,000 Japanese yen. The exchange rate on the purchase date is $0.007. When the account payable is paid, the exchange rate has risen to $0.008.
b. Vaughn Enterprises sells services and records an account receivable of 12,000 British pounds when the exchange rate is $1.55. Vaughan receives payment in pounds from the British buyer when the exchange rate is $1.60.
c. Bishop Chess Company records an account payable of 60,000 Swiss francs when the exchange rate is $0.65. At payment date, the exchange rate has fallen to $0.62.

Critical Thinking

Foreign Currency Transactions

13-45 In each of the following examples, determine the gain or loss resulting from foreign exchange transactions. All exchange rates are shown as the number of U.S. dollars required to obtain one unit of foreign currency.

a. Shipley Company purchases supplies and records an account payable of 82,000 Japanese yen. The exchange rate on the purchase date is $0.009. When the account payable is paid, the exchange rate has risen to $0.006.
b. Cameron Enterprises sells services and records an account receivable of 38,200 British pounds when the exchange rate is $1.38. Vaughan receives payment in pounds from the British buyer when the exchange rate is $1.44.
c. Bishop Chess Company records an account payable of 82,000 French francs when the exchange rate is $0.56. At payment date, the exchange rate has fallen to $0.51.
d. Describe how the firm might have hedged its foreign currency exposure by transactions to buy or sell foreign currencies in futures markets.

Critical Thinking

Foreign Currency Transactions: Unhedged Accounts Receivable and Payable

13-46 In each of the following cases, determine the amount of gain or loss to be reported in 1999 due to unhedged accounts receivable or payable that are denominated in foreign currencies. All exchange rates are stated as the number of U.S. dollars required to obtain one unit of foreign currency.

a. Asebrook Company recorded an account receivable of 10,000 British pounds in 1999 when the exchange rate was $1.50. At year-end, the exchange rate had risen to $1.60.
b. Baker Company recorded an account payable of 1,000,000 New Taiwan dollars in 1999 when the exchange rate was $0.04. At year-end, the exchange rate had risen to $0.05.
c. Hanno Company recorded an account receivable of 100,000 Canadian dollars in 1999 when the exchange rate was $0.75. At year-end, the exchange rate had fallen to $0.68.
d. Pfeiffer Company recorded an account payable of 50,000 Swiss francs in 1999 when the exchange rate was $0.60. At year-end, the exchange rate had fallen to $0.57.

e. In each of these cases (a through d), describe how the U.S. firm might have insulated itself from foreign exchange gains and losses by transactions in the foreign exchange forward market.

Foreign Currency Transactions and Hedging Activities

13-47 On October 1, 1999, the Keaton Company, a U.S. firm, sold merchandise to Chaplin, Inc., a British firm. The sales agreement specifies that Chaplin will make a payment of £500,000 to Keaton in 120 days on February 1, 1999. Relevant exchange rates are shown in the following table:

Date	Rate	$/£
October 1, 1999	Spot	$1.50
	30-day forward	1.48
	60-day forward	1.46
	90-day forward	1.42
	120-day forward	1.40
December 31, 1999	Spot	1.46
February 1, 2000	Spot	1.51

Required

a. Determine the amount of the account receivable and sales revenue to be recorded (in U.S. dollars) by the Keaton Company on the date of sale.
b. What amount of gain or loss would be reported by Keaton in 1999 and in 2000 if the foreign currency receivable is not hedged?
c. Describe how Keaton might hedge the above transaction in the forward market for British pounds. What is the amount of income or expense associated with the hedging transaction?
d. In retrospect on February 1, 2000, would it have been wise for Keaton to hedge the account receivable? Explain.

Interpreting Financial Statements: Foreign Currency Translation

13-48 Review Reebok's financial statements in Appendix E.

Required

a. Read Notes 1 and 13. Identify any unfamiliar or unusual terms. Match the terms presented in this chapter to the terms used by Reebok.
b. Does the firm's treatment of foreign currency translations seem to have any significant effect on its balance sheet? On its income statement?
c. What other impact might foreign currency translations have on the long-term success or failure of this firm? On other aspects of its financial statements? On other aspects of the firm's performance?

Foreign Currency Hedging

13-49 In Du Pont Corporation's 1994 annual report, Note 27 contained the following (partial) information:

Principal foreign currency exposures and related hedge positions on December 31, 1994, were as follows:

Currency (Dollars in millions)	Net Monetary Asset (Liability) Exposure	Open Contracts to Buy(Sell) Foreign Currency After Tax	Net After-Tax Exposure
British pound	$(1,428)	$1,427	$(1)
Dutch gilder	$ 273	$ (271)	$ 2
Italian lira	$ 205	$ (206)	$(1)

Required

Discuss the impact that hedging has had on Du Pont's financial statements.

Critical Thinking

Advantages and Disadvantages of Comprehensive Disclosures

13-50 a. Managers of U.S. firms sometimes allege that they are at a disadvantage when selling securities in international markets because U.S. disclosure and measurement standards are more comprehensive, stringent, and costly than are those of most other nations. Assume that these managers are correct and propose a solution to the problem.

b. Managers of non-U.S. firms sometimes argue that they are impeded from selling securities in U.S. financial markets because U.S. reporting standards are extensive and costly to implement. Propose a diplomatic solution to the problem, with due consideration to the costs and benefits of foreign and domestic business firms.

Translation of Foreign Currency Financial Statements

13-51 The balance sheet and income statement of Buchanen, Inc., a subsidiary of a U.S. company, is shown below. Buchanen, Inc. operates in New Zealand and prepares its financial statements in New Zealand dollars (NZ$).

Buchanen, Inc.
Balance Sheet and Income Statement
December 31, 2000
(NZ$ in millions)

Income Statement		Balance Sheet			
Revenues	NZ$ 1,200	Assets	NZ$ 1,500	Liabilities	NZ$ 600
Expenses	(900)			Paid-in capital	150
Net income	NZ$ 300			Retained earnings	750
			NZ$ 1,500		NZ$ 1,500

Supplementary information:
Exchange rates (US$/NZ$):

Average during 2000	.55
Spot rate, December 31, 2000	.60
Historical rate when capital stock was issued	.75
Beginning balance in retained earnings, in US$	$500.00

No dividends to shareholders were declared during 2000.

Required

a. Translate Buchanen's financial statements into U.S. dollars so that they can be consolidated with those of the U.S. parent firm.
b. Has the U.S. dollar strengthened or weakened relative to the New Zealand dollar during 2000? Explain how this change has affected Buchanen's translated balance sheet.
c. Explain why a translation adjustment is required in order to bring the translated balance sheet into balance.

Reconciliation of Income and Shareholders' Equity: The United States and the United Kingdom

13-52 Foreign companies whose shares are registered on U.S. security exchanges must file a description of significant differences between U.S. and domestic accounting principles with the SEC, as well as a reconciliation of net income and shareholders' equity under domestic and U.S. GAAP.

Antic Knights, plc, a British firm, included the following information in its SEC filings for 2000:

1. Summary of Differences Between United Kingdom and United States Generally Accepted Accounting Principles:
   (a) *Acquisition Cost*
   Under United Kingdom GAAP, certain acquisition-related costs can be immediately charged to retained earnings. Under United States GAAP, these costs are charged to the statement of earnings as incurred. Examples of such items include certain costs related to the closure of facilities and severances of terminated employees.
   (b) *Deferred Taxation*
   United Kingdom GAAP allows for no provision for deferred taxation to be made if there is reasonable evidence that such taxation will not be payable in the foreseeable future. United States GAAP requires provisions for deferred taxation be made for all differences between the tax basis and book basis of assets and liabilities.
   (c) *Goodwill and Other Intangibles*
   The Company writes off certain intangible assets, including goodwill, covenants not to compete, and favorable lease rights, directly to retained earnings in the year of acquisition. Under U.S. GAAP these intangible assets would be capitalized as assets and amortized over their estimated useful lives.
2. Reconciliations of Net Income and Shareholders' Equity:

Net Income Reconciliation
For the year ended
March 31, 2000
(Pounds in Thousands)

Net earnings before extraordinary items	£ 19,726
Amortization of goodwill	(10,292)
Acquisition costs	(3,012)
Deferred income taxes	(333)
Other	(1,895)
Estimated earnings, U.S. GAAP	£ 4,194

Shareholders' Equity Reconciliation
For the year ended
March 31, 2000
(Pounds in Thousands)

Shareholders' equity	£ 8,652
Goodwill	13,312
Deferred taxes	(509)
Other	1,172
Shareholders' equity, U.S. GAAP	£22,627

Required

a. For each of the indicated differences between U.S. and U.K. GAAP, indicate which method of accounting you consider to be more suitable to the needs of investor analysts. Explain your reasoning.
b. Based on the information provided, do you consider U.K. or U.S. GAAP to be more conservative? Explain.
c. Based on the explanations of differences between U.K. and U.S. GAAP, explain why each of the individual reconciling items is added (or subtracted) to convert to U.S. GAAP. (For example, why is goodwill subtracted in the income reconciliation and added in the shareholders' equity reconciliation?)

Critical Thinking

Reconciliation of Income and Shareholders' Equity: The United States and Chile

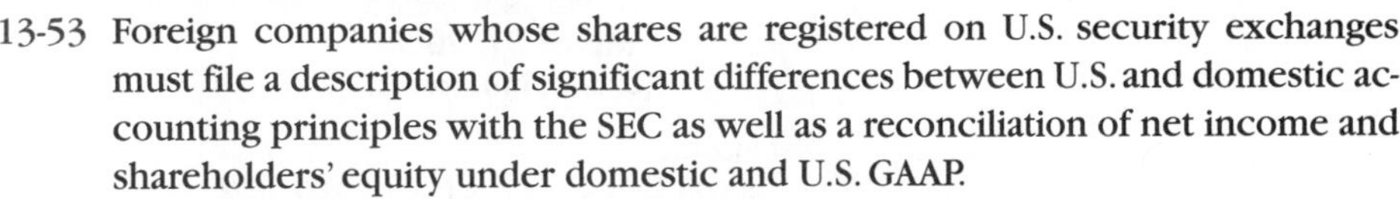

13-53 Foreign companies whose shares are registered on U.S. security exchanges must file a description of significant differences between U.S. and domestic accounting principles with the SEC as well as a reconciliation of net income and shareholders' equity under domestic and U.S. GAAP.

Goldplate Company, Inc., a Chilean firm, included the following information:

1. *Differences in Measurement Methods*

   The principal methods applied in preparing the accompanying financial statements that have resulted in amounts which differ from those that would have otherwise been determined under U.S. GAAP, are as follows:

   (a) *Inflation Accounting*

   The cumulative inflation rate in Chile, as measured by the Consumer Price Index, for the three-year period ended December 31, 2000, was approximately 85 percent.

   Chilean accounting principles require that financial statements be restated to reflect the full effects of loss in the purchasing power of the Chilean peso on the financial position and the results of reporting entities' operations. The method is based on a model in which net inflation gains or losses caused by monetary assets and liabilities exposed to changes in the purchasing power of local currency are calculated by restating all nonmonetary accounts of the financial statements.

   The inclusion of price-level adjustments in the accompanying financial statements is considered appropriate under the prolonged inflationary conditions affecting the Chilean economy.

   (b) *Revaluations of Property, Plant, and Equipment*

   Certain property, plant, and equipment are reported in the financial statements at amounts determined in accordance with a technical appraisal carried out in 1997. Revaluation of property, plant, and equipment is an accounting principle not generally accepted in the United States.

   (c) *Vacation Expense*

   The cost of vacations earned by employees is generally recorded by the Company on a pay-as-you-go basis. Accounting principles generally accepted in the United States require that this expense be recorded on the accrual basis as the vacations are earned.

(d) *Inventory Valuation*
Finished and in-process products are reported on the financial statements at the replacement cost of the raw materials included therein and therefore exclude labor and overhead, the practice of which is contrary to U.S. GAAP.

(e) *Write-Up of Noncurrent Asset*
Net income reported in the Chilean GAAP financial statements as of December 31, 2000, includes the effects of the reversal of a valuation allowance recorded in prior years to writing down the carrying value of disposable land to estimated market value.

2. Reconciliations of Net Income and Shareholders' Equity:

Net Income Reconciliation For the year ended March 31, 2000 (CH$ in thousands)		Shareholders' Equity Reconciliation For the year ended March 31, 2000 (CH$ in thousands)	
Net income, Chilean GAAP	CH$ 14,201,342	Shareholders' equity	CH$ 36,773,825
Depreciation on revaluation	43,188	Property revaluations	(4,259,726)
Provision for vacations	(58,984)	Inventory costing	67,592
Reverse asset write-up	(1,744,402)	Other	(2,154,501)
Other	627,904		
Net income, U.S. GAAP	CH$ 13,069,048	Shareholders' equity, U.S. GAAP	CH$ 30,427,190

Required

a. For each of the individual differences between U.S. and Chilean GAAP, indicate which method of accounting you consider to be the most useful to investor analysts. Explain your reasoning.

b. Based on the information provided above, do you consider Chilean or U.S. GAAP to be more conservative? Explain.

c. Discuss why each of the individual reconciling items is added (or subtracted) in converting from Chilean to U.S. GAAP.

Interpreting Financial Statements: Affiliated Firms

Critical Thinking

13-54 The PolyGram Group includes businesses around the world that are chiefly involved in acquisition, production, and marketing in the music industry, as well as the manufacture, sale, and distribution of prerecorded sound carriers, such as compact discs, cassettes, and records. In addition, PolyGram is engaged in activities with respect to music video, in the production of films and television programming, and in music publishing. Its income statements are summarized below (in millions of Netherlands guilders).

	1994	1993
Net sales	8,600	7,416
Direct costs of sales	(4,543)	(3,909)
Gross income	4,057	3,507
Selling, general and administrative expenses	(2,988)	(2,575)
Income from operations	1,069	932
Financial income and expenses	8	(5)
Income before taxes	1,077	927
Income taxes	(302)	(264)
Income after taxes	775	663
Equity in income of nonconsolidated companies	(9)	(20)
Group income	766	643
Minority interests	(28)	(29)
Net income	738	614

Required

a. Discuss any unusual terms or disclosure practices in PolyGram's income statement.
b. Discuss how and why PolyGram's income has been reduced due to minority interests and other interests in affiliated companies.
c. Did these interests have a significant effect on PolyGram's income? Why?
d. What other information would you like to have about PolyGram's interests in affiliated companies? Why?
e. Evaluate PolyGram's profitability. Consider its operating income separately from group income and from net income.

Critical Thinking

Interpreting Financial Statements: Effects of U.S. GAAP

13-55 Polygram's financial statements included the following additional disclosure (see preceding problem):

The calculation of Net income . . . substantially in accordance with U.S. GAAP, is as follows (in millions of Netherlands guilders):

	1994	1993
Net income per PolyGram's Consolidated Statements of Income	738	614
Adjustments to reported income:		
a. Amortization of goodwill	(27)	(26)
b. Amortization of intangible assets	(57)	(64)
c. Remeasurement of financial statements of entities in hyper-inflated countries	(13)	5
d. Other	5	5
Approximate net income in accordance with U.S. GAAP	646	534

Required

a. Discuss any unfamiliar terms used by PolyGram in this note.
b. How have the applications of U.S. GAAP affected PolyGram's reported net income? Do these differences seem significant? Why?
c. Reevaluate PolyGram's profitability (see preceding case). Does this new information change your assessment of PolyGram's profitability? How?
d. Why do you think PolyGram reports net income at higher levels in its primary financial statements and then at lower levels after applying U.S. GAAP?
e. Which of PolyGram's disclosures of net income is more conservative? Which is more comparable to other U.S. companies? Which would you prefer as a manager? As an investor? As a financial analyst? Discuss these differences.

Foreign Currency Effects

13-56 Boise Cascade Company is a major producer of paper, building, and office products. The company reported the following items related to foreign exchange gains and losses in its 1993 financial statements (dollars in thousands):

	1993	1992
Foreign exchange gain	$1,610	$6,590

Notes:

Foreign exchange gains and losses reported on the Statements of Income (Loss) arose primarily from activities of the Company's Canadian subsidiaries. On December 31, 1993, contracts for the purchase of 50,000,000 Canadian dollars were outstanding. Gains or losses in the market value of the forward contracts were recorded as they were incurred during the year and partially offset gains or losses arising from translation of the Canadian subsidiaries' net liabilities.

Required

a. The Note discussion indicates that the firm, through its Canadian subsidiaries, has ***net liabilities,*** in Canadian dollars. Explain the meaning of this term.
b. From the information provided, are you able to tell whether the U.S. dollar strengthened or weakened against the Canadian dollar during 1993? Explain.
c. Does Boise Cascade attempt to fully "hedge" its foreign currency transactions? Explain.

Internet

Foreign Currency Effects

13-57 Kimberly-Clark is a global corporation whose primary product is diapers and tissues. Access the EDGAR archives **(www.gov.sec/edaux/searches.htm)** to locate Kimberly-Clark's 1995 10-K. Answer the following questions based on its Note on Foreign Currency Related Issues.

a. What is the dollar impact of foreign currency transactions included in consolidated net income?
b. How does the company translate the financial statements of foreign operations other than those in hyper-inflationary economies?
c. How does the company translate monetary assets (accounts receivable and cash) of subsidiaries located in hyper-inflationary economies?
d. Determine the dollar impact on the company of the Mexican peso devaluation in 1995.

Financial Analysis in the U.S. and U.K.

13-58 Access the EDGAR archives **(www.sec.gov/edaux/searches.htm)** and locate the Schedule 14D1 filing (February 1, 1995) made by Cadbury Schweppes on the successful acquisition of Dr. Pepper/Seven-Up Companies Inc. *Hint:* Search on "Cadbury" or "Dr. Pepper." Examine the section that contains the financial statements of the U.K. corporation and locate the information on differences between U.K. GAAP and U.S. GAAP. In this section, the company has provided a GAAP reconciliation.

Required

a. What are the primary reasons for the differences in net income and shareholders' equity from U.K. GAAP to U.S. GAAP.
b. Explain the treatments of goodwill and trademarks under U.K. GAAP. How do these differ from U.S. GAAP?
c. Calculate the return on equity under both U.K. and U.S. GAAP. Explain how the different accounting standards have an impact on the computed ratios.

Financial Analysis in the U.S. and U.K.

13-59 Access the EDGAR archives **(www.sec.gov/edaux/searches.htm)** and locate the Schedule 14D1 filing made by either Amdura Corporation or FKI plc on March 22, 1995 (they are identical). *Hint:* You can search for this filing on the SEC database by inputting the name of either company. It was filed when FKI plc, a U.K. corporation, made a successful tender offer for Amdura Corp., a U.S. corporation. The Schedule 14D1 contains, among other things, the financial statements of FKI plc as per U.K. GAAP and a reconciliation of its net income and shareholders' equity as per U.K. GAAP to the U.S. GAAP equivalent.

Required

a. Calculate the return on equity of FKI plc per U.K. GAAP and per U.S. GAAP. Explain the major reasons for the difference.
b. Calculate the return on assets and operating income percentage of FKI per U.K. GAAP and U.S. GAAP, and explain the difference.
c. Compare the ratios of FKI plc with the return on equity, return on assets, and operating income percentage of Parker-Hannifin (access EDGAR for the raw data to compute the ratios), a U.S.-based competitor of FKI plc. Should one use the U.S. GAAP-based numbers or the U.K. GAAP-based numbers for FKI plc?

chapter

14 Additional Dimensions of Financial Reporting

LEARNING OBJECTIVES

1. Understand and interpret comprehensive income.
2. Interpret the financial statements of firms that have undertaken accounting changes.
3. Analyze information about operating segments.
4. Describe annual and interim reports.
5. Identify reports filed with the Securities and Exchange Commission (SEC).
6. Explain the efficient market hypothesis and its implications for accounting.
7. Describe the two major roles of financial accounting.
8. Understand the motivations for and methods of earnings management.

INTRODUCTION

This chapter deals with several important financial reporting issues that have not yet been fully addressed. These issues include comprehensive income, accounting changes, operating segment disclosures, annual and interim reports, reports filed with the SEC, the relationship between accounting information and stock prices, and a synthesis of the major roles that financial accounting information plays in our society. An understanding of these topics will make you a more sophisticated user of accounting information.

COMPREHENSIVE INCOME

A major focus of this text has been on net income and the long-standing conventional income statement. As of 1998, however, firms are required to disclose another important income measure: **comprehensive income.** The motivation for requiring disclosure of this new measure is that generally accepted accounting principles (GAAP) mandate that certain changes in the value of assets and liabilities be excluded from net income.

To illustrate, recall the treatment of marketable equity securities described in Chapter 6, "Current Assets." At year-end, the carrying value of securities classified as available-for-sale is increased or decreased to reflect current market value. However, that value change is not reflected in net income. Instead, the value change is included in a separate component of shareholders' equity. The Financial Accounting Standards Board (FASB) adopted this treatment due to the lobbying efforts of corporate managers. Managers prefer to exclude from income items that are volatile and that make income more difficult to control. The FASB reached a compromise: The securities are revalued, but the value change is excluded from net income until the securities are sold.

Many financial statement readers believe that this exclusion and several other similar ones reduce the usefulness of the net income figure. Because of this, the FASB now requires firms to report comprehensive income, which is defined as net income plus revenues, expenses, gains, and losses that are excluded from net income. These items include unrealized gains and losses on certain marketable securities, foreign currency items, changes in the market value of certain futures contracts, and changes in the additional pension liability provision.

Financial Statement Presentation

In displaying comprehensive income, firms can choose from the one-statement approach or the two-statement approach (a third approach is available, but the FASB discourages its use). The two-statement approach leaves the conventional income statement intact and a new statement, the statement of comprehensive income, is included. This statement starts with net income and the other items of comprehensive income are then added to net income. The final figure is comprehensive income. Exhibit 14-1 contains an example of the two-statement approach.

The one-statement approach extends the conventional income statement. Although the conventional format ends with net income, the extended statement includes the other items of comprehensive income to net income. The final figure of that statement would then be comprehensive income. Exhibit 14-2 illustrates the one statement approach.

EXHIBIT 14-1 Comprehensive Income: Two-Statement Approach

Bosch, Inc.
Statement of Income
Year ended December 31, 2001
(dollars in thousands)

Net sales	$250,000
Cost of products sold	150,000
Gross profit	100,000
Marketing and administrative expenses	40,000
Operating profit	60,000
Income taxes	25,000
Net income	$35,000

Bosch, Inc.
Statement of Comprehensive Income
Year ended December 31, 2001
(dollars in thousands)

Net income	$35,000
Other comprehensive income, net of tax:	
Foreign currency translation adjustment	4,000
Unrealized loss on securities	(5,000)
Comprehensive income	$34,000

EXHIBIT 14-2 Comprehensive Income: One-Statement Approach

Bosch, Inc.
Statement of Income and Comprehensive Income
Year ended December 31, 2001
(dollars in thousands)

Net sales	$250,000
Cost of products sold	150,000
Gross profit	100,000
Marketing and administrative expenses	40,000
Operating profit	60,000
Income taxes	25,000
Net income	35,000
Other comprehensive income, net of tax:	
Foreign currency translation adjustment	4,000
Unrealized loss on securities	(5,000)
Comprehensive income	$ 34,000

Assessment of Comprehensive Income Reporting

Differences between net income and comprehensive income arise solely because GAAP requires that the recorded value changes in certain assets and liabilities be excluded from net income. Many FASB critics argue that these exclusions are the result of undesirable political compromises by the FASB and reduce the usefulness of net income. The required disclosure of comprehensive income has the effect of reporting a figure that would equal net income if the FASB had not made those compromises. Thus, many financial statement readers view comprehensive income as a more useful number than net income. This suggests that analyses and ratio calculations that include net income should also be conducted using comprehensive income.

ACCOUNTING CHANGES

The term **accounting changes** includes three types of accounting events:

- A **change in accounting principle**,
- A **change in accounting estimate**, and
- A **change in reporting entity.**

Since the accounting for each type of change is different, they are discussed separately.

Change in Accounting Principle

In many situations, corporate managers are free to choose from several acceptable accounting methods. For example, LIFO or FIFO can be used for inventory valuation, and an accelerated or straight-line method can be used to calculate depreciation expense. Although managers can choose between alternative GAAP, once a method is selected, it should be used consistently from period to period. This enhances the interperiod comparability of financial statements. In other words, if a firm consistently uses the same accounting principles from one period to another, changes in the financial statement numbers over time will likely reflect changes in the underlying economics of the firm, rather than the effect of an accounting principle change.

Although the consistent use of accounting principles is desirable, firms do occasionally change from one principle to another. Because financial statement readers do not usually expect such changes, these changes are highlighted in the auditor's report. Since the existence of an accounting change dramatically alters the interpretation of financial statements, a review of the auditor's report should always be one of the first steps in the analysis of financial statements.

An accounting principle change can be accounted for in several ways. Each approach is used only in clearly defined circumstances.

General Rule To illustrate the general rule, consider a change in the depreciation method for a machine that originally cost $3,700, has an estimated salvage value of $700, and an estimated life of five years. Assume that during the first two years of the machine's life, the straight-line method was used. In the third year, the sum-of-the-years' digits method was adopted.

The general rule requires a **cumulative effect** adjustment. In the year of the change, the account balances are restated to show the amounts that would have appeared if the new method had been used all along. This requires a comparison of depreciation charges under the two methods.

Annual depreciation expense under the straight-line method is $600 [($3,700 − $700)/5], or a total of $1,200 for the first two years. Under the sum-of-the-years' digits method, total depreciation expense for the first two years would be $1,800:

	Depreciable Base		Fraction		Depreciation
Year 1	($3,700 − $700)	×	5/15	=	$1,000
Year 2	($3,700 − $700)	×	4/15	=	800
					$1,800

If the sum-of-the-years' digits method had originally been used, depreciation expense for the two years would have been higher by a total of $600. What effect would this have had on the accounting records at the beginning of year three? First, accumulated depreciation would have been higher by $600. Second, because depreciation expense would have been higher, net income and retained earnings would have been lower by $600. The analysis (which for simplicity ignores the tax effect) is as follows:

ASSETS	=	LIABILITIES	+	SHAREHOLDERS' EQUITY
Accumulated depreciation − $600				Retained earnings − $600 (Cumulative effect of accounting principle change)

The cumulative effect of $600 appears as the last item on the income statement in the year of the accounting principle change. Future years' depreciation expenses are based on the sum-of-the-years' digits method.

The general rule for reporting an accounting principle change results in two inconsistencies between the year of the change and prior years:

1. The cumulative effect of adopting the change is included in the adoption year's income. No comparable amount appears in prior or subsequent years' income.
2. Depreciation expense in the year of the change is based on the new method, while in prior years it was based on the old method.

Because of these inconsistencies, GAAP requires footnote disclosure of what net income would have been in the current and prior years had the new method been used. Many accountants refer to these as **pro forma amounts.** Because the pro forma amounts are based on the new accounting principle, valid comparisons can be drawn between the current and prior years. Valid comparisons can also be made between the pro forma amounts and the regularly reported results of future years.

Exhibit 14-3 contains a condensed income statement and a note from the 1997 financial statements of BE Aerospace, Inc. (BE), the world's largest manufacturer of commercial aircraft cabin interior products, such as aircraft seats, food and beverage preparation and storage equipment, and in-flight entertainment systems. In 1996, BE evaluated its accounting policy of capitalizing (recording as an asset) engineering costs incurred before a contract had been signed with a customer. This policy is rather liberal and results in higher reported asset values and higher reported income. In 1996, BE adopted the more conservative policy of expensing these costs. BE's new policy is more consistent with that used by most of its rivals. BE appropriately accounted for this accounting principle change by using the cumulative effect adjustment, which is included in the 1996 income statement.

Under the cumulative effect approach, intertemporal (across time) comparability of net income is compromised both by inclusion of the cumulative effect in 1996 net income and by the fact that a policy of capitalization was employed prior to 1996 and a policy of expensing was used starting in 1996. The note included in Exhibit 14-3 provides pro forma amounts that restate net earnings (loss) for 1996 and 1995, assuming retroactive application of the new (expensing) policy. Because the reported results for 1997 are based on the new policy, pro forma amounts are not necessary. Given that the reported 1997 figures are based on the new policy and the pro forma amounts for 1996 and 1995 are based on retroactive application of the new policy, the appropriate intertemporal comparisons are as follows (in thousands):

	1997	**1996**	**1995**
Net earnings (loss)	$13, 709	$(60,081)	$(35,398)

Reality Check 14-1 contains information about an accounting principle change made by Seaboard Corporation.

Exceptions Some accounting principle changes are accounted for **retroactively.** Under this approach, prior years' financial statements are restated to reflect the use of the new method. The obvious advantage of the retroactive approach is that the financial statements of the current and prior years are based on a common set of accounting principles. However, reissuing financial statements with numbers different from those that originally appeared may dilute the public's confidence in financial reporting.

The retroactive approach is only used in the following situations:

1. a change from LIFO to another inventory method,
2. a change in the method of accounting for long-term construction contracts,

3. a change to or from the full-cost method by firms in the extractive industries,
4. a change made by a firm issuing financial statements to the public for the first time, or
5. when required as part of the transition process for a new FASB standard.

The first three changes often result in large cumulative effects that would greatly compromise the interperiod comparability of financial statements. Consequently, these changes are accounted for by retroactive restatement. The fourth situation is one

EXHIBIT 14-3 Accounting Principle Change: Cumulative Effect Approach

BE Aerospace, Inc.
Consolidated Statement of Operations (Condensed)
(Dollars in Thousands)

	1997	1996	1995
Net sales	$412,379	$232,582	$229,347
Cost of sales	270,557	160,031	154,863
Gross profit	141,822	72,551	74,484
Other expenses	126,591	132,632	93,356
Earnings (loss) before income taxes and cumulative effect of accounting change	15,231	(60,081)	(18,872)
Income taxes	1,522	—	(6,806)
Earnings (loss) before cumulative effect of accounting change	13,709	(60,081)	(12,066)
Cumulative effect of change in accounting principle	—	(23,332)	—
Net earnings (loss)	$ 13,709	$ (83,413)	$ (12,066)

Note 2. Accounting Change. In fiscal 1996, the Company undertook a comprehensive review of the engineering capitalization policies followed by its competitors and others in its industry peer group. The results of this study and an evaluation of the Company's policy led the company to conclude that it should adopt the accounting method that it believes is followed by most of its competitors and certain members of its industry peer group. Previously, the Company had capitalized precontract engineering costs as a component of inventories, which were then amortized to earnings as the product was shipped. The Company now expenses such costs as they are incurred. While the accounting policy for precontract engineering expenditures previously followed by the Company was in accordance with generally accepted accounting principles, the changed policy is preferable.

The effect of this change in accounting for periods through February 25, 1995 was a charge of $23,332 ($1.44 per share); the effect of expensing engineering costs for the year ended February 24, 1996 was a charge of $42,114 ($2.60). The following table summarizes the pro forma net earnings (loss) and per share amounts for each period presented. Primarily as a result of this accounting change, inventories decreased by $65,446 as of February 24, 1996.

Pro forma amounts assuming the change in application of the accounting principle applied retroactively (unaudited) are as follows:

	Year Ended	
	February 24, 1996	February 25, 1995
Net loss	$(60,081)	$(35,398)
Net loss per share	$ (3.71)	$ (2.20)

REALITY CHECK 14-1

Seaboard Corporation reported the following financial information (dollars in thousands):

	1997	1996	1995
Earnings before cumulative effect of accounting change	$30,574	$2,840	$20,202
Cumulative effect of changing the accounting for inventories, net of tax expense of $1,922	—	3,006	—
Net earnings	$30,574	$5,846	$20,202

Assume that other than the cumulative effect, earnings were not materially affected by the change.

Required

Identify the earnings number for each year that would permit valid comparisons.

Solution

Because 1996 was the only year affected by the change, reported earnings for 1997 and 1995 can be used. For 1996, earnings before the cumulative effect should be used. The valid comparisons involve the following:

1997	$30,574
1996	2,840
1995	20,202

in which the general public has not previously seen the firm's financial statements. Accordingly, the public would be best served by a set of financial statements that is comparable across time periods. The fifth exception acknowledges that the FASB uses a variety of transition methods when issuing new standards.

Change in Accounting Estimates

Many financial statement figures are based on estimates. Depreciation expense and the book value of fixed assets, for example, are determined by estimates of useful lives and salvage values. As another example, uncollectible accounts expense and the net value of accounts receivable are based on estimates of the number of customers that will not honor their obligations to the firm.

An inherent aspect of estimates is that they do not always prove to be correct. Conceptually, changes in accounting estimates could be accounted for retroactively. That is, when an estimate proves faulty, prior years' financial statements could be restated. However, that treatment has been rejected by the accounting profession. For most firms of even modest size, a large number of estimates will miss their mark. The retroactive approach would result in firms continually restating financial statements, which would seriously compromise the credibility and usefulness of financial reporting.

Instead, changes in accounting estimates are accounted for **prospectively** by including them in the year of the change and in future years, if appropriate. To illustrate, assume that a machine is acquired for $14,000 in 1999. It has a salvage value of $2,000 and an estimated life of five years. Straight-line depreciation is used and the annual depreciation charge is $2,400:

$$\text{Annual depreciation expense} = \frac{(\$14{,}000 - \$2{,}000)}{5} = \$2{,}400$$

Assume that at the beginning of 2001 the machine's total useful life is now estimated to be eight years. Depreciation expense for 1999 and 2000 is not changed. The remaining depreciable base is depreciated over the remaining useful life of six years. Annual depreciation expense for 2001 through 2006 is $1,200:

Cost	$14,000
Less salvage value	(2,000)
Less depreciation to date	(4,800)
Remaining depreciable base	$ 7,200

$$\text{Annual depreciation expense} = \frac{\text{Remaining depreciable base}}{\text{Remaining life}}$$

$$= \frac{\$7{,}200}{6}$$

$$= \$1{,}200$$

The effect of changes in accounting estimates on net income must be disclosed in the notes to the financial statements. As a practical matter, although virtually all firms experience changes in accounting estimates, they are usually too small (immaterial) to require disclosure.

Change in Reporting Entity

A change in a reporting entity occurs when a firm changes the specific subsidiaries included in its consolidated financial statements (see Chapter 13, "Reporting Issues for Affiliated and International Companies"). This situation often arises when the parent first acquires the majority share of a subsidiary's voting stock.

The acquisition and consolidation of a new subsidiary essentially result in a different reporting entity. The new subsidiary might substantially change the consolidated group's size, scope, and scale of operations, as well as the nature of the products and services provided. Accordingly, the results of the new consolidated group cannot be validly compared to the results of the old group as previously reported.

A change in a reporting entity is accounted for retroactively. Prior years' financial statements are restated to reflect the past results of the new consolidated group. This approach ensures the comparability of the financial statements.

SEGMENT REPORTING

Many large corporations engage in a variety of different business activities and operate in various economic and geographic environments. They also serve many customers, both large and small, and financial statements provide figures covering all such groups. Many analysts, however, feel that they would benefit from more detailed information. They suggest that this information could assist them in making better estimates of a firm's risk and expected return. For example, a firm that generates 10 percent of its revenue and profit from software development and 90 percent from manufacturing breakfast cereal will have a different risk and return outlook than one that generates 10 percent of its revenue and profit from breakfast cereal and 90 percent from software development.

Accordingly, all publicly held corporations are required to make certain disclosures in financial statement notes. These disclosure requirements are summarized in the following sections.

Operating Segments

An **operating segment** is a component of a firm (a) that engages in business activities from which it can earn revenues and incur expenses, (b) whose operating results are regularly reviewed by the firm's chief operating decision maker, and (c) for which financial information is available. This definition is intentionally broad and recognizes that firms are organized in different ways. Some firms are organized around the products that are produced and distributed, which is the way many large diversified corporations are organized. Other firms are organized based on the type of customer. An auto parts distributor, for example, could have separate divisions to sell to professionals (repair shops) and to individual car owners (via its own retail outlets). Still other firms could be organized based on geography, with each region or country constituting its own segment.

Operating segments correspond to the organizational subunits that the firm's top management uses in evaluating performance and allocating resources. The advantage of this approach is that financial statement readers are provided with the same view of the firm and the same information that is used by top management. The disadvantage is that operating segment classifications across firms are not uniform, and interfirm comparisons of segment information is difficult.

For each major segment, firms must report

1. Profit or loss.
2. Total assets.
3. A number of other amounts, such as revenue from external customers and depreciation expense, but only if those amounts are included in the profit or loss measure used by the chief operating decision maker.

The measurement of each segment item listed above is to be the amount used by the chief operating decision maker. The calculation of these amounts need not comply with GAAP. Recall that for internal purposes, managers can use whatever information they find relevant. The FASB has now mandated that these internal measures be reported to the public (which includes a firm's competitors). Firms must also explain how the measurements are made and some of them must be reconciled to figures appearing on the GAAP-based financial statements.

Geographic Areas

A firm is also required to report information about its activities in different geographic areas. In particular, a firm must separately report revenue generated from its country of domicile and revenue generated in all foreign countries. A firm must also report long-lived assets located in the country of domicile and long-lived assets located in all foreign countries. If any of the above amounts attributed to an individual foreign country is material, separate disclosure is required.

Because political stability varies considerably from country to country, information about foreign activities is particularly helpful in assessing a firm's risk. The safety of a firm's assets in a relatively unstable country or the continuity of sales in such a country might be highly uncertain. This is an important consideration in estimating risk. For example, ICN Pharmaceuticals Inc. recently took a $172 million charge when the Yugoslav government defaulted on loan payments. ICN subsequently suspended sales in Yugoslavia, which accounted for about 30 percent of ICN's revenue.

Major Customers

A customer is considered to be a **major customer** if it accounts for 10 percent or more of a firm's revenue. Total revenue generated by each major customer must be disclosed as well as the operating segment that services the client; the customer need not be identified. This information provides insights into the riskiness of a firm's revenue stream. Greater risk is indicated if a few customers from one segment account for a large portion of revenue. If customers from that segment concurrently experience economic difficulties, the firm's revenue may suffer significantly. Moreover, a customer who accounts for a sizable portion of revenue may be able to demand significant concessions, which could have an unfavorable effect on the firm's future financial performance.

An Illustration

Exhibit 14-4 contains segment information for Global Enterprises, Inc., which has three operating segments:

1. **Chemical Specialties** produces chemicals for use by paper manufacturers and water-soluble polymers that enhance the storage and usage of liquid products.
2. **Food and Functional Products** produces items such as food gums used in processed meats and baked goods as well as fat substitutes.
3. **Aerospace** provides propulsion systems for virtually all space and military programs.

Based on sales and assets, the segments are generally of comparable size. To assess the relative profitability of the three segments, divide operating profit by assets. This is similar to the return on assets calculation discussed in Chapter 4, "The Income Statement." The results for 2001 are

- Chemical Specialties 23.1%
- Food and Functional Products 14.3%
- Aerospace 20.0%

Segment data can also help analysts to assess risks and future trends. For example, the success of Global's low-fat products will depend on consumer attitudes regarding their diets and their efforts to "eat right." In contrast, the aerospace segment's success will be determined by its capability to adapt to a post-Cold War environment. The trend in the profitability of the aerospace segment is quite favorable; its profit doubled in 2001 over the previous year.

Exhibit 14-4 also contains disclosures by geographic area. The majority of Global's sales take place in the United States, although about 38 percent of its sales occur in other countries. Thus, for example, the attitudes of consumers in both the United States and abroad will affect the success of Global's low-fat products.

EXHIBIT 14-4 Global Enterprises, Inc, Segment Reporting Disclosure

Operating Segment and Geographic Area Disclosures
(Dollars in Millions)

	Chemical Specialties	Food & Functional Products	Aerospace	Corporate & Other	Total
Operating Segments					
2001					
Net Sales	$ 900	$800	$ 700	$200	$2,600
Profit (Loss) from Operations	150	100	120	(50)	320
Total Assets	650	700	600	250	2,200
Depreciation	60	50	55	20	185
2000					
Net Sales	825	770	650	180	2,425
Profit (Loss) from Operations	130	80	60	(45)	225
Total Assets	630	675	580	225	2,110
Depreciation	55	45	50	15	165

Geographic Area	**U.S.**	**Foreign**	**Total**
2001			
Net Sales	$1,600	$1,000	$2,600
Long-Lived Assets	1,000	500	1,500
2000			
Net Sales	1,400	1,025	2,425
Long-Lived Assets	970	480	1,450

ANNUAL REPORTS

All publicly held corporations and many closely held ones issue their financial statements as part of an **annual report** to shareholders. Because these reports are a major means of communicating with shareholders, corporations take great care in their preparation. The reports are usually prepared on glossy paper, contain interesting photographs, and are sometimes quite lengthy. The 1997 annual report of Marsh & McLennan Companies, Inc., for example, is 57 pages long. Excerpts from two annual reports appear at the end of this text in Appendixes D, "Wendy's International, Inc.," and E, "Reebok International Ltd."

In addition to the financial statements and the related notes, annual reports include the following information:

1. an introductory letter by the chief executive officer highlighting the year's performance and commenting on prospects for the future,
2. a review of the types of businesses in which the firm is involved,
3. a financial summary (sales, net income, and so on) for each of the five or 10 most recent years,
4. management's discussion and analysis of the firm's liquidity, capital resources, and operations,
5. a statement by management acknowledging its responsibility to prepare the financial statements and maintain an adequate system of internal controls,

6. the auditor's report expressing an opinion on the fairness of the financial statements,
7. quarterly financial data,
8. stock price and dividend data, and
9. a listing of officers and directors, along with a limited description of their backgrounds.

Management's discussion and analysis (MDA) is one of the newest and most informative sections of the annual report. As noted in item 4, it includes a discussion of liquidity, capital resources, and operations. MDA contains an analysis of past performance and known trends. It also identifies the underlying economic causes of the observed trends.

In addition, MDA provides two types of information about the future. First, management may know of existing circumstances that will have an impact on future operations. For example, the planned sale of a firm's subsidiary will affect both operations and liquidity. Second, management might also comment on anticipated trends and their effect on the firm's future. An illustration of this type of analysis might be a sales forecast based on macroeconomic factors, such as an impending recession or higher interest rates.

Refer to the MDA section in Wendy's annual report (see Appendix D), which includes a discussion on trends in revenues, expenses, and income, as well as expectations about sales levels in 1998. A discussion of financial condition and liquidity is also provided.

INTERIM REPORTING

Annual financial statements are usually issued between one and three months after a firm's fiscal year-end. Given that firms' transactions occur on an ongoing basis throughout the year, many analysts feel that annual financial statements do not report information in a timely manner. Because of this, all publicly held corporations and many closely held companies report financial information on an interim basis throughout the year. Most firms undertaking such **interim reporting** do so quarterly.

Interim financial statements are usually highly abbreviated and contain only limited disclosures in notes. Moreover, they are not audited. Thus, although interim financial statements are more timely, they are not as comprehensive or as reliable as annual financial statements.

In general, interim financial statements are prepared based on the same accounting principles as a firm's annual financial statements. However, two exceptions exist. First, interim financial statements frequently require the use of additional estimates. For example, many firms do not undertake a physical count of inventory at the close of each quarter. Instead, the ending inventory amount and cost of goods sold are estimated.

The second exception concerns expense recognition. Some costs that are expensed for annual purposes are not *immediately* expensed for interim reporting if they clearly benefit more than one interim period. Instead, these costs are deferred (treated as an asset) and subsequently allocated as an expense to future interim periods.

The ski industry offers a good example. It would be reasonable for a ski area to have a fiscal year that runs from June 1 to May 31. Since May 31 is a low point in their operations, it is a natural time to tally results. Much of a ski area's repair and maintenance activities, however, take place over the ensuing summer months. In general, we know that repairs and maintenance costs are expensed immediately. However, given that the ski industry earns little revenue in the summer months and the repairs and maintenance costs will clearly benefit operations during the upcoming season, immediately expensing such costs will not result in the most useful interim financial information. Instead, these costs are deferred and allocated as an expense to future interim periods based on the revenue generated in those periods.

As the ski area example illustrates, the nature of some businesses is quite seasonal. Consequently, care must be exercised in projecting annual results from interim periods. The accounting profession encourages firms to include in their interim reports the results for the most recent 12-month period.

REPORTS FILED WITH THE SEC

As you know from Chapter 1, "Financial Accounting and Its Environment," the SEC has the legislative authority to regulate the financial disclosures of publicly held corporations. Although the SEC requires firms to file a number of different reports, two of these are of the most interest to us: 10-K reports and 10-Q reports.

A firm's **10-K report** includes virtually all the information contained in its annual report, plus some additional disclosures. These disclosures include information about litigation, executive compensation, and shareholdings by officers and directors. Because 10-K reports include such detailed disclosures, they are intended to meet the information needs of rather sophisticated investors. Accordingly, most firms send annual reports to shareholders and make 10-K reports available on request.

The second SEC report, the **10-Q report,** includes a firm's quarterly financial statements, plus some additional disclosures. These disclosures include information on litigation and defaults on debt securities. Firms usually send quarterly financial statements to shareholders and send 10-Q reports on request.

ACCOUNTING INFORMATION AND THE EFFICIENT MARKET HYPOTHESIS

Although accounting and finance researchers have now studied the **efficient market hypothesis (EMH)** for several decades, it remains rather controversial. This section describes the EMH and summarizes its implications for accounting.

The Efficient Market Hypothesis

The EMH states that publicly available information is fully reflected in share prices. That is, once a corporation releases information (for example, quarterly net income), that information is quickly and unbiasedly reflected in share prices. This implies that a trading strategy based on publicly available information will not be particularly successful.

Considerable evidence exists indicating that share prices react very quickly to accounting information. Exhibit 14-5 shows the results of a study that examined the number of extreme price changes that occured when a sample of firms released their earnings announcements. As can be seen, most of the price changes occurred within a few hours of the announcement. Thus, unless one acts very quickly, no especially large profits are available by trading based on reported earnings announcements.

Not all research evidence, however, is consistent with the EMH. Some studies have shown that sizable abnormal returns can be earned from an analysis of publicly available financial statements. These returns exceed typical transaction costs (such as brokerage commissions), suggesting that a net profit could be made.

Overall, the research evidence regarding the EMH is conflicting. As you progress through your business education, pay particular attention to new evidence that pertains to this issue.

EXHIBIT 14-5 Market Reaction to Earnings Announcements

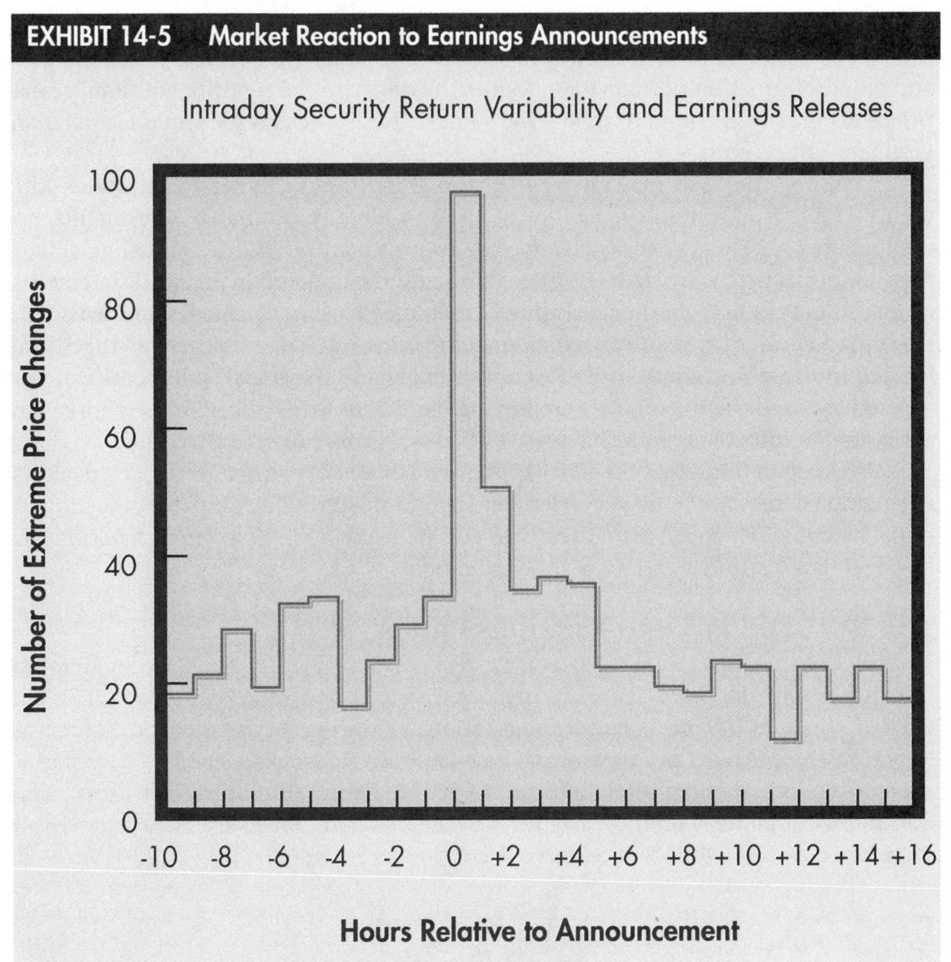

SOURCE: J. M. Patell and M. A. Wolfson, "The Intraday Speed of Adjustment of Stock Prices to Earnings and Dividend Announcements," *Journal of Financial Economics*, 1984, p. 240.

Implications of the EMH

The EMH has important messages for corporate managers and individual investors. Acceptance of the EMH should suggest to corporate managers that any attempt to affect their share price by using accounting ploys to influence reported earnings is not likely to be successful. For example, inflating earnings by selecting an income-increasing accounting principle will not fool financial statement readers. They will recognize that the increase in income was not due to improvements in the underlying profitability of the firm. Of course, rejection of the EMH could lead to a different inference.

Individual investors who accept the EMH would conclude that they are unable to earn abnormal profits by developing trading strategies based on publicly available information. Accordingly, selecting investments by analyzing annual reports will not prove profitable. The information in these reports is already reflected in share prices by the time the investor is able to obtain the report. These investors would be inclined to diversify their investments, perhaps by choosing mutual funds, which are investment vehicles that own shares in hundreds of corporations. By owning a small part of many companies, an investor's risk is reduced.

Investors who reject the EMH do not feel that share prices necessarily reflect all publicly available information. They feel that a careful analysis of financial statements and other information permits them to identify underpriced securities. Assuming that prices eventually gravitate to their "true values," these stocks represent a favorable investment opportunity.

Accepting the EMH may raise a question about the usefulness of financial statements. If financial statements cannot be used to identify profitable investments, are they of any use? The answer is clearly yes. Even though no individual will be able to earn abnormal profits by trading on the information contained in financial statements, all investors benefit from the disclosure of that information. Financial statements help stock markets identify relatively efficient companies. Capital resources can then be allocated to those firms, and overall wealth is expanded. Financial statements can also be used in corporate buyouts. By identifying inefficient firms (those firms whose managers are not effectively utilizing assets), takeover firms can select targets.

Also keep in mind that the EMH applies mostly to large, organized stock markets. Financial statements can be very useful in valuing closely held companies that are not publicly traded. Financial statements can also be used in credit-granting decisions, labor negotiations, and a variety of other situations.

The EMH and Price-to-Earnings Ratios

The price-to-earnings ratio (P/E ratio) was discussed in Chapter 10, "Shareholders' Equity." It is simply the price of a share of stock divided by earnings per share (EPS). The P/E ratio of large U.S. firms has averaged about 21 during the last decade. Some analysts view the P/E ratio as a measure of how expensive a stock is. The EPS stream is assumed to continue indefinitely into the future, and the P/E ratio reflects how many dollars investors are willing to pay for a $1 EPS stream. For example, a firm with a share price of $60 and EPS of $4 has a P/E ratio of 15:

$$\text{P/E} = \frac{\text{Price}}{\text{EPS}} = \frac{\$60}{\$4} = 15$$

Investors are willing to pay $15 for every dollar of earnings. This stock would be viewed as less expensive than one with a P/E ratio of 20. In this latter case, investors are paying $20 for every dollar of earnings.

Some investors recommend purchasing low P/E stocks. The rationale is that these stocks are cheap and have a great deal of upside potential. As you might guess, the research evidence regarding the success of this strategy is mixed.

In any event, recognize that P/E ratios vary among firms for several reasons. First, firms use different accounting principles, which systematically affect EPS. Everything else being equal, firms using accelerated depreciation report relatively low EPS. This results in a higher P/E ratio than that of firms using straight-line depreciation.

Variations in earnings growth are another reason why P/E ratios differ among firms. Recall the assumption that the EPS stream is expected to continue indefinitely. This assumption is not valid for many firms. In particular, firms with a large array of favorable investment prospects are likely to grow at relatively fast rates. The current EPS number for these growth firms understates the future EPS stream (the stream for which investors are actually paying), and the P/E ratio is therefore overstated for such growth firms.

In any given year, a firm's EPS might contain a transitory component, one that is not expected to persist into the future. For example, a firm will occasionally take a restructuring charge, which is a special charge that reduces net income. Accordingly, the current year's EPS understates the future earnings stream, and the P/E ratio is higher than it otherwise would be.

Interfirm differences in P/E ratios can be questionable guides for investment selection, however. Instead, differences in P/E ratios might simply reflect differences in accounting methods, earnings growth rates, and transitory earnings components.

An interesting illustration is provided by Electronic Data Systems (EDS). A dispute arose between EDS and one of its major customers regarding amounts due EDS for providing network management services. Litigation ensued and EDS took a charge of $200 million. Based on actual EPS of $1.50, its P/E ratio was:

$$P/E = \frac{\$52}{\$1.5} = 34.7$$

Eliminating the effect of this one-time charge results in an EPS of approximately $1.74. The adjusted P/E ratio would be 29.9.

$$P/E = \frac{\$52}{\$1.74} = 29.9$$

This is a more reasonable figure and illustrates how P/E ratios can be affected by transitory components of net income.

Reality Check 14-2 illustrates the effect accounting changes can have on P/E ratios.

THE ROLES OF ACCOUNTING

Throughout this text, we have emphasized the two roles that financial accounting plays. One role is to provide information useful for economic decision making. We saw how financial accounting information can be used in a variety of decision contexts, such as credit granting. Financial accounting's second role is to serve as a basis for engaging in contracts. That is, many contracts are based on financial statement numbers. This section summarizes these two purposes.

Informational Role

The **informational role** is emphasized by the FASB when it develops GAAP. In fact, the FASB has given considerable thought to the qualities that make information useful. Those qualities are summarized in Exhibit 14-6.

The two primary qualities that contribute to usefulness are relevance and reliability. **Relevance** refers to an item's capacity to make a difference in a decision. For example, few analysts would argue with the assertion that net income is relevant in business valuation. **Reliability** refers to an item's integrity. That is, does it measure what it purports to measure? The cash figure on the balance sheet is usually quite reliable, but pension obligations are considerably less reliable because of the many estimates involved in their calculation.

Some accountants question the helpfulness of these qualities in selecting accounting principles. In part, this is due to differences among financial statement users. For example, one user may find that expensing research and development (R&D) costs results in the most relevant information, while another user may feel that capitalizing R&D provides the best information. Such differences make it difficult for the FASB to choose the accounting method that is the most useful.

A Basis for Contracting

Serving as a **basis for contracting** is financial accounting's second role. Very frequently, firms enter into contracts that are defined in terms of numbers from the fi-

REALITY CHECK 14-2

Reality Check 14-1 contained the following information for Seaboard Corporation (dollars in thousands):

	1997	1996	1995
Earnings before cumulative effect of accounting change	$30,574	$2,840	$20,202
Cumulative effect of changing the accounting for inventories, net of tax expense of $1,922	—	3,006	—
Net earnings	$30,574	$5,846	$20,202

The following figures are on a per share basis:

	1997	1996	1995
Earnings before cumulative effect of accounting change	$ 20.55	$ 1.91	$ 13.58
Cumulative effect of changing the accounting for inventories, net of tax expense	—	2.02	—
Net earnings	$ 20.55	$ 3.93	$ 13.58
Price per share	$ 440	$ 266	$ 269

Required

a. Compute the P/E ratio for each year.
b. Which ratio is substantially different from the others?
c. What might explain the difference observed in part b?

Solution

a. The P/E ratios for the three years are

1997	1996	1995
$\frac{\$440}{\$20.55} = 21.4$	$\frac{\$266}{\$3.93} = 67.7$	$\frac{\$269}{\$13.58} = 19.8$

b. The P/E ratio in 1996 is approximately three times as large as the P/E ratio for the other two years.
c. The information provided indicates that the 1996 net income includes at least one significant transitory component: the cumulative effect of a change in accounting principles. This enables the calculation of a more meaningful 1996 P/E ratio that excludes the effect of the change. The modified P/E ratio is

$$P/E = \frac{\$266}{\$1.91} = 139.3$$

This modification actually enlarges the difference between the 1996 ratio and the other ratios. Consequently, an additional explanation must be sought. Earnings before the cumulative effect are much lower in 1996 than in the other years. Seaboard's low earnings in 1996 arose because the airline industry (Seaboard's customers) experienced a downturn and temporarily curtailed purchases from Seaboard. Although this had a very large effect on 1996 earnings, the stock price was not as dramatically affected.

EXHIBIT 14-6 Qualities of Useful Information

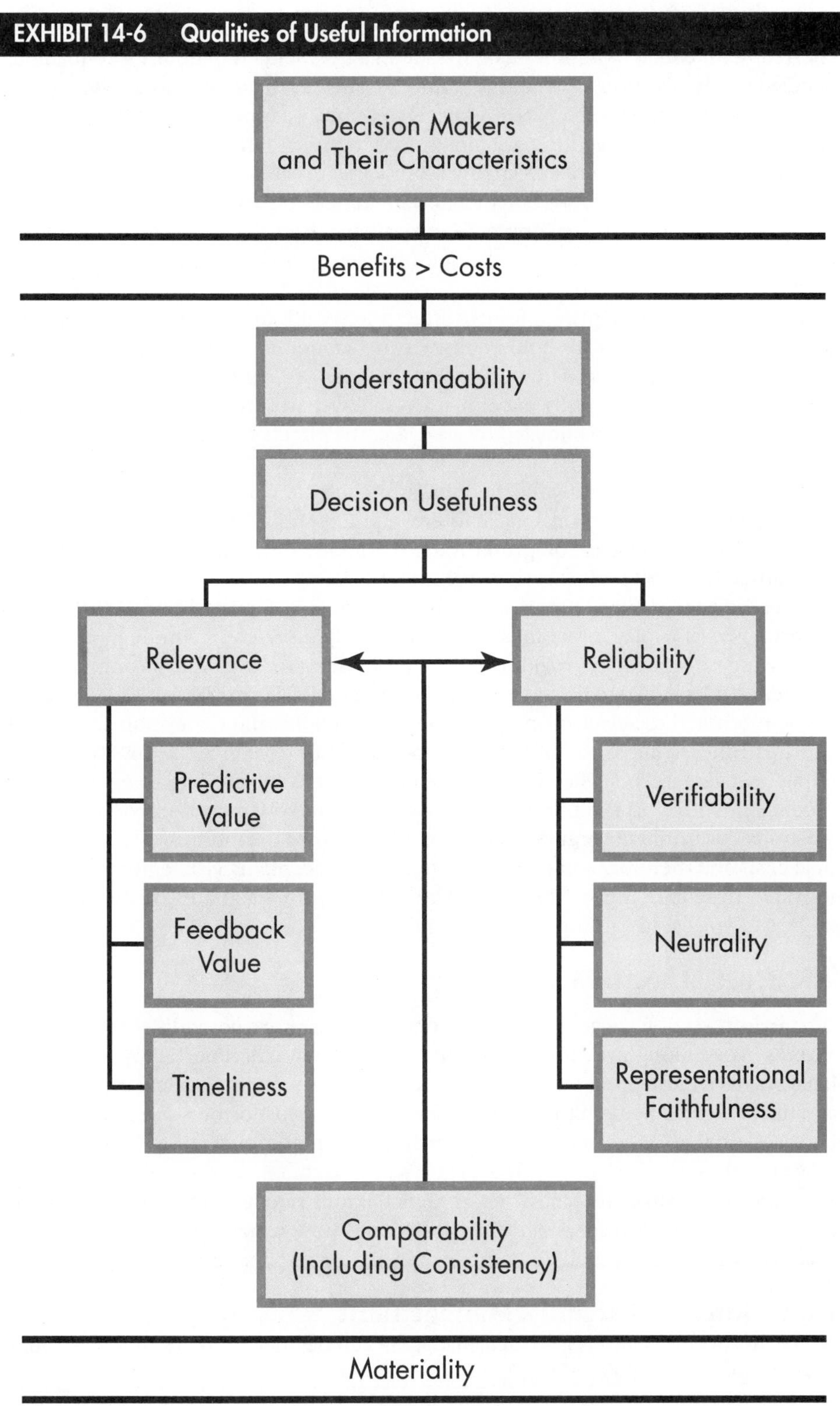

SOURCE: FASB Concepts Statement No. 2, "Qualitative Characteristics of Accounting Information." (Stamford, Conn., May 1980).

nancial statements. The compensation of top executives, for example, is often tied to reported net income. As another example, loan agreements require firms to maintain specified levels of various accounting numbers, such as the debt-to-total assets ratio.

Given that contracts are stated in terms of numbers appearing on financial statements, changing the accounting principles used to prepare those statements alters the terms of contracts. Of course, changing contract terms affects the wealth of the contracting parties. Thus, the adoption of a new, income-decreasing accounting principle may, for example, reduce the compensation paid to a firm's executives. This adversely affects their wealth, and since the corporation pays out less cash, the shareholders are benefited.

Because accounting principles can affect the wealth of various parties, some accountants feel that the FASB should consider the economic consequences of their accounting principle choices. They argue that the FASB is a regulatory body that should promote the public interest by maximizing social welfare. They further argue that social welfare can only be maximized by assessing the effects that accounting standards have on all parties.

The FASB has consistently rejected this approach. It believes that the effects of accounting principle choices on special interest groups should not influence the FASB's decisions. To do so would compromise the credibility of the financial reporting system. Rather, the FASB seeks "truth in accounting."

Because acceptable alternative accounting principles exist within GAAP, corporate managers also play a role in accounting principle selection. Although managers may have some interest in providing information useful for decision making, financial statement readers need to be acutely aware of other managerial motivations. Managers may be motivated to select/change accounting principles and to develop accounting estimates either to enhance their own compensation or to reduce the possibility of violating loan agreements. They may also be motivated to select accounting principles to reduce political costs. Political costs include taxes and other costs imposed on firms by various governmental regulations. Profitable firms are the most likely target for political costs and therefore some firms (particularly large, highly visible firms) might be motivated to reduce reported income. The next section elaborates on managers' incentives to engage in earnings management.

EARNINGS MANAGEMENT

The previous section suggested that corporate managers are not indifferent to the selection of accounting principles or to the earnings numbers reported by their firms. Managers have these preferences because accounting numbers (particularly earnings) can affect the well-being either of themselves, their firms, or both. Because of this, managers are motivated to engage in **earnings management**, which involves making accounting-related decisions that will result in favorable consequences for themselves and their firms. The following sections demonstrate how reported accounting earnings can affect managers and their firms, and how managers can undertake actions that will affect the income number reported on the financial statements.

Motivations for Earnings Management

The wealth of corporations and their managers can be affected by reported accounting earnings in the following ways:

1. Lending agreements typically place restrictions on borrowers stated in terms of accounting numbers. Restrictions include minimum levels of retained earnings

and current ratios, and maximum levels of debt-to-equity ratios. Higher reported net income reduces the likelihood that an agreement would be violated. Since violations can result in higher interest rates or other adverse consequences to the borrower, managers have an incentive to inflate reported earnings.

2. Managers' bonuses are often based on reported accounting earnings. Managers' personal wealth can therefore be increased by making accounting decisions that maximize the bonus.
3. Governments have the power to significantly affect the financial well-being of corporations through taxes, subsidies, antitrust actions, and a variety of other regulations and restrictions. Reported accounting earnings can affect the likelihood that a firm will reap a benefit or incur the cost of a governmental intervention. Because of this, some firms and their managers have an incentive to reduce reported income.
4. Stock market analysts pay close attention to a firm's earnings and the trend in earnings. Most valuation models place a positive weight on earnings growth. Consequently, corporations are motivated to report higher earnings, year after year. Also, analysts seek to minimize risk. Since highly variable earnings are a sign of riskiness, corporations seek to smooth peaks and troughs in reported earnings.
5. Earnings are also used as a basis for bargaining. When negotiating with an employees' union over wages and benefits, for example, a corporation's best interest might be served by reporting low earnings. The corporation can then claim that it doesn't have the financial resources to meet demands for higher employee compensation.

Methods of Earnings Management

GAAP provides corporate managers with a tremendous amount of discretion regarding accounting-related decisions and estimates. This latitude can be used by managers to shift income across years in order to achieve the objectives outlined in the previous section. Corporations can also time certain transactions in order to manage earnings. Specific earnings management tools include the following:

1. GAAP often permits a firm to choose its accounting methods from several acceptable alternatives. For example, earlier chapters of this book discussed three ways to account for inventory and three methods of depreciation. Managers seeking to maximize reported earnings would likely choose the FIFO inventory method (assuming a period of rising prices) and the straight-line method of depreciating fixed assets.
2. A variety of assumptions and estimates are needed to implement GAAP. For example, to actually calculate depreciation charges, estimates of useful lives and salvage values are needed. Other estimates required by GAAP include uncollectible accounts and product warranty liabilities. Managers often know considerably more about these issues than do

WHAT WOULD YOU DO?

As the chief financial officer for Bullet Enterprises, the chief executive officer (CEO) has asked your advice regarding an accounting principle change she is considering. Many firms in your industry have recently adopted LIFO. These adoptions were motivated by substantial increases in inventory costs. Under such conditions, LIFO can provide significant tax savings. Bullet's inventory costs have also risen, but not as much as your competitor's prices.

However, another issue concerns you. Your compensation package includes a bonus based on reported net income and the bonus is not activated unless net income exceeds $500,000. Your analysis shows that if LIFO is not adopted, net income will approximate $750,000. If LIFO is adopted, net income will be about $475,000. What would you tell the CEO?

the firm's auditors. Although managers' estimates must be reasonable, the range of reasonableness is fairly large.

3. Newly promulgated FASB standards usually provide a period of time, often two or three years, during which firms can initially adopt the new rules. Adoption dates selected by individual firms depend on the projected effects of the standard on the firm's financial statements (which could be in the billions of dollars), and on the firm's earnings management objectives.
4. During the past decade, numerous firms have taken large restructuring charges. These charges arise when firms revamp operations. They mostly include writing down assets and recognizing the severance benefits liability to employees who have been (or will be) terminated. Most restructurings take several years to complete. Restructuring charges can be an earnings management tool because of the many difficult estimates they entail.
5. Earnings can also be managed by cleverly timing certain transactions. For example, recall the accounting for securities classified as available-for-sale. Changes in the market value of these securities are not reflected in earnings while the securities are held. At the time securities are sold, the entire gain or loss (the difference between the historical cost and the selling price) is recorded. By carefully selecting to sell certain securities from its portfolio, a firm can predetermine if a gain or loss will be included in earnings.

Implications of Earnings Management

Accounting-related decisions (the selection of accounting principles and the development of accounting estimates) affect the well-being of corporations and their managers. The wide latitude provided by GAAP to corporate managers ensures that earnings management will continue to be practiced. As a result, the quality of information contained in the financial statements can be compromised. Financial statement readers must be diligent in their efforts to uncover these practices and intertemporal comparisons of financial statement numbers (such as the allowance for uncollectible accounts) can help. An examination of detailed disclosures in the financial statement notes is also important. Finally, a thorough knowledge of the firm and its industry is essential.

SUMMARY OF LEARNING OBJECTIVES

1. **Understand and interpret comprehensive income.**
Current GAAP excludes changes in the value of several assets and liabilities (e.g., marketable securities) from net income. Because of this, some financial statement readers believe that the usefulness of net income is compromised. Consequently, the FASB now requires firms to report comprehensive income, which includes net income and the value changes previously mentioned.
2. **Interpret the financial statements of firms that have undertaken accounting changes.**
Given that acceptable alternatives exist within GAAP, firms sometimes change accounting principles. Some changes are accounted for retroactively. That is, prior years' financial statements are restated to reflect the new principle, which ensures that the firm's financial statements are comparable across time periods. Most accounting principle changes, however, are accounted for by the cumulative effect approach; prior years' statements are not revised. The current year's income statement is based on the new method and it also includes the cumulative effect adjustment. Thus, interperiod comparability is compromised. Changes in accounting estimates are accounted for prospectively. That is, prior years' financial statements are not altered. The effect of the estimate change is reflected in the current and future years' income. Finally, changes in reporting entities are accounted for retroactively.
3. **Analyze information about operating segments.**
Firms are required to make disclosures in financial statements about their major operating segments. This information is intended to help analysts assess the risks and expected returns associated with each business segment.
4. **Describe annual and interim reports.**
Although this text focuses on financial accounting and the resultant financial statements, the broader context of financial reporting should be considered. Financial reporting includes financial statements as well as other financial information. Some of this information is contained in annual and interim reports, and includes the president's letter, management's discussion and analysis, and the auditor's report.
5. **Identify reports filed with the SEC.**
The most common reports filed with the SEC are 10-K and 10-Q reports. These reports contain, respectively, a firm's annual and quarterly financial statements, as well as more detailed disclosures. Relatively sophisticated analysts are the primary users of these reports.
6. **Explain the efficient market hypothesis and its implications for accounting.**
Despite considerable research effort, the validity of the EMH remains unsettled. Proponents believe that managers cannot fool the stock market with accounting gimmicks, and that investors cannot reap abnormal profits by using trading strategies based on publicly available information. Critics of the EMH believe that share prices do not reflect all publicly available information, and that profitable strategies based on that information can be developed.
7. **Describe the two major roles of financial accounting.**
First, financial accounting is designed to provide useful information for economic decision making. Second, many contracts are written in terms of accounting numbers. Because different accounting principles result in different accounting num-

KEY TERMS

bers, contract terms can be altered simply by changing accounting principles. Thus, corporate managers develop preferences for certain accounting principles. As a result, financial statement numbers are not necessarily unbiased, and they should be interpreted accordingly.

8. **Understand the motivations for and methods of earnings management.** The financial well-being of corporations and their managers can be significantly affected by reported accounting earnings. Because of this, corporations have an incentive to select accounting principles and make other accounting-related decisions in order to achieve their earnings management objectives.

QUESTIONS

14-1 Describe *comprehensive income*. How does it differ from net income?

14-2 Under what circumstances would a manager prefer comprehensive income or net income? An investor? A creditor?

14-3 How does comprehensive income differ from the concept of sustainable income, as described earlier in the text? Under what circumstances might an investor or creditor prefer sustainable income, as compared to comprehensive income?

14-4 Describe three different types of accounting changes. Under what circumstances should each be reported?

14-5 Discuss why financial statement users prefer a firm to consistently use the same accounting principles.

14-6 What is the financial statement user's first indication that an accounting change has occurred? Why should this source be examined first when reading a financial statement?

14-7 Discuss the general rule in reporting the effects of an accounting principle change. What is meant by a "cumulative effect" adjustment?

14-8 Under the general rule dealing with accounting principle changes, have the firm's retained earnings changed? How has the firm gained or lost some of its prior (accumulated) retained earnings? Why?

14-9 Discuss any inconsistencies that are introduced when accounting principle changes occur.

14-10 Are financial statements that include an accounting change more comparable with those of prior years or of subsequent years? Why?

14-11 Under what circumstances are prior years' financial statements retroactively restated? Why do you suppose these exceptions exist?

14-12 Why would a firm that is issuing its first public financial statements have more latitude in using retroactive adjustments for the effects of accounting changes?

14-13 Why does the FASB require that firms make retroactive adjustments when a new reporting standard has been issued?

14-14 When the effects of a change in an accounting estimate are recognized, can prior financial statements be restated retroactively? Why?

14-15 Where are the effects of changes in accounting estimates reported? Why should the financial statement user often not be aware of many of these changes?

14-16 In general, how are the financial statements changed when two firms merge or engage in some similar restructuring?

14-17 Why is a change in reporting entity shown as a retroactive adjustment and not as a prospective adjustment?

14-18 Identify three types of segment reporting. Where is this information reported? Why have such types of segment reporting been required?

14-19 Describe what is meant by an industry segment and the types of information that must be reported for each segment.

14-20 Why are the identifiable assets for each segment shown as part of segment reporting?

14-21 Why are profits for each segment shown as part of segment reporting?

14-22 Why are domestic and foreign operations separately disclosed? How would this information be helpful to an investor or creditor?

14-23 Why is information about a firm's major customers reported as part of the notes on the firm's segment? Why not use a threshold higher than 10 percent as the criterion for determining who is a major customer?

14-24 Describe why a firm with more foreign operations or more large customers (greater than 10 percent of its volume) might be viewed as having higher risk than a domestic company with many small customers (less than 10 percent).

14-25 Why does a firm's annual report contain so much information in such a variety of formats? Under what circumstances would a more condensed format be more useful?

14-26 Why are interim reports less reliable and less useful than annual reports? In what major ways do interim reports differ from annual reports?

14-27 Describe the efficient market hypothesis (EMH). How does it affect financial statement analysis as described in this text?

14-28 Assume that a firm changes from FIFO to LIFO during a period of rising prices. Would a proponent of the EMH predict an increase or decrease in the firm's share price as a result of the change in inventory valuations? Why?

14-29 Why do price-to-earnings (P/E) ratios differ between firms?

14-30 Describe financial accounting's two primary roles. Discuss the major criteria that financial accounting must adopt as part of its informational role? What other roles or criteria would you suggest? Why?

14-31 How do a firm's accounting principles affect contracts that are based on the financial statements?

14-32 Discuss how economic consequences can affect various users of financial statements. How should those who are affected by economic consequences participate in the development of accounting principles?

14-33 Why should financial analysts not be willing to accept all the information in a firm's financial statements at face value?

14-34 Identify the differences between relevance and reliability. Which would a manager emphasize? A financial analyst?

14-35 What is earnings management? Why would a manager engage in earnings management? Would an investor or creditor approve of such activities? Under what circumstances would an investor or creditor approve? Why?

14-36 Discuss each of the motivations for earnings management. Under what circumstances would you support the use of these techniques? Why?

14-37 Describe each of the methods used to manage earnings. Which seem appropriate and ethical? Why?

14-38 Identify some methods that might be used to manage earnings that were not described in this chapter. Are these new methods more appropriate or more ethical than the methods already described in the chapter? Why?

14-39 What are the implications of earnings management? As an external financial analyst, what can be done to combat earnings management?

14-40 The Sisters Coffee Emporium has been researching and developing new exotic coffee flavors and innovative coffee equipment. During 1998, it spent over $250,000 on R&D costs. It is now year-end and the company is preparing its balance sheet. Sisters would like the most relevant information to be reported to investors because the company is considering whether or not to capitalize the R&D costs.

a. Advise Sisters on the concepts of relevance and reliability and how the R&D expenditures should be handled.
b. Discuss the two primary concepts of accounting in the context of Sisters Coffee Emporium.

PROBLEMS

Comprehensive Income

Critical Thinking

14-41 IDQ's income statement data for the year ended November 30, 1999, is presented below (dollars in millions).

	11/30/99
Net sales	$340
Cost of goods sold	249
Gross profit	91
Selling, general, and administrative	40
Income before depreciation	51
Nonoperating income	2
Income before tax	53
Provisions for income tax	20
Net income	$ 33
Dividends	12
Unrealized gain on securities	10
Foreign exchange adjustement	3
Allowance for bad debts	13

Required

a. Review the annual income statement for the fiscal year ended 11/30/99. Identify any unusual items and any items that shouldn't appear on an income statement.
b. Using the data presented, prepare a statement of comprehensive income. Evaluate and discuss the differences between the income statement as originally shown and your statement of comprehensive income.
c. Compute a vertical analysis of each income statement. Comment on any differences in the return on sales ratio as derived from each statement.
d. Using the following balance sheet data, compute each ratio, and comment on any differences in the ratios as derived from each statement.
    i. Assuming average assets of $400 (million), calculate return on assets (ROA).
    ii. Assuming average shareholders' equity of $150 (million), calculate return on equity (ROE).

Critical Thinking

Comprehensive Income Trends

14-42 IDQ's income statement data for the years ended November 30, 2000 and 2001, are presented below (dollars in millions).

	11/30/00	11/30/01
Net sales	$1061	$1154
Cost of goods sold	792	830
Gross profit	269	324
Selling, general, and administrative	111	134
Income before depreciation	158	190
Nonoperating income	5	6
Income before tax	163	196
Provisions for income tax	64	76
Net income	$ 99	$ 120
Dividends	(10)	(12)
Foreign exchange adjustment	4	36
Unrealized loss on securities	(7)	(9)
Accumulated depreciation	(79)	(82)

Required

a. Review the annual income statements for each year. Identify any unusual items and any items that shouldn't appear on an income statement.

b. Using the data presented, prepare statements of comprehensive income for each year. Evaluate and discuss the differences between the income statement as originally shown and your statements of comprehensive income. Discuss the trends shown in net income and comprehensive income. Which are more helpful and useful for managers? For investors? Why?

c. Compute a vertical analysis of each income statement. Comment on any differences in the return on sales ratio as derived from each statement. Also comment on any differences in the trends shown by the ROS ratios.

d. Using the following balance sheet data, compute each ratio and comment on any differences in the ratios as derived from each statement.

   i. Assuming average assets of $420 and $390 (million) in 2000 and 2001 respectively, calculate return on assets (ROA) for each year. Evaluate the trends shown in each ratio.

   ii. Assuming average shareholders' equity of $150 and $135 (million) in 2000 and 2001 respectively, calculate return on equity (ROE). Evaluate the trends shown in each ratio.

Accounting Principle Change

14-43 Mesple Music, Inc. purchased musical instrument equipment on January 1, 1999, for $25,000. Mesple depreciated it on the straight-line basis over five years with no salvage value. However, on January 1, 2001, the company realized that the productive capacity of this equipment is declining, so it decided to change to the double-declining balance method of depreciation.

Required

a. Calculate depreciation expense for 1999 and 2000, using the straight-line method.
b. Calculate depreciation expense for 1999 and 2000, using the double-declining balance method. (Refer to Chapter 7, "Noncurrent Assets," for details on double-declining balance depreciation.)
c. Show the cumulative effect of the change in the year 2001 in terms of the effects on the balance sheet equation.

Accounting Principle Change

14-44 Central Air Conditioning, Inc. purchased machinery for installing air conditioners. The purchase price of the machine on July 1, 2000, was $35,000. The company chose a seven-year life, a sum-of-the-years' digits (SYD) depreciation, and no salvage value. Unfortunately, the weather during 2000, 2001, and 2002 was extremely mild and the machinery was not used as much as the company had thought. Therefore, it decided that the straight-line method would be more representative of the productive capacity of the machine, so it switched to the straight-line method on July 1, 2003.

Required (Ignore Income Tax)

a. Calculate depreciation expense, using SYD for the annual periods ending June 30, 2001, 2002, and 2003. (See Chapter 7 for a review of SYD depreciation.)
b. Calculate depreciation expense, using the straight-line method for the annual periods ending June 30, 2001, 2002, and 2003.
c. Show the cumulative effect of the change for July 1, 2003, in terms of the balance sheet equation.

Ratios: Accounting Change

14-45 Polymer Element Corporation presented the following (partial) income statements (dollars in thousands, except EPS):

	December 31		
	2000	1999	1997
Income from continuing operations after tax	$ 207,500	$ 195,400	$ 189,600
Cumulative effect of change in accounting principle	(25,000)	0	(45,000)
Net income	$ 182,500	$ 195,400	$ 144,600
Weighted-average common shares outstanding	146,000	146,000	146,000
Average total shareholders' equity	$3,650,000	$3,908,000	$2,892,000
Market price of stock	$20	$18	$16

Required

a. Calculate earnings per share (EPS) and calculate the P/E ratio for each year.
b. Calculate return on shareholders' equity for each year.
c. Revise the answers to parts a and b, adjusting the data for the cumulative effect of the change in accounting principle.
d. Comment on the impact these results might have on an investor's preferences or risks.

Calculating Depreciation

14-46 A firm has a computer that originally cost $37,500 with an estimated salvage value of $17,500 and an estimated life of five years. During the first two years, the firm used straight-line (SL) depreciation. In the third year, the sum-of-the-years'digits (SYD) method was adopted.

Required

a. Calculate the depreciation expense during the first two years under each method.
b. What would have been the effect, before taxes, on the accounting equation if SYD had been used during the first two years instead of SL?
c. Describe the general principle that must be followed to account for the difference.
d. What depreciation expense will be shown in the third and each subsequent year, using SYD?

Calculating Depreciation

14-47 A firm has a delivery truck that originally cost $55,000 with an estimated salvage value of $5,000 and an estimated life of 10 years. During the first two years, the firm used sum-of-the-years'digits (SYD) depreciation. At the beginning of the third year, straight-line (SL) depreciation was adopted.

Required

a. Calculate the depreciation expense during the first two years under each method.
b. What would have been the effect, before taxes, on the accounting equation if SL had been used during the first two years instead of SYD?
c. Describe the general principle that must be followed to account for the difference.
d. What is the depreciation expense that will be shown in the third and each subsequent year, using SL?
e. How would the financial statements be affected if a retroactive adjustment were the appropriate treatment? Does this difference seem important? Why?

Calculating Depreciation Expense

14-48 A copy machine was acquired at the beginning of 1998 for $12,000. It had a salvage value of $2,000 and an estimated life of five years.

Required

a. Calculate the annual straight-line (SL) depreciation.
b. Assume that at the beginning of the year 2000, the copy machine's total useful life is estimated to be eight years. What is the effect of this change in estimated useful life on net income each year?
c. What is the copy machine's book value at the end of 1998? 1999? 2000?
d. Using the original data, assume that at the beginning of 2001 it is determined that there will be zero salvage at the end of the fifth year. Assume that the original estimated useful life is still five years.
   i. What is the effect of this change in estimated salvage value on net income in each year?
   ii. What is the copy machine's book value at the end of the year 1998? 1999? 2000?
e. Using the original data, assume that both the change in estimated useful life and the change in salvage value occur as stated.
   i. What is the effect on net income in 2000 and 2001?
   ii. What is the copy machine's book value at the end of each year?
   iii. Do these effects seem so important that they would be separately disclosed in the notes? Why?

Calculating Bad Debt Expense

Integration of Concepts

14-49 Dandy's Discount Duds offers credit to all customers. It estimated that 15 percent of all such customers will not be able to pay their accounts. Dandy's credit sales in 2000 were $4,000,000. Its estimated bad debt expense was calculated at 15 percent of annual credit sales.

Required

a. What is the effect of estimated bad debts on net income in 2000?
b. In early 2001, Dandy discovered that half of its customers have been laid off because a major automaker closed two of its plants. Dandy found that 25 percent of its customers will not be able to pay their accounts. What impact will this new realization have on Dandy's income for 2001?
c. If a retroactive adjustment to 2000's net income were necessary, what other information is needed that is not shown in this problem?
d. Why is it appropriate that such adjustments to estimates be shown on a prospective basis?

Interpreting Financial Statements: Accounting Changes and Restructuring

14-50 Listed below are the income statements for Alco Standard Corporation, the largest distributor of copiers in North America (dollars in thousands):

	September 30 1994	1993
Revenues:		
Net sales	$7,925,784	$6,387,078
Dividends, interest, and other income	3,537	6,332
Finance subsidiaries	66,731	51,149
	7,996,052	6,444,559
Costs and Expenses:		
Cost of goods sold	5,884,819	4,799,757
Selling and administrative	1,765,483	1,378,814
Interest	43,802	40,189
Finance subsidiaries interest	27,978	23,662
Restructuring costs		175,000
	7,722,082	6,417,422
Loss from unconsolidated affiliate	(117,158)	(2,538)
Income from continuing operations before taxes	156,812	24,599
Taxes on income	86,203	16,984
Income from continuing operations	70,609	7,615
Loss from discontinued operations, net of tax		(7,515)
Net Income	$ 70,609	$ 100

Required

a. Study Alco Standard's income statement. Identify any unfamiliar or unusual terms.

b. Discuss Alco Standard's different reporting treatment in 1993 for its loss from discontinued operations and its restructuring costs.

c. As an investor, evaluate the two items in part b. What impact might they have on the company's future operations?

Recognizing the Effects of Accounting Changes

14-51 The Kellogg Company reported the following financial information (dollars in millions):

	1993	1992	1991
Earnings before cumulative effect of accounting change	$680.7	$682.8	$606.0
Cumulative effect of change in method of accounting for postretirement benefits other than pensions (net of tax benefit of $144.6)	—	(251.6)	—
Net earnings	$680.7	$431.2	$606.0

Assume that other than the cumulative effect, earnings for 1992 and 1991 were not materially affected by the change.

Required

a. Identify the most appropriate earnings figure for each year that leads to the most valid intertemporal comparisons.
b. These earnings figures, stated on a per share basis, are as follows:

	1993	1992	1991
Earnings before cumulative effect of accounting change	$2.94	$2.86	$2.51
Cumulative effect of change in method of accounting for postretirement benefits other than pensions (net of tax benefit of $144.6)	—	(1.05)	—
Net earnings	$2.94	$1.81	$2.51
Price per share	$56¾	$ 67	$65⅜

i. Compute the P/E ratio for each year.
ii. Why does the 1992 P/E ratio seem unusual?
iii. Compute a more meaningful P/E ratio for 1992.

Interpreting Financial Statements: Restructuring

14-52 Review Reebok's financial statements in Appendix E.

Required

a. Read Notes 2 and 12. Identify any unfamiliar or unusual terms.
b. Discuss Reebok's relationship with these firms. What impact did Reebok's actions have on the company's financial statements?
c. Why shouldn't these special charges be reported as retroactive adjustments so that the years are more comparable?

Change in Accounting Principles

14-53 Fitzer, Inc. reported the following data in its 1999 income statement (dollars in millions):

Income before cumulative effect of accounting changes	$1,093.5
Cumulative effect of change in accounting for postretirement benefits, net of income taxes	(312.6)
Income taxes	30.0
Net income	$810.9

Fitzer's notes include the following explanations:

In the fourth quarter of 1999, the Company adopted the provisions of SFAS No. 106, Employer's Accounting for Postretirement Benefits Other Than Pensions. This statement requires the accrual of the projected future cost of providing postretirement benefits during the period that employees render the services necessary to be eligible for such benefits. In prior years, the expenses were recognized when claims were paid.

The Company elected to immediately recognize the accumulated benefit obligation, measured as of January 1, 1999, and recorded a one-time pretax charge of $520.5 million ($312.6 million after taxes, or $0.93 per share) as the cumulative effect of this accounting change.

The Company adopted SFAS No. 109. The cumulative effect of the change increased net income by $30.0 million ($0.09 per share) and is reported separately in the 1999 Consolidated Statement of Income.

Required

a. Describe, in your own words, the accounting changes Fitzer included in 1999's net income.
b. Since these changes were all adopted in fiscal 1999, what is the effect of these changes on prior years?
c. Recalculate the effect on Fitzer's net income, assuming that neither change had been reported in 1999.
d. Why might Fitzer's managers have wanted to lump both changes in the same year? Why might they have wanted to recognize the postretirement change in 1999, rather than waiting until 2000?
e. Suppose Fitzer recorded a charge of $55,000,000 for restructuring the materials group in fiscal 1999. Why would managers want to lump several such changes into net income for the same year?
f. Write a short statement describing your view of management's motivations about recognizing accounting changes. Why is the timing associated with recognizing such changes so important to managers?

Interpreting Financial Statements: Restructuring

14-54 Bergen Brunswig Corporation reported the following information (dollars in thousands) in its 1993 consolidated earnings statement:

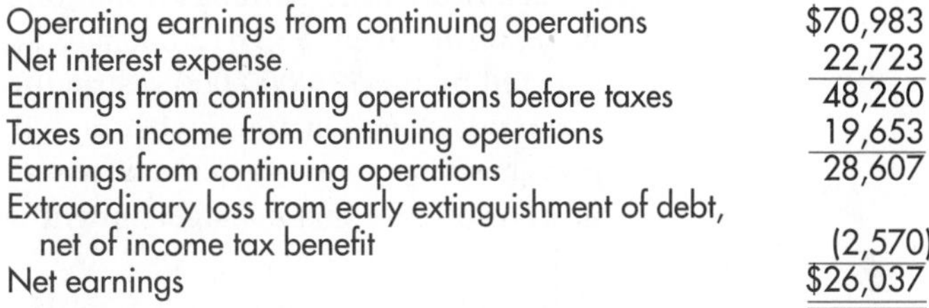

Operating earnings from continuing operations	$70,983
Net interest expense	22,723
Earnings from continuing operations before taxes	48,260
Taxes on income from continuing operations	19,653
Earnings from continuing operations	28,607
Extraordinary loss from early extinguishment of debt, net of income tax benefit	(2,570)
Net earnings	$26,037

Required

a. Comment on any unusual items in this income statement. Has Bergen Brunswig reported any accounting changes?
b. Bergen Brunswig's statements disclosed an item, earlier in the income statement, "Restructuring charge, $33,000,000." This item appeared only in the 1993 column, with nothing reported in the prior years. How do you suppose that this item related to operations of 1993 and to its continuing operations?
c. Note 12, Restructuring and Other Unusual Charges, disclosed the following new information:

During the fourth quarter of fiscal 1993, the Company approved a restructuring plan which consists of accelerated consolidation of domestic facilities into larger, more efficient regional distribution centers, the merging of duplicate operating systems, the reduction of administrative support in areas not affecting valued services to customers and the discontinuance of services and programs that did not meet the Company's strategic and economic return objective. The estimated pre-tax cost of the restructuring plan

(Continued)

is $33.0 million. The restructuring charge represents the costs associated with restructure, primarily abandonment and severance. For those activities or assets where the disposal is expected to result in a gain, no gain will be recognized until realized.

d. Did Bergen Brunswig have a choice on when to recognize the restructuring charge? Where would these costs have been reported if they were not listed in this category of costs?
e. How will the restructuring charges in 1993 affect Bergen Brunswig's future operations? How will these effects be reported in future years?
f. The same note disclosed another unusual charge:

    On June 18, 1993, the Company announced that a joint bid which the Company had made in April 1993 with the French Company, Cooperation Pharmaceutique Francaise, to acquire the largest French pharmaceutical distribution company, Office Commercial Pharmaceutique, had been withdrawn. Accordingly, expenses of $2.5 million, before income tax benefit of $1.0 million associated with the transaction, have been recorded in the fourth quarter of fiscal 1993.

    These expenses are not listed anywhere as a separate item in Bergen Brunswig's income statement. Why? Why must these costs be reported in 1993 and not in 1992 or 1994? Would your conclusions about the reporting of these costs change if you later found that Bergen Brunswig had reported in earlier years a separate section in its income statement called "Discontinued Operations"?
g. Bergen Brunswig's Earnings from continuing operations in 1992 and 1991 were, respectively, $53,012,000 and $58,061,000. How has this trend been affected by the $33,000,000 restructuring charge? If the company had not taken this charge in 1993, what would its earnings from continuing operations have been for 1993, and how would this affect the earlier trend? Why do you suppose that managers might want to take such a charge in 1993?

Accounting Principle Change: Cumulative Effect Approach

14-55 U. S. Shoe Corporation reported the following income statement information:

U.S. Shoe Corporation
Consolidated Statement of Earnings (Partial)
(Dollars in Thousands)

	1991	1990	1989
Earnings (loss) before cumulative effect of accounting change	($27,662)	$49,187	$12,965
Cumulative effect of accounting change related to product maintenance contracts, net of tax effect of $2,343	(3,621)	—	—
Net earnings (loss)	($31,283)	$49,187	$12,965

Note (3) Accounting Change (Adapted)

In December 1990, the Financial Accounting Standards Board issued a technical bulletin on accounting for product maintenance contracts such as those sold by the company's optical retailing group. The bulletin requires the defer-

> ral and amortization of revenue from the sales of such contracts on a straight-line basis over the term of the contract (one to two years). Under the accounting method previously followed by the company, a portion of the revenue earned from the sale of eyewear product maintenance contracts was recognized on the date of sale and the remainder was deferred and amortized on a straight-line basis over the term of the contract.
>
> Effective at the beginning of 1991, the company has elected to adopt this new accounting method for all contracts in place. The effect of this change is to increase the net loss in 1991 by $4.3 million, including $3.6 million, which is the cumulative effect of the accounting change.

If this change in accounting method had been in effect during 1990 and 1989, the effects would have been immaterial to net earnings.

Required

Evaluate the disclosures by U. S. Shoe Corporation. In what ways do these disclosures provide useful information to the readers of its financial statements?

Integration of Concepts

Effects of Retroactive Adjustment: Percentage-of-Completion Method

14-56 Ace Construction Company accounted for all its long-term contracts on a deferred basis; that is, all revenue and expenses were deferred until the completion of the contract when all the costs were known with certainty. Although this is a conservative approach, Ace has been having difficulty with its auditors and with the IRS over this approach. It now desires to shift to a percentage-of-completion method. Assume that only one such contract is to be changed at this time. This contract for $5,000,000 was initiated four years ago, and an equal amount of work was done each year. The contract work cost the firm $4,000,000.

Required

a. Show the effects of the $5,000,000 on the accounting equation, assuming that it was all reported as income in the final year.
b. Show the effects on the accounting equation of a retroactive adjustment to the firm's financial statements for each of the contract years. To answer this question, you may need to review Chapter 4, "The Income Statement."
c. Does this set of adjustments seem important to investors or financial analysts? Does it seem to be a useful adjustment that would be viewed as helpful by the readers of the firms' financial statements? Why?

Discussion of Accounting Changes

Integration of Concepts

14-57 Identify an accounting change (other than a change in depreciation method) that requires a cumulative adjustment. Create a numerical example of this accounting change and show the effects on net income and retained earnings during the year when the change occurs.

Discussion of Accounting Changes

Critical Thinking

14-58 Why would a change from FIFO, or some other inventory method, to LIFO not require a retroactive adjustment of a firm's financial statements? What would be the cumulative effect of such an adjustment?

Discussion of Accounting Changes

14-59 Discuss why the effects of a change in an accounting estimate are not reported using the "cumulative effects" rule. Discuss the differences between the "cumulative effects" method and the "prospective" method.

Discussion of How Estimates Are Used in Accounting

14-60 Review the prior chapters in this text and compile a list of at least five areas where estimates are required as part of the accounting measurement process. Determine through your review or through interviews with accounting professionals whether these estimates can generally be made in a reliable manner that requires limited adjustments in later years. In other words, what is the general long-term effect of using these types of estimates?

Various Accounting Changes

14-61 Match the following terms to the correct description. For each situation, describe in words (ignore the dollar amounts) what accounting treatments are required.

a. Change in accounting principle, cumulative effect reported
b. Change in reporting entity
c. Change in accounting estimate
d. Change in principle, retroactive effect reported

___ 1. Shipley Office Products, Inc. used equipment for three years and depreciated it on the straight-line basis. The original useful life was seven years, but after three years the company decided to change the original life to five years.

___ 2. American Shoe Corporation purchased all the outstanding stock of Faborini, Inc. in early 1998. American Shoe Corporation is preparing its comparative financial statements for the year ended December 1998.

___ 3. Sportscards USA decided to change its inventory costing method from LIFO to FIFO.

___ 4. The Second Time Through apparel shop has been owned by Homer Sampson. He wanted to raise capital to expand, so he decided to "go public" and offer the company stock for sale in the open market. At the same time, the company implemented an accounting change for postretirement benefits and calculated the cumulative effect of going from "pay-as-you-go" to estimating retirement benefits and accruing an expense each year.

Accounting Changes: LIFO to FIFO

14-62 The following consolidated financial statements, selected excerpts from the notes, and auditor's report for Zenith Electronics Corporation were obtained from the EDGAR database:

Consolidated Financial Statements

Zenith Electronics Corporation
Statements of Consolidated Operations and Retained Earnings (Deficit)

	Year Ended December 31		
	1997	1996	1995
	(In Millions, Except Per Share Amounts)		
Revenues			
Net Sales	$1,173.1	$1,287.9	$1,273.9
Costs, expenses, and other			
Cost of products sold	1,180.5	1,257.0	1,188.8
Selling, general and administrative (Note Four)	178.3	167.8	128.8
Engineering and research	42.9	46.7	43.5
Other operating expense (income), net (Notes One, Three, and Ten)	42.4	(26.3)	(30.1)
Restructuring and other charges (Note Seven)	-	9.3	21.6
	1444.1	1454.5	1352.6
Income			
Operating income (loss)	(271.0)	(166.6)	(78.7)
Gain (loss) on asset sales,	(4.6)	0.3	(1.7)
Interest expense	(25.5)	(15.1)	(19.9)
Interest income	0.9	3.6	1.8
Income (loss) before income taxes	(300.2)	(177.8)	(98.5)
Income taxes (credit) (Note Eight)	(0.8)	0.2	(7.7)
Net income (loss)	$ (299.4)	$ (178.0)	$ (90.8)
Per share			
Income (loss) per common share (Note Eighteen)	$(4.49)	$ (2.73)	$ (1.85)
Retained earnings (Deficit)			
Balance at beginning of year	$ (362.3)	$ (184.3)	$ (93.5)
Net income (loss)	(299.4)	(178.0)	(90.8)
Retained earnings (deficit) at end of year	$(661.7)	$(362.3)	$(184.3)

The accompanying Notes to Consolidated Financial Statements are an integral part of these statements.

NOTES TO CONSOLIDATED FINANCIAL STATEMENTS (Excerpts Only)

NOTE ONE—SIGNIFICANT ACCOUNTING POLICIES:

Principles of consolidation: The consolidated financial statements include the accounts of Zenith Electronics Corporation and all domestic and foreign subsidiaries (the Company). All significant intercompany balances and transactions have been eliminated.

Use of estimates: The preparation of financial statements in conformity with GAAP requires management to make estimates and assumptions that affect the reported amounts of assets and liabilities at the date of the financial statements and the reported amounts of revenues and expenses during the reporting period. Actual results could differ from those estimates.

Statements of consolidated cash flows: The company considers time deposits, certificates of deposit, and all highly liquid investments purchased with an original maturity of three months or less to be cash.

Inventories: Inventories are stated at the lower of cost or market. Costs are determined for all inventories using the FIFO method.

Engineering, research, product warranty, and other costs: Engineering and research costs are expensed as incurred. Estimated costs for product warranties are provided at the time of sale based on experience factors. The costs of co-op advertising and merchandising programs are also provided at the time of sale.

Impairment of long-lived assets: The company periodically assesses whether events or circumstances have occurred that may indicate that the carrying value of its long-lived assets may not be recoverable. When such events or circumstances indicate that the carrying value of an asset may be impaired, the company uses an estimate of the future undiscounted cash flows to be derived from the remaining useful life of the asset to assess whether or not the asset is recoverable. If the future undiscounted cash flows to be derived over the life of the asset do not exceed the asset's net book value, the company recognizes an impairment loss for the amount by which the net book value of the asset exceeds its estimated fair market value. See Note Three for additional information.

NOTE TWO—FINANCIAL RESULTS AND LIQUIDITY:

The company has incurred net losses of $299.4 million, $178.0 million, and $90.8 million in 1997, 1996, and 1995, respectively. For many years, the company's major competitors, many with greater resources, have aggressively lowered their selling prices in an attempt to increase market share. Although the company has benefited from cost reduction programs, these lower color television prices together with inflationary cost increases have more than offset such cost reduction benefits.

Since joining the company in January 1998, the new Chief Executive Officer, along with the rest of the company's management team has been developing a broad operational and financial restructuring plan. A broad outline of that plan has been presented to the company's Board of Directors in March 1998. The plan, which is designed to leverage the company's brand, distribution, and technology strengths, includes reducing costs, outsourcing certain components and products, disposing of certain assets, and capitalizing on the company's patented digital television technologies. Restructuring costs must be incurred to implement the plan.

Despite its negative cash flow, the company has been able to secure financing to support its operations to date, based on credit support from LGE. Between November 1997 and February 1998, the company (with the guarantee of LGE) entered into a series of new lending agreements with commercial lenders for unsecured lines of credit totaling more than $100 million, all of which has been drawn as of March 31, 1998.

Going forward, significant amounts of additional cash will be needed to pay the restructuring costs to implement the proposed business plan and to fund losses until the company has returned to profitability. Based on management's proposed plan, the company estimates that at least $225 million would be required to fund the company's restructuring costs and operations through the end of 1998 and that additional amounts could be required thereafter.

Although there is no assurance that funding will be available to execute the plan, the company is continuing to seek financing to support its turnaround efforts and is exploring a number of alternatives in this regard. LGE has agreed to provide up to $45 million in additional funding for one year from the date of the first borrowing, subject to LGE's right to demand repayment at anytime after June 30, 1998, and is secured by certain assets of the company. The company believes that this additional short-term financing, along with its current credit facilities, will be sufficient to support the company's liquidity requirements through June 30, 1998, depending on operating results and the level of continued trade support. In addition, the company is engaged in ongoing discussions with LGE concerning the company's business plan, and LGE is considering whether to provide additional long-term financial support. However, LGE has no obligation to do so. Any such support by LGE would be subject to a number of conditions, including the operating results of the company, third-party consents, Republic of Korea regulatory approvals, and other conditions. No decision has been made at this time by LGE or the company regarding additional financial support, and there can be no assurance that any additional financial support will be forthcoming from LGE.

In the absence of long-term financial support from LGE, there can be no assurance that additional financing can be obtained from conventional sources. Management is exploring alternatives that include seeking strategic investors, lenders, and/or technology partners; selling substantial company assets; or pursuing other transactions that could result in diluting LGE to a less than majority position. There can be no assurance that management's efforts in this regard will be successful.

Management believes that, under any restructuring scenario, the company's common stock would likely be subject to massive dilution as a result of the conversion of debt to equity or otherwise. There can be no assurances as to what value, if any, would be ascribed to the common stock in a restructuring. In addition, the company's subordinated debentures could suffer substantial impairment in a restructuring. Due to a number of uncertainties, many of which are outside the control of the company, there can be no assurance that the company will be able to consummate any operational or financial restructuring.

The company's independent public accountants have included a "going concern" emphasis paragraph in their audit report accompanying the 1997 financial statements. The paragraph states that the company's recurring losses and negative working capital raise substantial doubt about the company's capability to continue as a going concern and cautions that the financial statements do not include adjustments that might result from the outcome of this uncertainty.

Existing credit facilities are not expected to be sufficient to cover liquidity requirements after June 30, 1998, and the company is currently facing the prospect of not having adequate funds to operate its business. There can be no assurance that additional credit facilities can be arranged or that any long-term restructuring alternative can be successfully initiated or implemented by June 30, 1998, in which case the company may be compelled to pursue a bankruptcy filing in the absence of a proposed or pre-approved financial restructuring. The company will be required to obtain waivers under its financing arrangements for periods subsequent to June 30, 1998 and the lenders thereunder are under no obligation to provide such waivers.

Management believes that, despite the financial hurdles and funding uncertainties going forward, it has under development a business plan that, if successfully funded and executed as part of a financial restructuring, can significantly improve operating results. The support of the company's vendors, customers, lenders, stockholders, and employees will continue to be key to the company's future success.

NOTE THREE—IMPAIRMENT OF LONG-LIVED ASSETS:

During the fourth quarter of 1997, an impairment was recognized for the Consumer Electronics business because the future undiscounted cash flows of assets were estimated to be insufficient to recover their related carrying values. As such, the company recognized an expense of $53.7 million and established a valuation reserve for the write-down of the excess carrying value over fair market value. The fair market value used in determining the impairment loss was based upon management and third party valuations, including estimates of potential environmental liabilities. This FAS 121 charge is included in Other operating expense (income).

During the third quarter of 1997, the company recorded a charge of $10 million related to the impairment of certain long-lived assets that are to be disposed . The charge relates primarily to (i) assets that will be sold or scrapped as a result of the company's decision to phase out its printed circuit board operation (ii) assets that will be sold or scrapped as a result of the company's decision not to develop the proposed large-screen picture tube plant in Woodridge, Illinois and (iii) a building in Canada that was sold in December 1997. The amount of the charge is included in Other operating expense (income).

The impairment charges discussed above are based upon management's best estimates of the recoverability of long-lived assets and the fair value of the related assets. It is reasonably possible that the company's estimates of the recoverability of long-lived assets and the fair value will change. See Note Two for additional information.

NOTE FOUR—CHARGE FOR BAD DEBTS:

In November 1995, the company entered into a contract with a customer in Brazil to purchase TVs and TV kits and to assemble and distribute Zenith brand TVs in that country. In early 1997, this customer discontinued timely payments of its obligations and sought to renegotiate both the timing and the amount of the obligations to the company. While the company and this customer continued to negotiate in an attempt to reach a business solution, litigation was commenced by both parties in Brazil. The company had also initiated litigation against this customer in the United States. In late 1997, this matter was settled. The agreement provides that the company will make certain parts and components available to this customer and will receive an $11 million settlement payable in installments over 11 months. As a result of the above problems, the company recorded a $21.3 million bad debt charge during 1997 related to this customer, which reflects the company's estimated loss as of December 31, 1997. The bad debt charge affected the transferor certificate valuation allowance.

NOTE FIVE—ACCOUNTING CHANGES:

During 1997, the company changed its accounting policy for most tooling expenditures. The old policy was to charge most tooling expenditures to expense in the period acquired. The new policy is to defer the tooling charges incurred subsequent to March 29, 1997, over a 20-month period in order to more appropriately match the costs with their period of benefit. The accounting policy for picture tube tooling remains the same, which is to amortize that tooling over a four-year period. This change was accounted for as a change in accounting estimate effected by a change in accounting principle and will be accounted for on a prospective basis. The change decreased tooling expense by $8.9 million and decreased the loss per share by $.13 in 1997.

Effective January 1, 1996, the company changed its inventory costing method for its picture tube inventories from LIFO to FIFO. There has also been a strategic marketing shift in the company toward selling more larger-screen television sets and less smaller-screen sets. The picture tubes for the smaller-screen television sets are manufactured by the company and have been costed using LIFO. It is expected that the LIFO picture tube inventory pool will decrease and this decrease would create a LIFO liquidation resulting in a poor matching of current costs with current revenues. As a result, the company believes that the FIFO method is preferable as it will provide a more appropriate and consistent matching of costs against revenues. This change in accounting had no material impact on quarterly results and, as a result, quarterly information is not restated. The effect of this change in accounting principle was to reduce the net loss reported for 1996 by $2.7 million, or $.04 per share, The change has been applied to prior years by retroactively restating the financial statements. The effect of this change for 1995 was to reduce the net loss reported by $1.6 million, or $.03 per share.

REPORT OF INDEPENDENT PUBLIC ACCOUNTANTS

To the Stockholders of Zenith Electronics Corporation:

We have audited the accompanying consolidated balance sheets of Zenith Electronics Corporation (a Delaware corporation) and subsidiaries as of December 31, 1997 and 1996, as well as the related statements of consolidated operations, retained earnings, and cash flows for each of the three years in the period ended December 31, 1997. These financial statements are the responsibility of the Company's management. Our responsibility is to express an opinion on these financial statements based on our audits.

We conducted our audits in accordance with generally accepted auditing standards. These standards require that we plan and perform the audit to obtain reasonable assurance about whether the financial statements are free of material misstatement. An audit includes examining, on a test basis, evidence supporting the amounts and disclosures in the financial statements. An audit also includes assessing the accounting principles used and significant estimates made by management, as well as evaluating the overall financial statement presentation. We believe that our audits provide a reasonable basis for our opinion.

In our opinion, the consolidated financial statements referred to above present fairly in all material respects the financial position of Zenith Electronics Corporation and subsidiaries as of December 31, 1997 and 1996, and the results of their operations and their cash flows for each of the three years in the period ended December 31, 1997, in conformity with GAAP.

The accompanying consolidated financial statements have been prepared assuming that the Company will continue as a going concern. As discussed in Note Two to the financial statements, the Company has suffered recurring losses from operations and has negative working capital that raises substantial doubt about its capability to continue as a going concern. Management's plans in regards to these matters are also described in Note Two. The financial statements do not include any adjustments that might result from the outcome of this uncertainty.

As explained in Note Five to the financial statements, the Company changed its methods of accounting for tooling costs in 1997 and picture tube inventories in 1996.

Arthur Andersen LLP   Chicago, Illinois   March 27, 1998

Required

a. Review Zenith's income statement, notes, and auditor's report. Note any unusual terms. Trace all the information shown in each note (1-5) to the income statement. Trace the disclosures in the auditor's report to the notes and income statement.

b. Explain why the impact of the change in accounting method from LIFO to FIFO does not appear on the face of the income statement. How would this accounting change be more apparent? (*Hint:* Compare the 1996 data shown in the income statement to the original 1996 income statement as shown on page 607.)

c. Calculate Zenith's sustainable operating income for each year. Even though all the notes are not included above, assume that all the restructuring charges and the other operating expenses (income) as shown are not expected to continue. Also, make an adjustment reflecting the effects of the unusual bad debts as noted in Note 4.

d. Compare and contrast the sustainable operating income (see Chapter 4) with the operating income as reported in the income statement. How did your adjustments change the trend in Zenith's operating income? Does the adjusted data yield any more optimistic views of results expected in 1998 and 1999? Why?

e. The auditors raised questions about Zenith's capability to continue as a going concern entity. What evidence in the income statement supports their concerns? In the notes? Even though the balance sheet was not included above, what evidence about liquidity concerns supports the auditor's going concern issue?

f. What is Zenith's likely trend in net sales and net income? Is there any evidence that Zenith will even survive? What impact is the restructuring likely to have?

g. Even though the balance sheet, cash flow statement, and the remainder of the notes were not provided, what advice would you give to an investor in Zenith? To a manager? To a lender?

Internet

Identification of Accounting Changes

14-63 Locate the most recent 10-K filing by Bank One and Time-Warner from the EDGAR archives (www.sec.gov/edaux/searches.htm). Refer to the note on significant accounting policies in "Notes to the Financial Statements" to identify changes in accounting policies. Identify any changes the companies might have made in their methods of accounting. How have changes in accounting principles impacted their consolidated income statements?

Ethics

Possible Violation of Debt/Asset Covenant

14-64 Assume you have just conducted a preliminary analysis of your firm's 1999 financial statements. The firm has not prospered in recent years, and you are particularly concerned about violating a provision of a loan agreement you have with a local bank. Your firm has a $200,000, nine percent bank loan due in 2001. One provision of the loan agreement is that your firm's debt-to-total assets ratio does not exceed 50 percent. Your review of the 1999 financial statements indicates a ratio of 58 percent.

You are very confident that violation would result in a renegotiated interest rate of about 10.5 percent. Your firm would find meeting this higher interest charge to be quite difficult.

The only alternative to violating this provision that you can think of is to change depreciation methods. Currently, your firm uses double-declining-balance. You have calculated that changing to the straight-line method would reduce your debt-to-total assets ratio to 49 percent.

Required

a. How much additional interest expense would be incurred if the loan agreement is violated?
b. What are the ethical implications of this decision?

Segment Reporting

14-65 The following (partial) information was provided in the industry segment note in American Home Products Corporation's 1994 financial statements (dollars in millions):

	Years Ended December 31 1994	1993
Net sales:		
Health care products	$ 7,885.6	$7,369.1
Food products	997.3	935.8
Agricultural products	83.3	—
Consolidated total	$ 8,966.2	$8,304.9
Income before taxes		
Health care products	$ 1,839.9	$1,836.7
Food products	155.6	152.4
Agricultural products	16.8	—
Corporate	17.5	3.6
Consolidated total	$ 2,029.8	$1,992.7
Total assets on December 31:		
Health care products	$ 8,118.4	$5,165.3
Food products	558.8	504.4
Agricultural products	1,173.9	—
Corporate	11,823.7	2,017.7
Consolidated total	$21,674.8	$7,687.4
Net sales by geographic region:		
United States	$ 5,908.0	$5,695.8
Canada and Latin America	1,022.4	897.7
Europe and Africa	1,422.7	1,196.6
Asia and Australia	613.1	514.8
Consolidated total	$ 8,966.2	$8,304.9

Required

a. For each segment, calculate the return on assets (use end-of-year assets and operating profit) and calculate income before tax as a percent of sales.
b. Evaluate the performance of each segment. Regarding the products and services sold by each segment, comment on concerns and outlooks that an investor might have.
c. Comment on the company's sales in the different geographic regions. How could this impact the investor's evaluation of American Home Products' potential future performance?

Integration of Concepts

Evaluation of Segment Disclosure for Two Firms

14-66 Examine notes from the financial statements of two different companies to determine how they report segments of their operations. Evaluate the level of disclosure for each firm in terms of the usefulness and relevance of the notes provided by each firm.

Segment Reporting

14-67 TRW, Inc., is a global company that specializes in producing automotive, spacecraft, and information system products. The following (partial) segment data was reported (dollars in millions):

	December 31	
	1994	1993
Sales:		
Automotive	$5,679	$4,538
Space and defense	2,812	2,792
Information systems	596	618
Operating profit:		
Automotive	$476	$309
Space and defense	175	199
Information systems	96	74
Identifiable assets:		
Automotive	$3,481	$3,004
Space and defense	1,111	1,253
Information systems	622	752

Required

a. Calculate the return on assets of 1994 for each segment (use operating profit and ignore interest expense).
b. Calculate each segment's operating income as a percentage of sales.
c. Why is the segment-by-segment information important for an investor to have? Which ratio results will be most important to investors? Why?

Internet

Identification of Industry Segments

14-68 Locate the most recent 10-K filing by Gillette Corporation from the EDGAR archives (www.sec.gov/edaux/searches.htm). The "Notes to the Financial Statements" contains detailed segment information.

Required

a. Identify the major business (industry) segments in which Gillette is involved.
b. What is the percentage contribution of each segment to the company's net sales and profit from operations? Which is the most important business segment?
c. For which geographic areas does Gillette have a material presence? Which is the most profitable geographic area?
d. In your opinion, is Gillette a U.S. company or a global company?

Interim Reports

14-69 Falcon Amusements, Inc. chose September 30 as its year-end. Reported below are its quarterly income statements for fiscal 2000 and its annual income statement.

	Quarterly				
	10/1/99 12/31/99	1/1/00 3/31/00	4/1/00 6/30/00	7/1/00 9/30/00	Annual at 9/30/00
Net sales	$577,441	$571,930	$698,432	$818,034	$2,665,837
Cost of goods	118,563	126,471	134,587	174,259	553,880
Gross profit	458,878	445,459	563,845	643,775	2,111,957
Selling, general & administrative expense	303,755	377,096	393,309	428,588	1,502,748
Depreciation	52,055	51,622	52,651	53,044	209,372
Non-operating income	(114,062)	(17,251)	(14,845)	(3,315)	(149,473)
Interest expense	28,413	11,515	11,717	9,234	60,879
	270,161	422,982	442,832	487,551	1,623,526
Income before tax	188,717	22,477	121,013	156,224	488,431
Provision for income tax	51,614	6,412	36,499	44,521	139,046
Net income	$137,103	$ 16,065	$ 84,514	$111,703	$ 349,385

Required

a. Discuss briefly why Falcon is reporting quarterly information. Is it audited?
b. How does the annual audited information differ from the quarterly data?
c. Are there any obvious seasonal trends? Why might the cost of goods sold rise in the fourth quarter (aside from sales being higher)? *Hint:* Year-end adjustments. How might an investor be concerned about such trends and fluctuations?

Interim Reporting

14-70 International Dairy Queen's annual income statement for the year ended November 30, 1994, and its four quarterly income statements are presented below.

	Annual ending 11/30/94	11/30/94	2/24/95	5/26/95	8/25/95
Net sales	$340,833	$76,070	$67,530	$106,150	$115,361
Cost of goods sold	249,985	55,140	47,556	79,220	83,010
Gross profit	90,848	20,930	19,974	26,930	32,351
Selling, general, and administrative	40,495	10,331	12,352	11,136	13,418
Income before depreciation	50,353	10,599	7,622	15,794	18,933
Depreciation	0	0	0	0	0
Non-operating income	1,578	(56)	498	484	484
Income before tax	51,931	10,543	8,120	16,278	19,417
Provisions for income tax	20,510	4,160	3,210	6,430	7,670
Net income	$ 31,421	$ 6,383	$ 4,910	$ 9,848	$ 11,747

Required

a. Review the annual income statement for the fiscal year ended 11/30/94 and the quarterly income statements for the four quarters. Identify any unusual items.

b. Evaluate any seasonal trends in these quarterly statements.

c. Discuss why Dairy Queen would choose November 30 as its fiscal year-end.

Internet

Information Search

14-71 The SEC archives can be accessed at www.sec.gov/edaux/searches.htm.

Required

Locate the SEC disclosures for the corporate filings listed below. For each filing, answer the questions and identify who might use this information and why it is important to that user.

a. 10-K for Centurion Mines Corp (February 7, 1996)
   - The report was for which accounting year?
   - What industry is Centurion in and what is its Standard Industrial Classification number?
   - How many shares of stock were outstanding as of January 1, 1996?
   - When did Centurion's predecessor organization begin operations (from Section 1)?
   - What was the amount of net operating revenues?
   - Who audited Centurion's financial statements (from Section F2)?

b. 10-Q for SCI Systems Inc. (February 7, 1996)
   - The report is for which quarter of the fiscal year?
   - How many shares of stock were outstanding on January 23, 1996?
   - What was the amount of net sales for the three months ended January 24, 1995?

c. S – 8 for Campbell Soup Co. (February 6, 1996)
   - What securities were registered (be specific)?
   - What amount of securities were registered?
   - What was the proposed maximum offering price per share?
   - What was the amount of the registration fee?

d. DEF 14A for ADAC Laboratories (February 7, 1996)
   - What items of business were to be conducted at the 1996 annual meeting of shareowners (be brief)?

appendix

Accounting Procedures

LEARNING OBJECTIVES

1. Prepare and post journal entries.
2. Calculate account balances.
3. Prepare and post adjusting entries.
4. Prepare and post closing entries.
5. Generate balance sheets and income statements from general ledger accounts.

INTRODUCTION

This text focuses on conceptual accounting issues and the uses of accounting information. In contrast, this appendix summarizes the detailed procedures used by accountants to generate financial statements. Although, in theory, the basic accounting equation can be used to prepare financial statements, virtually all firms would find that approach to be extremely cumbersome. Far more efficient processes are needed by firms that have hundreds of different assets and liabilities and engage in thousands of transactions.

THE GENERAL LEDGER

Recall from Chapter 2, "The Basic Concepts of Financial Accounting," that the core of financial accounting is the analysis of transactions in terms of the basic accounting equation:

ASSETS = LIABILITIES + SHAREHOLDERS' EQUITY

The purpose of this analysis is to summarize the effects of different types of transactions on the equation's elements. In real business settings, this summarization is done in the **general ledger.** Although most accounting systems are computerized, at this stage we will illustrate a manual system. In such a system, the general ledger often takes the form of a loose-leaf notebook. Each page is assigned to a particular equation item (such as cash, inventory, accounts payable, or invested capital) and is referred to as an account.

Debits and Credits

To show increases and decreases in account amounts, plus (+) and minus (–) signs could be used. For several reasons, however, the accounting profession has discarded this alternative. Instead, each account is divided into a left-hand side and a right-hand side; increases are recorded on one side and decreases are recorded on the other.

For *all* accounts, the left-hand side is the **debit** side and the right-hand side is the **credit** side. For accountants, debit and credit have no meanings other than left and right, respectively. This can be a source of confusion. Many nonaccountants associate the term credit with something good. The accountant does not.

In actual business practice, general ledger accounts can take many forms. For simplicity, they are illustrated here using T-accounts. T-accounts for cash and accounts payable are shown as follows:

Cash			Accounts Payable	
Dr	Cr		Dr	Cr

The side of an account in which increases and decreases are recorded depends on the nature of the account. Increases in assets are recorded by debits, and decreases are recorded by credits. The rules for liabilities and shareholders' equity are the reverse: increases are recorded as credits, and decreases are recorded as debits. These rules are summarized in Exhibit A–1.

EXHIBIT A–1 Debit and Credit Rules

Assets		=	Liabilities		+	Shareholders' Equity	
Dr	Cr		Dr	Cr		Dr	Cr
+	–		–	+		–	+

The debit and credit rules are largely arbitrary. Accordingly, with one exception, do not look for any special logic in them. One aspect of the rules does make sense, however. Because assets appear on the opposite side of the basic accounting equation from liabilities and shareholders' equity, the debit and credit rules for assets are the opposite of the rules for liabilities and shareholders' equity. The reasoning for this is discussed later in the appendix.

An Example

Consider two illustrative transactions. First, shareholders invest $10,000 in a firm. In terms of the basic equation, this transaction increases cash and increases shareholders' equity (invested capital):

ASSETS	=	LIABILITIES	+	SHAREHOLDERS' EQUITY
Cash				Invested capital
+$10,000				+$10,000

In the general ledger, an increase in cash is recorded as a debit, and an increase in shareholders' equity is recorded as a credit. After the analysis, the amounts would appear as follows:

Cash			Invested Capital	
$10,000				$10,000

The second transaction involves a purchase of inventory for $2,000. This transaction increases inventory and decreases cash:

ASSETS		=	LIABILITIES	+	SHAREHOLDERS' EQUITY
Cash	Inventory				
−$2,000	+$2,000				

The decrease in cash is recorded as a credit, and the increase in inventory is recorded as a debit, as shown in these T-accounts:

As previously mentioned, the rules for assets (which appear on the left side of the equation) are the opposite of the rules for liabilities and shareholders' equity (which appear on the right side of the equation). This is no coincidence. By reversing the rules, the equality of debits and credits for each transaction (and in total) is assured. For example, when inventory is purchased for cash, inventory is debited and cash is credited for $2,000. The equality of debits and credits helps accountants identify and eliminate errors from the accounting process.

Balancing Accounts

To determine the net amount of cash, inventory, and so on at the end of an accounting period, the accounts must be **balanced.** This is done by totaling the debits and credits in each account and calculating their difference. This difference is shown on the side of the account that has the larger amount. These balances are the basis for the financial statements. The balanced cash account shows an $8,000 debit balance:

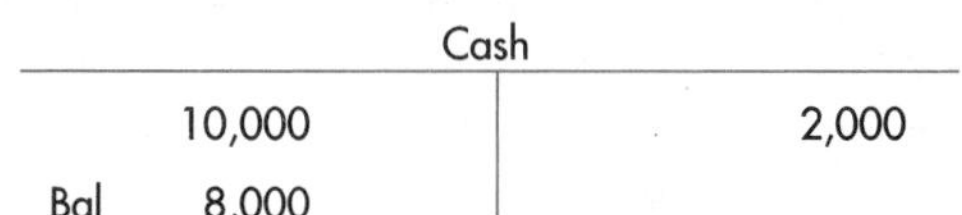

Chart of Accounts

Firms have a great deal of discretion in choosing their account titles and the number of accounts they employ. Accordingly, most firms develop a **chart of accounts**, which is essentially an index to the general ledger. It lists account titles and account numbers. Account numbers are often employed because they provide a firm's personnel with an efficient and unambiguous way to communicate. Exhibit A-2 illustrates a chart of accounts.

THE GENERAL JOURNAL

In the general ledger, the information about a given transaction is spread across two or more accounts. This makes it difficult for auditors and others to review all the in-

EXHIBIT A–2 Jacobs Golf and Tennis Chart of Accounts

Account	Account Number
Cash	110
Accounts Receivable	120
Prepaid Rent	130
Inventory	140
Equipment	150
Accumulated Depreciation	160
Accounts Payable	210
Unearned Revenue	220
Utilities Payable	230
Interest Payable	240
Notes Payable	250
Invested Capital	310
Retained Earnings	320

formation about a given transaction. The **general journal** is another major accounting record. It provides a chronological listing of all transactions and events. This enables the auditor to easily see all the accounts affected by a single transaction. As with the general ledger, the general journal in a manual system consists of a loose-leaf notebook.

Journal Entries

General journal entries are actually the first step in the *formal* financial accounting process. This step occurs after the accountant has conceptually analyzed the transaction in terms of the basic accounting equation, ascertained which accounts have increased or decreased, and translated the increases and decreases into debits and credits. A transaction's **journal entry** consists of

1. the date,
2. the account(s) to be debited,
3. the account(s) to be credited,
4. the amounts, and
5. an explanation.

For example, if shareholders invest $10,000 in a firm on January 1, cash is increased and shareholders' equity is increased. Translated into debits and credits, cash is debited and invested capital is credited. In journal entries, the debits are shown first, and the credits are indented and shown after the debits. The journal entry for the $10,000 investment would be

January 1

	Debit	Credit
Cash	10,000	
Invested Capital		10,000
To record shareholders' investment		

Notice that the journal contains two dollar columns. The one to the left is for debits and the one to the right is for credits.

Posting

To determine account balances, the amounts in the journal entries need to be placed in the general ledger. Transcribing the amounts from journal entries into the general ledger is called **posting.** From a procedural standpoint, transactions, events, and so on, are never initially entered into the general ledger. General journal entries are always prepared first and are then posted to the general ledger.

Summary

The accounting process includes the steps summarized in Exhibit A-3. We have covered the first four steps. Later in this appendix, we will cover the other steps in the accounting process.

EXHIBIT A–3 The Accounting Process

1. Identify transactions and events.
2. Analyze transactions and events in terms of the basic accounting equation.
3. Translate the transaction analysis into debits and credits.
4. Prepare journal entries and post to the general ledger.
5. Prepare and post adjusting entries.
6. Prepare the income statement.
7. Prepare and post closing entries.
8. Prepare the balance sheet.

AN ILLUSTRATION OF ACCOUNTING PROCEDURES

Chapter 2 provided a comprehensive example involving Jacobs Golf and Tennis (JG&T). JG&T began operations in January 2000 and engaged in a number of transactions. That example is used here to demonstrate the accounting procedures just discussed. The only difference between Chapter 2 and the treatment here is that we now assume that JG&T is organized as a corporation.

Transaction 1:	Shareholders invest $50,000.		
Analysis:	Increase cash; increase invested capital.		
Debits and credits:	Increase cash (an asset) by a debit; increase invested capital (an equity account) by a credit.		
Journal entry: January 1			
	Cash	50,000	
	Invested Capital		50,000
	To record investment by shareholders		
Transaction 2:	Borrowed $20,000 from a bank.		
Analysis:	Increase cash; increase notes payable.		
Debits and credits:	Increase cash by a debit; increase notes payable by a credit.		
Journal entry: January 1			
	Cash	20,000	
	Notes Payable		20,000
	To record note payable		

Transaction 3:	Paid in advance one year's rent of $12,000.		
Analysis:	Increase prepaid rent; decrease cash.		
Debits and credits:	Increase prepaid rent by a debit; decrease cash by a credit.		
Journal entry: January 1			
	Prepaid Rent	12,000	
	Cash		12,000
	To record prepayment of one year's rent		
Transaction 4:	Purchased inventory on account, $30,000.		
Analysis:	Increase inventory; increase accounts payable.		
Debits and credits:	Increase inventory by a debit; increase accounts payable by a credit.		
Journal entry: January 1	Inventory	30,000	
	Accounts Payable		30,000
	To record the purchase of inventory on account		
Transaction 5:	Purchased equipment for $25,000.		
Analysis:	Increase equipment; decrease cash.		
Debits and credits:	Increase equipment by a debit; decrease cash by a credit.		
Journal entry: January 1	Equipment	25,000	
	Cash		25,000
	To record purchase of equipment for cash		

At this point, journal entries have been prepared for all of JG&T's preliminary transactions. The next step is to post these entries to general ledger accounts. Exhibit A-4 contains general ledger accounts that reflect these postings.

EXHIBIT A–4 Jacobs Golf and Tennis General Ledger

Cash

Debit	Credit
1) 50,000	3) 12,000
2) 20,000	5) 25,000
Bal 33,000	

Prepaid Rent

Debit	Credit
3) 12,000	

Inventory

Debit	Credit
4) 30,000	

Equipment

Debit	Credit
5) 25,000	

Notes Payable

Debit	Credit
	2) 20,000

Accounts Payable

Debit	Credit
	4) 30,000

Invested Capital

Debit	Credit
	1) 50,000

REVENUE AND EXPENSE ACCOUNTS

Revenue and expense transactions affect the retained earnings component of shareholders' equity. For example, if a firm renders services in the amount of $100 to clients, on account, accounts receivable increases and retained earnings increases:

ASSETS	=	LIABILITIES	+	SHAREHOLDERS' EQUITY
Accounts Receivable +$100				Retained earnings +$100 (sales)

As you know from Chapter 2, the income statement summarizes the many types of revenue and expense transactions that affect retained earnings during a period. If all revenue and expense transactions were commingled in that one account, ascertaining the detailed amounts for each line item on the income statement would be quite difficult.

Consequently, general ledger accounts are established for each revenue and expense item desired on the income statement. Instead of initially debiting or crediting retained earnings for revenue and expense transactions, the revenue and expense accounts are used. These accounts are best viewed as **temporary accounts,** which are really components of retained earnings. Increases in revenues are shown as credits, while increases in expenses are treated as debits. Note that expenses reduce retained earnings; so increasing the debit balance in an expense account actually decreases retained earnings. Exhibit A-5 summarizes the debit and credit rules for revenue and expense accounts.

EXHIBIT A–5 Debit and Credit Rules for Revenue and Expense Accounts

Revenue		Expense	
Dr	Cr	Dr	Cr
−	+	+	−

To illustrate JG&T's revenue and expense transactions for January, 2000, assume that all transactions occur on January 15.

Transaction 6:	Rendered services to customers for $200 plus a promised future payment of $400.		
Analysis:	Increase cash; increase accounts receivable; increase service revenue.		
Debits and credits:	Debit cash by $200; debit accounts receivable by $400; credit service revenue by $600.		
Journal Entry: January 15	Cash	200	
	Accounts Receivable	400	
	Service Revenue		600
	To record service revenue		

The preceding entry is referred to as a **compound journal entry.** Its distinguishing characteristic is that more than one account is either debited or credited (or both). As with all journal entries, the total dollar amount of debits equals the total dollar amount of credits.

Transaction 7:	Received $100 from customers for services to be performed at a later date.		
Analysis:	Increase cash; increase unearned revenue (remember that unearned revenue is a liability).		
Debits and credits:	Debit cash; credit unearned revenue.		
Journal entry:			
January 15	Cash	100	
	Unearned revenue		100
	To record customers' prepayment of revenue		
Transaction 8:	Paid workers' salaries of $700.		
Analysis:	Decrease cash; decrease retained earnings via salary expense.		
Debits and credits:	Credit cash; debit salary expense.		
Journal entry:			
January 15	Salary Expense	700	
	Cash		700
	To record payment of salary expense		
Transaction 9:	Received a $120 utility bill for services already used. Payment was not immediately made.		
Analysis:	Utilities expense increases; utilities payable increases.		
Debits and Credits:	Debit utilities expense; credit utilities payable.		
Journal entry:			
January 15	Utilities Expense	120	
	Utilities Payable		120
	To record January utilities expense		
Transaction 10:	Sold, for $4,000 on account, inventory costing $2,200.		
Analysis:	Accounts receivable increases; sales increases; inventory decreases; cost of goods sold (CGS) increases.		
Debits and credits:	Debit accounts receivable; credit sales; credit inventory; debit CGS.		
Journal entry:			
January 15	Accounts Receivable	4,000	
	Sales		4,000
	To record a credit sale on account		
	CGS	2,200	
	Inventory		2,200
	To record CGS on credit sale		

Exhibit A-6 contains ledger accounts reflecting the posting of these entries.

ADJUSTING ENTRIES

As you know from Chapter 2, adjustments to the accounting records are typically needed before financial statements are prepared. The adjustments are needed to ensure that the account balances are correct and up to date. These adjustments result from interest accruals, depreciation, and a variety of other matters. Adjustments to the account balances are accomplished by journal entries. We now analyze the adjustments needed to correctly state JG&T's accounts as of January 31.

EXHIBIT A–6 Jacobs Golf and Tennis General Ledger

Cash

Debit	Credit
1) 50,000	3) 12,000
2) 20,000	5) 25,000
6) 200	8) 700
7) 100	
Bal 32,600	

Accounts Receivable

Debit	Credit
6) 400	
10) 4,000	
Bal 4,400	

Prepaid Rent

Debit	Credit
3) 12,000	

Inventory

Debit	Credit
4) 30,000	10) 2,200
Bal 27,800	

Equipment

Debit	Credit
5) 25,000	

Notes Payable

Debit	Credit
	2) 20,000

Accounts Payable

Debit	Credit
	4) 30,000

Unearned Revenue

Debit	Credit
	7) 100

Utilities Payable

Debit	Credit
	9) 120

Invested Capital

Debit	Credit
	1) 50,000

Retained Earnings

Debit	Credit

Service Revenue

Debit	Credit
	6) 600

Sales

Debit	Credit
	10) 4,000

Salary Expense

Debit	Credit
8) 700	

Utilities Expense

Debit	Credit
9) 120	

Cost of Goods Sold

Debit	Credit
10) 2,200	

Transaction 11: Incurred but did not pay interest expense of $133.
Analysis: Increase interest expense; increase interest payable.
Debits and credits: Debit interest expense; credit interest payable.
Journal entry:

Date	Account	Debit	Credit
January 31	Interest Expense	133	
	Interest Payable		133
	To record January interest expense		

Transaction 12:	Used $1,000 of prepaid rent.		
Analysis:	Increase rent expense; decrease prepaid rent.		
Debits and credits:	Debit rent expense; credit prepaid rent.		
Journal entry:			
January 31	Rent Expense	1,000	
	Prepaid Rent		1,000
	To record January rent expense		
Transaction 13:	Depreciation on equipment amounted to $208.		
Analysis:	Increase depreciation expense; decrease equipment by increasing the balance in the contra-asset account, accumulated depreciation.		
Debits and credits:	Debit depreciation expense; credit accumulated depreciation.		
Journal entry:			
January 31	Depreciation Expense	208	
	Accumulated Depreciation		208
	To record January depreciation expense		
Transaction 14:	Earned $50 of the $100 advance payment previously made by customers.		
Analysis:	Decrease unearned revenue; increase service revenue.		
Debits and credits:	Debit unearned revenue; credit service revenue.		
Journal entry:			
January 31	Unearned Revenue	50	
	Service Revenue		50
	To record revenue earned		

General ledger accounts with these postings appear in Exhibit A-7. The balances in the revenue and expense accounts are now correct and the income statement, contained in Exhibit A-8, can be prepared based on the revenue and expense accounts.

CLOSING ENTRIES

At this point, a problem exists in preparing JG&T's balance sheet. Since the revenue and expense transactions, which really affect retained earnings, were not recorded in that account, the balance sheet will not balance. Therefore, the amounts in the revenue and expense accounts must be transferred to retained earnings. This is done via closing entries.

JG&T's closing entries at the end of January appear in Exhibit A-9. Viewed in isolation, closing entries do not make a great deal of sense. However, keep in mind their purpose: to transfer balances from revenue and expense accounts to retained earnings. General ledger accounts that reflect the posting of these entries appear in Exhibit A-10. The balance now in retained earnings is that which would have been there if all the revenue and expense transactions were initially recorded in that account.

Note that after posting the closing entries, the balance in each revenue and expense account is zero. This is why they are called **temporary** (or **nominal**) **accounts.** Moreover, since the balances are zero, next month they will only reflect the revenue and expense amounts for February and not a cumulative amount beginning with January. This will enable the easy preparation of an income statement for the month of February.

EXHIBIT A–7 Jacobs Golf and Tennis General Ledger

Cash	
1) 50,000	3) 12,000
2) 20,000	5) 25,000
6) 200	8) 700
7) 100	
Bal 32,600	

Accounts Receivable	
6) 400	
10) 4,000	
Bal 4,400	

Prepaid Rent	
3) 12,000	12) 1,000
Bal 11,000	

Inventory	
4) 30,000	10) 2,200
Bal 27,800	

Equipment	
5) 25,000	

Accumulated Depreciation	
	13) 208

Notes Payable	
	2) 20,000

Accounts Payable	
	4) 30,000

Unearned Revenue	
14) 50	7) 100
Bal	50

Utilities Payable	
	9) 120

Interest Payable	
	11) 133

Invested Capital	
	1) 50,000

Retained Earnings	

Service Revenue	
	6) 600
	14) 50
Bal	650

Sales	
	10) 4,000

Salary Expense	
8) 700	

Utilities Expense	
9) 120	

Cost of Goods Sold	
10) 2,200	

Interest Expense	
11) 133	

Rent Expense	
12) 1,000	

Depreciation Expense	
13) 208	

EXHIBIT A–8 Income Statement

Jacobs Golf and Tennis
Income Statement
For the month ended January 31, 2000

Revenue		
Sales	$4,000	
Services	650	
Total revenue		$4,650
Expenses		
Cost of goods sold	2,200	
Rent	1,000	
Salary	700	
Depreciation	208	
Interest	133	
Utilities	120	
Total expenses		4,361
Net income		$ 289

EXHIBIT A–9 Closing Entries

Jacobs Golf & Tennis
General Journal

January 31		
15) Retained earnings	4,361	
Salary expense		700
Utilities expense		120
Cost of goods sold		2,200
Interest expense		133
Rent expense		1,000
Depreciation expense		208
To close expense accounts		
16) Service revenue	650	
Sales	4,000	
Retained earnings		4,650
To close revenue accounts		

DIVIDENDS

JG&T engaged in one more transaction in January. It declared and paid a $100 dividend to the shareholders. The analysis is as follows:

Transaction 17:	Paid dividend of $100.		
Analysis:	Cash decreases; retained earnings decreases.		
Debits and credits:	Debit retained earnings; credit cash.		
Journal entry:			
January 31	Retained earnings	100	
	Cash		100
	To record dividend		

The posting of this entry is also reflected in the general ledger accounts appearing in Exhibit A–10.

At this point, all transactions have been journalized and posted, and the revenue and expense accounts have been closed to retained earnings. A balance sheet based on the account balances in Exhibit A–10 can be prepared. It appears in Exhibit A–11.

OTHER PROCEDURAL MATTERS

One chapter cannot cover all of accounting's detailed procedures. However, a few additional items deserve attention.

Trial Balances and Worksheets

The equality of debits and credits implies that the total of all accounts with debit balances should equal the total of all accounts with credit balances. As a check on this, accountants prepare **trial balances** at various points in the accounting process.

A trial balance is simply a listing of general ledger accounts and their amounts. Two columns are used: one for accounts with debit balances and one for accounts with credit balances. Exhibit A–12 contains an illustration of a trial balance based on the account balances in Exhibit A–10. Note that the totals in the two columns balance.

An extended form of the trial balance is the **worksheet.** The worksheet serves two purposes. First, it includes a trial balance, so, accordingly, it provides a check on certain errors. Second, it serves as a testing ground for adjusting and closing entries. That is, prior to inserting the adjusting and closing entries into the general journal and ledger, many accountants test these entries in the worksheet, which is not a formal part of the accounting records. By doing this, errors in these entries can hopefully be eliminated before they are entered in the formal books of account. Worksheets are highly mechanical, so they are not considered further in this text.

Subsidiary Ledgers

This chapter has discussed only two formal accounting records: the general ledger and general journal. In actual practice, there are many more. One type of record is a **subsidiary ledger.** The purpose of a subsidiary ledger is to provide detailed information regarding a particular general ledger account.

Consider, for example, accounts receivable. This account indicates the total amount due from customers. Of course, firms also need to know the amount owed by each individual customer. Unfortunately, the accounts receivable account does not easily provide this information. The accounts receivable subsidiary ledger is designed to do this. Envision the subsidiary ledger as a separate loose-leaf notebook with a page (account) assigned to each customer.

To illustrate, assume that the Pine Company is owed a total of $700 from its three customers. Customer A owes $400, Customer B owes $200, and Customer C owes $100. As shown in Exhibit A–13, Pine's accounts receivable general ledger account shows a balance of $700. The subsidiary ledger, appearing in the lower half of the exhibit, shows the detail of each customer's indebtedness. Notice that the total of the subsidiary ledger accounts is $700, which agrees with the accounts receivable general ledger account.

Several other general ledger accounts, such as accounts payable and equipment, have subsidiary ledgers.

EXHIBIT A–10 Jacobs Golf and Tennis General Ledger

Balance Sheet Accounts

Cash

Debit	Credit
1) 50,000	3) 12,000
2) 20,000	5) 25,000
6) 200	8) 700
7) 100	17) 100
Bal 32,500	

Accounts Receivable

Debit	Credit
6) 400	
10) 4,000	
Bal 4,400	

Prepaid Rent

Debit	Credit
3) 12,000	12) 1,000
Bal 11,000	

Inventory

Debit	Credit
4) 30,000	10) 2,200
Bal 27,800	

Equipment

Debit	Credit
5) 25,000	

Accumulated Depreciation

Debit	Credit
	13) 208

Notes Payable

Debit	Credit
	2) 20,000

Accounts Payable

Debit	Credit
	4) 30,000

Unearned Revenue

Debit	Credit
14) 50	7) 100
Bal	50

Utilities Payable

Debit	Credit
	9) 120

Interest Payable

Debit	Credit
	11) 133

Invested Capital

Debit	Credit
	1) 50,000

Retained Earnings

Debit	Credit
15) 4,361	16) 4,650
17) 100	
Bal	189

Income Statement Accounts

Service Revenue

Debit	Credit
	6) 600
16) 650	14) 50
	Bal 0

Sales

Debit	Credit
16) 4,000	10) 4,000
	Bal 0

Salary Expense

Debit	Credit
8) 700	15) 700
Bal 0	

Utilities Expense

Debit	Credit
9) 120	15) 120
Bal 0	

EXHIBIT A–10 Jacobs Golf and Tennis General Ledger (Continued)

Interest Expense

	Debit	Credit
11)	133	15) 133
Bal	0	

Depreciation Expense

	Debit	Credit
13)	208	15) 208
Bal	0	

Rent Expense

	Debit	Credit
12)	1,000	15) 1,000
Bal	0	

Cost of Goods Sold

	Debit	Credit
10)	2,200	15) 2,200
Bal	0	

EXHIBIT A–11 Balance Sheet

Jacobs Golf and Tennis
Balance Sheet
January 31, 2000

Assets			Liabilities and Shareholders' Equity	
Cash		$ 32,500	Liabilities	
Accounts receivable		4,400	Accounts payable	$ 30,000
Prepaid rent		11,000	Utilities payable	120
Inventory		27,800	Interest payable	133
Equipment	$25,000		Unearned revenue	50
Less: Accumulated			Notes payable	20,000
depreciation	(208)	24,792	Total liabilities	50,303
			Shareholders' equity	
			Invested capital	50,000
			Retained earnings	189
				50,189
Total assets		$100,492	Total liabilities and shareholders' equity	$100,492

Special Journals

Preparing general journal entries for each transaction is a laborious, time-consuming process; account titles must be written and often the same amount must be written twice in the same entry. Because of this, accountants have devised streamlined journalizing procedures that make use of **special journals.** Special journals are constructed to achieve great efficiencies in journalizing transactions. Examples of special journals include sales journals, cash receipts journals, and cash payments journals.

Computerization

This appendix has emphasized manual (pen-and-ink) accounting systems, which are simple and straightforward. Accordingly, they help you envision the flow of information.

However, the vast majority of actual accounting systems are computerized and such systems have several advantages. First, they are able to process large numbers of

EXHIBIT A–12 Trial Balance

Jacobs Golf & Tennis
Trial Balance
January 31, 2000

	Debit	Credit
Cash	32,500	
Accounts receivable	4,400	
Prepaid rent	11,000	
Inventory	27,800	
Equipment	25,000	
Accumulated depreciation		208
Notes payable		20,000
Accounts payable		30,000
Unearned revenue		50
Utilities payable		120
Interest payable		133
Invested capital		50,000
Retained earnings		189
	100,700	100,700

EXHIBIT A–13 Pine Company General and Subsidiary Ledgers

General Ledger

Accounts Receivable

700	

Accounts Receivable Subsidiary Ledger

Customer A		Customer B		Customer C	
400		200		100	

transactions more quickly than manual systems. Consequently, they provide financial statements and other reports in a more timely manner. Second, they achieve a greater degree of accuracy than manual systems. Finally, they permit a greater amount of information (different reports) to be generated.

Computerized accounting systems require both hardware and software. Hardware consists of a computer's physical components, such as storage disks, monitors, keyboards, and central processing units. Computers range in size from laptop models to mainframe computers that can occupy an entire floor.

Software refers to coded instructions given to the computer, telling it how to process information. A set of instructions concerning one or more related tasks is called a *program*. Some firms develop their own programs for accounting tasks. Other firms rely on programs developed by software specialists. Many programs currently exist that enable small- and medium-sized firms to computerize their accounting functions quickly and inexpensively.

KEY TERMS

Balanced 620
Chart of accounts 620
Compound journal entry 624
Credit 619
Debit 619
General journal 621
General ledger 618
Journal entry 621
Posting 622
Special journals 632
Subsidiary ledger 630
Temporary (nominal) accounts 624
Trial balance 630
Worksheet 630

SUMMARY OF LEARNING OBJECTIVES

1. **Prepare and post journal entries.**
   Journal entries translate a transaction's basic accounting equation analysis into debits and credits. Because journal entries do not summarize the effects of transactions on the various financial statement elements, journal entries must be posted to general ledger accounts.
2. **Calculate account balances.**
   Account balances are determined by summing the debits in an account, summing the credits, and taking the difference.
3. **Prepare and post adjusting entries.**
   Adjusting entries are prepared at the end of a time period (usually a month, quarter, or year). Adjusting entries are needed because certain events might not have been reflected in the account balances. Typical examples include interest expense and depreciation expense. Adjusting entries update the account balances so that correct financial statements can be prepared.
4. **Prepare and post closing entries.**
   Revenue and expense transactions are initially recorded in revenue and expense accounts. This permits the preparation of a detailed income statement. Because these transactions ultimately affect retained earnings, closing entries are needed to transfer the balances in revenue and expense accounts to retained earnings.
5. **Generate balance sheets and income statements from general ledger accounts.**
   Financial statements can be prepared by simply transcribing the balances from the relevant general ledger accounts onto the appropriate financial statement.

QUESTIONS

A-1 Define the terms *debit* and *credit.*

A-2 Draw a diagram reflecting the parts of the accounting cycle, showing how journals, ledgers, and so on, are used to record transactions.

A-3 Define the term *posting.*

A-4 Discuss why a firm might use subsidiary ledgers.

A-5 Why are adjusting entries used?

A-6 Would a cash-based system have a need for adjusting entries? Why?

A-7 Why are closing entries used?

A-8 If a firm never prepared periodic financial statements, would it need to prepare adjusting or closing entries? Why?

A-9 What are some of the conditions that might cause a trial balance not to be "in balance"?

PROBLEMS

A-10 Describe each of the steps in the accounting process, as shown below:

1. Identify transactions and events
2. Analyze transactions and events in terms of the basic accounting equation.
3. Translate the transaction analysis into debits and credits.
4. Prepare journal entries and post to the general ledger.
5. Prepare and post adjusting entries.
6. Prepare the income statement.
7. Prepare and post-closing entries.
8. Prepare the balance sheet.

A-11 (Similar to Exercise 2-16) John Hasty opened his bakery on March 1, 1999. The following transactions took place in early March:

1. Deposited $10,000 into a checking account in the name of the Hasty Bakery.
2. Leased a small kitchen for one year at $500 per month. One month's rent was paid at this time.
3. Purchased kitchen equipment for $3,000 cash.
4. Purchased baking ingredients for $6,000 on account.
5. Obtained a $2,000, nine percent, one-year loan.
6. Rented a delivery truck for three years. The monthly payment of $200 is due at the end of each month. Nothing was paid in March.
7. Obtained a one-year insurance policy on the kitchen equipment. Paid the entire premium of $500.

Required

a. Prepare the journal entries to record these transactions.
b. Prepare any necessary adjusting entries (such as interest expense).
c. Post all journal entries to T-accounts.
d. Prepare a trial balance.
e. Prepare a balance sheet for the Hasty Bakery as of March 31, 1999.

A-12 (Similar to Problem 2-23) The following account balances are shown on November 30, 1999, for the Clever Bookstore:

Cash	$ 8,000	Accounts payable	$ 4,000
Accounts receivable	9,000	Salaries payable	2,000
Inventory	60,000	Notes payable	35,000
Supplies	3,000	J. Clever, capital	39,000
Total	$80,000	Total	$80,000

The following transactions occurred during December.

1. Paid workers the $2,000 owed them on November 30.
2. Made sales totaling $40,000. One-half of the sales were for cash. The other half were on account. The cost of goods sold was $25,000.
3. Purchased inventory on account, $15,000.
4. Collected in cash $22,000 of receivables.
5. Used supplies totaling $800.
6. Paid accounts payable of $12,000.
7. Paid December's interest on the note payable in the amount of $300.

Required

a. Prepare the journal entries to record these transactions.
b. Prepare any necessary adjusting entries.
c. Post all journal entries to T-accounts.
d. Prepare a trial balance.
e. Prepare a balance sheet for Clever Bookstore as of December 31, 1999.

A-13 (Similar to Problem 2-20) The following transactions all occurred on January 2 of the current year:

1. A company paid a $2,000 bill for a fire insurance policy that covers the current year and next year.

2. A company purchased for $200 a trash compactor that has an expected life of five years.
3. Two attorneys, working under a corporate structure, decide that a ski chalet at Vail is necessary to entertain current and prospective clients. At the same time, they are considering the addition of a third attorney. This new attorney has a ski chalet that she purchased five years ago for $120,000. Its current market value is $200,000.

Required

a. Prepare the journal entries to record these transactions. Record the acquisition of the ski chalet when the new attorney is hired and it is transferred to the corporation.
b. Prepare any necessary adjusting entries for the company's December 31 year-end (such as depreciation expense).
c. Post all journal entries to T-accounts.

A-14 (Similar to Problem 2-21) On June 1, a sole proprietorship was formed to sell and service personal computers. During the first six months, the following transactions occurred:

1. On June 1, invested $50,000 in the business.
2. On July 1, purchased a four-wheel-drive pickup truck for $22,000 (on account) that will be used in the business.
3. On September 1, paid fuel and repairs costs of $1,750 for the truck.
4. On December 31, the truck proves to be a "lemon" and it is sold to a used car dealer for $1,000.

Required

a. Prepare the journal entries to record these transactions.
b. Prepare any necessary adjusting entries for the company's December 31 year-end (such as depreciation expense).
c. Post the journal entries and accruals to T-accounts.
d. Prepare a trial balance.
e. Prepare a balance sheet for the December 31 year-end.

A-15 (Similar to Problem 2-22) Seaver & Co., a CPA firm, prepare their own financial statements with a December 31 year-end.

1. As of December 31, Seaver & Co. have rendered $20,500 worth of services to clients for which they have not yet billed the client, and for which they have not made any accounting entry.
2. Seaver & Co. owns equipment (computers, etc.) having an original cost of $12,000. The equipment has an expected life of six years.
3. On January 1, 1999, Seaver borrowed $15,000. Both principal and interest are due on December 31, 2000. The interest rate is 11 percent.
4. On January 1, 1999, Seaver rented storage space for three years. The entire three-year charge of $15,000 was paid at this time. Seaver correctly created a prepaid rent account in the amount of $15,000.
5. As of December 31, workers have earned $10,200 in wages that are unpaid and unrecorded.

Required

a. Record any necessary adjusting entries.
b. Post the journal entries to T-accounts.

A-16 (Similar to Problem 2-24) Susan's Sweets opened a candy shop on January 1.

1. Susan invested $100,000 in cash on January 1, 1999, and began business as a sole proprietorship.
2. Susan paid $20,000 for a six-month lease. The lease is renewable for another six months on July 1.
3. Susan purchased candy and other "sweetments" at a cost of $40,000 in cash.
4. Susan purchased store fixtures at a cost of $15,000, paying $5,000 in cash. These store fixtures have a useful life of five years, with no expected salvage value.
5. During the first month of operations, Susan's sales totaled $32,000. At the end of the first month, her outstanding accounts receivable were only $1,500. Her cost of sales was $9,500.
6. During the first month, her other operating expenses were $37,300 on account. She also paid herself a "salary" of $10,000, which was really a withdrawal.
7. Susan recorded depreciation for the first year.

Required

a. Prepare the journal entries to record these transactions.
b. Prepare any necessary adjusting entries (such as rent expense).
c. Post the entries to T-accounts.
d. Prepare a trial balance.
e. Prepare an income statement and balance sheet for Susan's Sweets to "tell the story" of the first month's operations.

A-17 (Similar to Problem 2-25) Susan's Shoe Shop opened on January 1. The following transactions took place during the first month:

1. Deposited $30,000 in the firm's checking account.
2. Purchased shoes, boots, socks, and other inventory for $45,000 on account.
3. Purchased display shelving, chairs, and other fixtures for $10,000 cash and $40,000 on account. Assume a useful life of five years.
4. Obtained a three-year, $20,000 bank loan at eight percent annual interest.
5. Paid $10,000 to two different creditors.
6. Signed an application for a one-year insurance policy and paid the year's premium of $2,400.
7. Paid three employees a monthly salary of $2,000 each.
8. Collected $35,000 from customers on account.

Required

a. Prepare the journal entries to record these transactions.
b. Prepare any necessary adjusting entries.
c. Post all journal entries to T-accounts.
d. Prepare a trial balance.
e. Prepare an income statement and balance sheet for Susan's Shoe Shop on January 31.

A-18 Matt's Ski Shop is in the process of acquiring a vehicle for the business. The following transactions took place in December, 2000:

1. Verbally agreed to purchase a used car from Slee-Z-Auto for $3,500.
2. Paid $400 for a warranty on the used car.

3. Took the car on a test drive, found it faulty, and told the salesperson to deliver a different car.
4. The sales manager kindly transferred the warranty to the second vehicle.
5. Paid $7,500 for the vehicle, which has a useful life of five years, and no salvage value.
6. Paid license and taxes of $475.
7. Bought new tires for $550.
8. On a cold winter morning, the car failed to start.
9. Purchased a new battery for $85.
10. Filed a warranty claim for the new battery.
11. Received $65 payment under the warranty.

Required

a. Prepare the journal entries to record these transactions.
b. Prepare any necessary adjusting entries.
c. Post all journal entries to T-accounts.

A-19 (Similar to Problem 2-29) Matt, the sole proprietor of Matt's Ski Shop, traveled to Switzerland to attend the Alpine Equipment Exposition. The following transactions occurred:

1. Paid $2,000 for airline tickets, hotel accommodations, and tour guidance from Hugo's U-Go Travel.
2. Changed the airline reservation.
3. Paid a $35 fee to change the reservation.
4. Arrived at the hotel and checked in.
5. Found his room to be next to the hotel laundry and facing the noisy loading zone. Furthermore, the room only had two cheap radios and no television!
6. Asked the hotel manager for a more suitable room.
7. Tipped the bellhop $5 after his luggage was moved.
8. Upon checking out of the hotel at the end of the week, found a $50 per day upgrade charge on his hotel bill.
9. Paid $257 for meals and phone charges on his hotel bill, but denied liability and responsibility for the upgrade charges.
10. The hotel manager insisted that the upgrade charges were Matt's responsibility, and that they would be added to his credit card balance.
11. Filed a complaint with Hugo's U-Go Travel and with the credit card issuer.
12. Received a refund of $200 from Hugo.
13. Received a credit for the upgrade charges from the credit card issuer.
14. Took films from the exposition to a photo shop for developing. Charges for developing and printing these films were expected to be $45.
15. Paid the $45 two weeks later.

Required

Prepare the journal entries for these related transactions.

A-20 (Similar to Problem 2-33) John's Anti-Mediation League (JAML) engaged in the following transactions in 1999:

1. On January 1, JAML borrowed $100,000 at six percent per year with interest due quarterly.
2. JAML paid a $1,000 kickback to a good friend who helped obtain the loan.

3. JAML had not yet paid any interest after the loan had been in effect for three months.
4. On June 30, JAML paid the interest due.
5. On July 1, JAML renegotiated the terms of the loan, which increased the interest rate to nine percent per year.
6. At the end of September, John paid the interest on the loan from his personal account.
7. At the end of December, JAML accrued the interest due.
8. On January 1, 2000, JAML paid the interest due to the lender and to John's personal account.

Required

a. Prepare the journal entries to record these transactions.
b. Post all journal entries to T-accounts.

A-21 Sue's Mediation League (SML) engaged in the following transactions in 2000:

1. On January 1, SML borrowed $250,000 at nine percent per year with interest due quarterly.
2. SML paid $1,000 to a good friend who helped obtain the loan.
3. SML had not yet paid any interest after the loan had been in effect for three months.
4. On June 30, SML paid the interest due.
5. On July 1, SML renegotiated the terms of the loan, which decreased the interest rate to six percent per year.
6. At the end of September, Sue paid the interest on the loan from her personal account.
7. At the end of December, SML accrued the interest due.
8. On January 1, 2001, SML paid the interest due to the lender and to Sue's personal account.

Required

a. Prepare the journal entries to record these transactions.
b. Post all journal entries to T-accounts.

A-22 (Similar to Problem 2-34) Sharon's Affairs and Parties (SAAP) engaged in the following transactions in 1999:

1. SAAP borrowed $150,000 at 10 percent per year to begin operations.
2. SAAP accrued the first month's interest on the loan.
3. SAAP accrued the second month's interest.
4. SAAP paid the interest due at the end of the second month.
5. Sharon loaned SAAP $10,000 at 24 percent interest per year.
6. SAAP accrued interest for the next month on both loans.
7. SAAP paid accrued interest at the end of the third month.
8. SAAP repaid Sharon's loan, along with a loan "cancellation" fee of $2,500.
9. SAAP accrued interest for the next month.
10. SAAP repaid the original loan, along with nine months accrued interest at the end of 1999.

Required

a. Prepare the journal entries to record these transactions.
b. Post all journal entries to T-accounts.

A-23 Hilger's Intimate Promises (HIP) engaged in the following transactions in 2000:

1. HIP borrowed $50,000 at eight percent per year to begin operations.
2. HIP accrued the first month's interest on the loan.
3. HIP accrued the second month's interest.
4. HIP paid the interest due at the end of the second month.
5. Hilger loaned HIP $10,000 at 24 percent interest per year.
6. HIP accrued interest for the next month on both loans.
7. HIP paid accrued interest at the end of the third month.
8. HIP repaid Hilger's loan, along with a loan "cancellation" fee of $1,500.
9. HIP accrued interest for the next month.
10. HIP repaid the original loan, along with nine months accrued interest at the end of 2000.

Required

a. Prepare the journal entries to record these transactions.
b. Post all journal entries to T-accounts.

appendix B

Careers in Accounting

INTRODUCTION

The field of accounting offers a variety of interesting and challenging career opportunities. In fact, *Money* magazine ranked accounting as the twenty-third most popular occupation. Accounting was rated high in short-term outlook, job security, and prestige. It was rated low in stress and strain. (Try telling that to a tax accountant on April 14!) This appendix describes possible accounting career choices.

Many individuals who begin their careers as accountants remain accountants throughout their work lives. Others use accounting as a stepping stone. For example, some members of congress are accountants, and at least one TV star (Bob Newhart) is a former accountant. Moreover, many chief executive officers have accounting backgrounds.

The American Institute of CPAs (AICPA) has compiled a summary of the placement results of recent college graduates. It shows the following:

	Bachelor's	Master's
Public accounting	27%	51%
Business/industry	28	18
Government	4	3
Other areas	10	2
Graduate school	2	3
Unknown	29	23
Total	100%	100%

Although this text concentrates on financial accounting, a wide array of employment possibilities are discussed here.

PUBLIC ACCOUNTING

CPA firms are the most visible employer of accountants. This visibility, in part, stems from the auditing relationship that CPA firms have with the very largest corporations. The financial statements of all publicly held companies are accompanied by an auditor's report, thereby providing CPA firms with significant publicity. Additionally, CPA firms have recently undertaken advertising campaigns costing millions of dollars. These firms regularly place advertisements in business publications such as *The Wall Street Journal* and *Fortune.* They also utilize television commercials. One firm has even aired a commercial during the Super Bowl.

CPA firms provide three primary services: auditing, tax preparation and planning, and management consulting. These services and the associated career opportunities are discussed in the following sections.

Auditing

As you know, a major role of CPA firms is to audit financial statements. The purpose of an audit is to ascertain if the statements comply with generally accepted accounting principles (GAAP). In essence, audits enhance the reliability of financial statements.

CPA firms generally have four hierarchical levels:

1. partners,
2. managers,
3. senior accountants, and
4. staff accountants.

Most CPA firms hire recent college graduates as staff accountants. These individuals have excellent educational backgrounds, but usually little or no practical experience. Accordingly, firms provide both formal and on-the-job training.

Staff accountants perform the "pick and shovel" work on an audit. Typical tasks include conducting test counts of inventory, sending letters to the client's customers to confirm accounts receivable, preparing and reviewing bank reconciliations, and verifying payroll withholdings. Computer-based tests and analyses are beginning to replace some of the drudgery associated with these tasks.

After two or three years of experience, many staff accountants are promoted to senior accountant. Senior accountants' responsibilities are much more interesting than those of staff accountants. Seniors play a major role in planning the audit. This entails specifying the audit tests necessary for a particular client. Seniors also supervise the fieldwork. That is, they oversee the staff accountants who perform the audit tests at the client's place of business.

After a total of five or six years of experience, some candidates are promoted to manager. Managers, along with senior accountants, participate in planning the audit. They supervise senior accountants and review the work of both senior and staff accountants. Managers also have significant interactions with the client's upper-level management. Many decisions, such as the timing of fieldwork, must be made jointly by the auditor and the client.

After a total of about 12 years of employment in large firms, successful candidates are promoted to partner. Less time is usually needed in smaller firms. Partners are ultimately responsible for the quality of an audit. They confer with the manager and senior accountant regarding difficult or sensitive problems. They are also the primary liaison with the client's top executives. In addition, a major part of their job entails practice development, such as getting new clients and retaining current clients. CPA firms are, after all, businesses that need clients in order to generate revenues and profits.

Tax

A major function of CPA firms is to assist clients with their taxes. Both individuals and business organizations, such as corporations, need this help. In general, CPAs provide two types of tax services. One is tax compliance which entails completing tax returns at year-end. The other service is tax planning which involves structuring transactions in order to minimize their tax effects.

Staff accountants and senior accountants are highly involved in tax compliance. Managers and partners review the work of staff and seniors and also provide clients with tax planning advice.

An increasingly important area is international tax. The globalization of business is prompting many corporations to conduct their affairs in more than one country. This requires knowledge of the tax laws of those countries, and the tax treaties among those countries.

Management Consulting

Members of CPA firms are widely recognized not only for their expertise in accounting, auditing, and taxes, but also for their overall business knowledge. Because of this, CPA firms offer a wide variety of consulting services to their clients. Perhaps the most prominent service is the installation of computerized information systems. Other services include employee benefits, mergers and acquisitions, and health care consulting.

CPA firms have been extremely successful in their consulting endeavors. For example, a recent survey by the AICPA showed that small businesses were three times more likely to seek advice from their CPA than from any other source.

Characteristics of CPA Firms

CPA firms can be described based on several characteristics. This section summarizes many important aspects of CPA firms.

Organizational Form CPA firms have traditionally been organized as sole proprietorships or partnerships. Recall that the owners of these organizations have unlimited legal liability. That is, their personal assets are available to meet all obligations of the business.

The individual states, which regulate the accounting profession, have been reluctant to permit accounting firms to organize as corporations. Many regulators feel that professionals (doctors, lawyers, accountants) should be fully responsible for their actions and should not enjoy the shield of limited liability provided by corporations.

An excellent counterargument exists, however. Consider a national CPA firm with offices in many cities. Let's assume that one of the firm's owners in the Boston office conducts a faulty audit and that the firm is sued. Should the personal assets of the firm's owners who work in, say, the Seattle office be available to satisfy any claims that may arise? These owners had nothing to do with the faulty audit, and might have only a passing acquaintance with the owner from the Boston office.

The accounting profession is currently seeking ways to limit the exposure of CPAs for damages arising from the actions of others. In many states, several organizational forms have recently become available to CPAs. Two of these are professional corporations and limited liability partnerships. Both of these organizational forms place limits on the liability of owners for acts committed by other owners. Owners, however, are still fully responsible for the consequences of their own acts. Professional corporations are typically used by accounting firms that conduct business in only one state. Limited liability partnerships are used by firms that operate in two or more states.

Size CPA firms vary dramatically in size. Many CPA firms consist of only an owner and maybe a few employees. In contrast, a number of CPA firms are extremely large international organizations. Exhibit B–1 contains a listing of the eight largest public accounting firms in the United States. The largest five firms are often referred to as the "Big Five." To gain an appreciation for their size, examine the columns labeled "Number of Professional Staff" and "Number of Offices." You can see that they are considerably larger than the other firms listed.

EXHIBIT B–1 Largest U.S. Public Accounting Firms

Rank by Revenue	Firm	FY97 U.S. Revenue ($mil)	% Chg.	No. of Partners	Non-Partner Prof'ls	No. of Offices	Practice Mix (%) A&A	Tax	MCS	Other
1	Andersen Worldwide	$5,445	21.0	1,673	32,319	95	20	14	66	0
2	PricewaterhouseCoopers	4,848	17.2	2,339	26,404	116	38	21	29	12
3	Ernst & Young	4,416	23.7	2,172	17,845	89	36	23	41	0
4	Deloitte & Touche	3,600	23.1	1,719	16,426	106	35	20	37	8
5	KPMG Peat Marwick	2,698	18.2	1,600	13,400	130	41	25	34	0
6	Grant Thornton	289	8.7	278	1,979	48	42	30	28	0
7	McGladrey & Pullen	270	5.5	381	1,883	64	33	22	23	22
8	BDO Seidman	240	13.7	217	1,337	42	51	26	23	0

SOURCE: *Public Accounting Report,* Copyright 1998 by Strafford Publications, Inc., 590 Dutch Valley Road, N.E., Atlanta, GA 30324-0729. 404-881-1141.

Of course, many medium-sized CPA firms exist. Without doubt, the public's best interest is served by a wide array of firm sizes. For example, small individual taxpayers (like us) might appreciate the personal attention (and relatively low fees) of a small or midsize firm. In contrast, a large international corporation will need the services of a large CPA firm that has multiple offices and specializes in international and domestic taxes and auditing.

The last three columns of Exhibit B–1 show the services emphasized by each firm. Most firms focus on accounting, auditing, and taxes. Only one firm, Arthur Andersen & Co., earns the majority of its revenue from management consulting services.

Compensation Exhibit B–2 summarizes salary information for several U.S. cities and the nation as a whole. Salaries vary considerably based on location. This variation reflects both the cost of living differences and supply and demand factors.

Based on levels within the firm, the biggest jump in compensation occurs between manager and partner. This makes sense, given that a manager is simply an employee of the firm, whereas a partner is an owner.

Exhibit B–2 contains averages for firms of all sizes. Compensation is usually higher in the larger firms. For example, partners in Big Five firms earn in excess of a quarter of a million dollars annually.

Overtime Employees of CPA firms have very demanding work schedules, largely due to the needs of their clients. All individual taxpayers must file their returns by April

EXHIBIT B-2 Public Accounting Salaries

	New York	Detroit	Denver	Nationwide
Entry level	$ 36,000	$ 35,000	$ 31,200	$ 31,600
Staff (1–2 years)	44,100	40,000	35,900	37,000
Senior (3–5 years)	59,300	50,000	44,500	44,800
Manager (6–9 years)	81,400	65,000	62,500	63,600
Partner (first year)	135,600	125,000	107,300	116,600

SOURCE: *Accounting & Finance Salary Survey,* 1998, by Source Finance.

15. Calendar year-end corporations must file their returns by March 15, and publicly held corporations with a calendar year-end must submit their audited financial statements by March 31.

Clearly, January through April are busy months for CPA firms. Employees of CPA firms work substantial overtime during this period. Average workweeks of 60 hours (or more) are common.

Fortunately, there can be a silver lining to the overtime cloud. Some firms provide a leisure bank. Overtime hours worked during busy seasons enable employees to take additional vacation days during slow seasons. Most firms also provide the option of monetary compensation for overtime hours.

Travel Large CPA firms have large clients, who have a number of geographic locations. Many employees of large CPA firms undertake some out-of-town travel. The auditing and management consulting staffs do most of the traveling. Although generalizations are difficult, two or three weeks of travel each year is a reasonable average. The tax staff usually travels considerably less.

CORPORATE (INDUSTRY) ACCOUNTING

Accountants who work in corporate settings perform a wide array of functions. The following sections describe general accounting, internal auditing, taxes, cost accounting, and budgeting.

General Accounting

Corporations are, of course, responsible for the preparation of their financial statements. This is a significant task, particularly for large corporations. Because of this, corporations employ many accountants to generate the information needed for financial statements.

Corporations are also subject to other reporting requirements. For example, lenders will sometimes ask for more detailed information than that found in financial statements. As another example, corporations must prepare SEC registration statements when they sell securities to the public. These and other requirements increase the need for general accounting personnel.

Internal Auditing

Virtually all large corporations, and many midsize ones, have internal audit staffs. A primary objective of an internal audit is the same as that of an external audit performed by public accountants: to help ensure the reliability of financial statements.

However, the role of internal auditing is somewhat broader. It also includes operational auditing, which assesses the effectiveness and efficiency of the corporation's operations. In part, this entails determining if internal policies are being followed. For example, many firms have a policy of paying quickly for purchases so that favorable discounts can be taken. Internal audits periodically assess if this policy is actually followed. Internal audits can also deal with much more complex issues, such as compliance with environmental laws and regulations.

Taxes

Tax accountants who work for corporations participate in the two primary tax-related activities of compliance and planning. Compliance can be quite complex for large corporations that operate in a number of jurisdictions. Federal tax returns must be completed, as well as multiple state returns. If the corporation operates in other nations, foreign returns must be compiled. Tax accountants are also responsible for returns related to payroll taxes, sales taxes, real estate taxes, and personal property taxes.

Tax planning is also a major responsibility for corporate tax accountants. The area of mergers and acquisitions is an increasingly important one for tax planning. It involves important issues such as these:

1. Should the target corporation's stock or the underlying assets be acquired?
2. Should the acquisition be funded by issuing stock, using available cash, or incurring new debt?

Careful attention to these questions can have a large impact on the amount of taxes paid.

Cost Accounting

It is crucially important for corporations to know the cost of the products and services that they produce. Without such knowledge, the profitability of different products and customers cannot be measured. This could result in unwise business decisions.

Calculating product costs in single-product firms is relatively straightforward. All manufacturing costs are related to that one product and are included in its cost. The task becomes much more difficult in multiproduct firms. In these firms, the same manufacturing facility is frequently used to produce several (perhaps many) products. Because of this, the cost of the facility must be allocated to the various products. The basis for such allocations is frequently not obvious, and cost accountants must decide how the costs are to be assigned to each product.

Cost accountants also accumulate information to help in controlling costs. For example, an important cost in many organizations is inventory handling costs, which include receiving, shipping, and storage costs. Knowing the amount spent on these activities is an essential ingredient to controlling the costs.

Budgeting

To be successful, corporations must identify goals and develop plans to achieve those goals. Budgets are quantitative expressions of corporate plans and reflect a corporation's expectations regarding future results. Realistic budgets help identify profitable opportunities. Moreover, the departure of actual results from budget targets will suggest areas in need of corrective action.

Accountants play a major role in budgeting. In conjunction with operating personnel, they develop forecasts of future operations. Accountants then trace through the effects of these forecasted operations on various financial statement items. For example, forecasts of sales and costs are a prerequisite for cash flow planning. That is, accountants will assess the impact and timing of forecasted sales and costs on cash to ascertain if future borrowings will be needed or if excess cash will be generated.

Personnel Policies

Corporations differ considerably regarding overtime, travel, training, and so on. Every situation is different, and job candidates should be careful to ask the necessary questions.

Compensation also varies, but surveys have been done that provide average salary figures. Exhibit B-3 contains entry-level averages for several types of corporate accounting positions. There is little variation across position categories, although there

EXHIBIT B-3 Corporate Accounting Salaries

	New York	Detroit	Denver	Nationwide
Entry level				
General accounting	$30,800	$30,000	$28,000	$27,600
Internal auditor	33,500	32,500	30,000	29,900
Tax accounting	35,300	32,500	23,200	30,700
Cost accounting	34,000	35,000	32,500	29,100
Controller	94,700	60,000	68,200	71,600

SOURCE: *Accounting & Finance Salary Survey*, 1998, by Source Finance.

are considerable geographic differences. The exhibit also contains average salaries for controllers, who are the chief accounting officers in corporations.

OTHER OPPORTUNITIES

Accountants are employed by many different organizations. Virtually all governmental units (federal, state, and local) rely on accountants to monitor their flow of funds. The Internal Revenue Service (IRS) employs a large number of tax accountants to interpret tax laws, provide assistance to taxpayers, and audit returns. Not-for-profit organizations, such as certain hospitals and charitable organizations, also need the services of accountants, who perform many of the same tasks in these organizations as those undertaken in corporations.

CERTIFICATION

Potential employers and the public at large have an interest in identifying competent accountants. To assist in this process, several professional organizations have established certification programs. For example, the Institute of Management Accountants operates the Certified Management Accountant (CMA) program. Other certification programs include Certified Internal Auditor (CIA) and Certified Fraud Examiner (CFE). Some certificate programs outside of the accounting field (Certified Financial Analyst) also require a knowledge of accounting.

To become certified, accountants submit their credentials for evaluation against standardized criteria established by the sponsoring organization. Most certificate programs require candidates to have a specified educational background, pass a rigorous exam, and have a certain amount of work experience. The following sections describe the two most well-known certificates: CPA and CMA.

Certified Public Accountant

The most widely known and widely held certificate is the CPA. In fact, becoming a CPA involves more than receiving the blessing of a private organization. CPAs, like doctors and lawyers, are licensed by the individual states. Each state has its own specific licensing requirements. This section provides a general overview of these requirements.

Education Most states require at least a baccalaureate degree and a specified array of accounting and related business courses. Many states require 21 to 27 semester hours of accounting. Courses might include intermediate financial accounting, intermediate managerial accounting, auditing, and taxes. Approximately 24 semester hours in other business courses, such as management, economics, finance, business law, and information systems, are also required.

There is a strong movement among the states to require 150 semester hours, rather than 120, for licensing. The rationale for this change is that both business in general, and accounting in particular, are becoming so complex that an adequate introduction to these topics requires 150 hours. The AICPA recommends the following allocation of semester hours:

General education	60–80
Education in business administration	35–50
Accounting education	25–40

The 150-hour requirement has been implemented or is being phased in by more than 40 states. Of course, all those CPAs who have 120 semester hours and are licensed prior to adoption of the 150-hour provision retain their licenses.

The CPA Exam All states require candidates to pass the Uniform CPA Exam, developed by the AICPA. The exam is given twice a year, on the first Wednesday and Thursday in May and November. It is an exhausting experience, taking $7\frac{1}{2}$ hours on Wednesday and eight hours on Thursday.

The exam has four parts:

1. Financial Accounting and Reporting
2. Accounting and Reporting—Taxation, Managerial, Governmental and Not-for-Profit Organizations
3. Auditing
4. Business Law and Professional Responsibilities

The most difficult aspect of the exam is its breadth. It is equivalent to taking a comprehensive final exam on approximately 12 courses during a two-day period. Obviously, candidates must spend a great deal of time preparing for this exam. Less than 20 percent of first-time candidates pass all parts. However, many candidates ultimately prove to be successful by retaking the parts they initially fail.

Work Experience Most states require one to three years of public accounting experience as a condition of licensing. Some states permit alternative work experiences, such as internal auditing. A few states have no experience requirement.

Other Requirements Many states require CPA candidates to pass an ethics exam. Most candidates complete a self-study course to prepare for this exam. Some states also have residency or employment requirements.

Nearly all states also require that their certificate holders engage in ongoing continuing professional education. This requirement usually involves 40 hours of training per year that is designed to enhance the competence of CPAs.

Career Implications Individuals are precluded from practicing public accounting without being a CPA. Thus, a CPA certificate is public accounting's entry requirement. (Keep in mind that you can work for a CPA firm without being a CPA.) However, in evaluating job candidates, many employers use easily implemented screening criteria, of which a CPA license is one. As a result, many CPAs are employed by corporations, governmental units, and other organizations.

Certified Management Accountant

The CMA program has four objectives:

1. to establish management accounting as a recognized profession by identifying the role of the management accountant and financial manager, the underlying body of knowledge, and a course of study by which such knowledge is acquired;
2. to encourage higher educational standards in the management accounting field;
3. to establish an objective measure of an individual's knowledge and competence in the field of management accounting; and
4. to encourage continued professional development by management accountants.

Education To become a CMA, a candidate must hold a bachelor's degree or a CPA certificate. Although the CMA program does not designate specific course work, the CMA exam, as a practical matter, effectively requires candidates to take a certain array of courses.

The CMA Exam The CMA exam is a four-part exam intended to measure candidates' knowledge of management accounting and financial management. In addition, the exam assesses candidates' abilities to analyze information and to communicate the results of that analysis. Ethical responsibilities are also addressed throughout the exam. The CMA exam's four parts are

1. Economics, Finance, and Management
2. Financial Accounting and Reporting
3. Management Reporting, Analysis, and Behavioral Issues
4. Decision Analysis and Information Systems

Candidates may register for any number of parts and take the parts in any order, but, the entire exam must be passed within three years. Each part takes four hours and the entire exam is given over a two-day period in mid-June and mid-December. Candidates who have passed the CPA exam are given credit for Part 2, Financial Accounting and Reporting.

Other Requirements CMA candidates must have two continuous years of management accounting experience or three years of auditing experience in public accounting. Holders of CMA certificates must meet a continuing professional education requirement that consists of 30 hours per year. Qualifying subjects include management accounting, corporate taxation, finance, computer science, systems analysis, statistics, management skills, insurance, marketing, business law, or other subjects relevant to the certificate holder's career development or employer needs.

WEB SITES

Numerous Web sites are available that provide information and advice about career opportunities and job search strategies. Many of these sites also provide lists of jobs and offer you the opportunity to put your resume on file. Some of these sites are

www.accountingnet.com
www.career.com
www.careermag.com
www.accountingstudents.com
www.studentcenter.com

Each of the Big Five firms has a Web site that describes, among other things, their career opportunities. These sites are

www.arthurandersen.com
www.dttus.com
www.ey.com
www.us.kpmg.com
www.pwcglobal.com/us

Finally, several very interesting sites regarding the accounting profession are available.

www.rutgers.edu/accounting
www.aicpa.org
www.fasb.org

THE FUTURE

As with many fields of endeavor, accounting faces continual change. Robert Half International, a leading employment agency specializing in accounting, has identified several factors that will affect accounting as we enter the 21st century. The following sections discuss these factors.

Computers

Computers are a fact of life for every accountant. Even very small organizations have computerized their accounting functions. The widespread use of computers is due to (1) the rapidly declining cost of computers, (2) the increased power of such computers, and (3) the availability of low-cost accounting software.

Accountants must be familiar with both hardware and software. College courses and continuing professional education classes address these issues. Since many computers operate in a similar fashion, most courses focus on software. The majority of software packages are user-friendly and require no knowledge of computer programming languages. These packages usually include readable instruction manuals, as well as on screen tutorials and help functions.

Although employers often provide training, they also look quite favorably on job candidates who already have some computer expertise. In fact, some employers pay a five to 10 percent premium to candidates who have experience with certain software packages.

Globalization

Businesses are now looking at the entire world as their marketplace. Both corporations and public accounting firms are expanding their international operations, creating the need for accountants with a global view. Accountants need to know the business practices, accounting procedures, language, and social customs of the countries in which their firms operate. Much of this knowledge is gained through experience, but some of it, including language training, can be obtained through formal classes.

Demographics and Personnel Policies

Perhaps the most noteworthy demographic trend in accounting is the increasing number of female accountants. More than half of recent accounting graduates were women. This suggests an increase in two-career couples. Managing two demanding work schedules and a family life is quite difficult. Because of this, organizations are becoming more flexible in their terms of employment. Part-time employment and job-sharing are more commonplace. Some public accounting firms have a partnership track that entails less than full-time work.

Although women comprise a majority of recent accounting graduates, men still dominate the upper levels in most firms (the "glass ceiling" effect). However, the trend is towards more equality. Although a few years ago only six percent of partners in large public accounting firms were female, current statistics indicate that women hold approximately 10 percent of partnership positions. This change is at least partially due to the formal mentoring programs established by firms to ensure that their female staff do not feel alienated and are given proper career guidance.

SUMMARY AND REVIEW

Accounting offers a variety of career opportunities, many of which are rather lucrative. Accountants are employed by public accounting firms, corporations, governmental units, and not-for-profit organizations. Accounting professionals engage in a variety of functions, such as financial accounting, taxes, cost accounting, and budgeting.

Certification is an important step in an accountant's career path. It is an indication of a candidate's qualifications. The most recognized certificate is the CPA. The CMA is, perhaps, the second most recognized certification.

The future job outlook for accountants is good. Demand for accountants is expected to be strong, and accountants continue to be respected by the business community. Accounting is also a road to the top of business organizations; many chief executive officers began their careers as accountants.

a p p e n d i x

The Time Value of Money

STUDYING THIS APPENDIX WILL ENABLE YOU TO

1. Determine the future value, or compound amount, of dollars that are invested or borrowed today.
2. Determine the value today, or present value, of dollars that are to be received or paid in the future.
3. Understand how the concept of present value is used to calculate interest expense.

INTRODUCTION

Many business transactions create financial assets and liabilities that represent cash inflows and outflows that will occur in future periods. For this reason, it is necessary to consider the concept of present and future values, or the **time value of money,** in order to determine how such transactions should be reported in the financial statements.

FUTURE VALUE

Money deposited to an interest-earning bank account will "grow" over time. For example, $1,000 deposited in an account earning 8% per year will amount to $1,080 ($1,000 × 1.08 = $1,080) after one year. If the total amount is left on deposit for a second year, it will grow to $1,166 rounded ($1080 × 1.08 = $1,166). Because the interest is not withdrawn from the account, in each successive year the account earns "interest on interest," and the account grows by a larger dollar amount each year. This notion of earning interest on interest is referred to as **compound interest.** The growth in the account balance can be depicted in the following way:

Initial deposit		$1,000
Amount in one year		$1,000 × (1.08) = $1,080.00
Amount in two years		$1,000 × (1.08) × (1.08)
	or	$1,000 × $(1.08)^2$ = $1,000 × (1.166) = $1,166

More generally, let *P* represent the initial deposit, let *i* represent the interest rate, let *n* represent the number of periods (e.g., years) over which the deposit is allowed to grow, and let *A* represent the **future value** of the deposit. The relationship may be written in the following way.

$$A = P \times (1 + i)^n$$

In our earlier example, $P = \$1{,}000$, $i = 8\%$, and $n = 2$, so

$$\begin{aligned} A &= P \times (1 + i)^n \\ &= \$1000 \times (1.08)^2 \\ &= \$1000 \times (1.166) \\ &= \$1{,}166 \end{aligned}$$

If the deposit were allowed to grow for 10 years, the future value would be \$2,159, i.e.,

$$\begin{aligned} A &= P \times (1 + i)^n \\ &= \$1{,}000 \times (1.08)^{10} \\ &= \$1{,}000 \times (2.159) \\ &= \$2{,}159 \end{aligned}$$

This simple formula may be used for any values of P (the initial deposit), i (the interest rate), and n (the number of periods) in order to obtain the future value of the deposit. The expression $(1 + i)^n$ is referred to as the **future value factor** because it converts the initial deposit to its future value for given values of i and n.

Future values frequently must be computed in business and finance, and special tables have been prepared showing the future value factors for various interest rates and numbers of periods. As a practical matter, financial calculators or personal computers are used to make these calculations. The tables included in this text are useful as a way of introducing you to the concepts of future values and present values. Exhibit C-1 contains future value factors, and you can use this table to verify the calculations that were made earlier. For example, refer to the 8% column in Exhibit C-1; the entries in this column show the future amounts for \$1 invested today at 8% per period. The factors for 1, 2, and 10 periods are 1.080, 1.166, and 2.159, respectively, the same as those used in our previous calculations.

PRESENT VALUE

In the preceding examples, we determined the future value of a cash deposit made today. Business decisions often require that we determine the value today, or **present value,** of an amount to be received or paid in the future. For example, suppose that we need \$10 million in three years to pay for new plant and equipment. How much would we need to deposit today in order to have \$10 million in three years, assuming that the interest rate is 10% per year? In this case we know the future amount (\$10 million), the interest rate (10%), and the number of periods (three years). We need to determine the value today, or the present value, of \$10 million to be paid three years in the future. Recall our earlier expression for calculating future values:

$$A = P \times (1 + i)^n$$

If we know A, the future value, and wish to determine P, the present value, we need only rearrange the expression as follows:

$$P = A \times 1/(1 + i)^n$$

EXHIBIT C-1 Future Value of $1

Periods	1%	2%	4%	6%	8%	10%	12%	14%	16%	18%	20%
1	1.010	1.020	1.040	1.060	1.080	1.100	1.120	1.140	1.160	1.180	1.200
2	1.020	1.040	1.082	1.124	1.166	1.210	1.254	1.300	1.346	1.392	1.440
3	1.030	1.061	1.125	1.191	1.260	1.331	1.405	1.482	1.561	1.643	1.728
4	1.041	1.082	1.170	1.262	1.360	1.464	1.574	1.689	1.811	1.939	2.074
5	1.051	1.104	1.217	1.338	1.469	1.611	1.762	1.925	2.100	2.288	2.488
6	1.062	1.126	1.265	1.419	1.587	1.772	1.974	2.195	2.436	2.70	2.986
7	1.072	1.149	1.316	1.504	1.714	1.949	2.211	2.502	2.826	3.186	3.583
8	1.083	1.172	1.369	1.594	1.851	2.144	2.476	2.853	3.278	3.759	4.300
9	1.094	1.195	1.423	1.689	1.999	2.358	2.773	3.252	3.803	4.436	5.160
10	1.105	1.219	1.480	1.791	2.159	2.594	3.106	3.707	4.411	5.234	6.192
11	1.116	1.243	1.539	1.898	2.332	2.853	3.479	4.226	5.117	6.176	7.430
12	1.127	1.268	1.601	2.012	2.518	3.138	3.896	4.818	5.936	7.288	8.920
13	1.138	1.294	1.665	2.133	2.720	3.452	4.363	5.492	6.886	8.599	10.699
14	1.149	1.319	1.732	2.261	2.937	3.798	4.887	6.261	7.988	10.147	12.839
15	1.161	1.346	1.801	2.397	3.172	4.177	5.474	7.138	9.266	11.974	15.407
16	1.173	1.373	1.873	2.540	3.426	4.595	6.130	8.137	10.748	14.129	18.499
17	1.184	1.400	1.948	2.693	3.700	5.054	6.866	9.276	12.468	16.672	22.186
18	1.196	1.428	2.026	2.854	3.996	5.560	7.690	10.575	14.463	19.673	26.623
19	1.208	1.457	2.107	3.026	4.316	6.116	8.613	12.056	16.777	23.214	31.948
20	1.220	1.486	2.191	3.207	4.661	6.728	9.646	13.743	19.461	27.393	38.338
21	1.232	1.516	2.279	3.400	5.034	7.400	10.804	15.668	22.575	32.324	46.005
22	1.245	1.546	2.370	3.604	5.437	8.140	12.100	17.861	26.186	38.142	55.206
23	1.257	1.577	2.465	3.820	5.871	8.954	13.552	20.362	30.376	45.008	66.247
24	1.270	1.608	2.563	4.049	6.341	9.850	15.179	23.212	35.236	53.109	79.497
25	1.282	1.641	2.666	4.292	6.848	10.835	17.000	26.462	40.874	62.669	95.396

In the present example, the future payment is known to be $10 million. The time period is three years, and the interest rate is 10%.

$$\begin{aligned} P &= A \times 1/(1 + i)^n \\ &= \$10{,}000{,}000 \times 1/(1.10)^3 \\ &= \$10{,}000{,}000 \times (.751) \\ &= \$7{,}510{,}000 \end{aligned}$$

In other words, if you were to deposit $7,510,000 into an account earning 10% interest, then the account balance would accumulate to $10 million at the end of three years. You can verify this result by using the future value factors in Exhibit C-1. Note that the future value factor at 10% for three periods is 1.331:

$$\begin{aligned} A &= P \times (1 + i)^n \\ &= \$7{,}510{,}000 \times (1.10)^3 = \$7{,}510{,}000 \times (1.331) \\ &= \$10{,}000{,}000 \text{ (rounded)} \end{aligned}$$

In financial terms, you would be equally as well off if you were to receive (or pay) $10 million in three years or to receive (or pay) $7,510,000 today.

In this case, the future value, A, is multiplied by a **present value factor,** $1/(1 + i)^n$, in order to obtain its present value. Exhibit C-2 contains present value factors. Notice that the future value factors in Exhibit C-1 and the present value factors in Exhibit

C-2 have a *reciprocal* relationship, i.e., present value factors are the inverses of future value factors.

$$\text{Present value factor} = \frac{1}{\text{Future value factor}}$$

For example, when $i = 8\%$ and $n = 2$

Present value factor = .857
Future value factor = 1.166
and .857 = 1/1.166

Let's use the present value factors in Exhibit C-2 to determine the present value of $100,000 to be received in five periods, assuming alternatively that the appropriate interest rate is 4, 8, and 12%. When interest rates are used to compute present values instead of future values, the interest rate is usually referred to as the **discount rate.**

Discount Rate (%)	Future Cash Receipt ($)	×	Present Value Factor for $n = 5$ (Exhibit C-2)	=	Present Value ($)
4	100,000	×	.822	=	82,200
8	100,000	×	.681	=	68,100
12	100,000	×	.567	=	56,700

EXHIBIT C-2 Present Value of $1

Periods	1%	2%	4%	6%	8%	10%	12%	14%	16%	18%	20%
1	0.990	0.980	0.962	0.943	0.926	0.909	0.893	0.877	0.862	0.847	0.833
2	0.980	0.961	0.925	0.890	0.857	0.826	0.797	0.769	0.743	0.718	0.694
3	0.971	0.942	0.889	0.840	0.794	0.751	0.712	0.675	0.641	0.609	0.579
4	0.961	0.924	0.855	0.792	0.735	0.683	0.636	0.592	0.552	0.516	0.482
5	0.951	0.906	0.822	0.747	0.681	0.621	0.567	0.519	0.476	0.437	0.402
6	0.942	0.888	0.790	0.705	0.630	0.564	0.507	0.456	0.410	0.370	0.335
7	0.933	0.871	0.760	0.665	0.583	0.513	0.452	0.400	0.354	0.314	0.279
8	0.923	0.853	0.731	0.627	0.540	0.467	0.404	0.351	0.305	0.266	0.233
9	0.914	0.837	0.703	0.592	0.500	0.424	0.361	0.308	0.263	0.225	0.194
10	0.905	0.820	0.676	0.558	0.463	0.386	0.322	0.270	0.227	0.191	0.162
11	0.896	0.804	0.650	0.527	0.429	0.350	0.287	0.237	0.195	0.162	0.135
12	0.887	0.788	0.625	0.497	0.397	0.319	0.257	0.208	0.168	0.137	0.112
13	0.879	0.773	0.601	0.469	0.368	0.290	0.229	0.182	0.145	0.116	0.093
14	0.870	0.758	0.577	0.442	0.340	0.263	0.205	0.160	0.125	0.099	0.078
15	0.861	0.743	0.555	0.417	0.315	0.239	0.183	0.140	0.108	0.084	0.065
16	0.853	0.728	0.534	0.394	0.292	0.218	0.163	0.123	0.093	0.071	0.054
17	0.844	0.714	0.513	0.371	0.270	0.198	0.146	0.108	0.080	0.060	0.045
18	0.836	0.700	0.494	0.350	0.250	0.180	0.130	0.095	0.069	0.051	0.038
19	0.828	0.686	0.475	0.331	0.232	0.164	0.116	0.083	0.060	0.043	0.031
20	0.820	0.673	0.456	0.312	0.215	0.149	0.104	0.073	0.051	0.037	0.026
21	0.811	0.660	0.439	0.294	0.199	0.135	0.093	0.064	0.044	0.031	0.022
22	0.803	0.647	0.422	0.278	0.184	0.123	0.083	0.056	0.038	0.026	0.018
23	0.795	0.634	0.406	0.262	0.170	0.112	0.074	0.049	0.033	0.022	0.015
24	0.788	0.622	0.390	0.247	0.158	0.102	0.066	0.043	0.028	0.019	0.013
25	0.780	0.610	0.375	0.233	0.146	0.092	0.059	0.038	0.024	0.016	0.010

As you might expect, the same future cash flow ($100,000 in this example) has differing present values, depending on the discount rate used. A larger discount rate produces a smaller present value. This is a sensible result because a higher interest rate indicates that interest earnings will be greater. Accordingly, the required initial deposit is smaller. The choice of a suitable discount rate to use in finding the present value of expected future cash flows requires considerable judgment. In general, discount rates that are used by lenders and investors vary directly with risk. For instance, riskier loans and investments require higher discount rates.

PRESENT VALUE AND SERIES OF FUTURE PAYMENTS

Imagine for a moment that you have won a million-dollar lottery and will receive payments of $200,000 at the end of each year for five years (5 years × $200,000 = $1 million). Could you use your lottery prize immediately to pay for a million-dollar house? You soon would realize that the lottery prize is worth less than $1 million because the payments will be received at various future dates. To find the prize's real value, you would need to determine the present value of each payment. Then you would add the present values of the individual payments in order to obtain the total present value. Assuming a 10% interest rate, the calculation is as follows:

Date of Payment	Cash flow ($)	×	Present Value Factor (Exhibit C-2)	=	Present Value ($)
End of:					
Year 1	200,000	×	.909	=	181,800
Year 2	200,000	×	.827	=	165,400
Year 3	200,000	×	.751	=	150,200
Year 4	200,000	×	.683	=	136,600
Year 5	200,000	×	.621	=	124,200
	Total		3.791		$758,200

This result shows that the series of five payments of $200,000 has a value today of $758,200, even though the total of the five payments is $1 million. In other words, if you were to receive $758,200 today and deposit this amount in a bank account earning 10% per year, you would be able to withdraw $200,000 at the end of each year for five years. In this sense, you would be just as well off receiving $758,200 immediately as if you received the five lottery payments (totaling $1 million) over five years. Instead of buying a million-dollar house today, you can only afford to spend $758,200.

In this lottery example, the cash flows are equal in dollar amount and are paid at the end of each period. The term **annuity** is used to describe equal cash flows over uniform time intervals. Such cash flow patterns are found frequently in business contracts. For this reason, special present value tables have been prepared for evaluating annuities. Exhibit C-3 contains present value factors for this purpose.

If we use the notation *S* to indicate the dollar amount of each of a series of cash flows and PVAF (*i* percent, *n* periods) to indicate the present value factor for an annuity of *n* periods at interest rate *i*, and if the interest rate is 10%, then your lottery winnings may be valued as follows using Exhibit C-3:

$$\begin{aligned} P &= S \times PVAF^{i}_{n} \ (i \text{ percent}, n \text{ periods}) \\ &= \$200{,}000 \times PVAF^{.10}_{5} \ (10\%, 5 \text{ periods}) \\ &= \$200{,}000 \times 3.791 \ (\text{from Exhibit C-3}) \\ &= \$758{,}200 \end{aligned}$$

EXHIBIT C-3 Present Value of an Annuity

Periods	1%	2%	4%	6%	8%	10%	12%	14%	16%	18%	20%
1	0.990	0.980	0.962	0.943	0.926	0.909	0.893	0.877	0.862	0.847	0.833
2	1.970	1.942	1.886	1.833	1.783	1.736	1.690	1.647	1.605	1.566	1.528
3	2.941	2.884	2.775	2.673	2.577	2.487	2.402	2.322	2.246	2.174	2.106
4	3.902	3.808	3.630	3.465	3.312	3.170	3.037	2.914	2.798	2.690	2.589
5	4.853	4.713	4.452	4.212	3.993	3.791	3.605	3.433	3.274	3.127	2.991
6	5.795	5.601	5.242	4.917	4.623	4.355	4.111	3.889	3.685	3.498	3.326
7	6.728	6.472	6.002	5.582	5.206	4.868	4.564	4.288	4.039	3.812	3.605
8	7.652	7.325	6.733	6.210	5.747	5.335	4.968	4.639	4.344	4.078	3.837
9	8.566	8.162	7.435	6.802	6.247	5.759	5.328	4.946	4.607	4.303	4.031
10	9.471	8.983	8.111	7.360	6.710	6.145	5.650	5.216	4.833	4.494	4.192
11	10.368	9.787	8.760	7.887	7.139	6.495	5.938	5.453	5.029	4.656	4.327
12	11.255	10.575	9.385	8.384	7.536	6.814	6.194	5.660	5.197	4.793	4.439
13	12.134	11.348	9.986	8.853	7.904	7.103	6.424	5.842	5.342	4.910	4.533
14	13.004	12.106	10.563	9.295	8.244	7.367	6.628	6.002	5.468	5.008	4.611
15	13.865	12.849	11.118	9.712	8.559	7.606	6.811	6.142	5.575	5.092	4.675
16	14.718	13.578	11.652	10.106	8.851	7.824	6.974	6.265	5.669	5.162	4.730
17	15.562	14.292	12.166	10.477	9.122	8.022	7.120	6.373	5.749	5.222	4.775
18	16.398	14.992	12.659	10.828	9.372	8.201	7.250	6.467	5.818	5.273	4.812
19	17.226	15.678	13.134	11.158	9.604	8.365	7.366	6.550	5.877	5.316	4.844
20	18.046	16.351	13.590	11.470	9.818	8.514	7.469	6.623	5.929	5.353	4.870
21	18.857	17.011	14.029	11.764	10.017	8.649	7.562	6.687	5.973	5.384	4.891
22	19.660	17.658	14.451	12.042	10.201	8.772	7.645	6.743	6.011	5.410	4.909
23	20.456	18.292	14.857	12.303	10.371	8.883	7.718	6.792	6.044	5.432	4.925
24	21.243	18.914	15.247	12.550	10.529	8.985	7.784	6.835	6.073	5.451	4.937
25	22.023	19.523	15.622	12.783	10.675	9.077	7.843	6.873	6.097	5.467	4.948

This is the same result as the one we obtained earlier by finding the present values of each payment and adding them to obtain the total present value of the series of five payments. In fact, the present value factors for annuities are equal to the sum of the present value factors for the individual cash flows. Refer to our previous calculation. The total of the five present value factors from Exhibit C-2 is the same as the present value factor for a five-period annuity from Exhibit C-3.

FUTURE VALUE AND SERIES OF FUTURE PAYMENTS

Firms sometimes arrange to make a series of cash payments over several periods to a special fund referred to as a **sinking fund.** The ending balance of the sinking fund is usually designated for a special purpose, such as the retirement of outstanding debt or the replacement of operating assets. To illustrate, let us continue with your imagined lottery winnings. Assume that you deposit in a retirement fund the $200,000 payments received at the end of each of the next five years. You expect to earn 10% each year. At the end of the fifth year, what would be the balance in your retirement fund? To find the future value of the fund, you would determine the future value of each deposit. Then you would add these future values in order to determine the total future value of your fund in the following manner (see next page).

Date of Deposit	Cash flow ($)	×	Future Value Factor (Exhibit C-1)	=	Future Value ($)
End of:					
Year 1	200,000	×	1.464	=	292,800
Year 2	200,000	×	1.331	=	266,200
Year 3	200,000	×	1.210	=	242,000
Year 4	200,000	×	1.100	=	220,000
Year 5	200,000	×	1.000	=	200,000
	Total		6.105		$1,221,000

Because each deposit is made at the end of the year, the first deposit earns interest for four years, the second deposit earns interest for three years, and so on. The last deposit is made at the end of the fifth (and last) year and so earns no interest at all. Since each of the cash flows is the same ($200,000), the cash flows are an annuity. That is, they are equal in dollar amount and are deposited each period. Because sinking funds with equal annual deposits are found frequently in business contracts, special future value tables have been prepared containing the appropriate annuity factors. Exhibit C-4 contains such factors.

EXHIBIT C-4 Future Value of an Annuity

Periods	1%	2%	4%	6%	8%	10%	12%	14%	16%	18%	20%
1	1.000	1.000	1.000	1.000	1.000	1.000	1.000	1.000	1.000	1.000	1.000
2	2.010	2.020	2.040	2.060	2.080	2.100	2.120	2.140	2.160	2.180	2.200
3	3.030	3.060	3.122	3.184	3.246	3.310	3.374	3.440	3.506	3.572	3.640
4	4.060	4.122	4.246	4.375	4.506	4.641	4.779	4.921	5.067	5.215	5.368
5	5.101	5.204	5.416	5.637	5.867	6.105	6.353	6.610	6.877	7.154	7.442
6	6.152	6.308	6.633	6.975	7.336	7.716	8.115	8.536	8.978	9.442	9.930
7	7.214	7.434	7.898	8.394	8.923	9.487	10.089	10.731	11.414	12.142	12.916
8	8.286	8.583	9.214	9.897	10.637	11.436	12.300	13.233	14.240	15.329	16.499
9	9.369	9.755	10.583	11.491	12.488	13.579	14.776	16.085	17.519	19.089	20.799
10	10.462	10.950	12.006	13.181	14.487	15.937	17.549	19.337	21.322	23.521	25.959
11	11.567	12.169	13.486	14.972	16.645	18.531	20.655	23.045	25.733	28.755	32.150
12	12.683	13.412	15.026	16.870	18.977	21.384	24.133	27.271	30.850	34.931	39.581
13	13.809	14.680	16.627	18.882	21.495	24.523	28.029	32.089	36.786	42.214	48.497
14	14.947	15.974	18.292	21.015	24.215	27.975	32.393	37.581	43.672	50.818	59.196
15	16.097	17.293	20.024	23.276	27.152	31.772	37.280	43.842	51.660	60.965	72.035
16	17.258	18.639	21.825	25.673	30.324	35.950	42.753	50.980	60.925	72.939	87.442
17	18.430	20.012	23.698	28.213	33.750	40.545	48.884	59.118	71.673	87.068	105.931
18	19.615	21.412	25.645	30.906	37.450	45.599	55.750	68.394	84.141	103.740	128.112
19	20.811	22.841	27.671	33.760	41.446	51.159	63.440	78.969	98.603	123.414	154.740
20	22.019	24.287	29.778	36.786	45.762	57.275	72.052	91.025	115.380	146.628	186.688
21	23.239	25.783	31.968	39.993	50.423	64.002	81.699	104.768	134.841	174.021	225.026
22	24.472	27.299	34.248	43.396	55.457	71.402	92.503	120.436	157.415	206.345	271.031
23	25.716	28.845	36.618	46.996	60.893	79.543	104.603	138.297	183.601	244.487	326.237
24	26.973	30.422	39.083	50.812	66.765	88.497	118.155	158.659	213.978	289.494	392.484
25	28.243	32.030	41.646	54.865	73.106	98.347	133.334	181.811	249.214	342.603	471.981

If we use the notation *S* to indicate the dollar amount of each of a series of future cash flows and FVAF (*i* percent, *n* periods) to indicate the future value factor for an annuity of *n* periods at interest rate *i*, and if the interest rate is 10%, then after five periods your retirement fund will amount to $1,221,000, computed as follows using Exhibit C-4:

$$
\begin{aligned}
\text{Future value} &= S \times \text{FVAF}^{i}_{n} \ (i \text{ percent}, n \text{ periods}) \\
&= \$\,200{,}000 \times \text{FVAF}^{.10}_{5} \ (10\%, 5 \text{ periods}) \\
&= \$\,200{,}000 \times 6.105 \ (\text{from Exhibit C-4}) \\
&= \$1{,}221{,}000
\end{aligned}
$$

In other words, $200,000 per year for five years at 10% interest has the same value as a single receipt of $1,221,000 at the end of five years. From our earlier example, recall that the same five-year $200,000 annuity has a present value of $758,200. From this, it follows that a single payment of $1,221,000 to be received in five years has the same value as $758,200 to be received immediately.[1]

At this point, you have acquired a useful set of tools for dealing with the time value of money. You are able to determine the future amount, or compound value, of an amount deposited today at a specified interest rate and number of time periods. Conversely, you are able to determine the value today, or present value, of an amount to be received at a specified future date, given the prevailing interest rate. Also, you are able to determine both the present value and the future value of an ordinary annuity or a series of periodic cash flows that are equal in dollar amount. The discussion of noncurrent liabilities in Chapter 9 will give you a chance to put these tools to good use.

This appendix has explained the time value of money and has illustrated the techniques of compound interest that are used widely in accounting for long-term financial assets and liabilities. Present value is the term used to denote the value today of cash to be received or paid in future periods. Future value is the term used to denote the expected maturity value of cash that is deposited (or otherwise invested) today at a specified rate of interest for a given number of future periods. Special tables have been constructed containing present value and future value factors for single cash flows, and the use of these tables has been illustrated in this appendix.

Business cash flows are often in the form of annuities, which are a series of cash flows that are equal in dollar amount and occur over uniform time intervals. Present value and future value calculations for annuities have been explained in the appendix. Special tables also have been constructed for evaluating annuities, and their use has been illustrated.

[1]The future value factor for five periods at 10% is 1.611 (from Exhibit C-1).

$$
\begin{aligned}
A &= P \times (1 + i)^{n} \\
&= \$758{,}200 \times (1.10)5 \\
&= \$758{,}200 \times (1.611) \\
&= \$1{,}221{,}000 \ (\text{rounded})
\end{aligned}
$$

KEY TERMS

Annuity 651
Compound interest 647
Discount rate 650
Future value 647
Future value factor 648
Present value 648
Present value factor 649
Sinking fund 652
Time value of money 647

SUMMARY OF LEARNING OBJECTIVES

1. **Determine the future value, or compound amount, of dollars that are invested or borrowed today.**
Compound interest calculations were explained using the following notation:

A = future value
P = present value
S = dollar amount of each of a series of cash flows (an annuity)
i = periodic interest rate
n = number of time periods

Future value, single cash deposit:

$$A = P \times (1 + i)^n \text{ (requires use of Exhibit C-1)}$$

Future value, series of equal cash flows (an annuity):

$$A = S \times FVAF^i_n \text{ (} i \text{ percent, } n \text{ periods) (requires use of Exhibit C-4)}$$

2. **Determine the value today, or present value, of dollars that are to be received or paid in the future.**
Present value, single future cash flow:

$$P = A \times 1/(1 + i)^n \text{ (requires use of Exhibit C-2)}$$

Present value, series of equal cash flows (an annuity)

$$P = S \times PVAF^i_n \text{ (} i \text{ percent, } n \text{ periods) (requires use of Exhibit C-3)}$$

3. **Understand how the concept of present value is used to calculate interest expense.**
When a firm borrows money, the amount received is the present value of the dollar amounts that will be repaid to the lender in the future. In other words, the future repayments are discounted at a suitable interest rate, to determine the present value of the loan. For this reason, interest expense is determined each period by multiplying the present value of the loan at the start of the period, by the interest rate that was used in discounting the future repayments.

QUESTIONS

C-1 Describe the concept of compound interest. In your own terms, why is a dollar today worth more than a dollar to be received three years from now?

C-2 Compare and contrast the concepts of future value and present value. Why might a decision maker prefer to use present values? Under what circumstances might future values be preferred?

C-3 Define an annuity. Under what circumstances can an annuity be a liability? Why might an analyst prefer to use the annuity concept in analyzing different liabilities?

C-4 In analyzing the benefits of two different annuities, will present values and future values yield a different ranking of the two annuities? Why? Describe the differences between each set of comparisons.

C-5 What basic information must be known before calculating the discounted cash flows associated with any liability?

C-6 Explain the concept of compound interest. In your discussion, explain why an initial deposit left in an interest-earning bank account for several years would earn larger amounts of interest in each successive year.

C-7 Discuss the different perspectives used to analyze the time value of money:
  a. Future value versus present value of a single amount
  b. Future value versus present value of a series of future payments (annuities)

C-8 When calculating a future value, if the interest rate increases from 12 to 18 percent, what happens to the future value? Why?

C-9 a. When calculating a present value, if the interest rate increases from 12 to 18 percent, what happens to the present value? Why?
  b. Is there any inconsistency between your answer to this question and your answer to Question 9A-8? Why or why not?

C-10 a. Identify the basic types of information that you must have in order to calculate the time value of money.
  b. Which of these information elements is more objective (can be determined with greater precision)?
  c. How will subjective estimates of some of these factors affect your interpretation and use of present and future values?

C-11 Could an analyst use either present or future values and still get the same rankings or preferences for two alternative projects? Why?

C-12 Assuming that an analyst's conclusions or investment decisions will be the same under either present or future values, why are present values preferred for most analytical purposes?

EXERCISES

Future Value Calculations

C-13 Calculate the future value of the following cash flow streams, assuming a 10 percent annual interest rate in each case:
  a. Deposit $10,000 in a certificate of deposit for three years.
  b. Deposit $10,000 in a savings account at the end of year 1 and an additional $10,000 at the end of year 2. What is the balance in the account at the end of the second year?
  c. Make five deposits of $10,000 in a savings account on December 31 of each year. What is the balance at the end of the fifth year? At the end of the fourth year?

Present Value Calculations

C-14 Calculate the present value of the following cash flow streams, assuming a 12 percent interest rate in each case:
  a. A certificate of deposit will mature in one year that will be worth $ 10,000 at that time.
  b. A $100,000 bond will mature in three years.
  c. An insurance payout agreement will provide $30,000 at the end of each of the next three years.

Future Value Calculations

C-15 You have just discovered a 1957 Corvette that the owner will sell you in three years for $25,000. How much must you deposit in your savings account each year for three years in order to be able to buy the Corvette? Assume that all deposits are at the end of the year and that the Corvette will be purchased at the end of the third year. Also, assume an interest rate of eight percent.

Present Value Calculations

C-16 At the end of five years, you are guaranteed to receive $20,000. At each of the specified interest rates, what is the present value of this future promise?

a. Assume annual compounding at 12 percent.
b. Assume annual compounding at six percent.
c. Why is the present value different at different interest rates? Discuss these differences. Without making any further calculations, would the present value at 16 percent be higher or lower than the present value at 12 percent. Discuss why this must be so.

Present Value Calculations

C-17 A firm expects to make future payments on its warranty obligations of $300,000 per year for the next five years. What is the present value of this liability?

a. Assume an interest rate of 12 percent.
b. Assume an interest rate of six percent.
c. Why should a reader of financial statements be concerned about the interest rate that the firm may have used in calculating the present values of various financial contracts?

PROBLEMS

Time Value Calculations

C-18 Evaluate each independent situation using the appropriate table and an interest rate of 12 percent.

a. You would like to relax and not work for the next six years, but you would like to withdraw $25,000 at the end of each year. How much must you have in your investment account now to be able to do this?
b. You would like to have $100,000 upon graduation. How much should you invest in a fund at the end of each year for the next four years?
c. Your firm signs a contract to repay $1,000,000 in five years. How much will the firm receive today in exchange for this promised future payment?
d. You have found some wonderful mountain property. You're thinking if you could invest a single sum of $50,000 for five years you might be able to buy a parcel of land that costs $70,000. However, the land cost is expected to appreciate compounded at four percent per year. Can you afford the land?

Time Value Calculations

C-19 Evaluate each independent situation, using the appropriate table and an interest rate of eight percent.

a. A retirement fund is set up to pay $15,000 per year for the next 20 years. How much is in the fund at the beginning?

b. A company is required, as part of their loan restrictions, to set up a sinking fund account (an investment account) and invest $5,000 at year-end for four years. How much will be in the fund at the end of four years to provide for the debt payoff? Identify two alternative ways of using the tables to calculate your answer.

c. How much should you invest now to have $60,000 at the end of nine years? Would your answer be different if interest is compounded semiannually during these nine years?

d. How much will your fund grow to in 10 years if you invest $20,000 today? Would your answer be different if interest is compounded semiannually during these 10 years?

Annuity Necessary to Meet Future Cash Objective

C-20 A firm promises to pay its CEO a bonus of $1,000,000 on her retirement at the end of eight years. How much must the firm put aside at the end of each year at an interest rate of 10 percent in order to meet its commitment? Identify two alternative ways of using future value tables to analyze this problem.

Future Value of Annuity Deposits

C-21 A large chemical firm has just lost a major lawsuit and now must make 20 payments of $1,000,000 at year-end to the survivors of its chemical factory explosion. Using an eight percent interest factor, how much must be in the fund to provide for these payments?

Present Value Calculations

C-22 Calculate the present value of the following cash flows, using a 10 percent interest rate:

a. Your rich uncle promises to give you $1,000,000 in 10 years, when you are more mature and able to handle such sums.

b. Your rich aunt promises to give you $3,000,000 in 20 years, when she is sure you are mature enough to handle such sums.

c. Evaluate which of the two promises you prefer, and describe why you prefer it.

Present Value Calculations

C-23 Calculate the present value of the following cash flows, using an eight percent interest rate:

a. Your rich uncle promises to give you $100,000 for each of the next five years, and $1,000,000 at the end of the tenth year.

b. Your rich aunt promises to give you $3,000,000 in 20 years, when she is sure that you will need the money!

c. Evaluate which of the two promises you prefer, and describe why you prefer it.

Present Value Calculations

C-24 Calculate the present value of the following cash flows, using a 12 percent rate of interest:

a. Your rich uncle promises to give you $100,000 for each of the next five years, $200,000 for the following five years, and $1,000,000 at the end of the tenth year.

b. Your rich aunt promises to give you $3,000,000 in 20 years, when she is sure that she will have enough money to afford this gift.

c. Evaluate which of the two promises you prefer, and describe why you prefer it.

Present Value Calculations

C-25 Calculate the present value of the cash flows associated with a life insurance policy that you inherited, using a 10 percent interest rate.

a. The life insurance policy offers a payout option of $300,000 at the end of each of the next three years.

b. A second option, under the same policy, is to receive $100,000 at the end of each year, for the next 12 years.

c. Identify which option you prefer, and describe why you prefer it.

Present Value Calculations

C-26 Calculate the present value of the cash flows associated with the retirement options under your pension plan, using an eight percent interest rate.

a. One retirement option under the pension plan is to receive 90 percent of your current annual salary of $80,000 at the end of the year, for life, which is expected to be 20 years.

b. Another option is to receive a lump sum distribution of $1,300,000 immediately.

c. A third option is to receive five annual (year-end) payments of $300,000.

d. Evaluate which option you prefer and describe why you prefer it.

Present Value Calculations

C-27 Calculate the present value of the cash flows associated with the retirement options under your pension plan, using a 10 percent interest rate.

a. One retirement option under the pension plan is to receive 90 percent of your current annual salary of $100,000 at the end of the year, for life, which is expected to be 20 years.

b. Another option is to receive a lump sum distribution of $1,000,000 immediately.

c. A third option is to receive five annual (year-end) payments of $250,000.

d. Evaluate which option you prefer and describe why you prefer it.

Present Value Calculations

C-28 Calculate the present value of the cash flows associated with a life insurance policy that you inherited, using a 12 percent interest rate.

a. The life insurance policy offers a payout option of $500,000 at the end of each of the next four years.

b. A second option, under the same policy, is to receive $245,000 per year, for each of the next 12 years.

c. Identify which option you prefer and describe why you prefer it.

Present Values: Interpreting Financial Statements

C-29 Refer to Wendy's financial statements in Appendix D. Review the financial statements to determine how and where present value calculations may have been used.

Required

a. Were present value calculations disclosed?

b. If the present value calculations were not separately disclosed, discuss areas where you infer that such calculations must have been used.

Present Values: Interpreting Financial Statements

C-30 Refer to Reebok's financial statements in Appendix E. Review the financial statements to determine how and where present value calculations may have been used.

Required

a. Were present value calculations disclosed?

b. If the present value calculations were not separately disclosed, discuss areas in which you would infer that such calculations must have been used.

appendix D

Wendy's International, Inc.

Management's Review and Outlook

RESULTS OF OPERATIONS

1997 Overview

Wendy's International Inc. (the company) concluded another successful year in 1997, with average sales increases in both the Wendy's and Tim Hortons (Hortons) concepts. In addition, the Wendy's domestic company operating margin expanded to 14.8% in 1997 from 13.3% for 1996. Management remained focused on long-term strategies to deliver continued success for the company and to enhance long-term shareholder value. Several strategic actions were initiated to position the company for continuing success. These initiatives include:

- In February 1998, the Board of Directors approved a plan to repurchase up to $200 million in Wendy's common stock over the next 18 to 24 months. Thereafter, the company plans to make additional stock purchases to offset the dilutive impact of the employee stock option grants.

- The continuation of the successful program to buy and sell Wendy's restaurants within the system, however, going forward the company anticipates the gains from franchising company operated restaurants to be markedly lower than levels of the last three years. Gains in 1998 are expected to be in the $10 million to $15 million range.

- Several operations-related actions initiated in the fourth quarter of 1997 which included plans to close or franchise 82 underperforming company operated restaurants, remove salad bars from the majority of Wendy's company operated restaurants, provide for the disposition of surplus property and develop a plan to accelerate new restaurant growth in 1999 and beyond.

- A decision made in the fourth quarter of 1997 to implement a new enterprise-wide information technology system and a new store management system to replace several different systems developed over the years. As part of this plan, various assets were written down to reflect net realizable values.

- A decision, effective December 28, 1997, to change the accounting for pre-opening costs for new restaurants to a policy of expensing these costs as they are incurred. Existing deferred costs were written off. Previously, the company had followed a policy of amortizing pre-opening costs over the first 12 months of new restaurant operations.

The impact of these initiatives was a non-recurring charge of $72.7 million pretax ($50.0 million after tax), substantially all non-cash. These charges are included in general and administrative expenses in the Consolidated Statement of Income (see Note 2 to the consolidated financial statements and the "general and administrative expenses" discussion below). The company reported basic earnings per share (EPS) of $.99 for the year, and diluted EPS of $.97. Without the impact of the initiatives mentioned above, basic EPS was $1.37 and diluted EPS was $1.33. This represents a 12% increase, before non-recurring charges, in diluted EPS compared with $1.19 in 1996 and $.88 in 1995. Net income in 1997, before the initiatives, increased 16% to $181 million compared with $156 million in 1996 and $110 million in 1995.

Retail Sales

Retail sales includes sales from company operated Wendy's and Hortons restaurants, bakery sales to Wendy's franchisees and warehouse sales of dry goods and supplies to Hortons' franchisees. Retail sales increased 5.4% to $1.7 billion in 1997 from $1.6 billion in 1996 which compared with a 7.2% increase over 1995. The largest component of retail sales was generated from Wendy's domestic company operated restaurants which increased 5.9% in average unit net sales in 1997, compared with 3.4% in 1996. The average number of Wendy's company operated domestic restaurants decreased 46 in 1997, increased 15 in 1996, and increased 37 in 1995. The bakery and warehouse sales increased 23.2% in 1997 and 9.3% in 1996, reflecting increases in the number and average sales of Wendy's and Hortons' franchised restaurants serviced. International company operated Wendy's are primarily concentrated in Canada, where average unit sales increased 7.7% in local currency.

The following chart reflects average net sales per domestic Wendy's restaurants for the last three years:

	1997	1996	1995
Company	**$1,111,000**	$1,049,000	$1,014,000
Franchise	**$1,017,000**	$978,000	$974,000
Total domestic	**$1,042,000**	$998,000	$986,000

The improvement in average Wendy's domestic restaurant sales reflects the continued emphasis on quality plus everyday value, effective marketing campaigns, the addition of Fresh Stuffed Pitas to the permanent menu and the focus on restaurant operations.

The average number of transactions in domestic company operated Wendy's increased approximately 2.8% in 1997 compared with 1.1% in 1996 and .4% in 1995. Domestic selling prices increased 1.4% during the year, while 1996 and 1995 increased .7% and .2%, respectively. This is consistent with the company's continued emphasis on its everyday value strategy in the extremely intense competitive environment.

Franchise Revenues

Included in franchise revenues are royalty income from franchisees, rental income from properties leased to franchisees, gains from franchising Wendy's company restaurants and franchise fees. Franchise fees include charges for various costs and expenses of the company related to establishing a franchisee's business, and include initial equipment packages for the Hortons franchises. Reserves against collection of these franchise revenues are also provided. Management reviews reserves on an ongoing basis and believes there are adequate levels for franchise-related receivables. Adjustments to reserves established in prior years are reflected in general and administrative expenses.

Royalties, before reserves, increased $19.6 million or 12.9% in 1997, and $11.6 million or 8.3% in 1996. An average of 239 more franchise domestic Wendy's restaurants were open in 1997 compared with an average of 177 more in 1996. Hortons' royalties increased 17.6% in 1997 and 17.7% in 1996, reflecting the increase in the number of franchise restaurants open in addition to positive same-store sales growth in local currency of approximately 8% in 1997 and 5% in 1996.

Pretax gains from franchising Wendy's restaurants amounted to $80.5 million in 1997 for 228 restaurants, compared with $63.2 million in 1996 for 179 restaurants and $37.8 million for 120 restaurants in 1995. Additionally, pretax gains resulting from the sale of properties which were previously leased to franchisees by Wendy's amounted to $475,000 in 1997, $3.4 million in 1996 and $3.8 million in 1995. Franchise fees were $36.2 million in 1997, $35.1 million in 1996 and $40.6 million in 1995.

Rental income from restaurants leased to franchisees increased $20.7 million in 1997 compared with an increase of $12.7 million in 1996, reflecting an additional number of restaurants being leased to franchisees. At the end of 1997, 1,679 restaurants were leased to franchisees, versus 1,366 in 1996 and 1,219 in 1995. Of these, Hortons leased 1,046 to franchisees in 1997, 904 in 1996 and 815 in 1995.

Cost of Sales and Restaurant Operating Costs

Wendy's cost of sales for all domestic restaurants decreased to 59.1% of Wendy's domestic retail sales in 1997 from 60.1% in 1996 and 58.7% in 1995. Domestic food costs, as a percent of domestic retail sales, were 28.9% in 1997, 30.0% in 1996 and 29.1% in 1995. The reduction in food costs reflected a reduction in french fry costs, the favorable impact of new products such as Fresh Stuffed Pitas and the benefit of a 1.4% increase in selling prices. The increase in 1996 reflected unfavorable delivered prices primarily for chicken and bacon in addition to the popularity of chicken products during 1996 resulting in a higher proportion of retail sales from chicken.

Wendy's domestic labor costs were 26.3% of domestic retail sales in 1997, compared with 26.0% in 1996 and 25.6% in 1995. The increase reflects higher restaurant labor costs due to pressure on wage rates. This continues to be driven by demand throughout the industry for labor to provide quality service to customers. In 1997 and 1996, labor rates were also impacted by minimum wage increases. The company continues to control labor costs by adherence to its labor guidelines. Sales per labor hour increased to $26.66 in 1997 reflecting a 3.3% increase in productivity following a 1.7% increase in 1996.

Wendy's domestic company restaurant operating costs remained constant in 1997, and increased $20.1 million in 1996 and $12.6 million in 1995. Wendy's domestic restaurant operating costs as a percent of domestic retail sales were 26.1% in 1997, 26.6% in 1996 and 26.2% in 1995. The reduced percentage in 1997 reflected lower marketing expenditures and the leveraging benefit of higher average sales. Rent, salaries and benefits, maintenance and expenditures related to food safety were higher in 1996 compared with 1995.

The Wendy's domestic company operating margin was 14.8% for 1997, compared with 13.3% in 1996 and 15.1% in 1995. The improvement in 1997 reflects favorable food cost and restaurant operating costs as discussed above. The following chart details the margin.

	1997 % of Sales	1996 % of Sales	1995 % of Sales
Retail sales	**100.0%**	100.0%	100.0%
Cost of sales	**59.1**	60.1	58.7
Company restaurant operating costs	**26.1**	26.6	26.2
Domestic company operating margin	**14.8%**	13.3%	15.1%

Cost of sales for the Wendy's bakery and Hortons' warehouse operations increased $33.8 million in 1997 and $12.3 million in 1996, reflecting additional sales to franchisees due to the increased number of restaurants serviced and higher average sales per restaurant.

Operating Costs

Operating costs include rent expense related to properties subleased to franchisees and cost of equipment sold to Hortons franchisees as part of the initiation of the franchise business. Training and other costs necessary to ensure a successful Hortons franchise opening, costs to operate and maintain the warehouse and bakery operations are also included in operating costs. Costs that can not be directly related to generating revenue are included in general and administrative expenses. Depreciation on properties owned and leased to franchisees is included in depreciation expense.

Rent expense increased $5.8 million in 1997 and $4.6 million in 1996 reflecting the growth in the number of properties being leased and then subleased to franchisees. In 1996, the higher rent expense was offset by lower cost of equipment and related expenses reflecting fewer new store openings by Hortons Canadian franchisees during 1996. There were 955 total restaurants leased by the company and then subleased to franchisees in 1997 versus 815 in 1996 and 692 in 1995.

General and Administrative Expenses

General and administrative expenses were $233.0 million in 1997 compared with $136.5 million in 1996 and $136.4 million in 1995. The increase in 1997 reflects several non-recurring charges in the fourth quarter in connection with the strategic initiatives outlined above (see Note 2 to the consolidated financial statements). These charges totaled $72.7 million pretax ($50.0 million after tax) and were substantially non-cash. The company identified 82 underperforming Wendy's restaurants of which 64 will be closed and 18 will be franchised. Of the closures, 56 restaurants are domestic, seven are in Canada and one restaurant is in the United Kingdom. The plan also includes charges for the disposition of surplus property. A charge of $35.0 million was recorded for this initiative. Also in the fourth quarter 1997, a decision was made to implement a new enterprise-wide information technology system and a new store management system. A charge of $15.7 million was recognized for the write down to net realizable value of existing information systems.

The company changed the accounting treatment for pre-opening costs at year-end 1997 to begin expensing such costs as they are incurred. Previously, the company was deferring pre-opening costs to be amortized over the first 12 months of the new restaurant's operations. The write off of the balance of pre-opening costs was $6.0 million. A decision was made to remove salad bars from most company operated Wendy's restaurants and assets were written down $7.1 million to reflect this. The balance of $8.9 million included reserve provisions for various legal and international contingencies and other asset write downs.

Excluding the non-recurring charges, general and administrative expenses increased $23.8 million in 1997. This primarily reflected increases in salaries and benefits and other investments to expand Wendy's and Hortons in existing markets, introduce the Hortons concept to the United States, and further develop Wendy's outside North America. Reserves originally provided for Hortons' environmental issues were reduced $2.9 million in 1997 and $6.6 million in 1996.

General and administrative expenses in 1996 were approximately equal to 1995 with normal increases in annual merit-based compensation in 1996 offset by adjustments to environmental reserves for Hortons and by a 1995 expense for a Hortons benefit plan which ended that year.

Special Charges

Special charges for 1995 included the profit sharing contributions which occurred while Hortons was a private company, professional fees incurred to effectuate the Hortons transaction, reserves for contingencies, and costs related to organizing Canadian operations to blend the Wendy's and Hortons concepts. The Hortons transaction was accounted for as a pooling of interests in 1995.

Interest

Net interest expense decreased in 1997 primarily as a result of higher interest income of $25.3 million compared with $16.2 million in 1996 and $10.2 million in 1995. Interest income increased in 1997, 1996 and 1995 primarily as a result of an increase in notes receivable taken for restaurant dispositions. Interest expense was $28.9 million in 1997, $23.0 million in 1996 which includes distributions on the company-obligated mandatorily redeemable preferred securities and $20.5 million in 1995. Interest expense was reduced in 1995 due to debt retirements but increased in 1997 and 1996 reflecting additional borrowings in December 1995 and September 1996.

Income Taxes

The effective income tax rate for 1997 was 40.5% compared with 38.8% for 1996 and 33.3% for 1995. The increase in 1997 resulted from certain non-deductible foreign losses which did not result in tax benefits and somewhat higher state taxes. The increase in 1997 and 1996 also reflects the income generated by Hortons in Canada, which has a higher tax rate than domestic operations. A tax benefit of $6.6 million related to Canadian operations was realized in 1995 pursuant to further successful developments related to the 1993 Canadian reorganization.

FINANCIAL POSITION

Overview

The company maintains a strong balance sheet to support system growth. Total assets were approximately two-and-one half times liabilities and the debt-to-equity ratio was 21% at year-end 1997 compared with 23% in 1996 and 41% in 1995 (company-obligated mandatorily redeemable preferred securities are excluded from the debt-to-equity ratio). Standard & Poors and Moody's have given the company debt ratings of BBB+ and Baa-1, respectively.

Total assets increased $160.2 million or 9.0% over 1996 primarily due to an increase in notes receivable and additions to property and equipment for restaurant development. Notes receivable were $192.6 million at year-end 1997, an increase of $62.6 million over 1996 which was primarily due to restaurant dispositions. Total cash and cash equivalents amounted to $234.3 million at year-end 1997 compared with $219.0 million at year-end 1996. Return on average assets was 13.4% in 1997, or 17.2% excluding the non-recurring charges of $72.7 million, compared with 17.6% in 1996.

Common shareholders' equity increased 12.1% in 1997. On a per share basis, equity increased to $8.95 per share in 1997 from $8.16 per share in 1996. The company's return on average equity was 11.5% in 1997, or 15.7% excluding the non-recurring charges, compared with 16.6% in 1996. In 1996, the company raised $200 million by issuing company-obligated mandatorily redeemable preferred securities. These securities have characteristics of both traditional debt and traditional preferred securities, and are classified between long-term liabilities and common shareholders' equity on the company's balance sheet.

Reserve balances related to royalty receivables and other franchise-related receivables, which are primarily recorded in accounts and notes receivables, were $7.8 million and $8.7 million at December 28, 1997 and December 29, 1996, respectively.

Cash Flow

Cash provided by operating activities increased 17.6% to $223.4 million in 1997, compared with $189.9 million in 1996 and $164.9 million in 1995. In all three years, cash provided by operating activities was primarily used for capital expenditures, dividend payments, debt repayment and acquisitions of franchised restaurants.

Cash proceeds of $68.0 million were realized in 1997 from the sale of Wendy's company operated restaurants to franchisees, while $67.1 million was provided in 1996 and $39.0 million was provided in 1995. Over the last three years, the company used $112.1 million to acquire Wendy's franchised restaurants and $50.8 million to purchase competitors' concepts to be converted to Wendy's or Hortons. The company issued $200 million in company-obligated manditorily redeemable preferred securities in 1996 and $200 million of long-term debt in 1995. The company also repaid $204.5 million in long-term obligations during the last three years.

During 1997, capital expenditures amounted to $294.6 million. New restaurant expenditures amounted to $197.4 million; $47.3 million was spent for improvements to existing restaurants; and $49.9 million was spent for other additions. These included Hortons' expenditures of $34.9 million for new restaurant development, which are leased to franchisees. Current plans are to open about 375 new Wendy's restaurants, of which approximately 100 will be company operated Wendy's sites, and 200 new Hortons in 1998. Capital expenditures are expected to be approximately $285 million in 1998 including approximately $87 million for Hortons. The Board of Directors approved a plan to repurchase up to $200 million in Wendy's common stock over the next 18 to 24 months. Thereafter, the company plans to make additional stock purchases to offset the dilutive impact of employee stock option grants. Cash flow from operations, cash and investments on hand, possible asset sales, and cash available through existing revolving credit agreements and through the possible issuance of securities should provide for the company's projected cash requirements through 1998, including cash for capital expenditures, future acquisitions of restaurants from franchisees, stock repurchases or for other corporate purposes.

Tim Hortons

Hortons is the second largest quick-service restaurant chain in Canada and at year-end 1997 had 1,578 restaurants open. The company believes there are significant opportunities to expand the Hortons concept throughout Canada and the United States. In 1997, 213 new Hortons were opened, including 57 in the United States. The concept is extremely flexible and includes standard units with a bakery, both with and without drive-through windows, double-drive through buildings, and various other satellites, kiosks and carts. In addition, combination units shared with Wendy's are utilized. Future expansion in Canada is anticipated to be primarily through franchising and the company plans to open about 160 Canadian Hortons in 1998. Hortons will also continue development in the United States, and plans to open 40 stores in 1998.

Hortons is primarily a franchise operation in Canada and financial success depends on developing new stores and increasing average unit sales. This results in royalties, rental income and revenue from warehouse sales. The average unit same-store sales increased approximately 8% in local currency during 1997. As a result of this, and new development, royalties increased 18%, rental income increased 18% and warehouse sales increased 25% over 1996. In total, Canadian systemwide Hortons sales advanced 19% during the year.

International Wendy's

Canada is the company's largest international market and makes up the majority of company operated international restaurants. Canadian Wendy's average restaurant sales for company operated restaurants increased 7.7% in local currency in 1997, following a 1.4% increase in 1996. In 1997, 19 Wendy's opened in Canada, bringing total restaurants to 245 at year end. Included in these restaurants are combination units featuring Wendy's and Hortons which have proven successful with 46 units open at the end of 1997. In 1998, the company plans to open 25 Wendy's restaurants in Canada.

At year-end 1997, there were 387 international Wendy's open outside Canada, with 86 restaurants opened in 1997. International growth outside Canada continues to be primarily through franchising, but real estate joint ventures and company operated units are also planned. The company plans on opening 75 new Wendy's in international markets outside North America in 1998 and intends to increase international development in future years.

Inflation

Financial statements determined on a historical cost basis may not accurately reflect all the effects of changing prices on an enterprise. Several factors tend to reduce the impact of inflation for the company. Inventories approximate current market prices, there is some ability to adjust prices, and liabilities are repaid with dollars of reduced purchasing power.

MANAGEMENT'S OUTLOOK

Management is committed to increasing shareholder value over time. The initiatives implemented to dispose of underperforming restaurants, write down underperforming assets, establish appropriate reserve levels and, accelerate restaurant development, are all consistent with management's long-term focus. Likewise, management believes the new enterprise-wide information systems and a new store management system will position the company for future information technology challenges. Management believes the common share repurchase program is in the best interest of the company and shareholders.

The company intends to adhere to its long established strategies of exceeding customer expectations, fostering a performance-driven culture, delivering a balanced message of brand equity plus value in advertising and creating a healthy restaurant system. The company believes that its success depends on providing quality products and everyday value, not in discounting products. Menu variety is also an important part of customer satisfaction. Restaurants are remodeled on a recurring basis to maintain a fresh image and increase convenience for consumers. When combined with effective marketing, the goal of these initiatives is to increase the number of transactions and average sales per restaurant.

New restaurant development continues to be very important. Both Wendy's and Hortons restaurant concepts are underpenetrated in domestic and international markets. The company intends to grow aggressively, but responsibly, focusing on the markets with the best potential for sales and return on investment. Each new company owned unit must meet minimum operational and financial requirements before being approved for development. A total of 584 new restaurants were added in 1997. Current plans call for approximately 575 new units to open in 1998. Of these, approximately 375 are planned as Wendy's restaurants and 200 are planned to be Hortons. While the majority of units will continue to be traditional sites, special sites, such as shopping malls and universities, will contribute to this growth. The company plans to accelerate the new unit development growth rate beginning in 1999 and expects to open about 675 new units in 1999. During 1998 resources will be allocated to manage the increased development.

The company will continue its strategy to enhance the overall health of the Wendy's system by acquiring restaurants from, and selling restaurants to, franchisees where prudent. The company does not expect the gains generated from selling company restaurants to be as significant to overall earnings as in recent years. Gains in the past three years were $81 million in 1997, $67 million in 1996 and $42 million in 1995. In 1998, these gains are expected to be in the $10 million to $15 million range.

The strength and vitality of the franchise community is an essential part of the continued success of the company. Various strategies have been developed to assist individual franchisees and the overall franchise system. The goal of these strategies is to encourage responsible new restaurant development, add new franchisees, enhance minority representation, increase royalty income, and maintain a high royalty receivable collection rate. The company will continue to maintain appropriate reserves against franchise receivables.

The company is optimistic about development of Hortons in the United States, but the concept does not yet enjoy the superior brand recognition it has in Canada. The entire domestic quick-service industry is competitive and there are many established baked goods outlets. The company plans to build consumer awareness and traffic for Hortons.

The company remains optimistic about long-term opportunities for international operations. Most of Wendy's development outside North America is with franchisees who are affected by economic conditions, such as those recently experienced in Southeast Asia. Europe and the Middle East also remain very challenging. Likewise, although the Canadian economy remains strong, the Canadian dollar has weakened in recent months and Wendy's company operations and Hortons franchise operations were impacted. The company does not believe these conditions change the long-term potential of the international business, but they could influence short-term results.

Year 2000

The company has completed an assessment of year 2000 compliance. The year 2000 issue concerns the ability of date sensitive software to properly recognize the year 2000 in calculating and processing computer system information. The company has initiated a plan to install a new enterprise-wide information system and a new store management system, which will include new software that is year 2000 compliant. The company has made an assessment that some existing software will need to be modified since it will not be replaced by the new information systems. The modification is expected to cost $3 million to $4 million, of which $1 million has been expensed in 1997, and the remainder will be expensed over the next two years. The new information systems are estimated to cost approximately $70 million to $80 million, a substantial portion of which will be capitalized. The company anticipates timely completion of these projects which should mitigate the year 2000 issue. However, if the new information systems are not implemented on a timely basis and if modifications to existing systems can not be accomplished on a timely basis, there would be adverse financial and operational effects on the company. The amount of these effects can not be ascertained at this time.

Recently Issued Accounting Standards

Financial Accounting Standards Number 130 - "Reporting Comprehensive Income" was issued in June 1997. This statement requires the reporting of comprehensive income and its components in a full set of general-purpose financial statements. Additionally in June 1997, Financial Accounting Standards Number 131 - "Disclosures about Segments of an Enterprise and Related Information" was issued. This statement provides information about operating segments in annual financial statements and requires selected information about operating segments in interim financial reports. It also requires certain related disclosures about products and services, geographic areas and major customers. These statements are effective for years beginning after December 15, 1997. The company is in the process of evaluating the impact of these statements.

Safe Harbor Statement

Certain information contained in this annual report, particularly information regarding future economic performance and finances, plans and objectives of management, is forward looking. In some cases, information regarding certain important factors that could cause actual results to differ materially from any such forward-looking statement appear together with such statement. In addition, the following factors, in addition to other possible factors not listed, could affect the company's actual results and cause such results to differ materially from those expressed in forward-looking statements. These factors include competition within the quick-service restaurant industry, which remains extremely intense, both domestically and internationally, with many competitors pursuing heavy price discounting; changes in economic conditions; consumer perceptions of food safety; harsh weather, particularly in the first and fourth quarters; changes in consumer tastes; labor and benefit costs; legal claims; risk inherent to international development (including currency fluctuations); the continued ability of the company and its franchisees to obtain suitable locations and financing for new restaurant development; governmental initiatives such as minimum wage rates, taxes and possible franchise legislation; and other factors set forth in Exhibit 99 to the company's Form 10-K filed with the Securities and Exchange Commission.

WENDY'S DOMESTIC AND INTERNATIONAL RESTAURANTS

	Total Wendy's			Wendy's Company Operated			Wendy's Franchised		
	1997	1996	1995	**1997**	1996	1995	**1997**	1996	1995
Open at beginning of year	**4,933**	4,667	4,411	**1,315**	1,311	1,264	**3,618**	3,356	3,147
Opened	**371**	343	333	**97**	89	98	**274**	254	235
Closed	**(97)**	(77)	(77)	**(15)**	(10)	(14)	**(82)**	(67)	(63)
Acquisitions within the system	**261**	283	203	**33**	104	83	**228**	179	120
Dispositions within the system	**(261)**	(283)	(203)	**(228)**	(179)	(120)	**(33)**	(104)	(83)
Open at end of year	**5,207**	4,933	4,667	**1,202**	1,315	1,311	**4,005**	3,618	3,356

Consolidated Statement of Income

Years ended December 28, 1997, December 29, 1996 and December 31, 1995

(In thousands, except per share data)	1997	1996	1995
Revenues			
Retail sales	$1,651,689	$1,566,888	$1,461,880
Franchise revenues	385,641	330,256	284,400
	2,037,330	1,897,144	1,746,280
Costs and expenses			
Cost of sales	1,026,026	976,666	890,363
Company restaurant operating costs	389,534	379,404	351,062
Operating costs	63,175	54,710	60,216
General and administrative expenses (Note 2)	232,983	136,461	136,424
Depreciation and amortization of property and equipment	95,638	88,957	80,573
Other (income) expense	6,899	(683)	2,595
Special charges			49,672
Interest, net	3,604	6,812	10,230
	1,817,859	1,642,327	1,581,135
Income before income taxes	219,471	254,817	165,145
Income taxes	88,972	98,869	55,075
Net income	$ 130,499	$ 155,948	$ 110,070
Basic earnings per common share	$.99	$1.23	$.93
Diluted earnings per common share	$.97	$1.19	$.88
Dividends per common share	$.24	$.24	$.24
Basic shares	131,595	126,461	118,934
Diluted shares	140,738	133,684	130,164

See accompanying Notes to the Consolidated Financial Statements.

Consolidated Balance Sheet

December 28, 1997 and December 29, 1996

(Dollars in thousands)	1997	1996
Assets		
Current assets		
Cash and cash equivalents	$ 234,262	$ 218,956
Accounts receivable, net	66,755	53,250
Notes receivable, net	13,897	11,003
Deferred income taxes	31,007	15,760
Inventories and other	35,633	37,994
	381,554	336,963
Property and equipment, net	1,265,500	1,207,944
Notes receivable, net	178,681	118,994
Goodwill, net	51,346	51,636
Deferred income taxes	15,117	12,938
Other assets	49,482	52,959
	$1,941,680	$1,781,434
Liabilities and Shareholders' Equity		
Current liabilities		
Accounts payable	$ 107,157	$ 108,629
Accrued expenses		
Salaries and wages	31,377	24,741
Taxes	21,615	18,502
Insurance	30,899	30,337
Other	14,415	18,874
Current portion of long-term obligations	7,151	6,681
	212,614	207,764
Long-term obligations		
Term debt	205,872	197,622
Capital leases	43,891	44,206
	249,763	241,828
Deferred income taxes	81,017	62,956
Other long-term liabilities	14,052	12,114
Commitments and contingencies		
Company-obligated mandatorily redeemable preferred securities of subsidiary Wendy's Financing I, holding solely Wendy's Convertible Debentures	200,000	200,000
Shareholders' equity		
Preferred stock, authorized: 250,000 shares		
Common stock, $.10 stated value per share, authorized: 200,000,000 shares Issued: 115,946,000 and 113,148,000 shares, respectively	11,595	11,315
Capital in excess of stated value	353,327	312,570
Retained earnings	839,215	740,311
Translation adjustments and other	(18,191)	(5,712)
	1,185,946	1,058,484
Treasury stock, at cost: 129,000 shares	(1,712)	(1,712)
	1,184,234	1,056,772
	$1,941,680	$1,781,434

See accompanying Notes to the Consolidated Financial Statements.

Consolidated Statement of Cash Flows

Years ended December 28, 1997, December 29, 1996 and December 31, 1995

(In thousands)	1997	1996	1995
Cash flows from operating activities			
Net income	$130,499	$155,948	$110,070
Adjustments to reconcile net income to net cash provided by operating activities			
Depreciation and amortization	104,529	94,981	84,452
Deferred income taxes	802	23,394	(4,393)
Gain from restaurant dispositions, net	(80,460)	(63,190)	(37,810)
Loss (gain) on other asset dispositions, net	60,416	(124)	760
Net reserves for receivables and other contingencies	352	(8,855)	15,424
Changes in operating assets and liabilities net of effects of acquisitions and dispositions of restaurants			
Accounts and notes receivable	(21,101)	(3,443)	(11,091)
Inventories and other	(1,476)	(6,476)	(1,245)
Accounts payable and accrued expenses	6,391	(6,956)	7,370
Decrease (increase) in other assets	12,048	(571)	(3,243)
Other changes, net	11,402	5,220	4,603
Net cash provided by operating activities	223,402	189,928	164,897
Cash flows from investing activities			
Proceeds from restaurant dispositions	68,017	67,140	38,994
Proceeds from other asset dispositions	25,876	30,951	19,139
Capital expenditures	(294,552)	(307,284)	(217,532)
Acquisition of franchises	(10,226)	(59,119)	(42,746)
Principal payments of notes receivable	17,265	11,576	1,418
Other investing activities	(7,359)	(5,253)	12,990
Net cash used in investing activities	(200,979)	(261,989)	(187,737)
Cash flows from financing activities			
Proceeds from issuance of trust preferred securities		200,000	
Proceeds from issuance of term debt			285,410
Proceeds from issuance of common stock	30,567	12,192	20,653
Principal payments on long-term obligations	(6,089)	(29,434)	(169,017)
Dividends paid on common stock	(31,595)	(30,436)	(24,565)
Payments on amounts due officer, net		(63,221)	(5,057)
Other financing activities		(4,211)	1,904
Net cash (used) provided by financing activities	(7,117)	84,890	109,328
Increase in cash and cash equivalents	15,306	12,829	86,488
Cash and cash equivalents at beginning of period	218,956	206,127	119,639
Cash and cash equivalents at end of period	$234,262	$218,956	$206,127
Supplemental disclosures of cash flow information			
Interest paid	$29,186	$30,556	$19,939
Income taxes paid	79,941	71,840	53,364
Debt converted to common stock		98,714	84
Capital lease obligations incurred	6,811	6,156	7,717
Notes receivable from restaurant dispositions	70,839	53,231	39,070
Acquisition of franchises			
Fair value of assets acquired	19,106	64,803	67,291
Cash paid	10,226	59,119	42,746
Liabilities assumed	8,880	5,684	24,850

See accompanying Notes to the Consolidated Financial Statements.

Consolidated Statement of Shareholders' Equity

Years ended December 28, 1997, December 29, 1996 and December 31, 1995

(In thousands)	1997	1996	1995
Common stock at stated value			
Balance at beginning of period	$ 11,315	$ 10,399	$ 10,179
Exercise of options	280	103	220
Conversion of subordinated debentures		813	
Balance at end of period	11,595	11,315	10,399
Capital in excess of stated value			
Balance at beginning of period	312,570	199,804	171,888
Exercise of options, including tax benefits	40,757	14,865	27,832
Conversion of subordinated debentures		97,901	84
Balance at end of period	353,327	312,570	199,804
Retained earnings			
Balance at beginning of period	740,311	614,799	529,294
Net income	130,499	155,948	110,070
Dividends paid	(31,595)	(30,436)	(24,565)
Balance at end of period	839,215	740,311	614,799
Translation adjustments and other	(18,191)	(5,712)	(4,511)
Treasury stock, at cost	(1,712)	(1,712)	(1,712)
Shareholders' equity	$1,184,234	$1,056,772	$818,779
Common shares			
Balance issued at beginning of period	113,148	103,993	101,787
Exercise of options	2,798	1,031	2,200
Conversion of subordinated debentures		8,124	6
Balance issued at end of period	115,946	113,148	103,993
Treasury shares	(129)	(129)	(129)
Common shares issued and outstanding	115,817	113,019	103,864
Common shares issuable upon conversion of exchangeable shares	16,450	16,450	16,450
Common shares issued and outstanding, including exchangeable shares	132,267	129,469	120,314

See accompanying Notes to the Consolidated Financial Statements.

Notes to the Consolidated Financial Statements

NOTE 1 SUMMARY OF SIGNIFICANT ACCOUNTING POLICIES

Description of business

The company's principal business is the operation and franchising of quick-service restaurants serving high-quality food. At year-end 1997, the company and its franchise owners operated 5,207 restaurants under the name "Wendy's" in 50 states and in 33 other countries and territories. Additionally, the company and its franchise owners operated 1,499 restaurants under the name "Tim Hortons" in Canada and 79 units in the United States.

Fiscal year

The company's fiscal year ends on the Sunday nearest to December 31.

Basis of presentation

The Consolidated Financial Statements include the accounts of the company and its subsidiaries. All intercompany accounts and transactions have been eliminated in consolidation.

Certain reclassifications have been made for prior years to conform with the 1997 presentation.

For purposes of the Consolidated Statement of Cash Flows, the company considers short-term investments with original maturities of three months or less as cash equivalents.

The preparation of financial statements in conformity with generally accepted accounting principles requires management to make estimates and assumptions. The most significant of these estimates are related to reserves for receivables, workers' compensation claims, income taxes, useful lives of long-lived assets and contingencies. These affect the reported amounts of assets and liabilities and disclosure of contingent assets and liabilities at the date of the financial statements and the reported amounts of revenues and expenses during the reporting periods. Actual results could differ from these estimates.

In 1995, special charges included the profit sharing contribution made to the sole shareholder of Hortons (prior to acquisition) of $29.6 million, and legal, accounting, and other professional fees of $4.0 million to effectuate the Hortons transaction. Also, reserves of $13.5 million for environmental issues and contingencies, and miscellaneous costs to organize Canadian operations to blend the Wendy's and Hortons concepts were included.

Inventories

Inventories, amounting to $19.3 million and $17.0 million at December 28, 1997 and December 29, 1996, respectively, are stated at the lower of cost (first-in, first-out) or market, and consist primarily of restaurant food items, new equipment and parts, and paper supplies.

Property and equipment

Depreciation and amortization are recognized using the straight-line method in amounts adequate to amortize costs over the following estimated useful lives: buildings, up to 40 years; leasehold improvements, up to 25 years; restaurant equipment, up to 15 years; other equipment, up to 10 years; and property under capital leases, the primary lease term. Interest cost associated with the construction of new restaurants is capitalized, while certain other costs, such as ground rentals and real estate taxes, are generally expensed as incurred.

Property and equipment, at cost, at each year end consisted of the following:

(In thousands)	1997	1996
Land	$ 335,258	$ 319,284
Buildings	601,616	532,682
Leasehold improvements	313,229	333,239
Restaurant equipment	394,702	420,288
Other equipment	84,039	70,141
Capital leases	74,566	74,268
	1,803,410	1,749,902
Accumulated depreciation and amortization	(537,910)	(541,958)
	$1,265,500	$1,207,944

Goodwill

Goodwill is amortized using the straight-line method over periods ranging from 10 to 40 years which, for leased restaurants, includes the original lease period plus renewal options, if applicable. The company periodically reviews goodwill and, based upon undiscounted cash flows, recognizes impairments when a permanent decline in value has occurred. Accumulated amortization of goodwill was $21.7 million and $19.2 million at December 28, 1997 and December 29, 1996, respectively.

Notes receivable

The carrying amount of notes receivable approximates fair value.

Pre-opening costs

Effective December 28, 1997, the company recorded a special pretax charge of approximately $6.0 million to reflect the decision to write off all existing pre-opening costs and to thereafter expense such costs as incurred. The company did not separately state this change ($2.5 million pretax) as a cumulative effect of a change in accounting principle due to the immaterial effect of the change. Previously, the company capitalized certain operating costs incurred prior to the opening of a new restaurant and amortized such costs over a one-year period (see Note 2).

Capitalized software development costs

The company capitalizes internally developed software costs which are amortized over a seven-year period. At December 28, 1997 and December 29, 1996, capitalized software development costs, net of accumulated amortization amounted to $1.0 million and $6.6 million, respectively (see Note 2).

Advertising costs

The company expenses advertising costs as incurred.

Franchise operations

The company grants franchises to independent operators who in turn pay technical assistance/franchise fees which may include equipment, royalties, and in some cases, rents for each restaurant opened. A technical assistance/franchise fee is recorded as income when each restaurant commences operations. Royalties, based upon a percent of monthly net sales, are recognized as income on the accrual basis. The company has established reserves related to the collection of franchise royalties and other franchise-related receivables and commitments (see Note 10).

Franchise owners receive assistance in such areas as real estate site selection, construction consulting, purchasing and marketing from company personnel who also furnish these services to company-operated restaurants. These franchise expenses are included in general and administrative expenses.

Foreign operations

At December 28, 1997, the company and its franchise owners operated 245 Wendy's restaurants and 1,499 Tim Hortons restaurants in Canada. Additionally, 387 Wendy's restaurants were operated by the company and its franchise owners in other foreign countries and territories. Assets and liabilities are translated at the year-end exchange rates and revenues and expenses are translated at average exchange rates for the period. Resulting translation adjustments are recorded as a component of shareholders' equity. The functional currency of each foreign subsidiary is the respective local currency.

Net income per share

During 1997, the company adopted Financial Accounting Standards Number 128 – "Earnings per Share". All prior year earnings per share amounts have been restated.

Basic earnings per common share is computed by dividing net income available to common shareholders by the weighted average number of common shares outstanding during each period. Diluted computations include dilutive common share equivalents and company-obligated mandatorily redeemable preferred securities, when dilutive, and the elimination of related expenses, net of income taxes.

The computation of basic and diluted earnings per common share for each year end is shown below:

(In thousands except per share amounts)	1997	1996	1995
Income for computation of basic earnings per share	$130,499	$155,948	$110,070
Interest savings on assumed conversions	6,034	2,759	4,727
Income for computation of diluted earnings per share	$136,533	$158,707	$114,797
Weighted average shares for computation of basic earnings per share	131,595	126,461	118,934
Incremental shares on assumed issuance and repurchase of stock options	1,570	2,749	3,107
Assumed conversions	7,573	4,474	8,123
Weighted average shares for computation of diluted earnings per share	140,738	133,684	130,164
Basic earnings per share	$.99	$1.23	$.93
Diluted earnings per share	$.97	$1.19	$.88

NOTE 2 NON-RECURRING CHARGES

In the fourth quarter of 1997, the company initiated several strategic actions that resulted in pretax charges of $72.7 million, which are included in general and administrative expenses in the Consolidated Statement of Income. The charges were primarily to establish the proper value of nonproducing or underperforming assets. The company identified 82 underperforming Wendy's restaurants of which 64 will be closed and 18 will be franchised. This plan also includes a provision for disposition of surplus property. A charge of $35.0 million was provided to write down the assets to disposal value. Also in the fourth quarter, a decision was made to implement a new enterprise-wide information technology system and a new store management system. A charge of $15.7 million was recognized to write down the existing information system to net realizable value. A decision to remove salad bars from most company operated Wendy's restaurants resulted in an asset write down of $7.1 million. All of the aforementioned assets are to be disposed of by December 31, 1998.

The company changed the accounting treatment for pre-opening costs at year-end 1997 to begin expensing such costs as they are incurred. Previously, the company deferred pre-opening costs to be amortized over the first 12 months of the new restaurant's operations. The write-off of the balance of pre-opening costs was $6.0 million. The remaining $8.9 million includes provisions for various legal and international contingencies and other asset write downs.

NOTE 3 TERM DEBT

Term debt at each year end consisted of the following:

(In thousands)	1997	1996
Notes, unsecured, and Mortgages Payable with a weighted average interest rate of 8.1%, due in installments through 2010	$ 13,518	$ 5,023
6.35% Notes, due December 15, 2005	96,815	96,524
7% Debentures, due December 15, 2025	96,502	96,464
	206,835	198,011
Current portion	(963)	(389)
	$205,872	$197,622

The 6.35% notes and 7% debentures are unsecured and unsubordinated. They are not redeemable by the company prior to maturity.

In 1995, the company entered into interest rate swaps to manage its exposure to interest rate fluctuations on the 6.35% and 7% securities issued in 1995. The company reflects realized and unrealized gains and losses on hedging instruments as an adjustment to the carrying value of the hedged asset or liability. Accordingly, realized losses related to these interest rate swaps amounting to $3.6 million and $3.4 million, respectively, have been recorded as a reduction of the carrying value of the notes and debentures and will be amortized to interest expense over the term of the related debt.

Based on future cash flows for all term debt, the fair value was approximately $214 million at December 28, 1997 and $191 million at December 29, 1996.

The combined aggregate amounts of future maturities for all term debt are as follows:

(In thousands)	
1998	$ 963
1999	981
2000	1,017
2001	935
2002	1,017
Later years	201,922
	$206,835

The company has unused contractual lines of credit aggregating $200 million from various financial institutions, generally at their respective prime rates.

Net interest expense for each year consisted of the following:

(In thousands)	1997	1996	1995
Total interest charges	$ 18,936	$ 20,257	$ 20,456
Distributions on trust preferred securities	9,973	2,772	
Interest income	(25,305)	(16,217)	(10,226)
	$ 3,604	$ 6,812	$ 10,230

NOTE 4 COMPANY-OBLIGATED MANDATORILY REDEEMABLE PREFERRED SECURITIES

In 1996, Wendy's Financing I (the trust) issued $200,000,000 of $2.50 Term Convertible Securities, Series A (the trust preferred securities). Wendy's Financing I, a statutory business trust, is a wholly-owned consolidated subsidiary of the company with its sole asset being $202 million aggregate principal amount of 5% Convertible Subordinated Debentures due September 15, 2026, of Wendy's (the trust debenture).

The trust preferred securities are non-voting (except in limited circumstances), pay quarterly distributions at an annual rate of 5%, carry a liquidation value of $50 per share and are convertible into the company's common shares at any time prior to the close of business on September 15, 2026, at the option of the holder. The trust preferred securities are convertible into common shares at the rate of 1.8932 common shares for each trust preferred security (equivalent to a conversion price of $26.41 per common share). The company has executed a guarantee with regard to the trust preferred securities. The guarantee, when taken together with the company's obligations under the trust debenture, the indenture pursuant to which the trust debenture was issued, and the applicable trust document, provides a full and unconditional guarantee of the trust's obligations under the trust preferred securities.

Based on the quoted market price, fair value of the trust preferred securities was approximately $215 million at December 28, 1997 and $208 million at December 29, 1996.

NOTE 5 LEASES

The company occupies land and buildings and uses equipment under terms of numerous lease agreements expiring on various dates through 2086. Terms of land only and land and building leases are generally for 20 to 25 years. Many of these leases provide for future rent escalations and renewal options. Certain leases require contingent rent, determined as a percentage of sales, when annual sales exceed specified levels. Most leases also obligate the company to pay the costs of maintenance, insurance and property taxes.

At each year end capital leases consisted of the following:

(In thousands)	1997	1996
Buildings	$ 74,566	$ 74,268
Accumulated amortization	(34,967)	(35,188)
	$ 39,599	$ 39,080

At December 28, 1997, future minimum lease payments for all leases, and the present value of the net minimum lease payments for capital leases, were as follows:

(In thousands)	Capital Leases	Operating Leases
1998	$ 10,014	$ 49,868
1999	8,567	46,210
2000	7,007	42,134
2001	6,223	38,369
2002	5,882	35,682
Later years	49,451	222,939
Total minimum lease payments	87,144	$435,202
Amount representing interest	(37,065)	
Present value of net minimum lease payments	50,079	
Current portion	(6,188)	
	$ 43,891	

Total minimum lease payments have not been reduced by minimum sublease rentals of $3.6 million under capital leases, and $229.3 million under operating leases due in the future under noncancelable subleases.

Rent expense for each year is included in company restaurant operating costs and amounted to:

(In thousands)	1997	1996	1995
Minimum rents	$56,512	$50,806	$45,142
Contingent rents	13,737	12,817	9,709
	$70,249	$63,623	$54,851

In connection with the franchising of certain restaurants, the company has leased land, buildings and equipment to the related franchise owners. Most leases provide for monthly rentals based on a percentage of sales, while others provide for fixed payments with contingent rent when sales exceed certain levels. Lease terms are approximately 10 to 20 years with one or more five-year renewal options. The franchise owners bear the cost of maintenance, insurance and property taxes.

The company generally accounts for the building and equipment portions of the fixed payment leases as direct financing leases. The land portion of leases and leases with rents based on a percentage of sales are accounted for as operating leases.

At each year end the net investment in financing leases, included in other assets, consisted of the following:

(In thousands)	1997	1996
Total minimum lease receipts	$ 24,708	$ 33,531
Estimated residual value	3,308	4,615
Amount representing unearned interest	(12,497)	(17,727)
Current portion, included in accounts receivable	(888)	(931)
	$ 14,631	$ 19,488

At each year end assets leased under operating leases consisted of the following:

(In thousands)	1997	1996
Land	$136,288	$116,181
Building	314,155	234,870
Equipment	43,468	27,626
	493,911	378,677
Accumulated amortization	(102,995)	(73,308)
	$390,916	$305,369

At December 28, 1997, future minimum lease receipts were as follows:

(In thousands)	Financing Leases	Operating Leases
1998	$ 2,456	$ 38,982
1999	2,288	37,332
2000	2,226	35,942
2001	2,058	33,761
2002	1,952	29,869
Later years	13,728	115,318
	$24,708	$291,204

Rental income for each year is included in franchise revenues and amounted to:

(In thousands)	1997	1996	1995
Minimum rents	$39,643	$35,267	$28,612
Contingent rents	55,968	39,622	33,542
	$95,611	$74,889	$62,154

NOTE 6 INCOME TAXES

The provision for income taxes at each year end consisted of the following:

(In thousands)	1997	1996	1995
Current			
Federal	$54,114	$50,658	$ 51,641
State and local	7,254	4,290	3,864
Foreign	26,802	20,527	3,963
	88,170	75,475	59,468
Deferred			
Federal	(3,421)	14,235	7,724
State and local	265	1,258	(476)
Foreign	3,958	7,901	(11,641)
	802	23,394	(4,393)
	$88,972	$98,869	$ 55,075

The temporary differences which give rise to deferred tax assets and liabilities at each year end consisted of the following:

(In thousands)	1997	1996
Deferred tax assets		
Lease transactions	$ 4,012	$ 4,049
Reserves not currently deductible	30,523	13,597
Foreign operations	11,842	12,464
All other	5,230	2,696
	51,607	32,806
Valuation allowance	(4,734)	(2,585)
	$46,873	$30,221
Deferred tax liabilities		
Lease transactions	$ 5,854	$ 7,615
Property and equipment basis differences	35,582	34,886
Installment sales	33,334	18,215
All other	6,996	3,763
	$81,766	$64,479

Deferred tax assets for foreign operations have been established primarily for net operating loss carryovers and excess capital allowances. In 1996 and 1997, the deferred tax assets related to non-Canadian foreign operations are offset by a valuation allowance.

A reconciliation of the statutory U.S. Federal income tax rate of 35 percent to the company's effective tax rate for each year is shown below:

(In thousands)	1997	1996	1995
Income taxes at statutory rate	$76,815	$89,186	$57,801
Effect of foreign operations	8,891	6,090	(2,993)
State and local taxes, net of federal benefit	4,888	3,606	2,209
Canadian restructuring benefit			(3,936)
Other	(1,622)	(13)	1,994
Income taxes at effective rate	$88,972	$98,869	$55,075

NOTE 7 STOCK OPTION AND SHAREHOLDER RIGHTS PLANS

The company has various stock option plans which provide options for certain employees and outside directors to purchase common shares of the company. Grants of options to employees and the periods during which such options can be exercised are at the discretion of the compensation committee of the Board of Directors. Grants of options to outside directors and the periods during which such options can be exercised are specified in the plan applicable to directors and do not involve discretionary authority of the Board. All options expire at the end of the exercise period. Options are granted at the fair market value of the company's common shares on the date of grant and no amounts applicable thereto are reflected in net income. The company makes no recognition of the options in the financial statements, except in the earnings per share computations, until they are exercised. Pro forma disclosures are provided as if the company adopted the cost recognition requirements under Financial Accounting Standards Number 123 (SFAS 123) – "Accounting for Stock-Based Compensation."

On August 2, 1990, the Board of Directors adopted the WeShare Stock Option Plan (WeShare Plan), a non-qualified stock option plan to provide for grants of options equal to 10 percent of each eligible employee's earnings, with a minimum of 20 options to be made to each eligible employee annually. An aggregate of 5.4 million common shares of the company have been reserved pursuant to the WeShare Plan.

The options have a term of 10 years from the grant date and become exercisable in installments of 25 percent on each of the first four anniversaries of the grant date. On July 30, 1997, August 1, 1996 and August 3, 1995, approximately 572,000 options, 896,000 options and 785,000 options were granted to eligible employees at an exercise price of $27.13 per share, $17.38 per share and $18.31 per share, respectively.

In addition, the Board of Directors also adopted the 1990 Stock Option Plan (1990 Plan) on August 2, 1990, and amended the 1990 Plan on August 1, 1991, February 23, 1994 and February 20, 1997. An aggregate of 18.5 million common shares of the company have been reserved for issuance to key employees and outside directors under the 1990 Plan, as amended.

On July 30, 1997, August 1, 1996 and August 3, 1995, approximately 1.6 million options, 1.4 million options and 1.3 million options were granted under the 1990 Plan at an exercise price of $27.13 per share, $17.38 per share and $18.31 per share, respectively.

The following is a summary of stock option activity for the last three years:

(Shares in thousands)	Shares Under Option	Weighted Average Price Per Share
Balance at January 1, 1995	9,654	$11.52
Granted	2,262	18.28
Exercised	(2,200)	9.39
Canceled	(414)	14.78
Balance at December 31, 1995	9,302	13.52
Granted	2,994	17.77
Exercised	(1,031)	11.82
Canceled	(518)	16.16
Balance at December 29, 1996	**10,747**	**14.74**
Granted	**2,239**	**26.78**
Exercised	**(2,798)**	**10.92**
Canceled	**(485)**	**18.04**
Balance at December 28, 1997	**9,703**	**$18.46**

Options exercisable to purchase common shares totaled 4.4 million, 5.1 million and 4.2 million at December 28, 1997, December 29, 1996 and December 31, 1995, respectively. Shares reserved under the plans at each year end were 15.4 million in 1997, 12.0 million in 1996 and 12.5 million in 1995.

The fair value of each option granted during 1997 is estimated on the date of grant using the Black-Scholes option-pricing model with the following assumptions: (1) dividend yield of 1.1%, (2) expected volatility of 28%, (3) risk-free interest rate of 5.8% and (4) expected life of four years.

The weighted average fair value of options granted during 1997, 1996 and 1995 was $7.73, $4.70 and $4.49, respectively.

The following tables summarize stock options outstanding and exercisable at December 28, 1997:

(Shares in thousands)	Options Outstanding		
Range of Exercise Prices	Options Outstanding	Weighted Average Remaining Contractual Life	Weighted Average Exercise Price
$ 5 – $15	2,927	5.3	$12.97
15 – 17	2,201	8.5	17.35
17 – 19	2,273	7.5	18.36
19 – 28	2,302	9.5	26.60
$ 5 – $28	9,703	7.5	$18.46

(Shares in thousands)	Options Exercisable	
Range of Exercise Prices	Options Exercisable	Weighted Average Exercise Price
$ 5 – $15	2,626	$12.70
15 – 17	595	17.30
17 – 19	1,090	18.31
19 – 28	43	21.00
$ 5 – $28	4,354	$14.81

Had compensation expense been recognized for stock-based compensation plans in accordance with provisions of SFAS 123, the company would have recorded net income and earnings per share as follows:

(In millions, except per share data)	1997	1996	1995
Net income	$126.3	$153.5	$109.4
Basic earnings per common share	$.96	$1.21	$.92
Diluted earnings per common share	$.94	$1.17	$.88

The impact of applying SFAS 123 in this pro forma disclosure is not indicative of future amounts. SFAS 123 does not apply to grants prior to 1995, and additional grants in future years are anticipated.

The company has a Shareholder Rights Plan (Rights Plan) under which one preferred stock purchase right (Right) was distributed as a dividend for each outstanding common share. Each Right entitles a shareholder to buy one ten-thousandth of a share of a new series of preferred stock for $100 upon the occurrence of certain events. Rights would be exercisable once a person or group acquires 15 percent or more of the company's common shares, or 10 days after a tender offer for 15 percent or more of the common shares is announced. No certificates will be issued unless the Rights Plan is activated.

Under certain circumstances, all Rights holders, except the person or company holding 15 percent or more of the company's common shares, will be entitled to purchase common shares at about half the price that such shares traded for prior to the announcement of the acquisition. Alternatively, if the company is acquired after the Rights Plan is activated, the Rights will entitle the holder to buy the acquiring company's shares at a similar discount. The company can redeem the Rights for one cent per Right under certain circumstances. If not redeemed, the Rights will expire on August 10, 2008.

NOTE 8 ACQUISITIONS

During 1997, the company acquired 25 Wendy's restaurants in the Salt Lake City market for cash and notes totaling $18.7 million. Eight other restaurants were also acquired in 1997.

Additionally, the company acquired 31 Rax restaurants in Ohio, West Virginia and Kentucky for $9.1 million. These sites were converted to Wendy's and Tim Hortons restaurants.

During 1996, the company acquired 41 Wendy's restaurants in the New York market for cash of $20.6 million and 52 Wendy's restaurants primarily in the South Carolina market for cash of $27.5 million. Eleven other restaurants were acquired for $11.0 million during 1996.

In addition, the company acquired 40 Roy Rogers restaurants in the New York area for $17.7 million and 44 Hardee's restaurants in the Detroit market for $24.0 million. These sites were converted to Wendy's and Tim Hortons restaurants.

On December 29, 1995, the company acquired all of the stock of 1052106 Ontario Limited (Ontario), formerly 632687 Alberta Ltd., the parent company of the Tim Hortons restaurant chain, for 16.45 million shares of a Canadian subsidiary of the company exchangeable for 16.45 million common shares of Wendy's International, Inc. The exchangeable shares may be exchanged at any time until December 29, 2005, at which time they must be exchanged. Tim Hortons is the leading franchisor of bakery and coffee shops in Canada. The transaction was accounted for as a pooling of interests. In connection with the acquisition, $4.0 million in professional fees to effectuate the transaction were incurred.

Additionally during 1995, the company acquired 33 Wendy's restaurants in the Little Rock market for cash of $37.0 million and 47 restaurants in the Pittsburgh market for $4.0 million cash and notes of $23.0 million. Three other restaurants were acquired for $1.7 million during 1995.

NOTE 9 DISPOSITIONS

The company franchised 228, 179 and 120 Wendy's restaurants during 1997, 1996 and 1995, respectively. These transactions resulted in pretax gains of approximately $80.5 million, $63.2 million and $37.8 million in 1997, 1996 and 1995, respectively, and are included in franchise revenues.

Notes receivable related to dispositions were $166.7 million at December 28, 1997 and $103.4 million at December 29, 1996.

NOTE 10 COMMITMENTS AND CONTINGENCIES

At December 28, 1997 and December 29, 1996 the company's reserves established for doubtful royalty receivables were $2.0 million in both years. Reserves related to possible losses on notes receivable, real estate, guarantees, claims and contingencies involving franchisees totaled $5.8 million at December 28, 1997 and $6.7 million at December 29, 1996. These reserves are included in accounts receivable, notes receivable and other accrued expenses.

The company has guaranteed certain leases and debt payments of franchise owners with average annual obligations of $9.2 million over four years. In the event of default by a franchise owner, the company generally retains the right to acquire possession of the related restaurants.

The company is self-insured for most workers' compensation, general liability and automotive liability losses subject to per occurrence and aggregate annual liability limitations. The company is also self-insured for health care claims for eligible participating employees subject to certain deductibles and limitations. The company determines its liability for claims incurred but not reported on an actuarial basis.

The company has entered into long-term purchase agreements with some of its suppliers. The range of prices and volume of purchases under the agreements may vary according to the company's demand for the products and fluctuations in market rates.

The company and its subsidiaries are parties to various legal actions and complaints arising in the ordinary course of business; many of these are covered by the company's self-insurance or other insurance programs. It is the opinion of the company that the ultimate resolution of such matters will not materially affect the company's financial condition or earnings.

The company continues to complete environmental assessments of properties where appropriate. The amount of obligation to be incurred is uncertain, however the company believes such obligations to be immaterial to the financial position and results of operations of the company.

The company has completed an assessment of year 2000 compliance. The year 2000 issue concerns the ability of date sensitive software to properly recognize the year 2000 in calculating and processing computer system information. The company has initiated a plan to install a new enterprise-wide information system and a new store management system, which will include new software that is year 2000 compliant. The company has made an assessment that some existing software will need to be modified since it will not be replaced by the new information systems. The modification is expected to cost $3 million to $4 million, of which $1 million has been expensed in 1997, and the remainder will be expensed over the next two years. The new information systems are estimated to cost approximately $70 million to $80 million, a substantial portion of which will be capitalized. The company anticipates timely completion of these projects which should mitigate the year 2000 issue. However, if the new information systems are not implemented on a timely basis and if modifications to existing systems can not be accomplished on a timely basis, there would be adverse financial and operational effects on the company. The amount of these effects can not be ascertained at this time.

NOTE 11 RETIREMENT PLANS

The company's retirement program covers substantially all full-time employees qualified as to age and service. The program includes a contributory defined benefit pension plan and a defined contribution plan for management and administrative employees. The defined benefit pension plan allows for employee contributions and provides a matching benefit from the company in addition to a basic benefit which is independent of employee contributions. The pension plan also provides for a guaranteed rate of return on employee account balances. The defined contribution plan provides for an annual discretionary contribution which is determined each year by the Board of Directors. The defined contribution plan allows for 401(k) contributions, acceptance of qualified rollovers, a loan feature, and a choice of four investing options, one of which is common stock of the company. In addition, the retirement program includes a noncontributory defined benefit pension plan for all eligible crew employees and shift supervisors of the company.

The company also has supplemental retirement plans for certain key employees to replace benefits otherwise not available from the pension and profit sharing plans due to the limitations imposed under the Internal Revenue Code.

The funded status of the pension plans for each year end consisted of the following:

(In thousands)	1997	1996
Accumulated benefit obligation:		
Vested	$(43,839)	$(38,120)
Nonvested	$ (4,467)	$ (4,394)
Projected benefit obligation	$(51,360)	$(45,197)
Fair value of plan assets	53,659	48,705
Unrecognized net loss	2,959	355
Unrecognized prior service costs	76	3,466
Minimum pension adjustment	(739)	
Prepaid pension cost	$ 4,595	$ 7,329

In determining the present value of benefit obligations, discount rates of 6.75% and 7.25% were used in 1997 and 1996, respectively. The expected long-term rate of return on assets used was 8.5% in 1997 and 1996. The assumed rate of increase in compensation levels was 8.0% for 1997 and 1996. Plan assets as of December 28, 1997 consisted of debt and equity instruments and cash equivalents.

Net periodic pension cost for each year consisted of the following:

(In thousands)	1997	1996	1995
Service cost	$ 4,583	$ 4,478	$ 3,756
Interest cost on projected benefit obligation	3,575	3,105	2,903
Return on plan assets	(7,743)	(5,161)	(8,580)
Net amortization	4,902	1,930	5,533
	$ 5,317	$ 4,352	$ 3,612

The company provided for profit sharing and supplemental retirement benefits of $4.4 million, $4.3 million and $3.6 million for 1997, 1996 and 1995, respectively.

A minimum pension liability equal to the excess of the accumulated benefit obligation over the fair value of plan assets and liabilities already accrued is reflected in the balance sheet by recording an intangible asset and reducing shareholders' equity.

The company had an agreement with the former Chairman of the Board which, as a result of his death in 1996, required the company to expense $1.3 million under this agreement in 1996.

NOTE 12 ADVERTISING COSTS

The Wendy's National Advertising Program, Inc. (WNAP) is a not-for-profit corporation which was established to collect and administer funds contributed by the company and all domestic franchise owners. WNAP is not a consolidated subsidiary of the company. These contributions total 2% of net sales and are used for advertising programs designed to increase sales and enhance the reputation of the company and its franchise owners. Since 1993, the domestic system has agreed to increase national advertising spending from 2% to 2.5% of net sales. During 1997, 1996 and 1995, the company contributed $32.4 million, $31.8 million and $30.3 million, respectively, to WNAP. These contributions were recognized in company restaurant operating costs. At December 28, 1997 and December 29, 1996, the company's payable to WNAP amounted to $2.3 million and $2.5 million, respectively.

The advertising program utilized by Hortons, known as the Ad Fund, is similar in operation to WNAP. Hortons' franchisees and company operated units are required to contribute 4% of gross sales to the Ad Fund.

Total advertising expense of the company, including amounts contributed to WNAP, the Ad Fund, local advertising costs and other marketing and advertising expenses, amounted to $60.9 million, $62.2 million and $62.1 million in 1997, 1996 and 1995, respectively.

NOTE 13 SEGMENT REPORTING

The company operates exclusively in the food-service industry. The following presents information about the company by geographic area. There were no material amounts of revenues or transfers among geographic areas.

(In thousands)	United States	International	Corporate	Total
1997				
Revenues	$1,593,409	$443,921		$2,037,330
Income before income taxes	232,708	66,677	$(79,914)	219,471 [1]
Total assets	1,617,867	287,114	36,699	1,941,680
1996				
Revenues	$1,514,819	$382,325		$1,897,144
Income before income taxes	255,791	64,804	$(65,778)	254,817
Total assets	1,482,094	270,328	29,012	1,781,434
1995				
Revenues	$1,402,918	$343,362		$1,746,280
Income before income taxes	240,765	48,921	$(124,541)	165,145
Total assets	1,215,810	266,672	26,679	1,509,161

[1] *Includes charges of $72.7 million ($50.0 million after tax), see Note 2.*

NOTE 14 SUBSEQUENT EVENT

On February 4, 1998, the company's Board of Directors approved a program for the repurchase of up to $200 million of the company's outstanding common shares over the next 18 to 24 months. Thereafter, the company plans to purchase shares each year in an amount to offset the dilutive effect of employee stock option grants.

NOTE 15 QUARTERLY FINANCIAL DATA (UNAUDITED)

Quarter (In thousands, except per share data)	First 1997	First 1996	Second 1997	Second 1996	Third 1997	Third 1996	Fourth 1997 [1]	Fourth 1996
Revenues	$458,884	$409,883	$540,215	$491,911	$525,501	$506,575	$512,730	$488,775
Gross profit[2]	107,884	87,964	159,818	135,937	146,788	132,204	144,105	130,259
Net income (loss)	24,637	19,454	56,996	49,304	52,968	46,941	(4,102)	40,249
Basic earnings per common share[3]	.19	.16	.43	.39	.40	.36	(.03)	.31
Diluted earnings per common share[3]	.19	.16	.42	.38	.39	.36	(.03)	.30

[1] *Includes charges of $72.7 million ($50.0 million after tax), see Note 2.*
[2] *Total revenues less cost of sales, company restaurant operating costs, and operating costs.*
[3] *Amounts have been restated, see Note 1.*

Management's Statement of Responsibility for Financial Statements

To Our Shareholders

Management is responsible for the preparation of the financial statements and other related financial information included in this Annual Report. The financial statements have been prepared in conformity with generally accepted accounting principles, incorporating management's reasonable estimates and judgments, where applicable.

The company maintains a system of internal accounting controls designed to provide reasonable assurance that assets are safeguarded, that transactions are executed as authorized, and that transactions are recorded and reported properly. The control system is supported by written policies and procedures, appropriate divisions of responsibility and authority and an effective internal audit function. Even effective internal controls, no matter how well designed, have inherent limitations, such as the possibility of human error or the overriding of controls. Further, changes in conditions may have an impact on the effectiveness of controls over time.

The company assessed its internal control systems for the year ended December 28, 1997, using the criteria for effective internal controls as described in *Internal Control – Integrated Framework* issued by the Committee of Sponsoring Organizations of the Treadway Commission. This in-depth review focused on the effectiveness and efficiency of operations, the reliability of financial reporting and compliance with applicable laws and regulations. Similar reviews were performed concurrently at Tim Hortons and Wendy's Restaurants of Canada. Based on this assessment, the company believes that, for the year ended December 28, 1997, its system of internal control met those criteria.

The company engages Coopers & Lybrand L.L.P. as independent public accountants to perform an independent audit of the financial statements. Their report, which appears herein, is based on obtaining an understanding of the company's accounting systems and procedures and testing them as they deem necessary.

The Board of Directors has an Audit Committee composed entirely of outside directors. The Audit Committee meets periodically with representatives of internal audit and Coopers & Lybrand L.L.P., and both have unrestricted access to the Audit Committee.

Gordon F. Teter

Gordon F. Teter
Chairman, Chief Executive Officer and President

Frederick R. Reed

Frederick R. Reed
Chief Financial Officer, General Counsel and Secretary

L A Laudick

Lawrence A. Laudick
Senior Vice President, General Controller and Assistant Secretary

Report of Independent Accountants

To The Shareholders of Wendy's International, Inc.

We have audited the accompanying consolidated balance sheet of Wendy's International, Inc. and Subsidiaries as of December 28, 1997 and December 29, 1996, and the related consolidated statements of income, shareholders' equity, and cash flows for the years ended December 28, 1997, December 29, 1996 and December 31, 1995. These financial statements are the responsibility of the company's management. Our responsibility is to express an opinion on these financial statements based on our audits.

We conducted our audits in accordance with generally accepted auditing standards. Those standards require that we plan and perform the audit to obtain reasonable assurance about whether the financial statements are free of material misstatement. An audit includes examining, on a test basis, evidence supporting the amounts and disclosures in the financial statements. An audit also includes assessing the accounting principles used and significant estimates made by management, as well as evaluating the overall financial statement presentation. We believe that our audits provide a reasonable basis for our opinion.

In our opinion, the financial statements referred to above present fairly, in all material respects, the consolidated financial position of Wendy's International, Inc. and Subsidiaries as of December 28, 1997 and December 29, 1996, and the consolidated results of their operations and their cash flows for the years ended December 28, 1997, December 29, 1996 and December 31, 1995, in conformity with generally accepted accounting principles.

Coopers & Lybrand L.L.P.

Columbus, Ohio
February 4, 1998

Corporate/Shareholder Information

Wendy's International, Inc.
Stock Symbol/Exchange:
WEN (NYSE)

1997 Data:

Stock price range: $19.625 - $27.9375
Dividend: $.24
Diluted EPS: $.97
Diluted EPS before non-recurring charges: $1.33
Shareholders' equity per share: $8.95
Capitalization: 17% debt, 83% equity
Cash and cash equivalents: $234 million
Shares outstanding: 132.3 million
Market capitalization: $3.0 billion
Systemwide sales:
- Wendy's: $5.23 billion
- Tim Hortons: $772 million
- Total: $6.00 billion

Number of Units:
- Wendy's: 5,207
- Tim Hortons: 1,578
- Total: 6,785

Quick-service restaurant (QSR) market share:
- Wendy's — 12.8% (U.S. hamburger)
- Tim Hortons — 10.4% (Canada)

Common Shares

Wendy's shares are traded primarily on the New York Stock Exchange. Options in Wendy's shares are traded on the Pacific Stock Exchange. At March 2, 1998, the Company had approximately 93,000 shareholders of record.

Comparison of Five-Year Cumulative Total Return

Assumes $100 invested 12/31/92 in Wendy's stock, S&P 500 and industry peer group (dividends reinvested).

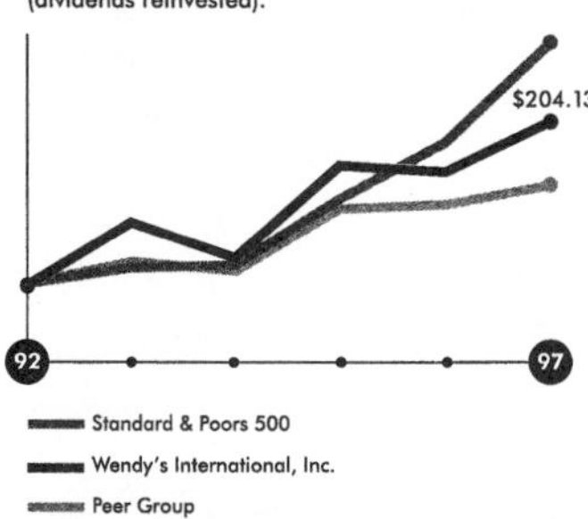

Market Price Of Common Stock

1997	High	Low	Close
1st Quarter	$23.375	$19.875	$20.625
2nd Quarter	26.625	19.625	25.9375
3rd Quarter	27.9375	21.000	21.250
4th Quarter	24.1875	19.8125	24.0625

1996	High	Low	Close
1st Quarter	$22.500	$17.125	$18.125
2nd Quarter	20.000	16.750	18.625
3rd Quarter	22.250	16.750	21.500
4th Quarter	23.000	18.250	20.875

Stock Split History

September 1977 .... 4-for-3
June 1978 .... 2-for-1
March 1981 .... 3-for-2
November 1982 .... 3-for-2
March 1984 .... 4-for-3
March 1985 .... 4-for-3
May 1986 .... 5-for-4

(Example: 100 shares of Wendy's common stock purchased in 1976 equaled 1,333 at 12/31/97)

Dividend History

Wendy's quarterly dividend is currently $.06 per share. Wendy's has paid 79 consecutive dividends. Additional information on dividends can be obtained by contacting the Investor Relations Department at the Corporate Office.

Debt Rating

Standard & Poors ...... BBB+
Moody's Baa-1
(As of 12/31/97)

Annual Meeting

The Annual Meeting of Shareholders of Wendy's International, Inc. will be held at 10:00 a.m., April 29, 1998, at the Aladdin Shrine Temple, 3850 Stelzer Road, Columbus, Ohio 43219. Shareholders are cordially invited to attend.

Form 10-K

The Company's Annual Report on Form 10-K will be sent free of charge upon request to the Investor Relations Department at the Corporate Office.

Corporate Governance

- The majority of the Board Membership Committee and the committee chairperson are outside directors.
- The Compensation Committee is comprised of all outside directors.
- The Audit Committee is comprised of all outside directors.
- Members of the board of directors have broad, diverse and relevant backgrounds in senior management positions, the restaurant industry, retail, finance and legal.
- A policy against the payment of greenmail is in place.

Certified Public Accountants

Coopers & Lybrand L.L.P.
Columbus, Ohio

Legal Counsel

Vorys, Sater, Seymour and Pease LLP
Columbus, Ohio

Product Information

A complete nutritional and ingredient information brochure for Wendy's products is available by writing to the Consumer Relations Department at the Corporate Office.

Company Brochures

For a copy of Wendy's environmental or code of conduct brochures, write to the Corporate Office.

Shareholder Inquiries

Inquiries regarding address corrections, lost certificates, dividends, direct deposit, changes of registration, stock certificate holdings, dividend reinvestment, and other shareholder account matters should be directed to Wendy's transfer agent, American Stock Transfer & Trust Company.

Transfer Agent And Registrar

American Stock Transfer & Trust Company
Shareholder Services Department
40 Wall Street, 46th Floor
New York, NY 10005
1-800-937-5449
1-800-278-4353 (Dividend reinvestment)
http://www.amstock.com

Financial Information

Investor Relations

General inquiries:
Marsha Gordon
Shareholder Relations Specialist
(614) 764-3019 Fax: (614) 764-3330
email: marsha_gordon@wendys.e-mail.com

Analysts, portfolio managers and financial media:
John D. Barker
Vice President, Investor Relations
(614) 764-3044 Fax: (614) 764-3330
email: john_barker@wendys.e-mail.com

Information Requests and Shareholder Newsline

A recorded message system allows you to request printed financial information, dividend reinvestment information and listen to current news releases and prior day common stock closing price.
(614) 764-3105

Internet

Visit Wendy's website at **http://www.wendys.com** where you will find investor information, news releases, advertising, product, franchising and nutritional information, as well as information about The Dave Thomas Foundation for Adoption.

Investor information is also available:
http://www.investquest.com

Videotapes

Two videotapes are available for investment clubs and other interested groups. A corporate identity video or a financial update video is available by writing or calling (614) 764-3105. Please specify which video you would like to receive.

General Information

Consumer inquiries, concerns, store locations and information requests
(614) 764-3100
(Ask for Consumer Relations)

Media inquiries
Denny Lynch
Vice President, Communications
(614) 764-3413

Franchise inquiries
Wendy's: (614) 764-8434
Tim Hortons: Canada — (905) 339-6283
U.S. — (614) 791-4202

Corporate Offices

Wendy's International, Inc.
4288 West Dublin Granville Road
P.O. Box 256
Dublin, Ohio 43017-0256
(614) 764-3100

Tim Hortons
874 Sinclair Road
Oakville, Ontario L6K 2Y1
(905) 845-6511

Tim Hortons — U.S. Office
4150 Tuller Road, Suite 236
Dublin, Ohio 43017-5014
(614) 791-4200

Dividend Reinvestment And Stock Purchase Plan

Wendy's shareholders of record may elect to have cash dividends automatically reinvested in additional shares of Wendy's through the Dividend Reinvestment and Stock Purchase Plan. Additional shares may also be purchased by investing voluntary cash payments of $20 to $20,000, but not more than a total of $20,000 annually. Automatic monthly deduction from your bank account is also available. Participation is entirely voluntary. All fees associated with stock purchases made under the Plan are paid for by Wendy's International, Inc. As of March 2, 1998, 69 percent of all registered shareholders were participants.

To receive an informational brochure/enrollment form, please contact American Stock Transfer & Trust Company at the address or telephone number listed on page 40.

Wendy's Supports NAIC

Wendy's is proud to be a corporate member of the National Association of Investors Corporation (NAIC). The NAIC, a not-for-profit organization with over 630,000 members, provides a program of investment information, education and support for individual investors and investment clubs. Wendy's participates in several NAIC-sponsored programs during the year, including the Low Cost Investment Plan, Own Your Share of America, Investor Information Reports (green sheets), the National Investors Expo and regional investor fairs. Visit the Wendy's booth at the following investor fairs in 1998:

March 14	Phoenix, AZ
April 4	Columbus, OH
April 18	Portland, OR
May 30	Madison, WI
October 15-17	San Jose, CA

NAIC's Low Cost Investment Plan

NAIC members may purchase their initial share of Wendy's stock through NAIC's Low Cost Investment Plan. For information contact:

National Association of Investors Corporation (NAIC)
711 West Thirteen Mile Road
Madison Heights, MI 48071
(248) 583-6242

printed on recycled paper with a 10 percent post-consumer content

appendix E

Reebok International Ltd.

financial results and corporate information

selected financial data

AMOUNTS IN THOUSANDS, EXCEPT PER SHARE DATA

YEAR ENDED DECEMBER 31,	1997	1996	1995	1994	1993
Net sales	$ 3,643,599	$ 3,478,604	$ 3,481,450	$ 3,280,418	$ 2,893,900
Income before income taxes and minority interest	158,085	237,668	275,974	417,368	371,508
Net income	135,119	138,950	164,798	254,478	223,415
Basic earnings per share	2.41	2.06	2.10	3.09	2.58
Diluted earnings per share	2.32	2.03	2.07	3.02	2.53
Cash dividends per common share	—	.225	.300	.300	.300

DECEMBER 31,	1997	1996	1995	1994	1993
Working capital	$ 887,367	$ 946,127	$ 900,922	$ 831,856	$ 730,757
Total assets	1,756,097	1,786,184	1,651,619	1,649,461	1,391,711
Long-term debt	639,355	854,099	254,178	131,799	134,207
Stockholders' equity	507,157	381,234	895,289	990,505	846,617

The earnings per share amounts prior to 1997 have been restated as required to comply with Statement of Financial Accounting Standards No. 128, "Earnings Per Share." For further discussion regarding the calculation of earnings per share, see Note 1 to the Consolidated Financial Statements.

On June 7, 1996, Reebok completed the sale of substantially all of the operating assets and business of its subsidiary, Avia Group International, Inc. ("Avia"); accordingly, subsequent to that date, the operations of Avia are no longer included in the Company's financial results. 1997 results include an income tax benefit of $40,000 related to the conclusion in 1997 of outstanding tax matters associated with the sale of Avia. 1997 also includes total special after-tax charges of $39,161 relating to restructuring activities in the Company's global operations.

Financial data for 1995 includes total special after-tax charges of $44,934, of which $33,699 relates to the sale of Avia and $11,235 relates to facilities consolidation, severance and other related costs associated with the streamlining of certain segments of the Company's operations.

Financial data for 1993 includes a special after-tax charge of $7,037 related to the sale of Ellesse U.S.A., Inc. and Boston Whaler, Inc.

management's discussion and analysis

OF RESULTS OF OPERATIONS AND FINANCIAL CONDITION

THE FOLLOWING DISCUSSION CONTAINS FORWARD-LOOKING STATEMENTS WHICH INVOLVE RISKS AND UNCERTAINTIES. THE COMPANY'S ACTUAL RESULTS MAY DIFFER MATERIALLY FROM THOSE DISCUSSED IN SUCH FORWARD-LOOKING STATEMENTS. PROSPECTIVE INFORMATION IS BASED ON MANAGEMENT'S THEN CURRENT EXPECTATIONS OR FORECASTS. SUCH INFORMATION IS SUBJECT TO THE RISK THAT SUCH EXPECTATIONS OR FORECASTS, OR THE ASSUMPTIONS UNDERLYING SUCH EXPECTATIONS OR FORECASTS, BECOME INACCURATE. FACTORS THAT COULD AFFECT THE COMPANY'S ACTUAL RESULTS AND COULD CAUSE SUCH RESULTS TO DIFFER MATERIALLY FROM THOSE CONTAINED IN FORWARD-LOOKING STATEMENTS MADE BY OR ON BEHALF OF THE COMPANY INCLUDE, BUT ARE NOT LIMITED TO, THOSE DISCUSSED BELOW AND THOSE DESCRIBED IN THE COMPANY'S 1997 ANNUAL REPORT ON FORM 10-K UNDER THE HEADING "ISSUES AND UNCERTAINTIES".

operating results 1997

Net sales for the year ended December 31, 1997 were $3.644 billion, a 4.7% increase from the year ended December 31, 1996 sales of $3.479 billion, which included $49.4 million of sales from the Company's Avia subsidiary that was sold in June 1996. The Reebok Division's worldwide sales (including Greg Norman) were $3.131 billion in 1997, a 5.0% increase from comparable sales of $2.982 billion in 1996. The stronger U.S. dollar has adversely impacted Reebok Brand worldwide sales comparisons with the prior year. On a constant dollar basis, sales for the Reebok Brand worldwide increased 8.3% in 1997 as compared to 1996. The Reebok Division's U.S. footwear sales increased 3.0% to $1.229 billion in 1997 from $1.193 billion in 1996. The increase in the Reebok Division's U.S. footwear sales is attributed primarily to increases in the running, walking and men's cross-training categories. The increase in sales in these categories was partially offset by decreases in Reebok's basketball, outdoor and women's fitness categories. The underlying quality of Reebok footwear sales in the U.S. improved from last year. Sales to athletic specialty accounts increased approximately 31%, and the amount of off-price sales declined from 7.6% of total Reebok footwear sales in 1996 to 3.2% of total Reebok footwear sales in 1997. The Reebok Division's U.S. apparel sales increased by 37.2% to $431.9 million from $314.9 million in 1996. The increase resulted primarily from increases in branded core basics, licensed and graphic categories. The Reebok Division's International sales (including footwear and apparel) were $1.471 billion in 1997, approximately equal to the Division's International sales in 1996 of $1.474 billion. The International sales comparison was negatively impacted by changes in foreign currency exchange rates. On a constant dollar basis, for the year ended December 31, 1997, the International sales gain was 6.4%. All International regions generated sales increases over the prior year on a constant dollar basis. For International sales, increases in the running, classic and walking categories were offset by decreases in the basketball and tennis categories. Generally in the industry there is a slowdown in branded athletic footwear and apparel at retail, and there is a significant amount of promotional product offered across all distribution channels. As a result of this situation and the expected ongoing negative impact from currency fluctuations, it will be difficult to increase reported sales for the Reebok Brand in 1998.

Rockport's sales for 1997 increased by 14.5% to $512.5 million from $447.6 million in 1996. Exclusive of the Ralph Lauren footwear business, which was acquired in May 1996, Rockport's sales increased 7.3% in 1997. International revenues, which grew by 46.0%, accounted for approximately 21.0% of Rockport's sales (excluding Ralph Lauren Footwear) in 1997, as compared to 16.0% in 1996. Increased sales in the walking and men's categories were partially offset by decreased sales in the women's lifestyle category. The decrease in the women's lifestyle category was the result of a strategic initiative to re-focus the women's business around an outdoor, adventure and travel positioning and reduce the product offerings in the refined women's dress shoe segment. Rockport continues to attract younger customers to the brand with the introduction of a wider selection of dress and casual products. The Ralph Lauren footwear business performed well in 1997 and is beginning to generate sales growth in its traditional segments, reflecting the benefits of improved product design and development and increased distribution. Rockport plans to expand the current product line of Ralph Lauren Polo Sport athletic footwear during 1998 with additional products which will be available at retail during 1999.

The Company's gross margin declined from 38.4% in 1996 to 37.0% in 1997. Margins are being negatively impacted by both start-up costs and initially higher manufacturing costs on the Company's new technology products (DMX 2000 and 3D Ultralite). In addition, the decline reflects a significant impact from currency fluctuations as a result of the stronger U.S. dollar and a decrease in full-margin at-once business as a result of an over-inventoried promotional retail environment. The Company estimates that 100 basis points of the margin decline is due to currency. Looking forward, the Company expects margins to continue to be under pressure through at least the first half of 1998. However, the Company believes that if the technology product line expands and gains greater critical mass and with improving production capabilities, the new technology products are capable of generating margin improvement.

Selling, general and administrative expenses decreased as a percentage of sales from 30.6% in 1996 to 29.4% in 1997. The reduction is primarily due to the absence of certain advertising and marketing expenses associated with the 1996 Summer Olympics. In addition, non-brand building general and administrative infrastructure expenses declined. Research, design and development expenses increased 27.0% for the year and retail operating expenses increased in support of new store openings. At December 31, 1997, the Company operated 157 Reebok, Rockport and Greg Norman retail stores in the U.S. as compared to 141 at the end of 1996.

As described in Note 2 to the Consolidated Financial Statements, the Company recorded special pre-tax charges of $58.2 million relating to restructuring activities in the Company's global operations. The restructuring should enable the Company to achieve operating efficiencies, including improved inventory management, credit management, purchasing power and customer service and should provide the organization with access to a single global data base of company, supplier and customer information. The restruc-

management's discussion and analysis

OF RESULTS OF OPERATIONS AND FINANCIAL CONDITION

turing initiatives should also improve logistics, allow the Company to focus its spending on those key athletes and teams who are more closely aligned with its brand positioning and produce cost savings once completed during 1999.

Interest expense increased as a result of the additional debt the Company incurred to finance the shares acquired during the 1996 Dutch Auction share repurchase.

As described in Note 14 to the Consolidated Financial Statements, the Internal Revenue Service notified the Company in August 1997 that it had approved the Company's tax treatment of certain losses related to the sale of its Avia subsidiary. Accordingly, the Company recorded a tax benefit in the quarter ended September 30, 1997 totaling $40.0 million. Excluding the favorable impact of this special income tax credit, the Company's effective tax rate was 33.2% in 1997, as compared with 35.4% in 1996. The decrease in the rate is attributable to a change in the mix of the earnings between domestic and international subsidiaries. The Company expects its effective tax rate in 1998 to be further reduced to 31.0% - 32.0% as a result of the change in geographic mix of earnings and ongoing efforts to improve cash flow through various tax planning initiatives.

The $10.5 million increase in other expense in 1997 relates primarily to currency losses due to the stronger U.S. dollar.

Year-to-year earnings per share comparisons benefited from the Company's share repurchase programs including the Dutch Auction share repurchase which was completed in August 1996. Weighted average common shares outstanding (dilutive) for the year ended December 31, 1997 declined by 15.0% to 58.3 million shares, as compared to 68.6 million shares for the year ended December 31, 1996.

The Company's footwear and apparel production operations are subject to the usual risks of doing business abroad, such as import duties, quotas and other threats to free trade, foreign currency fluctuations, labor unrest and political instability. The Company believes that it has the ability to develop, over time, adequate substitute sources of supply for the products obtained from present foreign suppliers. If, however, events should prevent the Company from acquiring products from its suppliers in Indonesia, China, Thailand or the Philippines, or significantly increase the cost to the Company of such products, the Company's operations could be seriously disrupted until alternative suppliers are found.

For several years, imports from China to the U.S., including footwear, have been threatened with higher or prohibitive tariff rates, either through statutory action or intervention by the Executive Branch, due to concern over China's trade policies, human rights, foreign weapons sales practices and its foreign policy. Further debate on these issues is expected to continue in 1998. However, the Company does not currently anticipate that restrictions on imports from China will be imposed by the U.S. during 1998. If adverse action is taken with respect to imports from China, it could have an adverse effect on some or all of the Company's product lines, which could result in a negative financial impact. The Company has put in place contingency plans which should allow it to diversify some of its sourcing to countries other than China if any such adverse action occurred. In addition, the Company does not believe that it would be more adversely impacted by any such adverse action than its major competitors. The actual effect of any such action will, however, depend on a number of factors, including how reliant the Company, as compared to its competitors, is on production in China and the effectiveness of the contingency plans put in place.

The European Union ("EU") imposed import quotas on certain footwear from China in 1994. The effect of such quota scheme on Reebok has not been significant because the quota scheme provides an exemption for certain higher-priced special technology athletic footwear, which exemption is available for most REEBOK products. This exemption does not, however, cover most of Rockport's products. Nevertheless, the volume of quota available to Reebok and Rockport in 1998 is expected to be sufficient to meet the anticipated sales for ROCKPORT products in EU member countries. If, however, such quota is not sufficient, there could be an adverse effect on Rockport's international sales.

In addition, the EU has imposed antidumping duties against certain textile upper footwear from China and Indonesia. A broad exemption from the dumping duties is provided for athletic textile footwear which covers most REEBOK models. If the athletic footwear exemption remains in its current form, few REEBOK product lines will be affected by the duties; however, ROCKPORT products would be subject to these duties. Nevertheless, the Company believes that those REEBOK and ROCKPORT products affected by the duties can generally be sourced from other countries not subject to such duties. If, however, the Company was unable to implement such alternative sourcing arrangements, certain of its product lines could be adversely affected by these duties.

The EU also has imposed antidumping duties on certain leather upper footwear from China, Thailand and Indonesia. These duties will apply only to low cost footwear, below the import prices of most Reebok and Rockport products. Thus the Company does not anticipate that its products will be impacted by such duties.

The EU continues to review the athletic footwear exemption which applies to both the quota scheme and antidumping duties discussed above. The Company, through relevant trade associations, is working to prevent imposition of a more limited athletic footwear exemption. Should revisions be adopted narrowing such exemption, certain of the Company's product lines could be affected adversely, although the Company does not believe that its products would be more severely affected than those of its major competitors.

Various other countries have taken or are considering steps to restrict footwear imports or impose additional customs duties or other impediments, which actions affect the Company as well as other footwear importers. The Company, in conjunction with other footwear importers, is aggressively challenging such restrictions. Such restrictions have in some cases had a significant adverse effect on the Company's sales in some of such countries, most notably Argentina, although they have not had a material adverse effect on the Company as a whole.

management's discussion and analysis

OF RESULTS OF OPERATIONS AND FINANCIAL CONDITION

operating results 1996

Net sales for the year ended December 31, 1996 were $3.479 billion, approximately equal to the net sales for the year ended December 31, 1995 of $3.482 billion. Excluding Avia sales, net sales for the year ended December 31, 1996 were $3.429 billion, 2.3% higher than the $3.352 billion for the same period in 1995. The Reebok Division's worldwide sales were $2.982 billion in 1996 and $2.984 billion in 1995. Growth in this Division's U.S. apparel sales as well as growth in their International sales was offset by a decrease in U.S. footwear sales. U.S. footwear sales of the Reebok Division decreased 12.7% to $1.193 billion from $1.367 billion in 1995. The decrease was due primarily to decreases in substantially all categories other than walking and soccer which had increases in sales. U.S. apparel sales of the Reebok Division increased by 42.0% to $314.9 million from $221.7 million in 1995. The increase resulted from increases in licensed and branded apparel, particularly in T-shirts, all purpose bottoms, warm-ups, tops and outerwear. International sales of the Reebok Division (including footwear and apparel) were $1.474 billion in 1996, an increase of 5.7% from $1.395 billion in 1995. Strong apparel sales and increases in footwear sales of basketball, walking and classic products were partially offset by decreases in the running, cross-training and outdoor footwear categories. The stronger U.S. dollar adversely impacted sales comparisons with the prior year. On a constant dollar basis for the year ended December 31, 1996, the International sales gain was 8.8%. On a local currency basis, thereby eliminating the impact of changes in foreign currency exchange rates, the United Kingdom, Japan, Korea and South Africa had increases in sales whereas there were decreases in sales in France, Canada and Belgium and in the Division's sales to certain Latin American distributors.

Rockport's sales for 1996 increased by 21.6% to $447.6 million from $368.1 million in 1995. This increase reflects an emphasis on Rockport's walking technology and the successful introduction of new products in 1996. Increased sales in the men's casual dress and performance walking categories were partially offset by decreased sales in the women's lifestyle and outdoor categories. Rockport's 1996 results include the Ralph Lauren footwear business. In May 1996, Rockport entered into a licensing arrangement for the North American license for Ralph Lauren footwear and also acquired Ralph Lauren Footwear, Inc., the former North American footwear licensee for Ralph Lauren. Rockport is expected to acquire the Ralph Lauren footwear licensing rights for the rest of the world over the next several years. Sales of Ralph Lauren footwear were $31.9 million in 1996 for the seven month period from May 1996 (the date of acquisition) through December 1996. Rockport's International business increased by 21.0% in 1996. Exclusive of sales of Ralph Lauren footwear, Rockport's International sales accounted for 16% of its total sales during 1996.

For the year ended December 31, 1996, the Company's sales include $49.4 million of sales of Avia, a decrease of 61.9% from the $129.6 million of sales of Avia for 1995. On June 7, 1996, Reebok completed the sale of substantially all of the operating assets and business of Avia. Accordingly, subsequent to that date, the operations of Avia are no longer included in the Company's financial results.

Gross margins declined from 39.3% in 1995 to 38.4% in 1996. The decline in margins includes the effect of costs incurred with respect to new products and technologies. These costs include the impact of start-up tooling, shorter production runs and increased air freight. The margin decline also reflects a substantial shift in the overall mix of the U.S. business due to increased apparel sales and decreased footwear sales. U.S. apparel sales in 1996 accounted for 20.8% of the Reebok business in the U.S. as compared to 14.0% in 1995. Since U.S. apparel sales contribute lower gross margins than the U.S. footwear business, the shift in domestic mix negatively impacts overall gross margins. International margins were negatively impacted in 1996 as compared with the prior year due to a strong U.S. dollar as against most international currencies.

Selling, general and administrative expenses increased as a percentage of sales from 28.7% in 1995 to 30.6% in 1996. Advertising and marketing expenses increased by $66.2 million during 1996 with approximately $30.0 million of that increase attributable to Reebok's Olympic participation. Continued investment in brand-building expenses, including product development, retail presence, sports marketing and on-field presence also contributed to the increase. In addition, retail operating expenses increased in support of the U.S. retail store expansion. At December 31, 1996, the Company operated 141 U.S. Reebok, Rockport and Greg Norman retail stores as compared to 117 at the end of 1995. Primarily all of these U.S. retail stores are located in factory direct outlet malls.

Amortization of intangibles decreased due to the write-down in the fourth quarter of 1995 of the carrying value of Avia to estimated fair value on sale.

Minority interest represents the minority shareholders' proportionate share of the net income of certain of the Company's consolidated subsidiaries.

Interest expense increased from $25.7 million in 1995 to $42.2 million in 1996 as a result of increased borrowings to fund the purchase of approximately 17.0 million shares of the Company's common stock in connection with the Company's Dutch Auction self-tender offer which was completed in August 1996.

Year-to-year earnings per share comparisons benefited from the Company's share repurchase programs and the repurchase of shares pursuant to the Dutch Auction. Weighted average common shares outstanding (dilutive) for the year ended December 31, 1996 declined to 68.6 million, compared to 79.5 million shares for the year ended December 31, 1995.

Reebok brand backlog

The Reebok Brand backlog (including Greg Norman apparel) of open customer orders for the period January 1, 1998 through June 30, 1998 was essentially flat as compared to the same period last year. On a constant dollar basis, the Reebok Brand back-

management's discussion and analysis

OF RESULTS OF OPERATIONS AND FINANCIAL CONDITION

log increased 3.4%. North American backlog for the Reebok Brand, which includes the U.S. and Canada, increased 2.8% and the International backlog decreased 5.7%. On a constant dollar basis, the International backlog increased 4.4%. Reebok U.S. footwear backlog increased 2.1% and Reebok U.S. apparel backlog (including Greg Norman apparel) decreased 1.7% as compared to the same period last year. Management believes the slowdown in the Reebok Division's domestic footwear and apparel bookings is the result of retailers becoming more cautious in placing future orders, given current market conditions. The Company continues to see improvement in the shape of the Reebok Brand U.S. footwear order book, with athletic specialty backlog up 57% for the next six months and the volume channel down 11%. The percentage changes in open backlog are not necessarily indicative of future sales trends. The reasons for this are that many orders are cancelable, sales by company-owned retail stores can vary from year-to-year and the ratio of orders booked early to at-once shipments can vary from period to period. For example, the percentage of Reebok U.S. footwear futures to total Reebok U.S. footwear sales was approximately 87% in 1997 as compared to 78% in 1996.

liquidity and sources of capital

The Company's financial position remains strong. Working capital was $887.4 million at December 31, 1997 and $946.1 million at December 31, 1996. The current ratio at December 31, 1997 was 2.5 to 1 compared to 2.8 to 1 at December 31, 1996. The decline in the current ratio is primarily the result of the medium-term notes of $50.0 million due in 1998, which were previously classified as long-term debt, being classified as a current liability at December 31, 1997 and the pre-payment of $100.0 million of long-term debt during 1997.

Accounts receivable decreased by $28.8 million from December 31, 1996, a decrease of 4.8%. This is the result of the Reebok Division reducing the average days sales outstanding in U.S. receivables by 7 days as compared to last year end. Inventory increased by $19.2 million, or 3.5% from December 31, 1996. U.S. footwear inventories of the Reebok Brand increased 24% at year end in dollars versus a year ago but only 5% in pairs, reflecting higher average per unit costs due to the inclusion of a greater percentage of technology products and a greater percentage of on-time delivery from the Far East factories as they began to catch up with demand, given the general slowdown in the industry. Reebok U.S. apparel inventories were down 23.7% and Reebok retail outlet inventories were down 12% despite adding ten additional stores over the course of the year and achieving same store sales increases of 7.3% in 1997.

During the year ended December 31, 1997, cash and cash equivalents decreased $22.6 million and outstanding borrowings decreased by $138.7 million. The Company elected to make prepayments of $50.0 million in February 1997 and $50.0 million in May 1997 on its long-term debt facility used to fund the Dutch Auction share repurchase in August 1996. Cash provided by operations during 1997 was $126.9 million, as compared to cash provided by operations of $280.3 million during 1996. The change in operating cash flow year-to-year is attributable to improved inventory management practices which had a significant impact in reducing 1996 inventory levels from the prior year thereby generating significant cash in that year. Cash generated from operations, together with the Company's existing credit lines and other financial resources, is expected to adequately finance the Company's current and planned 1998 cash requirements. However, the Company's actual experience may differ from the expectations set forth in the preceding sentence. Factors that might lead to a difference include, but are not limited to, future events that might have the effect of reducing the Company's available cash balances (such as unexpected operating losses or increased capital or other expenditures), as well as future events that might reduce or eliminate the availability of external financial resources.

As a result of the current industry conditions and the Company's near-term business outlook, the Company has announced plans to further restructure its operations in order to manage its business more efficiently in the near-term. Key initiatives will include simplifying and flattening the organizational structure by eliminating management layers, combining and redefining business units and centralizing operations. The intention is to focus the business on fewer near-term opportunities, postpone certain longer-term investments, and simplify the process flows to gain greater efficiencies. As a result of this effort, the Company expects to take a special charge in the first quarter of 1998 of between $25 million to $35 million on a pre-tax basis. The on-going effect of the restructuring will be to reduce operating costs to a level more commensurate with the anticipated short-term business outlook.

The Company has conducted a comprehensive global review of its computer systems to identify the systems that could be affected by the "Year 2000" issue and has developed an implementation plan to address the issue. During 1997, the Company started its global implementation of SAP software which will replace substantially all legacy systems. The Company presently believes that, with modifications to existing software and converting to SAP software, the year 2000 issue will not pose significant operational problems for the Company's computer systems as so modified and converted. The Company expects the global implementation of SAP to be substantially completed by 1999 and the implementation is currently on schedule. However, if such modifications and conversions are not completed timely or effectively, the year 2000 problem could have a material impact on the operations of the Company.

Lawsuits arise during the normal course of business. The Company does not expect the outcome of any existing litigation to have a significant impact on its financial position or future results of operations.

The Company enters into forward currency exchange contracts and options to hedge its exposure for merchandise purchased in U.S. dollars that will be sold to customers in other currencies. Realized and unrealized gains and losses on these contracts are included in net income except that gains and losses on contracts which hedge specific foreign currency commitments are deferred and accounted for as a part of the transaction.

management's discussion and analysis

OF RESULTS OF OPERATIONS AND FINANCIAL CONDITION

The Company also uses forward currency exchange contracts and options to hedge significant intercompany assets and liabilities denominated in other than the functional currency. Contracts used to hedge intercompany balances are marked to market and the resulting transaction gain or loss is included in the determination of net income.

Foreign currency losses realized from settlements of transactions included in net income for the year ended December 31, 1997 were $8.1 million. Realized gains and losses from settlements of transactions for the years ended December 31, 1996 and 1995 were not significant. The Company has used forward exchange contracts and options as an element of its risk management strategy for several years.

At December 31, 1997, the Company had forward currency exchange contracts and options, all having maturities of less than one year, with a notional amount aggregating $357.9 million. The contracts involved twelve different foreign currencies. No single currency represented more than 20% of the aggregate notional amount. The notional amount of the contracts intended to hedge merchandise purchases was $165.3 million. Deferred gains (losses) on these contracts were not material at December 31, 1997 and 1996.

The Company uses interest rate swap agreements to manage its exposure to interest rate movements by effectively converting a portion of its variable rate long-term debt from floating to fixed rates. These agreements involve the exchange of variable rate payments for fixed rate payments without the effect of leverage and without the exchange of the underlying principal amount. Interest rate differentials paid or received under these swap agreements are recognized over the life of the contracts as adjustments to interest expense. At December 31, 1997, the notional amount of interest rate swaps outstanding was $245.0 million.

Financial instruments which potentially subject the Company to concentrations of credit risk consist principally of cash equivalents and hedging instruments. The Company places cash equivalents with high credit major financial institutions and, by policy, limits the amount of credit exposure to any one financial institution.

The Company is exposed to credit-related losses in the event of non-performance by counterparties to hedging instruments. The counterparties to these contracts are major financial institutions. The Company continually monitors its positions and the credit ratings of its counterparties and places dollar and term limits on the amount of contracts it enters into with any one party.

consolidated balance sheets

AMOUNTS IN THOUSANDS, EXCEPT SHARE DATA

DECEMBER 31	1997	1996
assets		
CURRENT ASSETS:		
Cash and cash equivalents	$ 209,766	$ 232,365
Accounts receivable, net of allowance for doubtful accounts (1997, $44,003; 1996, $43,527)	561,729	590,504
Inventory	563,735	544,522
Deferred income taxes	75,186	69,422
Prepaid expenses and other current assets	54,404	26,275
Total current assets	1,464,820	1,463,088
Property and equipment, net	156,959	185,292
NON-CURRENT ASSETS:		
Intangibles, net of amortization	65,784	69,700
Deferred income taxes	19,371	7,850
Other	49,163	60,254
	134,318	137,804
Total Assets	$ 1,756,097	$ 1,786,184
liabilities and stockholders' equity		
CURRENT LIABILITIES:		
Notes payable to banks	$ 40,665	$ 32,977
Current portion of long-term debt	121,000	52,684
Accounts payable	192,142	196,368
Accrued expenses	219,386	169,344
Income taxes payable	4,260	65,588
Total current liabilities	577,453	516,961
Long-term debt, net of current portion	639,355	854,099
Minority interest	32,132	33,890
STOCKHOLDERS' EQUITY:		
Common stock, par value $.01; authorized 250,000,000 shares; issued 93,115,835 shares in 1997, 92,556,295 shares in 1996	931	926
Retained earnings	1,145,271	992,563
Less 36,716,227 shares in treasury at cost	(617,620)	(617,620)
Unearned compensation	(140)	(283)
Foreign currency translation adjustment	(21,285)	5,648
	507,157	381,234
Total Liabilities and Stockholders' Equity	$ 1,756,097	$ 1,786,184

THE ACCOMPANYING NOTES ARE AN INTEGRAL PART OF THE CONSOLIDATED FINANCIAL STATEMENTS.

consolidated statements of income

AMOUNTS IN THOUSANDS, EXCEPT PER SHARE DATA

YEAR ENDED DECEMBER 31	1997	1996	1995
Net sales	$ 3,643,599	$ 3,478,604	$ 3,481,450
Other income (expense)	(6,158)	4,325	3,126
	3,637,441	3,482,929	3,484,576
COSTS AND EXPENSES:			
Cost of sales	2,294,049	2,144,422	2,114,084
Selling, general and administrative expenses	1,069,433	1,065,792	999,731
Special charges	58,161		72,098
Amortization of intangibles	4,157	3,410	4,067
Interest expense	64,366	42,246	25,725
Interest income	(10,810)	(10,609)	(7,103)
	3,479,356	3,245,261	3,208,602
Income before income taxes and minority interest	158,085	237,668	275,974
Income taxes	12,490	84,083	99,753
Income before minority interest	145,595	153,585	176,221
Minority interest	10,476	14,635	11,423
Net income	$ 135,119	$ 138,950	$ 164,798
Basic earnings per share	$ 2.41	$ 2.06	$ 2.10
Diluted earnings per share	$ 2.32	$ 2.03	$ 2.07
Dividends per common share	$ —	$ 0.225	$ 0.300

THE ACCOMPANYING NOTES ARE AN INTEGRAL PART OF THE CONSOLIDATED FINANCIAL STATEMENTS.

consolidated statements of stockholders' equity

DOLLAR AMOUNTS IN THOUSANDS

	Common Stock Shares	Common Stock Par Value	Additional Paid-in Capital	Retained Earnings	Treasury Stock	Unearned Compensation	Foreign Currency Translation Adjustment
BALANCE, DECEMBER 31, 1994	117,155,611	$ 1,172	$ 167,953	$ 1,428,058	$ (603,241)	$ (2,598)	$ (839)
Net income				164,798			
Adjustment for foreign currency translation							12,475
Issuance of shares to certain employees	43,545		1,558			(1,558)	
Amortization of unearned compensation						1,008	
Shares repurchased and retired	(6,639,600)	(66)	(182,569)	(42,835)			
Shares retired	(67,200)	(1)	(1,385)	(554)		1,940	
Shares issued under employee stock purchase plans	161,377	2	4,253				
Shares issued upon exercise of stock options	361,400	4	6,004				
Put option contracts outstanding		(15)		(39,108)			
Premium received from unexercised equity put options			3,233				
Income tax reductions relating to exercise of stock options			953				
Dividends declared				(23,353)			
BALANCE, DECEMBER 31, 1995	111,015,133	1,096	0	1,487,006	(603,241)	(1,208)	11,636
Net income				138,950			
Adjustment for foreign currency translation							(5,988)
Treasury shares repurchased					(14,379)		
Issuance of shares to certain employees	43,278			1,505		(55)	
Amortization of unearned compensation						292	
Shares repurchased and retired	(18,931,403)	(190)		(672,900)		688	
Shares issued under employee stock purchase plans	157,134	2		4,042			
Shares issued upon exercise of stock options	272,153	3		6,930			
Put option contracts expired		15		39,825			
Income tax reductions relating to exercise of stock options				2,385			
Dividends declared				(15,180)			
BALANCE, DECEMBER 31, 1996	92,556,295	926	0	992,563	(617,620)	(283)	5,648
Net income				135,119			
Adjustment for foreign currency translation							(26,933)
Issuance of shares to certain employees	9,532			431		(431)	
Amortization of unearned compensation						566	
Shares repurchased and retired	(313)					8	
Shares issued under employee stock purchase plans	151,210	1		4,362			
Shares issued upon exercise of stock options	399,111	4		10,040			
Income tax reductions relating to exercise of stock options				2,756			
BALANCE, DECEMBER 31, 1997	93,115,835	$ 931	$ 0	$ 1,145,271	$ (617,620)	$ (140)	$ (21,285)

THE ACCOMPANYING NOTES ARE AN INTEGRAL PART OF THE CONSOLIDATED FINANCIAL STATEMENTS.

consolidated statements of cash flows

AMOUNTS IN THOUSANDS

YEAR ENDED DECEMBER 31	1997	1996	1995
CASH FLOWS FROM OPERATING ACTIVITIES:			
Net income	$ 135,119	$ 138,950	$ 164,798
Adjustments to reconcile net income to net cash provided by operating activities:			
Depreciation and amortization	47,423	42,927	39,579
Minority interest	10,476	14,635	11,423
Deferred income taxes	(17,285)	(6,333)	(1,573)
Special charges	55,697		62,743
Changes in operating assets and liabilities, exclusive of those arising from business acquisitions:			
Accounts receivable	(13,915)	(107,082)	16,157
Inventory	(47,937)	77,286	(29,531)
Prepaid expenses	(28,613)	22,650	7,841
Other	24,458	11,042	(18,830)
Accounts payable and accrued expenses	20,759	67,769	(25,327)
Income taxes payable	(59,257)	18,419	(55,553)
Total adjustments	(8,194)	141,313	6,929
Net cash provided by operating activities	126,925	280,263	171,727
CASH FLOWS FROM INVESTING ACTIVITIES:			
Payments to acquire property and equipment	(23,910)	(29,999)	(63,610)
Proceeds from business divestitures		6,887	
Net cash used for investing activities	(23,910)	(23,112)	(63,610)
CASH FLOWS FROM FINANCING ACTIVITIES:			
Net borrowings (payments) of notes payable to banks	27,296	(36,947)	2,426
Proceeds from issuance of common stock to employees	17,163	13,362	11,216
Dividends paid		(20,922)	(23,679)
Repayments of long-term debt	(156,966)	(1,290)	(112,445)
Net proceeds from long-term debt		632,108	230,000
Proceeds from premium on equity put options		717	3,233
Dividends to minority shareholders	(3,900)	(7,426)	(2,885)
Repurchases of common stock		(686,266)	(225,470)
Net cash used for financing activities	(116,407)	(106,664)	(117,604)
Effect of exchange rate changes on cash	(9,207)	1,485	5,944
Net increase (decrease) in cash and cash equivalents	(22,599)	151,972	(3,543)
Cash and cash equivalents at beginning of year	232,365	80,393	83,936
Cash and cash equivalents at end of year	$ 209,766	$ 232,365	$ 80,393
SUPPLEMENTAL DISCLOSURES OF CASH FLOW INFORMATION:			
Interest paid	$ 59,683	$ 38,738	$ 23,962
Income taxes paid	115,985	77,213	152,690

THE ACCOMPANYING NOTES ARE AN INTEGRAL PART OF THE CONSOLIDATED FINANCIAL STATEMENTS.

notes to consolidated financial statements

DOLLAR AMOUNTS IN THOUSANDS, EXCEPT PER SHARE DATA

1
summary of significant accounting policies

BUSINESS ACTIVITY
The Company and its subsidiaries design and market sports and fitness products, including footwear and apparel, as well as footwear and apparel for non-athletic "casual" use, under various trademarks, including REEBOK, the GREG NORMAN Logo and ROCKPORT and footwear under RALPH LAUREN and POLO SPORT.

PRINCIPLES OF CONSOLIDATION
The consolidated financial statements include the accounts of the Company and its subsidiaries. All significant intercompany transactions and accounts are eliminated in consolidation.

USE OF ESTIMATES
The preparation of financial statements in conformity with generally accepted accounting principles requires management to make estimates and assumptions that affect the amounts reported in the financial statements and accompanying notes. Actual results could differ from those estimates.

RECOGNITION OF REVENUES
Sales are recognized upon shipment of products.

ADVERTISING
Advertising production costs are expensed the first time the advertisement is run. Media (TV and print) placement costs are expensed in the month the advertising appears. Advertising expense (including cooperative advertising) amounted to $164,870, $201,584 and $157,573 for the years ended December 31, 1997, 1996 and 1995, respectively.

ACCOUNTING FOR STOCK-BASED COMPENSATION
In 1996, the Company adopted Statement of Accounting Standards No. 123, "Accounting for Stock-Based Compensation" ("Statement 123"). As permitted by Statement 123, the Company continues to account for its stock-based plans under Accounting Principles Board Opinion No. 25, "Accounting for Stock Issued to Employees," and provides pro forma disclosures of the compensation expense determined under the fair value provisions of Statement 123.

CASH EQUIVALENTS
Cash equivalents are defined as highly liquid investments with maturities of three months or less at date of purchase.

INVENTORY VALUATION
Inventory, substantially all finished goods, is recorded at the lower of cost (first-in, first-out method) or market.

PROPERTY AND EQUIPMENT AND DEPRECIATION
Property and equipment are stated at cost. Depreciation is computed principally on the straight line method over the assets' estimated useful lives. Leasehold improvements are amortized over the shorter of the lease term or the estimated useful lives of the assets.

INTANGIBLES
Excess purchase price over the fair value of assets acquired is amortized using the straight line method over periods ranging from 5 to 40 years. Other intangibles are amortized using the straight line method over periods ranging from 3 to 40 years.

FOREIGN CURRENCY TRANSLATION
Assets and liabilities of most of the Company's foreign subsidiaries are translated at current exchange rates. Revenues, costs and expenses are translated at the average exchange rates for the period. Translation adjustments resulting from changes in exchange rates are reported as a separate component of stockholders' equity. Other foreign currency transaction gains and losses are included in the determination of net income.

For those foreign subsidiaries operating in a highly inflationary economy or having the U.S. dollar as their functional currency, net nonmonetary assets are translated at historical rates and net monetary assets are translated at current rates. Translation adjustments are included in the determination of net income.

INCOME TAXES
The Company accounts for income taxes in accordance with FASB Statement No. 109, "Accounting for Income Taxes" ("Statement 109"). Tax provisions and credits are recorded at statutory rates for taxable items included in the consolidated statements of income regardless of the period for which such items are reported for tax purposes. Deferred income taxes are recognized for temporary differences between financial statement and income tax bases of assets and liabilities.

NET INCOME PER COMMON SHARE
In 1997, the Financial Accounting Standards Board issued Statement No. 128, "Earnings Per Share" ("Statement 128"). Statement 128 replaced the calculation of primary and fully diluted earnings per share with basic and diluted earnings per share. Unlike primary earnings per share, basic earnings per share excludes any dilutive effects of options, warrants and convertible securities. Diluted earnings per share is very similar to the previously reported fully diluted earnings per share. All earnings per share amounts for all periods have been presented, and have been restated, to conform to Statement 128 requirements.

RECENTLY ISSUED ACCOUNTING STANDARDS
During 1997, the Financial Accounting Standards Board issued Statement No. 130, "Reporting Comprehensive Income" ("Statement 130"). The Company will adopt the provisions of Statement 130 during fiscal 1998. At that time, the Company will be required to disclose comprehensive income. Comprehensive income is generally defined as all changes in stockholders' equity exclusive of transactions with owners such as capital investments and dividends.

In June 1997, the Financial Accounting Standards Board issued Statement No. 131, "Disclosures About Segments of an Enterprise and Related Information" ("Statement 131"), which is required to be adopted for years beginning after December 15, 1997. Management of the Company does not expect the adoption of Statement 131 to have a material impact on the Company's financial statement disclosures.

notes to consolidated financial statements

DOLLAR AMOUNTS IN THOUSANDS, EXCEPT PER SHARE DATA

RECLASSIFICATION

Certain amounts in prior years have been reclassified to conform to the 1997 presentation.

2
special charges

The financial results for 1997 include special pre-tax charges of $58,161 ($39,200 after tax or $0.67 per diluted share) relating to restructuring activities in the Company's global operations. The restructuring charge relates to facilities consolidation and elimination, asset write-downs, personnel related expenses and the termination or restructuring of certain underperforming marketing contracts that no longer reflect the Company's brand positioning. The restructuring activities include reducing the number of European warehouses from 19 to 3; establishing a shared services company that will centralize European administrative operations; and implementing a global management information system. The charge will cover certain one-time costs, of which approximately 70% will affect cash. In connection with the plan, the Company may incur other additional costs that are not recognizable at this time or cannot be reasonably estimated. The components of the charge are as follows:

	ORIGINAL	1997 UTILIZATION	BALANCE DEC. 31, 1997
Marketing contracts	$ 25,000	$ —	$ 25,000
Fixed asset write-downs	16,500	(9,600)	6,900
Employee retention and severance	9,200	(800)	8,400
Termination of leases	6,500	(700)	5,800
Other	961	—	961
	$ 58,161	($ 11,100)	$ 47,061

The fixed asset write-downs relate to assets that will be abandoned or sold.

The restructuring should enable the Company to achieve operating efficiencies, including improved inventory management, credit management, purchasing power and customer service and should provide the organization with access to a single global data base of company, supplier and customer information. The restructuring initiative should also improve logistics, allow the Company to focus its spending on those key athletes and teams who are more closely aligned with its brand positioning and produce cost savings once completed during 1999.

In 1995, the Company recorded a special pre-tax charge of $72,098 ($44,934 after tax or $0.56 per diluted share) principally related to the adjustment of the carrying value of Avia to its estimated fair value on sale. Actual amounts recorded in 1996 did not differ materially from the Company's estimates.

3
dutch auction self-tender stock repurchase

On July 28, 1996, the Board of Directors authorized the purchase by the Company of up to 24.0 million shares of the Company's common stock pursuant to a Dutch Auction self-tender offer. The tender offer price range was from $30.00 to $36.00 net per share in cash. The self-tender offer commenced on July 30, 1996 and expired on August 27, 1996. As a result of the self-tender offer, the Company repurchased approximately 17.0 million common shares at a price of $36.00 per share. Concurrent with the Dutch Auction share repurchase, the Company's Board of Directors elected to suspend subsequent declarations of quarterly cash dividends on the Company's stock. Accordingly, the last dividend declared was for shareholders of record as of September 11, 1996. Suspension of the dividend will conserve substantial cash which the Company plans to utilize to reduce debt incurred as a result of the share repurchase.

4
property and equipment

PROPERTY AND EQUIPMENT CONSIST OF THE FOLLOWING:

DECEMBER 31	1997	1996
Land	$ 9,037	$ 29,283
Buildings	75,380	75,044
Machinery and equipment	221,114	204,354
Leasehold improvements	48,663	48,757
	354,194	357,438
Less accumulated depreciation and amortization	197,235	172,146
	$ 156,959	$ 185,292

5
intangibles

INTANGIBLES CONSIST OF THE FOLLOWING:

DECEMBER 31	1997	1996
Excess of purchase price over fair value of assets acquired (net of accumulated amortization of $8,098 in 1997 and $6,326 in 1996)	$ 25,481	$ 27,696
Other intangible assets:		
Purchased technology	52,827	52,827
Company tradename and trademarks	47,254	49,092
Other	13,699	13,693
	113,780	115,612
Less accumulated amortization	73,477	73,608
	40,303	42,004
	$ 65,784	$ 69,700

notes to consolidated financial statements

DOLLAR AMOUNTS IN THOUSANDS, EXCEPT PER SHARE DATA

6
short-term borrowings

The Company has various arrangements with numerous banks which provide an aggregate of approximately $1,053,000 of uncommitted facilities, substantially all of which are available to the Company's foreign subsidiaries. Of this amount, $407,328 is available for short-term borrowings and bank overdrafts, with the remainder available for letters of credit for inventory purchases. In addition to amounts reported as notes payable to banks, approximately $317,718 was outstanding for open letters of credit for inventory purchases at December 31, 1997.

On August 23, 1996, in conjunction with the repurchase of its shares pursuant to the Dutch Auction self-tender offer, the Company entered into a new credit agreement underwritten by a syndicate of major banks. The agreement included a $750,000 revolving credit facility, expiring on August 31, 2002 which replaced the Company's previous $300 million credit line. The balance of the facility was a $640,000 six-year term loan (see Note 8).

On July 1, 1997, the Company amended and restated the credit agreement. The amendment reduced the revolving credit portion of the facility from $750,000 to $400,000. The revolving credit facility is available to finance the short-term working capital needs of the Company as well as support the issuance of letters of credit for inventory purchases, if required. At December 31, 1997 and December 31, 1996, there were no borrowings outstanding under the revolving credit portion of this agreement. As part of the agreement, the Company is required to pay certain commitment fees on the unused portion of the revolving credit facility as well as comply with various financial and other covenants. As part of the amendment, the commitment fees the Company is required to pay on the unused portion of the revolving credit facility as well as the borrowing margins over the London Interbank Offer Rate on the used portion of the revolving credit facility were reduced. The amendment further removed or relaxed various covenants. All other material terms and conditions of the credit agreement remained unchanged.

The Company utilizes a commercial paper program under which it can borrow up to $200,000 for periods not to exceed 270 days. This program is supported, to the extent available, by the unused portion of the $400,000 revolving credit facility. At December 31, 1997, the Company had no commercial paper obligations outstanding.

The weighted average interest rate on notes payable to banks was 7.1% and 5.5% at December 31, 1997 and 1996, respectively.

7
leasing arrangements

The Company leases various offices, warehouses, retail store facilities and certain of its data processing and warehouse equipment under lease arrangements expiring between 1998 and 2007. Minimum annual rentals under operating leases for the five years subsequent to December 31, 1997 and in the aggregate are as follows:

1998	$ 35,809
1999	30,196
2000	20,319
2001	12,268
2002	8,308
2003 and thereafter	15,756
Total minimum lease obligations	$ 122,656

Total rent expense for all operating leases amounted to $45,827, $46,751 and $40,602 for the years ended December 31, 1997, 1996 and 1995, respectively.

8
long-term debt

LONG-TERM DEBT CONSISTS OF THE FOLLOWING:

DECEMBER 31	1997	1996
Variable Rate Term Loan due August 31, 2002 with interest payable quarterly	$ 497,398	$ 640,000
Medium-term notes, bearing interest at rates approximating 6.75%, due May 15, 2000, with interest payable semiannually on May 15 and November 15	100,000	100,000
6.75% debentures due September 15, 2005, with interest payable semiannually on March 15 and September 15	98,953	98,803
Medium-term notes, bearing interest at rates approximating 6%, due July 15, 1998, with interest payable semiannually on February 15 and August 15	30,000	30,000
Medium-term notes, bearing interest at rates approximating 6%, due February 11, 1998, with interest payable semiannually on February 15 and August 15	20,000	20,000
Bank and other notes payable	14,004	17,980
	760,355	906,783
Less current portion	121,000	52,684
	$ 639,355	$ 854,099

notes to consolidated financial statements

DOLLAR AMOUNTS IN THOUSANDS, EXCEPT PER SHARE DATA

On August 23, 1996, the Company entered into a $1,700,000 credit agreement underwritten by a syndicate of major banks of which $950,000 was available in the form of a six-year term loan facility for the purpose of financing the Company's acquisition of common stock pursuant to the Dutch Auction self-tender offer (see Note 3). Based on the number of shares tendered, the Company borrowed $640,000 from this facility. The undrawn portion of $310,000 was immediately canceled upon funding of the share repurchase. The credit agreement included various covenants including restrictions on asset acquisitions, capital expenditures and future indebtedness, and the requirement to maintain a minimum interest coverage ratio. Under the terms of the agreement there are various options under which the interest is calculated. On July 1, 1997, the Company amended and restated the credit agreement. This amendment left the remaining portion of the six-year term loan of $522,398 (as of December 31, 1997) on substantially the same payment schedule, after adjusting for the $100,000 in optional prepayments made in 1997. The amendment also removed or relaxed covenants pertaining to restrictions on asset acquisitions and sales, capital expenditures, future indebtedness and investments and reduced the borrowing margins charged by the banks on the variable rate term loan. All other material terms and conditions of the credit agreement remain unchanged.

At December 31, 1997 and December 31, 1996, the effective rate of interest on the variable term loan was approximately 6.19% and 6.20%, respectively. In addition, the Company is amortizing fees and expenses associated with the credit agreement over the life of the agreement.

Maturities of long-term debt during the five-year period ending December 31, 2002 are $121,000 in 1998, $95,576 in 1999, $185,000 in 2000, $110,000 in 2001 and $147,398 in 2002.

9
employee benefit plans

The Company sponsors defined contribution retirement plans covering substantially all of its domestic employees and certain employees of its foreign subsidiaries. Contributions are determined at the discretion of the Board of Directors. Aggregate contributions made by the Company to the plans and charged to operations in 1997, 1996 and 1995 were $13,696, $11,755 and $11,644, respectively.

10
stock plans

The Company has stock plans which provide for the grant of options to purchase shares of the Company's common stock to key employees, other persons or entities who make significant contributions to the success of the Company, and eligible members of the Company's Board of Directors. The Company has elected to follow Accounting Principles Board Opinion No. 25, "Accounting for Stock Issued to Employees" ("APB 25") and related interpretations in accounting for its employee stock options. Under APB 25, as long as the exercise price of the Company's employee stock options equals the market price of the underlying stock on the date of grant, no compensation expense is recognized.

Under the 1994 Equity Incentive Plan, options may be incentive stock options or "non-qualified options" under applicable provisions of the Internal Revenue Code. The exercise price of any stock option granted may not be less than fair market value at the date of grant except in the case of grants to participants who are not executive officers of the Company and in certain other limited circumstances. The exercise period cannot exceed ten years from the date of grant. The vesting schedule for options granted under the 1994 Equity Incentive Plan is determined by the Compensation Committee of the Board of Directors. The 1994 Equity Incentive Plan also permits the Company to grant restricted stock to key employees and other persons or entities who make significant contributions to the success of the Company. The restrictions and vesting schedule for restricted stock granted under this Plan are determined by the Compensation Committee of the Board of Directors. The Company also has an option plan for its Directors. Under this plan, a fixed amount of options are granted annually to all non-employee Directors. Grants of options under the Directors plan vest in equal annual installments over three years.

The Company has two employee stock purchase plans. Under the 1987 Employee Stock Purchase Plan, eligible employees are granted options to purchase shares of the Company's common stock through voluntary payroll deductions during two option periods, running from January 1 to June 30 and from July 1 to December 31, at a price equal to the lower of 85% of market value at the beginning or end of each period. Under the 1992 Employee Stock Purchase Plan, for certain foreign-based employees, eligible employees are granted options to purchase shares of the Company's common stock during two option periods, running from January 1 to June 30 and from July 1 to December 31, at the market price at the beginning of the period. The option becomes exercisable 90 days following the date of grant and expires on the last day of the option period. Accordingly, no options are outstanding at December 31, 1997 and 1996. During 1997, 1996 and 1995, respectively, 151,210, 157,134 and 161,377 shares were issued pursuant to these plans.

In June 1990, the Company adopted a shareholders' rights plan and declared a dividend distribution of one common stock purchase right ("Right") for each share of common stock outstanding. Each Right entitles the holder to purchase one share of the Company's common stock at a price of $60 per share, subject to adjustment. The Rights will be exercisable only if a person or group of affiliated or associated persons acquires beneficial ownership of 10% or more of the outstanding shares of the Company's common stock or commences a tender or exchange offer that would result in a person or group owning 10% or more of the outstanding common stock, or in the event that the Company is subsequently acquired in a merger or other business combination. When the Rights become exercisable, each holder would have the right to purchase, at the then-current exercise price, common stock of the surviving company having a market value of two times the exercise price of the Right. The Company can redeem the Rights at $.01 per Right at any time prior to expiration on June 14, 2000.

At December 31, 1997, 13,705,700 shares of common stock were reserved for issuance under the Company's various stock plans and 70,105,308 shares were reserved for issuance under the shareholders' rights plan.

notes to consolidated financial statements

DOLLAR AMOUNTS IN THOUSANDS, EXCEPT PER SHARE DATA

THE FOLLOWING SCHEDULE SUMMARIZES THE CHANGES IN STOCK OPTIONS DURING THE THREE YEARS ENDED DECEMBER 31, 1997:

	NUMBER OF SHARES UNDER OPTION		
	NON-QUALIFIED STOCK OPTIONS	OPTION PRICE PER SHARE	WEIGHTED AVERAGE EXERCISE PRICE
Outstanding at December 31, 1994	5,879,575	$ 8.75–$39.77	$ 22.83
Granted	1,361,502	28.75– 36.75	34.90
Exercised	(361,400)	8.75– 33.25	16.75
Canceled	(722,760)	11.38– 39.77	30.57
Outstanding at December 31, 1995	6,156,917	8.75– 38.88	24.96
Granted	4,436,947	26.75– 41.63	31.32
Exercised	(272,153)	8.75– 37.02	25.41
Canceled	(406,005)	11.38– 37.02	31.10
Outstanding at December 31, 1996	9,915,706	8.75– 41.63	27.54
Granted	1,205,704	33.75– 49.25	35.51
Exercised	(399,111)	8.75– 36.75	25.72
Canceled	(534,680)	24.00– 41.63	33.14
Outstanding at December 31, 1997	10,187,619	$ 10.63–$49.25	$ 28.26

At December 31, 1997, the exercise prices for outstanding options ranged from $10.63–$49.25. Within that range, 2,771,254 options were outstanding between $10.63 and $19.37. All of these options were exercisable at December 31, 1997. The weighted average exercise price and average remaining contractual life of these options is $17.43 and 2.5 years, respectively. Additionally, 7,416,365 options were outstanding between $20.46 and $49.25. Included in this range are 1,552,954 options exercisable at a weighted average exercise price of $30.23. The weighted average exercise price and average remaining contractual life of these outstanding options is $32.33 and 8 years, respectively.

Shares granted in 1996 include a July grant to certain senior executives made in conjunction with the Dutch Auction. The options do not begin to vest until the end of 1998, and vesting extends for a period of up to five years ending in December 2002. These option grants provide that if an optionee sells before the end of 1998 any shares acquired through the exercise of options which were held prior to the Dutch Auction, the optionee will forfeit an identical number of shares subject to option under the July 1996 grant. In addition, during 1996 the Company reinstituted December as the month in which it grants its annual stock options to employees. The 1995 and 1994 annual employee option grants were issued in February 1996 and March 1995, respectively.

At December 31, 1997, 1996 and 1995, options to purchase 4,324,208, 3,983,278 and 3,956,545 shares of common stock were exercisable, and 3,032,790, 1,225,051 and 3,369,311 shares, respectively, were available for future grants under the Company's stock equity plans.

Pro forma information regarding net income and earnings per share is required by Statement 123, which requires that the information be determined as if the Company has accounted for its employee stock options granted subsequent to December 31, 1994 under the fair value method of that statement. The fair value for these options was estimated at the date of grant using a Black-Scholes option pricing model with the following weighted-average assumptions for 1995, 1996 and 1997, respectively: risk-free interest rates ranging from 5.2% to 7.7%; dividend yields of .89%, .68% and .0%; volatility factors of the expected market price of the Company's common stock of .27 in 1995 and 1996 and .35 in 1997; and a weighted-average expected life of the option of 4.2 years.

For purposes of pro forma disclosures, the estimated fair value of the options is amortized to expense over the options' vesting period.

THE COMPANY'S PRO FORMA INFORMATION FOLLOWS (IN THOUSANDS, EXCEPT FOR EARNINGS PER SHARE INFORMATION):

	1997	1996	1995
Pro forma net income	$ 127,506	$ 134,017	$ 163,404
Pro forma basic earnings per share	$ 2.31	$ 2.03	$ 2.09
Pro forma diluted earnings per share	$ 2.23	$ 2.00	$ 2.07

The weighted average fair value of options granted in 1997, 1996 and 1995 is $13.09, $10.76 and $11.63, respectively.

Because Statement 123 is applicable only to options granted subsequent to December 31, 1994, its pro forma effect will not be fully reflected until 2001.

11
acquisition of common stock

On October 19, 1995, the Board of Directors authorized the repurchase of up to an additional $200,000 in Reebok common stock in open market or privately-negotiated transactions. This authorization was in addition to the share repurchase programs of $200,000 each adopted by the Company in July 1992, July 1993 and October 1994. As of December 31, 1997, the Company had approximately $129,800 available for future repurchases of common stock under these programs.

During 1996 and 1995, the Company issued equity put options as part of its share repurchase program. These options provided the Company with an additional source to supplement open market purchases of its common stock. At December 31, 1997 and 1996, no shares of outstanding common stock are subject to repurchase under the terms and conditions of these options.

notes to consolidated financial statements

DOLLAR AMOUNTS IN THOUSANDS, EXCEPT PER SHARE DATA

12
business acquisitions and divestitures

On May 23, 1996, the Company finalized a long-term exclusive footwear licensing arrangement with Ralph Lauren to design, develop, manufacture, market and distribute men's, women's and children's footwear under the Ralph Lauren label. The agreement requires payment of certain annual minimum amounts for royalties and other compensation. The territory for the license initially includes North America and is expected to expand worldwide as existing Ralph Lauren licenses expire subject to reaching agreement with Ralph Lauren as to business plans for the additional territories. In conjunction with the licensing arrangement, Reebok's subsidiary, The Rockport Company, Inc., acquired Ralph Lauren's prior licensee for the U.S. and Canada, Ralph Lauren Footwear, Inc.

On June 7, 1996, Reebok completed the sale of substantially all of the operating assets and business of its subsidiary, Avia Group International, Inc.

13
financial instruments

The following methods and assumptions were used by the Company to estimate the fair value of its financial instruments:

Cash and cash equivalents and notes payable to banks: the carrying amounts reported in the balance sheet approximate fair value. Long-term debt: the fair value of the Company's medium-term notes and debentures is estimated based on quoted market prices. The fair value of other long-term debt is estimated using discounted cash flow analyses, based on the Company's incremental borrowing rates for similar types of borrowing arrangements. Unrealized gains or losses on foreign currency exchange contracts and options: the fair value of the Company's foreign currency exchange contracts is estimated based on current foreign exchange rates. Fair market value of interest rate swaps: the fair value of the Company's interest rate swaps is estimated based on current interest rates.

THE CARRYING AMOUNTS AND FAIR VALUE OF THE COMPANY'S FINANCIAL INSTRUMENTS ARE AS FOLLOWS:

	CARRYING AMOUNT		FAIR VALUE	
DECEMBER 31	1997	1996	1997	1996
Long-term debt	$ 760,355	$ 906,783	$ 759,049	$ 881,372
Unrealized gains on foreign currency exchange contracts and options	4,619	173	6,256	1,394
Interest rate swaps	0	0	344	1,420

FOREIGN EXCHANGE FORWARDS AND OPTIONS

The Company enters into forward currency exchange contracts and options to hedge its exposure for merchandise purchased in U.S. dollars that will be sold to customers in other currencies. Realized and unrealized gains and losses on these contracts are included in net income except that gains and losses on contracts which hedge specific foreign currency commitments are deferred and accounted for as a part of the transaction. The Company also uses forward currency exchange contracts and options to hedge significant intercompany assets and liabilities denominated in other than the functional currency. Contracts used to hedge intercompany balances are marked to market and the resulting transaction gain or loss is included in the determination of net income.

Foreign currency losses realized from settlements of transactions included in net income for the year ended December 31, 1997 were $8.1 million. Realized gains and losses from settlements of transactions for the years ended December 31, 1996 and 1995 were not significant. The Company has used forward exchange contracts and options as an element of its risk management strategy for several years.

At December 31, 1997, the Company had option and forward currency exchange contracts, all having maturities of less than one year, with a notional amount aggregating $357,913. The contracts involved 12 different foreign currencies. No single currency represented more than 20% of the aggregate notional amount. The notional amount of contracts intended to hedge merchandise purchases was $165,324. Deferred gains (losses) on these contracts were not material at December 31, 1997 and 1996.

INTEREST RATE SWAPS

The Company uses interest rate swap agreements to manage its exposure to interest rate movements by effectively converting a portion of its variable rate long-term debt from floating to fixed rates. These agreements involve the exchange of variable rate payments for fixed rate payments without the effect of leverage and without the exchange of the underlying principal amount. Interest rate differentials paid or received under these swap agreements are recognized over the life of the contracts as adjustments to interest expense.

During the fourth quarter of 1996, the Company entered into several amortizing interest rate swaps with a group of financial institutions having an initial notional value of $320,000 and expiring on December 31, 2000. The notional amount of the swaps is reduced each year in accordance with the expected repayment schedule of the Company's variable rate term loan. The terms of the swaps require the Company to make fixed rate payments on a quarterly basis whereas the Company will receive variable rate payments based on the three month U.S. dollar LIBOR. At December 31, 1997 and 1996, the notional amount of interest rate swaps outstanding was $245,000 and $320,000, respectively. In January 1998, the Company entered into additional interest rate swaps in the amount of $150,000 with respect to the variable rate term loan.

CONCENTRATIONS OF CREDIT RISK

Financial instruments which potentially subject the Company to concentrations of credit risk consist principally of cash equivalents and hedging instruments.

The Company places cash equivalents with high credit financial institutions and, by policy, limits the amount of credit exposure to any one financial institution.

The Company is exposed to credit-related losses in the event of non-performance by counterparties to hedging instruments. The counterparties to these contracts are major financial institutions. The Company continually monitors its positions and the credit ratings of its counterparties and places dollar and term limits on the amount of contracts it enters into with any one party.

notes to consolidated financial statements

DOLLAR AMOUNTS IN THOUSANDS, EXCEPT PER SHARE DATA

14
income taxes

THE COMPONENTS OF INCOME BEFORE INCOME TAXES AND MINORITY INTEREST ARE AS FOLLOWS:

	1997	1996	1995
Domestic	$ (32,783)	$ (12,720)	$ 14,292
Foreign	190,868	250,388	261,682
	$ 158,085	$ 237,668	$ 275,974

THE PROVISION FOR INCOME TAXES CONSISTS OF THE FOLLOWING:

	1997	1996	1995
CURRENT:			
Federal	$ (34,314)	$ 1,961	$ 3,998
State	(324)	4,534	13,878
Foreign	64,413	83,921	83,450
	29,775	90,416	101,326
DEFERRED:			
Federal	(8,940)	(1,705)	(1,594)
State	(1,900)	(689)	(3,112)
Foreign	(6,445)	(3,939)	3,133
	(17,285)	(6,333)	(1,573)
	$ 12,490	$ 84,083	$ 99,753

During 1992, the Company recorded a write-down in the carrying value of its Avia subsidiary in the amount of $100,000 with no corresponding tax benefit recognized in that year due to the uncertainty concerning the ultimate deductibility of the charge. In June 1996, substantially all of the operating assets and business of Avia were sold. After the sale, in December 1996, the Company requested a pre-filing determination from the Internal Revenue Service ("IRS") regarding the deductibility of certain losses pertaining to the sale of Avia. In August 1997, the IRS notified the Company that it had approved the Company's tax treatment concerning the deductibility of the Avia losses and accordingly, a corresponding reduction in income taxes totaling $40,000 was recorded in the third quarter of 1997 and is reflected in the current federal and state provisions.

Undistributed earnings of the Company's foreign subsidiaries amounted to approximately $405,265, $517,309 and $410,402 at December 31, 1997, 1996 and 1995, respectively. Those earnings are considered to be indefinitely reinvested. Upon distribution of those earnings in the form of dividends or otherwise, a portion would be subject to both U.S. income taxes and foreign withholding taxes, less an adjustment for applicable foreign tax credits. Determination of the amount of U.S. income tax liability that would be incurred is not practicable because of the complexities associated with its hypothetical calculation; however, unrecognized foreign tax credits would be available to reduce some portion of any U.S. income tax liability.

INCOME TAXES COMPUTED AT THE FEDERAL STATUTORY RATE DIFFER FROM AMOUNTS PROVIDED AS FOLLOWS:

	1997	1996	1995
Tax at statutory rate	35.0%	35.0%	35.0%
State taxes, less federal tax effect	1.5	1.7	2.7
Effect of tax rates of foreign subsidiaries and joint ventures	(4.3)	(1.6)	(2.0)
Tax benefit from Avia losses	(25.3)		
Amortization of intangibles	0.4	0.4	0.4
Other, net	0.6	(0.1)	0.1
Provision for income taxes	7.9%	35.4%	36.2%

Net deferred income taxes reflect the net tax effects of temporary differences between the carrying amount of assets and liabilities for financial reporting purposes and the amounts used for income tax purposes.

DEFERRED TAX ASSETS ARE ATTRIBUTABLE TO THE FOLLOWING TEMPORARY DIFFERENCES AT DECEMBER 31

	1997	1996
Inventory	$ 30,238	$ 35,212
Accounts receivable	24,973	23,085
Liabilities	26,714	9,661
Depreciation	6,117	5,528
Other, net	6,515	3,786
Total	$ 94,557	$ 77,272

notes to consolidated financial statements

DOLLAR AMOUNTS IN THOUSANDS, EXCEPT PER SHARE DATA

15
earnings per share

THE FOLLOWING TABLE SETS FORTH THE COMPUTATION OF BASIC AND DILUTED EARNINGS PER SHARE:

	1997	1996	1995
NUMERATOR:			
Net Income	$ 135,119	$ 138,950	$ 164,798
DENOMINATOR:			
Denominator for basic earnings per share — weighted-average shares	56,162	67,370	78,317
Dilutive employee stock options	2,147	1,247	1,170
Denominator for diluted earnings per share — adjusted weighted-average shares and assumed conversions	58,309	68,617	79,487
Basic earnings per share	$ 2.41	$ 2.06	$ 2.10
Diluted earnings per share	$ 2.32	$ 2.03	$ 2.07

16
operations by geographic area

NET SALES TO UNAFFILIATED CUSTOMERS, NET INCOME AND IDENTIFIABLE ASSETS BY GEOGRAPHIC AREA ARE SUMMARIZED BELOW:

	1997	1996	1995
NET SALES:			
United States	$ 2,000,883	$ 1,935,724	$ 2,027,080
United Kingdom	661,358	566,196	492,843
Europe	510,981	623,209	642,622
Other countries	470,377	353,475	318,905
	$ 3,643,599	$ 3,478,604	$ 3,481,450
NET INCOME:			
United States	$ 83,894	$ 41,522	$ 52,314
United Kingdom	50,441	60,050	74,175
Europe	(567)	21,854	28,138
Other countries	1,351	15,524	10,171
	$ 135,119	$ 138,950	$ 164,798
IDENTIFIABLE ASSETS:			
United States	$ 938,027	$ 887,217	$ 813,935
United Kingdom	372,526	391,865	291,825
Europe	278,606	282,057	311,903
Other countries	166,938	225,045	233,956
	$ 1,756,097	$ 1,786,184	$ 1,651,619

There are various differences between income before income taxes and minority interest for domestic and foreign operations as shown in Note 14 and net income shown above. Sales or transfers between geographic areas are not material.

17
contingencies

The Company is involved in various legal proceedings generally incidental to its business. These include a lawsuit filed by a former distributor in Brazil in which the plaintiff has asserted a claim for damages in excess of $50,000. While it is not feasible to predict or determine the outcome of these proceedings, management does not believe that they should result in a materially adverse effect on the Company's financial position, results of operations or liquidity.

reports

report of ernst & young llp, independent auditors

BOARD OF DIRECTORS AND STOCKHOLDERS
REEBOK INTERNATIONAL LTD.
STOUGHTON, MASSACHUSETTS

We have audited the accompanying consolidated balance sheets of Reebok International Ltd. and subsidiaries as of December 31, 1997 and 1996, and the related consolidated statements of income, stockholders' equity, and cash flows for each of the three years in the period ended December 31, 1997. These financial statements are the responsibility of the Company's management. Our responsibility is to express an opinion on these financial statements based on our audits.

We conducted our audits in accordance with generally accepted auditing standards. Those standards require that we plan and perform the audit to obtain reasonable assurance about whether the financial statements are free of material misstatement. An audit includes examining, on a test basis, evidence supporting the amounts and disclosures in the financial statements. An audit also includes assessing the accounting principles used and significant estimates made by management, as well as evaluating the overall financial statement presentation. We believe that our audits provide a reasonable basis for our opinion.

In our opinion, the consolidated financial statements referred to above present fairly, in all material respects, the consolidated financial position of Reebok International Ltd. and subsidiaries at December 31, 1997 and 1996, and the consolidated results of their operations and their cash flows for each of the three years in the period ended December 31, 1997, in conformity with generally accepted accounting principles.

Ernst + Young LLP

BOSTON, MASSACHUSETTS
FEBRUARY 2, 1998

report of management

FINANCIAL STATEMENTS

The management of Reebok International Ltd. and its subsidiaries has prepared the accompanying financial statements and is responsible for their integrity and fair presentation. The statements, which include amounts that are based on management's best estimates and judgments, have been prepared in conformity with generally accepted accounting principles and are free of material misstatement. Management has also prepared other information in the annual report and is responsible for its accuracy and consistency with the financial statements.

INTERNAL CONTROL SYSTEM

Reebok International Ltd. and its subsidiaries maintain a system of internal control over financial reporting, which is designed to provide reasonable assurance to the Company's management and Board of Directors as to the integrity and fair presentation of the financial statements. Management continually monitors the system of internal control for compliance, and actions are taken to correct deficiencies as they are identified. Even an effective internal control system, no matter how well designed, has inherent limitations — including the possibility of the circumvention or overriding of controls — and therefore can provide only reasonable assurance with respect to financial statement preparation. Further, because of changes in conditions, internal control system effectiveness may vary over time.

The Company maintains an internal auditing program that monitors and assesses the effectiveness of the internal control system and recommends possible improvements thereto. The Company's accompanying financial statements have been audited by Ernst & Young LLP, independent auditors, whose audit was made in accordance with generally accepted auditing standards and included a review of the system of internal accounting controls to the extent necessary to determine the audit procedures required to support their opinion on the consolidated financial statements. Management believes that, as of December 31, 1997, the Company's system of internal control is adequate to accomplish the objectives discussed herein.

REEBOK INTERNATIONAL LTD.,

PAUL FIREMAN
CHAIRMAN,
PRESIDENT AND CHIEF
EXECUTIVE OFFICER

KENNETH WATCHMAKER
EXECUTIVE VICE PRESIDENT
AND CHIEF FINANCIAL OFFICER

quarterly results of operations

(UNAUDITED)

AMOUNTS IN THOUSANDS, EXCEPT PER SHARE DATA

YEAR ENDED DECEMBER 1997	FIRST QUARTER	SECOND QUARTER	THIRD QUARTER	FOURTH QUARTER
Net sales	$ 930,041	$ 841,059	$ 1,009,053	$ 863,446
Gross profit	356,229	323,511	370,211	299,599
Net income	40,184	20,322	73,968	645
Basic earnings per share	.72	.36	1.32	.01
Diluted earnings per share	.69	.35	1.26	.01
YEAR ENDED DECEMBER 1996				
Net sales	$ 902,923	$ 817,572	$ 970,080	$ 788,029
Gross profit	351,132	312,268	380,530	290,252
Net income	48,415	19,813	50,612	20,110
Basic earnings per share	.65	.27	.76	.36
Diluted earnings per share	.64	.27	.75	.35
Cash dividends per common share	.075	.075	.075	.000

Net income for the fourth quarter of 1997 includes a special charge of $18,000 after taxes, or $0.31 per diluted share, for the restructuring of a number of marketing contracts.

Net income for the third quarter of 1997 includes a tax credit of $40,000, or $0.68 per diluted share, as well as a special charge of $21,161 after taxes, or $0.36 per diluted share, for facilities consolidation and elimination, asset adjustments and personnel-related expenses associated with global restructuring activities.

On June 7, 1996, Reebok completed the sale of substantially all of the operating assets of its subsidiary Avia. Accordingly, subsequent to that date, the operations of Avia are no longer included in the Company's financial results.

The earnings per share amounts are presented to comply with Statement of Financial Accounting Standards No. 128, "Earnings Per Share." For further discussion regarding the calculation of earnings per share, see Note 1 to the Consolidated Financial Statements.

shareholder information

independent auditors

Ernst & Young LLP
200 Clarendon Street
Boston, MA 02116

transfer agent and registrar

BankBoston, N.A. is the Transfer Agent and Registrar for the Company's common stock and maintains the shareholder accounting records. The Transfer Agent should be contacted on questions of changes in address, name or ownership, lost certificates and consolidation of accounts. When corresponding with the Transfer Agent, shareholders should state the exact name(s) in which the stock is registered and certificate number as well as old and new information about the account.

BankBoston, N.A.
c/o Boston EquiServe
Post Office Box 8040
Boston, MA 02266-8040
Phone: (781) 575-3400
Facsimile: (781) 828-8813
Toll-free number outside Massachusetts: (800) 733-5001
http://www.equiserve.com

form 10-k

For a copy of the Form 10-K Annual Report, filed with the Securities and Exchange Commission, write to:

Office of Investor Relations
Reebok International Ltd.
100 Technology Center Drive
Stoughton, MA 02072

web site

http://www.reebok.com

corporate headquarters

Reebok International Ltd.
100 Technology Center Drive
Stoughton, MA 02072

annual meeting

The Annual Meeting of Stockholders will be held at 10:00 a.m., local time, on Tuesday, May 5, 1998 at BankBoston, Second Floor Long Lane Conference Room, 100 Federal Street, Boston, Massachusetts.

Shareholders of record on March 11, 1998 are entitled to vote at the meeting.

stock information

The Company's common stock is quoted on the New York Stock Exchange under the symbol RBK. The following table, derived from data supplied by the NYSE, sets forth the quarterly high and low sales prices during 1997 and 1996.

	1997		1996	
	HIGH	LOW	HIGH	LOW
First	52⅞	40⅝	31⅜	25⅜
Second	49⅞	37⅛	33¾	26
Third	52¼	43⅝	36⅞	29¼
Fourth	49½	27⅝	45¼	32½

The number of record holders of the Company's common stock at February 20, 1998 was 7,050.

REEBOK, the Vector Logo, THE PUMP, DMX, the Human Rights Logo and HEXALITE are registered trademarks, and HYDROMOVE, ATTACK LIFE, PRO FUNCTION and 3D ULTRALITE are trademarks of Reebok.

ROCKPORT is a registered trademark and UNCOMPROMISE is a trademark of The Rockport Company, Inc.

GREG NORMAN is a registered trademark and the Greg Norman Logo is a trademark of Great White Shark Enterprises, Inc.

RALPH LAUREN and POLO SPORT are registered trademarks of Polo/Ralph Lauren Corporation.

Portions of this Annual Report are printed on recycled paper.

DESIGN: BELK MIGNOGNA ASSOCIATES, NEW YORK
PHOTOGRAPHY: (PAGES 1–5) DAVIES + STARR, (PAGES 14, 16) ROB HOWARD
QUOTE OPPOSITE PAGE 12: ©1997 THE ECONOMIST NEWSPAPER GROUP, INC. REPRINTED WITH PERMISSION. FURTHER REPRODUCTION PROHIBITED.

glossary

A

accelerated depreciation A depreciation method that recognizes greater depreciation in an asset's earlier years and results in less income. This is widely used for federal tax purposes.
account A category created in order to group similar transactions for the purpose of recording activity and providing information.
accounting The systematic process of measuring the economic activity of an entity to provide useful information to those who make business and economic decisions.
accounting changes Includes a change in accounting principle, a change in estimate, and a change in reporting entity.
accounting information system The processes and procedures required to generate accounting information.
Accounting Principles Board (APB) Predecessor to the FASB.
accounts payable Unwritten obligations arising in the normal course of business. Accounts payable typically result from the purchase of inventory, supplies, and services.
accounts receivable Credit sales that have not yet been collected. The relevant amount is the estimated cash to be generated from collections of the accounts. See *allowance for uncollectible accounts* and *net realizable value* for related terms.
accounts receivable as a percent of sales A liquidity ratio used to assess a company's collection procedures and working capital management. Calculated as gross accounts receivable divided by sales.
accrual basis of accounting Records revenues when goods or services have been earned, regardless of when cash is received. Records expenses when incurred, regardless of when cash is distributed.
accrued expenses (liabilities) A current liability that represents services already consumed, but no cash has been paid.
accumulated benefit obligation The amount of pension benefits, calculated under actuarial and present value assumptions, that employees have earned to date, based on current salary levels.
accumulated depreciation The total amount of depreciation that has been recognized to date on a long-lived asset. It is presented as a "contra-asset" account that is subtracted from the asset's cost to determine its net book value.
accumulated postretirement benefit obligation The actuarial present value of the future postretirement benefits that employees and retirees have earned to date.
acid-test ratio See *quick ratio.*
acquisition A business combination in which a buyer firm acquires more than 50 percent of the voting stock of an investee firm, and thereby controls the investee.
actuarial assumptions Assumptions about future events based on historic data such as employee turnover, service lives, and longevity that are used to estimate future costs such as pension benefits.
adjusting entries Journal entries entered into the accounting records typically before financial statements are prepared. Adjusting entries are needed to ensure that the account balances are correct and up to date.
adjustment A change in the accounting equation to record accruals, deferrals, and other estimates so that the equation reflects changes in assets, liabilities, and equities. Could also refer to an *adjusting entry.*
administrative expenses Support function expenses consisting of senior managers' salaries, accounting and auditing costs, insurance, depreciation of administrative offices, and so on.
advances from customers See *unearned revenue.*
aging method Refers to classifying accounts receivable by the number of days they are past due; for example, zero to 30 days, 31 to 60 days, 61 to 90 days, more than 90 days, and so on.
allowance for uncollectible accounts An overall estimate of the accounts receivable amounts that will not be collected. Presented as a contra-asset account that is subtracted from accounts receivable.
amortization The periodic recognition of the consumption (expense) of an intangible asset.
annual report The annual report includes financial statements as well as notes to the statements, management discussion, and the independent auditor's report.
annuity Equal cash flows over uniform time intervals.
APB See *Accounting Principles Board.*
arms-length transaction Transactions that are conducted by independent parties, each acting in their own self-interest.

asset management ratios Show the composition of the firm's assets, as well as changes in the composition of assets over time.

assets Valuable resources that an entity owns or controls. They represent probable future economic benefits and arise as a result of past transactions or events.

associating cause and effect An application of the matching principle where a clear and direct relationship or link exists between an expense and its associated revenue. See *matching principle.*

audit An evaluation of the credibility of a firm's financial statements by independent CPAs. The audit opinion is the product of the audit and reflects the auditor's professional judgment regarding whether the financial statements are presented in accordance with GAAP.

audit opinion An auditor's report expressing an opinion as to whether the financial statements were prepared according to GAAP. See *audit.*

authorized shares Shares of stock that the firm is permitted to issue according to its corporate charter.

available-for-sale securities An investment for which unrealized gains and losses are not included in net income.

average cost method A method for determining the per unit cost of inventories by summing the beginning inventory cost plus all purchases and dividing by the number of units available for sale.

average exchange rate Refers to converting one country's currency into a different monetary unit. The average exchange rate over a month or a year can be used to make the foreign currency translation, as compared to using the *current exchange rate.*

B

balance sheet A financial statement that shows, at a specified time, a firm's financial condition, which is determined by its assets, liabilities, and owners' equity. Also referred to as *statement of financial position.*

bank reconciliation An accounting procedure that explains any differences between a firm's cash balance as determined by the firm and the firm's cash balance as determined by the bank.

basic accounting equation A simple three-element equation that corresponds to the balance sheet. The equation is Assets = Liabilities + Owners' Equity, where Owners' Equity is synonymous with Shareholders' Equity.

basis of comparison Assessing a firm's economic condition by establishing a reference or benchmark for the firm's financial information. Benchmarks include the firm's prior performance, industry averages, and that of other firms.

big bath An occurrence when a firm reports large accounting losses in a single year that do not truly reflect the performance or profitability of the firm. The losses are created by accounting treatments that are motivated by reasons such as favorable bonuses for management in a subsequent year.

bond or bonds payable Liability in the form of a note, issued to investors.

book value An asset's cost less its accumulated depreciation.

bottom line See *net income.*

budgets Quantitative expressions of corporate plans and expectations of future results.

buildings See *plant.*

business combination The general term for the activity in which one firm takes over or assumes control over another firm. Forms of business combinations include mergers, consolidations, and acquisitions.

C

capital Conventional terminology for sole proprietorships that denotes the owners' interest in the assets of the business.

capital gains (or losses) Result from increases (or decreases) in the market price of stocks over the period they are held by investors.

capital lease A lease agreement that is treated like an installment purchase (sale) of an asset. Capital leases increase the amounts of reported long-term assets and long-term debt for the lessee. The lessor records a receivable and eliminates the leased asset from its accounting records.

capital structure An analysis of a firm's strategy for financing its assets with relative amounts of debt and equity.

capitalize Record expenditures related to an asset's acquisition, installation, or refurbishment as part of the cost of the asset. The carrying (book) value of the asset is increased by these costs.

carrying value The historical cost of an asset less its accumulated depreciation.

cash and cash equivalents Includes currency, bank deposits, and various marketable securities that can be turned into cash on short notice. These amounts are available to meet the firm's cash payment requirements.

cash basis of accounting Records revenue when cash is received and records expenses when cash is distributed.
cash flows from financing activities Cash flow transactions to obtain or repay owners' investments, bonds, and long-term loans. Reported on the *statement of cash flows.*
cash flows from investing activities Cash flow transactions for acquiring or disposing of long-term assets and long-term investments. Reported on the *statement of cash flows.*
cash flows from operating activities (CFOA) The net cash increase (decrease) resulting from the firm's operating activities. Reported on the *statement of cash flows.*
cash interest coverage ratio Shows the relationship between all cash available to pay interest and the interest actually paid. Calculated as CFOA plus interest and taxes paid divided by interest paid.
cash return on assets A ratio to analyze a firm's profitability and financial returns. Calculated as cash flow from operating activities plus interest paid divided by average total assets.
change funds Cash funds to enable cashiers to make change for their customers. Included in cash on the balance sheet. See *petty cash.*
change in accounting estimate Refers to a change in an estimate that underlies financial statement amounts. Includes changes in useful lives and salvage values of fixed assets.
change in accounting principle A change by a reporting entity in the accounting principles used to prepare its financial statements.
change in reporting entity A change in the subsidiaries that comprise a consolidated group.
chart of accounts Lists account titles and account numbers that serve as an index to the general ledger.
charter Formal registration document filed with the state of incorporation that includes the corporation's business purpose and authorizes the firm to issue one or more types of ownership shares. Referred to as a "corporate charter."
closing entries Transfer the amounts in the revenue and expense (nominal) accounts to retained earnings.
CMA (Certified Management Accountant) Professional certification program administered by The Institute of Management Accountants.
collateral Specific assets pledged for security as part of a loan agreement. The creditor may have the right to seize the collateral in the event of loan default by the borrower.
collection period The average length of time it takes to collect a receivable. Calculated by dividing accounts receivable by average sales per day.
commitments Agreements with suppliers, customers, employers, or other entities that relate to "not yet completed" transactions and consequently have not been recognized in the accounts. When significant, they should be disclosed in the notes to the financial statements.
common size income statements A vertical analysis that measures and reports all the components on the income statement as a percentage of net sales. This technique allows comparability across periods and firms.
common stock The basic type of stock ownership that typically entitles the stockholder to vote on corporate matters and share in profits. Common shareholders are the true residual owners of the corporation.
common stock equivalent Securities and stock options that can be converted to common stock.
compensating balances Deposits or funds that a firm agrees to keep in accounts with a lender that pay little or no interest. The lender usually earns interest on such funds, which is not paid to the borrower.
composition analysis The starting point for any analysis of capital structure. It provides a description of the relative amounts of capital obtained from each major source of financing. See *asset management ratios* or *capital structure..*
compound interest The process of earning interest on interest from previous periods.
comprehensive income Includes all changes in owners' equity except for investments by owners and distributions to them.
conservatism principle When doubt exists about the accounting treatment for a given transaction, the alternative that reports lower asset values and lower net income is usually selected.
consolidated financial statements Reports that combine financial position, cash flows, and operating results for all firms that are under the parent company's control.
consolidation A business combination in which a new corporation is created to acquire the stock or the net assets of two or more existing companies. The

original companies then cease to exist as separate corporations.
contingencies Conditions which may result in gains and losses and that will be resolved by the occurrence of future events.
contra account An account that is used solely to record and accumulate reductions in the balance of its related account. A contra account balance is subtracted from the balance of the related account.
contra-equity account A negative equity account or a deduction from another shareholders' equity account. For example, *treasury stock* is always shown as a deduction from shareholders' equity. See *contra account.*
contributed capital The portion of shareholders' equity that arises from direct contributions (investments) from the owners.
convertible bonds Bonds that entitle the bondholder to exchange the bonds for a specified number of shares of stock at a specified future time.
convertible preferred stock Preferred shares that may be exchanged for common shares at a specified future time.
copyright Granted by the federal government to convey the exclusive right to use artistic or literary works for a period of 75 years.
corporation A separate accounting and legal entity, apart from its owners (shareholders), granted the right to exist under its charter by individual states.
cost accounting Determines product costs and other relevant information used for managerial decision making.
cost method of accounting The parent company recognizes income on its financial statements from the subsidiary only when the subsidiary declares a dividend.
cost of goods sold The direct cost of acquiring or manufacturing a product that has been sold.
cost of goods sold percentage Cost of goods sold divided by net sales.
coupon rate The stated interest rate in a bond contract. Also referred to as the *nominal, stated,* or *face* rate.
CPA (Certified Public Accountant) A public accountant licensed by a state board. The CPA exam is administered by the American Institute of Certified Public Accountants.
CPA firms Provide the three primary services that comprise public accounting: auditing, tax preparation, and management consulting.
credit The right-hand side of an entry in the double-entry accounting system.
cumulative effect The usual approach for implementing a change in accounting principle. The cumulative effect is included in the current year's net income.
cumulative preferred stock Shares that accumulate dividends when dividends are not declared by the firm. Accumulated dividends must be paid before any dividends can be paid to common shareholders.
currency forward market Market in which foreign currencies are bought and sold for future delivery.
current assets Includes cash and other assets that will typically be converted to cash or be consumed in one year or one operating cycle (if greater than one year).
current exchange rate Refers to converting financial amounts expressed in terms of one country's currency into a different monetary unit. The current exchange rate at the end of a month or a year can be used to make the foreign currency translation, as compared to using the *average exchange rate.*
current liabilities These include trade accounts payable and other short-term obligations that will be due in one year or one operating cycle, if greater than one year. These also include the *current maturities of long-term debt.*
current maturities of long-term debt The portion of long-term debt due within the upcoming period.
current ratio The most popular liquidity ratio, calculated by dividing all current assets by all current liabilities.

D

date of declaration Date the firm has obligated itself to make a dividend payment. On that date, owners' equity (retained earnings) is decreased and liabilities (dividends payable) is increased.
date of payment The date the actual dividend payment is made. Cash and dividends payable (liability) are reduced.
date of record The date that determines who will receive the dividend. The investor that holds the stock on that day will be paid the dividend.
debit The left-hand side of an entry in the double-entry accounting system.
debt management ratios Analysis of the balance sheet that focuses on the composition of a firm's debt including long-term notes, bonds, and lines of credit.
debt securities Investments in debt instruments such as commercial paper or bonds. These instruments provide evidence of indebtedness and can be negotiated (sold).

debt-to-assets ratio A primary indicator of a firm's debt management and leverage position that employs percentage composition analysis. Calculated as total debt divided by total assets.
declining-balance methods (DB) Accelerated depreciation method where depreciation expense is calculated by multiplying an asset's book value at the beginning of the year by a percentage equal to a multiple of the straight-line method rate.
deferred tax liability A liability for income taxes due in future periods.
defined benefit plan A pension plan specifying the benefits that employees will receive at retirement.
defined contribution plan A pension plan that specifies the periodic amount, usually a percentage of an employee's current salary, that the firm agrees to contribute to a pension fund.
denominated Refers to the conversion of financial amounts expressed in one country's currency into a different monetary unit. For example, yen might be denominated in U.S. dollars.
deontology The consequences of the act do not solely dictate its correctness; the nature of the act itself influences its correctness.
depletion The allocation of the cost (using up) of natural resources, which is systematically expensed over time.
deposits-in-transit Bank deposits delayed by processing. These cash receipts have been recorded in the firm's accounting records.
depreciable basis Cost of an asset less its estimated salvage value.
depreciation The decline, over time, of the service potential of long-lived tangible assets, most notably plant and equipment. Because this service potential is consumed, a periodic expense is recorded.
depreciation expense An expense that is reported gradually and systematically over the asset's useful life or until its disposal. Depreciating an asset is an attempt to allocate the original cost as an expense to the periods that benefit from the asset's use.
dilutive The effect on earnings per share (EPS) when common stock equivalents are used in the EPS calculation.
direct approach A method for preparing and displaying the cash flow statement where cash from operating activities is calculated on the basis of all cash flows with customers, suppliers, employees, and other operating activities. Contrast with *indirect approach.*
direct rates Used to indicate the rate at which U.S. dollars are translated into foreign currencies. Direct rates specify the number of units of U.S. dollars that are equivalent to one unit of the foreign currency. See *indirect rates.*
discontinued operations A segment of a company that has been sold, abandoned, or disposed that represents a distinct major line of business. Such a segment is reported apart from operating income as discontinued operations on the income statement.
discount on bonds A bond is issued below its *face* amount, indicating that the coupon rate is lower than the market rate for similar bonds (such as risk, maturity). See *par value* and *premium on bonds.*
discount rate An interest rate used in calculating the present value of money. This rate is often not explicit and is derived by taking the risk of the investment and prevailing market rates into account.
discounted note A noninterest-bearing note where the interest charge has been deducted from the principal in advance.
discounts taken Savings in the form of a percentage deducted from the purchase price of goods and services offered by the seller to induce early payment.
dividends Distributions of assets, usually cash, that the corporation elects to make periodically to its stockholders.
double-declining-balance method A declining-balance method using a multiple of 200 percent of the straight-line rate.
double-entry accounting An accounting method in which transactions are recorded by entering equal amounts in the left-hand (debit) side and right-hand (credit) side.
double taxation A form of taxation in which income taxes are paid by corporations on their earnings, which are taxed a second time when shareholders pay taxes on the dividends that they received from corporations.

earnings See *net income.*
earnings management Involves accounting-related decisions that result in favorable consequences to firms and their managers.
earnings per share (EPS) Indicates the net income earned by each share of outstanding common stock.

earnings quality The sustainability of currently reported earnings in future periods. Also relates to the *conservatism principle.*
economic assumptions Related to pension accounting, these assumptions include the assumed interest rate used to discount future pension benefits, and the anticipated rate of return on pension plan assets.
economic value The market value of a company's stock.
efficient market hypothesis Proposes that all publicly available information is reflected in security prices.
entity assumption An assumption that accounting records of a business entity are kept distinct from the entity's owners. This allows the owner to assess the status and performance of the business on a stand-alone basis.
equipment Resources that include office desks and chairs, tools, drill presses, robots, computers, x-ray and other scanners, podiums, and so on. Equipment and *plant* are major resources of many organizations.
equity capital Represents ownership interests in the corporation in the form of stock bought by investors. Equity capital is not a liability to be repaid at a future date.
equity method of accounting A method in which the parent company recognizes its share of the subsidiary's reported income (or loss) on its financial statements and adjusts the basis of the investment (asset) in the subsidiary.
equity securities Represent ownership interests in the form of stocks issued by corporations. This interest is reported on the balance sheet as an asset (investments).
ex dividend stock A stock that subsequent purchasers will not be entitled to receive the previously declared dividend for but that investors on the date of record will receive.
executory contracts Contracts formed merely by an exchange of promises. No substantive exchange of cash or services has occurred to meet the "past transaction" criterion for the contract to be recognized for financial accounting purposes.
expected return An increase in the investor's wealth, in the form of increased market value of the investment and dividends, that is anticipated over a set amount of time.
expenses The consumption of resources as a result of conducting business for the purpose of generating revenues and profits.
external expansion Occurs as firms take over, or merge with, other existing firms.
externally acquired goodwill The amount that a firm pays in excess of the net assets of another business that the firm acquires. The excess is recorded as *goodwill,* an asset on the balance sheet.
extraordinary items Events and transactions that are unusual in nature (not typical of the firm's operations) and infrequent in occurrence (not expected to recur in the foreseeable future). These items are reported apart from operating income on the income statement.

F

factor Selling accounts receivable for cash.
factor receivables Obtaining funds from a factor or lender by pledging or transferring accounts receivable to the factor.
FASB See *Financial Accounting Standards Board.*
FIFO (first in, first out) A method for valuing inventory that assumes the goods "first in" are those "first out" as they are sold or used in a production process.
financial accounting Provides financial statements, prepared following GAAP, to decision makers external to the business.
Financial Accounting Standards Board (FASB) A private organization that issues Statements of Financial Accounting Standards (SFAS) that currently are the most authoritative source of GAAP. The FASB is empowered by the SEC to set GAAP.
financial leverage ratio See *debt-to-assets ratio.*
financing activities Describes a firm's sources of cash through borrowing or equity transactions. Its category is shown on the cash flow statement.
finished goods Completed inventory items that are awaiting sale.
fiscal year A financial reporting period that may be different from the calendar year. A firm uses a fiscal year because it is conventional to their industry and more convenient to their production or sales activity.
fixed asset turnover A ratio that analyzes how effectively a firm is utilizing its productive capacity (fixed assets). This is calculated by dividing sales by the average book value of property, plant, and equipment.
fixed assets Tangible, long-lived assets, primarily property, plant, and equipment.
foreign currency transactions Transactions that are settled with a nondomestic currency.

foreign exchange rage Specifies the number of U.S. dollars (from a U.S. perspective) that are needed to obtain one unit of a specific foreign currency.
forward rate The rate of exchange for future delivery of foreign currencies.
franchise Rights to market a particular product or service, typically within a geographic area. These rights have economic value.
free cash flow Cash flow from operating activities less cash needed to replace productive resources.
full cost method Capitalizes, as an asset, the exploration costs of both successful and unsuccessful natural resource sites. Used in accounting for mining and oil and gas exploration.
functional currency The currency a company uses to conduct its business.
future value The concept that money earns interest over time and the value of money will be greater in the future as interest accumulates with the principal amount.
future value factor Using multiplication, converts the initial deposit to its future value.

G

GAAP See *generally accepted accounting principles.*
GAAS See *generally accepted auditing standards.*
gains Profits realized from activities that are incidental to a firm's primary operating activities.
general journal The entry point of transactions to the accounting records. It provides a chronological listing of all transactions and events.
general ledger Contains accounts and balances that summarize a firm's transactions.
general purpose Meets the common information needs of a variety of financial statement users.
generally accepted accounting principles (GAAP) The most widely used accounting treatments for financial reporting. The FASB, with SEC support, sets GAAP.
generally accepted auditing standards (GAAS) Developed by the accounting profession to provide guidance in the performance of an audit.
going concern concept The assumption underlying accounting and auditing that a firm will continue doing business in the future.
goodwill The amount paid in excess of the fair market value of an acquired firm's identifiable net assets. Goodwill should not be confused with *internally generated goodwill* that results from reputation, location, and client lists.
gross margin Revenues less cost of goods sold. Important to any retailer or manufacturer as a source of operating profit. See *gross profit (margin) percentage.*
gross profit See *gross margin.*
gross profit (margin) percentage A profitability measure calculated as gross profit (margin) divided by revenues.

H

hedge Entering into a contract to buy or sell foreign currencies in the forward market in order to protect against the risks of foreign exchange rate fluctuations.
hedging contract A contract to buy or sell foreign currencies in the forward market to protect against the risks of foreign exchange rate fluctuations. Also referred to as a *hedge.*
historical cost The exchange price on the date of acquisition of the asset, usually indicated by the amount of cash that changed hands.
horizontal analysis A trend analysis where components of the current year's financial statements are compared to components of a prior year's statements.
hybrid securities A security that is neither clearly debt nor clearly equity. Instead, it combines certain features of both types of securities. See *convertible bonds.*

I

immediate recognition An expenditure is expensed immediately because it has no discernible future benefit.
income statement A financial statement that summarizes the firm's earnings during a specified period of time. It contains at least two major sections: revenues and expenses. Also referred to as *statement of earnings.*
income taxes Expenses based on the firm's earnings imposed by the federal, state, and local governments and by foreign jurisdictions.
indentures Provisions and restrictions attached to a bond that make the bond more attractive for investors.
indirect approach A method for preparing and displaying the cash flow statement where the cash from operating activities is calculated indirectly by adding or subtracting various noncash adjustments to the reported net income. Contrast this approach with *direct approach.*

indirect rates Used to indicate the rate at which foreign currencies are translated into U.S. dollars. Indirect rates specify the number of foreign currency units that are equivalent to one U.S. dollar. See *direct rates.*
informational role The objective of accounting designed to provide information useful for decision making.
intangible asset Noncurrent assets that lack physical substance. Intangible assets often consist of legal rights including patents and copyrights. Intangibles are important resources controlled by the organization and in some cases may be the most important resource.
intangibles Type of long-term asset representing nonmaterial rights or contractual privileges, such as patents, copyrights, and so on.
intercompany receivables and payables Receivables and payables of a parent company and its subsidiary(s). They are eliminated in consolidation reporting.
intercompany sales Sales of a parent company and its subsidiary(s). They are eliminated in consolidation reporting.
interest-bearing note A debt instrument (note) that pays interest at a stated rate for a stated period.
interest cost In pension accounting, this is the interest on the projected benefit obligation. In accounting for postretirement benefit obligations other than pensions, it is the beginning of the year accumulated benefit obligation multiplied by the discount rate.
interest expense The firm's cost of borrowing money from creditors. Often simply referred to as *interest.*
interim reporting (interim reports) Reporting financial results more frequently than once a year.
internal auditing Performed within the firm to ensure the reliability of financial statements. Internal audits also assess the effectiveness and efficiency of the corporation's operations.
internal expansion Occurs as firms invest in new plant and equipment, research, and other productive assets in order to serve growing markets or to extend the scope of their operations into new products and markets.
internally generated goodwill The unrecognized, unreported costs incurred that enhance the value of the organization. Examples of value include good reputation and customer base, successful relationships with suppliers, skilled labor force, talented management, and so on.
inventory Items that have been purchased or manufactured for resale to customers.
invested capital Amounts received by a corporation upon sale of its stock to investors. Includes par value and paid-in capital.
investing activities Describes a firm's uses of cash to acquire other assets. This category is shown on the cash flow statement.
investor ratios Indicates a firm's performance with regard to its shares' market value. Primarily of interest to owners or investors.
issued shares Shares of stock that have been issued to investors.

J

journal entry An entry that appears in the general journal and consists of the date, the account(s) to be debited, the account(s) to be credited, the amounts, and an explanation.

L

lease An agreement where the *lessor* conveys to the *lessee* the right to use property, plant, and equipment for a designated future period.
lessee The user or renter of property in a lease agreement.
lessor The owner of property in a lease agreement.
leverage Financing a large proportion of asset acquisitions with long-term debt, as opposed to equity, that results in leveraged returns (profits) to the common equity shareholders.
liabilities Obligations of the entity to convey something of value in the future. They are probable future sacrifices of economic benefit that arise as a result of past transactions or events.
license The right to engage in a particular activity.
LIFO (last in, first out) A method for valuing inventory that assumes "last in" purchases of inventory are those first sold or first used in the production process.
liquidate Refers to how quickly the firm's inventory and other assets can be apportioned in order to raise cash as demanded by creditors and owners.
liquidity Refers to how quickly the firm's current assets can be converted to cash.
liquidity ratios Group of ratios used to evaluate the firm's short-term solvency and how effectively it manages its working capital.

losses Losses realized from activities that are incidental to a firm's primary operating activities.
lower of cost or market (LCM) Required method of valuing inventory under GAAP where market is defined as current replacement cost.

M

major customers A customer from which an organization generates 10 percent or more of its revenue.
managerial accounting Provides information that is custom-tailored, detailed, and proprietary for a firm's managers to make operating decisions.
market rate The "cost of money" (interest), as determined by the monetary market forces (supply and demand).
market-to-book value ratio Indicates the relationship between the market's valuation of the firm and the book values shown in the firm's financial statements. Calculated as the quoted price per share on a stock exchange divided by the firm's asset value per share.
market value The replacement cost of an asset. Also, the market price of a marketable security.
marketable securities A debt or equity security that is readily marketable on a securities exchange registered with the SEC, some foreign exchanges, or if its price is available through the National Association of Securities Dealers Automated Quotations Systems (NASDAQ) or the National Quotation Bureau.
matching principle A principle underlying expense recognition indicating that all resources consumed in generating revenue should be recorded in the same time period as the revenue. This accrual basis approach provides a better portrayal of a firm's performance as reflected on the income statement.
materiality principle States that separate disclosure is not required if an item is so small that knowledge of it would not affect the decision of a reasonable financial statement reader. A guideline used by auditors and accountants to determine whether a particular item or cost will have a potential significant effect on a decision.
maturity date Date on which the principal of a note becomes due.
merger A business combination in which the buyer firm acquires either the stock, or the assets and liabilities, of an investee firm. The investee is then dissolved, and no longer exists as a separate corporation.
minority interest in consolidated subsidiaries The book value of a subsidiary's outstanding shares of stock that are not under the control of the parent.
mortgage payable A loan agreement where the title to real property is secured by the lender to manage the risk of loan default by the borrower. The payable is a liability for the borrower.
multiple-step income statement Calculates certain subtotals for the reader such as gross profit and operating income.

N

natural resources Assets such as mines containing gold, silver, copper, or other minerals, wells containing oil or gas, and timberlands. Natural resources are also called "wasting assets."
net assets The excess (residual) amount of assets over liabilities measured by an entity's accounting. Net assets are equivalent to owners' equity as shown by rearranging the basic accounting equation: Owners' Equity = Assets ÷ Liabilities. Also referred to as *net worth*.
net book value The initial (recorded) cost of an asset less the accumulated depreciation. Also referred to as the *carrying value* of an asset.
net income Amount by which total revenues exceed total expenses. The *bottom line* on the income statement.
net income percentage A profitability ratio that indicates the proportion of net income earned on every sales dollar. Calculated as net income divided by sales.
net loss Amount by which expenses exceed revenues.
net of tax Indicates that expected tax effects have already been considered as part of a particular calculation or figure. Indicates that taxes have been deducted from a particular financial component.
net profit See *net income*.
net realizable value The estimated cash to be collected from an asset.
net sales Gross sales revenue less any allowances or discounts.
net worth See *net assets*.
nominal account Revenue and expense accounts that are initialized to zero when the amounts are transferred to retained earnings at the end of the reporting period. Also referred to as a *temporary* account.

nonbusiness organizations Any organization that does not have a profit objective or motivation. May refer to a *nonprofit* or *not-for-profit organization.*
noncash investing and financing activities A category of investing and financing activities that does not involve cash flows.
noncurrent assets Long-term assets that are used in the conduct of the business. The replacement cycle for a noncurrent asset is greater than one year.
noncurrent liabilities Liabilities that represent obligations, typically from long-term borrowing that generally require payment over periods longer than a year.
noninterest-bearing note A debt instrument (note) that does not explicitly pay interest but is usually bought at a discount.
note A written promise to pay signed by the debtor. The obligation to pay has arisen from past borrowing transactions.
note payable A formal written agreement with a fixed repayment date(s) that the debtor signs in order to borrow funds from banks or other lenders. Notes payable may be either interest bearing or noninterest bearing and can usually be further negotiated by the owner.
notes to the financial statements Information that clarifies and extends the material presented in the financial statements with narrative and detail.
number of days sales in accounts receivable A liquidity ratio that indicates how quickly the firm is "turning" or "cycling" its accounts receivable. A high number indicates poor management of accounts receivable. It's calculated as ending accounts receivable divided by sales per day.
number of days sales in ending inventory (NDS) A liquidity ratio used to measure inventory levels. A low number indicates efficient inventory levels. Calculated as ending inventory divided by cost of goods sold per day.

O

obligations for warranties Liabilities resulting from offering assurances of repairs, replacements, and/or refunds in the event of product failures or customer dissatisfaction.
on account Purchases or sales on credit.
operating activities Activities involved with completing the ordinary day-to-day transactions needed to carry on business.
operating capacity The ability of a firm to produce goods or services that can be assessed by analyzing the firm's tangible and intangible noncurrent assets.
operating cycle The time needed to purchase raw materials, manufacture inventory, sell the inventory, and collect cash from the customer.
operating income Gross margin or gross profit less all other operating expenses.
operating income percentage A profitability ratio calculated by dividing operating income by sales revenues. Also called operating income ratio.
operating lease A lease agreement treated as an ordinary rental, where the asset is merely used by the lessee and rental payments are reported as expense.
operating segment A component of a firm (a) that engages in business activities from which it may earn revenues and incur expenses, (b) whose operating results are regularly reviewed by the firm's chief operating decision maker, and (c) for which financial information is available.
opportunity cost A cost that exists as a result of lost profits due to more profitable alternative investments being precluded by less profitable investments currently undertaken.
other items (net) A component of pension expense that includes amortization of the transition amount, prior service cost, and gains and losses.
outstanding checks Checks that are included in the accounting records but not shown on the bank statement.
outstanding shares Issued shares that are not held in treasury by the issuing firm. Only outstanding shares are eligible for dividends.
overhead Manufacturing costs other than direct labor and materials.
owners' equity Represents the owners' interest in the assets of the business. It is the residual amount that equals assets minus liabilities. See *basic accounting equation.*

P

paid-in capital Term used to describe a component of shareholders' equity. Represents the difference between amounts invested by shareholders and the par value of their investment.
par value (bonds) The amount due on the bond's maturity date.
par value (stock) Stated amount per share for legal purposes. Usually the amount is minor and represents a fraction of the market value, or issued amount, of the stock.
parent The term applied to the buyer company in a business combination.

partnership An unincorporated business owned by more than one owner and operated under a legal contract (partnership agreement) among the partners. Partnerships are not separate legal entities apart from their owners, but they are separate accounting entities.

patents Granted by the federal government to convey the exclusive right to use a product or process for a period of 17 years.

pay-as-you-go The method used prior to 1993 for accounting of nonpension postretirement benefits, where expenses were reported on the cash basis, and no obligations were recognized for future payments.

pension Benefits (compensation) provided by firms to their retired employees.

percentage composition (analysis) Refers to a ratio analysis of financial statement data based on the relative proportions of column totals. See *vertical analysis.* Contrast with *horizontal analysis.*

percentage-of-completion Recognizes a portion of the revenue, cost, and profit each year according to the percentage of the job completed.

percentage of PPE depreciated (age) Equals accumulated depreciation divided by PPE (gross) and indicates the age of PPE.

petty cash (fund) Small quantity of funds kept on hand for incidental expenditures requiring quick cash. These funds are included in the cash amount on the balance sheet.

plant Includes office, retail or factory buildings, warehouses or supply depots, or hospitals and health clinics. Along with equipment, plant is a primary productive resource of any organization.

political costs Costs that are imposed on firms by the political process. Examples include taxes and costs to implement regulations.

pooling of interests The accounting treatment used in a business combination when firms combine by an exchange of voting stock. These combinations are interpreted as a "uniting of ownership interests" rather than a purchase of one firm by another.

posting Transcribing the amounts from journal entries into the general ledger.

preferred stock Equity capital shares that have priority over common shares with regard to dividends and distributions of assets in the event of firm liquidation.

premium on bonds The amount by which a bond is bought and sold above its *face* amount. See *par value* and *discount on bonds.*

prepaid expenses Unexpired assets that have been paid for in advance and represent the rights to future benefits. Prepaid expenses are classified as current assets.

prepaid rent A prepaid expense representing the right to occupy property.

present value The value today of an amount to be received or paid in the future.

present value factor Using multiplication, this converts a future value to its present value.

price-to-earnings (P/E) ratio Widely used investor ratio that indicates the relationship between market prices and earnings. Calculated as the stock's market price per share divided by its earnings per share.

principal The original or base amount of a loan or investment.

privatization Selling government-owned or -controlled enterprises to private investors.

pro forma amount Hypothetical or projected amount. Synonymous with "what if" analyses. Pro forma statements indicate what would have happened under specified circumstances.

profit See *net income.*

profitability ratios Group of ratios that analyze the return on investment to the owners and the level of gross and net profit margins being generated by revenues.

projected benefit obligation The amount of pension benefits that employees have earned to date, based on the expected future salary levels.

property Usually represents land on which the firm's offices, factories, and other facilities are located. May also be used generically to refer to factories, warehouses, and so on.

prospectively The method of accounting for changes in estimates whereby past financial statements are not affected. The change impacts only future periods.

quality of income ratio A cash ratio calculated by dividing cash from operating activities by net income.

quality of sales ratio A liquidity ratio that indicates the proportion of sales revenue that has generated cash in the current year. Cash sales are considered high-quality sales while credit sales are low-quality sales. Calculated as cash received from customers divided by sales.

quick ratio A liquidity ratio that only considers those current assets that may be available quickly. Calculated as cash plus cash equivalents plus net receivables divided by current liabilities. Also referred to as the *acid-test ratio.*

R

raw materials Materials, components, or ingredients that have not yet entered the manufacturing process. They are shown as inventory on the balance sheet.
realize Recognizing a gain or loss in the financial statements.
recognition Recording a transaction in the accounting records.
relevant Information that makes a difference in the decision making process.
reliable Information that is free from error and bias.
research and development costs Costs incurred to generate new knowledge or to translate knowledge into a new product or process. According to GAAP, these costs should be expensed immediately.
residual interest See *net assets.*
residual owners Refers to constituents who have a secondary or "final" ownership interest in an organization. Often refers to shareholders who take a secondary position relative to bondholders or preferred shareholders.
residual value See *salvage value.*
restrictive covenants Limitations imposed by a creditor on a debtor's actions. Covenants are often based on accounting measurements of assets, liabilities, and/or income.
restructure The term used to describe corporate downsizing and refocus of operations. The total estimated costs of restructuring should be expensed in the current year.
retained earnings The portion of shareholders' equity that reflects the increase (or decrease) in the shareholders' interest from revenue and expense transactions.
retroactively The method of accounting for accounting principle changes whereby past years' financial statements are restated to reflect the use of the new method.
return on assets (ROA) ratio A profitability ratio that indicates the rate of return on the firm's assets. It is used to compare the firm's rate of return with alternative investments that could be undertaken. Calculated as net income plus interest expense times one minus the tax rate, all divided by average total assets.
return on equity (ROE) ratio A profitability ratio used to relate net income to shareholders' equity.
return on plan assets As related to pension accounting, it is a reduction in pension expense because of the return that is expected on the plan's assets. The reduction is based on anticipated, not actual, return.
return on shareholders' equity ratio A ratio that links the income statement and the balance sheet by dividing net income by average shareholders' equity.
revenue Inflows of assets (or reductions in liabilities) in exchange for providing goods and services to customers (sales, for example) or inflows from collecting interest, rent, royalties, and so on.
revenue recognition principle States that revenue should be recognized in the accounting records when the earnings process is substantially complete and the amount to be collected is reasonably determinable.
risk The uncertainty surrounding estimates of future cash flows.

S

sale Delivery of goods or services in exchange for cash or other consideration.
sales return Items returned by customers for credit or other adjustment. Usually defective or unacceptable merchandise.
salvage value The estimated amount a firm expects to receive when an asset is sold at the end of its useful life. Also referred to as *residual value.*
Securities Exchange Commission (SEC) Created by the Securities Exchange Act of 1934, the SEC has the power to set accounting principles and financial disclosure requirements for firms with securities traded on public exchanges.
security As related to debt, it is synonymous with collateral. As related to investments, it is synonymous with publicly traded stocks and bonds (securities).
selling expenses A category of expenses shown on the income statement related to marketing and other selling activities.
service cost As related to pension accounting, service cost (normal cost) is the present value of future pension benefits that employees earned during the current year. As related to accounting for postretirement benefit obligations other than pensions, it is the amount of the accumulated benefit obligation that was earned by employees during the current year.
service lives The working years of employees prior to retirement, as used in accounting for postretirement benefit obligations.
SFAS See *Statements of Financial Accounting Standards.*
shareholders' equity Represents the shareholders' interest in the assets of the firm. It is the residual amount that equals assets minus liabilities. See *basic accounting equation.*

single-step format Refers to an income statement format where all revenues are shown in one category, and all expenses are shown in another category, without calculating intermediate subtotals. Contrast with *multiple-step income statement.*
single-step income statement Summarizes all revenues in one section and all expenses in another.
sinking fund A fund that is designated for a special purpose, such as the retirement of outstanding debt or the replacement of operating assets.
sole proprietorship A business owned and usually operated by the same individual. The owner and business are not separate legal entities but are separate accounting entities.
specific identification method A method for determining the cost of inventory by maintaining the identity and cost of each item, usually by serial number or other code, such that each item or unit can be tracked throughout the holding and selling process.
spot rate The rate of exchange for immediate delivery of foreign currencies.
statement of cash flows A financial statement that reports the sources and uses of cash by a firm during a specified period. Three major activities of the firm are reported: operating, investing, and financing. This statement is intended to provide information about a firm's ability to generate cash.
statement of earnings A financial statement that summarizes the firm's earnings during a specified period of time. It contains at least two major sections: revenues and expenses. Also referred to as the *income statement.*
statement of financial position A financial statement that shows, at a specified time, a firm's financial condition, which is determined by its assets, liabilities, and owners' equity. Also referred to as the *balance sheet.*
statement of owners' equity A financial statement that summarizes the changes that took place in owners' equity over a period of time.
statement of shareholders' equity A financial statement that summarizes the changes that took place in shareholders' equity over a period of time.
Statements of Financial Accounting Standards (SFAS) The primary sources of GAAP. The statements provide explicit accounting treatment for financial transactions. Currently they are created by the FASB.
stock dividend Additional shares of stock are received by investors in the form of a dividend. Retained earnings is reduced and invested capital is increased.
stock option Rights to purchase a firm's stock at a specific price over some designated future period.
stock split An exchange of shares of a firm's stock for existing outstanding shares that usually results in more shares issued.
straight-line method (SL) A depreciation method that allocates an equal amount of expense to each year in an asset's life.
subsidiary The term applied to the investee firm in a business combination when the firm continues to exist.
subsidiary ledger Provides detailed information regarding a particular general ledger account.
successful efforts method Immediately expenses the cost of unsuccessful oil and gas sites. Only the costs directly associated with locating and developing successful sites are capitalized.
sum-of-the-years'-digits method (SYD) An accelerated depreciation method where the numerator is the number of useful remaining years and the denominator is the sum of the years' digits in the asset's useful life. The denominator is calculated as $[N \times (N-1)]/2$, where N is the number of years in the asset's life.
sustainability Describes the ability of an organization to continue its operations and achieve its objectives. Can relate to the *going concern concept.*
systematic and rational allocation Method used to implement the matching principle where costs that cannot be directly linked to specific revenue transactions are recognized as an expense in the years it helps generate revenue.

T

T-account A form of ledger page used to record (or illustrate) the entry of debits and credits into ledger accounts.
tax accounting Encompasses the two functions of tax compliance and tax planning. Tax compliance involves the process of completing tax forms and the calculation of a firm's tax liability. Tax planning entails providing advice about the effects that business transactions will have on the firm's tax liability.
tax benefit A reduction in taxes, or a tax credit or refund, due to a particular action or expense incurred by a taxable entity.
tax compliance Entails completing tax returns at period end or year-end.
tax planning Involves structuring transactions so as to minimize their tax effects.
taxes payable Represents unpaid taxes that are owed to a governmental unit and will be paid within a year.
temporary differences A situation in which book accounting and tax accounting measurements differ and will be offset by opposite deviations in later periods.

time value of money The concept that funds (money) earn interest over time. This implies that a dollar to be received a year from now is worth less than a dollar received today.

times interest earned ratio A calculation that indicates the relative risk of bankruptcy or other default. "Times interest earned" indicates the "cushion" or margin of safety that the firm enjoys in meeting its interest expenses. It is calculated as earnings before interest and taxes divided by interest expense.

trade receivables See *accounts receivable.*

trademarks Words, symbols or other distinctive elements used to identify a particular firm's products.

trading securities Securities held by firms for brief periods of time that are intended to generate profits from short-term differences in price.

transactions The exchange of resources between the firm and other parties.

translation adjustment The process of converting monetary units stated in terms of one country's currency into a different monetary unit. See *foreign currency transactions* and *foreign exchange rate.*

treasury stock Repurchased outstanding shares of a firm's own stock.

trend analysis Comparing financial numbers across periods of time.

trial balance A listing of all general ledger accounts and their balances for the purpose of verifying that total debits equal total credits.

10-K report Mandatory report filed by a company on an annual basis with the SEC.

10-Q report Mandatory report filed by a company on a quarterly basis with the SEC.

U

unearned revenue Advance payments from customers for the right to receive goods or services in the future. The advance payment is recorded as a liability until the goods are delivered or the services are rendered to the customer.

unrealized gain (loss) on marketable securities The difference between a security's historical cost and its market value.

unrealized inventory profits Inventory that has been transferred among a parent company and its subsidiary(s). Profits related to these inventories that have not been sold to outside entities are removed from the consolidated financial statements.

users of financial statements Interested parties with an economic interest in the firm that need financial information. Typical users include the firm's owners, creditors, managers, employees, customers, and suppliers. Some users obtain information directly from the firm, others rely on quarterly and annual reports.

utilitarianism Judges the moral correctness of an act based solely on its consequences. The act that maximizes overall favorable consequences should be taken.

vertical analysis Examines the composition of elements on the income statement (balance sheet) as a percentage of net revenues (total assets).

vertical percentage analysis Refers to a ratio analysis of financial statement data. Is based on relationships between a target figure (like total revenues or total assets) and other figures shown on the same report. It's often used to examine capital structure or other financing relationships. See *percentage composition analysis.*

vested benefit obligation Indicates the amounts to which employees have irrevocable rights, even if they leave the firm prior to retirement.

W

warranty obligations Represent the firm's estimated future costs to fulfill its obligations for repair or refund guarantees of products sold or services provided prior to the balance sheet date.

wasting assets Assets such as mines containing gold, silver, copper, or other minerals, wells containing oil or gas, and timberlands. Wasting assets are also called "natural resources."

weighted average Each level of outstanding shares of common stock is weighted by the fraction of a year that it stayed constant.

working capital Current assets minus current liabilities.

work-in-process Consists of manufactured or assembled items that are partially completed at the balance sheet date.

worksheet An extended form of the trial balance.

company index

K

L

M

N

O

P

Q

R

S

T

U

V

W

Z

web index

subject index

B

C

D

E

F

K

L

M

N

O

P

T